11-10-03

Best wishes —

Duval E Culbertson [signature]

Compliments of —
Arlington Resort Hotel
& Spa
Hot Springs National Park, Ark.
New Year's Eve 2003

LEO and VERNE

The Spa's Heyday

ORVAL E. ALLBRITTON

Illustrations
by
Nan Merchant

Garland County Historical Society
Hot Springs, AR 71901

ABOUT THE AUTHOR

Orval E. Allbritton, a native of Hot Springs, graduated from Lakeside High School and attended Arkansas Law School after earning an A.A. at Little Rock Junior College (now UALR). Now retired, he was formerly with the Federal Bureau of Investigation and was also a claims specialist with Crawford Insurance Company. A member of the Garland County Historical Society's Board of Directors, Allbritton has contributed numerous articles for the Society's annual publication, "The Record."

ISBN 0929604-87-3

In Memory

of

Norma Freeman Allbritton

Vernal Snell Ledgerwood

Leo Patrick McLaughlin

PREFACE

Any history of Hot Springs National Park, Arkansas would be incomplete and remiss without a close scrutiny and study of what many people refer to as the McLaughlin Era. The time referred to was named after the flamboyant mayor and long time political boss, Leo P. McLaughlin. The name, McLaughlin Era, however, is really a misnomer as there was another individual equally powerful and important in the operation of the political machine which controlled Garland County politics for over twenty years--he was Verne S. Ledgerwood, the consummate politician.

Many people born in this county the last half of the twentieth-century may be unfamiliar with the names of Leo P. McLaughlin and Verne S. Ledgerwood. They, also are probably unaware of the tremendous influence these two men had on controlling and shaping the image that Hot Springs presented to the nation for many years, an image that was not always pleasing or flattering, but one that was most interesting.

One man craved and loved the spotlight of public attention and desired to be in the forefront of all publicity. The other was content to stay shrouded dimly in the background and pull the strings to insure the machine functioned smoothly.

McLaughlin and Ledgerwood were very successful politicians. Both were dedicated to Hot Springs and neither ever wanted to live anywhere else. Neither coveted or sought a higher political office, yet both would probably have been successful had they done so. One might say that both men were products of this area, McLaughlin having lived his entire life in the city, save a few months in the army, and Ledgerwood was brought to Hot Springs when only a few months old. They lived, worked, played and died here. Their lives are forever entwined with the threads of the history of the Spa City.

The two grew up together, excelling in athletics on the various school teams. They both entered the field of law as their profession. Their political careers were enmeshed so tightly one might assume they were the closest of cronies. This was not so. While they were cordial toward each other most of the time, they were not friends, and their association in their adult years was strictly a business arrangement. Sadly, in the end there was a coldness existing between the two. One man died with few friends, despised by many of the citizens he had governed and only the loyalty of his sisters remaining. The other was honored by the Bar Association, friends and acquaintances.

But this is not only the story of these two individuals who influenced the lives of so many people and local events during the period known as The Great Depression, but it is about the beautiful mountain city known as Hot

Springs. It covers the period from the time the McLaughlin family came to the area in the late 1870s until the wide open and illegal gambling, which existed here, was closed down in 1967. The story covers the wildness of the little town's frontier appearance and frequent street gunfights, which still excite us, to the modern city which rose from the ashes and debris of several devastating fires and floods, to the plush gambling casinos crowded by the thousands of visitors who flocked here, first by stagecoach, then by train and car. People of immense wealth journeyed here for entertainment as well as those less fortunate folks who were seeking relief of ailments through the God given thermal waters. It was a wonderful place where the rich frolicked, played golf and fished, and rubbed elbows with the gangsters of Chicago and New York who vacationed, attended the fights at the old Auditorium, and joined the locals in open admiration of the big-league ball players training at Whittington and Majestic parks. But it was also a place that attracted con-men who preyed on the weak and the gullible.

Where else than Hot Springs was it better demonstrated about how difficult it sometimes becomes to rid a city and county of government corruption when good people allow the manipulating of the ballot boxes to take place? And a main prevailing thought throughout this work is how through politics and even bribery a city and county could defy the State Constitution for nearly eighty years by permitting illegal and wide open gambling. And yet there should be no condemnation of those who *honestly* tried to run and work in the clubs. The writer is the first to acknowledge that many of those were some of the most civic minded people we had. It is not our intention to cast aspersions on them or any of their defendants, many of whom are fine productive citizens.

This, then, was Hot Springs' heyday. For those of us who were fortunate enough to grow up in Hot Springs during this era we can reflect back to those times and honestly admit that Leo and Verne added a little spice and zest to our lives. Had fate decreed, we might have been born and raised in many places that were mundane and boring. Hot Springs, Arkansas certainly wasn't one of those!

Orval E. Allbritton
Hot Springs, Arkansas
July 2003

INTRODUCTION AND ACKNOWLEDGMENTS

Being born and growing up in Hot Springs in the era of 1920-1945 had a marked effect upon my life, a natural curiosity and thirst for history. Listening to stories, many exaggerated, others vague, of the early Hot Springs days of terrible fires and floods; the dozens of saloons, deadly street gunfights, of moonshine and bootlegged whiskey, visiting mobsters and gangsters in big shiny black cars, stuffed ballot boxes, stolen elections, celebrities galore, and wide-open illegal gambling, all piqued my imagination and sparked my interest, bringing up the question: Were there other places of similar history and composition as the Spa?

The older the writer becomes and the wider his knowledge, the more resounding the answer. "No, Hot Springs is unique, unparalleled and one of a kind." I can think of no more interesting place to call home than the Valley of the Vapors.

It had not been the author's original intention or purpose to write a book or a partial history of the Spa. However, reading such works as Dee Brown's, *The American Spa, Hot Springs, Arkansas*, referred to as a "compact history," and Dr. Francis J. Scully's *Hot Springs, Arkansas And Hot Springs National Park*, called a "medical history," which he expanded to include such information as conventions, pageants, pioneers, civic groups, early property and land disputes, postal receipts and bank deposits, left unanswered questions. While both of those works have filled a particular void in the life of our city, the writer realized that these did not really focus on the most important asset the Spa had in its growth over the many years--its hardy, devoted people, its sometimes shady past and the politics which motivated the everyday life in the city.

Sir John Robert Seeley wrote in his *Growth of British Policy*, "History is past politics and politics present history." From its earliest days politics played a major role in the city's development!

Given encouragement by the late Inez Cline, Garland County Historian and Garland County Historical Society Director, Bobbie Jones McLane, a fifth generation resident, I embarked on what I believed to be a two-year project. After over five years of research and writing I have satisfied my curiosity and hopefully that of others.

Here then is a documented version of many known and unknown events and occurrences which were important, at least when they happened, of the people involved and the politics which influenced them. By documenting this work it was our hope to minimize the errors which sometimes occurs by the retelling and reliance solely on memory.

A project such as this is not a one person endeavor and the author is indebted to a host of people, organizations and offices. While it is impossible to name all those who have so generously contributed of their time and knowledge it behooves me to try.

At the top of the list of assistance is the Garland County Historical Society which has provided a base of operations, use of their files, scrapbooks, Municipal Court and Police Court Records, newspaper microfilm of almost a hundred years history, oral tapes from the Leo P. McLaughlin Life and Times Project, and its wonderful photographic files.

John Wells and his great staff at the Garland County Library, made me feel at home as I used the facilities, especially the new microfilm reader, for weeks on end.

The personnel of the Circuit, Chancery and Probate records at the Garland, Saline and Hot Springs County office were most accommodating. So was the Montgomery County Circuit Court's office. Karen Landac of the Pulaski County Chancery Clerk's office was most patient and helpful in obtaining records from longtime storage. The office of Assistant City Manager Lance Hudnell was most helpful in locating city records which we felt were needed in the researching of this subject. The Rapides Parish Records at Alexandria, Louisiana was successful in locating a little known and long ago forgotten marriage license involving Leo P. McLaughlin. The United States Federal Court Clerk of the Western District of Arkansas was most cooperative and helpful in helping us locate an important case file at the National Archives in Fort Worth, Texas, and we are grateful for their assistance.

Many hours of research were conducted at the Arkansas History Commission in Little Rock and we truly thank Russell Baker and the fine support staff for their help.

The writer is deeply appreciative of the time and information provided from personal and taped interviews of knowledgeable individuals. Those included former Governor Sidney McMath; former FBI Special Agent and Garland County Sheriff Clay White; former club owners Jack Pakis and James Evelyn Young; former Chairman of the Garland County Elections Committee and member of the "McLaughlin Grand Jury, Jacob King; Attorney Norwood Phillips, Jr., relative by marriage to the McLaughlin family; former County Judge and State Senator Q. Byrum Hurst; niece of Judge Verne S. Ledgerwood, Dora Jane Ledgerwood Ellis; former Garland County Sheriff and State Senator Eugene "Bud" Canada; and former newspaperman, the late Roy L. Bosson of Athens, Texas.

And the writer would be remiss if our thanks did not extend to our daughter and son-in-law, Rebecca and Karl Cunningham, of Mena, who made the task easier by keeping our computer updated and operational!

Several members of the Garland County Historical Society have rendered special help for which the writer is most appreciative. Nathalie Martin helped us secure some needed baptismal records. Bob Brown, a former photographer for the Associated Press furnished us some previously unpublished photos. Mark Palmer made helpful suggestions and provided some rare pictures. Our thanks to each of these.

There are always expenses involved in extensive research and this was no exception. We wish to convey our appreciation to Dorothy Morris and the Morris Foundation working in conjunction with the Garland County Historical Society who had confidence in the project by providing a grant.

We know the reader of this work will be delighted with several drawings which depict scenes long faded into the past but which activate the memory as one reads the event. Those sketches have been contributed by a most talented member, Nan Merchant. Thank you, Nan.

The only person, other than the writer, to have read every word of the manuscript is Bobbie Jones McLane, Executive Director of the Garland County Historical Society. Her encouragement and help in making corrections and constructive suggestions have been most valuable and appreciated. Our work was made easier by her support!

Lastly, the GCHS is most fortunate in having a person of the caliber and talent as Wendy Bradley Richter, Archivist at Ouachita Baptist University, and Co-Editor of *The Record*. Even with her multitude of duties she agreeably took on the job of editing and setting up this work and for which we are forever indebted.

FOREWORD

Hot Springs is my hometown. I moved to Hot Springs from Columbia County, Arkansas, on my tenth birthday. I had lived on a farm. My friends and my acquaintance with people were limited to kinfolks and close neighbors. Hot Springs was a new world, a metropolitan area, populated by people with many national origins: Irish, Jewish, Italians, Syrians, Greeks, and Southerners. I became acquainted with them all, friends with their children. We went together in grade school and high school right on up to the time that we marched off to war. There were the Dowds, Longinottis, Lockwoods, Pappases, Mattars, Smiths and Browns.

Hot Springs was a notorious, wide-open town. A multi-million dollar gambling operation was its life, entertainment was its lure, civic corruption was its distinction. But unlike Las Vegas and other cities, gambling in Hot Springs was against the law.

Gambling itself is a lure to the unwary, a temptation to the weak, an addictive poison to the gullible. Innocent people are victimized, families are impoverished and children left to go hungry when the head of a family, drawn to the gaming table like a moth to a lighted lamp, throws away his paycheck or exhausts his savings on a throw of the dice, a turn of the wheel, or a deal of the cards. But the most sinister evil of illegal gambling is the very existence of those in authority, the elected officials, who further their own personal interests and private gain, rather than protect the rights of the citizens they are duty-bound to represent. Gambling powers have to control law enforcement, or the lack thereof, for their own security and the protection of their illegal operations.

This was the condition that existed in Hot Springs for a quarter of a century. The city machine was controlled by the mob, which in turn controlled the election commissions that selected the judges and clerks for the party primaries and the general elections. Election judges and clerks were recruited from casinos, bars, bookies, and allied businessmen. Thus, the outcome of any election in the city or county was "fixed," since a sufficient number of "magicians" in the polling places and "magic" in the ballot box ensured victory for the mob's slate of selected candidates.

The political bosses in Hot Springs picked the judges, the prosecuting attorney, the mayor, the chief of police, the sheriff, the constable, and grand juries---all those involved with law enforcement responsibilities.

Any citizen who dared to run for office, opposing a candidate anointed by the machine, was subjected to "reasoning and persuasion" as to the error of his ways. This, failing, the recalcitrant was subjected to certain sanctions.

Perhaps, for example, this advocate of law and justice might have a mortgage, with payments due, that might be purchased and the mortgage foreclosed, or his business could be investigated and closed for some obsolete ordinance violation. If these "gentle" tactics were not productive, this "trouble-maker" would be arrested, locked up, and subjected to a kangaroo court with punishment administered by policemen acting as "security guards" in the jail.

Not only did the machine control the elections and poll tax registration, it also controlled the process of selecting petit jurors, supposedly the "twelve good men and true" who were judges of the facts in civil or criminal cases and those serving on grand juries, were empowered to indict any "violators" of the law.

Reprisals were directed against those who did not "get along by going along," who cast an unfriendly vote in the ballot box, voted wrong in the jury verdict, or were "getting out of line." Even though reprisals were carried out quietly without any publicity the local press was "not nosy" about "such things." These punitive actions were known and spread around and about the city— in the bars, brothels, bathhouses, in the lobbies of the hotels, in the casinos, and the bookie organizations— all places where prosperity hung by the thread of approval by those in power.

In the winter season, Hot Springs could have in residence more gangland warlords than New York, Chicago, or Las Vegas. The "big boys" came and went, in and out of town: Al Capone, Lucky Luciano, Pretty Boy Floyd, the Barkers, and other underworld characters. As frequent visitors, they were big tippers, free spenders, high rollers. Owney Madden had become a permanent resident of Hot Springs, marrying the postmaster's daughter, after he was given the option by a rival mob in New York to either leave town or run the risk of being found in the Hudson River wearing "concrete shoes." Although I am unaware of any illegal activities in which he was involved on the local scene, he apparently maintained his connections and was a contact for visiting Dons of the criminal world and other displaced mobsters looking for a stake.

In 1946, the city bosses were more powerful, more deeply entrenched than before the war. The returning GIs were appalled that the people of Hot Springs and Garland County were denied "free elections where the citizen could cast his ballot freely without fear and intimidation and have that vote counted as cast; and the Constitutional right of a fair and impartial trial by jury."

A 1942 federal grand jury reported that "every provision required by the State's statutes for the preservation and protection of the ballot was wholly ignored and violated." A later grand jury report summarized the conditions in Hot Springs in the summer of 1946, "the extent of graft and corruption in this city is unbelievable. It has touched our school system, our social, religious, and business lives" (Cunningham, *Youth at the Helm*, p. 78).

With a determination to confront these abuses, the GIs organized with military precision and fielded a candidate for every county and judicial district office in the Democratic primaries of July, 1946. I was a candidate for Prosecuting Attorney for the 18th Judicial District.

The campaign was mean, tough, and hard-fought. The political bosses tightened the screws, meeting with all city and county employees, people working the gambling houses and hotels, and businessmen who were dependent upon the tourist trade. Not only were they instructed to get their families and relatives of voting age to the polls and advise them to vote for the administration's candidates, they were told that the administration would know how they voted, so their jobs, dependent on the largess, were at stake.

The vote on Election Day was the largest ever cast in Hot Springs, twice or double the number of votes cast in the previous election. The GIs went "over the top," making a clean sweep. They captured every elective office in Garland County, plus the office of prosecuting attorney, and circuit judge in the 18th Judicial District.

Thus, the freedom of the ballot box was returned to the people of Garland County so the right of dissent and political participation was restored. Thereafter, they could vote for whom they chose without fear or intimidation and have their vote counted as cast.

The Seventh Amendment to the Constitution of the United States mandates that the right of trial by jury be preserved. This requires that a jury be fairly selected from a cross-section of the community, that they have no interest in the outcome of the case, and that they take an oath to, well and truly, try the case based upon the evidence. After the election, this inalienable right was restored.

The review by Orval Allbritton of the rule by McLaughlin and Ledgerwood of Hot Springs is well researched and excellently written. I lived, experienced, the period which he so vividly describes, from the time I was a paperboy on the streets of Hot Springs to the period when I joined the United States Marine Corps.

His Hot Springs story calls up a drumbeat of thoughts and memories which saddens me, but when I look on Hot Springs today, the wonderful people, and the prospects for the future, my spirits are lifted, and I am gladdened.

The people of Hot Springs are in control of their own destiny, and they are on course for becoming a nationally recognized resort, where people may come with their families for recreation, rest, and rejuvenating of family ties.

Sid McMath

Sid McMath

THE PIONEERS

The McLaughlins

At its height, the potato famine swept across Europe, completely decimating the economy of Ireland. Entire families and villages were wiped out. During the period 1845-1847, more than 700,000 people died of starvation and disease.[1] As the misery increased, hundreds of thousands began a migration to other countries. Farms and shops that had been owned by the same families for hundreds of years were sacrificed to obtain fares to Australia, South America and the United States.

When the famine commenced John Henry McLaughlin was but a small boy, having been born in March 1842.[2] There was a large concentration of McLaughlins in Offaly County near the small town of Tullamore, and it is believed that this is the area in which John Henry lived. His father, William McLaughlin, was described as a "raiser of horses." No doubt it was a painful experience for William to have to dispose of his herd of fine horses, but for the family to survive it was a necessity. The livestock and farm did bring funds to buy passage for his family with enough to get a start in the New World.[3]

The three main ports of entry at that time for Irish immigrants were Boston, New York and Philadelphia. There is some evidence to suggest that the McLaughlins landed in the latter port and possibly settled in Maryland.[4] It is possible that William McLaughlin began to raise horses while in Maryland and could even have spent the Civil War years in that capacity. There is no evidence to conclude that John Henry McLaughlin and his two brothers, Frank and Michael, had any military service in the Union Army, although they would have been approaching military age when Fort Sumpter was fired upon.[5]

The trail of the McLaughlin family is picked up shortly after the war when

---

[1] *The World Book Encyclopedia*, Vol. 9, 1962, p. 338.

[2] *Caruth Funeral Home Records*, published 1989, p. 4. Also, Department of Commerce Census - Population - 1900. This record indicates his birth being 3/1/1841. Census Records - 1880 reflect J. H. McLaughlin born 1838.

[3] U. S. Census - 1900, indicates J. H. McLaughlin's arrival was in 1850. Other records suggest 1848 was the year of entry. It is possible that William came first in 1848 and then sent for his family in 1850.

[4] *Philadelphia Naturalization Records*, p. 449, does indicate that William McLaughlin, John H., and Michael were processed at Philadelphia 11/02/1848.

[5] The 1910 Census had a question, "Are you a survivor of the Union Army, The Confederate Army or Navy?" The question was not answered on John Henry McLaughlin's summary and we must believe that he was not in service for this conflict.

the family appears at Memphis, Tennessee. While many families were left broke and destitute by the war, they seemed to have come through the hard times in good financial condition. By 1876 John Henry and his brother Frank were operating a "staple and fancy" grocery store at 368 Main Street in downtown Memphis.[6] Younger brother, Michael, was employed in a blacksmith shop.[7]

When John Henry was thirty-one years-old, he married a nineteen year-old Irish girl, Bridget Adela Russell. Her family had migrated to America at the close of the Civil War.[8] There appears to be no information as to how John Henry and Bridget met or where they were married. It is entirely possible it was an arranged marriage, which was common among Irish families of that day. While in Memphis they resided out of the downtown area on Raleigh Road. Their first two children were born while in Tennessee: Mary Anna in May 1875, and John William in September 1876.[9]

After a few years of partnership, John Henry and Frank differed on how the grocery business should be conducted. As is the usual case with strong opinionated brothers, they had a parting of the ways. Frank pulled out of the partnership and entered another grocery business at 116 Beale Street in Memphis. It was known as Mahlon and McLaughlin.[10]

A relative of John Henry, who had just come back from a visit to Hot Springs, Arkansas, began to tell of unusual opportunities available in the small town two hundred miles to the west of Memphis. He related exciting things that were taking place, and described the incomparable beauty of the area. The small health resort had been a very difficult trip for travelers prior to 1875. The building of the Hot Springs Railroad, commonly known as "The Diamond Jo" made it much easier. This was a narrow gauge line connecting Hot Springs to the Iron Mountain Railroad at Malvern. Before that time travelers enroute to the spa had to take the El Paso stage coach from Malvern. Not only was it known as a rough trip, but one full of danger of being held up by road agents.[11] Now, hundreds of people were flocking to the area. New hotels, bath houses and stores were being built. The little town had suffered

---

[6] *Sholes Memphis City Directory, 1876, and Memphis City Directory - 1877*, p. 93. The late Roy Bosson once told this writer that he had heard the McLaughlin family may have come to Tennessee from either North or South Carolina, but was not certain.

[7] *Sholes City Directory* - 1879.

[8] It is believed that Bridget's father was named James Russell. The McLaughlin's second son, James Russell, was apparently named in honor of her father.

[9] *U. S. Census - 1900, Hot Springs Township, City of Hot Springs.*

[10] *Sholes Memphis City Directory - 1878.*

[11] Two stage robberies occurred in 1874 that were credited to the James-Younger gang. See Larry Rhodes' article in the *Senior Edition*, Hot Springs, Arkansas, February 1999.

The "Diamond Jo" - early 1880s

much damage to its downtown area from a disastrous fire which had occurred 5 March 1878 and had left over one thousand people homeless.[12] The small wooden structures of the downtown sector offered little resistance to the windswept flames. The fire had started about 2:00 o'clock in the morning and had burned almost uncontrolled for eight hours.[13] As block after block of houses and buildings were consumed, the inadequacy of the small fire department became apparent. In spite of this blow and setback, people were still flocking to the Spa seeking the curative benefits of its hot thermal waters. Others came looking for entertainment at the card tables and roulette wheels.

The small city had been incorporated in 1876, when 467 persons signed a petition as an application that was presented to then County Judge J.W. Jordan. It seemed that the citizens had taken this action to curtail and protect themselves from some of the undesirables who had infested their community as the petition sets forth: *Your petitioners would state and show your honor that our community, or town is now being flooded with lewd and immoral characters who infest our streets day and night and by their obscene carriage and vulgar language render it absolutely disagreeable for persons of respectability to be on the streets and more especially on the Holy*

---

[12] Mamie Ruth Stranburg Abernathy, *History, People, Places & Events, 1997*, p. 10. (Hereinafter cited as *Timeline*)

[13] *Hot Springs Illustrated Monthly*, March 1878.

Sabbath; on account of which many on that day are denied the privileges of attending the services of the various churches, and that your petitioners believe that this state of facts will prove very detrimental, if not to our morals in fact at home to our moral reputation abroad. Those acting on behalf of the citizens were A. Curl, P.J. Gavin and James B. Wood.. The petition was certified 5 April 1876 by County Judge J.W. Jordan. The first mayor was I.W. Carhart, who was commissioned by Governor A.H. Garland, for whom the county was named.[14]

J.H. McLaughlin had been intrigued by his relative's description and made an inspection trip to the resort and returned to Memphis favorably impressed. While Bridget may have had some reservations toward moving to a smaller and more primitive home, she was a dutiful Irish wife and let her husband make that decision. In the latter part of 1878 he sold his business and moved his small family to Hot Springs.[15]

VALLEY STREET.

---

[14] Council Records of City of Hot Springs. Early volumes at Garland County Library. First volume, Chapter l, begins 2 April 1878. The above is summarized in an article in the *Sentinel-Record*, 15 June 1958.

[15] Most accounts agree with the date of 1878 as being the year the McLaughlins arrived at Hot Springs. The single exception is an article appearing in the *Sentinel-Record & New Era* 1932, "Centennial Edition" p. 18, indicating their arrival as 1877. Both Memphis City Directories 1877 and 1878 reflect he was still operating a grocery store in that city. Early land records of Garland County reflect J.H. McLaughlin purchased property on 30 September 1878 under a Quit Claim deed from Owen O'Donnell with final transaction completed 25 April 1879.

No doubt the little town of Hot Springs must have appeared shabby to the McLaughlin family. After all, they were moving from a modern city of 40,000 people to one less than a tenth that size and lacking many conveniences of the larger town. All water was from springs and wells and the Hot Springs Water Company would not be operational until 1882.[16] It was not an inviting scene with many of the burned out structures standing as stark reminders of the ravages of the recent fire. Yet the town showed the vital signs of progress as debris was being removed and new building was taking place.

There were no paved streets and the main thoroughfares, Central and Valley, had a large creek flowing southward through the town. In summer there was a haze of dust caused by wagon wheels and horses. In the winter the streets turned to mud and many merchants kept planks of lumber to lay across mud holes to assist their customers in reaching their businesses. As the water from the thermal springs entered the creek, making contact with cold water, there was a mist and fog rising from the creek bed that hovered over the valley generally until the morning's sun rays burned the vapors away. A series of structures called bath houses had been built on the east side of Central (then known as Valley) with the rear of the buildings being pressed against the foot of Hot Springs Mountain. No less than eleven foot-bridges spanned the creek and allowed pedestrians to cross to their favorite bathing spot.

The business houses in the downtown area for the most part, occupied the west side of the street, although a few were on the east side. The latter caused land disputes with the government for many years. Some of the new replacements were being constructed of wood. It would take another conflagration before many people would be convinced it was safer and wiser to build with fire resistant materials. There was a small mule-pulled trolley line operating in the downtown area. It only ran from Cartwright's Corner (Spencer's) to the junction of Park and Whittington Avenues, but was of great help to those infirmed. A short time later the line would extend several blocks north on Park Avenue to Castle Park where a car barn was built to house the small trolley cars.

It was easy for John Henry to see by walking down Central Avenue that the merchants had faith in the economy of the town. Every where he looked he could see signs they were gearing up for the expected tourist trade. It was evident that a "thirsty" visitor would not have to walk or look far for a drink as there were twenty saloons between the Malvern Crossing and the Junction of Park and Whittington. Several of those had gambling operations in the rear or perhaps on the second floor. Hotels and restaurants were springing up. He also noticed a number of grocery stores locating in the downtown area. This partially persuaded him to search for a location elsewhere. A vacant one-story

---

[16] *Timeline*, p. 11.

HOT SPRINGS HOTEL.

frame building on the southwest corner of Malvern and Church Street caught his eye. It was only a few years old and in a good state of repair. It had a large storeroom at the rear with a loading dock where cattle feed and bulk groceries could easily be placed in wagons. But the best thing, was the owner had a house adjacent to the store and was willing to sell both. Between the south side of the store and the house was a curbed and guttered well.[17] A deal was struck and the McLaughlins settled into life in a small town.

John Henry McLaughlin had made either a very wise or a very lucky selection for his new grocery business. Malvern Avenue became one of the centers of business in the growing town. The road led into the county linking the farming area east of town, Lawrence and Price Station, and communities as far away as Magnet Cove. Many people found it convenient to trade with J.H. McLaughlin, as he became known. It had been a good move as the family began to prosper almost from their first day in their new home. The year 1878 ended with Bridget seven months pregnant and awaiting the birth of her third child, Elizabeth McLaughlin, who first saw light on 28 February 1879.

---

[17] *The Sanborn-Perris Insurance Maps of Hot Springs - 1886,* show the house to evenly front with the store on Malvern Avenue. The ones of 1890 and 1892 reflect the house abutting and possibly connecting to the store on the south side, but set back from the street by several feet.

The Ledgerwoods

William H. Ledgerwood was born in the western farmlands of Illinois, just twenty miles east of Keokuk, Iowa, 20 October 1837.[18] His parents had immigrated to this country from Scotland in the early 1830s. About 1850, William H. Ledgerwood and his family moved to southeastern Kansas and settled in Greenwood County. The farm was just a few miles from the bustling prairie town and county seat of Eureka on the banks of the Fall River. Eureka, in the late 1880s, had a wide dirt main street with brick buildings housing the mercantile stores. The tree-surrounded county court house towered over all the buildings save the Greenwood Hotel, a large three-story structure that had been built in 1883.[19] The Ledgerwoods were able to homestead four-160 acre tracts of land and began to grow corn.[20] Unfortunately, growing corn had been easier and more profitable in Illinois than Kansas.

William courted and married a seventeen year-old girl, Permelia Ann Welch, born 3 November 1844. This marriage produced five sons, W.H. Ledgerwood, 28 March 1861; James E., David E., and John J. Ledgerwood, born in 1873, although there is some question as to the accuracy of this date, and Albert O.

Life was hard and difficult in this area during the Civil War as the Kansas Jayhawkers and Bushwhackers roamed the land freely preying on farmers, stealing crops and livestock and seemingly uncaring of the fate of the citizens of that area.

After the war ended it was necessary for William to hire out as a wagon master to pilot several wagon trains to California.[21] He had gone west several years before, looking for gold.[22] On the long journey, he allowed his beard to grow and since it was definitely reddish in color to many on the wagon train he became known as "Red Beard." Even though several wagon trains came under attack by Indians, neither of his were threatened.

As the first of his trains passed near Ft. Bridger, Wyoming, and into Utah, he began making plans. All wagon masters of that day were familiar with the story of the Mountain Meadow Massacre which occurred in southern Utah in 1857, when a joint attack of Piute Indians and Mormons dressed as Indians

---

[18] *U. S. Census - 1910, Garland County, Arkansas,* and dates on tombstone, Greenwood Cemetery, Hot Springs, Arkansas.

[19] Information from Alfred Ferguson with the Greenwood County, Kansas Historical Society, Inc., 5 March 1999.

[20] Life and Times of Leo McLaughlin Project, taped interview with Verne S. Ledgerwood by Felicia Denny, August 7, 1980. There were three cassette tapes of the interview of Ledgerwood. (Hereinafter cited as LAT Ledgerwood)

[21] LAT Ledgerwood, op cit.

[22] Ibid.

William "Red Beard" Ledgerwood
Courtesy of Dora Jane Ledgerwood Ellis

Dora Snell Ledgerwood
Wife of J.J. Ledgerwood and mother of Verne S. Ledgerwood

***J. J. Ledgerwood**, Father of Verne S. Ledgerwood,*
and Dora Jane Ledgerwood
Courtesy of Dora Jane Ledgerwood Ellis

attacked a train of sixty wagons. When the first charge came the wagons were circled and for four and one-half days the pioneers withstood attack after attack. The Mormons then donned their regular attire and appeared to the besieged under a white flag claiming to be intercessors. They told the travelers if they would give the Indians their livestock and wagons and hand over their weapons, the Mormons would escort them to safety at Cedar City. Running low on water and ammunition the emigrants made the fatal decision to lay down their arms and to comply with the offer. As soon as they were disarmed "every man from the wagon train was murdered and then every woman and every child deemed old enough to carry the tale" was turned over to the Indians to rape and butcher. This dastardly attack took the lives of over 120 people, who had primarily come from Marion, Crawford, Carroll and Johnson counties, Arkansas.[23]

An investigation revealed that a Mormon missionary named Parley Pratt had taken up with a woman named Eleanore McLean, wife of Hector McLean. The spurned Hector began tracking the two and killed Pratt near Van Buren, Arkansas. Word reached Salt Lake City of Pratt's murder and the first train entering Mormon territory happened to be the ill-fated one from Arkansas, and their revenge was taken on completely innocent people. Even though the Arkansas State Legislature and the U.S. Congress pressed to bring the killers to justice only one Mormon was ever tried and convicted. The individual was John D. Lee who had bargained with the emigrants for their arms and he appeared to have been sacrificed by the Salt Lake City authorities. And that was twenty years after the massacre. Lee was taken to Mountain Meadows, "seated on his own coffin and shot."[24] For several years wagon trains had avoided Utah, unless escorted by Federal troops.

William Ledgerwood did not intend to be surprised, and stopped his wagon train east of Salt Lake City. He sent an invitation to the titular head of the Mormon religion, Brigham Young. Young and a couple of his aides came to the encamped wagons and were treated to a fine supper. No doubt he could see that this was a very large group and all the men were heavily armed. "Red Beard" told his guests they were just passing through and hoped there would be no difficulty. They had a friendly supper and Brigham Young said he hoped their trip would be safe and uneventful. The train proceeded on to its

---

[23] A very good account of this tragedy is by Bob Lancaster and can be read in *Arkansas Times*, 15 September 1994, p. 40. In a Commentary to *The Arkansas Democrat-Gazette*, 10 October 1999, James A. Everett, entitled "Utah Massacre Still Has Hint of Hypocrisy," states that the Mormon Church, for several years following the massacre, presented bills to the United States Government for "the care of the surviving orphaned children."

[24] Ibid.

destination without trouble.[25]

While the five sons of William H. Ledgerwood were growing to manhood and running the farm, their mother, Permelia, was suffering from rheumatism, especially during the cold Kansas winters. Mrs. Ledgerwood became acquainted with an old Indian who lived in the area. He, too, had suffered from rheumatism and told her of the "wonderful hot springs in the mountains of Arkansas." He told how his aches and pains were greatly relieved by bathing in the hot waters emanating from the thermal springs. The Indian strongly recommended Permelia going there for a while.[26] He was a good salesman and William, who was between a couple of his wandering trips, bundled up his wife and two of the sons carried them by wagon to Eureka where they caught the Union Pacific Railroad to Pittsburgh, Kansas, transferring to the Kansas City Southern. At Van Buren, Arkansas they made connections to Little Rock and reached Malvern via the Iron Mountain Railroad. There they took the short ride to Hot Springs on "The Diamond Jo."

This was at a time before many of the bath houses had been built and many people bathed in the pools and the creek, which flowed down Valley (Central).[27] After several weeks at Hot Springs the Ledgerwoods returned to Kansas. Permelia very much rejuvenated and feeling quite fit. Her family was astonished and delighted. She began to tell them of the beauties of the wonderful mountain resort that had seemed so much alive with the many visitors from all over the world.

By 1888, the Ledgerwood clan was firmly established in Greenwood County, Kansas. But, they were struggling with the uncertainty of farming. One year it was too much rain. The next, not enough. Then when a good crop came in, the price of corn was so low that all of their labor seemed to have been in vain. They were discouraged. Especially John J. Ledgerwood. He believed there was a better life for his family somewhere else.

John J. Ledgerwood had married a local Kansas girl, Dora Snell, who had been born in Illinois. She had given birth to a son, Archie E., on 22 May 1885. Their second son, Vernal Snell Ledgerwood, was born 19 April 1889, just two months before the family decided to leave Kansas.[28]

This decision had come about as a result of a family meeting at which time the four boys expressed their disappointment with farming in general. Because

---

[25] Taped interview with Trice Ellis, Jr., and Dora Jane Ledgerwood Ellis, by Orval Allbritton, 2 July 1998.

[26] LAT Ledgerwood.

[27] Ibid., tape 1, side 1.

[28] LAT Ledgerwood and *Caruth Funeral Home Records,* Pub. Hot Springs, Arkansas 1989, p. 91.

the Ledgerwood family was so gregarious it was pretty much understood that what the majority wanted, all would agree. After much discussion it was decided to sell out and move to some place more pleasant and with better weather, but where? For several years Permelia had painted such beautiful word pictures of her trip to Hot Springs, it seemed a foregone conclusion that the mountain spa would be their destination. One of the boys was to remain behind until he could dispose of all land and buildings. The others loaded their wagons with furnishings and clothing and set off for Arkansas. They shipped the wagons and horses to Malvern and started overland toward Hot Springs, from that city, early one morning in 1889.

Approaching Hot Springs on the Malvern Road, near the present Hot Springs Country Club, John J. noticed a house for rent. A few days later he leased it and the Ledgerwoods settled in until other accommodations in town could be secured.

Church, School and Donuts

One of the first people Bridget McLaughlin met after arriving in Hot Springs was Father Patrick H. Garaghty, parish priest at St. Mary's Catholic Church. Bridget was a devout parishioner and had served in the church all of her life. She wanted her family to be faithful in their worship. Garaghty had come to this country with his parents from County Longford, Ireland.[1] He had been ordained to the ministry at Emmettsburg, Maryland, and had trained at Mt. St. Mary's Seminary. With his good looks, bright smile and wavy hair he became a common sight on the streets of early Hot Springs, as he sought new converts and members. Any Irish families arriving in the Spa could expect an early visit from the parish priest. An invitation to Mass and reminder of their religious obligation was generally sufficient to expect the errant church member to attend. Bridget steered the McLaughlin family into the life of the church and they became valued members.[2]

John Henry's grocery and feed business was booming to the point of his being unable to handle it alone. Since his children were to small too work, he wrote his younger brother Michael and offered him a job. Michael accepted the invitation and moved into the family home next to the store.

More children followed: James Russell, born in 1882; Leo Patrick, 5 June 1888; Stella Margaret, February 1890; Dorothy Irene, 28 February 1892; and George Joseph, 2 January 1894. Bridget now had eight children ranging in age from one to twenty. The two older boys, John William and James Russell, were worked into clerking in the growing grocery business. With John Henry's brother Michael, he had adequate help. Bridget was still struggling with all the household duties, cleaning, laundry and cooking for a house full of people. Help was forthcoming as a young Irish lass, Elizabeth "Bettie" Flanagan, who may have been a distant relative of the family, moved in about 1887 and became an important part of the household.[3] Both Bettie Flanagan and Michael McLaughlin were so well thought of by John Henry and Bridget McLaughlin they were named as God-parents at the christening of one of the subjects of this volume, Leo Patrick McLaughlin. The ritual was performed at St. Mary's by Father P. H. Garahty, 1 July 1888.[4]

When the McLaughlins arrived in Hot Springs in 1878 a concern of many of the local citizens was the lack of proper educational facilities. Several of the leading residents set about to solve the problem. Prior to this time

---

[1] *Centennial*, "A Century at St. Mary's," Hot Springs, Arkansas, 1969, p. 5.

[2] Ibid.

[3] *Spring's Directory of the City of Hot Springs - 1887.* Spring & Swazie, Publishers, St. Louis, p. 38.

[4] Records of St. Mary's Church, Hot Springs, Arkansas.

subscription schools had offered "reading, writing and arithmetic" courses. The Hot Springs Special School District was voted into being in 1881.[5] A school was opened in a renovated warehouse on Cottage Street. About this same time plans were being made by the Sisters of Mercy to start a school. The St. Mary's Academy was opened in 1882 on Whittington Avenue.[6] It was situated on a pie-shaped lot bounded by Walnut and Willow and adjacent to St. Mary's Convent.[7]

Without any objection from John Henry, Bridget started sending the children to St. Mary's. She believed they received better training in the parish school than public, and it was only ten or twelve blocks away. Probably her opinion began to change in the mid-1880s. Maybe not so much from a scholastic stand-point as one of danger. It seems as if several gunfights in the downtown sector of Hot Springs caused a number of citizens to worry about their children when passing through that area. Some of the fights were from drunken brawls and occurred around saloons and generally at night when no children were present. There were several, however, that happened in broad daylight and sent the entire city into an uproar.

St. Mary's Academy

The McLaughlin children attended school here.

---

[5] Mamie Ruth Abernathy, "History of Hot Springs Special School District # 6 of Garland County, 1881-1985," *The Record, 1985*.

[6] *Centennial*, "A History of St. Mary's."

[7] Sanborn-Perris Maps, Hot Springs, 1890, # 12.

One of the first involved a dentist, T.F. Linde, who was serving as both Mayor and Police Judge, and Charles Matthews, editor of *The Hot Springs Daily Hornet.* Mayor Linde was particularly upset with some crusty editorials written by Matthews accusing him of being "tough" on people who spit on the sidewalks or raced their horses down Central Avenue, but of being lax on enforcing laws against the gambling elements in town. Matthews was not armed when the two met on Central Avenue (then Valley Street), but that made little difference to Linde who began firing his pistol in the direction of the newspaperman. Matthews was hit by three bullets, one striking him in the wrist, and a wound to the shoulder, but he was still able to wrestle the pistol from the mayor. Linde, like the Boy Scouts, believed in being well-prepared, quickly produced a second revolver and began spraying the street with bullets striking a street peddler and a city councilman, who had come out of his store to see what was going on.[8] While the shooting caused a great deal of comment Mayor Linde was not removed from office or charged with the wounding of three men. It was treated as just another day in early Hot Springs.

T. F. Linde

The conflict with T.F. Linde did not frighten Charles Matthews from writing his very abrasive editorials and his next confrontation occurred on August 1, 1882, involving Dewitt C. Rugg, part-owner of the Arlington Hotel. Matthews, using the *Hornet's stinger,* had accused Rugg of paying a bribe to a man to testify before a United States Senate hearing that there were no hot water springs on the land the Arlington Hotel was built on since the government had claimed all land having such springs to be owned by the federal government. Matthews pointed out it was obvious to anyone walking down Central Avenue, (Valley) in those early days, they could observe water bubbling from the hillside and see vapors rising from the springs around the Arlington. Rugg, running into Matthews on Central Avenue a few days later, drew his pistol and took a shot at Matthews, but fortunately missed.

Matthews broadened his scatterload approach to the evils he perceived in Hot Springs and continued to attack D.C. Rugg and his partner Samuel W.

---

[8] *The Record* - 1993, "Charles Matthews: Editor with a Gun," Dale T. Schoenberger, reprint from *True West* magazine, January 1993.

Fordyce, a very powerful and wealthy man who also had an interest in the Arlington Hotel. Joining the duo of hotel men was the chief gambler in town, Frank Flynn, who operated The Office Saloon and had a gambling club in the Arlington. Flynn cared less that the Arlington was built on government land, but he was irate over charges by the editor concerning his gambling activities. Matthews referred to the three men as "the Arlington Gang."[9] That accusation was to cost him his life in a gunfight, again on Central Avenue, on September 22, 1882. Matthews was confronted by Sam Fordyce, who maintained his office in the Hot Springs Opera House, the two meeting near the DeSoto Valley Springs. Fordyce was carrying a club, some described it to be a heavy cane, as well as a gun. Fordyce began to strike Matthews with the club as Matthews tried to get out of the way and Fordyce tried to shoot the fleeing editor. Fordyce followed Matthews, continuing to strike him with the club. Finally Matthews, who had been knocked to the ground, was able to pull a pistol from his pocket, fired at Fordyce, but missed. An armed D.C. Rugg suddenly appeared on the scene and began to shoot at Matthews who retreated out into the street. Matthews turned his attention toward Rugg firing at his assailant and one shot hit Rugg, but was not fatal. Rugg, obviously in pain, began to holler, "He got me. Run him down boys, run him down." Matthews was also hit. Next on the scene was Frank Flynn who came out of his saloon carrying a long barrel pistol. He calmly leveled the gun across his arm to steady his aim and fired and Matthews, mortally injured, fell face down into the muddy street. Fordyce, Flynn, and Rugg were charged with manslaughter and tried separately. Flynn and Rugg, who had fired the fatal shots were acquitted. Fordyce, who had prompted the confrontation was fined two hundred dollars.[10] Life seemed cheap at Hot Springs in those early days!

Another gunfight became known as the Flynn-Doran war. This conflict occurred in the spring of 1884, but had its beginning two years before. Frank Flynn had settled in Hot Springs in the 1870s and through tough management and tactics, as a gambler toward anyone attempting to encroach on his "territory" became known as the "Boss Gambler." His principal site of gambling was The Office Saloon located on upper Central Avenue. Every gambling operation, no matter how big or small, had to have his sanction as he paid off city officials for the privilege of operating. His favors were known to be hard and expensive. When a newcomer by the name of Jim K. Lane opened two gambling clubs, The Monarch and the Palace, Flynn became a very unhappy individual.[11] He marched to Lane and ordered him to close within "twenty-four hours." Lane refused. The following day Flynn returned

---

[9] *Ibid.* Also, The Hot Springs *Daily Hornet*, 25 1882.
[10] Ibid.
[11] Mary D. Hudgins, "The Flynn-Doran Battle," *The Record* - 1973, p. 41.

22 September 1882

"The Arlington Gang" - including De Witt C. Rugg and Samuel W. Fordyce - guns down Hot Springs Daily Hornet *editor Charles Matthews over an editorial he had written*

with several men and proceeded to destroy much of Lane's gambling equipment. Since Flynn was backed by city authorities, Lane had no alternative but to close his clubs, and left town. But, he was not done.

Two years later, Lane met up with a tough and "totally courageous and honorable man," as described by Frank "Omaha" Borman, an opinion that others failed to share. The man was a former Confederate officer and gambler, Major S.A. Doran. He had been involved in gambling activities and had killed a young man, Eugene Whitfield, his landlord, at Memphis in 1880. Doran was next heard from when he became involved in a shooting scrape at Sherman, Texas, killing a policeman.[12] After hearing Lane's story, Doran offered to hire-on and reopen the gambling halls at Hot Springs which Lane still owned and were vacant. Lane accepted the offer. Arriving in Hot Springs Doran did as he had agreed. It was not long before he was approached by Frank Flynn who sized him up as being a man he could not bluff or intimidate. As it turned out, Flynn's impression was correct. Flynn offered to hire or pay-off Doran. Doran was polite, but refused the offer. From this point, things got worse, much worse, and tension began to mount. The two club operators began to hire gunmen out of the Southwest to act as dealers who worked around the gambling tables armed and with Winchester rifles within quick reach. Everyone was packing a gun. Flynn and Doran met on Central in one duel and exchanged shots. Doran was unhurt. Flynn was wearing a protective device referred to as a "coat of mail," and was struck in the chest causing him to "spit blood for several days."[13] A few days later Flynn and two of his men were discovered by the management of the Arlington Hotel to have set up a "snipers nest" in one of the hotel's front rooms overlooking one of Doran's saloons. Word quickly spread through the town and people wondered just how long the peace would hold?

The answer was not long in coming as one morning, Frank Flynn and two of his brothers, Billy and John, were riding on Central Avenue in a cab and as they passed the Monarch Club, several of the Dorans, brandishing Winchester rifles and shotguns, opened fire on the Flynns. The driver of the buggy was shot from his seat and killed and two gamblers were fatally shot. Frank Flynn and two bystanders, one a customer in a barber shop, were wounded. The Chief of Police, Thomas Toler, a fearless individual, arrived on the scene quickly, armed with a shotgun and a revolver, and arrested all the gamblers in sight. A vigilante group rounded up others and placed them on trains to Malvern, telling them not to come back.[14] One of the Doran gang, a gunman from Texas, Ed Howell, refused to leave town, which decision was a bad one

---

[12] *Daily Arkansas Gazette*, 10 February 1884, p. 1.

[13] Ibid., p. 49.

[14] Ibid., p. 50.

In February 1884, gamblers Frank Flynn and his brothers, Billy and John, are ambushed by Major S.A. Doran and his men on Central Avenue. Three men were killed in what became known as the Flynn-Doran War.

on his part. He began to brag to his friends that he intended to shoot Chief Toler on sight. Word quickly reached Toler who knew Howell hung out around the Opera House Bar. He went there and waited for Howell to appear. When he did Toler shot him dead. The inquest ruled the killing as justifiable.

A few years later, on 16 March 1899, the granddaddy of all street gunfights took place on Central, a few doors north of Cartwright's Corner (Spencer's). Even the fabled "Shootout at the O.K. Corral" in Tombstone, Arizona a few years earlier, at which three men were killed, paled in comparison. In fact, there were two gunfights that day in the Spa, both involving police officers and county deputies. The first was harmless and caused no damage, but scattered several visitors and townspeople who were out and about on the street near Mobb's (Schneck's) Drug store. The friction was naturally over control of gambling and an upcoming mayor's election.

In the second fray that day, which occurred in front of Lemp's Beer Depot near where the Marquette Hotel is located, Police Chief Tom Toler, Sergeant Thomas Goslee, Detective Jim Hart, of the police department and Johnny O. Williams, son of sheriff R.L. Williams, and Lewis Hinkle, bartender and beer-wagon driver, were killed. Ed Spear, a part-time deputy, had his throat slashed from ear to ear and two bystanders were wounded by stray shots.[15] Spear and Chief Deputy Coffey Williams, the sheriff's brother, accounted for three of the dead, Sheriff Bob Williams a fourth. It was a volatile happening, and reports widely circulated by the newspapers shocked the entire country. Again, no one was convicted of any of the killings.

The killings and shootings on the main thoroughfare in Hot Springs were not well-received by the many business people who had devoted so much energy and money in advertising that the Spa was a safe and wonderful place. Following the deadly gunfight, visitors in the Spa headed for the trains in droves. Assurances from the city fathers that "everything was alright and there was nothing to worry about," did little good to stem their departure, as most people believed that anywhere that gun battles between law enforcement officers took place was somewhere to avoid. It also was not good news to the parents of children who traversed Central Avenue on their way to and from school. Bridget would rethink her decision to send her children to St. Mary's.[16]

---

[15] For a full review of this tragedy read Orval E. Allbritton's, "City Drenched in Blood," in *The Record - 1996*, or a two-part series in *The Sentinel-Record*, Hot Springs, Arkansas,16-17 March 1999, based on the same article. Amazingly, Ed Spear recovered from his throat being slashed and lived fifty more years.

[16] It is known from an old photograph taken about 1896 and reproduced in the Sentinel-Record. 29 June 1936, that Will and Leo McLaughlin attended St. Mary's along with other well known Spa residents Holden Blahut, Ed B. Mooney and Vince Picchi. St. Mary's was sold to a Negro organization, The Royal Circle of Friends, to be used as a sanitarium for "destitute Negroes," *Sentinel-Record*, 1 November 1921.

John Coffee Williams

Johnny O. Williams
(Son of Sheriff R.L. Williams)

Courtesy of Mark Palmer

By 1889 John Henry McLaughlin had acquired most of the block on Malvern Avenue between Church and Creek Streets. When he opened his business eleven years before, his store and a cobbler's at the south end of the block had been the only commercial undertakings for over a block. Gradually, he had been able to purchase a couple of small dwellings and two shot-gun houses. He had these razed and erected several rental buildings for businesses. By 1890 they were occupied by a meat market, a saloon and a variety store.[17]

Malvern Avenue was changing by leaps and bounds. New businesses were locating there. A large new hotel, The Park, was constructed, plush enough to rival the Arlington and Eastman. It was equipped with bowling alleys, a casino, and a wonderful dance floor. The Armour Packing Company erected a large building at the edge of the railroad yard, equipped with walk-in ice boxes. Two furniture stores moved to the area, each claiming to have the largest and most modern stock in the state. Several building craft supply houses located there, a plumbing, and an electrical and a painting supply house opened. With the influx of new business two restaurants arrived and naturally a couple of saloons to slake the thirst of workmen getting off work. The Peoples Steam Laundry, employing fifty workers, built a modern plant less than a block from John Henry's store. These new businesses replaced several saloons, where nightly drunken brawls occurred and a couple of houses of prostitution. One of those had been operated several years at Malvern and Gulpha and was run

[17] Sanborn-Perris Maps, February 1890, #10.

16 March 1889 – Another street gunfight, this time between the police department and sheriff's office over the control of gambling, resulted in the deaths of five men

by Gracie Lane, a madam, who was the wife of Jim Lane, owner of the Monarch and Palace saloons located on Central.[18] When Frank Flynn ran Jim Lane out of town, Gracie closed her establishment and followed her husband to New Orleans. The so-called cleaning-up of the neighborhood and all the new business on Malvern Avenue reflected that the wheels of commerce were spinning for the people of Hot Springs.

As his business increased, so did his wealth. John Henry McLaughlin's name appeared in the top third of a ranking of "one hundred citizens who own two thirds of all the real estate in the city."[19] With his family increasing, his brother Michael, and housekeeper Bettie living with them, he was being urged by Bridget to seek larger and more comfortable living quarters. Besides, Bridget was not happy with the number of saloons operating in the neighborhood, some of which stayed open late into the night. Drunken brawls and even shootings sometimes disturbed their sleep. She especially was not pleased when a noted Hot Springs madam, Josie Belmont and her girls, moved into a rooming house only one-half a block from their store. Belmont, a divorcee from Georgia, had been low-key with her activities at first, working alone. Then she hired several young girls who identified themselves to the census taker as being "seamstress and dress-makers" while Josie brazenly listed her own occupation in the city directory as "Madam."[20]

There seemed to be no doubt as to what was going on with men entering the building at all hours of the day and night. You didn't have to draw a diagram for Bridget. She had growing and inquisitive sons and she wanted to move them away from the temptations of the neighborhood. With her imploring, John Henry McLaughlin conceded the house had become crowded and they began looking for a new home. Toward the turn of the century, the McLaughlins bought a large plot of land on the southwestern part of the wide intersection of Malvern and Grand. There were some tenant houses on the property fronting on Grand that would remain for several years but John Henry began to build a large two-story frame home well back from the street and on a hill. It was to be one of the finest in that section of town.

The appearance of Hot Springs to the Ledgerwood family in 1889 must have been totally different from the impression the McLaughlins had of it in 1878. The scars from the devastating fire in the downtown area were healed and

---

[18] U. S. Census - 1880, Garland County, D-119, and *Hot Springs City Directory* 1883-1884, p. 94.

[19] *Daily Sentinel*, Hot Springs, 4 May 1889.

[20] *Maloney Directory - Hot Springs - 1897, and U. S. Census - 1900,* Hot Springs Township, City of Hot Springs, Ward - 2. Josie Belmont operated her house of prostitution on Malvern for several years. Finally about 1909 she moved her girls to the West End Club at the end of Whittington Avenue where she reigned for several years.

covered over. On some streets electric lights had appeared, replacing the old gaslights. Many new buildings had arisen from the ashes to project a view of a modern city. Quite imposing was the Army and Navy Hospital which had been built by the Federal Government and which sat high on a hill looking down on the business district. On upper Central Avenue was the Opera House, a magnificent structure. On its stage appeared many of the name performers of that day. Political rallies and speeches were delivered from its broad stage. William Jennings Bryan, "The Silver-Throated Orator," a frequent visitor to the Spa, made several rousing speeches, his clear voice resonating to the highest balcony seats. School graduating classes proudly trooped across the stage receiving their awards and diplomas. And it was within this building that the Assemblies of God first organized.

And there had been other improvements. The trolley lines had been extended and were electric. Gas and water lines were buried beneath many of the streets and shortly, the government began building an archway over Hot Springs Creek, which was completed in 1884 and was a help with the frequent flooding problems and reduced the unpleasant odors emanating from the stream.

As the Ledgerwood men looked around for employment they could scarcely miss the competitions of the various businesses of the city. This was evident from the advertisements of several general merchandise stores. Simon Mendel and his brother, owners of the Queen City Store, proclaimed, "We are driving prices way down to rock bottom." R.A. Cartwright's Globe Store countered and stressed at his establishment "a great reduction in all clothing lines." J.A. Townsend seemly apologized that his store was moving to another location and would favor the buyer as "I have determined for the next two months, to give a real benefit to all customers," by reducing prices. It certainly seemed to be a buyers market, but it so often does.[21]

But the competitive spirit did not stop with the food and clothing stores, it even infected the newspapers of the city as they vied for patronage. *The Hot Springs Daily Sentinel's* editor, J.G. Higgins, claimed to be the "only paper in the City receiving daily a telegraphic news report." J.L. Wadling, editor of *The Hot Springs Daily News*, put a guilt trip on the political leanings of people by saying his paper was "the leading Democratic paper in the City of Hot Springs and County of Garland." T.K. Kimbell, owner and editor of *The Hot Springs Daily Graphic*, in effect said "us, too," as he stressed his paper was "Democratic in politics," and seemed to indicate it really was not important as his paper always did a "superior job."[22]

John J. Ledgerwood and his family did not tarry very long in the rental

---

[21] *Hot Springs Daily News*, 22 December 1887 and many other issues.

[22] Charles Cutter, *Cutter's Guide*, - Hot Springs - 1890.

dwelling on the Malvern Road. He did not have any desire to farm any longer and intended to get a job or make one for himself in town. John J. and his brother James E. bought a bakery on upper Central Avenue, but shortly would move it to 222 Ouachita, where they remained for several years. The building on Ouachita was a two-story frame building with the bakery located on the ground floor. A widow, Mrs. Sammons, rented an apartment on the second floor. John and James became long time partners, and employed their brother, Albert O., as a baker, for several years. A fourth brother, David opened and operated The Plateau Barber Shop for a number of years.[23]

As stated previously, the Ledgerwood family tended to be clannish, working and playing together. Just how much is demonstrated by how close they chose to live together. Albert lived at 612 Orange Street, John J.'s family was at 610 Orange, and James at 608. Brother David was just down the street and around the corner on Woodbine. Father William and Mother Permelia, resided with John J. and Dora S., and their three sons, Archie, Verne, and Cecil, who was the only son born in Hot Springs a couple of years after they arrived in the Spa City.[24]

While the bakery business was very competitive, the energetic brothers were successful in their operations and were able to expand by buying out the City Bakery at 648 Central Avenue. That bakery was in a high traffic area of the city. The brothers were quick to capitalize on its location and opened, in connection with the bakery, a grocery and a confectionery.[25] They widened their business interests when they began to bottle and distribute carbonated drinks, cider, ginger-ale and mineral water under the name of *Red Lythia Water.*[26] The biggest break for the Ledgerwoods came shortly after the turn of the century when the two brothers signed with an Atlanta-based company the right to bottle and distribute its little known product--Coca-Cola--which became an instant hit in the area as well as all over the world.[27] The future looked bright for John and James.

The two brothers suffered a considerable setback, by fire, at their business on Ouachita Friday 22 February 1895. The following morning's paper reported, "The fire originated in the bakery of *Ledgerwood Bro's., on Ouachita Avenue, from one of the ovens becoming too hot.*"[28] It proved to be a disastrous happening as the building and contents burned to ashes before the fire

---

[23] *Mahoney's Hot Springs City Directory - 1897,* p. 102.

[24] Ibid.

[25] *Hemming Directory Co.'s Vol I, Hot Springs City Directory - 1903,* p. 210, and other sources.

[26] Ibid., p. 19.

[27] LAT Ledgerwood. Verne Ledgerwood stated that his father allowed him to bottle the first bottle of Coca-Cola in Hot Springs. He was a teenager.

[28] *Hot Springs Sentinel,* 23 February 1895, p. 1.

department arrived. The fire was driven by strong winds, spreading to the adjacent Tennessee Wagonyard, owned by C. Rugg, and consuming its barn and stables. Before the fire fiend was extinguished three people died and over twenty-five buildings were destroyed. Mayor R.L. Williams lost several business rentals and six cottages.[29]

Naturally, John J. and James felt remorse over the fire, much beyond their own loss. But this was in an age when people were understanding that fires and accidents did occur. It was not a very litigious society. And besides, this musically talented family had contributed to the excitement, enjoyment and pleasure of the community by organizing the Ledgerwood Bro's Band. This group played concerts in the park, for parades, at political rallies and other functions. They met and practiced on the second floor of the bakery. Three of the brothers, John J., James E., and Albert O., played one or more instruments in the band. It generally had between sixteen and twenty players and was accorded to be the first organized band in Hot Springs. A music teacher, H.M. Morris, was hired to work in the bakery and became the leader of the band and was known all over town as "Professor."

As the small children of the Ledgerwood family reached school age they were shuttled off to school. Archie, Verne, Cecil, cousins Hugh, Fay, and Ruth probably all attended Quapaw School, which was only a few short blocks from their homes. Quapaw was a two-story frame building located between Market and Chapel Streets and hosted grades one through eight.

If Vernal Ledgerwood and Leo Patrick McLaughlin had never previously met, they certainly did in 1904 as both were in the ninth grade at Central School. This school was located at Garden and Laurel Streets two or three blocks east of Malvern. In more recent years the land was occupied by Goldstein School. Central was the first brick school in the district and was two stories high.

Since Hot Springs was not a large place in 1904, it is possible that the two boys were already acquainted. Both were interested in athletics and they could have seen each other at one of the major league baseball exhibition games in the spring when the teams were here training. Or they may have come into contact while driving one of the delivery wagons for their fathers' business. Leo loved horses all his life and preferred the delivery wagon to clerking in the store. Verne on the other hand preferred running the bottling equipment, but made deliveries when needed. The course, thus was set and these two were destined to a closer and much better acquaintance.

---

[29] Ibid.

Calamity, Athletics and Graduation

It was only six or seven blocks from where Verne Ledgerwood lived on Orange Street to Central School on Garden, but was referred to as being "across town." It was rather a nice walk on a warm autumn or spring day, but it was a beastly one in bad weather. The school wasn't on a car line, the nearest being on Malvern Avenue, and if one rode the trolley there still remained a three block walk. Most kids walked and it became a social time and one of getting acquainted. Everyone carried books and a lunch pail or sack with sandwiches. While there was a rule about not leaving campus, it was not always followed. Leo McLaughlin sometimes ran down to his father's store and made a sandwich from bologna or ham and ate with his brothers Will and Russell. But, there was a danger in doing this. If his dad and brothers were extra busy he would be given the job of making a delivery and he would be late getting back to class. Some teachers were understanding, others were not. Verne Ledgerwood would sometimes steal away to the bakery on Central to eat, and he generally had no difficulty in getting back on time. He was a good student and most of the teachers liked Verne and gave him a little extra latitude. As freshmen they had not begun to be noticed much by the other students as perhaps being a bit above average. On Saturdays, like other boys their age, Leo and Verne were expected to work in the family business.

The month of February 1905 had been extremely cold, with sleet, snow, freezing rain and frigid winds whistling down the canyons and valleys of the Spa. But by the twenty-third of the month the bad weather seemed to moderate and there was a promise that spring might not be too far away. The streets were busy, hotels were filling up and the Spa was gearing up for a winter-spring season that promised to be a record setter. Then, out of the blue, calamity struck the bustling town once again.

About 3:45 in the early morning hours of 15 February 1905 a fire started in the Grand Central Hotel, a large two-story frame structure on Chapel Street, just to the rear of the Central Methodist Church. Strong winds swept the blaze across the street, igniting boarding, rooming houses and private dwellings.[1] The flames engulfed the Methodist Church, a structure designed with stores at ground level fronting onto Central with the sanctuary on the second level. This was where Dora Ledgerwood took her family to church. The flames then leaped Central Avenue catching a building just south of the Whittington Stearns Building and burned south as far as Plateau and South Border, and east along Oak and Elm (Broadway). As the flames ignited one building after another and raced southward, Garland County Sheriff R.L. "Bob" Williams realized the jail and county court house were in its path. He made

[1] *The Hot Springs Daily News*, 16 February 1905.

arrangements to transfer the twenty-seven prisoners to the city jail.[2] Through quick thinking, Williams was able to save the county's tax records. Both jail and court house were burned to the ground and some county records were lost forever. Sweeping north and west the flames gobbled up Quapaw School, nearly all the commercial buildings on Ouachita, and many residences on Orange and Hawthorne. The devastation and damage was unbelievable. Block after block was leveled and turned into debris and ashes. The flames did not discriminate between the rich and the poor: it wiped out everything in its path, and was not extinguished for five hours. Some of the city's finest residences went up in smoke that morning. Bernard Gross, the mortician, Dr. R.H. Taylor, Dr. A.F. Sanders, Dr. F.A. Peak, Dr. Leonard Ellis, Dr. Rodgers, Sheriff R.L. Williams and Frank Flynn, the old gambler, all lost beautiful and spacious homes.

The city was stunned. *The Sentinel-Record* headlines read, "Acres of Ruins," and the *Hot Springs Daily News* proclaimed, "Appalling Calamity, One-Fourth of City Destroyed By Fire This Morning in Four Short Hours."

More than a thousand persons were left without a place to sleep or rest. Many had barely escaped being trapped by the raging flames and had only the clothes upon their backs. Sadly, there were a few who had not escaped and perished in the intensity of the fire.[3]

The Ledgerwood family suffered heavy losses. The building housing the bakery on Ouachita and its contents were destroyed and very little was saved by John and James. David E. lost his barber shop and its contents at 713 Central. Both James and John lost their residences on Orange.[4] David lost his on Woodbine. Like a thousand others, they, too, were homeless.

Mayor George R. Belding called a meeting at the City Auditorium of city officials and people of the community. He appointed a relief committee and asked C.N. Rix, President of the Arkansas National Bank to be the financial chairman, a wise choice. Rix agreed.[5]

An appeal was made by the mayor to those who had not suffered loss. "On account of the appalling disaster in our midst, I ask all citizens to throw their homes, boarding houses and hotels open to those unfortunates free of charge, who are without protection and without shelter, until arrangements can be made for their comforts."[6]

The response was heart warming. Several of the lodges--Odd Fellows, Knights of Pythias and Woodmen of the World--invited the homeless to avail

---

[2] Ibid., col. 5. The jail and court house were on Oak Street where the old Hot Springs Central High was built in 1915, is located.

[3] Ibid., p. 1, col. 5.

[4] *The Sentinel-Record*, 28 February 1905, p. 4.

[5] Ibid., 26 February 1905, p. 1.

[6] *Hot Springs Daily News*, 27 February 1905, p. 1.

themselves of their meeting facilities in which to stay for a short time. William Shannon, with the Essex Park Racetrack and also part owner of the Kentucky Club, said their buildings were open to those needing to get out of the weather. Mr. Condon, Manager at Oaklawn Park said, "Us, too."[7]

Donations poured in to the relief committee in torrents. Mr. Augustus Busch, chairman of the Anheuser-Busch Brewing Company, gave $1,000. Not to be out-done by its competitor, Pabst Brewing Company also gave $1,000. Then Busch raised the ante, donating another $500. Oaklawn Park gave $500. The gambling clubs opened their purses, The Southern Club, Arkansaw Club, and the Kentucky Club, each gave $500, and the Indiana Club $250. All the large hotels responded: the Eastman, the Waverly, and the Arlington, each donated $250; and the Waukesha $200. Individuals and churches contributed. The John Henry McLaughlin family, never known for being very charitable, donated $50 in groceries.[8]

After the first shock passed, people began to seek temporary housing until their homes could be rebuilt. Some camped out alongside West Mountain in tents provided by the Army-Navy Hospital and some sent by Governor Jeff Davis from National Guard stores. The Ledgerwoods were part of this group for awhile.[9]

Only two days passed from the date of the fire until cleaning up of the debris and rebuilding began. One paper reported, "Phoenix-like [a bird of mythology which raised from its ashes] a new and greater Hot Springs promises to rise from the gray ashes that now mark the site of hundreds of homes and business houses. The sound of the hammer and saw were heard in the burned district yesterday morning."[10]

J.H. McLaughlin had to admit his thirty year-old son had been right. For sometime Will had been trying to convince his father he needed to diversify the business. Will had become tired of the grocery business. It took long and hard hours of work to run the business. Being the eldest son he was expected to open the store at 5:30 in the morning. That was in time to catch some of the early laundry workers who would stop and buy nick-knacks and sandwich meats for their lunches. Too, the farmers from east of town arrived early with their fresh produce or freshly butchered beef or pork.

Will had made a study and comparison of the grocery business to others. He saw that the employees of other businesses, in many cases, did not have to report for work until 8:00, and none put in the late hours that were necessary in the grocery business. His father was slow to adapt to Will's idea. After all,

---

[7] Ibid.

[8] Ibid., p. 1, col. 3.

[9] Trice Ellis, Jr. and Dora Jane Ledgerwood Ellis, 2 July 1998.

[10] *The Sentinel-Record*, 28 February 1905, p. 1, col. 1.

raising horses and the grocery business was all he knew. Will pointed out that there was considerable loss in handling produce. Potatoes had to be turned and if one tuber was going bad it had to be thrown away before it affected the others. The ice boxes of that day kept fresh meat only a few days and it was sometimes necessary to discount some that was beginning to turn color. A snag or tear in a sugar or meal sack could mean a loss of profit. Hardware, on the other hand he told his father had a long shelf life and normally did not lose its value. It certainly didn't take the time or care that fresh produce took. J.H. was unconvinced, but permitted Will and Russell to clean out a corner of the store and to buy some items on a trial basis. Will stocked the corner with kegs of nails, hardware cloth, strap hinges, nuts and bolts, that he knew farmers used, tools of various kinds and some leather harness, such as plow reins and horse collars. In the feed shed, he kept sheets of metal roofing and screen wire. Gradually the farmers began to buy some of their tools and needs at McLaughlin's. When they asked for something he didn't have, Will immediately ordered it. John Henry looked on with an interested, but doubting eye. Then, the big fire struck. Three of the hardware stores on Ouachita Avenue--R.E. Johnson, T.G. Evans and Hamp Williams--were wiped out.[11] The need for tools and building material in the city was immediate and at an all time high. John Henry watched as people trooped in and out buying up the hammers, saws and other tools and all of the building material. No longer in doubt, the green light was turned on for Will to order more stock by his approving father. John Henry would not turn loose of his grocery business, but he was now totally supportive of Will in his hardware endeavor.

The fire had scattered the Ledgerwood family who had lived so near each other. The bakeries were relocated at 321 Ouachita and 744 Central. John and James had rebuilt their bottling plant at 506 Orange Street and had purchased more modern equipment. John J. built a new, roomy two-story house at 215 Woodbine. James moved out on south Central near the city limits. David moved to 615 Ouachita and had located his barber shop opposite from the one that burned on Central. Albert O. still worked at the bakery and had moved his family near Sixth and Garland, in South Hot Springs.[12]

Two of the brothers ventured into local politics. David was elected City Treasurer, a job that permitted him to continue his barber trade. John J., a man of great common sense, had been persuaded by a number of people in the First Ward to run for the city council and he was elected alderman.[13]

When school opened in the fall of 1907, there seemed to be something a bit

---

[11] Ibid., p. 1, cols. 5-6.

[12] Polk's *Hot Springs City Directory - 1905-1906*, p. 176.

[13] Ibid., p. 19.

special about the class destined to graduate the following spring. The faculty was quick to recognize and acknowledge the intelligence of the group and urged them on to greater accomplishments. The class had started the year with a total of twenty-four students but dropped to twenty-two shortly, eighteen girls and four boys.[14] Leo McLaughlin and Vernal Ledgerwood composed half of the boys; Granville Burrow and Myron Townsend, the other half. Remember, this was in an era when it was thought a sixth or seventh grade education was sufficient. It was considered alright for fifteen and sixteen year-old boys to drop out of school and get a job and help support their families. No stigmatism was attached to such an action.

No one in the McLaughlin family had gone to school more than eight years. Leo's older brothers, Will and Russell, had dropped out to start working full time in the family business. His two older sisters, Mary Anna and Elizabeth, both destined to be old maids and who today might be considered to be couch-potatoes because of their inactivity, had quit school after St. Mary's. Leo probably was motivated to stay in school for three reasons. First, he never really enjoyed clerking in the store and preferred other activities to escape having to spend his time there. Second, he was enjoying activities at school, especially athletics. And, finally, he wanted to do something with his life beside shop-keeping and he needed time to figure out what?

Verne Ledgerwood had his eyes set on a goal and was motivated to remain in school. His sights were set higher than the bakery or bottling works. He was also good at athletics and enjoyed the competition they afforded. He, unlike Leo, had a plan. He wanted to study law, not as many men did by working in a law office and learning from another lawyer. He wanted to go to law school after graduating from high school. Besides, this was a fun-time and a fun class to be in. Even the class-adopted yell proclaimed its push toward graduation.[15]

Class Yell

"It's hurry or worry!
No time to wait!
Either flurry or scurry!
This class of '08!
Ever foremost - hard to excel
Too busy graduatin'
To stop to yell."

Verne and Leo were involved in nearly all school activities, except Girl's

---

[14] *The Thermometer - 1908*, p. 37. The beginning enrollment is given on p. 30. A group picture shows twenty-two and a *Sentinel-Record*, article, 21 October 1951 lists twenty-two.

[15] Ibid.

Glee Club, and they were even roped into one of their productions. They were Business Managers for the first school annual, *The Thermometer - '08*. Verne was secretary of the Hot Springs High School Athletics Association and captain of the baseball team. His cousin Hugh, a well-liked junior, was captain of both the football and basketball teams.

Leo was President of the Senior Class, and was known to many of his acquaintances as "Irish," a hint as to his family's origin. In a class play, "The Spinsters Return," performed on the stage of the City Auditorium, by the Girls Glee Club, Leo was persuaded to play a role, "Professor Dinkenspiel," and Verne played "His Assistant."[16]

However, it was in football that Central High stood out, even though this was only the second year for that sport. Seven games were played and Hot Springs won five and lost two, one to Little Rock, 6-5. Three of the games won were against colleges, Ouachita, Henderson and Hendrix.[17] Since the school had no field the home games were played at the Arkansas State Fairgrounds on south Central.

McLaughlin was acclaimed the best fullback in the state. Leo was nearly six feet tall and weighed a solid 186 pounds, far more than most linemen he had to charge through.[18] Verne Ledgerwood ran the team from the quarterback post and was declared, "the fastest quarterback in the association."[19]

The game of basketball was introduced to the city of Hot Springs on 31 December 1907, News Year's Eve night, at the Bijou Skating Rink at Central and Olive[20]. The referee was none other than the great baseball player destined for the Hall of Fame, Honus Wagner. It had come about by a trip made to Little Rock by three Hot Springs students, Verne and Cecil Ledgerwood, who was a sophomore, and Elbert Fulton, a junior. Verne had heard about a game to be played in Little Rock one Saturday early in December. He told his father, John J., of their interest in going and Mr. Ledgerwood encouraged them. Giving them some money he said, "If it looks like a game the school might be interested in, then buy a ball and a couple of goals." The boys brought the equipment back home. Immediately after the last football game was played that year basketball practice began. Once again Ledgerwood and McLaughlin were in the thick of things. Verne played what now is known as point-guard or play maker. Leo, the tallest player on the team, played center. Twelve games were played and the local five lost only to Hendrix College.

Leo McLaughlin was proclaimed by *The Thermometer* as being "the best all-

---

[16] Ibid., p. 70.

[17] Ibid., p. 77.

[18] Statistics on height and weight obtained from Department of Veterans Affairs, file XC-21-231-799 - Leo Patrick McLaughlin.

[19] *The Thermometer '08*, article by Edward Buchanan, p. 77.

[20] Ibid.

around athlete in the State," describing his football and basketball accomplishments and those at a track meet held in Little Rock.

The publication also listed Verne's accomplishments and called him "the best guard in the State" and called attention to "his clear head work and foresight at quarter-back." One could certainly make a case that the editorial staff of *The Thermometer* was biased in their praise of McLaughlin and Ledgerwood. But, while it is conceded that the publication flowered-up the athletic prowess of the two young men, they must have been exceptional in their ability to learn and master new games just being introduced to this area.

But school was not all academics and sports, although they were a major part. There was quite a social life, a whirl of parties and picnics at Castle or Riverside Parks and fun evenings riding the Leapy-Dip and other carnival rides at Whittington Park, or roller-skating at the Bijou Rink. There were movies and live productions at the Airdome Theater off of Prospect, where you could cheer the hero and hiss the villain. A fun afternoon could be spent with a visit to Happy Hollow. Norman McLeod, the owner, had made a living catering to the visitors and town folks alike with his live donkeys, bear and oxen. A few cents would provide a lifetime memory in the form of one of his posed photographs. And, of course, girl dating! Because of the high ratio of girls to boys, the competition between the fairer sex for attention from the males must have been rather fierce. Some senior girls gave up on dating a senior boy and looked to the class below.

McLaughlin--tall, dark, and handsome--had many admirers. Even in high school, he was the best-dressed young man with cardigan sweaters and pleated trousers. Ledgerwood was always neat and with his wavy hair was a favorite of the girls. He conceded McLaughlin's edge over the other boys, and once remarked, "Leo was tough competition with the gals."[21] Before the school year was over Leo and "Pretty Peggy" Estelle Holland were an item. Peggy's father was a real estate agent in the Spa. In the Senior Limerick column a clue was dropped as it read, "As big, as a giant, handsome too, As a lawyer, some day, Peggy he'll woo."[22]

At the start of his last year Verne was drawn to a new Senior who had just moved in to the area from Texas, Mathilde Chimene. She was described as having dark dreamy eyes which held Verne "in a spell."[23] They spent considerable time together until mid-semester.

But late in the school year Verne was to meet the love of his life, a freshman, Bess Wakelin. He told the story that one day the students were lined up to enter the building. Verne was wearing a small beanie-cap with an insignia on

---

[21] Ibid.

[22] *The Thermometer '08*, p. 36.

[23] Ibid.

it. All of a sudden, a cute, slender built girl flashed by on a dare from some of her classmates and grabbed the beanie. All the students roared in laughter at the prank. It took Verne a couple of seconds to regain his composure and he took off after the girl and quickly overhauled her and recovered his cap. He told the girl, "You do that again and I am going to paddle you." Predictably, a few days later, the same girl grabbed his cap and once more he chased her and ran her down. Before the eyes of twenty or thirty students he proceeded to paddle the girl. That evening, Verne told his mother about the incidents and that he had paddled her. Dora was not pleased with her son's action and reprimanded him. "You go apologize to that girl and bring her by, I want to meet her."[24] Verne thought his mother made this last request to make certain that he had made the apology.

Verne, who had great respect for both his parents, did as his Mother requested and brought Bess Wakelin by their home. "My mother had always wanted a daughter and that was the darnest thing I ever saw," Ledgerwood said. "They immediately hit it off and became close friends." After Bess had left, Dora Ledgerwood told her son, "This is it, this is it. There's no need for you to look any further, that's the girl for you, and don't you let her get away." Verne said he certainly wasn't ready to get married, but he and Bess corresponded while he was away in college and he began to see some of the qualities in her that his mother had first spotted.[25]

Bess Wakelin was an all-state player. She is second from left.

Courtesy of Dora Jane Ledgerwood Ellis

---

[24] LAT Ledgerwood.

[25] Ibid.

Shortly before graduation, Leo McLaughlin confided to Vernal Ledgerwood he was undecided about what he was going to do after school ended. Leo knew he was expected to work in the family grocery, but he did not want to wind up as a clerk or a store owner. He indicated to Verne an interest in studying law. Ledgerwood invited him to go to the University of Arkansas the following fall and room with him. He told Leo he planned to attend Fayetteville one year to get his pre-law courses and the following year intended to transfer to Tulane University in New Orleans, because the law school was touted to be the finest in the South.[26] Leo agreed to the plan.

In the second semester, the Class of 1908 moved from the crowded Central School with other high school classes into a new building on Oak Street that was still under construction. Late in May 1908, with the new auditorium still bare of seating, twenty-two seniors marched across the stage at the City Auditorium and received their diplomas. "But we were the first class to graduate from the new building," Verne Ledgerwood said. It had been a roller-coaster year--it had gone so quickly and they perhaps felt a bit sad as Longfellow once expressed it, "Nothing now is left but majestic memories."

[26] Ibid.

College Versus Politics

The fall of 1908 found Vernal S. Ledgerwood and Leo P. McLaughlin entering the University of Arkansas at Fayetteville. It was not an easy trip from Hot Springs to the northwestern part of the state where the university was located. Via train it was necessary to go to Little Rock, transfer to Van Buren and lastly to Fayetteville. Travel by road was long and tedious and generally took two days. That was out of the question for busy students trying to squeeze a long weekend for a visit home. Besides, neither owned an automobile.

Because the two young Hot Springs men did not intend to attend the University of Arkansas but one year, their major was unlisted and only the general courses of study were selected. They were enrolled as "special students."[1]

Ledgerwood adapted to college life very quickly. Leo McLaughlin did not: he was miserable. He was not happy with his surroundings or courses of study and he may have even been a bit homesick. After two weeks, following a sleepless night, Leo told Verne, "I'm dropping out of college and going home. I want to go down and see if I can get into politics."

Ledgerwood had been aware of Leo's discomfort for the past two weeks and tried to encourage his roommate. "Leo, if you go home now you'll blow a chance to get an education, why don't you give it another chance?"

McLaughlin was firm, "My mind is made up. Besides, I can get an education later."

"But, of course," Ledgerwood would later recall, "He never did."[2]

Verne Ledgerwood completed his freshman year at Fayetteville. He came home in the spring and worked in the bottling plant that summer. Leo McLaughlin had left him without a roommate but he knew he had one for the coming college year.

Allen Thurman Davies was a junior in high school when Verne graduated and he had just finished school when Ledgerwood came back to Hot Springs for the summer. Davies' father, R.G. Davies, had come to Hot Springs in the mid-1870s, and set up a law practice. He had lived at Sunnyside Plantation near Lake Village, Arkansas and still had family there. As an attorney of

---

[1] Letter from Cassandra McCraw, Reading Room Supervisor, University Libraries Special Collections, University of Arkansas, 17 July 1998, in response to an inquiry by the author. Many publications and articles about Leo P. McLaughlin made the same error in assuming he graduated from the university instead of staying "only two weeks." Local historians as Dr. Scully and Mary Hudgins gave credence to McLaughlin having graduated from that institution. They were in good company as *The Kansas City Star* and *Colliers Magazine* erroneously credited him in having obtained a law degree, just to mention a few.

[2] LAT Ledgerwood.

considerable ability, he had been one of the lawyers selected to draw up the first Charter for the City of Hot Springs in 1876.[3] Davies was elected as the first city attorney for the city of Hot Springs and had been a member of the vigilante group that herded the gamblers onto trains and ordered them not to return following the Flynn-Doran clash.[4]

A.T. Davies had been given the nickname "Sunny" in high school, possibly because he talked so much about the plantation in south Arkansas. Later, in adult life the nickname changed to "Sonny." Sonny and Verne had become close personal friends in high school. They had made careful plans concerning their advanced legal education and even that they wanted to be law partners when they got out of college.[5] Davies had an aunt who lived in New Orleans, near Tulane, where they wanted to attend. He had corresponded with her telling her of their plans and she invited both Davies and Ledgerwood to live and board at her house. The two gratefully accepted.

For the next three years Ledgerwood applied himself and studied hard. The harder he worked the more interested in law he became. He took voluminous notes and because of the completeness, accuracy and clarity of his notebooks, he became the focal point for groups studying for exams. He said, "I didn't know anyone in New Orleans and didn't run around, so I had little else to do."[6]

Bridget McLaughlin may have been disappointed when Leo returned home after staying at Fayetteville only two weeks. But, she no doubt got over the disappointment quickly as being the old mother-hen she was, she liked to have all her chicks home at roosting time. And she did have them, all eight children at home. Including she and John Henry, they now had ten people living under one roof. Even though it was quite a large house it, no doubt at times seemed filled with people. John Henry's brother, Michael, had lived with them when they first moved to the new house. But as the boys got larger and more of them were able to assist in the store, Michael began to look around for something else to do. Also, he may have had the same problem that their brother Frank did when he was a partner in the store at Memphis. He and John Henry may have begun to get on each other's nerves. Since much of his work at the store was in the meat market he was acquainted with the management at Armour Packing Company, just up the street on Malvern. About 1903 he got a job with that firm and moved out of the mansion to a rooming house near the packing company.[7]

---

[3] Ibid.

[4] From obituary of R. Geddes Davies, *Hot Springs New Era*, 20 February 1933.

[5] LAT Ledgerwood.

[6] Ibid.

[7] *Hemming Directory, Vol. 1, Hot Springs City Directory - 1903*, p. 224.

Bridget McLaughlin

Bridget ruled her family with an "iron hand." She did not want her eight children to marry– only Leo, Stella, and George defied her.
Courtesy of Norwood Phillips, Jr.

Also, Bettie Flannagan had departed from the McLaughlin home. She had been a lot of help to Bridget as the kids were growing up. She had lived for awhile in a couple of rooms on the second floor of the carriage or garage house at the rear of the main dwelling which faced Hill Street.[8] But with the work load getting lighter, she was no longer needed. Bettie had been the confidant for the girls with their little secrets, and assisted them with their clothes and hair. She had also been the target for the younger boys pranks, which she good-naturedly endured. Bettie had met a man by the name William A. Garland and for awhile they had an on-again, off-again romance. Once they had even taken out a license to get married but for some unknown reason no wedding took place.[9] At any rate, she left the McLaughlin household.

Anyone acquainted with Bridget did not doubt that she ruled her home. Within the confines of the walls of the mansion, her word was law. Oh, she was too wise to interfere with John Henry and his business. He was too good a provider. Through his shrewd management the wealth of the family had greatly increased. He had replaced the frame store building at Creek and Malvern with a modern two-story brick building. They now owned an entire block on Malvern, property on Ouachita Avenue, and a two-story building in downtown Hot Springs on Central at Prospect. When John built that building

[8] LAT Ray Cross.

[9] Marriage Records, Garland County Clerk's Office, Book 2, p. 20.

he had his name placed near the top and it was, and is today, known as The McLaughlin Building. Besides the commercial buildings, John Henry had purchased several houses that were rental units. The rental properties kept a nice cash flow to support the ten people living in the home.

Little is known about what took place behind the walls of the McLaughlin home because the family was a bit strange and very private. Late in the evenings, on warm days, John Henry could be seen sitting on the large front porch in his rocker talking with Will and Russell and sometimes Bridget. A large circular watering trough was located in the intersection in front of the McLaughlin home. Farmers would water their stock there upon entering town and then again as they left. Sometimes John Henry would holler at someone he knew and many times the acquaintance would come and sit on the steps and visit. But few people were ever invited into the home and the McLaughlins certainly never entertained. They seemed content in the company of each other.

There were a number of stories and rumors concerning the family, but it seemed to be common knowledge that when Bridget learned of one of her children becoming interested in a person of the opposite sex she became very interfering in their lives. She watched each budding romance with a suspicious eye. In the event the other individual was not of the Catholic faith, Bridget began a systematic crusade to hammer away and demonstrate the lack of religious compatibility between the two young people. This religious intolerance was not lost upon any suitors. They generally withered under her relentless attack, and in the words of Omar Khyam, they simply "folded their tents and stole away into the night." If the other party was of the same faith, she began a campaign of pointing out any unflattering traits or faults of that individual, until the two broke up. There is no single known instance when she ever encouraged any of her children to seek a mate and/or to marry. And, so far as any of her offspring having children--no way. Rumors persisted for years that there was a strain of insanity in her family background and she did not want it cropping up in the lives of her children. She had little to worry about in this respect from her four eldest children. Mary Anna was never seen in the company of a male companion and it was rumored about town that she was subject to seizures and seldom ventured out of the house. Elizabeth was probably the most obedient, and docile to her Mother's wishes, and had no beaus. Although likeable at times she was a bit dull and content to spend most of her time with Bridget and in her sisters' company. Will was engrossed in the operation of the store and was pleased to be increasing the amount of hardware stock. John Henry, whose health was on the decline, was permitting Will more say into the operation of the store. Will was prone to wander down on Malvern at times and join some cronies at one of the saloons for a few drinks. Generally he held his liquor quite well, but there were recorded instances when he over did his drinking and was brought home by some friendly policeman. And occasionally, his name appeared on the police or municipal court blotter, but this occurred mostly after his father had passed away.[10] This did not seem to bother Bridget very much, although she may have reprimanded him when he sobered up. Just as long as he was not out searching for a wife, his infrequent drinking bouts were forgiven. Both John and Bridget thought Will was wasting his time when he decided to run for alderman of the Second Ward. They may have been surprised at the easy victory he had over his opponent. Will knew a lot of people, especially in the Second Ward and, they showed their regard for him at the polls.

James Russell seemed to be a stay-at-home type, however this may have been due to his lack of stamina. He had poor health and his doctor didn't seem to be able to diagnose what was wrong with him in the early stages of what turned out to be tuberculosis. His health seemed to be the only thing that ever worried the family about his life. It wasn't the four eldest children that concerned Bridget so much, it was the four youngest.

While Leo was attempting to fit himself into the adult world, his sister Stella graduated from high school with the Class of 1909.[11] Stella was quite an attractive young lady. She had brown hair (which she would dye yellow in later years), a trim figure, and dressed quite stylishly for a high school girl. Her teachers reportedly said of her conduct, that she talked a great deal in school. She had many teen-age flirtations and seemed to be popular with some of the other students, especially a young fellow-classmate, Earl Sauls, who was involved with Stella in many school activities. They liked each other's company and he may have manifested a romantic interest in Stella. Bridget's reputation concerning potential suitors of her daughters' affection discouraged what some thought was a special friendship between the two young people. Many people in Hot Springs recognized Stella and Irene as they rode their beautiful saddle horses about town and made striking figures with their modern riding habits. They were considered to be excellent young horsewomen and were on occasion hired by Christopher J. Ledwidge, owner of the St. Louis Riding Stables, which at that time was located across the street from the Arlington Hotel, on the site of the present hotel. The stable catered to a high-type clientele and had some very fine steeds for rent. "Whenever a horse show was held at Oaklawn Park or somewhere else, my father would hire the McLaughlin sisters to show his horses. They were quite good," Leon

---

[10] John William was picked up by a couple of policeman one night and was charged with being Drunk and Disorderly and was arrested. At that time his brother, Leo, was the City Attorney. Hot Springs City Jail Docket, p. 29, 28 January 1921.

[11] Hot Springs Senior Yearbook - 1909, and *Sentinel-Record,* 21 October 1951.

Ledwidge later said.[12]

The next sibling, George, dropped out of school in the tenth grade. He had never enjoyed school and was not as good a student as Leo, Stella and Irene, the latter who graduated in 1913.[13] He had an intense interest in baseball. When the Boston Red Sox or Pittsburgh Pirates were in town for spring training, George had a habit of disappearing from school or the family store and mysteriously reappearing at one of the ball fields on Whittington. He was quite awed by the big-leaguers and their level of play. Baseball was George's first love, years later it would be Fannie.

Leo may have believed when he returned home from his short stay in college he would be treated like the return of the prodigal son from the Bible, and be feted and dined by his family. If he expected John Henry to run out and kill the fatted calf he was in for a rude awakening. It was not John Henry's character to let one boy loaf-around while his other sons were working. His philosophy was "Work should be shared." If a boy lived and ate at home, he worked! Leo was no exception and was put to work. He could clerk in the store and make deliveries as his younger brother George was doing. When the two younger boys were not busy they could clean the stables for the delivery horses, located behind the store along Hot Springs Creek and the stable for the carriage and saddle horses, on Hill Street, at the rear of the McLaughlin home.

That wasn't what Leo had in mind. He wanted to become a lawyer and get in politics and there were only two ways to go about it and he had already blown the path involving college. He knew he had given the first only a faint-hearted chance, and possibly he may have even been a bit disappointed with himself. Now he must go the other route if his dreams were to be fulfilled. He would have to work as an assistant to a practicing attorney until he was able to prepare himself to take the oral Bar Exam before the Arkansas Supreme Court. He became acquainted with a fine lawyer, George P. Whittington who had an office in the Arkansas National Building at the corner of Central and Reserve. Whittington had graduated from the University of Virginia.[14] He had brought his family to the Spa and had a good law practice.

Whittington liked the young man, however, he did not need or want an assistant. He did have a suggestion or two. He would be glad to impart some of his legal knowledge in return for Leo's running some errands for him to the Court House and the Police Court. And, too, he suggested Leo enroll in Judge

---

[12] Life and Times of Leo P. McLaughlin, interview of Leon Ledwidge, by Jean Ledwidge, 28 July 1980.

[13] Hot Springs Senior Yearbook - 1909.

[14] Life and Times of Leo P. McLaughlin, recorded interview of David Whittington, son of George Whittington.

Alonzo Curl's study group. This was a local group of young aspiring men who met with Alonzo Curl and studied the proper handling and filing of legal forms and documents, which makes up a large part of the legal world. Leo McLaughlin agreed. During 1909, McLaughlin clerked in the family store and applied himself to studying law under George P. Whittington and attending Alonzo Curl's study group.

First Victory and Tragedy at the Court House

In 1910, the Democratic Party in Garland County was a fractured organization. The leadership was constantly bickering and arguing among themselves. Some candidates were disillusioned and were complaining about how the handling of elections and especially the counting of votes was conducted. They complained that they could not get a fair count because their opponent had hand-picked judges at a number of the polls. The allegations bore a lot of truth. The split first occurred in 1906, and had not gotten any better.[1] This issue was kept alive before the public by Lee Evans and a famous controversial person named "Umbrella" Bill McGuigan. The old saying "the squeaking wheel gets the grease" certainly applied here. After much wrangling, the party finally made amends in a meeting held 25 March 1910. A special sub-committee chosen "for their fairness" and composed of C.V. Teague, Seward Erickson, G. Dillard, John J. Ledgerwood, Frank Childs, Frank Walker and J.M. Roberts, submitted a report. They provided a list of judges for the various polls, carefully selected not to favor any candidate running for office. Further, the committee recommended that any regular candidate would be given the right "to request the judges to permit some well known Democrat to represent his interests when the votes are being counted." Only a few changes were needed to conclude the meeting in a very harmonious manner.[2] The rift in the party seemed healed.

There was a big scramble to file for the many offices as it appeared the election would be more honestly run and the votes accurately recorded. George Whittington was an incumbent State Representative and quickly filed. There was an opening for a second representative to be elected from the district. Strangely, the two positions were thrown open and as many that wanted to enter the race could. All were lumped into one group and the voters could vote for two candidates and the two having the most votes would be nominated to the general election in the fall. Of course, election in the Democratic Primary was generally tantamount to election as the party was that dominant. W.W. Waters, who had served Hot Springs as mayor several years before announced. So did J.L. Wadley, William Hirschman and A.W. Lindsey.

Whittington, a very shrewd political analyst, encouraged Leo McLaughlin to announce. "With five already in the race you stand a good chance of slipping in. Some of those in the race have run several times and the voters may like a new face. Think it over and if you decide I'll help you get your petition and file. We can even travel in the county together, if you like."

---

[1] *Hot Springs Sentinel-Record*, 26 March 1910.

[2] Ibid.

McLaughlin had told Ledgerwood that he was coming home and get in to politics, but this was not the office he had in mind. However, it would be a start and Whittington had assured him he would help him. It was probably a surprise to many when Leo announced for State Representative. He barely qualified for the age limit to run for state office. Even the local newspaper referred to his youth: "Leo P. McLaughlin is a young Hot Springs product just out of high school."[3]

The field closed out with six men vying for two positions. McLaughlin knew a lot of people did not know him. He was well-known in the Second Ward where he had lived all his life and where the family business was located. He knew he had to get out and circulate to become better known. He asked the newspaper if he could make a statement and was given the green light. He worked for several hours on a short statement: "To The Voters of Garland County: I am a candidate for representative in the Democratic Primary election on July 16, and I want your support. I have entered this race in response to a petition signed by many good Democrats, asking me to run. I am the only candidate called out by a petition. This petition set forth that the young men should be given a share in the public affairs while they are young and ambitious and this opinion has met the approval of not only the young men, but the fathers of the young men as well. I am very much gratified at the assurance of hearty support extended me from all sides. I feel justified in my ambition to represent Garland County as I was born and educated here, and all the interest I have is centered here. It is but natural to expect that my every effort would be to promote the welfare of the county. I am thoroughly acquainted with the wants and needs of the people of this city and county and if I am elected I will go into office free to represent the whole people and not owned or controlled by any faction. If you do the honor to make me one of your representatives in the next legislature I shall be in readiness at all times to advocate such measures as may be considered to [Be in] the best interest of the people of Garland County. Respectfully, Leo M'Laughlin[4]

It turned out to be a fast summer for Leo McLaughlin as he spent little time clerking at the store and more time campaigning with George Whittington.

John Henry McLaughlin's health seemed to be deteriorating. With Leo out campaigning most of the time John Henry worked to fill the void created by Leo's absences. He never said much about Leo running for office but would brighten up when some customer would comment they intended to vote for Leo.

Leo didn't have much of a platform on which to run and he was not very well-acquainted with the issues of the day, but listening to Whittington he was

---

[3] *The Sentinel-Record,* 17 July 1910, p. 1.
[4] Ibid., 10 July 1910, p. 1.

learning. As they stopped at county stores groups would gather around the soft-drink boxes and it was customary to buy everyone a five-cent Coca-Cola, or perhaps a big orange soda-pop. That obligated them to at least listen and kept their attention long enough to pass out some campaign cards and answer a few questions. Leo's main topic was on "Local Option" stating that he was in favor of each county voting on the state-wide Prohibition law.[5] "Local Option" was always a safe, popular and favorite topic taken by politicians when they did not have much to say, just as it is today. The voters seemed to take to the young man who gave an appearance of complete honesty.

Not only were the campaigns hot the summer of 1910, but the weather was scorching. The fans at the McLaughlin store on Malvern just stirred up the hot air. John Henry McLaughlin was waiting on a customer when he became faint and started to sag to the floor. Russell, having seen his father's discomfort, rushed and held him up and helped him to a chair. Will quickly brought a dipper of water and an ice compress and applied to his forehead. The sixty-nine year old McLaughlin revived shortly. After a call to Bridget by one of the boys they were told to bring him home and she would summon their family doctor. John Henry was feeling better by the time the doctor arrived. After examining him, the doctor told Bridget he was working too hard for a man his age and especially in the heat. He suggested a few weeks of vacation. John Henry gave in to Bridget's insistence of going to Mountain Valley for a rest. She had told her husband that Will, Russell and George could handle the store. John Henry said there was one condition in him going to Mountain Valley and that was that they come back in town on election day as "I intend to vote for my boy."

Election day opened July 16 with a light rain falling. The rain cooled the temperatures enough that a good turnout of voters resulted. That night there was a pressing crowd in the halls and about the grounds of the Garland County Court House. Leo McLaughlin was one of these. He may have been fearful that his race had fallen short. Odds had been against him. As boxes of ballots were brought in and the results were chalked up on the large black board there would be groans from one side and cheers from the other. Much of the county vote was late coming in, but with each box Leo's hopes soared. By 2:00 a.m., when the final city votes came in the handwriting was on the wall. He was a winner! McLaughlin won the First, Second, Third, Fifth and Sixth Wards. Whittington was second to Leo in those Wards and won the fourth with McLaughlin coming in second. The two were ecstatic. When the final county vote was chalked up, Whittington had nosed by McLaughlin by twenty-four votes and the two had far out-distanced the other four

---

[5] Ibid.

candidates.[6] The final count showed George at 843 to Leo's 819. The nearest competitor was W.W. Waters with 641.[7] Leo P. McLaughlin had just tasted his first political victory, and he loved it.

It was a nice morning 17 August 1910. Verne Ledgerwood sat on the front porch of his parents' home at 215 Woodbine, the one they had built following the fire of 1905. The two-story dwelling faced the rear of the Garland County Courthouse across a large vacant lot where the old National Guard Armory and now the Senior Citizens Center is located. Just two years before, on that same open field, the Hot Springs Airship Company had built a seventy-five foot long dirigible. The company had been headed and funded by Dr. W.H. Connell, S.J. Erickson and the publisher of *The Hot Springs New Era*, John A. Riggs. Several Hot Springs citizens had invested in the venture, even the two owners of the Ledgerwood Bros. Bakery. The builder, Joel T. Rice, of Royal, Arkansas had convinced them with his drawing that the airship would fly. It was named "The Arkansas Traveler." Unfortunately it was not destined to travel far as there was no aluminum to build the under carriage and steel was used. It was far too heavy and the craft had gotten off the ground only twenty-five feet when it settled back to earth. Riggs and Rice moved the operation to New York, and while the airship briefly flew, it failed there, also.

Verne Ledgerwood had been told by his father not to come to work until after lunch as the bottling equipment was being worked on that morning. He would be leaving soon to go to New Orleans for his third year in college and he was glad at the chance to visit with his mother.[8]

As Mrs. Ledgerwood rocked back and forth, chatting with her son, sitting in a porch swing, the two were completely unaware that a life and death drama was about to be enacted just up the street.

Garland County Sheriff Jake Houpt had been victorious in the Democratic primary winning a second term nomination of office, but not without dispute or controversy. His opponent, T.J. Richards had claimed irregularities in boxes of the Fifth Ward. The claim was denied.[9] Houpt's brother, Sid, acted as chief deputy.

Three or four days before, the sheriff had received a call from the sheriff of Clark County asking his assistance and to be on the lookout for two brothers, George and Oscar Chitwood, whose real names were Smith, and who were wanted for stealing some horses. Sheriff Houpt ordered their arrest and he and Sid had gone to the Chitwood home in Ragweed Valley, which was in Lincoln Township in the western part of the county. The two brothers were

---

[6] Ibid.

[7] Ibid., 24 July 1910.

[8] LAT Ledgerwood.

[9] *The Sentinel-Record*, 10 July 1910, p. 1.

not there at that time.[10]

Two days later the Chitwoods showed up in Hot Springs and reportedly had been seen at the Williams Wagon Yard near the courthouse, and then later at a nearby bar. Sheriff Houpt sent his brother, Sid, to find them and summon them to his office. W.B. Steed was about to leave the wagon yard when he saw the Chitwoods saddling their ponies as Sid Houpt walked up. "Boys," Sid Houpt said, "Jake wants to see you at his office."[11] The two men led their mounts across the street, tied them to a post on the westside of Hawthorne Street and went in.

Sid Houpt had just returned to the sheriff's office when he and his brother were joined by Garland County Clerk Robert Mooney. Sid stepped to a side room for just a minute and as he came out he saw the Chitwood brothers had come in. One of the suspects addressed Jake Houpt, "What do you want with us?"

Tossing some papers on his desk Houpt replied, "I have a warrant for your arrest."

The words were hardly out of the sheriff's mouth until the Chitwoods whipped out their revolvers covering the two Houpts, and ran down the hall and out the north entrance of the courthouse to where their horses were tethered on Hawthorne Street. Sheriff Houpt picked up a pistol and took off after the fleeing men. Sid Houpt, who did not have a gun, secured a .38 revolver from the collector's office and ran in pursuit. As the two officers stepped from the door they saw the Chitwoods starting to mount their horses. Witnesses stated that the two wanted men began firing at the pursuing officers and described it as a "fusillade of fire."[12] The lawmen returned the gunfire until their ammunition was almost exhausted.

When the Chitwoods swung out onto Ouachita Avenue, a paved street, they spurred their mounts and the steel shod hoofs slid on the iron car rails. Both horses fell. Sid Houpt fired his last shot striking Oscar Chitwood in the elbow and as he had exhausted the ammunition in his pistol ran into the courthouse for more. Sheriff Jake Houpt ran toward George Chitwood, who had fallen from his horse, and Chitwood had dropped his pistol but picked it up and ran behind a trolley which had been stopped by its operator, Ben Green, awestricken at the scene taking place before him. Houpt pursued, ordering Chitwood to throw up his hands and surrender. Both men were aiming their weapons at each other. Chitwood fired a split second before Houpt. The bullet struck Sheriff Jake Houpt under the right arm, ranging downward and

---

[10] Ibid., 18 August 1910, p. 1.The record reflects the warrants were issued in Amity, Clark County, charging the Chitwoods with being horse thieves.

[11] Ibid., 25 August 1910.

[12] Ibid., 18 August 1910.

17 August 1910
A gunfight occurred on Ouachita Avenue between cattle rustlers George and Oscar Chitwood and Sheriff Jake Houpt and his brother, Sid. George Chitwood and Sheriff Houpt were killed.

puncturing his lungs. George Chitwood, also hit, staggered behind the trolley car just as Deputy Sid Houpt rejoined the fray. He fired one shot at George Chitwood who was already mortally wounded and the accused rustler collapsed to the pavement.[13] Sid Houpt grabbed a buggy and took off toward South Hot Springs, in the direction the wounded Oscar Chitwood had fled on his horse.

When the shooting first commenced, Dora Snell Ledgerwood and her son Vernal were quietly talking. The gunfire could plainly be heard and they could see people scurrying about around the courthouse grounds. Verne jumped up from the porch swing and dashed in the house, reappearing in a few seconds with a shotgun and shells he had bought the week before. Dora tried to keep him on the porch but he brushed by her, loading the weapon as he ran. He later said, "In those days it was expected that citizens would go to the aid of their officers, if needed. I got there just in time to see one of the Chitwoods riding off with Deputy Houpt in hot pursuit."[14]

Sheriff Jake Houpt died two days later and his body was taken for burial to Ten Mile Cemetery near Lonsdale.[15]

The day before Houpt's burial, fugitive Oscar Chitwood surrendered to two farmers, John Bryan and J.A. Coleman, both of Ragweed Valley. These two turned Chitwood over to two deputies, Ben Murray and John Rutherford. The officers claimed a reward that had been taken up by citizens incensed over the killing of Sheriff Houpt. The money was to encourage the capture of Oscar Chitwood. The two farmers disputed the claim of the lawmen and filed suit. The two deputies then claimed it had been their intention to give the money to the widow of Sheriff Jake Houpt.[16]

In a hearing before Judges A. Curl and Henry Evans, witnesses were called and it was decreed, "the money subscribed for capture of Oscar Chitwood is not due anybody."[17] He had turned himself in.

With Oscar Chitwood in custody the matter should have been all over with the exception of the murder trial. It was a sad chapter in the history of Garland County. However, it was to have an even sadder, strange, bizarre and sordid ending.

---

[13] Ibid., also *The Sentinel-Record*, 25 August 1910.

[14] LAT Ledgerwood.

[15] *The Sentinel-Record*, 21 August 1910, p. 1. The sheriff must have had a premonition that he was dying as he requested that election fraud charges he had filed against some individuals be dropped.

[16] Ibid., 25 August 1910.

[17] Ibid., 11 September 1910.

Seated, Reb Houpt. Standing, left to right: Bud, Henry, Sid, Cal, and Jake. Sid replaced his brother Jake as sheriff when Jake was killed by the Chitwood brothers.

A few days after the shootings and the deaths of Sheriff Houpt and accused horse thief George Chitwood, Sid Houpt was appointed to fill the vacancy left by his brother's demise. A committee headed by Senator Hamp Williams, Representative George Whittington, Judge James B. Wood, Coroner Dr. J.P. Randolph, Assessor Rube Gilliam and Alderman Walter W. Little appeared before Governor Donaghey and presented a petition signed by 1,500 citizens requesting the appointment of Sid Houpt.[18] Five days later, 28 August, the Garland County Democratic Central Committee met and voted to name Sid Houpt to the 12 September ballot in place of his deceased brother, Jake.[19]

The Houpt name was well known to voters of Garland County. Between the three Houpts--Reb, Jake, and Sid--and a bitter opponent, R.L. "Bob" Williams, they dominated the sheriff's office from 1886-1914. Reb Houpt and Bob Williams had gone head-to-head for the office of sheriff a number of times. Williams had won three straight terms from 1886-1892. Reb Houpt then won three terms of his own, one as tax collector and two as sheriff, until he was suspended by the circuit court for malfeasance. Williams came back in

---

[18] Ibid., 23 August 1910.
[19] Ibid., 28 August 1910.

898 and was suspended the following year. He returned as sheriff from 1902-908, when he was again suspended with Reb Houpt being appointed to fill is term. Jake Houpt was then elected and served until his death in August 910.[20]

In the fall election Sid Houpt prevailed in a very close race with Republican 'J. Prichard. Houpt barely edged Prichard in the city vote and squeaked by the county to win the office..[21]

In that same election Leo P. McLaughlin and George Whittington easily on their respective positions. The night following the election, when all the allot boxes had been brought in and the votes counted, the entire Democratic ticket claimed victory.

It had been a number of years since a wild demonstration and torchlight arade had followed an election, but both sides were ready to cut-loose, and ut-loose, they did. Both democrats and republicans believed the vote ounting was honest and even losing was not as painful if a candidate believed e ballots had been counted fairly. All the democratic winners, friends and apporters led the way. They piled in automobiles gaily decorated with merican flags and red, white and blue bunting. Many who could not get in e cars rode the running boards waving small flags. They started down Ouachita, then up Central and Park, blowing their horns, ringing noisy owbells, and some singing and some shouting at the tops of their voices. The utomobiles were followed by buggies, carriages and men on horseback. The inners were followed by the defeated republican candidates and followers. hey too, had American flags, but from their vehicles banners were displayed s a gesture of good sportsmanship. Some read, "It was on the square, now oost the state fair." Others stated, "We didn't beat them, but we had them ared."[22] Many of the celebrants, both democrats and republicans, found their ay into the bars and saloons and the celebrations went on into the wee hours f the morning. No brawls or fights were reported, but if there were the police ist looked the other way.

For Leo McLaughlin, it was an exhilarating time and he was enjoying the restige that comes with being a winner. He was watching and learning from thers.

Sheriff-elect Sid Houpt and his family left Hot Springs on a holiday vacation few days before Christmas. They intended to visit family and friends in exas and Oklahoma. Sid had gone through a very stressful four months. irst, his brother had been killed, and that was followed by the election which e narrowly won. And then, he had to attend to the Harry Poe execution 2

[20] Arkansas Officials, Garland County Officials, pp. 149-150.
[21] *Sentinel-Record*, 13 September 1910.
[22] Ibid., 15 September 1910.

September 1910. Poe was a convicted rapist who had been condemned to die on the gallows. Before his death, Sheriff Jake Houpt had set the date and time for the hanging. This, and one other, were believed to be the only lega hangings in the history of Garland County.[23]

Shortly after the election he had appointed Ben Murray as his chief deputy Since deputy Row Brown intended to visit his relatives in Dardanelle during the holidays, Houpt hired John Rutherford as a deputy and jailer, four days before Christmas.

There had been much tension in the city following the killing of Jake Houpt After Oscar Chitwood was safely in custody the tension subsided somewhat With the unusually large number of witnesses who saw the gunfight there seemed to be little doubt that Oscar Chitwood would be convicted. The onl question was would he be given life or death. That was one reason the gallow and enclosure had not been dismantled.

It therefore was a surprise to citizens of the Spa to wake up to headlines i the paper, "Oscar Chitwood Shot and Killed by Men." Deputy John Rutherford claimed Chitwood was taken from him by fifteen to twenty arme and masked men who shot the prisoner to death within the confines of the enclosure where Harry Poe had been hanged. Rutherford further stated he sav forty to fifty masked men lined up near the courthouse.[24] Rutherford's story at first believed, began to come apart as several witnesses in the vicinity an on all sides of the courthouse upon hearing gunfire rushed to their windows They said they saw neither a mob or "fifteen to twenty men," much less "fort to fifty masked men." In fact, they did not see anyone!

A coroner's inquest was ordered and a jury was appointed. This include some of the best-known and well-regarded citizens of the Spa: Ham Williams, F.M. Sigler, Frank Joplin, Albert O. Ledgerwood, John J Ledgerwood, James E. Ledgerwood, D.C. Russey, Carlton Taylor, E.T Housley, Robert Kirby and Eugene Thornton. After hearing many witnesses including a number of inmates in the jail at the time, and taking over 500 page of testimony, stories and rumors began to seep from the courthouse.[25] *Th Sentinel-Record* dedicated almost the entire front page of 28 December to summary of the testimony given to the coroner's jury.

By mid-morning of 29 December the cries of "Extra, Extra, read all abou it," rang up and down Central, Ouachita and Malvern. Large headline proclaimed "Three Ordered Apprehended, Deputy Sheriffs Rutherford an

---

[23] Ibid., 3 June 1913. Clarence A. Schumann was convicted of killing his wife in Ju 1912. The headline in the morning papers following the execution, I DIE A CHRISTIAN.

[24] Ibid., 27 December 1910..

[25] Ibid., 24 January 1911, p. 2.

Murray and a Third Man May be Held for Murder."[26]

By afternoon the excitement of the morning began to fade. Then the voices of newsboys could be heard again crying, "Extra - Extra." Headlines larger than those of that morning spread across the page, "Officers Arrested." The account stated Ben Murray and John Rutherford had been arrested and charged with the murder of Oscar Chitwood and been taken to Little Rock for safe-keeping.[27]

The third suspect was never indicted and it was only speculation as who it might be. Some thought it to be one of the Houpt brothers, as several prisoners testified Chitwood had plead as he was being removed from the courthouse, "Please Mr. Houpt don't kill me, give me my trial."[28] The Houpts had been able to give their location as being elsewhere when the crime took place.[29] Other people thought the "third man," might be Deputy Sanders who Rutherford had relieved, but he too, had an alibi.

The criminal trial of Rutherford lasted eight days, plus the deliberations by the jury of twelve hours. The jury finally came out with a verdict of "not guilty."[30] Somehow, to the public, it was not a satisfying verdict. If John Rutherford was not guilty, who was responsible? Prosecuting Attorney J.B. Wood had approached the case on a conspiracy theory, but was unable to convince the jury.

The fall-out from the trial was punishing, especially to Rutherford, Murray and the Houpt family. Many of the people who had supported the Houpts over the years were disturbed because no one was brought to account for the crime of killing Oscar Chitwood.[31]

---

[26] Ibid., 29 December 1910, first Extra Edition.

[27] Ibid., 29 December 1910, second Extra edition.

[28] Ibid., 27 May 1911.

[29] Reb and Henry Houpt admitted as to being about the jail the evening before the killing but went home about 8:00 p.m. Their story was confirmed by a farmer, Will Oxford.

[30] *Sentinel-Record*, 28 May 1911. Ben Murray would not be tried for this crime.

[31] LAT Ledgerwood. "Enough suspicion hung over this trial to hurt the entire family politically." Sid Houpt was indicted by a Grand Jury for malfeasance his first full year in office and Charles Webb was appointed by the court to fill the vacancy.

Law Credentials and the Passing of a Patriarch

Leo Patrick McLaughlin could not help but be a bit excited as he went to Little Rock to attend his first swearing in of the Arkansas State Legislature. The Thirty-Eighth General Assembly was scheduled to run from January 12, 1911 to May 13, 1911. They took his picture along with all the other legislators and hung them on a wall of the capitol. He was a very young man to be holding such an important position. It was a heady sensation.

Within a few days he wondered what he had gotten into. It was such a confusing process, the filing of forms and bills, the committees and other meetings in "smoke-filled rooms," where pressure was applied by some of the senior legislators to support this bill or that bill. There was the urging by some "if you support my bill, I'll support yours--maybe." Leo discovered he was almost totally dependent upon George Whittington to ascertain the status or worth of a bill or perhaps which way he should vote. He and George would go to Little Rock on an early train on Monday morning and stay until Friday afternoon, at which time they would return home. In effect, he had very little impact on the legislature and had no desire to seek that office again. The most important thing coming out of the legislative meetings for Leo, was meeting several of the "movers and shakers" of state government who would become important contacts in later years. And in future years he would proudly refer to "My stint in the State Legislature."

McLaughlin returned to Hot Springs at the end of the session and learned there was a vacant office on the third floor of the Arkansas National Bank Building. It was very near the office of George Whittington and since he was so dependent on the older attorney, he rented it.[1] Not too much later an office adjoining Whittington's became available and he made the short move and even had a connecting door leading into the older lawyer's space.[2] McLaughlin would maintain an office on this floor for over forty years. The sign on the door, *Leo P. McLaughlin, Esq., Attorney at Law,* looked impressive. He was now a full fledged attorney, or at least that was what it said on the door and how his acquaintances referred to him. But was he really? A few doubted, and some even questioned his qualifications. Over the years he handled many divorce cases and some clients would not have slept well at night had they thought there was any question concerning his licensing--why, they might even be living in sin if their divorce was not legal.

A few years later, 1915, during a race for city attorney, a political opponent, Peyton T. Jordan, asked this question in a political ad, "Can Leo McLaughlin

---

[1] *Polk's Southern Directory, Hot Springs - 1912,* p. 263.

[2] LAT David Whittington. He stated that the door between the two offices generally remained open throughout the day.

represent the city in the Supreme Court?" Mr. Jordan answered his own question, "No, he can not practice in the Supreme Court." He then proceeded to present the copy of a letter from P.D. English, Clerk of the Supreme Court, November 24, 1915, advising that "Leo P. McLaughlin, according to the records in this office, has never been admitted to the bar of this court."[3]

Establishing a precedent on what he would do in answer to a political accusation, McLaughlin lashed back citing a lone appearance before the Supreme Court on behalf of the City of Hot Springs. At that appearance was a fully qualified Hot Springs Attorney from Hot Springs, Floyd Huff.[4] Did Leo ride Huff's coat-tails for that hearing? He then went on the attack accusing Jordan, who had recently moved to Hot Springs, of having tried only one case in Garland County Circuit Court and had a lawyer assisting him.[5]

But what does the record really reflect after so many years have passed? Various newspapers and books have stated as a fact that Leo McLaughlin had impeccable credentials as to his educational and professional background. More than one article has clearly indicated McLaughlin to hold a law degree from the University of Arkansas. Other sources have been a bit more reserved. What is myth and what is fact and truth? In researching this matter the writer contacted several sources including the University of Arkansas and the Arkansas Supreme Court. As previously stated, the University of Arkansas confirmed that McLaughlin entered school in 1908, but never finished that year. In the 1900-1940 era, graduates of the University of Arkansas Law School automatically were admitted to the bar and licensed to practice. Those studying under the tutelage of a licensed member of the bar could take an oral examination by the Arkansas Supreme Court and if passing, was admitted to the bar to practice law. A law student graduating from an out-of-state law school was also permitted to take an oral examination by the Arkansas Supreme Court.

At our request, Ava Hicks, Assistant Librarian with the Arkansas Supreme Court, researched the questions, "Was Leo P. McLaughlin admitted to practice law before the Supreme Court of Arkansas, and is there a record of him having been licensed by the State of Arkansas or Arkansas Bar Association to practice law?"

Ms. Hicks later advised she had made contact with Chris Thomas with the Current Board of Law Admissions and Examiners. He reported that the name of Leo P. McLaughlin did not appear in their past records. Denise Parks with

---

[3] *Sentinel-Record*, 7 December 1915, p. 2.

[4] When Peyton Jordan pointed out that Leo P. McLaughlin had his poll tax only four months before McLaughlin announced for the State Legislature, Leo responded that he had lived in Hot Springs all twenty-one years of his life and he was not able to buy a poll tax until he turned twenty-one, seemingly a sound argument.

[5] *Sentinel-Record*, 8 December 1915, p. 4.

Office of Clerk of the Arkansas Supreme Court, had five books registering the names of those licensed to practice before the Supreme Court in the early decades of the twentieth century. The name Leo McLaughlin does not appear in those records.[6]

We have been informed that it was a very "lax time" as to monitoring those who opened a law office and "hung out their shingle." Leo McLaughlin had the sponsorship of George Whittington, a well-respected lawyer, and that must have been good enough for Leo to begin practicing law. It appears that he just never got around to qualifying himself and the fact became lost over the years. He made no apparent effort to ever set the matter straight. At least the citizens of the Spa accepted him as being qualified to practice law.[7] When he became mayor several years later, no one dared question his qualifications. In later years, various publications, newspapers and magazines, would often cite the mayor was "a graduate of the University of Arkansas and had earned a degree in law." Others would even elaborate that he had been a star on the University's football team. But no one had the nerve to correct it back then.

Down in the bayou state of Louisiana, Tulane University was graduating a very fine law class in the spring of 1912. From its ranks would come a United States Senator, two District Court Judges, the mayor of the city of New Orleans, several corporate presidents and a number of very good lawyers.[8] Vernal Snell Ledgerwood was one of these. He ranked second in his graduating class. The Dean of the law school tried to persuade Ledgerwood to accept a fellowship of study at an eastern university and to return to Tulane to teach. But Verne was only interested in getting back to Hot Springs. It was his plan to open a law office and be joined the following spring by Sonny Davies, who was a grade behind him. Davies would not be lonesome his final year at Tulane as joining him from Hot Springs was another law student, Samuel Garrett.

When Ledgerwood returned home he moved back in with his parents at 215 Woodbine. A few weeks later he appeared before the Arkansas Supreme Court in Little Rock and took and passed the Arkansas Bar Examination.[9]

****

---

[6] Arkansas Supreme Court Library, Ava Hicks, 1 July 1999.

[7] In a discussion with a senior member of the local bar association the writer was told that in all probability Leo McLaughlin was voted by the Garland County Bar Association to practice before the local courts and that he restricted his practice to this level.

[8] LAT Ledgerwood.

[9] Ibid.

On 16 May 1912 the McLaughlin family lost its patriarch, John Henry McLaughlin. Bridget, his wife, was awakened about 1:00 o'clock in the morning by struggling noises coming from her husband. She quickly summoned their family doctor and awakened the house. By the time the physician arrived the old Irishman had passed away. The doctor told them his death was a result of heart failure, he was seventy years-old.[10] John Henry McLaughlin was laid to rest in Calvary Cemetery two days later. He had been considered a shrewd buyer and seller and he had a good name among the many farmers who bought from and sold to him.

This field at Whittington Park was used by several major league teams in the spring as a training site. It became the home of the Hot Springs Bathers (Class D, Cotton States League) in 1938, and lights were installed.

[10] *Sentinel-Record*, 16 May 1912, p. 1.

Summer Fun, Con-Games and Disaster, Again!

The summer of 1912 was a dry one. For almost forty days it did not rain and the weather was scorching. Not only was it dry from the stand point of the weather, but also from a business one. Neither Verne Ledgerwood or Leo McLaughlin had much business as they were just beginning their law practices. Leo did have an edge on Verne. His brother, John William (Will), had been appointed the administrator of his father's estate, which was sizeable. Will had been his father's bookkeeper for several years and had looked after the rental properties and it was no big deal to him. He, of course, used his younger brother Leo to handle any legal matters involving the estate, such as rental agreements, transfer of property or titles and drawing up of Quit Claim Deeds. And Leo did have a certain amount of overflow business George Whittington was able to funnel his way. Small cases which did not interest Whittington were given to Leo for handling. And Whittington acknowledged that Leo did have a certain talent for handling divorce cases and the clients generally seemed pleased. Sometimes upon interviewing a potential client, Whittington would summon Leo in to his office, introducing him as "My associate," although no actual partnership existed. Since McLaughlin occupied the adjacent office and the door was kept open the client just assumed they were in business together. Leo McLaughlin always made a very favorable impression as he was a very nice- looking young man, fashionably-dressed and friendly. This was especially true of clients of the female gender.

That summer both Leo McLaughlin and Verne Ledgerwood were members of the first baseball team in the Spa to carry the name, "Bathers." The team was not a member of any organized league, but played teams from Little Rock, Pine Bluff and what was known then as "saw-mill teams." Those were teams being sponsored by mills or businesses. Some of the players on the "Bathers" that year were L. Longinotti, Elbert Fulton, "Shorty" Strock, Rawson, McQuintes, Whisenant, and Hinkle. The team played their home games at Whittington Park. This was the very image of small ballparks throughout the country, with plank clad fencing enclosing the playing area with a central grandstand behind home plate, topped with a corrugated iron roof. A chicken wire screen or netting was draped from the roof to the ground to protect fans from batted or thrown balls. Open air bleachers stretched along both foul lines. Signs painted on the outfield walls suggested fine places to eat or shop, where to fuel your car, or perhaps the best place to get a haircut.

Before the advent of lighted or night baseball the games during the week started late in the day and hopefully all innings could be played before the game was called on account of darkness. That was no problem with games played on Sunday afternoons. They generally started about two o'clock, which gave people time to get home from church and eat before heading for the ballpark. That is, unless a preacher had a long-winded sermon, and when that

Hot Springs Bathers - 1916

Leo McLaughlin is second from left, Verne Ledgerwood, third from left, back row.

Courtesy of Dora Jane Ledgerwood Ellis

occurred one could see ball fans checking their watches at frequent intervals as a hint to the preacher it was time to "wind it up." And there were some preachers whose sermons pointed out that going to the movie houses and ball diamonds on Sundays amounted to "sin." Those ministers who had substantial contributors in their congregations who were ball fans were careful to skirt around this topic.

A concessionaire was always on hand to sell soft drinks on a hot afternoon. If he did not have a cooler box, a number-three washtub with a twenty-five pound block of ice kept the cokes cold for the afternoon. These could be purchased for five cents. Pre-prepared sandwiches, wrapped in wax paper were for sale of those who had not had time to eat before coming to the ballpark. Peanuts and popcorn, previously bagged, were only a nickel. Sometimes a vendor might have a large watermelon iced down and a big slice could be purchased for a dime and eaten at a picnic table nearby. And, admission to the game was only twenty-five cents for adults and a dime for the young fans. The funds were used to buy equipment and pay for the occasional road trip the team would make. It could be a fun and economical outing. As an added attraction the Ledgerwood Band might put in an appearance to the delight of all, with a mini-concert of peppy tunes and marches. Transportation to and from the game by trolley was only seven cents each way, and transfers to the Park, Malvern, Central and South Hot Springs lines were free. Generally when a game broke up, fans could expect two or three trolleys to be lined up to take the crowd away. Those having to wait for another car could stroll through the park enjoying the music coming from the carousel and merry-go-round, or take a few minutes and watch roller-skaters whirling around the floor to a Viennese waltz. Before another trolley arrived a couple might meander through the park or cross the street and tour the Alligator or Ostrich Farms, these were always popular attractions. Weeknights there was dancing at an open air pavilion. A boy could take his best girl out to the ball game and perhaps spend no more than a dollar or two and have an enjoyable time.

Hot Springs was really hopping at this time. The city had a very liberal-minded administration. W.W. Waters had been elected mayor on a liberal ticket. He had been around Hot Springs since 1877, having arrived here as a young man and worked at the old Sumpter Hotel as a clerk. He gradually increased his standing in the community and operated a grocery store near the Junction.[1] Waters was elected mayor in 1895 and served one two-year term. He was a democrat by politics but formed one-half of an unusual partnership with Charles N. Rix, President of the Arkansas National Bank, a staunch republican. Besides a difference in politics, Waters and Rix differed in coming from opposite sections of the country, Waters from "rebel territory" near Spartanburg, South Carolina, and Rix from deep in "Yankee-land" where he had fought with the Union Army and attained a rank of Captain. Many of Rix's friends still fondly referred to him as Captain. But the two got along in business, owned one of the bath houses, and had a genuine regard for each other. Serving with Waters in his administration was J.A. Stallcup, city attorney, and Jack Archer, police judge.[2]

In the spring election of 1912, Leo McLaughlin won the city attorney's position, beating James P. McConnell. He was the youngest candidate ever--he was barely twenty-two years old.

When the "Wild Year,"–1913, as many later called it--rolled around, Hot Springs was as open as any town in the country. Gambling and prostitution were attractions designed to separate the thousands of visitors from their money and introduce it into the economy of the city. It gave those who were here taking the baths extra-curricular activities with which to amuse themselves.

Plush gambling clubs and casinos had sprung up. There was the Southern

---

[1] Those growing up in Hot Springs knew the "Junction" to be at the Columbian Memorial, a tri-cornered, open structure in the intersection of Park, Whittington and Central Avenues. It was a trolley transfer point and scene of several large holiday celebrations. In effect, though, there were other "junctions"--Central and Malvern, Central and Ouachita, etc.

[2] *Polk's Southern Directory - Hot Springs - 1912.*

Club, operated in its infancy by Charles Dugan and Dan Stuart and later taken over by Sam Watt, a nephew of Garland County Sheriff Bob Williams, and W.S. Jacobs, a long-time gambler from Tennessee. It was located across Central Avenue from the Arlington Hotel. The Kentucky Club, just south of the Southern was owned and operated by William T. Shannon and his wife.[3] Close by was The Ohio Club being run by William S. Jacobs and a junior partner, John Coffee Williams, a younger brother of Sheriff Williams.[4] A few more doors south was the very fine Indiana Club operated by Charles Bryan and Art Slavin.[5] Over at the corner of Spring and Broadway was one of the older, but quite well-known sporting houses, The Arkansas Club, (sometimes spelled Arkansaw Club). Several smaller clubs were also in operation and struggled for business. Those included The Texas Club run by some of the Akin boys and The West End Club, located at the end of the car line on Whittington, with the gambling operation under the management of Sam Maxwell and the Inn and other entertainment in the hands of Josie Belmont and her girls who had moved over from Malvern Avenue.

There was no central direction of the gambling activities city-wide, as each club made its own deal with the "city fathers" and "paid what the freight would bear." Mayor Waters and his Chief of Police James Leonard supposedly had the say on who would be or would not be permitted a gambling operation inside the city. Since Sheriff R.L. "Bob" Williams had the complete and final word who in the county might operate or not, it was necessary for the city administration not to step on Williams' toes lest he exercise his constitutional authority. Williams had a little game going of his own in the county. Gambling was permitted at Mountain Valley for a short while, then Ozark Lithia Springs and the old Chicago Club near where Club Belvedere now is located. The agreement of dividing "the spoils" of the county came to light in an address to a special called grand jury by Circuit Judge C.T. Cotham.[6] Few of the local folks were shocked.

The above-mentioned grand jury hearing had been brought about by complaints of visitors being conned or "fleeced" out of their money by various and complicated scams. One visitor, Frank P. Fox, of Indianapolis, Indiana, had lost $20,000 in cash in a con-game. Fox was extremely wealthy and the con-men figured Fox would be so embarrassed he would not complain to the authorities and even if he did, they believed the local law enforcement officials would back them up. A big mistake! Fox went ballistic. He was a personal friend of William J. Burns, founder of the Burns

---

[3] *New Era*, 11 February 1913.
[4] Ibid., 12 March 1913.
[5] *Sentinel-Record*, 28 March 1913.
[6] Ibid., 25 March 1913.

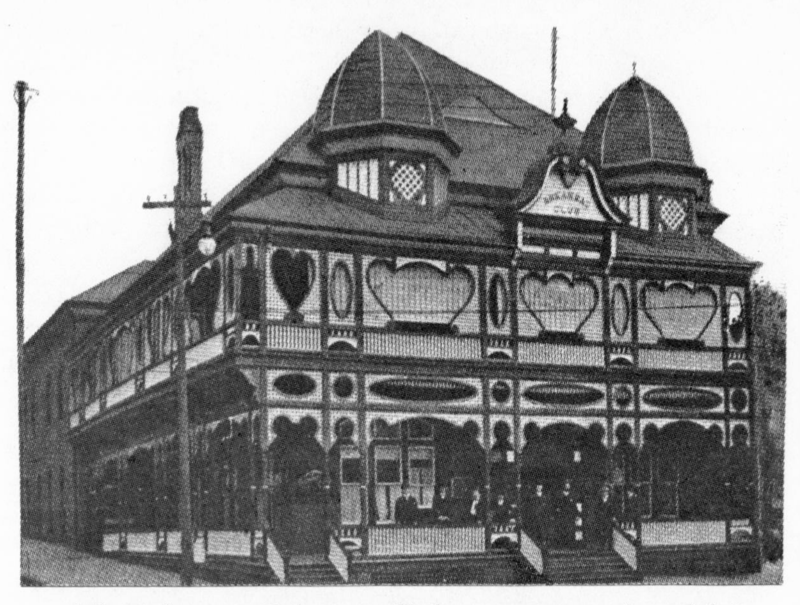

The Arkansas Club was called a "men's sporting club."
It was located on the southeast corner of Broadway and Spring Street, and was bought by the Elks' Club ca. 1915

Southern Club – 1913
For many years the Southern Club was the Spa's premier gambling house

Indiana Club - 1913
Several cons and swindle games occurred here, helping give the Spa a bad reputation

International Detective Agency and had once done a big favor for Burns, and a call by Fox brought Burns detectives to the Spa by the droves. Another call brought his personal attorney, John Hickey, from Indianapolis who associated his wealthy client with two fine Hot Springs attorneys, Will H. Martin, a former prosecuting attorney and his partner, Hartley Wootton. They then established close contact with the assistant prosecuting attorney, George Whittington. As the story began to unfold and be published in the press throughout the country other victims who had been conned here began to come forth.[7] Mayor Waters took little action at first until prodded by Sheriff Williams. The mayor was like the little Dutch-boy with his finger in the dike trying to hold back the tide. The scene before him was like standing on shore and gazing at the ocean, there seemed to be no end. Complaints continued to pour in. Spectacular arrests began to be made with George Whittington following the wife of "Big Charlie" Wilks to Little Rock and arresting her husband; and the exciting grabbing of "The Brass Kid," from under the

---

[7] *The Record* - 1997, pp. 14-83. An article entitled "Big Charlie, The Fixer and The Brass Kid," by Orval E. Allbritton, sets forth in detail the various scams.

"protective custody" of the Chicago Police Department by Garland County Deputy Sheriff Walter Wheatley, followed by a mad car chase down Michigan Avenue and across the state line into Indiana outside the jurisdiction of the Illinois authorities. Then there were the trials and tribulations of Wheatley trying to get "The Brass Kid" back to Arkansas to face trial. All of these events appeared as front-page coverage and almost read as an adventure story or a soap opera. The business community began to be upset by the unfavorable publicity and image projected upon the city. Judge C.T. Cotham had enough, and summoned the grand jury in a special meeting. The colorful aliases of the participants came to light and caught the imagination of the public: Charles Wilt, alias "Big Charlie;" Ed Spear, alias "The Fixer;" Jack Porter, alias "Handsome Jack;" Walter P. Worth, alias "The Harmony Kid;" Joe Denton, alias "The Baltimore Plunger;" and the most famous, J.P. Coon, alias James H. Ward, alias "The Brass Kid."[8]

With the unfavorable publicity attending the "fleecing" stories and Hot Springs filling up with crooks and con-men, W.W. Waters tried to close down the gambling for a "cooling-off" period. Much to his chagrin, he discovered several of his police officers had "cut their own deal" with the gamblers and disobeyed him and had permitted the continuing of their illegal operations. It was completely out of control. Sheriff Bob Williams was being pressured by threats of a special called grand jury and did not want to be charged with malfeasance of office by not doing his duty. Too, his own family, regular members of St. Luke's Episcopal Church, were urging him to take action. After a stormy meeting with Waters, Williams gave the clubs an ultimatum, "Close down within forty-eight hours or your gambling equipment will be seized and burned."[9] Some of the clubs believed Williams was posturing for the public and press. They quickly discovered he wasn't, as he and his deputies seized a wagon load of gambling equipment and burned it on the court house grounds.[10] This was quickly followed by raids on the large clubs. As gamblers watched a pick-ax slice through an expensive roulette wheel, reality set in: Williams was serious. Bob Williams even raided and shut down the Ohio Club in which his brother Coffey was a partner. Stunned, the gambling clubs began to close their doors. One newspaper described the scene as "the gloomiest day of the year."[11]

Mayor Waters was faced in the democratic primary that spring by two opponents, Hamp Williams and John A. Riggs. Hamp Williams was a well-known business man operating a large hardware store on Ouachita Avenue

---

[8] Ibid.

[9] *New Era*, 11 February 1913.

[10] *Sentinel-Record*, 10 February 1913.

[11] *New Era*, 10 February 1913.

and had opened the first Ford automobile agency in Hot Springs. He had been an advocate for an open town, but had changed his mind as the con-racket stories unfolded. Riggs was publisher of the *New Era*, President of the Lopez Medicine Company, and was one of the leading advocates for women's suffrage. It was a formidable array facing Waters, and he and his supporters--especially the gambling community who threw hundreds of dollars into the election--campaigned extremely hard. He barely escaped by beating his adversaries by only ten votes. It had been a narrow victory and people believed the open-town policy would continue. Everyone figured Waters was "home-free," and would have no opposition in the general election. Waters was thus surprised on the last day to file for office, when Dr. Jacob W. McClendon walked into the clerk's office and presented himself as running as the Peoples Party candidate.

Jacob McClendon was a man cut from a different bolt of cloth than most politicians, "a cat of a different color." He was a strong-willed individual, had an extremely fine medical practice, and was one of the leading surgeons in Hot Springs. What really made him so unique was his honesty, a seemingly unusual trait for one in politics. But, of course, even though he was elected mayor five terms and was never beaten, he never claimed to be a politician. He was once described as a man whose "integrity has never been questioned by even his bitterest enemies."[12] McClendon, neither a dyed-in-the-wool democrat or a moss-back republican, drew his support across party lines. Those who knew him were aware of the fact his actions were not always popular and that he always did what he considered "to be the right thing," regardless of the consequences. There were no polls in those days and even had there been, McClendon would have still have done what he believed to be best. He promised the town that if he was elected there would be a complete housecleaning of the police department, which had appeared very shady on the matter of the con-game issue. Mayor Waters completely under-estimated his opponent and was stunned when the returns came in showing McClendon to be the new mayor. McClendon was true to his word and from the police department kept only two men, appointing Tom Ellison chief. He also warned all saloons that he meant for them to comply with the Sunday closing law, and if they didn't believe him, just try him.[13] There were few takers.

Things could not be much worse for the gambling community. With Bob Williams, supported by Judge C.T. Cotham, shutting down the clubs, and Dr. McClendon winning the mayor's race, their last hope was gone and many left town. The remainder had to get jobs elsewhere. With the clubs gone and the heat on, the con-men, too, packed up and left. That is, those who were not

---

[12] *Sentinel-Record*, 13 April 1921.

[13] Ibid., 14 November 1913.

sent to the penitentiary like J.P. Coon, "The Brass Kid."[14] Charlie Wilts, "Big Charlie,"had talked two prominent Hot Springs attorneys and some of his gambling friends in going on his bail for $10,000. They might as well have gathered a crowd to watch and burned the money on the courthouse grounds as they were never to see "Big Charlie" again. The signers of the bond wiggled and squirmed every way they could trying to keep from paying the $10,000 pledged. Circuit Judge Cotham ordered it paid--they appealed to the Supreme Court. The Supreme Court ordered it paid--they appealed for a Governor's pardon. The Governor, after holding a hearing at Hot Springs at the Arlington Hotel and listening to the bond signers and a host of citizens who believed the lawyers and gamblers who had signed the bond, should pay-up, denied the pardon, tried to hold a straight face as he got back on his train, and probably laughed all the way back to Little Rock at the lawyers and gamblers getting conned.[15] A few days later Sheriff Williams sold property the signers had pledged.

Ed Spear, "The Fixer,"a local fixture, had narrowly averted conviction by a jury vote of 11-1. When it was discovered the dissenting juror had slipped out of the Moody Hotel late one night, where the jury had been sequestered by order of the court, and was gone several hours, an irate prosecuting attorney and judge ordered him jailed. Spear was tried again in September 1913, this time in Mt. Ida, where another hung jury verdict resulted.[16]

Robert L. Williams

Williams was the most powerful political force in Hot Springs before Leo P. McLaughlin. He was elected sheriff nine times and mayor once.

Courtesy of Mark Palmer

---

[14] The" Brass Kid" proved to be an elusive individual. He "conned" the Arkansas State Penitentiary into believing he was insane and was transferred to the State Hospital at Little Rock. He promptly "conned" two attendants into believing he would send them $200 if they permitted him to escape. He was not seen again for ten years, then brazeningly reappeared at Hot Springs, was recognized, and sent back to the State Penitentiary to complete his sentence.

[15] *Sentinel-Record,* 11 July 1914.

[16] Ibid., 7 September 1913.

Ed "The Fixer" Spear

It appeared that Ed Spear, "The Fixer," was out of the woods. Unfortunately for him, W.H. Martin, who had been acting as a Special Prosecutor, had been given a federal appointment as United States Attorney for the Eastern District of Arkansas. Martin's memory was long and he had not forgotten his old adversaries, Spear and "Handsome Jack" Porter, and filed charges against them for fraudulently using the mails in the con-games they pulled, and sent U.S. Marshals to arrest them. That trial was in Federal District Court and before a Federal-selected jury. This was a different ball game and this time the two were convicted and sentenced to the Federal Penitentiary at Atlanta, Georgia.[17]

A lot had happened in Hot Springs the first eight months of 1913, nearly all disturbing to the community. There were the con-games; the gambling shut-downs; the trials; a flood in downtown Hot Springs; a gas explosion in the basement of Mattar Brothers Auction House and the injuring eleven people and destroying several buildings; the last legal execution in Garland County;[18] the lynching of an accused rapist of Garland Huff, daughter of Floyd Huff, a prominent attorney; and the suicide of Sheriff Bob William's brother, John Coffey Williams, who had taken part in the big shootout in 1899. Each of these had been troubling and disconcerting.

W. H. Martin

In the April elections of that year, Police Judge Jack Archer was reelected to office, but because of ill health passed away 1 July 1913.[19] Verne Ledgerwood's name was put before the

---

[17] U. S. Congressman Jay Dickey's office was able to locate the complete penal files on Ed Spear and Jack Porter, now located in the National Archives.

[18] *Sentinel-Record*, 2 June 1913. This was the hanging of Clarence A. Schumann, who admitted killing his wife, Lulu, "in a fit of jealous rage." Not long afterward the Arkansas State Legislature passed a bill requiring all executions to be performed by the State.

[19] Hot Springs Funeral Records. Also, commented on in *Sentinel-Record*, 9 November 1913.

council as a possible replacement for Archer. Many of the aldermen were personally acquainted with the young attorney and everyone knew his father J.J. Ledgerwood. His sponsor was Judge Thurston P. Farmer, a well-regarded citizen, who many years before had "set a precedent as a young attorney and established a splendid record as police judge."[20] The measure passed unanimously and no one could foresee Ledgerwood's career would far surpass everyone's who ever held that bench.

Yes, much had happened in the first eight months of 1913, but the worst was yet to come!

For sometime James Russell McLaughlin, the second-eldest son of John and Bridget, had been suffering greatly from his respiratory problems. He no longer had stamina to work at the store and the least effort brought on fits of coughing. When his complexion turned sallow, two conferring physicians recommended his going to Manitou Springs, Colorado and entering a sanitorium for treatment of his tuberculosis. His mother, Bridget, and sister, Elizabeth, accompanied him there and stayed several days. They received word after their return that Russell had a turn for the worse. Bridget sought comfort and advice from their new parish priest the Reverend William J. Carroll, who arrived in Hot Springs in August 1913.[21] She was most heartened when word was received that Russell was "out of danger."[22] Mary Anna prevailed upon her family to permit her to visit her ill brother in Colorado and they assented. She stayed near Russell for two weeks, visiting, taking short walks, and reading to him every day.[23] She barely got out of Colorado before the winter snows arrived.

The Ed Spear trial in Mt. Ida was winding down on September 5, when word was received, "Hot Springs is burning." Nothing struck fear into the citizens of the Spa like hearing the word, "fire." Fire had decimated the downtown area in 1878. Fire had cost lives and destroyed eighteen blocks on Ouachita, Orange and Hawthorne in 1895. A large section of the city was laid waste by fire and lives had been lost in 1905, and some areas had not completely recovered by 1913, when the cry of "fire" was again heard.

The origin of the worst fire in the history of the State of Arkansas occurred in an apartment of a rooming house on Church Street. The tenant was a laundress who left a charcoal heating iron unattended for a few minutes. During that time, a piece of laundry, an ironing board cover, a blowing curtain or some fabric was ignited and within minutes the room was totally engulfed in flames. By the time the fire department was summoned the house was a

---

[20] *Sentinel-Record*, 23 November 1913.

[21] *Centennial - St. Mary's,, p. 21.*

[22] *Sentinel-Record*, 2 November 1913.

[32] Ibid., 23 November 1913.

After the fire - 5 September 1913

rolling ball of flame and had caught an adjacent home, and was quickly spreading to other wooden structures.[24] As building after building burst into flames it became apparent the small fire department would be unable to contain the fierce conflagration. A call was placed to Little Rock to send "additional equipment." The capitol city responded by dispatching Captain B.S. Harmon, a six-man crew, and a large pumper truck.[25]

As flames cut through buildings in just minutes, dynamiting was tried. This method of fire fighting had been unsuccessful in large fires at Chicago and Cleveland and during the earthquake and fire at San Francisco. It was not successful at Hot Springs, either. The first building to go up by this means was People's Laundry. The flames merely feasted on the carcass of the blown-up buildings and moved westward. Other attempts were tried with the same result.

Will McLaughlin, at his store on the corner of Church and Malvern, had a "front-row seat" to the start of the fire. As he watched the flames move his way he told his brother George and a helper to hitch two wagons and bring them to the rear loading dock. They began to load them with the best merchandise and several onlookers began to help them. Brother Leo arrived just as the Public Utility complex across the street caught fire. When flames leaped the street and caught the roof of the McLaughlin store on fire, Will called a halt in his attempt to save all of the stock and ordered everyone to

---

[42] Ibid., 7 September 1913.

[25] *Arkansas Gazette*, 7 September 1913.

move to safety. From a safe distance they watched as the hardware store and fourteen of their rental units became nothing but fuel for the fiery inferno.[26]

Horrified, crowds watched as flames, estimated to be one hundred feet in height, enveloped the business district on Malvern, destroying the large Park Hotel and Bath House, Peters Brothers Grocery, Pappas Confectionery, five saloons, Battles Drug Store, Plunkett Jarrell Grocery Company and many others.

Like a giant threshing machine, the flames mowed down the Iron Mountain passenger and freight depots, the Ozark Sanitarium and the beautiful high school building, only five years old. As the flames raced up and down Orange, Hawthorne, and Woodbine, houses built since the fire of 1905 went up in flame and smoke.

The Ledgerwood Bottling Works, which had been rebuilt since the last fire, again became the fire's victim. So did the Ledgerwood home. John J. Ledgerwood was heard to exclaim, "If I didn't have bad luck, I wouldn't have any luck at all." It was the third time in twenty-five years that he had lost both his business and his home. One thing was different, however, when he saw the fire spreading he pulled his two delivery wagons in and he and his three boys were able to save almost all the house furnishings, clothes and some of the business equipment. They fled to the safety of West Mountain.[27]

The Garland County Court House, only eight years-old at the time of the 1913 fire, was badly "gutted." Many records were lost.

---

[26] Ibid., 7 September 1913.

[27] Trice & Dora Jane Ledgerwood Ellis.

Nothing seemed to stop the progress of the conflagration as the flames crossed Central at Market. They threatened to turn toward the business district on the main thoroughfare. A heroic effort was made by the combined fire departments and they were successful in diverting the flames along Ouachita. The fire department could not be faulted as the water system failed once the utility plant and pumps were destroyed. There just wasn't any water in the mains. Without water how do you stop a fire? How, indeed?

The Moody Hotel, which burned in 1905, again was destroyed. So was the Garland County Court House. Many beautiful homes burned that day and left hundreds homeless. The fire had reached the foot of West Mountain when a God-sent rain began to fall on the tortured city and cool down the fire. At last, the fire fiend appeared satiated. Nearly sixty smoldering blocks of blackened ruins were left as a stark reminder of the ravages of fire. Blackened chimneys and walls stood like tombstones in a cemetery. It was to be a long and sleepless night for hundreds.

At least Leo McLaughlin and his family had an unscathed and undamaged house. The Ledgerwoods did not.

Dora Snell Ledgerwood had been in failing health for several months. She had tried to keep up her activities at Central Methodist Church but there were many days she did not feel like going. The local doctors seemed baffled about her condition and finally acknowledged their helplessness and inability to improve her health. The doctors suggested that she journey to Baltimore, Maryland and enter the John Hopkins Hospital for evaluation and treatment. She and John J. were getting ready to make the trip when the fire occurred, destroying their home and business. Dora knew her husband was shouldering a great responsibility with trying to get his business going again and rebuilding the house. The boys, Archie, Verne, and Cecil were helping every way they could. When the doctor told Dora she should not waste any further time in getting to the clinic in Baltimore she told John J. that she would go, but for him to stay and to look out for the family. She said she would be alright as she knew she would be getting the best of care, and would not be as much of a burden if she was in the hospital. John J. would not hear of her making the trip alone and hired a young lady, Anna Crow, to accompany her and keep him advised of her progress.[28] The news from Baltimore of the examination would not be good news--but, few things were in 1913!

---

[28] Ibid., 2 November 1913.

Following the fire everyone recognized Hot Springs was in big trouble. It was in desperate straits. As the welcomed rain arrived, cooling the fire, darkness enveloped a tired and sorely wounded city where nearly 5,000 persons were left homeless.[1] Some would find shelter with relatives in undamaged sections of town. Others were taken in by some of the hotels and boarding houses. But still others were walking the streets with glazed and stunned expressions on their faces. Mayor McClendon made an appeal for homes to "throw open their doors" to the unfortunates. The city had no electricity or water: the utility plant stood in ruins. Communication was a big problem as telephone lines were down all through the burned area affecting service throughout the city. There was no public transportation as trolley lines were down on Malvern, South Central and South Hot Springs, and of course, there was no power to run the trolleys. The Hot Springs Fire Department was crippled with no water in the mains and thousands of feet of fire hose burned and damaged by falling walls. That night, by the glow of tallow candles at the Business Mens League, Mayor Jacob W. McClendon opened a crucial and important meeting. Present were all twelve of the city council, the executive committee of the Business Mens League composed of Hamp Williams, John Barrett, Simon Cooper and Martin A. Eisele. This group was to operate as the official Relief Committee. George Belding, secretary of the State Fair Association, was elected to handle all publicity for the committee and Hamp Williams was elected to head the committee. It was agreed to call a mass meeting of the citizens for the following morning at the City Auditorium. How word got around the city of the meeting is amazing, but over five hundred people were waiting to get in the Auditorium before 10:00 o'clock.

President Hamp Williams, who had again lost his business and home, opened the meeting: "This is the saddest meeting I ever presided over. We are called here to devise ways and means for providing for the needy and distressed, of which there are thousands in Hot Springs today."

Mayor McClendon announced he had received many messages from cities, clubs and individuals throughout the country offering aid. Such offers were encouraging. People were concerned and cared about what happened to Hot Springs and its people.

A relief fund was established and the first person donating was Frank P. Fox, a visitor and the man who had been swindled out of $20,000 at the Indiana Club, in Hot Springs. He gave $200.[2]

Realizing a huge amount of aid was needed, the committee agreed to accept

---

[1] *Arkansas Gazette*, 7 September 1913.
[2] *Arkansas Democrat*, 7 September 1913.

Governor George W. Hays' offer for two companies of militia to be dispatched from Conway and Beebe.[3] Little Rock Mayor Charles N. Taylor, who had accompanied Governor Hays, was greatly touched with sympathy for the many homeless people he saw poking with sticks into the ruins and ashes of their former homes, hoping to find anything left of value. He pledged to mount a fund raising drive at Little Rock and hastened back to start the relief effort.[4] Before leaving the mass meeting of citizens, Mayor Taylor and officials of the Rock Island and Iron Mountain Railroads were given a standing ovation for their help and offer of contributions. Governor Hays ordered the State Guard to make tents and other equipment available to the homeless.[5] It was learned at that meeting visitors staying at the hotels about the city had contributed over $1,000.

Help was coming from everywhere--everywhere that is, but the Federal Government. Hot Springs, a Government Reservation, had received aid from the small fire fighting force at the Army-Navy Hospital because it had been a neighbor-helping-neighbor sort-of-thing. But in its great need, the city surrounded on all sides by the reservation could not depend on its government for help. Today, the President and Members of Congress would be falling over each other to tour such a sight as the burned out city presented. They would arrive in droves, bringing dozens of reporters and photographers to record the event, long before the ruins stopped smoldering. As soon as the cameras stopped flashing they could not return to Washington fast enough to start pouring millions of dollars into the rebuilding of the city. As the politicians of today would modestly say–"It is the humane thing to do." What you would not hear is "it would be politically correct." But such were not the times in 1913. The citizens of Hot Springs were strong people, and not quitters for they had been tested by fire--more than once!

It was a time of cooperation and working together. The Southwestern Telephone and Telegraph Company loaned what poles they had in stock so that the city might rebuild the electrical service.[6] The Eastman and Arlington Hotels had small generating power plants and permitted the utility company to connect the systems to restore power in parts of the city.

The Central Methodist Church, which had burned in the fire of 1905 while located at Central and Chapel Streets, had built a new building, opening on Easter Sunday of 1909, at the intersection of Olive and Central. Unfortunately, they had moved into the path of the fire of 1913 and the congregation was again homeless. The First Baptist Church made available its facilities for the

---

[3] Ibid.

[4] *Arkansas Gazette*, 7 September 1913.

[5] *Sentinel-Record*, 14 September 1913.

[6] Ibid.

mid-week service and owners of the Princess Theater offered its property fo
Sunday morning services.[7]

Individuals and firms improvised to get back into business. Hamp Williams
whose hardware store on Ouachita Avenue had burned a second time, knew
what to do. He erected a large tent across the street on a vacant lot, ordered
building supplies, and opened business two days after the fire. So did C.N
Anderson, a blacksmith, setting up his tent operation on Hawthorne. H
McCafferty, a well-known undertaker, lost a new building in the fire, but had
saved his rolling stock. He erected a tent and ordered new stock and continued
service for his clients. His home and a rental dwelling had both been
destroyed. His insurance agent, John Henry Reece, had a vacant apartment and
McCafferty was able to domicile his family there.

The Hot Springs Street Railway cleared their tracks of debris and put two o
the old mule pulled trolleys back into operation. These were quite popula
with tourists who came to Hot Springs to view the ruins.

Within a few days following the fire every contractor in town had work
orders to keep his crew busy for a year. Carpenters, bricklayers, steel framers
roofers, cabinet makers and painters poured into the city looking for work
and there was plenty of it. The work went on so long that many of the out-of
town workers brought their families in, entered their children in schools and
discovered they liked the town so well they stayed.

As researchers dig back into the records of the Spa city, looking at it
colorful history and its past trials and tribulation caused by fire, flood o
depression, it is the opinion of this writer that they would surely agree th
recovery from the fire of 1913 was Hot Springs' finest hour!

Everywhere one looked on Malvern Avenue there was activity. Burned and
twisted metal, brick, charred beams and other debris was being cleaned and
hauled away. The city had decided not to rebuild the power plant on it
original location at the northwest corner of Malvern and Church Street.
Instead, it would be rebuilt along Hot Springs Creek at Belding Avenue.

Second Ward Alderman Will McLaughlin had fought hard in a specia
council meeting to include much of the second ward in "the extension of th
fire limits."[9] This was an ordinance requiring all buildings, business or persona
dwellings, within specific areas to be rebuilt with fire resistant materia
Nothing would improve the looks of the city so much as the new bric
structures. Will McLaughlin had also introduced a bill requiring enlarging o
water mains. He asked that twenty-four inch mains replace twelve-inch main

---

[7] *Central Church Souvenir Booklet*, Paul Douglas Printers, Memphis, 1914.
[8] Ibid.
[9] Ibid.

and twelve-inch mains replace six-inch mains.[10] In the future, these would enhance the fire-fighting capabilities of the city.

Will and Leo McLaughlin contacted their former tenants to ascertain if they were willing to rent from them again if the building they had occupied for their business was restored. All but two assured the McLaughlins they would lease from them again. With this assurance and before any insurance settlements were made, they employed contractors to begin. The first two buildings would replace the original store on the southwest corner of Malvern and Church, and the other would be on the east side of Malvern. Both would be two-story brick buildings.[11]

There was one major change: there would be no more McLaughlin Grocery and Hardware, as it had been known for the past three or four years. The McLaughlin family was out of the grocery business and only hardware and queensware would be sold. It might have been different if Russell McLaughlin was well and able to operate the grocery. But he wasn't. He was far away in Colorado and very ill.

John J. Ledgerwood did have a great burden on him--a very ill wife, his home in ashes, and his business in ruins. To top it off his brother and partner, James had decided to move to California in 1912. James and Ellen, his wife, had their home burned in 1895 and 1905. Ellen, who was born in Nebraska and had no family locally, had enough and encouraged James to see if life might be a bit easier out west. They regretted leaving their family and their church. They were charter members of Orange Street Presbyterian Church and had seen it grow from twelve members to a sizeable congregation. James explained the situation to John J., who was understanding, and the two decided to retain their partnership in the event the California move proved to be a mistake. James moved his family to the Los Angeles area[12] and by good luck and a successful relationship with the Coca-Cola Company was able to get a franchise for that area. When the big fire occurred at Hot Springs, that settled the issue for good: James and his family would be returning only for visits. Their son, (William) Hugh Ledgerwood, a very well-liked young man who graduated at Hot Springs in 1909 remained for several years. He worked as a bookkeeper for the Security Bank.[13] Hugh courted and married Flora Diffee, 11 June 1911.[14] They resided on Amber and Plateau Streets. In a second marriage, Hugh would marry Minnie MacKenzie of Nova Scotia.[15]

---

[9] *Sentinel-Record*, 10 September 1913.
[10] Ibid., 14 September 1913.
[12] *Polks - Hot Springs City Directory - 1912*, p. 245.
[13] *Polks - Hot Springs Directory - 1915-1917.*
[14] Garland County Marriage Records, Book R, p. 183.
[15] *Sentinel-Record, 6 July 1917.*

Vernal S. Ledgerwood and Bess Wakelin Ledgerwood
Courtesy of Dora Jane Ledgerwood Ellis

When Verne Ledgerwood returned from college in 1912, he learned his mother Dora and Bessie Wakelin had grown quite close. Bess did little thoughtful things for her older friend, and had shared some of Verne's letters with his mother. Bess' mother had died several years before and her father, a cobbler, had raised her and her brother Joe in a house on Whittington. Upon Verne's return he discovered Bess to be grown up and they started to date as "steadies." With Dora's health rapidly declining, Bess spent more and more time around the Ledgerwood home and she was able to make Verne's mother more comfortable. The two young people became engaged about the first of July 1913, when Verne was appointed Police Judge by the city council. Before that time his law practice was not providing an income large enough to support a wife. They set a date to marry around Christmas.

Then the fire struck, upsetting everyone's lives. John J. was able to rent a house at 457 West Grand for his family and a building at 700 West Grand for his bottling works.[16] Dora was a wise woman and was much aware that her condition was worsening. Upon her return from Johns Hopkins, the fire and fight in her eyes were gone, and the family realized her time was short. With John J. having to attend to the rebuilding of his business and home he had to hire someone to stay with Dora. Bess suggested to Verne that they move up

[16] Bell Telephone Directory, September 1913.

the date of their wedding and she could move in and take care of Dora. Since they had been invited to reside in the Ledgerwood home anyway, her suggestion made sense.

On a cold, raw winter's day, 12 November 1913, Vernal Snell Ledgerwood, age 24, and Bess E. Wakelin, age 20, were married.[17] Bess became to her mother-in-law, Dora, as Ruth was to Naomi, in the *Bible*. She looked after Dora's needs until her mother-in-law was called by death 14 March 1914 and she was laid to rest in Greenwood Cemetery. Dora's church paid homage to her in it's *Souvenir Booklet*, with these words: "When the year was at the spring and her day at high noon, Mrs. Dora Ledgerwood passed through Glory's morning gate to walk in Paradise."

The Ledgerwoods

Left to right: Vernal S., Cecil, Archie, Hugh, J.J., James E.

Courtesy of Dora Jane Ledgerwood Ellis

[17] Garland County Marriage Records, Book P, p. 145.

Mayor-Council Conflict and Stella's Disappointment

Hot Springs slipped quietly into the year 1914, perhaps with a furtive glance over its shoulder at what was undoubtedly the worst year of its entire history. It was a much-changed town from the one that had started 1913, with its brothels and gambling halls operating flagrantly before its populace, protected by a corrupt city administration and its law enforcement agencies. A new administration was at the helm of the city promising reform. It was not perfect, but was more honest in its dealings. Almost one-fifth of the Spa lay in burned waste, but showing promise of a new day as homes and businesses were arising from the ashes. Plans for a bigger and better high school were underway. The Garland County Court House was being rebuilt.

The city was beset with many problems, all costing money. And the coffers were bare, so bare in fact, that at one point Mayor McClendon loaned the city $17,000, interest-free, to meet its obligations. McClendon had not only lost his home in the fire, but The Diamond Jo Sanitarium, which he owned and operated. However, he always made time to work on the city's problems.

In spite of Dr. Jacob W. McClendon's generous attitude with the city, the interest-free loan and the fact he never took a salary, donating it all to charity, he had detractors. Normally a new chief executive is given time by the council to institute a new agenda before coming into conflict with him. Not so, with this council. What is normally referred to as the honeymoon period, was never accorded to McClendon. In fact, even before he was sworn in to office the old council, mostly composed of the same individuals carried over to the present council, was working against him. He had the audacity to run as an independent defeating W.W. Waters, a democrat, and they were all democrats. It was known to the council that McClendon intended to appoint S.A. Buchanan as his secretary, and to combine that office with the job of police clerk which would effect a savings to the city. All previous mayors, including W.W. Waters, had a secretary. This mattered little to the council in its opposition to the newly elected mayor. In an almost shady meeting called the night before McClendon was to take office, the council in a mean-spirited move, abolished the office of the mayor's secretary.[1] The motion for this action was made by councilman C.J. "Pike" Horner, who was leaving the council and was followed by supporters of defeated Mayor W.W. Waters. The council must have been day-dreaming to think this type of behavior would go unnoticed by the voters. The move by the council had not been very well-

---

[1] *Sentinel-Record*, 8 April 1913, pp. 1-2.

eceived by the public.[2] An outcry and clamor occurred. It must have slipped he minds of the councilmen who had elected Dr. McClendon as mayor, and lso themselves. The voters! Had the aldermen miscalculated? The answer was wift in coming. The council was quickly privately and publicly reminded. The *entinel-Record* reported the following morning: "There were many protests esterday from the public because of the action of the old city council in bolishing the office of secretary to the mayor."

Then, in an editorial, Editor John H. Higgins really scored the council and ung them out to dry, writing: "When the city council, through a resolution, ttempted to repeal an ordinance, and thus upset the plans of Mayor IcClendon, the municipal law making body not only showed its teeth to the ew mayor but showed its ignorance to the people. How different from the ttitude of the city council was the attitude of Mayor McClendon in his plea or harmony and cooperation?"[3]

A politician is never more sensitive than at a time when a combination of ublic outrage and the spotlight of critical press coverage focus on his nisdeeds. It makes pussycats out of lions. Like it or not, Jacob W. McClendon vas mayor, elected and supported by a majority of the voters and the leading ocal newspaper. Members of the council no doubt, did not enjoy the riticism, but they understood the message from the people, loud and clear, nd the second meeting was reflective of their change in attitude as the papers eported, "City Council and Mayor Together."[4]

But the mayor and council would have other clashes.[5] There would always e differences of opinion. After all, the council was composed of dyed-in-the-vool democrats who did not always agree among themselves and the mayor, vho was a strong-willed person and had been elected on the Peoples Party icket. Even with these differences the city came through the crisis caused by he fire of 1913 and great hurdles were crossed by the council and mayor, ogether. And really, the kindly, well-intentioned mayor and voters would have he last word, as not a single councilman would still be in office at the end of)r. McClendon's tenure as mayor.

The democratic primary was to be held in December of 1914. Voters did not now if Dr. McClendon would cross-over and become a Democrat or not. He ad not announced his intentions to run again as an Independent in the pring. The remnants of the gambling establishment encouraged former nayor W.W. Waters to represent their interest and he entered the primary. His

---

[2] Ibid, 10 April 1913, p. 5. One banker called Mayor McClendon, approved his ppointment of S.A. Buchanan, and offered to pay $120 a month toward keeping Buchanan in he mayor's office.

[3] Ibid., 9 April 1913, p. 2.

[4] Ibid., 15 April 1913, p. 3.

[5] Ibid., 2 May 1913,. p. 1.

opponent would be Harry Jones, owner and manager of the Majestic Hotel.[6]

Harry Jones was a unique individual. His was truly a success story, a rags-to-riches tale. He had come to Hot Springs as a mere lad and secured a job as a stock-boy at the Majestic Hotel. The owner recognized Jones to be an honest, hard-working, and unselfish person, and promoted him as time went by. When Jones became manager he was very instrumental in the hotel becoming one of the better hostelries in the Spa. Jones, saving and investing his money carefully, was able to buy the hotel from his employer when he expressed a desire to sell-out.

Jones, like Dr. McClendon, was not a politician in the true sense of the word, but he loved Hot Springs and was very concerned with its future.. He was a moderate or middle-of-the-road democrat. He recognized that the bread-and-butter of Hot Springs was the thermal water and the thousands of visitors it brought in supporting the hotels, restaurants and downtown businesses. Gambling provided entertainment and relaxation for the visitors' amusement. But the gambling and loose money attracted the con-men and flim-flam artists who preyed on tourists and gave the city a bad name and reputation. This, he did not like. Jones could live with the gambling if properly controlled. He could not live with the undesirable element gambling always seemed to attract.

On the same democratic primary ticket was a contest for police judge, the position held by Vernal Ledgerwood. He, of course, announced early for the office. So did another young attorney, Dennison (Dan) S. Barnes.[7]

Barnes and Ledgerwood had become well-acquainted as anyone practicing law had to try cases in police court, and the two had become friendly. Dan Barnes had worked for awhile as a clerk for the Plunkett-Jarrell Grocery Company.[8] His parents were R.D. and Ruth Barnes and he lived with them on Parker Street. Dan began to study a little law and took the bar exam, passed, and started practicing law. He was not very successful and decided he would try for an elected office. Barnes told Verne Ledgerwood he had nothing against him personally, but wanted and needed the job as police judge. In an unusual and gentlemanly agreement the two pacted for a low-key and dignified campaign. There would be no name-calling, no speech-making and a minimum of political ads.[9] It would save both of them money and they would remain friends if it did not get personal. This must have been an unusual happening, especially for Hot Springs politics. Verne Ledgerwood's ad merely

---

[6] Ibid., 1 December 1914.

[7] Ibid.

[8] *Polks Southern Directories - Hot Springs - 1912.*

[9] *Sentinel-Record,* 1 December 1914.

tated, "His Record is His Endorsement."[10]

In the primary Harry Jones defeated W.W. Waters 784-535. Ledgerwood vas victorious over Barnes 828-513.[11]

For sometime, S.E. Dillon, superintendent of the public utilities, had been ırging the city fathers to embark upon a more venturesome path. He told hem that he was certain that the installation of a modern street lighting ystem in the downtown area would help make Hot Springs into a modern ınd attractive city. Up until that time, low-powered street lights cast their eeble glow only a short distance leaving areas of the downtown blocks dark ınd in shadows. At times, he explained, it was difficult to find one's way along he sidewalks without stumbling over rough portions of the concrete hidden n the dark. The business community and the Business Men's Club were upportive and the mayor and city council went along with the movement. Construction began in the summer of 1914.

As the end of the year approached, plans began to be formulated for a huge celebration and turning on the lights. Everyone wanted it to take place before Christmas, and December 23 was selected. It would be called the "White Way" celebration and a committee was elected with Gus Strauss, a businessman, chairman. Strauss immediately invited Governor George W. Hays to come and bring the dedicatory address. Other important people were nvited--t would be a time to show off the new Hot Springs.

The two daily newspapers, *The Sentinel-Record* and *The New Era*, came up with a plan for the public to nominate and vote on a queen for the occasion.[12] A ballot was printed in the papers each day and when filled out would be a vote for the young lady of the reader's choice. The newspapers admitted that "every effort is being made to have this a popularity contest without being nterfered with through the use of financial means in behalf of the candidates."[13]

Over fifteen young ladies were nominated and one of those was Stella McLaughlin. Stella was twenty-three years old, very attractive, and quite well-known for being a horsewoman. She was often seen riding one of the family's beautiful saddle horses about town. She still had some friends from her school days and several of these set out to help get her elected "White Way" Queen. Her eldest sister, Anna, began a telephone campaign on Stella's behalf. She called acquaintances of the family reminding them of the ballots in each day's paper and urged them to fill out the forms, turn them in and vote for her sister. She called the parishioners of St. Mary's Church and asked for their

[10] Ibid., 3 December 1914.
[11] Ibid., 4 December 1914.
[12] Ibid., 16 December 1914, p. 1.
[13] Ibid.

Stella McLaughlin was an attractive young woman as well as an excellent horsewoman

support.

Judges selected to count the ballots for the contest were M.A. Eisele, George Callahan and M. Rose, superintendent of the Federal Reservation. These three men would meet every two or three days and count the accumulated votes. When the first vote was reported Stella was well-pleased as she had recorded 1,203 votes, far above her two nearest opponents, Juanita Gilliam with 464 and Ruby White with 412. Stella had no sure thing as her as the two front-runners behind her were also well-known.

Juanita C. Gilliam was eighteen years-old and had grown up around Hot Springs, was personable and a very talented musician. She was a singer, described as having a very fine contralto voice and good skills on the piano and often was hired by some of the hotels around the holidays to entertain. While Ruby White was not an entertainer, she was quite well-known in the business sector as being a stenographer at the William J. Little Agency, and was quite popular with the younger set. Her father had died several years before and her mother, Willie White, ran a furnished room place on south Central.[14]

Stella grew more confident when the second report reflected she was still in the lead and had doubled the vote over the second runner, Ruby White.[15]

---

[14] *Polks Southern Directory - Hot Springs - 1915.*

[15] *Sentinel-Record*, 17 December 1914.

What apparently was unknown to Stella was that the supporters of Juanita Gilliam had also been calling their friends and picking up the ballots and holding them for several days before turning them in. This was revealed just before the contest ended, three days before the planned celebration. When that vote was published, Juanita had surged ahead of Stella, 7,852 to 6,324. Ruby White was third with 4,888.[16] Stella was crushed and hopes of recognition as queen were dashed away. She would never forgive Juanita and her friends for denying her the victory. But all was not lost. It was announced that the three finalists would be presented with "beautiful silver sets" by George Belding, from the Business Mens Club. Each girl would be able to appoint two maids to attend them and they would be seated on the speaker's stand erected in The Triangle (Como Square). Stella chose her sister Anna, who had aided her so faithfully, and her best friend, Florence Moody.[17]

In spite of terrible weather conditions--very cold temperatures and freezing rain--a huge crowd lined the parade route and filled The Triangle. Motorists had been encouraged to bring their automobiles and join the parade and there was a fierce traffic jam, before the event, during and afterwards.

When Mrs. William G. Maurice crowned Juanita Gilliam with a beautifully-lighted electric crown and quoted from the *Bible*, "God said let there be light; and there was light," the switch was thrown and The Triangle and Central Avenue was flooded with bright lights. At this, The Ledgerwood Band, with a full corps of thirty members, "struck up Dixie, and immediately there was a volcano of noises and shouts."[18]

The Sentinel-Record reported the next morning the celebration "Surpasses in enthusiasm anything ever held in the City of Hot Springs."

What a difference a year could make! Just one year before Hot Springs was staggering from the valley of despair caused by a monster of a fire and at the end of 1914 the city was on the move again and it seemed everyone's spirit had soared to the mountain top.

[16] Ibid., 20 December 1914.
[17] Ibid., 24 December 1914.
[18] Ibid.

Hunting, Fishing and Dancing

Verne Ledgerwood was becoming a sportsman. He had always had a grea interest in the outdoors, hunting and fishing, but had not always had the tim to devote to it that he would have preferred. Police Judge was just a part-tim job, generally conducted in the mornings. In the afternoons he would atten to his law practice with his partner A.T. "Sonny" Davies. It took both jobs t provide a living for the young couple. Not until Davies, an electe representative to the legislature, introduced a bill to elevate the police court i Garland County to the level of a municipal court would Ledgerwood hav time to devote to his hobbies of hunting and fishing. Under state law municipal judge could not practice law on the side. Clients coming t Ledgerwood for legal help were referred to his partner Davies and the sometimes split the fee.[1]

Ledgerwood and several other sportsmen in the area spent many days at duck and fishing camp on Lake Chicot, in southeast Arkansas. Some of h companions were J. Freeman, W.H. Martin and his son Tom K. Marti George Ryan, Douglas Hotchkiss, Tom Garen and others.[2]

The Ledgerwood Brothers
Left to right: Archie, Verne, Cecil
Courtesy of Dora Jane Ledgerwood Ellis

---

[1] LAT - Ledgerwood.

[2] *Sentinel-Record,* 27 November 1922, and many others.

He and brothers Cecil and Archie, fished the Ouachita and Saline Rivers. 'hey hunted the bottoms along the Saline for squirrels and ducks. During bird eason they could be found following their dogs in the western areas of ;arland and Montgomery counties.

Verne and Bess had a fairly active social life as both had grown up in Hot prings and had many friends. They were not of the trendy-set, attending nany of the dances and balls at the Arlington and Eastman Hotels. When the .ew Como Hotel was opened by Al Reynolds, dances were regularly held on he roof garden during nice weather. Bess and Verne would meet their friends here for light dining and dancing in the cool breezes the roof-top provided.[3]

On Saturday nights during cool or cold weather they could be found neeting with their friends at Schneck's Drug Store at Central and Prospect. everal couples would sit around the marble-top, wire-leg tables, or on the ounter stools, dangling their feet and enjoying fellowship and refreshments f ice-cream, sundaes, and cokes from the great old soda fountain that became o well known to so many generations of people. The refreshments were riced to fit the young couples' limited budgets. Laughter and friendship was he order of the day and even when their meeting was long they had no fear f being asked to leave by George Schneck, the proprietor. Sometimes the adies would go to one of their homes to continue the visit. Often, the men vould adjourn upstairs over the drug store to a doctor's office where there vas an old open-faced piano and the group would try their hand at some of he barbershop quartets favorites such as *Sweet Adeline*, and *The Church in the Wildwood*.[4] "None of us had much money, but it was a fun-time," Verne .edgerwood would later say.

The society editor for *The Sentinel-Record*, Mrs. D.A. Crockett, wife of David Crockett, County Supervisor, working from her home at 120 Garland Avenue, ut in long hours trying to keep up with the fast moving social scene in the pa City. Her work more than tripled during the winter and spring season as he town was flooded with socialites, high-level politicians, and industrial iants of the country. Each hotel was proud to boast and publicize its guest nd new arrivals list. Her column was carefully perused by the socially inclined o see what each debutante, or matron, was wearing and how the ballrooms vere decorated. Those who attended such functions eagerly searched the olumn to determine if their name was mentioned and in what connection. It vas a way of knowing what was going on about town.

Each holiday season Hot Springs became awash in the flood of parties, lances and social affairs. The Arlington Hotel always had both formal and nformal dances, Christmas Eve parties and a huge New Year's ball. These

---

[3] LAT Ledgerwood.

[4] Ibid.

were times when some of Hot Springs' social-set had the opportunity to rub elbows with some of the country's most important people. The visitors and local set matched up quite well with the dignitaries present and the celebrations were sometimes described as having "a spirit of conviviality and merriment."[5] Leo P. McLaughlin was seen many times at these functions. He seldom brought anyone, but occasionally his sister Stella would attend and they were seen dancing well into the evening, sometimes with each other. McLaughlin loved to dance with the beautiful Juanita Gilliam, but only if Stella wasn't around. She still had not forgiven Juanita for defeating her for the White Way Queen honor. Leo was quite popular and in the event he saw some lady whose husband was not affording her the opportunity to get on the dance floor he would gallantly ask permission of the man to ask his wife for a dance. He was a good dancer and through his attention to some of the neglected ladies, became a favorite at the balls. But he had a fault--when the check came Leo was a master at waiting for someone else to pick it up. This was a trait he would exhibit most of his life.

The large hotels competed with each other for the most sought-after dance of the season. They left no stone unturned. A race and scramble was on to assemble the best orchestra and the most renowned conductor. The Arlington boasted Professor Richard J. Barton, while the Eastman countered with Professor R. John Graham and the Majestic touted Walter Cain.[6] These three were regulars for many seasons and there were always local disagreements as to which one was best. It was generally agreed, however, they were all very good.

Sunday concerts were held in the rotunda at the Arlington and reportedly were "completely filled."[7] There, classics were performed, such as Rossini's *William Tell*, and popular music such as Victor Herbert's *The Debutante*.[8] Local vocal talents were utilized like Jane Finley or Juanita Gilliam, "The White Way" Queen. The numbers performed by the locals were reportedly "enthusiastically received."

The Eastman Hotel, often referred to as the Monarch of the Glen, usually did not open until January in time for the expected deluge of winter visitors. There was always an inaugural ball to set the opening of the season. The manager, W.E. Chester, who would later manage the Arlington, tried to make each inaugural ball something special to remember. Gala colored lights and decorations were strung about the lobby and dance floor.[9]

---

[5] *Sentinel-Record*, 2 January 1915.
[6] Ibid., 12 January 1915, p. 3.
[7] Ibid.
[8] Ibid., 17 January 1915, p. 3.
[9] Ibid., 19 January 1915, p. 7.

A special program was planned at the Majestic Hotel by the United)aughters of the Confederacy to commemorate the birthday of Robert E. Lee nd as a memorial to the fallen heroes of the South. The memorial address vas delivered by Judge C.T. Cotham, a very fine speaker. A lengthy musical rogram followed including vocal solos by Juanita Gilliam and Louise Iorner.[10]

But celebrations, parties and dances were not restricted to the large hotels. everal of the smaller hotels put on programs that were a bit less formal than hose of the larger hostelries but were just as entertaining. Dances were held t the Moody, Great Northern and Marquette and were quite well-attended, ometimes by some of the same people who went to the larger hotels.

Home affairs were popular during this time. Mayor Jacob McClendon and is wife, a newly-elected Worthy Matron of the Order of the Eastern Star, eld a large New Years Drop-In party in their newly-rebuilt home on Pleasant treet. It was described as "a perfect bower of greenery, cut flowers, potted lants and other decorative effects." A musical program was presented and ncluded the very busy, and popular Juanita Gilliam and Mrs. Ki Davies. Over ne hundred guests showed up.[11]

A dancing party for "the younger set," was held by Mr. and Mrs. Walter)odson and Mr. and Mrs. Harry Jackson at the Jackson home.[12]

There were all sorts of functions for the entertainment of the home folks. ilver Tea affairs with refreshments and accompanied by miniature programs of music and readings were provided for the guests' entertainment. Church hoirs showed up at the birthday party of some worthy church member and ard parties were used for the benefit of homeless children. Card parties were opular with college girls visiting home during the summer or holidays. Besides being entertaining these functions provided the platform to catch up on the latest gossip of who was dating whom or who was about to get narried.

The Sunshine Club, a group of benevolent ladies, met, had fun, games and nusic, and accumulated various materials for needy families. The Musical Art Club, which met monthly in the music-room at the Buckstaff Bath House, rovided programs for members and invited guests.[13]

The larger hotels had social directors whose job it was to see that their mportant guests' names were reported to the newspapers' society editor-- that s, unless that individual did not desire any publicity. Occasionally a movie star,

---

[10] Ibid.

[11] Ibid., 2 January 1915.

[12] Ibid., 17 January 1915.

[13] Many sources, including *Sentinel-Record*, 2, 6, 15, 17, 18, 19 January 1915, to name . few.

or other well-known person, who was seeking only relaxation and not publicity, would ask the hotel management for anonymity and their request was heeded. Also, especially in later years, mobsters and gangsters from Chicago and New York would appear on the scene and would want only privacy. They were generally big spenders and the hotels were pleased to accommodate them.

Others did not mind the attention or publicity. United States Senator J. Hamilton Lewis, of Illinois, was a regular guest at the Arlington and visited the Spa quite often. He always had complimentary words concerning the hot thermal baths he had taken and proclaimed he never felt better.[14] He was quoted quite often and the testimony of such important people was used in promotional literature sent out by the hotels advertising their establishments.

Many of the visitors were quite wealthy, traveling in their own private railroad cars which were parked in the yards of the Iron Mountain or Rock Island Railroad yards. Two of these were Mr. and Mrs. James Hobart Moorer, the Diamond Match King who stayed in the Spa three weeks or longer during twelve different years.[15] Another was Jay Gould.

Each January generally saw Albert B. Gaines, President of the New York Hotel Company, which operated the Arlington and Eastman Hotels, show up for a visit. Sometimes he would be accompanied by Col. Lyman T. Hay, general manager of the two palatial hostelries.[16]

Festivities were held on each holiday, each hotel or group trying to outdo each other. The events around Valentine's Day, Washington's birthday, and of course, the St. Patrick's Day balls kept the social editor busy at her typewriter keeping the Spa, and its guests, informed of these colorful functions.

Vernal Ledgerwood enjoyed his job as police judge and later as municipal judge. In his early days, he learned that his salary and the expenses of the court had been set by the council as coming from the fines imposed upon those engaged in prostitution. He admitted at this time in his life, he wasn't very much of a church-going person, but he did believe he was a fairly moral man and the source of money for his salary was troublesome and disagreeable to him.[17]

He approached Mayor McClendon with his concern. Ledgerwood told the mayor that the city needed to provide funds for its court system from some other source, or, as he said, "I'm going to let the women go without fines."[18]

---

[14] *Sentinel-Record*, 19 January 1915.
[15] Ibid.
[16] Ibid., 15 January 1915.
[17] LAT Ledgerwood.
[18] Ibid.

J.W. McClendon was a strong moral person and understood the judge's concern and promised to look into the matter. A few days later the council was able to transfer funds with Ledgerwood's salary coming from the general revenue.

With a State Prohibition option law voted into place in 1915, some of the citizens of the Spa set about to gather petitions to address the county court to allow the "sale of intoxicating liquors of all kinds."[19]

Petitions were available in many of the businesses downtown. Workers from some of the saloons and bars fanned out across the city gathering signatures and addresses. Several thousand people gave their signatures and their names were printed in the daily newspapers.

The measure was placed on the ballot and became law after a favorable vote. Wards voting for the measure were permitted licenses to sell the intoxicants, those not for the measure were considered "dry."

[19] *Sentinel-Record*, 3 January 1914, pp. 8 and 9.

When Mama is Unhappy, Everybody is Unhappy

Leo P. McLaughlin won his third nomination as city attorney in December of 1915. It appeared he would face no opponent in the April election. Some of his acquaintances began to note changes in Leo's behavior. Perhaps his margin of victories over his opponents had increased his confidence until he was becoming almost cocky and acting as if he was unbeatable. Some people began to think McLaughlin had become too arrogant and others noted that if they expressed a difference of opinion, he took it as a personal affront and would sometimes berate the individual. If a difference of opinion was made public he would attack the person in front of others or even in the newspapers, sometimes writing long abusive columns. At times the attacks were vicious and ugly. Leo P. McLaughlin rarely admitted he had erred or had made a mistake. It just was not his nature. He disliked criticism, and disliked anyone who directed any criticism toward him.

In one incident McLaughlin was so upset with Gus Buchanan, secretary to Mayor McClendon, he wrote a long scathing letter to the newspapers. Buchanan had expressed his disagreement concerning the city attorney's handling of a matter relating to the illegal use of city water by the contractor who was in the process of rebuilding the Moody Hotel. Judge Ledgerwood had already heard the case and declared N.M. Moody was guilty of the misuse of water and issued a fine of $120.[1] Moody disagreed and instead of appealing the fine to the circuit court, complained to Leo McLaughlin. Acting as city attorney, McLaughlin compromised the matter for sixty dollars.[2] Buchanan thought McLaughlin had overstepped his authority since the court had already imposed the fine and he wanted the matter to be heard by the council. McLaughlin successfully blocked the hearing of the matter until Alderman Rigsbee signed a request that it be included on the council's agenda. The council, trying not to take sides between the two temperamentals, McLaughlin and Buchanan, tabled the issue.[3] McLaughlin took the council's action as complete vindication of his handling. He overlooked the fact that several of the councilmen had voted to table the matter simply because the city attorney had already committed the city and they wanted to be rid of a troublesome matter and move on with the city's business. It certainly had not been their intention to convey the idea they were approving McLaughlin's action which had cost the city money. The city attorney and the mayor's secretary needed to work together but from this point on, they were bitter enemies. But this was peanuts compared to the blunder he made in 1916.

---

[1] *Sentinel-Record*, 7 March 1915.
[2] Ibid., 6 March 1915.
[3] Ibid., 2 March 1915.

For several years Dr. Edwin F. Winegar of Hot Springs had been working on an idea that would have made the city into the world's greatest health resort. Dr. Winegar proposed to build a modest health sanitarium in the Spa at a cost of a quarter of a million dollars. After visiting the Battle Creek, Michigan Sanitarium he enlarged his plans to an expected cost of a half million dollars.[4]

Before he could move on his new plan, Dr. Winegar came into contact with a wealthy man from New York, Col. R. Onffroy. Onffroy, a natural- born Frenchman, had come to this county twenty-seven years before and had been involved in several large ventures and financial investments. Winegar explained his plans to Col. Onffroy who encouraged him "to reach for the stars." Onffroy had been to many of the large resorts and sanitariums in Europe and he explained to Winegar that Hot Springs had the natural beauty coupled with the wonderful thermal waters to become the world's finest health center. The two men enlarged the plans and had draftsmen draw a diagram of how they dreamed the sanitarium and supporting facilities would appear. Onffroy was quite certain they could raise the estimated nine million dollars necessary from eastern interests.

The area projected for the plan encompassed thirteen and one-half acres in downtown Hot Springs. The boundaries ran along the west side of Central and Ouachita Avenues from Prospect to Market Streets and to where the two side streets intersected just past the Levi Memorial Hospital. The area created a large triangle. It would be necessary to obtain options on every piece of property in the proposed area. It would require the city to close and forego its rights over Chapel and Crown Streets.[5]

The project called for local support and some of the most prominent citizens were called upon to serve on what was to be known as the Sanitarium Committee: E.N. Roth, Chairman, W.W. Little, C.N. Rix, Ed Johnson, M.J. Henderson, M.C. Tombler, J.H. Avery, C.C. Sparks, George R. Belding, Dr. S. Blaisdell, Sam Blumenstiel, J.T. Jones, Captain Smith, A.J. Murphy and William Steifel. It was the duty of this committee to work with the property owners arriving at fair values and obtaining options on the land involved. Because of the reputations of the men selected to the committee there was a high respectability as citizens knew these individuals were the builders of Hot Springs.

The project was so huge it boggled the mind. The Spanish-Romanesque architecture captured the eye as the drawing of the project was widely circulated. The eight-story hotel was designed to accommodate six hundred guests. The sanitarium had accommodations for three hundred patients. There

---

[4] Francis J. Scully, *The Record - 1960.*

[5] Records of Hot Springs City Council, 16 January 1916.

was designed into the front of the complex, space for sixty businesses, all fronting onto Central-Ouachita Avenues which could be leased or rented. Tennis courts, swimming pools, pavilions, pagodas, fountains and walks beautified the landscape. A large club house, cafe, theater, ball room and casino were planned for the convenience and entertainment of the visitors.[6]

The Sanitarium Committee called a mass meeting for December 30, 1915, at the Business Men's League and urged every property owner and business man to attend. The plan was carefully outlined that the values placed on the property within the triangle would be liberal and options would be solicited at higher value than "the market price today or larger than it has ever been in Hot Springs."[7]

Mayor McClendon and the city council pledged their cooperation. So did County Judge Mooney. The city was asked to purchase frontage along Central Avenue and the county was to use its grading and highway equipment to widen the street.[8]

Within days several owners having property in the designated area, generally respected by the citizenry of the Spa, Col. D.C. Rugg, Dr. A.U. Williams, E.N. Roth, L.D. Cooper, J.T. Jones, Cooper and Watt partnership, C.N. Rix, and others promptly signed the options. Within a few weeks only two pieces of property remained in the triangle on which the committee had no signed option. The first was in the seven hundred block of Central, a well-known and popular landmark cafe, the Hot Springs Confectionery, more commonly known as Jim and George's. It was owned and operated by Jim Fotioo and George Antonio.[9] These men feared that the sanitarium venture might fall through and the committee might sell the property to others. When assured that this would not occur and they were given a waiver that should that happen they would have first option to return to the establishment, Jim and George were convinced and signed the option.

That left only one piece of property to conclude the local end of the transaction and the options were to be rushed to Chicago for review by the financiers. The piece of property holding up the entire matter was a two story building at the corner of Central and Prospect known as the McLaughlin Building, owned by Bridget McLaughlin, mother of city attorney Leo McLaughlin. When members of the committee tried to talk with Mrs. McLaughlin they were informed that her son, attorney Leo P. McLaughlin was handling the matter. Leo's attitude toward the committee was almost juvenile

---

[6] *Arkansas Gazette*, 25 February 1917.

[7] *Sentinel-Record*, 30 December 1915.

[8] Ibid., 26 January 1916.

[9] This cafe opened in 1906 and operated until 29 May 1953, and had a "continuous operation of 47 years." It was operated as a 24-hour restaurant and its name in later years was The Lafayette, but locals still referred to it as "Jim and George's."

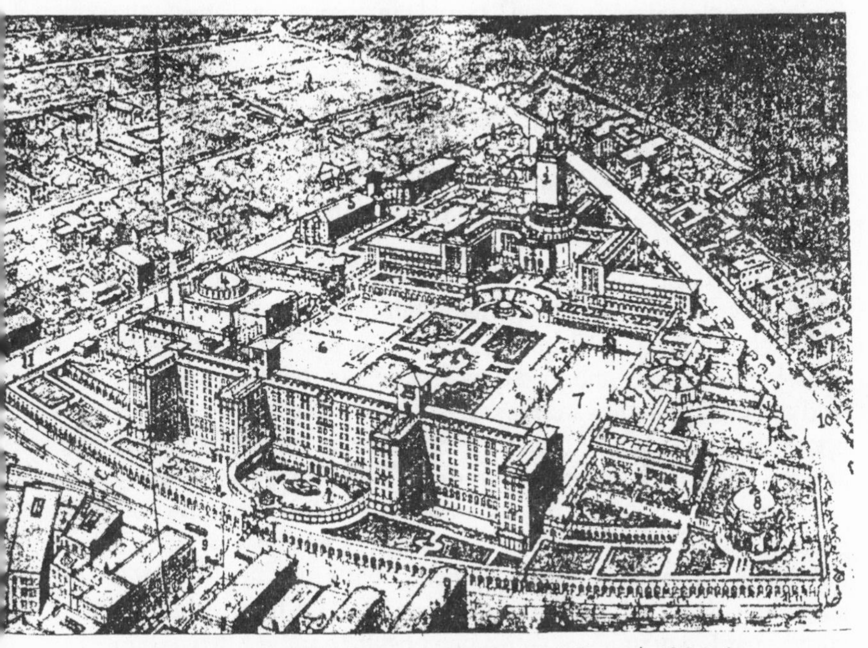

1. Hotel. 2. Sanitarium & Doctor's Offices. 3. Bath House. 4. Club-Casino. 5. Dormitories. 6. Tennis Courts. 7. Swimming Pool. 8. Drinking Pavilion. 9. Central Ave. 10. Prospect Ave. 11. Market St.

The proposed sanitarium project was "scuttled" by Leo P. McLaughlin's stubbornness

and unforgivable. In fact, at times he was downright rude and sometimes would not return calls left for him. Possibly there were one or more individuals on the committee that Leo did not like, or who had opposed him on some other matter, or had voted against him and he was not a person who was able to politely confront someone that had opposed his opinion. For the great and overall good of the project, Leo McLaughlin could not forget some grudge he had for someone on the committee. He acted as if he believed he was playing a game of poker and was holding an unbeatable hand.

Requests were made to Leo McLaughlin for permission to discuss the subject with his mother. McLaughlin refused.[10] Various members of the committee tried to talk with McLaughlin in an attempt to ascertain his objection to signing the option and also to convey to him that he was holding up the most beneficial project that had ever been presented to Hot Springs. He finally told them the tenant held a lease on the building for a year. The committee had run into this problem more than once and told Leo they offered "to accept the option subject to the conditions of the lease which you may have with your tenant."[11] They told him they would "amend the option." Bridget's son said he'd have to study their offer. More delay!

When the committee re-contacted Leo McLaughlin he informed them that his mother had "an outstanding option" to sell, but would not tell the committee who the individual was.[12] He next told them his mother had an offer of $27,200 for the property. The committee assured him that was not a problem. Leo was running out of excuses and the committee was running out of patience.

Time passed and other members of the committee tried to talk with him and did discuss the subject with George Whittington, whose opinion they knew McLaughlin valued. Whittington sensed that Leo McLaughlin was backing himself into a corner and tried to warn him, but the city attorney thought he held all the chips in the game he was playing. He came up with another reason not to sign, telling the committee they had no assurance the property would ever be used for sanitarium purposes. The committee offered to give a "provision to the effect that the sanitarium will be erected on the blocks proposed to be used for sanitarium purposes, it cannot be taken advantage of."[13] Will McLaughlin, Leo's brother, could sense the frustrations of the committee and tried to discuss the issue with his brother but was told, "I know what I'm doing." Leo remained obstinate and refused to budge.

People who had supported McLaughlin for city attorney began to wonder at his resistance to the sanitarium project and the thin reasons he gave for not permitting his mother to sign. Several were calling for action by the city to condemn the property and get on with the project. They just failed to see who would be in charge of the condemnation procedure--Leo McLaughlin, city attorney, and up to this time had never indicated he would have removed himself from that position should litigation become necessary. Anyone who thought that one out quickly decided that wasn't going to take place. E.N. Roth, Chairman, had already called on the city to condemn the property under

---

[10] *New Era*, 15 January 1916.
[11] Ibid.
[12] Ibid.
[13] Ibid.

the public right of eminent domain law but nothing was taking place at city hall.

Leo McLaughlin was smug in his position and believed he held the upper hand. Had he looked around and been realistic he might have even seen he had just painted himself in a corner, and that he was out on the proverbial limb and Roth and the committee were getting ready to saw it off.

Leo McLaughlin's playhouse was turned upside down on 15 January 1915 when the *Hot Springs New Era* hit the street that afternoon. A two-column article on page one cited a letter that had already been mailed to Bridget McLaughlin, from and signed by the entire Sanitarium Committee. In large headlines above the letter it stated, "FINAL OFFER MADE TO MRS. McLAUGHLIN." It outlined in detail the efforts of the committee to deal with her son Leo and how each of his concerns had been answered and addressed. It told of their repeated requests to speak directly with her which had been "refused by your representative." There was no mistake in the tone of the letter--it let Bridget know they did not intend to allow her piece of property to block such a large and beneficial project for Hot Springs.

When the letter mailed by the committee reached the McLaughlin home on Malvern, the peace and stillness of the community was shattered. Bridget exploded! Leo had not kept her apprised of what was going on and to have some of the foremost citizens of the city have to write a letter to communicate with her was unthinkable. Furiously she tried to reach Leo at his office but was told by George Whittington's secretary Mona O'Dwyer, her son had left for the day. She called Will at the hardware store and was informed he had not seen Leo all day. She started to tell Will what the letter was about and he said, "I know, it's on the front page of the *New Era*." His mother was aghast to think that the letter had now been made available for the eyes of everyone in the city. She told Will to send George home with a copy of the paper. As Bridget read and reread the account in *The New Era*, her temperature went up.

The great southern humorist, Jerry Clower, had an expression he occasionally used concerning his wife when something displeased her, "When Mama is unhappy, everybody is unhappy." And mama Bridget was a very unhappy person. By the time Leo McLaughlin got home, his brothers and sisters were tip-toeing around the house, staying mainly to their rooms and out of their mother's path. Bridget was not quick to loose her temper, but she was in a real boil and no one wanted to cross her. Leo had just walked into a fire storm.[14] He had messed-up first rate.

---

[14] LAT Mary Hudgins, a taped interview 1980. Most people that knew Leo McLaughlin agreed that he wasn't a heavy drinker, although a few claimed that on occasions McLaughlin would go on a bender. Hudgins had an office in the First National Building for several years and stated that on more than one occasion LPM would lock himself in his office

It must have been a very interesting weekend in the large McLaughlin home on the hill. Bridget was too embarrassed to even attend the church services at St. Mary's. She was aware that many in the congregation had supported the sanitarium project. Indeed, what were they saying behind her back? Bridget could not face them and she placed the blame squarely where it belonged--on Leo. His reasons and excuses were not acceptable to Bridget. This was one time in his life that he was completely subdued. He had always respected his mother.[15] She had given him the ball to carry and he had fumbled. Bridget told Leo he was out of the game--she would handle the matter from then on.

On Monday morning, January 17, Bridget tried to call E.N. Roth only to learn that the chairman was enroute to Chicago to meet with the promoters of the project. She was put in touch with Charles Rix, President of the Arkansas National Bank. She told Rix she wanted to sign the option and Rix told her he would send attorney A.J. Murphy to her with the proper papers. The following day Bridget McLaughlin signed the option on the property at Central and Prospect. Fearing some delay might occur in the city being made aware she had signed the agreement she telephoned John A. Riggs, publisher of *The New Era*, and let him know so that he could apprise the readers of his papers. The headlines that evening read, "M'LAUGHLIN OPTION IS SIGNED TODAY."[16]

To make matters worse, the revised option which Leo's mother had signed was turned down by the promoters in Chicago. The Committee again called for condemnation procedures on the McLaughlin property.

Unfortunately the delay and blocking tactics by Leo McLaughlin in the acquisition of the land had severe ramification and contributed to the demise of the project. It had been hoped that the demolition and construction would be accomplished for the 1918-19 winter season. Much of the financing had been obtained and it appeared that the project was set to begin, but the lengthy delay in getting the land options signed pushed the time too close to an approaching world disaster. The country was on the verge of being dragged into the war being fought in Europe and the country was beginning to get on a war-footing. The pledged funds were diverted to the manufacturing of war materials. Materials necessary in large construction, including heavy steel, became non-existent. The noble vision of Dr. Winegar in making Hot Springs the world's greatest health resort faded into oblivion, never to be revitalized again. Leo McLaughlin had helped to scuttle the project, whether intentionally

---

with the lights out and the elevator man would bring him food and drink, and sometimes he would remain there several days. Possibly this may have been one of the times he sought solitude from his irate mother as he later sought solitude from his wrecked martial affairs.

[15] LAT Ledgerwood. Verne Ledgerwood marveled at the respect Leo had for his mother and said that many times he used her as a sounding board for his ideas.

[16] *New Era*, 18 January 1916.

or through ignorance, although he would later deny it. As he always craved praise for things he accomplished on behalf of the city, he certainly deserved a large share of the blame for blocking a wonderful project that would have changed Hot Springs forever.[17] But, Leo would not escape completely.

As a young city attorney, Leo P. McLaughlin lost his first race to Sam McConnell

[17] Francis J. Scully, *The Record - 1960.*

Following the scenario of the sanitarium option signing, Leo McLaughlin was not very popular with many citizens who had supported the project, and because of that he was not very visible. Many people who had always been friendly in their greetings to McLaughlin turned their backs or acted as if they didn't see him. He, in turn, had been embarrassed by his mother dismissing him from the further handling of the case and because of the publicity attending the signing everyone in town knew the story. He would have liked the issue to be over and forgotten, but it wasn't.

There were several people who were still upset that McLaughlin had caused such a delay in the sanitarium project. One, Fred W. Vaughan, who had worked hard on the project, poured out criticism on Leo's sore head. Others were interested in creating some opposition for him in the city's April election. Leo had won the democratic primary in December, which usually was tantamount to election in Garland County. As the group sought a viable candidate, a young lawyer, James S. (Sam) McConnell, almost unnoticed, filed for the position of city attorney.[1]

McConnell had come to Hot Springs from Little Rock several years before, and had served a short time as assistant postmaster in 1904-1905. He had also been connected with the county school system prior to entering the legal profession. McConnell was very active in civic and fraternal matters and served as the Grand Chancellor of the Arkansas Domain of the Knights of Pythias.[2] Mayor McClendon had paid honor to him because of his having been instrumental in bringing several large conventions to Hot Springs.

Leo McLaughlin scarcely paid any attention to McConnell entering the race. First, McConnell was running as an independent candidate and the only person who had been successful as an independent in several years was an exception, Dr. Jacob W. McClendon, who the voters viewed as a totally honest man. And second, McConnell was very inexperienced in politics and appeared to have very little support base. McLaughlin was almost ignoring McConnell's candidacy until he learned of a meeting held 29 February by "by a few of my personal and political enemies."[3] Leo suddenly became focused. He threw out charges against his unnamed "personal and political enemies," who he claimed were "calling for another meeting for Thursday night," for the purpose of creating some opposition for him and "did not have the nerve to sign it [the ad announcing the meeting] so the names of those present were withheld from the public." He claimed the meeting was because of his stand on the

---

[1] *Sentinel-Record*, 23 February 1916.

[2] Ibid.

[3] Ibid., 1 March 1916, a paid political ad by Leo McLaughlin.

anitarium project, then he reversed himself and said it wasn't that at all, but ecause, "They oppose me because they are my enemies and they are using his as a shield, not having nerve enough prior to this to come out open and ust say what they thought about me." He might have been very surprised at what some of the people were saying.

McLaughlin, after stating it wasn't about the sanitarium project, proceeded o justify his handling of his mother's property and that the delay was omeone else's fault. He tried to portray himself in his political advertisements s being maligned, mistreated and misunderstood.

Changing tactics he became accusatory and threatening, "I understand from heir resolution they expect to have a meeting and let him (a candidate they night choose) run up their coat tails, and I desire to serve notice on him now, hat if he has the nerve to enter the ring upon his own merits that he had etter look out, because this fight will be hot and furious. The fight is on and am in it to the finish, regardless of who my opponent is."[4]

Leo was flailing about trying to guess what the citizens committee was lanning and attempted to bully and bluff any other attorneys from entering he race. Had he waited a day he would have had the answers.

The papers reported there was no reason for a meeting since Sam McConnell had announced for the city attorney's office and the Citizens Committee would endorse and support him. Also, it explained in unmistakable anguage the reason they were throwing their support to McConnell: "The pposition to Leo McLaughlin has grown out of the sanitarium project, the McLaughlin property within that district having been denied the committee n the terms that others signed options. --- When there was a movement ledged itself to condemnation proceedings against the McLaughlin property, nd in anticipation of this suit in the courts, it was generally conceded that McLaughlin as city attorney would not be the proper person to represent the ity."[5]

With the endorsement of McConnell, Leo suddenly had a target. To be more precise, three targets: the candidate; the committee; and the committee's representative, F.W. Vaughan.

In later years, the campaign ads for Leo McLaughlin's political races generally had more finesse than those penned by Leo, as the latter ones were written by Verne Ledgerwood. When Leo handled his own ads he sometimes gave them the scatter gun treatment--firing at anybody and everybody he believed to be his enemy. Most generally he got into a name- calling contest, avoided the issues, and became very personal.

Surprising even his closest supporters, Leo suddenly became the champion

---

[4] Ibid.

[5] Ibid., 2 March 1916.

for the sanitarium project. "I hope that the money can be secured, because *we all* want the sanitarium," he said.[6] And, "I will do all in my power to aid the promotion of the sanitarium project or any other project that will benefit the welfare of *my* hometown."[7] Did Leo sound a bit repentant? Probably not, but after all, he was a politician, and he wanted to tell the voters what they wanted to hear, even if it wasn't his real feelings. He was doing a complete "flip-flop."

In a speech at Fagan Park on Ash Street in the second ward, McLaughlin charged that Sam McConnell had been indicted by a Federal Grand Jury for embezzlement.[8] He had completely overlooked or failed to mention that McConnell had been cleared of those charges. McConnell's supporters quickly contacted former postmaster J.W. Howell and several of the jurors who completely vindicated him.[9]

Now it was McConnell's turn--his and Fred Vaughan's, who replied for the Sanitarium Committee: "Mr. McLaughlin," said Fred Vaughan, "is simply begging the question when he charges that certain members of the Sanitarium Committee are using the 'sanitarium proposition as a shield' to create prejudice against him. The committee simply desires the defeat of McLaughlin for the office of city attorney as a business expediency, because he cannot in good faith serve the city in that capacity and maintain his present attitude toward the sanitarium project--*he cannot bark with the dogs and run with the hare.*"[10]

In one political advertisement McLaughlin had referred to his opponent, Sam McConnell, and friends as "amateur politicians." McConnell did not let that pass as he retorted, "Mr. Leo P. McLaughlin has characterized me and all the people who support me for City Attorney as amateur politicians. I presume he considers himself as a professional. It is one of the characteristics of a professional politician that he can take 182 cases in which the Police Judge has assessed fines and settle them after they have been appealed from the Police Court."

McConnell then took step-by-step how ninety-eight of those cases never reached the Circuit Court docket.[11]

On and on the fight went. The nearer to election the rougher the rhetoric became. McLaughlin, sensing a possibility that some democrats might cross-over and vote for his Independent opponent, became threatening. He urged them to remain loyal to the party. Such voters, he announced, might be disfranchised.[12]

---

[6] Ibid., 28 March 1916.
[7] Ibid.
[8] *New Era*, 3 April 1916.
[9] Ibid., 30 March 1916. Also, *Sentinel-Record*, 31 March 1916.
[10] *Sentinel-Record*, 4 March 1916.
[11] *New Era*, 1 April 1916.
[12] *Sentinel-Record*, 31 March 1916.

Up until the last Leo P. McLaughlin thought he was going to win. He had never lost a race and had always had strong support in every ward and he could visualize nothing that he had done to let him believe he would not win.

At the city hall the evening of the city wide election a large crowd had assembled to get the results. As ward after ward reported, Leo began to have an uneasy feeling. He was behind in every ward, except his home ward, the second. The vote was close, 516-489, only because of the lopsided vote for Leo in the second ward, 170-92, but it was not enough. Leo's bubble had burst--McConnell had defeated the twenty-seven year-old city attorney. As he and brother Will trudged their way homeward that night, he probably felt as faded as the wilted boutonniere in his lapel.

When the vote was analyzed it was discovered that almost two hundred democratic voters who had supported the aldermen in their wards had not voted at all in the city attorney's race. They apparently had taken McLaughlin's threat seriously about the crossover voting, but refused to cast their vote for him. But Leo was not the only McLaughlin to feel the backlash of the voter's ire: his brother Will lost his second ward seat to an opponent. For the time being, the McLaughlins were out of office.

Leo McLaughlin was smarting from his loss of the city attorney's position when the family received word that his brother James Russell was very ill in Colorado. Since Russell had been sent to a sanitarium at Manitou Springs four years before, he had been back home for only two short visits. His health continued to decline and his mother and sisters alternated visits to keep up his spirits. Bridget was preparing to journey there to see him when word was received he had passed away on 24 April 1916.[1] His mother took the loss very hard and blamed herself that she had not gone earlier, delaying until after Leo's election was past. The one who was truly crushed by Russells's death was his older sister Anna (Annie).[2] The two had been very close and had corresponded regularly. She had tried to keep him abreast of the news from Hot Springs and mailed him clippings of various happenings. Services were held at St. Mary's and Russell was buried at Calvary Cemetery in the family plot near his father.

Anna was so distraught her sister Elizabeth took her to Colorado Springs in May to rest. They were joined several weeks later by sister Stella and the three remained there until August with Anna returning much improved.[3]

The school district election in the late spring of 1916 seemed lackluster and "with very little special enthusiasm."[4] However, it was to provide a spark of interest that set the town talking for days. The race was between three fine citizens, Hy Covington, Dr. Barry and Judge C.T. Cotham, with Covington and Cotham being the eventual winners.

Dr. Jacob W. McClendon and Leo P. McLaughlin had cooperated and worked well together as mayor and city attorney. There had been a few differences, but those were generally trivial. McClendon had even endorsed McLaughlin in his second race for office. Then had come the item that caused them trouble--McLaughlin's obstinate position in blocking the sanitarium project which Mayor McClendon believed would have been so beneficial for the entire city of Hot Springs. He had thrown his support to McLaughlin's opponent Sam McConnell.

McLaughlin took McClendon's opposition as a personal affront, as he historically did when anyone opposed him. After any sort of setback, defeat, or rejection he complained bitterly to his acquaintances and family. Listening to him this time was his younger brother George, who took up the cry. Unfortunately George was sometimes crude in his remarks and let his mouth

---

[1] *Sentinel-Record*, 26 April 1916.
[2] Ibid, 16 July 1916.
[3] Ibid, 9 September 1916.
[4] Ibid., 21 May 1916.

override his brain. He began to badmouth Dr. McClendon behind his back, and even bragged he was going to shoot the mayor on sight. Word soon reached the mayor who was no coward, but thirty years older and much slower than George McLaughlin. He had no intention of allowing George to bully or beat him up. McClendon armed himself with a revolver.

On the evening of the school election Dr. McClendon, a resident of the second ward, went to the polling precinct to cast his vote. Sitting at one of the tables was Leo McLaughlin's brother George, acting as one of the clerks. McClendon's Scottish temper flared when he spotted McLaughlin and he approached him angrily saying, "You said I defeated your brother for office and that you were going to shoot me."[5]

As the twenty-two year-old McLaughlin got to his feet and started toward the advancing mayor George saw McClendon's hand reach to an inside coat pocket and come forth with a cocked and aimed six-shooter. McLaughlin wisely stopped his rush toward the city executive and two of the poll judges, Guy Woolston and George North, who had been watching the confrontation sprang toward McClendon and "soon wrested the pistol from him."[6]

McClendon was charged "with intent to kill George McLaughlin."[7] Some of the mayor's detractors tried legal action to remove him from office, at least until the case could be heard. Circuit Judge Scott Wood ruled that McClendon could remain in office as mayor. An appeal was made to the Arkansas Supreme Court; it sustained the circuit court and McClendon continued as mayor until the trial later that year.

When the issue finally came to trial it had been thoroughly hashed and rehashed by residents of the spa. Both men, McClendon and George McLaughlin, were quite well-known. McLaughlin played on a local ball team but was considered lazy by many who knew him. He had a knack of disappearing when work was needed to be done. He could be likable at times, but also had the reputation of being surly, a bully and braggart and he had little sympathy in his corner when the trial began. On the other hand, Dr. J.W. McClendon was always polite, and friendly. He spoke to everyone and treated both supporters and opponents with the same courtesy. The mayor was seen daily strolling from his office in the Thompson Building to City Hall trailed by his always present faithful dog Blue.

After hearing the evidence the jury was out but a short time. It had reached a verdict of guilty very quickly. There was no question that the enraged mayor had drawn a gun on George McLaughlin. It was on the issue of penalty that disagreement arose. The judge had instructed the jurors for the reduced charge

---

[5] Ibid.

[6] Ibid.

[7] Ibid., 20 November 1916.

of "aggravated assault," and said, "It can be considered in making up the verdict, with a fine set by law of no less than $50.00 and prison time not to exceed one year."[8] Several of the jurors jumped at that. They wanted imprisonment for J.W. McClendon "of but one minute in jail." Others thought that might not be enough time and they felt the mayor should serve at least one hour of time.[9] When the verdict was read by the jury foreman, George McLaughlin angrily stormed out of the court room.

As the sentence was pronounced Judge Wood turned to Sheriff Brad Smith and said, "Sheriff I now remand the defendant into your custody for the purpose of incarceration in the county jail of servitude of one hour."[10]

Sheriff Smith replied with a broad smile, "Yes sir, your Honor." Then to the Mayor, "Dr. McClendon would you please accompany me to your cell?" As they started to leave the court room Col. Murphy, McClendon's attorney, said to his client, "Jake, I can file an appeal if you want." He too, was grinning. It was reported that half of the jury was waiting in the sheriff's office for the mayor to be released an hour later, each wringing his hand as he came out of the cell. He emerged in jovial spirits and asked, "Has the city of Hot Springs ever had a convict as mayor before? Or am I the first?"

Elizabeth Sylvester was described as a "pioneer of the county," and resided in a modest frame cottage facing East Grand Avenue at the intersection of Spring Street. In some manner she came to believe that someone had buried treasure on her property many years before and she was determined to locate it, but needed help to find it. Some acquaintance told her to get in touch with J.M. "Doc" Phillips, who was a professed "treasure hunter," and had been about Hot Springs for several weeks. Had the woman been thinking, she could have determined by looking at the run-down appearance of Phillips that he was not very successful in his chosen profession. Mrs. Sylvester contacted the down and out Phillips and explained her belief in treasure being buried on her property. This was right down the alley for Doc Phillips. He persuaded Mrs. Sylvester to let him sleep on the couch in the front room of her house and feed him while he worked out a plan to recover the treasure she believed to be buried in her yard. She was soon to rue the day that she permitted the mentally unbalanced Phillips to move in.

Neighbors began to notice that if one of them ventured near the Sylvester property Doc Phillips turned ugly, ordering them away. When no attention was paid to him he suddenly appeared with a pistol in his hand. Mrs. Sylvester

---

[8] Ibid.

[9] Ibid.

[10] This was late in the year and Brad Smith won an election over Thomas Hanley who had been appointed to fill the unexpired term of Sheriff Charles Webb, who was killed. The account of that shooting follows. *Sentinel-Record*, 30, November 1916.

ater said that she noticed Phillips sometimes "went into spells" and said "he was under the control of spirits."[11] After several people complained Garland County Sheriff Charles C. Webb, who was serving his first term, decided he needed to look into the complaints. He sent Deputy Sheriff John Young and Constable W.R. Downen, to the scene to talk with Elizabeth Sylvester concerning the problem. She told the men that Doc Phillips had been in a terrible rage all day and suggested that the men leave and that when he calmed down she would telephone and they could come back and confront him. They left and reported to Sheriff Webb.

That night Charles Webb received a call to the effect Doc Phillips was causing further trouble and threatening the neighbors. Webb, deputies Dave Young and Henry Houpt were taken to the scene on East Grand by John Turner, who was known to everyone as "Dear Brother."[12]

As the men started to go up to the house, Phillips suddenly appeared on the porch dressed only "in his union suit" and holding a pistol in his hand. Draped from his shoulder was a cartridge belt and holster. Phillips warned the lawmen not to come closer. Webb tried to reason with"Doc Phillips, however the man became more threatening. Amazingly there was not a weapon among the four lawmen.[13] Webb seldom carried a gun and encouraged his officers to do likewise. John Turner was sent after some guns. When he returned he had several pistols and additional men, Jimmy Rowles, Joe Lookadoo, Police Captain Reb Houpt and later George Witherow.[14] Some of these were armed with rifles and shotguns.

Further efforts were made to coax Doc Phillips from the house but he answered the officers with profanity and threats. Sheriff Webb made the fatal decision, "I'll lead the way in. I've got a wife and family and I don't want to die, but we must get that crazy man."[15]

Flanking the Garland County Sheriff as they approached the porch, were two very experienced and fearless officers, Dave Young and Reb Houpt. Both had been under fire before. Due to the hot weather all the windows of the house were open as well as the front door. Opening the screen door the trio of officers entered the dark hallway of the house. They had reason to believe that Phillips was in the living room or the first room to the right as they were entering. That door was closed. Houpt, standing to one side of the door, turned the knob and threw the door open. As the door swung inward,

---

[11] *Sentinel-Record*, 11 July 1916.

[12] Ibid., p. 2. Turner operated the Delmar Hotel at Market and Quapaw for several years.

[13] Ibid.

[14] Based on *Sentinel-Record* reports of 11 and 12 July 1916. Some facts were corrected in the latter edition.

[15] *Sentinel-Record*, 11 July 1916. Statement to reporter by witness Wade Allen.

"Phillips thrust a pistol out of the darkness" and opened fire. The first bullet from the .41 caliber revolver struck Sheriff Webb in the head as he was in a crouching position preparing to enter the room. Webb dropped to his knees and then to the floor, fatally wounded. Phillips continued to fire with the second bullet striking Dave Young in the groin and the wounded deputy staggered out the front door.[16] Houpt, who had seen the muzzle flashes from Phillips' gun, stuck his own weapon in the doorway and blazed away into the darkness, spraying the room with bullets. Pistol empty, he exited the house behind Dave Young who was being loaded into a car to take him to the hospital. As Houpt told the armed men outside what had occurred they opened fire with pistols, Winchester rifles and shotguns. Phillips returned fire from two windows, then every thing became quiet.

About an hour after the initial attack the men outside decided to try again, hoping that Sheriff Webb was just wounded and still alive. This time the sortie was to be led by Reb Houpt with George Witherow and Henry Houpt on each side. As they reached the porch Reb reached toward his brother to push him out of line of fire when Phillips opened fire from inside. When that occurred a fusillade of fire came from those around the house and Henry Houpt was struck in the hip by a bullet.[17] Reb Houpt always believed his brother had been struck by gunfire from the posse and not that coming from Doc Phillips.[18] Reb Houpt and George Witherow stuck their weapons, one a shotgun, in a front window and emptied them into the room.

One final shot came from inside the house, apparently at an automobile traveling down Spring Street, then silence.

A third attempt was made to enter the house to recover the body of Sheriff Webb. This job was performed by Deputy Row Brown, Doc Walz, Jimmy Rowles and Joe Lookadoo. Brown had no weapon and only a "small search light," having left his service revolver at Morris Drug Store that afternoon. This time they entered the dark and silent house from the rear, going down the narrow hallway, and checking each side room. They found Webb's body in the hall and brought it outside. Someone exclaimed he saw some movement on the part of the sheriff and brought hope to the onlookers, when he declared he was alive. That notion was quickly dispelled when Drs. J.P. Randolph and J.W. Smith, who were on the scene, examined the body and pronounced Charles Webb to be dead.

The lawmen in the house entered the front room where Phillips had last been known to be. The room was in complete disarray caused mainly by the many bullets coming in the windows and through the thin frame walls. Cotton

---

[16] Ibid., 12 July 1916.
[17] Ibid., 11 July 1916.
[18] Ibid., 12 July 1916.

stuffing protruded from bullet holes in the upholstery. Toward the rear of the room was a couch, which the madman had used as a bed. The body of Doc Phillips "was seen hanging across the foot."[19] He had two wounds, neither fatal had they been quickly treated. He had been struck in the knee, severing a large blood vessel and he had bled to death over several hours.

Burial services were held at First Baptist for Charles Webb. Rev. Dana Terry paid tribute to his bravery as did members of The Moose, Odd Fellows and Modern Woodman of the world. He was buried in Greenwood Cemetery.

Thus ended a very tragic and sad chapter in the history of Hot Springs and Garland County.

---

[19] *Sentinel-Record*, 11 July 1916.

Drumming, Leo P. McLaughlin and the Dictagraph

The last twenty years of the nineteenth century and the early years of the twentieth century saw Hot Springs develop into the greatest health Spa in the nation. Thousands of people arrived each year crippled with arthritis and rheumatism and after a course of the hot mineral water baths many left much improved. Others suffering from various kinds of venereal disease were helped. Such success stories were spread far and wide by those who had benefitted from the treatment they had received. That good news brought other sufferers by the droves. Everyone in the city, hotels, restaurants, drug stores, laborers and especially the doctors were prospering. Unfortunately when such conditions exist there are always those who are motivated by greed, who devise schemes and plans to short-cut the established system to gain an unfair edge on their competition. In this case they were called drummers.

Drumming was not invented at Hot Springs, however, it was brought to a new level, or perhaps one might say to a new low, and was to cause criticism of the Spa all over the country. While the system of drumming became very complex and complicated, to deceive the public and police, its elements were simple, "You bring me a customer/client and I'll split my fee with you."[1] In even simpler terms it was the old "kick-back racket at its worst." The practice developed when men calling themselves physicians, though they had neither the education, creditials or skills needed for the profession, sought means to have unsuspecting visitors directed to their offices for treatment. Some referred to themselves as "Doctor," others called themselves "Professor," though neither had any special qualifications for the treatment of the ill or afflicted. They tried to devise all sorts of medically and scientific sounding names for their treatments to entice patients. Professor Mitt Cooper advertised his treatment as The Cooper Electric and Massage Institute and claimed it cured "Neuralgia, Headache, Paralysis, Nervousness, Chronic Rheumatism, and all diseases Peculiar to Women."[2] And then there was The Keeley Institute operated by C.I. Stephens and R.M. Huntington, M.D., whose speciality was directed toward those who wanted to cure the "Liquor, Opium and Tobacco Habits." These fellows were Heaven-sent to the alcoholics as the institute advertised their patients "had little suffering" and "Liquor patients *given all the liquor they want.*"[3] W.H. Walz, Manager of Fisher's Specific--whatever that meant--offered "Permanent cures" for many ailments, using procedures with mystifying and deceiving names, The Gold System, The

---

[1] A very fine article, "The Drumming Evil," appears in *The Record - 1977*, researched and written by Mary D. Hudgins.

[2] *Hot Springs City Directory - 1892.*

[3] Ibid.

Double Chloride of Gold, and The Silver Chloride Method. It was no wonder the visitors quickly became confused and many times welcomed the help of shysters.

Even the bath houses got caught-up in the competition. The Maurice offered treatment by Professor Francis F. Hellwig, Masseur and Electrician. The Superior Bath House sounded pious and honest in their advertisements as it let it be known its owners were Rev. Robert Proctor and Dr. S.S. Wilson. The encouragement to bathe there was set forth by the management as they claimed "best results are obtained by bathing near the spring."[4] What they failed to tell was the thermal water came from a central collecting pool and was distributed to all bath houses, those near and far from the springs. All of this must have been most distressful to the poor visitor who was seeking treatment for his aches and pains.

Since the charlatans and quacks were unable to compete with qualified and medically-trained doctors they employed drummers to meet the trains, engage people in conversation finding out the reason for their visit and recommending the unqualified man as the "best practitioner in town." They would take the unsuspecting visitor to a hotel, who would pay the drummer a fee, and direct the party to certain drug stores where they knew they would be paid for their services. At times there would be a hundred or more drummers in and about the depots, each with an automobile or buggy to whisk the newcomer to lodgings and medical treatment described to be the "best in town." Even reputable doctors were caught up in the frenzy and to meet the competition began to hire drummers of their own.[5] The competition between drummers developed so sharply they had to expand their field of opportunity. Some would journey to Benton and board the return train to Hot Springs using the time to meet and convince the incoming visitors that only Dr. "So and So" could meet their medical needs and that such and such hotel was the only place to stay while in Hot Springs. When the trains became crowded with drummers some would go to Little Rock and some as far away as Memphis or St. Louis which would give them adequate time to work the crowd before they arrived at the spa. It was a lucrative trade and people who had not been to the resort were easily fooled by these friendly-appearing and glib-tongued drummers. If one of the visitors had been referred by his hometown physician to one in Hot Springs with whom he was acquainted with, the visitor was sometimes told, "Oh, I think he is out of town and won't be back for a couple of weeks," or "Has he been able to get his license back to practice?" Sometimes they would disparage some reputable doctor by saying, "Is he still practicing? Has he quit drinking so heavily? I understand

---

[4] *Hot Springs City Directory - 1897.*

[5] *Hot Springs Daily News*, 23 February 1889.

he's been considering the cure." Unfortunately, these ploys, deceits and lies worked on people who had never been to Hot Springs, and money they had and which they intended to use to benefit their health was siphoned off by quacks and unscrupulous people.

As stories of the rip-offs reached St. Louis, Chicago and other large cities headlines began to appear in some of the leading papers warning people of the problem in the small resort. Headlines such as "Paradise of Quacks," or "A Confidence Game That Would Put To Shame the Three-Card Monte Sharp," and "Physicians' Drummers Lay For Sick Visitors on Railroad Trains." Such publicity did absolutely nothing to instill confidence in prospective visitors.

One article described the swindlers one might run in to at Hot Springs: "By far the worst of these sharks is the quack doctor. He has no principle, no conscience and he robs the invalid by methods that would make a road agent turn green with envy." And indeed, Hot Springs did abound with quacks and unscrupulous drummers.

As word began to be spread by "the victims shamelessly robbed," notice finally reached the Federal Government. Efforts to ascertain the conditions at the federal Reservation was reported by one newspaper": Information of an appalling character as to the practices of quack doctors and drummers at Hot Springs, Ark., has come into the possession of the Interior Department. Outrages have been committed by these fiends in human guise, the diabolism of which is almost beyond conception. The proof which the officials of the department now have is however, such as to leave no room for doubt, and if the perpetrators are not sent to the penitentiary, as a result of their preying upon the sick, ignorant and weak-minded, it will be because there is no law to punish them."[6] And, therein lay the truth to the problem-- there were no laws to meet the specific problem! And certainly the laws that did exist were not being enforced.

The Interior Secretary sent a special investigator, Will J. Zevely, to look into the situation. His very detailed report is most revealing, "These drummers are the shrewdest people in the country. I am advised that they are successful, not only with people unaccustomed to travel, but that even two United States Senators have fallen victim to their wiles."[7]

Physicians and hotels who did not employ persons to drum business were losing a great deal of money to those who did. They began to complain to the city administration to stop the drummers. Several city ordinances were passed trying to regulate the problem. One even required that drummers wear metal

---

[6] *St. Louis Globe Democrat*, 22 September 1898.

[7] Ibid. Taken from an article titled "Startling Facts About Hot Springs Rascality, Quack Doctors and Runners."

badges identifying themselves as drummers.[8] Another law restricted the area around the depot platforms as being "off-limits" for drummers. These laws had little effect as the resourceful drummers easily circumvented these roadblocks. The railroads tried to help by passing out circulars warning passengers to beware of the drummers. Still, people were being hoodwinked by the crafty drummers.

A Federal Medical Board was established to approve and license doctors. Any doctor or hotel employing drummers were banned from utilizing any of the bath houses or hot waters.[9] These men were authorized to screen the credentials of all physicians engaged in treatment of persons needing or requiring the hot mineral baths.

Later that year a list of approved physicians was made public.[10] Out of the 116 applications submitted to the examining board only 79 were approved as having the requisite, or educational qualifications. The list was posted in every bath house with instructions that, "No doctor whose name is not on this list can have patients bathed except such as hereafter secure approval of the department."

Physicians appearing on the list were warned, "If detected in drumming business directly or indirectly they will be cut off."[11]

An effort by the State of Arkansas to legislate and regulate the medical profession and drumming at Hot Springs was enacted and called the Gannt Act. It was so broad in its scope covering malpractice that ten local physicians fell into its clutches, including Dr. C.T. Drennen, who was on The Federal Medical Board. When the matter reached the bench of Federal District Judge Trieber, he granted an injunction prohibiting the enforcing of the Gannt Law.[12]

Several doctors whose expertise and credentials were suspect and not approved sought redress in federal court. Little help was to come from that quarter.

When the City of Hot Springs attempted to control drumming by requiring all doctors engaged in the practice to license and list their drummers a loud hue and cry arose. It was discovered that some of the most prominent doctors in town were employing multiple drummers to bring in clients. Dr. J.S. Horner had to admit to having no less than eleven active drummers; Dr. A.U.

---

[8] *The Record - 1977*, Mary Hudgins, p. 91.

[9] *Sentinel-Record*, 17 March 1903. Secretary of the Interior Hitchcock appointed Lt. Col. Blair D. Taylor, Dr. C. Greenway and Dr. Travis Drennen to the local Medical Board.

[10] *Daily News*, 6 October 1903.

[11] *Bulletin of the Department of Interior*, 31 October 1904, signed Martin A. Eisele, Supt. Hot Springs Reservation and approved by E. A. Hitchcock, Secretary.

[12] *Sentinel-Record*, 30 December 1903.

Williams was credited with ten, and Dr. Blaydes with eight and so on.[13]

With the doctors who refused to drum and through the efforts of Dr. J.M. Keller, a Medical Society, a branch of the State Society and the American Medical Association, was organized with Dr. W.H. Barry as its president.[14]

Dr. O.H. Burton, Treasurer of the Garland County Medical Society, published a reward of $1,500 for information leading to the conviction of physicians engaged in drumming.[15]

One of the most notorious drumming doctors, Samuel C. Van Leer, sued both Reservation Superintendent Martin Eisele and members of the Federal Board for $50,000 damages and requested an injunction to restrain the board from further interfering with his business by preventing him from prescribing the hot waters for his patients. Federal Judge Trieber dismissed the suit.[16]

Another individual active in doctor drumming was Dr. James Fulton, who was fined for violations on several occasions.[17]

Probably the most active of all the drumming physicians was Dr. Ernest B. Rider, who kept his office open six days a week and advertised that he would meet patients on "Sunday by appointment."[18] Rider was very aggressive and used a number of drummers to funnel patients to his practice. He had a habit of being confrontational, resulting in his being arrested on several occasions.[19]

It, therefore, is not surprising that with such tension existing between the forces who drummed business and those who opposed it, that violence was bound to occur.

Rider's constant antagonism finally led to a serious encounter with another physician, Dr. A.U. Williams, who had reversed his own stand on drumming and had become totally opposed to it.

The difficulty took place inside the Kempner Building near the elevator. There were no witnesses to the altercation, but apparently the two men met by chance, and exchanged sharp words, and a scuffle ensued. People on the street were unaware of the conflict until they saw "Dr. Williams emerge from the building, bleeding profusely from three wounds about the face and hand."

---

[13] List of Drummers in Conformity to an Ordinance passed by the City of Hot Springs found in the files of Dr. Francis Scully, now located in the Garland County Historical Archives.

[14] *Courier-Journal*, 27 March, year unknown, found in Dr. Keller's Scrapbook, # 12, pages 15-16, in possession of National Park Service.

[15] *Daily News*, 6 August 1906.

[16] *Arkansas Gazette*, 3 November 1905. Van Leer advertised himself as a "Specialist," and as an "Eclectic."

[17] *Sentinel-Record*, 8 November 1905.

[18] *Hot Springs City Directory - 1915.*

[19] *Sentinel-Record*, 14 November 1905, 11 April 1906; *Daily News*, 15 March 1916, 19 March 1906, 3 August 1906, and others.

Dr. Rider was able to get to his office and had been stabbed with a knife and was bleeding from a wound to the abdomen and intestines.[20] He was removed to the Cecil Sanitarium. After treatment for his wounds Dr. Williams accompanied police to the station and from his description of the fracas the officers were of "the general opinion that Rider was the aggressor."[21] Rider refused to give a statement.

The affair was splashed in local and statewide newspapers and led one editor to sum it up with the comment, "A man who is afraid of thunder and can't dodge lightening had better keep out of the doctor squabbles."[22]

Other instances of violence occurred. The editor of the *Citizens Daily Bulletin*, W.T. Amis, wrote an article reporting a visitor George P. Molden of Superior, Wisconsin having been drummed by "Dutch" John Dashner to the Brockway Hotel and then was taken to Dr. Fulton's, who in turn referred him to the Palace Bath House, each collecting a fee. Word reached the Reservation Superintendent who cut off the hot water from the bathing facility since Dr. Fulton was not an approved doctor.[23] Amis followed that with other articles about Dr. Fulton.

Fulton went looking for Amis and a report reached the ears of Sheriff R.L. "Bob" Williams that Fulton intended to kill the editor. The Sheriff ran into Fulton on Central Avenue in front of Webb Brothers store. Williams asked for Fulton's gun and he refused to give it up. Williams, who was unarmed, tried to persuade Fulton to surrender the weapon. With the help of Calvin and Charles Webb "they relieved Fulton of a large gun."[24]

One of the *Bulletin's* reporters, F.T. Lynch, was attacked and beaten by C.C. Lemly, a well-known druggist, over a story he had written. The story obtained from a detective working for the Federal Medical Board, named Lemly as providing the names of several doctors to visitors, all known to be engaged in drumming. Lemly was infuriated by the article and called up the editor and characterized the story as "a damned lie and the detective who furnished the information as the progeny of doubtful parentage."[25] Lemly was arrested and charged for assault and battery.

The drumming doctors, hotels and drummers struck again. Detective J.L. Boone, had been employed by the Federal Medical Board to gather evidence and "had made life unbearable for the *drummers*" by arresting those working around the railroad depots. The drummers secured a sympathetic deputy Howell to serve a warrant issued by Justice Archer, charging Boone with

---

[20] *Daily News*, 10 May 1907. This was an EXTRA publication.
[21] *Sentinel-Record*, 11 May 1907.
[22] *Orear's Yellow Jacket*, 19 May 1907.
[23] *Citizens Daily Bulletin*, 29 June 1907.
[24] Ibid., 25 July 1907.
[25] *Citizens Daily Bulletin*, 20 August 1907.

perjury against some of the drummers.[26] Charges against Boone were dismissed and he resumed his anti-drumming crusade and almost single handedly brought the system to a mere crawl. His activity was hurting the quack doctors and their drummers hard and they struck back. A.R. Lynch, a drummer and his employer, Dr. Fulton, were so incensed with Boone they sought him out and surprised him. Dr. Fulton held a shot-gun on Boone while Lynch took the detective's gun from him. Then Boone, standing "with his hands elevated above his head was beaten with his own weapon wielded by Dr. Fulton." Boone was knocked to the ground and Fulton continued to strike him. The assault was stopped on the "prostrate officer in the pursuit of his duty as bystanders grabbed Fulton as Lynch ran off."[27] One newspaper labeled the attack as "One of the most dastardly and cowardly attempts made upon an officer in the pursuit of his duty recently recorded in the history of Hot Springs."

A mass meeting of "indignation" was called by the Garland County Medical Society, and resolutions were passed "with one dissenting vote of the attack on J.L. Boone."[28]

With the public outraged, Dr. Fulton was charged and convicted in Police Court of aggravated assault and fined $50 and sentenced to jail for ninety days.[29] Fulton's days at Hot Springs were numbered as his welcome had worn out. His accomplice, A.R. Lynch, fled the confines of Garland County and the warrant sworn out for his arrest went unserved.

For a time drumming seemed to go underground and the adverse publicity affecting the city diminished. Then the practice began to grow with the intervening years, "because the State Laws and Federal rules to stamp out this evil had up until then, 1915, proven ineffective."[30]

All of these activities served to harm the reputation of the city as being a resort of the highest level. The local Medical Board, in a secret meeting elected a committee to deal with the growing problem. Three outstanding men served: Dr. W.T. Wooten, Dr. William H. Deadrick and Dr. A.H. Tribble After careful consideration the committee hired a very fine attorney, William G. Bouic, who also was an assistant prosecuting attorney, to conduct an investigation designed to rid the city forever of drumming. Bouic advised wha

---

[26] *Sentinel-Record*, 23 August 1907.
[27] *Daily News*, 24 January 1908.
[28] Ibid., 25 January 1908.
[29] *Sentinel-Record*, 30 January 1908.
[30] From a seven page memoranda by William G. Bouic, entitled, *The Cleaning Up of Bad Situation in the Medical Profession*. The value of the paper is that Bouic was involved in the cleanup first-hand. It is undated and was submitted to the Garland County Historical Societ by attorney Richard W. Hobbs, 19 July 1991. Hobbs advises that Bouic was his first law partn and served as prosecuting attorney for the Eighteenth Judicial District.

e believed was necessary to gather the evidence needed and the committee agreed to raise the money"--with the understanding that work and results of he investigation were to be kept secret until same had been completed.[31] urther, "the movement was not to be directed against any one doctor but gainst the entire profession or anyone willing to pay for patients."

Bouic pointed out, "This was imperative, (maintaining secrecy) as the onditions which had existed for years reached into quarters which were then nknown. Any discussion of the work would have resulted in a complete ailure."[32]

Bouic decided the only way to get the evidence needed was to set up what s commonly referred today as a "sting operation." A small hotel was leased nd a man hired "for the purpose of drumming his patrons to any doctor villing to pay."[33] The attorney knew he needed some people to operate the ting that were not known to the community and hired the Burns Detective gency, who had been so active in the con-game investigations of 1913. Four peratives were sent to Hot Springs, bringing with them a couple of Dictagraph machines. These were early recording devices, not previously nown to have been used in the Spa.

At that time W.G. Bouic occupied a suite of offices, 311-312 in the Arkansas National Bank Building. Attorneys James E. Hogue and Leo P. McLaughlin vere his neighbors, sharing rooms 308-310. McLaughlin occupied the latter oom and shared a semi-vacant entry room with Hogue. That room adjoined Bouic's 311, an office seldom used. Bouic was aware that Leo McLaughlin epresented three or four of the hotel drummers but believed for a fee McLaughlin might "throw in with the anti-drumming group." He was well cquainted with Leo, but approached him cautiously, first feeling him out vithout revealing who Bouic represented. He discovered McLaughlin to be eceptive to the idea. Apparently Leo saw nothing unethical or there being a ossible conflict of interest in moving to the anti-drumming side of the ledger. After all, a fee was a fee, and Leo was always practical where money was nvolved.

The Burns detectives installed a microphone in Leo's outer office with the vire running to the receiver in Bouic's seldom used room, where one of the perators would record the conversations.[34] The installation was of crude

---

[31] Ibid., p. 4.

[32] Ibid.

[33] Ibid. Some evidence exists that the Plaza Hotel was the one involved, whereas nother source suggests that it may have been a small boarding house on Spring Street. It is ossible that both were used.

[34] *Sentinel-Record*, 26 September 1916. Apparently the "workmanship" was not of high uality as when the device was discovered it was described as "merely dangling there" apparently ot noticed by any who were interviewed.

Leo P. McLaughlin interviewed drummers using the first Dictagraph machine in Hot Springs

esign as the microphone reportedly dangled above a desk, but apparently ent unnoticed since this was reportedly the first ever used in Hot Springs.

For a period of several weeks Leo McLaughlin would call his drumming lients to his office on the pretext that he needed information on how the rumming was carried on. He would question them not only about how they perated but who they represented and how the payoffs were made.[35] To ncourage the drummers McLaughlin pointed out that the bill, restricting hem from operating on the depot platforms, was under review by the rkansas Supreme Court. He told them until that decision was made final he ad an agreement with Police Judge Verne Ledgerwood that if any drummers ere arrested on the platforms the most the judge would fine them was ten ollars.[36] It is apparent in reviewing the transcripts that the drummers had onfidence in Leo McLaughlin as he artfully led them to reveal how they pproached visitors and skillfully manipulated them into going to a certain otel or rooming house. Then, when the visitor inquired or asked for a ecommendation as to a good physician the drummer many times would take he visitor to a drug store, often times Lemley's, and introduce him to a harmacist saying, "This gentleman is looking for a good doctor, can you ecommend one to him?" The druggist would then write on a piece of paper he names of four or five doctors, all who were known to be drummers, and end the individual on his way. When the visitor showed the doctor the slip f paper referring him to the physician the doctor would know to whom he wed a fee. One system frequently used was that the doctor would take an nvelope to the druggist, representing his fee, and leave one, which the ruggist would place in the cash register and the drummer could pick it up at nytime. No names would appear on any of the transactions except the riginal recommendation which also contained other names.[37] Sometimes the rummer would call the doctor and say, "I need to see you a few minutes, when would be convenient?" In the privacy of the physician's office the octor would check his ledger to determine which clients that particular rummer had sent to him and he would then pay the drummer. There were no witnesses to the system but the doctor and drummer--and they weren't telling.

---

[35] From Dr. Francis Scully's files. Some transcribed copies of the Dictagraph Records appear in the file and he probably obtained them from the National Park Records-- hereinafter referred as Dictagraph Records.

[36] Ibid.

[37] Dictagraph Records. From tapes involving admitted drummers George Watts, John Frank Williams and Mac McCollam. The drummers had a vocabulary all their own. "Cold-turkey," referred to taking a visitor in who was on a depot platform. "Fruit" was the money they derived from the kick-back, "Boob" referred to a non-local person. "Sucker" was the visitor who fell for the ploy and "Bull" was any police watching the depots.

Leo McLaughlin interviewed several small hotel owners who practiced drumming, including L.L. Asbury, owner of the Marion Hotel on Whittington Avenue and Clyde Denton, operator of the New Lindell Hotel located in the 300 block of Ouachita. Each of these interviews were quite revealing and insightful into their operations and added a great amount of evidence which could be used. Thus, nearly seven hundred pages of evidence was accumulated.

Evidence began to mount as the lynch-pin of the covert operation, J.M. Carter, a recovering drug addict, later referred to as "Gabby," who had been hired by the Burns Detective Agency, provided affidavits of his activities as hotel manager and drumming people to various doctors.[38] He even posed in several as a visitor who was drummed by a Mr. Kinney, and taken to Dr. Lanning, treated with medication and a course of baths.[39]

Keeping such a widespread and complicated operation secret proved to be impossible as the Medical Committee sought donations to fund the project. The anti-drumming group had under-estimated the number involved in drumming. It was initially believed that the number of physicians practicing drumming numbered only ten or twelve doctors, when in fact almost forty were so involved. Thus, when a couple of the doctors who drummed were contacted for donations to the anti-group for expenses being incurred in the covert operation "the cat was out of the bag." The names of the Committee, W.G. Bouic and their operative J.M. Carter became known.[40]

Word of the discovery quickly spread through the drumming community. When it was learned that Carter had furnished affidavits attesting to the fact that several physicians were involved in drumming, as well as druggists, hotels and boarding houses, fear was rampant. The drumming forces sought some type of damage control, not only to protect what, to them had been a profitable means of livelihood, but to keep them out of jail.

Dr. W.G. Choate, who was deeply involved in drumming and had treated several patients referred to him by Carter, persuaded J.M. Carter to go to Memphis on pretense it was a business trip to drum up other clients for him. It was really a ploy to get Carter out of town while the drumming forces tried to assess and investigate the situation. Carter became suspicious when he was accompanied by Al Williams, operator of the Sumpter House, also a drummer, who worked for Choate. Carter slipped away from Williams and returned to Hot Springs, bringing four visitors for the Gayso Hotel (part of the old

---

[38] *New Era*, 26 September 1916.

[39] From Affidavit of J.M. Carter taken at New Orleans, Louisiana, 26 September 1916. This is on file at the National Park Service and a copy is in Dr. Francis Scully's files at GCHS Archives. Hereinafter cited as Affidavit-Carter.

[40] Memo - Bouic, p. 5.

Goddard Hotel) which had been under management of G.H. Hall. Carter learned that in the two days he was gone, "Hall had become suspicious and afraid of what was taking place, had sold out and left the city."[41] The situation was now reaching a dangerous status.

When Dr. Choate learned that Carter had returned to Hot Springs he contacted Carter and asked him to accompany him to the Public Drug Store at the corner of Ouachita and Market Streets. Although suspicious, Carter agreed. He stated they were followed by three men he later identified as Dick Baird, Johnnie Clements and "Skinny" Ellision. When they reached the drug store he told, "Hall had said I had made affidavits against certain doctors and Choate said that he would kill me before I could put him out of business."

The men surrounded Carter and all had drawn pistols, except Ellision, and told him "that I would have to sign a statement that they would prepare or be killed. Dr. Choate dictated a statement to a young lady who had slipped in the drug store through the back way. The group had the names of each of the physicians Carter had given affidavits on as being drummers and providing data to implicate them. They forced Carter to sign each statement revoking the testimony he had furnished in the affidavits, all the while surrounding him as "they stood there with drawn guns, telling me they would kill me."[42]

The group knew of Carter's weakness for drugs as they put him in an automobile and began giving him one-quarter grain tablets of morphine. He was taken to Little Rock where Johnnie A. Clements, who operated Clements Rooms at 708½ Central, bought tickets for two for New Orleans. "All during the trip," he said, "he gave me morphine tablets."

Carter arrived at New Orleans on September 19th, "full of drugs" and remained under their influence until the 21st.[43] Clements was getting ready to put Carter on a boat for Cuba, to get him "out of the country," when Carter began to come to his senses and gave his captor the slip.[44] Carter found a telegraph office and immediately dispatched a telegram to W.G. Bouic informing him where he was and that he had been forced to leave Hot Springs. Bouic and Leo McLaughlin were elated as they had desperately been trying to locate Carter for several days as they were aware much of their case hung on him. Bouic realized that by that time Clements, and possibly others, were searching for Carter. He reasoned, quite probably, "Carter's life was in danger." Dr. Charles H. Garrett, originally of Hot Springs, was at that time interning at one of the leading hospitals in New Orleans. Bouic called him and told him the situation. Garrett immediately went to where J.M. Carter had said

---

[41] Affidavit - Carter.
[42] Ibid.
[43] Ibid., p. 2.
[44] Memo - Bouic, p. 5.

he would be, and upon locating him, whisked him away to the hospital and telephoned Bouic that he had found Carter. He said he would keep Carter at the hospital until Bouic could come after him.[45]

Bouic and Leo McLaughlin left for New Orleans, although they told everyone they were headed to Memphis.[46] The two spa attorneys decided that Carter might be safer in New Orleans for the time being and rented him a room at 702 N. Rampart Street. An affidavit was secured from him as to what had happened as they intended to take it back to show Circuit Judge Scott Wood how the drumming forces were playing "hardball." They told Carter to lay low and they would send for him when he was needed for the Grand Jury.[47]

While the two lawyers were gone from Hot Springs a "bombshell" burst over the drumming forces. On September 25, the microphone to the Dictagraph machine was found in the "outer room where Attorneys Hogue and McLaughlin hold forth in the Arkansas National Bank Building." When told of the discovery James E. Hogue was "indignant,"and claimed he knew nothing about it.[48] Had Bouic and McLaughlin arranged for the discovery of the recording device in order to "flush-out," their quarry? This would have removed the "heat," so far as Carter was concerned. The records are silent as to who discovered the Dictagraph or this aspect of the case.

Reservation Superintendent Parks took possession of the machine and it became known that the gathering of evidence had been underway for many weeks and was directed against those doctors engaged in drumming.[49]

The discovery of the Dictagraph struck fear into the drumming community as no one was aware who had been recorded, what had been said, or who all had been implicated. Judge Scott Wood poured more oil on the fire by convening the Grand Jury on the same day the story broke about discovery of the recording device. Bouic lost no opportunity and requested the "drumming evil" be gone into.

When this occurred the drumming forces "began to hold meetings at various hotels in the city with the view of discussing action they would (need to) take in the event they were indicted." What was unknown to these drummers, hotel men and physicians was the Burns agents had discovered their plans and planted their dictagraphs in the meeting locations. Bouic later said, "When this became known panic existed among them."

---

[45] Ibid. Bouic stated that had Dr. Garrett not been able to get Carter before the "Drumming forces," this important link would probably never been available to those in charge of the investigation."

[46] *New Era*, 26 September 1916.

[47] Affidavit of J.M. Carter.

[48] *Sentinel-Record*, 26 September 1916.

[49] *New Era*, 26 September 1916.

The depots were suddenly deserted as many drummers, fearing indictment by the Grand Jury, packed their bags and left town leaving no forwarding address. Several physicians, possessing doubtful credentials, quacks, and "make-believe doctors," learning of these developments concluded there were greener pastures elsewhere and quickly closed their offices and left town. Dr. W.G. Choate, who had been one of the most aggressive drumming physicians, moved to Tulsa, Oklahoma. Dr. Henry N. Hardister, who operated from the Sumpter-Little Building, suddenly decided he was needed in Dallas, Texas and moved. Dr. Ernest Rider sought better pickings at Kansas City. Two years later he would be in similar trouble in another city. The exodus continued.

When it became known that a meeting of hotel men and drummers, which had been held at the Sumpter House, had been recorded, more panic resulted. The manager Albert H. Williams and his son, turned the operation of the hotel over to Mrs. E. Marie Wright, and the two men hastily left for parts unknown.[50] Dick Baird took his family to Paris, Texas, hoping to escape indictment. Leon Gilkey gave up the operation of the Gilkey Hotel and headed to Detroit. Bouic let it be known that a complete recording had been made of a meeting at the Putman Hotel and it was being furnished the Grand Jury. Others hurriedly packed and left before they could be subpeonaed. A few would eventually venture back and would find Hot Springs was a town of forgiving citizens!

Real concern set in when W.G. Bouic, now acting in his official capacity as assistant prosecuting attorney, told the press, "We have evidence of drumming against no less than twenty-three physicians in Hot Springs. Of this nature we have convicting evidence against eighteen. There are also at least seven of the city's prominent drugstores involved in this investigation."[51] He laid before the reporters a sordid tale of how visitors were victimized and how even several of the bath houses were involved. It was not a pretty picture of the beautiful and pristine city nestled in the mountains of Arkansas.

With this evidence laid out in the press, the dam broke. Physicians, hotel men, druggists and bath house people became fearful of their indictment, possible prison time, and began looking for an escape. Some hurried to their lawyers to ascertain how much trouble they were in. Others went direct to Bouic and McLaughlin offering "to make open confessions with the view of getting such leniency as a confession might bring." Many of these were prominent men who had gotten caught up in the act of drumming because of the competition the practice afforded.[52] They had not intended for it to get out of hand, but they had gradually sank deeper in the mire of the evil system. The

---

[50] *Sentinel-Record,* 3 October 1916.
[51] Ibid.
[52] Memo - Bouic, p. 6.

very least they could expect was to face professional embarrassment.

When the Grand Jury began to sift through the evidence on doctor drumming and perjury charges, indictments were returned against a large number of people. Several of the leaders in the drumming movement "accepted suspended sentences on grounds that they would never practice drumming again in this county or state."[53]

Leo McLaughlin, working as an assistant prosecuting attorney, helped prepare the cases involving physicians. In an effort not to compromise his ethics he carefully avoided the cases connected with the hotel men, some of whom he had represented.[54]

The back of the drumming evil was broken. It would never revive again, although there would be scattered instances where a taxi-cab driver would "drum" someone to one of the smaller hotels or boarding houses and would be paid. For thirty-five years the practice of drumming had cast a shadow over the medical community of Garland County and it took an intense effort to defeat it--it surely had not gone without a fight.

---

[53] Ibid.

[54] *Sentinel-Record*, 3 October 1916.

The City Commission and Another Disappointment for Leo

Nineteen-seventeen was very different from other years because of the number of elections that were held in the resort city. By the first week in April, voters trekked to the polls no less than four times. It had been usual for the Democratic party to hold a primary election during the month of December, prior to the city elections scheduled for April. For some obscure reason the primary was held in early February. At that time lawyer Alonzo Curl, ran against Police Judge Verne Ledgerwood with the outcome predictable as Ledgerwood posted a wide margin of votes, 692-238.[11] While there was little fireworks produced by the judicial race, quite a flap occurred in the mayor's race. Candidates for the mayor's nominee position included George Belding, Secretary of the Business Men's League and former mayor. His opponent was a hardware dealer from South Hot Springs, R.A. "Bob" Sigman. Almost from the start the two--both democrats--went at each other like two pit-bull dogs in a fight over a bone. Sigman referred to Belding and his supporters as "curbstone henchmen," and claimed his opponent had promised the police and fire chiefs jobs to enough people to fill the city auditorium.[2] Sigman said there were two things going on in Hot Springs that he would provoke the law against, "One is boot-legging, the other is the gambling dive."[3] George Belding, questioning his opponent's courage, "in a red-hot address at city auditorium countered he had offered $100 to any one who could get Bob Sigman to attend the meeting and knew when he made the offer it would never have to be paid." Belding classified his opponent's publicity man "As a person with poison dripping from his heart, who has wallowed in the mire and who is now feeling the effects of a mis-spent life."[4] The two pounded each other for days and called each other almost ever name but a child of God.

When all the smoke, fire and rhetoric had cleared George Belding had defeated R.A. Sigman 583-319, for the Democratic nominee.[5] But the war had not been won, only the first battle had been fought.

It was elections such as this that caused John A. Riggs to seek another form of municipal government for Hot Springs, one not so fraught with partisan politics, mud-slinging and name calling.

John Andrew Riggs was a most amazing person. He had been born 5 November 1866 at Quincy, Illinois. For several years he had lived at Wichita, Kansas where he formed a partnership in the Lopez Medicine Company.

---

[1] *Sentinel-Record*, 16 February 1917.
[2] Ibid., 14 February 1917.
[3] Ibid.
[4] *Sentinel-Record*, 17 February 1917.
[5] *Sentinel-Record*, 16 February 1917.

While visiting Hot Springs he recognized the opportunities the area afforded and opened up a branch of his company here. For years the business occupied the upper floors of a brick building at Spencer's corner. He and his wife, Ida Louisa Callahan Riggs, fit quite well into the social, business and political community of the Spa. He became publisher of the *Hot Springs New Era*, a daily afternoon paper, and used the power of the press to express his support or opposition on various local issues over the years. He ran for, and was elected State Representative.

Riggs was an advocate of women's suffrage and became their champion in Arkansas by using his office as State Representative to espouse their cause and later sponsored legislation to aid their crusade. He invested in the ill-fated plan to build airships at Hot Springs and when there was a hint that oil might be pooled beneath the rocky soils of Garland County organized an oil exploration company. Unfortunately, the results of the drilling proved as disappointing as the airship venture.

Believing the mayor-aldermanic form of city government to abound with partisan politics, waste and inefficiency, he came up with an unsuccessful attempt to have Hot Springs declared a city of no government and that it be placed under the direct control of the United States Congress, similar to that of the District of Columbia. He reasoned that with the Federal Reservation surrounding the city it would qualify in this respect. What was appealing to the public about his view was that the federal government would have a greater responsibility of financing the city's operation since so much of the area in and about the city afforded no taxes for the city's support. The Spa was deeply in debt, principally caused by the fire of 1913, during which all its utilities were destroyed and had to be completely rebuilt. Therefore, any financial help would be most welcome. Riggs' plan was flawed, of course. No one at City Hall or the Court House wanted federal authorities telling them how to run their county and city, and strong opposition to the plan arose. Businessmen feared what regulations they might have imposed upon them in event of federal intervention. They need not have worried as Congress was not interested in the plan.

But Riggs was not daunted or discouraged. He and George A. Callahan came up with a plan to change the municipal government to a city manager-commission form of government. It would have four commissioners and a mayor elected, and a city manager hired by the five-man commission. The two men had talked at length with Mayor W.S. Shaw, of Minor, North Dakota, who sold them on the system of having each elected commissioner responsible for one part of the city's operation: one over the police, one over the fire department, the street department, etc. Riggs was also hopeful that a non-partisan form of government might reduce the friction always existing between the major political parties. He believed this to be divisive and non-productive. The plan calling for the hiring of a city manager, was supposedly non-political. While the idea was appealing, the removal of partisan politics from the spa's city government at that time was wishful thinking and Riggs' voice was like one crying into the wind. The plan did pass the state legislature with the option of any first class city being able to select its own destiny through the ballot box.[6] When the voters went to the polls in early March the city-commission form was adopted by a narrow margin. But as editor John G. Higgins so accurately pointed out, "Forms of government do not amount to so much as the men in control."[7]

Naturally the city council members had campaigned to retain the mayor-aldermanic system, but to no avail. Mayor McClendon took the opposite approach. Realizing that he might be put out of a political job, he believed the new idea of the city-manager form of municipal government might be worth trying, and he supported the measure.

Then came the third election of the year, called an "elimination primary." It was to provide a slate on which the new candidates for commissioners would run on. As many as wanted to could file for a commissioner's position. That election was to be followed by a runoff, to be held two weeks later.[8] At that time the mayor and four commissioners would be elected.

George Belding, who seemed to have run in vain when he won the nomination of the Democratic party, decided to enter the race for mayor. His first opponent to announce was George A.Callahan, who had rendered considerable aid to John A. Riggs in getting the city manager-commission bill passed. Riggs was related to Callahan by marriage and fully supported his candidacy.[9] It had been doubtful that Dr. Jacob W. McClendon would seek another term as mayor but his friends persuaded him to enter[10]. No doubt when his announcement was made both George Belding and George Callahan flinched and realized that the odds had just changed--McClendon did not run for office like any other politician. McClendon did not deal in personalties and seldom mentioned his opponents. His message was clear and unmistakable. In his announcement Dr. McClendon gave a very down to earth assessment of his beliefs and love for Hot Springs. He said, "I'm an American citizen, free-born and I'm not glued to the earth. I'm not akin to the man who stands still. I believe that when a man gets into an office he should leave it in a better condition than he found it.

"I represent no class or clique. My plain creed embraces alike the best interests of labor and the president of a bank. My sole object is to make Hot

---

[6] *New Era*, 26 February 1917.

[7] *Sentinel-Record*, 20 March 1917.

[8] *Ibid.*

[9] *Sentinel-Record*, 4 March 1917, 6 March 1917. A large number of businessmen signed a petition in support of George A. Callahan.

[10] Ibid.

Springs the greatest resort on earth, which it should have been years ago. I would like to see Hot Springs conducted along the constructive, independent, fearless and public spirited lines. If you think you are safe in voting for my policies, all well and good. I thank you." This was McClendon, pure and simple, what you saw was what you got.

The public was surprised as so many well-known men threw their hats into the ring and announced for the position of commissioner. A total of sixteen filed for the elimination primary. Since the voting was to be done city wide a citizen would be able to cast eight votes and the final eight would move on to the runoff.

Leo P. McLaughlin, who had missed politics terribly, came to a conclusion that he was known well enough city wide to be elected one of the commissioners. Leo's ego led him to believe that out of the sixteen candidates he could easily make the cut of eight to the runoff.[11]

Even though the election was touted to be non-partisan it was believed that because of his affiliation with the Democratic party and having beaten R.G. Sigman in the Democratic Primary George Belding was the odds on favorite. As usual Dr. McClendon was difficult to figure but was able to nose out George Belding 484 votes to 446. Callahan was third with a respectable 325 votes. Thus the runoff for mayor was set with McClendon and Belding.

Dr. Jacob W. McClendon
served as mayor for the aldermanic and commission forms of government. He had just won his fifth term of office when he died.
Drawing by Harry Cloud

---

[11] *Sentinel-Record*, 20 March 1917.

In the commissioners race there were some real surprises, especially for Leo P. McLaughlin, as he finished twelfth in a sixteen-man race and with voters able to vote for eight men. It was a crushing blow for Leo. Just how could McLaughlin lose so badly? He certainly had name recognition. His only respectable showing was in the Second, his home ward, and finished behind Hamp Williams there.[12] It appeared the voters were still remembering Leo's part in losing the sanitarium project. He was certainly a disappointed candidate. For several days he was not seen around the streets and sulked in his loss. He need not have worried, though, it would be the last election that Leo P. McLaughlin would ever lose!

In the runoff election on 3 March, George Belding was again expected to win as many expected him to pick up the majority of the votes for Callahan. Once again the political experts had miscalculated. Dr. McClendon, who seldom spent money on political ads and never promised city jobs to supporters, merely shook hands and listened to people and their problems, nosed out his opponent 823-765. Four well-known men with good civic reputations were elected commissioners, Hamp Williams, Frank Stearns, E.N. Roth and M.A. Eisele.[13]

On the same ticket was an unopposed race for the new Municipal Judge for a term of four years. Verne Ledgerwood's good and close friend, State Representative Allen T. "Sonny" Davies, had entered a bill in the legislature creating a municipal court at Hot Springs and which had passed. When many voters see an unopposed office they merely strike through it or leave it blank. Out of the total of 1,588 voters in that election, 1,566 marked their ballot for Vernal Ledgerwood.[14]

John A. Riggs had designed the city manager-commission government in hopes it would remove politics from elections of the municipal government at Hot Springs. He may not have realized the removing of politics from the Spa was even a greater task than a small child in taking a bone out of the grasp of a Doberman-pincher. At that stage in the history of the resort it was impossible!

---

[12] Ibid., 21 March 1917, p. 6.
[13] Ibid., 4 April 1917.
[14] Ibid. Also, LAT - Ledgerwood.

Hot Springs Goes to War: So Does Leo P. McLaughlin, Reluctantly

By the time President Woodrow Wilson signed a declaration of war against Germany in April 1917, the country was already gearing up for the expected conflict. For several months a majority of the public believed it was a foregone conclusion that the United States was being rapidly dragged into the European struggle which had raged for over three years. At first America tried to stay neutral and isolated but too many incidents like the sinking of the Luisitania accelerated the path to its entry of the war.

On the day the president signed the declaration of war, the organization of a Hot Springs company of men began. It was planned to tender the volunteer company to join a "new regiment in this state."[1] The first volunteers signing at the Spa were, J.W. Alford, Jr., Tate Brown, Robert Triffit, Charles Triffit, Frank Jobe, Ralph Barnett, Luther Scarbrough, Will Johnson, Robert Nix, Lee Echard, Fred Lee and William Hilpret.[2] Within a few days they would be joined by others.

By September men were leaving Hot Springs en route to training camps in large numbers. Company C and the Ambulance Corp of the third Arkansas Regiment, totaling 192 men, left town via train, en route to Fort Logan Roots where they would spend about three weeks of basic training and then would pass on to Camp Beauregard, a new facility near Alexandria, Louisiana, where they were to receive their final preparation for duty in France.[3] Small groups of ten to fifteen men left regularly, some ordered to Fort Dodge, Iowa, or Camp Pike, Arkansas and others to Camp Beauregard, Louisiana.[4]

Some men with special skills or talents sought commissions to enter the service. Cecil H. Ledgerwood, younger brother of Judge Vernal S. Ledgerwood was interviewed in Washington, D.C. for "a splendid appointment in the government military service."[5] Shortly after Cecil had graduated from high school in 1910, he entered a partnership with Loyd S. Williamson. This firm was first located on Third Street, then moved to 144 Central Avenue, operating as Plumbing, Gas Fitting and Heating Contractors.[6] The firm was doing quite well when the fire of 1913 tripled its business. Cecil Ledgerwood's skills and knowledge of pipe fitting was to put him "in charge of certain engineering and sanitary lines of defense."[7] He was commissioned

---

[1] *Sentinel-Record*, 7 April 1917, p.8.
[2] Ibid.
[3] Ibid., 11 September 1917, p. 3.
[4] Ibid., 31 August 1918.
[5] *Sentinel-Record*, 23 June 1917.
[6] *Polks Southern Directory - Hot Springs, 1917.*
[7] *Sentinel-Record*, 23 June 1917.

a lieutenant.[8]

Several Hot Springs men were either commissioned when they entered service or received promotions afterwards. A few were Lt. Colonel Phillip Sisney, Major Birkett Williams, Captains Hartley Wootton, Gilbert Hogaboom, Walter Pollard, Garnett Eisele, Joe P. Randolph, John W. St. Clair, Warren Townsend and W.A. Johnson.

Quite a number of physicians from the resort volunteered or were drafted and received commissions of varying ranks. Some were Dr. Earl Sanders, Dr. J.W. Bush, Dr. Lautman, Dr. Loyd Thompson, Dr. F. Earl Diemer, Dr. W.K. Smith, Dr. A.C. Prichard, Dr. H. King Wade, Dr. J.H. Smith, Dr. O.H. King, and Dr. C.G. Coffee.

Some of the Spa's well-known young men sported first and second lieutenants' bars; Edwin Dillon, Richard Lawrence, Jesse Gilliam, L.D. Cooper, Jr., Troy Teague, M.J. Sullivan, Miller Belding, Robert Thornton, Dwight Boxer, James Weaver, James Cook, Felix Katz, H.H. Jarrett, Arthur Frisby, Julian Corrington, Frank Posey, Percy Scholem, A.G. Cooper, A.T. "Sonny" Davies, and Wayne Moore.[9]

Many of the above were volunteers, but some were drafted under the national subscription act. On May 19, 1917, the United States Congress passed a selective service law to raise armies for the war. Under this act a total of 24,234,021 men registered and of that number 2,810,296 men were inducted.[10] The draft board of Garland County was headed by W.W. Gentry, L.E. Sawyer and L.W. Miller.[11] An Exemption Board was also appointed by President Wilson and was composed of County Clerk Allen Hotchkiss, Sheriff Brad O. Smith and County Health Officer Dr. John S. Woods.[12]

The young men of Garland County lined up to register on 5 June 1917. Vernal S. Ledgerwood was number 68. His brother Cecil followed with number 69. Cousin Hugh got to the sign-up table late that same day and logged in as 902. Leo P. McLaughlin and brother George were numbered 297 and 298.[13] John William McLaughlin, who was forty years-old, did not have to register until the third call in September 1918.

By the end of July 1917, the national draft lottery drawing had been held and published in newspapers across the country. Young men eagerly scanned the first numbers drawn to ascertain how high on the priority list they might be.

---

[8] Ibid., 19 October 1918, p. 2.

[9] Ibid., 31 August, 1918, p. 8.

[10] *The World Book Encyclopedia, Vol. 4, - 1962,* pp. 263-264.

[11] *Sentinel-Record,* 14 September 1918.

[12] Ibid., 28 June 1917.

[13] Microfilm of Selective Service Registrants of Local Board for County of Garland and State of Arkansas.

A mill-foreman, Finis Jack Lawson, holding number 258, was the first man drafted in Garland County. John Clarence Horner, Daniel L. Kelly, Roy Fickle and brothers Elmer and J. Franklin Witherspoon, followed.[14]

When the army announced it was establishing an officers training school for young Americans, and solicited applications, several local boys applied. Tests were to be given at Leon Springs, Texas, located a few miles northwest of San Antonio. Leo McLaughlin announced, as he was leaving for Chicago on a business trip, that when he returned in "about ten days" he would enter the Officer's Training camp at Leon Springs.[15] What caused McLaughlin to change his mind is unknown. It does not appear from his army file that he ever took the test necessary to apply for a commission. As his friends and acquaintances left for service it seemed as if he became more determined to remain at home. In later years political opponents sometimes referred to him as having been a "slacker," an unflattering term applied to those who tried to avoid military service. In World War II, the term applied to those acting in similar manner was "draft dodger." Leo McLaughlin stoutly resented the implication, but as will be seen, there was some justification for the referral.

A.T. "Sonny" Davies, law partner of Verne Ledgerwood, applied for the officer training program and while at Leon Springs went over to a new branch of service, the Army Aviation Corps, and along with twenty-six other young men also took the examination for that branch of service. When he returned to Hot Springs a few days later, he was notified he had passed both the test for the officer's training program and also the "very trying examination for enlistment in the Aviation Corps of the United States Army." Only two others passed the examination with Davies.[16] He accepted the commission in the aviation service and distinguished himself during the war.

But, it wasn't just men who were volunteering for overseas duty. Many women enrolled in the Red Cross nursing classes, held at Leo N. Levi Hospital. Practicing physicians such as Dr. Purdom, Dr. Tribble, Dr. Drennan, Dr. Short, Dr. Wootton and Dr. Chestnutt taught basics from emergency first aid to hygiene and bacteriology, and how to take care of battle wounds. Twenty-six of these ladies enlisted for overseas duty, namely, Lila Rix, Mrs. Robert Neill, Rose Goslee, Mrs. S.D. Weil, Maud Henderson, Mrs. Scott Wood, Mrs. Hal Bailey, Mrs. C.N. Roberts, Gladia Russell, Carrie Price, Gertrude McQueenie, Etta Seals, Mrs. Delaney, Mrs. J. C. Bohl, Fay Barnett, Alma Holiday, Mrs. James Chestnut, Mrs. J.C. Horner, Louise Johnson, Mrs. E. T. Cook, Kate C. Rummel, Mrs. J.M. Proctor, Hattie Glades, Mrs. Warren

[14] *Sentinel-Record*, 28 July 1917, p. 8.
[15] Ibid, 4 August 1917.
[16] *Sentinel-Record*, 11 August 1917.

Murphy, May Jones Nowhill and Kate Martin.[17] Due to the fact their training was only four weeks before the end of the war none probably served, but they had shown courage in their committment!

Herbert Hoover held the position of Food Administrator when the United States entered the World War. His job was to make certain that the production and distribution of food for American military personnel, civilians, and allies would be adequate. As he began to set up a giant network to funnel foodstuff into the war effort Hoover searched the country for dependable men to administer the program on the state level. He selected and appointed Hamp Williams of Hot Springs to head the food program in the state of Arkansas. This was certainly a compliment to the ability of the Spa resident and businessman. He did not let Hoover down for his confidence.[18] When sugar came in to short supply, Williams encouraged the growing of sorghum. As the country began to run short of wheat he urged farmers to increase production of that crop. In 1917, Garland County produced 5,257 bushels of wheat and increased it to 10,604 bushels a year later.

Herbert Hoover was also instrumental in instituting the pledge card campaign to conserve food in this country.[19] This was a program to enlist the aid of hotels, boarding houses, cafes and restaurants in observing "meatless" and "wheatless" days on Tuesdays and Wednesday of every week.

The pledge read: "Believing it imperative that we do all within our power to assist our country at this critical time in winning this war by the proper conservation of food and that strict adherence to the general plan, of observing meatless and wheatless days, as outlined by the Federal Food Administration, Washington, D. C., we, the undersigned restaurant and hotel proprietors of the City of Hot Springs, Arkansas, agree and hereby pledge ourselves to serve no pork, mutton or beef on Tuesday of each week, and on Wednesday of each week no wheat bread or wheat products of any kind, thereby observing strictly one "meatless" and one " wheatless" day of each week. It is also agreed that any violation of this pledge will be promptly reported to the chairman of this committee as well as the name of any patron objecting to this ruling."

A pledge card was placed in the window or on the door of each establishment cooperating with the program. Violators were subjected to their names being published in the local press.[20]

---

[17] Ibid., 1 October 1918, p. 2.

[18] *Sentinel-Record*, 17 August 1917.

[19] Ibid., 28 October 1917.

[20] Ibid., 9 December 1917. Not all cities did as well as Hot Springs on the wheatless -meatless days. The *Sentinel-Record* reported 20 December 1917, that those days were "reported an almost failure in Oklahoma City as only fifteen percent of the people were following the guidelines."

The Food Administration set guidelines for the amount of profit each business was entitled to on scarce and rationed items. Businesses were forewarned they should expect regular inspection of their books and which were to be made by a staff of auditors of J.R. Britton of Little Rock.

When profiteering was discovered a penalty of several days of closure of the business resulted. Also, a sign was displayed on the business in large black letters, "Closed for Profiteering," and another pledge card signed by the owner pledging to abide by the rules in the future.[21] Sometimes the auditing was so strictly done that it revealed such minor infraction as a store owner overcharging by ten cents on a barrel of flour. Occasionally an innocent proprietor was summoned, as was the case of C.J. Burch, 1302 Central Avenue. When the auditor had completed his work he gave a statement to the newspapers, "The summons was in error and investigation of the books of Mr. Burch showed he had abided faithfully by the rules of the administration and he was to be commended for his patriotism."[22] This was still in a time when the government could make a mistake and apologize for the wrong committed.

The general public was asked to rely on voluntary compliance with rationing orders issued monthly by the Food Administration. This worked well until the middle of 1917, when sugar was first rationed to retailers according to the number of customers they had. The retailers then rationed their own customers.[23] Sometimes inequities occurred with this system, as some merchants played favorites with some of their better customers. Understandably, this practice occasionally resulted in charges of unfairness.

During the summer of 1918 a number of serious sugar shortages occurred. Local Food Administrator, C.N. Russ issued a statement on July 20, that the city of Hot Springs was completely out of sugar. Russ had issued a warning to "all hotels, and restaurants, all city, county and state institutions, hospitals, saw mills, logging camps, boarding houses that feed as many as twenty five a day that they must purchase their sugar requirements with federal issued certificates, and had to be filed by July 15."[24]

A couple of months before, the city and eating establishments had completly exhausted tea and sherbert supplies.[25]

The soft drink industry was hit particulary hard as evidenced by the sale of Vapor City Bottling Works. This company was owned by Brad O. Smith, who had been elected Garland County Sheriff. After struggling with material

---

[21] Ibid., 7 December 1918.
[22] Ibid.
[23] *The American Peoples Encyclopedia*, Spencer Press, 1952, Vol. 16, p. 518.
[24] *Sentinel-Record*, 3 July 1918, p. 8.
[25] Ibid., 14 May 1918.

shortages and labor problems, he issued a statement, "The demands of the sheriff's office is so great and the operation of the bottling company so costly I have decided to sell the business to Ledgerwood Brothers, pioneers in the bottling business here."[26]

J.J. Ledgerwood was glad to acquire Vapor City Bottling Works as he explained, "Due to the scarcity of glass for bottles and the rapidly increasing cost of everything, the demand of the business in Hot Springs was not sufficient to support two such businesses."[27] There were times that the lack of sugar greatly reduced the Ledgerwood output of soft drinks, and bakery products.

Rallies were held, city- and county-wide, to sell Liberty Bonds to finance the war. The leading businessmens' organizations took the forefront and pushed hard to meet each quota set up for Garland County. Both the Ledgerwood and McLaughlin families participated and purchased bonds. As a rule Hot Springs and Garland County over subscribed their goals and quotas.

Patriotic rallies were held by farmers in the county. One, at Hemp Wallace, had hundreds of people on hand and they participated in singing rousing songs to set the tone for the event. *America, Arkansas, The Star Spangled Banner* and *Dixie,* rang across the countryside. Short speeches, "The Farmer's Obligation to the Government and How to Meet It," and "Lunches for School Children," followed by "Farm Loans," were delivered in patriotic fashion.[28] And always, there were prayers to protect the boys, "over-there."

Another idea of Herbert Hoover, which was to have a big effect on Hot Springs and Garland County, was a loose-knit organization he inspired, called the "Four Minute Men." These were men in the community who were willing to appear at different functions and deliver a four-minute speech. Generally the speech was based on data furnished by the Food Administration informing and encouraging the public to greater effort to support the war program.

The speakers appeared regularly at the Princess, Royal and New Central theaters. The Garland Bar Association encouraged their members to become involved and dispatched their members into the county with programs held in each township, generally at schools. Some of those taking part were James McConnell, T.E. Rutherford, John D. Haskins, Dan S. Barnes, Leo P. McLaughlin, C.T. Cotham, James L. Graham, John Lewis, Arthur Cobb, W.G. Bouic, George P. Whittington, L. E. Sawyer, Tom Martin, W.H. Martin and others[29]. During the middle of September 1917, they appeared at Crystal Hill,

---

[26] Ibid., 19 June 1919. Vapor City had contracts with Hires Root Beer and the Nehi brands of soda-pop.

[27] Ibid.

[28] *Sentinel-Record,* 2 August 1918.

[9] Ibid., 18 September 1917.

Walnut Grove, Mazarn, Meyer Creek and Fourche Loop Schools. Mt. Tabor Church invited a speaker and other churches picked up the idea. Kellaro Store in the Mt. Valley Township requested a speaker and they were placed on the schedule.

Others besides attorneys were involved in the Four Minute Men. Several ministers, school officials and business men used their talents--men such as Rev. C.E. Hickok, David A. Crockett, Rev. F.M. Wylie, Walter Ebel and Rabbi A.B. Rhine.[30]

The press reported the short inspirational talks were well received. The theaters started to play the *Star Spangled Banner* at the conclusion of the Four Minute Men's brief address creating audience participation. Rabbi Rhine, speaking on the subject of "Who Our Enemy Really Is," closed his address with a tribute to "Old Glory," and "urged loyalty to the nation's 'starry banner.' While the strains of the national anthem, are being played," he said, "let us pay the respect due our flag and as one rise in tribute to the greatest flag the world has ever known."

It was a time that everyone was encouraged to participate in the war effort. Prayers were said daily in the schools for the service men and for their safe return. Shades of Madelyn Murray O'Hair! And, it was unthinkable to start the day without a pledge of allegiance to the flag. At that time not even the most liberal or worst radical person would have dared suggested the "burning of the flag." It would have been extremely dangerous and injurious to his health to have done so.

As the war advanced, the ranks of young men around Hot Springs thinned. The National Board in Washington requested the local selective service board to advise as to what "where considered non-essential employment at Hot Springs."[31] This was not a duty that members of the local board enjoyed as it practically placed a bullseye on each registrant falling into that category. The board set about the task and wired Washington the following jobs were considered non-essential: "pool hall proprietors, cigar clerks, waiters, elevator boys, chauffeurs, department store clerks, fountain dispensers, cigar makers, city salesmen, porters, ushers and ticket collectors in movie houses, and hotel clerks."[32]

Several of the city officials, especially those married, were placed in lower classifications, such as 3-A.[33] Verne Ledgerwood was one of these. Near the end of the war he had been moved up and notified he would be "in the next

---

[30] Ibid., 28 October 1917.
[31] Ibid., 14 September 1918.
[32] Ibid.
[33] Ibid., 8 May 1918, p. 3.

lraft." Luckily the war ended before he had to report.[34]

Leo P. McLaughlin had lost any exuberance, if he ever had any, for entering he military service. As hundreds of young men marched off to war he was noved up on the eligibility list. When he was summoned for a pre-induction physical on 24 January 1918, it had become serious--to him at least--and Leo knew he was just a step away from becoming a part of the growing military force. He easily passed the physical examination by Dr. John S. Wood.[35]

But what was Leo to do? He was almost on the threshold of being inducted. A plan evolved, if he could defeat city attorney James S. McConnell, in the city election scheduled for early April, he might be dropped to a 3-A classification as most city officials were. McLaughlin was always willing and able to enter the political arena. True, McConnell had defeated him two years before, however since he had been in office the city attorney had made some mistakes and had made some enemies. He now had chinks in his armor and Leo knew how to exploit them.

McLaughlin was aware of the fact that McConnell had erred big time in confronting C.N. Russ, Secretary of the Merchants Association, with an accusation that the merchants were not having their printing needs done in Hot Springs. Russ, in a long and detailed letter, published in the paper jumped on the subject like a frog on a June-bug. He said that McConnell was "like the kettle calling the pot black." Russ pointed out that McConnell's own stationery had the Democrat Printing and Lithograph Company's logo imprinted on it.[36] That company was located in Little Rock. He continued, citing other things McConnell was responsible for. The city attorney also came into criticism when Mayor McClendon referred to "the present city paving on Central Avenue as graft and of poor quality." The statement was in reference to the paving bill having been vetoed by McClendon and the city attorney telling the Commissioners they could override his veto, which they did.[37] McClendon, as usual, had considerable support and McConnell came out looking like damaged goods.

Even though the office of city attorney no longer revolved upon the question of party lines, Leo reminded voters McConnell had been and still was a republican, which, in that era in Hot Springs, was not a good thing. McConnell admitted to being a republican and pointed out that Leo P. McLaughlin and late entry Sam Garrett, all were "on the same footing as we are running as independents."[38] However the damage had been done. The

---

[34] LAT Ledgerwood.

[35] Veterans Administration File 350/211P, XC-21-231-700, Order 329, Report of Physical Examination, 1/24/18.

[36] *Sentinel-Record*, 16 June 1916.

[37] Ibid., 7 September 1917.

[38] Ibid., 2 April 1918, p. 8.

majority of voters in Hot Springs were democratic and the thought of voting for someone that acknowledge he was a republican was abhorrent.

Of the three candidates, McLaughlin was by far the most experienced campaigner. This time he did not dwell negatively on McConnell's faults and failures, but on what he would do if elected. It was a new twist for Leo, and it worked.

The voter turnout was light, only 823 votes cast. McConnell won the First Ward, but by only one vote, and the Sixth Ward by thirty-three votes. He was behind Leo by only six votes in both the Fourth and Fifth Wards. Again it was the Second Ward that threw its support to McLaughlin and when the vote was counted McConnell probably felt swamped as Leo polled 161-48. Garrett came in a distant third with a total of 158 votes. McLaughlin won by a total of 87 votes, thanks to his home ward.[39]

McLaughlin had been notified several weeks before the election he was due to be called up and that he would have to report for duty at Camp Beauregard, Louisiana about May 25. He knew from taking his physical in January that the deadline was rapidly approaching. He was hoping to win the city attorney's election and be placed in a lower classification.[40] He argued with the board over drafting him and "not reducing him to class 3, as he was an office holder."[41] When they would not rescind the summons he filed an appeal with the Exemption Board. Their decision was the same, but they did agree to get a ruling from the Adjutant General over the district. General Loyd England replied, "Electors to office after being subject to the draft made no difference." Leo plainly did not want to go to war and appealed the decision of the Adjutant General. The result was the same, Leo was ordered for a review by the local board and J.R. Housley signed McLaughlin as being "physically qualified for general military service."[42]

While Leo P. McLaughlin acquiesced to the draft board and prepared to enter the armed forces he again became a controversial figure. He turned to the City Commissioners, asking for an "indefinite leave of absence, and the privilege of naming who should succeed him in the office during his absence."[43] He told the commissioners he had looked up the law and he "was certain he had the right to name a competent attorney to look after this business for him during the remainder of the term." The commissioners were caught off balance by the request and wanted to study the matter for a few days. Leo was in a hurry and in no mood to wait. Catching the commissioners

---

[39] James S. McConnell would soon leave Hot Springs and move to Nashville, Arkansas where he would become involved in real estate and insurance.

[40] *Sentinel-Record*, 8 May 1918, p. 3.

[41] Ibid.

[42] VA File, 2 May 1918.

[43] *Sentinel-Record*, 14 May 1918, p. 2.

off guard he made an end-run and out maneuvered them by announcing he had appointed O.H. Sumpter to serve in his place. He said, "When a city official is unavoidably absent from his duties he has the right to name the man who shall serve in his place, according to numerous decisions of the supreme court."[44] A small uproar occurred as members of the bar differed in opinion on the legality of the situation. Three of the Commissioners reported they would dispute the appointment of Sumpter and threatened to take the matter to the courts for settlement.[45] After a few days cooler heads prevailed and the Commissioners decided to let Sumpter's appointment stand. After all, Sumpter was a very good and experienced attorney. It was just the manner that McLaughlin had taken that galled them.

What was not known at the time was the agreement that McLaughlin and Sumpter had privately made between them and it would not be revealed for a couple of years. It would be the root-cause and reason for a spectacular fist fight between the two men on a downtown street.

Leo P. McLaughlin reluctantly left Hot Springs a few days later and entered the army at Camp Beauregard, May 27, 1918.[46]

Camp Beauregard, Louisiana, was a "tent city" during World War I
Leo P. McLaughlin and other local boys took their basic training here

---

[44] Ibid., 16 May 1918, p. 8.
[45] Ibid., 17 May 1918, p. 8.
[46] VA File.

The Reluctant Doughboy, and the One-Day Honeymoon

Camp Beauregard was located in central Louisiana, mainly in Grant Parish. In 1918 it was a sprawling, much undeveloped area of several thousand acres. Two railroads traversed the area: one, the Kansas City Southern linking Winfield and Alexandria; the other, connecting Monroe and Alexandria. In 1918 only three small communities existed in the area, Dry Prong, Bentley and Pollock. The nearest city where service men could go on leave and enjoy themselves, was Alexandria.

The camp was a growing city of temporary wooden structures and tents housing several thousand men. Several elongated buildings served as mess halls, shower facilities and a base hospital. All the streets were dirt, which were being constantly ground to a reddish-grey powder from the thousands of feet marching to and fro. A large tank wagon watered the main streets to reduce the flying dust in an attempt to aid the men's breathing. It didn't rain often during the summer, but when it did the streets became a sea of mud until the sun dried them out. Then it was just a short time until there were two or three inches of dust to again swirl up and assail the nostrils of any living being.

Henry Ford, one of the inventors of the assembly line production, must have approved the techniques employed by the army. Recruits, in droves, were hurried through the process. The men were run through for hair cuts and their heads were shaved to keep down lice. They were given physicals and vaccination shots to prevent a myriad of diseases. Stacks of olive green scratchy uniforms and heavy high top shoes to be worn with canvas leggings were doled out to each man. And that was only a start. Men stood in line for the showers and the mess halls where food was dumped on metal trays. Food items intermingled to the extent potatoes became unidentifiable from bread pudding, and everything was hidden under a greasy-looking gravy. A scoop of ice cream quickly melted from the hot tray it was dumped upon. For the boys who had been raised in poor homes the meals probably seemed good. But those who were used to eating well, thought the meals were far below "Mom's home cooking."

Some of the training areas were in scrub brush with thorns so long and so sharp they could penetrate a heavy military shoe. Men with injuries from the thorns could expect a visit to the base hospital as infection often and quickly set in.

And the vermin--the pesky flies that swarmed about one's head or the mean little sand fleas that constantly sought haven in recruits' shoes and boots and had a bite far belying its size. While the chiggers and red-bugs were a class below the Arkansas variety, they caused small sores and severe itching and the small packs of greasy, smelly pink salve dispensed by the hospital gave the service men a distinct odor. The ticks equaled those in Arkansas, there just seemed to be millions more in the sandy loam brush country of Louisiana.

The soldiers were warned to tap their shoes on the floor each morning before putting them on as it might be an unpleasant and painful surprise when a sand-scorpion, which had sought refuge during the night, curled his stinger into a toe or a foot. But of all the insects with which Camp Beauregard was most blessed, it was the mosquitoes that were most hated. The little winged terrors swarmed from the swamps, bogs and pools of stagnant water by the millions. Spraying and treating the breeding places may have helped control the problem, but you couldn't prove it by those plagued by the fierce insects. The ferocity of their attacks was maddening as men tried to forget the aches and pains of tired and sore muscles from their training as they tried to grab a few hours sleep, tossing and turning on the narrow canvas cots. Sounds of cursing and swatting of the pesky little varmints could be heard throughout the barracks each night.

Camp diseases were a very real fear of all trainees. The great density of population in army camps with crowded living conditions contributed substantially to the infection rate. Camp Beauregard stood high on the list of camp related deaths. In one week 202 soldiers died there from influenza and pneumonia. During 1917 and 1918 the Spanish flu reeked havoc throughout the world. The U.S. Army had a total of 50,301 illness-related deaths.[1] Hundreds of thousands died throughout the world from the highly infectious flu-bug.

Leo McLaughlin knew something about the Spanish flu. It had made a swath through Hot Springs in 1917-1918, and a number of citizens died as a result of the severity of the disease and lack of medical knowledge to effectively treat it. Leo's eldest sister, Mary Anna, had succumbed to the disease in February 1917.[2] This very well may have contributed to Leo's fears of being inducted into the army where the flu was so rampant.

It was a drastic change in any recruit's life. Some adapted and adjusted well, others did not. Leo P. McLaughlin was one of the latter. Leo was not cut out for the military life. He was a square peg trying to fit into a round hole. When he was inducted at Camp Beauregard on May 27th, he was introduced into a totally strange and uncomfortable world. He was pushed, hurried and ordered about. The only persons to whom he had been receptive in bossing him were his father, who was dead, and Bridget, his mother, who was two hundred miles away. He was a most reluctant soldier, his past and future behavior would attest to that fact. His drill sergeant was unprepared and unused to the

---

[1] Surgeon General's First Time Statistics Showing Deadly Results of Epidemic, 2 February 1919. Of the total, 32,165 were in camps and 18,136 in the expeditionary forces.

[2] *Caruth Funeral Home Records*, p. 104, lists her name as May Anna. The 1880 Census reflects her name as Mariana. Other sources, including her tombstone in Calvary Cemetery, gave Mary Anna, which is believed to be correct.

prima dona recruit he was to meet in McLaughlin. His first assignment was to Company G of the 156th Infantry.

By the end of two weeks his actions and lack of cooperation caused his drill sergeant to order him to the base hospital. He had been given a physical the day after he arrived and all three of the examining doctors had pronounced him to be both physically and mentally fit.[3]

On reporting to the hospital, Captain Thomas M. Rives, examined Leo McLaughlin and marked his chart, "Under observation for *mental disease*. No disease found." Apparently the doctor believed the soldier was under a bit of stress and decided a couple of days rest might benefit him. Captain Rives dismissed McLaughlin with a return to duty slip for June 13th.[4]

Leo P. McLaughlin was a troubled man of thirty years. He had not wanted to be in the army and he was having difficulty in adjusting to the rugged life of a soldier. Also, he had left a problem at Hot Springs, unknown to his family and close acquaintances, and he did not know how to handle it.

The next event in the life of Leo P. McLaughlin had two versions, based on who was telling the story. Fortunately, part of the scenario can be documented and the secret hidden for over eighty years has now come to light.

Prior to his entry into the army Leo had been seeing Juanita Gilliam, who had won the Whiteway Queen contest, on the sly. He realized if his mother got wind of their relationship she would do everything possible to break them up. They had been meeting at the Eastman or Arlington Hotels, where Juanita was sometimes engaged to sing for some function or benefit and would spend hours together, dining and dancing. After the function Leo would sometimes escort Juanita to her home on Hawthorne Street. Their evasive tactics were successful and caused very little talk about Hot Springs and word failed to reach Bridget to alert her of a possible romantic affair. She was aware Leo loved going to dinners and dances, but was totally uninformed of Leo's and Juanita's rendezvous.

One source said that it was known to a few that Leo was "madly in love with someone," but was unable to remember or tell who that person was. Others said it was merely one of Leo's many flings with young women, with whom he seemed to be enamored and involved with over many years of his life.

In the event he was "madly in love" with Juanita, as some believed, he would have been aware that any attempt to marry in Hot Springs would be met with strong objections from his mother. The matter would quickly become known once a license was applied for and Bridget was certain to learn of their intent. Not only would she berate him but would have the Parish Priest admonishing

---

[3] VA File, Form - Physical Examination at Place of Mobilization, Camp Beauregard 28 May 1918.

[4] VA File, Forms - Admission and Dispositions Forms, 10 June 1918.

him the marriage would not be sanctioned by the Church as Juanita was not a member of the Catholic faith. Juanita and her family attended the Methodist church, but were not regular members. Bridget controlled the purse strings of the family and provided a comfortable home for her remaining children and demanded allegiance. She expected no less from Leo.

Part of Leo's resistance to induction into the army could have included a genuine fondness for Juanita and not wanting to be separated from her. It would be a reasonable assumption as there were thousands of other men in that category.

Also, it has been suggested by some that Leo and Juanita had been more than just good friends, that she was pregnant when he went to Camp Beauregard, he was highly troubled with the situation, and feared his Mother learning about their relationship. Later developments, especially the secretiveness of the affair, lent some credence to this theory. In the event this was the truth, Juanita may have been pressuring Leo to marry her quickly before he was sent overseas in order to give their baby his name. Bridget surely would have gone into orbit had she known this.

There is documentation attesting to the fact that Juanita arrived in Alexandria, Louisiana on or about June 18, 1918. Leo obtained a short-time pass to go to town on Wednesday June 19, and met Juanita. The two then went to the Rapides Parish Clerk's office and secured a marriage license from R.M. Bitherwick.[5]

Having been around municipal government for several years as city attorney, Leo knew just the place to get married which would not involve the church. They went to City Judge Levin L. Theroe to perform the ceremony.[6] To demonstrate just how secretly McLaughlin wanted to keep the marriage, one only need to examine the names of those who witnessed the ceremony. None appearing on the license, other than the bride and groom, were from Garland County even though there were a number of acquaintances of both Leo and Juanita in training at Camp Beauregard, though not invited to participate either as a best man or witnesses. The witnesses were perhaps office holders in the court house or city hall as several had Cajun sounding names, which were common to the area.

Because Leo's pass was only for a few hours he had to return to the base and left Juanita at an Alexandria hotel. The events that follow certainly are bizarre and unusual for a mature man just marrying a beautiful girl. Had something gone amiss on the brief, one-day honeymoon? He was due to

---

[5] State of Louisiana, Parish of Rapides, Clerk's Office, Thirteenth District Court, # 3962, Vol. 45, Page 140. Hereinafter cited as Rapides Parish Marriage Records.

[6] Ibid.

140

No. 396 ✓

State of Louisiana
Parish of Rapides

THIRTEENTH JUDICIAL DISTRICT COURT
CLERK'S OFFICE

Be It Known, That in order to obtain and put of record the data as required by Act No. 104, of the General Assembly of the State of Louisiana, July 8th, 1912, the following questions must be answered by the party making application for a Marriage License:

Name of Man? Leo P. McLaughlin

Age? 30 Residence? Hot Springs Ark

Name of Father? J. H. McLaughlin Living? no

Residence?

Name of Mother? Bridget McLaughlin Living? yes

Residence? Hot Springs Ark

Previously Married? no Name of former wife, if any?

Former Wife, dead or alive?

Race? Caucasian

Name of Woman? Miss Juanita Gilliam

Age? 21 Residence? Hot Springs Ark

Name of Father? W. C. Gilliam Living? yes

Residence? "

Name of Mother? Mamie Gilliam Living? yes

Residence? "

Previously Married? no Name of former husband, if any?

Former Husband, dead or alive?

Race? Caucasian

(Sign Here) Leo P. McLaughlin

No. 3962 140

Marriage License

STATE OF LOUISIANA, PARISH OF RAPIDES
CLERK'S OFFICE, THIRTEENTH DISTRICT COURT

To any Ordained Minister of the Gospel, Judge or to any Justice of the Peace, Greeting:

YOU ARE HEREBY AUTHORIZED AND EMPOWERED TO UNITE IN THE BOND OF

Matrimony and Holy Wedlock

Mr. Leo P. McLaughlin. (white)

AND

Miss Juanita Gilliam (white)

both residents of the State aforesaid, and to solemnize and to celebrate said Marriage between said parties according to the laws and customs of this State, and to make your return hereof as the law directs, and this your authority for so doing.

Given under my hand and seal of office, this 19 day of June 1918

A. R. Hetherwick
Clerk of District Court.

State of Louisiana, Parish of Rapides:

I hereby certify that I have on this day, in pursuance of the foregoing license celebrated and solemnized a marriage between:

Mr. Leo P. McLaughlin

and Miss Jaunita Gilliam

agreeable to the laws and customs of the State of Louisiana.

In faith whereof, I have, together with the parties and undersigned witnesses, signed this present on this 19th day of June, 1918

THREE WITNESSES:

R. B. Webster
Leo W. Moreau
D. Lemoine

Leo P. McLaughlin
Juanita Gilliam
Leon L. Hesse
City Judge

report for training the following morning and was acting very strange. By the time he was due for muster he was "frothing from the mouth." Was it real, or put-on? Was the stress of his marriage of a few hours so great Leo couldn't handle it? Later, some boys from Hot Springs, who were in training at Beauregard, would tell their families back home that Leo had eaten soap to gain this appearance. His drill sergeant tried to talk with Leo and making no sense from what he was saying ordered him to the base hospital where he was confined to "the psychiatric ward."[7] His admittance chart was documented, "Under observation for mental incapacity. No disease found."[8]

Was Juanita aware of Leo's condition or aware of his "feigning?" Was she a partner in the ploy? The records do not reveal this information. One of Leo's acquaintances, upon learning of his confinement to the hospital, and not being aware of his marriage the day before, called the McLaughlin family home at Hot Springs about 11:00 p.m. on the night of June 20, and reported his admittance to the base hospital and advised that Leo appeared "seriously ill."[9]

Bridget McLaughlin and Stella packed and left Hot Springs the following morning aware only that Leo was ill. Undoubtedly, it must have been a very interesting encounter between Bridget and Stella McLaughlin and Juanita Gilliam McLaughlin, who they were unaware was visiting Leo at the base hospital at Camp Beauregard. Much more startling to them must have been the news that Leo and Juanita had been married two days before. How indeed, did Leo break the news of his marriage, or was it Juanita who dropped this tid bit of news on the two McLaughlin women? Bridget was probably steaming toward Leo and coldly polite toward Juanita. Stella was the opposite, she boiled in anger at both. She disliked Juanita, who had defeated her badly in the Whiteway contest and for which she never forgave her. She tried to ignore Juanita while in her company, and did not relish having her as a sister-in-law. Stella refused to be in the company of Juanita any longer, and was so incensed at Leo for marrying her enemy, she stayed at the base only one day, returning home. Bridget's immediate dislike of Juanita stemmed from the fact that she and Leo had been married and that the union would not be sanctioned by the church. She had also discouraged any of her children from marrying because of possible insanity in their bloodlines. And, now Leo was acting as if he was mentally deficient. Even though her son was thirty years of age this was a matter she did not trust to his handling. Before Stella left, Bridget instructed her to contact George Whittington and apprise him of the facts and get his

---

[7] *New Era*, 29 March 1927, p. 6. This is from a reprint of an affidavit of Dr. Loyd Thompson, who was stationed at Camp Beauregard at the time and who was one of three examining physicians of Leo P. McLaughlin.

[8] VA File, 20 June 1918, Register No. 14321.

[9] *Sentinel-Record*, 21 June 1918, p. 2.

opinion concerning an annulment of the marriage because of Leo's mental state. She may have believed Juanita had trapped her son in marriage, but also that Leo did not know what he was doing. Is it possible she may have encouraged her son to keep up the mental farce? Especially until she heard from their attorney, George Whittington. News of the marriage could not be kept secret as there were too many local men on the base in training so the wedding was leaked to the press, but only with the scantiest of details.[10]

Instead of saying that Leo was confined to the hospital "Under observation for mental incapacity," the family reported he had been hospitalized for "heat prostration," which phrase does not appear anywhere in his army medical file.[11] In the event Leo had become overheated it certainly was not from being overworked or from the army training. Maybe being near the beautiful Juanita Gilliam, now Juanita McLaughlin, had sent his temperature soaring a few degrees.

After a period of several weeks in the psychiatric ward, McLaughlin was continuing to behave abnormally. The attending physician could discover no neurological findings to cause Leo to act in this manner. As required after a period of thirty days a report was filed with the base commander, who in turn appointed a board of three medical officers to examine what had become known at the base hospital as "The McLaughlin Case."[12]

When the medical panel examined McLaughlin they reported, "We observed the following manifestations: the rolling of the eyes, protruding of the tongue; slobbering at the mouth, incoherent speech, failure to recognize me, [Dr. Lloyd Thompson] whom he had previously known in Hot Springs and whom he had seen and recognized upon his arrival in camp, a twitching of the muscles of the body and a jerking of his arms and legs. At the conclusion of our examination it was the unanimous opinion of the board of medical officers that Leo P. McLaughlin was malingering and feigning insanity, in order to escape military service, there being no abnormal neurological findings which would account for the symptoms above mentioned."[13]

The base commander drew only one conclusion from the medical panel's report. McLaughlin was malingering! On July 29, Leo McLaughlin was discharged from the base hospital and ordered back to duty.[14] The unit to which Leo had initially been assigned had finished its basic training and was preparing to leave for France.[15] Of the sixty days Leo had spent at Camp

---

[10] *Sentinel-Record*, 22 June 1918, p. 2. The small article stated, "The announcement of the wedding came in the nature of a distinct surprise."

[11] Ibid.

[12] *New Era*, 29 March 1927, affidavit of Dr. Lloyd Thompson.

[13] Ibid.

[14] Veterans Administration File, 29 July 1918.

[15] *Sentinel-Record*, 13 August 1918, p. 2.

Beauregard less than three weeks had been devoted to training, the remainder of time he had been confined to the hospital. He was reassigned to the 114th Field Signal Battalion.[16]

Bridget McLaughlin had returned to Hot Springs after spending several weeks near her son while he was in the hospital. She had been unable to dissolve the marriage in Louisiana.[17] Bridget may have encountered some resistence from her son if he discerned her purpose to dissolve his marriage. As he would be leaving for France shortly, Bridget would work on Juanita at Hot Springs, and perhaps her family. Leo's sister, Elizabeth, spent a few days visiting Leo even after his Mother had departed. Apparently Elizabeth got along much better with Juanita than did Bridget or Stella, and they shared visitation time with Leo. Elizabeth left Alexandria a few days before her brother was discharged from the hospital and everyone knew Leo was headed for more training. Juanita, too, left for Hot Springs as it became apparent Leo McLaughlin would be headed for Europe by the middle of August despite his efforts to remain in this country.[18]

While the war was waging in Europe, life went on in Hot Springs. Families proudly displayed the blue-star banners in the windows of their homes reflecting that someone from that household was serving time in the military. Some, sadly, displayed a gold star reflecting a father or son had been killed in the line of duty. One young man from the Spa, Warren Townsend, lost his life on the battlefield in France and members of American Legion Post 13, at Hot Springs, named the post in his honor.[19] Wives and mothers dreaded receiving one of the black bordered Western Union or Postal Telegraph wires from the War Department with the message beginning, "We regret to inform you...." Lists of those from all over the country, whose lives had been lost in the war, were published periodically in the local press. These were closely scanned by readers to determine if any of the casualties was known to them. Even worse on the families was being told their loved one was "missing in action," and the sheer agony of maybe never knowing what had happened to their family member.

As the war machine demanded more soldiers, men were constantly being called up. As this occurred, adjustments in the labor force became necessary.

---

[16] VA File, 29 July 1918.

[17] Clerk of Court, Rapides Parish, Alexandria, 6 December 1999. The definitive work, *Long on Domestic Relations*, 3rd Edition,, Joseph R. Long, Bobbs-Merrill Co., Indianapolis, 10th printing 1948, Section 210 reflects the grounds for annulment as incompetency, fraud or duress.

[18] *Sentinel-Record*, 9 August 1918, p. 2.

[19] Captain Richard Warren Townsend, of Company H, 357th infantry, died on September 13, 1918, as a result of leading his men in a charge on a German machine gun nest. He was buried at the American cemetery, Toul, Sebastapool, France. Taken from a letter from his brother, Pvt. Myron Townsend, published in the *Sentinel-Record*, 30 January 1919.

This included changes in city offices. Several police officers and firemen were called into service. Then, there were other changes. Charles Weaver, who had held the city manager's job from the begininning of the commission form of government, submitted his resignation. There was just too great a hassel to meet payrolls on the limited income of the city. He was replaced with George R. Belding, secretary to the Business Men's League. Belding was allowed to continue holding his position with the league which also paid him a salary. The city reduced his income as manager from $2,500 to $2,100 per year because of his involment with the league.[20]

With the city still struggling with its finances, W.H. Watson, City Treasurer and Belding had to juggle the city's monetary obligations each week. If one department was fully paid, others would run short, creating unhappy employees.[21] There had been times in the past few years when the city had to resort to issuing scrip, a method of payment not always in favor of employees.[22] Of course, this system is no longer legal. Once when payday came and went without checks, the fire department demanded its pay and Chief Loyd Tate said, "We desire to put the citizens on notice that unless we are all paid on or before Friday morning, Sepetember 15, at 9:00 o'clock, the entire personnel of the fire department will quit the service."[23] It is to be noted that the striking of police or firemen is no longer legal. Other methods of protests, such as the "blue-flu" are sometimes used by the departments.

Mayor McClendon was trying to arrange a loan for the money-strapped city when the Business Men's League came to the rescue. The business community of the city had suffered greatly, along with all the citizens from two devastating fires in the past eleven years, and they certainly did not want to see a walk-off of the city's firefighters leaving the stations and equipment unmanned. This civic-minded group of business men arranged so that the firemen could cash their warrants (scrip) and an announcement was made that George Callahan and George Belding and a committee, "had gone out among the business interests and received pledges to take up the scrip of the fire department at par."[24]

The city's financial pain was not lessened when military authorities at Camp Pike gave an "arbitrary order that unless the houses of immorality of the city were closed the government would issue some sort of edict against soldiers spending their weekends here."[25] Each of the houses of prostitution and their inmates paid fines to operate their business. The press reported, "the city's

---

[20] *Sentinel-Record*, 31 August 1918, p. 2.
[21] Ibid., 10 September 1916.
[22] Ibid., 7 September 1916.
[23] *Sentinel-Record*, 12 September 1916.
[24] Ibid., 15 September 1916.
[25] Ibid., 2 August 1918, p. 8.

strong box will miss the usual fines."[26] There seemed to be little effort to clos the "houses" but they were urged to clean up their act, and to become le conspicuous.Another major loss of city revenue had been the closing of th Spa's thirty-one saloons because of Prohibition and the tax they generated.

People at home, just as the boys in service, also suffered losses. Mayor an Mrs. Jacob W. McClendon, lost their only child in a tragic accident. Willia McClendon, age ten, was involved in a two-bicycle accident with young Bil Moncrief. The two youngsters collided, spilling both boys onto the groun William McClendon received bumps and bruises and was able to ride his bil to his father's office were he was patched up and thought to be alright. Th night he went into convulsions and died.[27] The blow to the McClendons w particularly hard as both were of advanced age and would bear no oth children.

Some service men were fortunate in being assigned to nearby camps an were able to come home frequently. Many were even assigned for the duratic of the war at one of these facilities. One of these was George McLaughli younger brother of Leo. George entered the army shortly after his brother. H was assigned to the supply depot at Camp Pike, near North Little Roc Suprisingly, he adapted to military life much better than his older brother an seemed suited for the job, having worked in his family's store from an ear age and understood stocking goods and taking inventories. As a result h gained the approval of his superiors and was quickly promoted to the rank corporal and a few months later to sergeant.[28] He was able to visit his fami quite often and was released shortly after the Armistice.[29]

Some of the young officers assigned to Camp Pike were invited to atten special events at the Spa and would journey over for a weekend. When a dan was given in honor of Anne Bertner, at the Como Hotel, Lieutenants Di Lawrence, Walter Jackson, Sam Kroon, Rue Long and Captains Hartl Wootton and Garnett Eisele, showed up.[30]

A group of local girls gave a volunteer program for benefit of the Na League and which was held at a packed house at the Princess Theater. Th stage was decorated with Japanese flowers. Dancers were Misses Zena Horne Dixie Lee Cotton, Gladys Van Leer, Elizabeth Deaderick, Ruth Thoma Willie and Helen Greer. Classical dances, including ballets were performed.

It was a time when the service men and locals made the best of a taxi situation.

---

[26] Ibid.

[27] *Sentinel-Record*, 16 August 1918.

[28] Ibid, 21 July 1918, p. 2., and 27 October 1918, p. 3.

[29] Ibid., 8 January 1919.

[30] Ibid., 16 September 1917, p. 6.

[31] Ibid., 4 September 1917.

What Became of the Gilliam Family?

William C. Gilliam had arrived in Hot Springs in the early 1890s, and as a oung man had been employed by J.F. Joplin, who operated a grocery store t 330 Ouachita Avenue.[1] When he was twenty-one years-old he met and narried eighteen year-old Mamie Hardy, whose family had settled in Hot pring County near the Social Hill community. The couple were married on December 23, 1893, by Reverend S.M. Fisher. They had three known children, esse J., Juanita C. and Nellie F.

William Gilliam, or as he was best known, Will, worked for awhile as a clerk or Golden Brothers Grocers at 708 Central. He was hired by Max Mayer, resident of Little Rock based Scott-Mayer Commission Company, as a alesman. Gilliam worked out of their local warehouse at 5 Malvern Avenue until it was moved to 205-207 Elm.[2] W.C. Gilliam became actively engaged n the Masonic Sumpter Lodge at Hot Springs and served as its Worshipful Master 1907-1908.[3]

As the children got older, Mamie, in order to supplement the family's ncome, entered into a partnership with Frances (Fannie) Smith, as dressmakers and they operated a couple of years under the business name of Smith-Gilliam. The two women rented space in the Sumpter-Little Building on Central Avenue, believing a downtown address would benefit their business. Mamie's skill with the sewing machine and needle was probably esponsible for the beautiful dresses and gowns her daughter Juanita wore when performing at the Arlington and Eastman Hotels.

Jesse Gilliam, the eldest of the three children, was a member of the Hot Springs High School graduating class of 1912. After getting out of school he obtained a job as cashier at the Citizen Electric Company. When war broke out, he entered the army in 1917 and rose to the rank of lieutentant.

It is a most interesting and puzzling question as to what became of the entire William C. Gilliam family, and especially Juanita, following her marriage to Leo P. McLaughlin, and her return to Hot Springs in August 1918.

It is only speculation as to what occured from the middle of August 1918, when Juanita returned home, until she left the Spa two weeks later leaving a ecord that she made only one return trip to Hot Springs. The last notice of he family as complete is on August 31, at which time a local newspaper eported, "Mrs. W. C. Gilliam, Mrs. Leo McLaughlin, Miss Pete Gilliam and Miss Stella Hardy left this week for Colorado in order to spend the remainder

---

[1] *Maloney City Directory - Hot Springs, Arkansas* - 1903.

[2] *Hot Springs City Directory - 1903.*

[3] *History of Sumpter Lodge Number 419, Free and Accepted Masons, published 1928.* Both William C. and son Jesse, appeared on the membership roll up to 1919, then both disappear.

of the summer."[4] No reason, other than to spend the remainder of the summer, was given and it was a bit uncommon to journey to that area so late in the summer as snowfall sometimes comes early in the Rockies. Still, it might have been only a vacation, although there are no other recorded notices of the Gilliam family going on such a trip. Could it have been to get Juanita and Leo's marriage annulled or possibly for the purpose of obtaining a divorce? There is some reason to believe this was the case as Juanita returned to Hot Springs for a brief time to star in the Elk's Club production of "The Jollies of 1919." In the newspaper announcements and the program of the production lists her several times as "Miss Juanita Gilliam," along with the other star, "Mrs." Ki Davies.[5] Had Bridget been successful in persuading the Gilliam family to go the route of obtaining an annullment or divorce whereby Juanita retained her maiden name, and freed her son, Leo from a marriage not sanctioned by the church? It is even possible Bridget funded the journey and stay, as the Gilliams were not wealthy people? Or again, could it have been that Juanita, as some suspected, was pregnant and was seeking an abortion? Leo's mother, Bridget, in order to gain their cooperation, would probably have discussed with Juanita and Mamie Gilliam the suspected fault in the McLaughlin-Russell bloodline.

And maybe, the report in the newspaper was simply to throw off nosey friends and acquaintances as to where they were going and for what purpose.[6] Whatever, the trail ends, so far as the Gilliam family is concerned with the news article of August 31, and the brief appearance of Juanita in the Elk's Ministrel of 1919. Apparently W.C. Gilliam left the employ of the Scott-Mayer Commission Company, where he had worked so long, however, his destination is unknown. Thinking perhaps that William C. Gilliam had sought a transfer with his company to Little Rock, to remove his family from an embarrassing situation, searches of records in that city failed. No further mention has been discovered of any member of this family in any legal or local publications.

Since no records have been located in Colorado, it is quite possible they did not go there. Because Mamie Hardy Gilliam was from Social Hill, the possibility existed that a dissolution of the marriage might have been sought in Hot Spring County. No such luck. How about Saline, Pulaski or Lonoke County, where Mamie's brother Dr. S.T. Hardy resided? No records appear in the County Clerk's, or Chancery Clerk's offices of those counties.

---

[4] *Sentinel-Record*, 31 August 1918, p. 2.

[5] Ibid, 19 March and 24 March 1919.

[6] All efforts to locate either an annulment, divorce, or birth of a child in Colorado, have failed. Vital Records at Colorado Springs searched records from 1918-1950, but was unable to locate any information, 12 December 1999.

When Leo McLaughlin was discharged from the army in 1919, he indicated on an exit form that he was unmarried and unless Leo deliberately lied, his marriage and Juanita's had been dissolved at the time. Arkansas death records through 1948 fail to reveal any of the immediate Gilliam family–W.C., Mamie, Jesse, or Juanita Gilliam McLaughlin--as having expired in this state. This was a family who was well-known and active in the city of Hot Springs, and had been for years. What had become of them? Searches of church membership rolls and contact with an official of Sumper Lodge 419 have furnished no leads. Everything, timing, and circumstances point to the unfortunate and brief marriage of Leo P. McLaughlin and Juanita Gilliam as being the reason the Gilliam family family left Hot Springs, leaving no trace, only questions!

The question of what happened to the Gilliam family would remain a mystery for many years. The writer searched old musty records, sought assistance from several state agencies, all to no avail. Then, accidentally he ran across a letter in the files of the late Inez Cline, Garland County Historian, which shed a little light. The letter was dated July 23, 1976, and was from from a lady in Washington, D.C. inquiring of any information regarding a Madison Carroll Gilliam who had lived around Lightfoot Springs in Clark County and operated a sawmill. The inquirer, Valeria Hardy, mentioned that her cousin Juanita Gilliam, had been involved in an affair with one of the mayors of Hot Springs and the adults of the family had all talked in "whispers," when the children were around. (Of course, Leo McLaughlin would not become mayor until 1927) According to that lady the Gilliam family moved to Phoenix in the early 1920s because Juanita's younger sister, Iveanne, had tuberculosis. In all probability the move to a drier climate was only one reason the family left. Bridget McLaughlin, Leo's mother, would have been willing to pay the expenses of the Gilliam family to leave Hot Springs and disentangle her son from a marriage which she had not sanctioned.

Leo P. McLaughlin's signal unit departed Camp Beauregard, Louisiana shortly after the middle of August 1918. It traveled by rail to New Jersey where it embarked on the former German liner, <u>Levithan</u> and arrived in France shortly after September first.[7]

Most of the hastily trained American units were given several weeks of additional training before going to the fronts and into the trenches.

Before the 114th Field Signal Battalion could be assigned to the front, the Armistice was signed on November 11, 1918. Celebrations broke out all over the world. Early on that morning, all over America, newsboys were crying,

---

[7] *Sentinel-Record*, 8 September 1918. Leo wrote his mother and advised they "arrived safely." Ironically, another Hot Springs boy, Alfred Brooks, arrived at the same time, but McLaughlin and Brooks were not destined to meet for several months.

"Extra, Extra, Peace at last."[8]

A.T. "Sonny" Davies had arrived in Paris on November 10. He had been reassigned to a new airfield near the Swiss border. When he arrived in Paris, his luggage was missing and he decided to stay a day or two hoping it would catch up to him. He, therefore, was in the French capitol when the Armistice was announced. He wrote his mother, he had never seen "the joy in peoples faces like there was during the wild celebration which followed."[9]

With the war ending the troops on the front line that had been under fire had priority of going home over those not having been engaged with the enemy. Leo McLaughlin's unit camped with thousands of other troops in a "tent city" near Yerres, France. This was only twelve miles west of Paris and gave the troops the opportunity of visiting the fabled city. McLaughlin and W.G. Bouic, who had occupied an office next to Leo's in the Arkansas National Building, ran into each other. The two Spa residents were happily surprised to see each other and sat down and addressed Christmas cards home. Both sent one to the *Sentinel-Record.*[10] They then began their wait for the return of their respective units to the U.S.A.

Meanwhile, back home, it was politics as usual. Garland County Sheriff Brad O. Smith was facing reelection in November 1918. His campaign was hard-hitting and he claimed he had "been the particular target of the bootlegger and the gambler because he had enforced the law."[11] Smith had worked closely with Circuit Judge Scott Wood and gambling was at a near stand still. Brad Smith's opponent in the fall race was Tom Bledsoe, who was considered very strong in the city. Judge Wood drew attorney James L. Graham as an opponent and Prosecuting Attorney John Haskins faced attorney B.H. Randolph. For "the first time in the history of Garland County, two candidates made a sincere effort to win an election whose names were not printed on the ballot." Randolph and Graham were qualified by petitions to the Secretary of State as independent candidates, but Secretary Tom Terrell "refused to place their names among those certified for the election."[12] Naturally, the Garland County Commissioners, all Democrats, gave no help to the two independents and refused to place their names on the ballot. However, the commissioners in Montgomery County had the names printed. As a result, Graham had no chance for circuit judge against Wood and Haskins easily defeated Randolph.[13] The two losers and their supporters would forever believe the local commissioners had sabotaged the election before it

---

[8] *Hot Springs New Era*, 11 November 1918.
[9] *Sentinel-Record*, 4 December 1918, p. 2.
[10] Ibid., 21 December 1918, p. 3.
[11] *Sentinel-Record*, 3 November 1918.
[12] Ibid., 6 November 1918.
[13] Ibid., 13 November 1918, p. 8.

ever took place.

In the city elections in the early spring of 1919 the position of two city commissioners were to be contested. Four candidates filed: George P. Sheppherd, Will McLaughlin, both former city councilmen, and W.W. Gentry and Harry Jones. The men were restricted from campaigning, "under the terms of the (city commission form of government) act," although each man could express his views and opinions to the press.[14] It was a rather low-key election with Gentry and Jones being victorious. Will McLaughlin came in a disappointing fourth with only 381 votes and 159 of those were from his home ward.[15] The voters seemed unforgiving, remembering the part his family had played in scuttling the sanitarium issue. Will was through with politics personally and he would run no more.

---

[14] Ibid., 8 March 1919, p. 4.
[15] Ibid., 9 April 1919, p. 6.

With the war powers at the peace table and the thousands of soldiers awaiting transport home, there was a struggle beginning throughout America which would last for a decade and a half. It was called Prohibition or the federally-enforced law against the manufacture and sale of alcohol. Garland County was right in the middle of the struggle. It was an old story.

In the 1890s neither the national Democratic or Republician parties would consider prohibition in their platforms even though there was a strong sentiment and growing support for the measure throughout the country. This gave rise to the Prohibition Party. Strength was added to the movement when it was joined by another common-minded group, the Anti-Saloon League, led by a Bible-thumping, hatchet-wielding crusader, Carrie O. Nation.[1]

Carrie believed in taking her fight direct to the object of her scorn. She looked upon herself to be divinely inspired for her "hatchetations" and "crusades."[2] She struck fear into the hearts of grizzled barkeeps and saloon operators just by her six-foot appearance, clutching her Bible with one hand and swinging her hatchet with the other. Tavern operators tried to close and bar their doors when this large imposing woman, dressed from head to foot in black, came marching down the street at the head of an army of women, singing hymns, carrying axe handles, hoes and torches. Even the police in many cities shied away, not wanting to get mixed up with a group such as this. The threat of jail did not halt Carrie Nation, for during her career, she had been arrested over thirty times. On several occasions a frenzied driven mob of women, had literally wrecked a saloon while the owner helplessly looked on. There were instances when a bar had been set on fire and the flames spread to other businesses. But, no matter, there was no apology from Carrie, as she believed she was just carrying out her divine purpose in life.

She had appeared in Hot Springs in 1905, and tried to work up a crowd at Happy Hollow Springs, and did cause quite a commotion, but apparently she did not get the following she wanted or needed. One saloon operator had a sign painted, "All Nations are Welcome Here, Except Carrie." Even after her death in 1911, there were crusades to halt the sale of liquors. The Anti-Saloon League did much to get local towns and communities to go "dry."

In 1913 the League started a national movement to add an amendment to the Constitution to prohibit the manufacture and sale of alcoholic beverages. It failed when voted on by the House of Representatives in 1914. Another opportunity came along in the guise of the World War. During the war the army's great need for grain helped cause the food-control bill to push forward

---

[1] *The World Book Encyclopedia - 1958*, Vol. 13, p. 24.
[2] Ibid., Vol. 14, pp. 284-287.

the Amendment, which was passed. No whiskey was to be manufactured after September 8, 1917, and no beer made after May 1919. After July 1919, no saloon could operate legimately.[3] As the deadline approached, the stocks of bars, saloons and liquor stores were quickly depleted from their shelves by people "stocking-up." Newspapers, making a survey reported "shelves have been swept bare." There were those who seldomed imbibed but who hoarded a few bottles for the reason you never could tell when a person might need some "snakebite medicine."

At Hot Springs, as the city's thirty-one saloons prepared to close their doors, one owner, John A. "Jack" Goodine, whose saloon was at 825 Central Avenue, recived a strange call. The caller, Robert Gardner, was manager of a small circus, which wintered in the Spa. "Jack, we know you haven't long to remain in business," said Gardner, "so we thought we'd call and offer sympathy and learn at the same time if you cared to treat." Gardner explained he had some elephants who loved beer better than almost anything.

Goodine was game and invited Gardner to bring his elephants into town for a treat. Two hours later, patrons of Goodine's who were "bellied" up to the bar were astonished when Gardner appeared in the door followed by two large elephants. Those who had their feet on the bar-rail immediately moved away as the room suddenly became extremely crowded by the huge pachyderms. Gardner explained that there were three more of the huge creatures on the sidewalk. Goodine took a tub and filled it with beer and carried it out on the sidewalk where the contents were quickly slurped up by the thirsty elephants. The papers reported "By this time Central Avenue was jammed with people and all traffic stopped."

While the ban may have been a misfortune to the saloon men it became an immediate boon and opportunity to other groups--the moonshiners and bootleggers. This type of activity had been illegal for many years, but was practiced principally to evade the payment of government tax and for personal consumption. This type of whiskey production in the early days was looked upon by the country folks, so engaged, as a household necessity and they believed the government had no right to prevent them from making their liquor. Some of the men and boys who became involved in this illegal business did so because the money they made was "good," in spite of the risk involved, and there was a large and willing market. Too, it was far easier work than trying to eek out a living on a rocky and soil-depleted hillside farm, even if such activity was illegal. Those who did come up with a successful corn crop had no worry about selling their product for it brought far more for "corn squeezings," than for corn meal. In fact, a New Orleans newspaper was quoted that the corn and grain market in Arkansas was being calculated by

---

[3] Ibid., Vol. 14, pp. 717-718.

30 June 1919

Since after 1 July 1919 no saloon could legitimately operate, John A. "Jack" Goodine treated Jack Gardner's five "beer-thirsty" elephants, rather than pouring it out.

buyers by the gallon instead of by the bushel.

Almost all areas of Garland County became involved in this illegal activity. From Jessieville, Beaudry and the Dark Corner area in the northeast to the Little Mazarn in the west, and from Ragweed Valley in the west to Lonsdale and Price Station in the east and the Jack Mountain area of the south, dozens of lazily curling smoke columns revealed the location of wild-cat stills.

Enacting the law was one thing; enforcing it was quite another. From the very onset, the law was not popular and had resistance from many quarters. Federal authorities immediately encountered difficulties in enforcing the law. They found a lack of cooperation on the part of local law enforcement officials, many who had friends and relatives living in the county, some of whom were engaged in the illegal activity. To the federal government, the task was overwhelming. One young man questioned by a Garland County Grand Jury as to why he wanted to make liquor, drawled, "Well, everybody out our way is doin' it."[4] And, that was probably not far from the truth.

To encourage better cooperation from local law enforcement agencies the government offered incentives in the form of bonus and rewards for turning in the location of stills, seizure of illegal made liquor and the apprehension of moonshiners and bootleggers. These were welcomed by the low paid officers and after warning their kin-folk to desist operations and with this monetary encouragement, results were almost instantly noted as the arrests greatly increased. In fact, court records reflect that in one year 1,293 violators of the liquor laws appeared before Judge Ledgerwood for a hearing or referral to the Grand Jury.

Impressed at the number of liquor related cases, Judge Verne Ledgerwood, a tee-totaler himself, commented, "The prohibition law has not been a success. In my opinion it never will be. Public sentiment makes or breaks any law, and public sentiment is against bone-dry prohibition. The best that officers can hope to accomplish is keeping down as much as possible the flagrant violation of that law."[5]

As the pressure of law enforcement was brought to bear on the illegal manufacture of liquor, the wily moonshiners became more inventive in hiding and disguising their wildcat stills. In May 1921, Sheriff Downen and his deputies discovered a "novel still" on Kerly Creek, south of Hot Springs. It was one constructed of hardwood, with the exception of the worm and bottom of the pot which were of copper. The slogan "aged in wood" could well have been changed to "distilled in wood." Following a well worn path leading away from the still the officers arrived at a house where a family of ten

---

[4] *Sentinel-Record*, 27 December 1925, Sec.II, p. 1.
[5] Ibid.

lived. Several arrests were made.[6]

Officers were sometimes led to stills by smoke emanating from the fires necessaryto distill the whiskey, but on occassion theywere misled. Byaccident officers found a still hidden in a family's smokehouse. The farm was situated six miles north on the Little Rock highway.[7] Officers were unbelieving when the owner said he didn't know it was there.

Another unusual find was one located by Garland County deputies Godwin, Van Sickle and Guest seven miles south of Hot Springs. A steel burial casket served as the pot of a moonshine distilling plant. It was concealed in a ravine between Shady Grove Road and Gulpha Creek.[8]

A still located just off of Thornton Ferry Road was a "cheap-job," as described by officers, as it was constructed out of an old oil barrel.[9] A similar made still, but of far greater capacity, was destroyed in Whittington township.[10] It had twelve barrels.

A double galvanized pot still was destroyed by Deputy Sheriff Will Lowe and Deputy U.S. Marshal Henry Rowe and they arrested four men. It was located twelve miles north of the city on the old Akin Road.[11] Several drunk and staggering hogs led the officers to follow a stream, just off Shady Grove Road and they discovered a small still hidden in a hollow log. The swine had gotten into the mash and became intoxicated, but apparently the "porkers" were forgiven by the 'revenuers' for their indiscretion and were not taken in.[12]

At one time the Garland County Court House halls were lined with stills which officers had brought in as evidence. One young man who ventured into the courthouse, upon seeing the stills, thought they were for sale and upon asking in one of the clerk's office was referred by an employee, with tongue in cheek, to "see Sheriff Brad Smith, he might sell you one."

It was a strange and crazy time and citizens well known and respected in the community were caught up either in the moonshine operations or the selling or bootlegging of the illegal whiskey. People were even making home brew and cooking mash on their cookstoves and mixing gin in their bath tubs. Many small garage stills were found and the owners charged. A well known former deputy sheriff, Ben Murray, was arrested on bootlegging charges and held for a Federal Grand Jury.[13] A former Garland County Sheriff, Sid Houpt, Sr., who lived on the Mill Creek Road, was charged with operating a still on his land,

---

[6] Ibid., 9 May 1921.
[7] Ibid., 29 April 1922, p. 1.
[8] Ibid., 8 December 1922.
[9] Ibid., 19 December 1925
[10] *Sentinel-Record*, 24 November 1925.
[11] *New Era*, 17 November 1926.
[12] *Sentinel-Record*, 30 July 1925.
[13] Ibid., 5 April 1927.

even though he stoutly denied it was his.[14] A Baptist minister in the Buckville area was convicted in Federal Court on moonshining.[15] It came as a big surprise to the sexton of Greenwood Cemetary when a mourner, placing flowers on a loved-one's grave, discovered a still on the backside of the graveyard.[16]

There was a prominent Central Avenue restauranteur at Hot Springs who was suspected of bootlegging. This gentleman was not into home-brewed whiskey as the sheriff's raid on his home revealed. He bootlegged only the 'good stuff.' Three cases of bonded liquor, three large barrels of wine and five smaller containers of sour wine were found.[17] He paid a $400 fine and was placed on probation. Five officers raided a cleaning and pressing shop on Third Street and charged the owner with bootlegging and selling moonshine bythe drink.[18] There were thrilling automobile chases as the moonshiners tried to bring their illegal contraband into the city for sale. City officers Bob Moore and Joe Scott had two exciting races at high speeds through the city streets in one week, apprehending several bootleggers.

Well-intentioned people got caught up in trying to help enforce the Prohibition laws by joining a vigilante group such as the Ku Klux Klan, which had its own views of justice. At first the Klan's objectives were patriotic, but as time went on it took on a sinister nature. The congregation of a Lonsdale church was startled one Wednesday night in 1922, when the church doors were suddenly flung open to admit thirty hooded and robed members of the Klan. As the robed ones lined the front and walls of the church, Rev. J. Ellsworth Coombs, a guest speaker from the Christian Church at Hot Springs, was starting his message, and was handed a statement with orders to read it. It was a warning "against bootleggers in Garland County and notifying the 'leggers' that the Klan would conduct an active campaign to bring their business to an end."[19] What result this visit had is not known and it is unknown if any of these hooded ones took part in a similar sortie the following night into the Dark Corner area that had fatal consequences. A group of citizens had met at a school house to see a movie film, and which was attended by Garnett Braughton, county school supervisor and the same Rev. J. Ellsworth Coombs, who had been at Lonsdale, when the meeting was interrupted by several hooded figures. This time there would be an unfortunate confortation. Three moonshiners, two young men and the other sixty-one years of age, set up an ambush outside the school house. One of the

[14] Ibid., 5 December 1922. Also, 24 November 1922.
[15] Ibid., 21 April 1921.
[16] *Sentinel-Record*, 2 December 1921.
[17] Ibid., 22 December 1922.
[18] Ibid., 2 December 1921.
[19] Ibid., 16 November 1922.

December 1922

The Ku Klux Klan tried to frighten people into quitting the "home-making" of moonshine liquor. A party of the secret society invaded church services at Lonsdale

Klan members, Jeff Howell, who was later identified as being on the petit jury, was killed and two others, John Newkirk and J. Wheatley, a jockey, were wounded. The event was a shock to Hot Springs as five car loads of the Klan had driven out from the city. The Garland County Sheriff's office and Hot Springs Police Department swarmed into the Jessieville area and arrested forty of the male citizens, "for questioning". The prisoners were brought to town and introduced to "police methods of interrogation."[20] Even though the three moonshiners responsible for the ambush--Al Baldwin, Travis Conros and Tom Talley--confessed and were sentenced to prison, the action had put a damper on Klan activities in the area, and their enthusiasm for this type of vigilante action waned. The Klan tried to improve its image by donating money to a school fund and other worthwhile activities, however it began to fade in its influence and its membership roll began a decline.[21] Many of the better known businessmen who had been attracted by the secret organization began to see its dark side and quietly quit attending the meetings and contributing to its operation. While moonshining had its humorous side, it could be a deadly and fatal game.

Trying to apprehend the illegal operators of a still, Federal Prohibition Enforcement Officer Jesse Johnson, was killed from ambush.[22] This type of violence tended to make officers searching for stills and their wary operators in unfamiliar territories a bit trigger-happy. When officers approaching a still detected any sign of resistence on the part of the moonshiners the lawmen generally shot first and asked questions later.

A very unfortunate affair involving moonshiners occurred in eastern Garland and northwestern Hot Spring Counties in January 1919. Garland County Sheriff Brad O. Smith received a tip of a sizeable moonshine operation on the Garland-Hot Spring County line. Believing the tip to be genuine, he notified Sheriff Tom Bray at Malvern. The two coordinated the operation meeting near Price Station, on the Rock Island Railroad, after midnight 24 January 1919. In addition to the two county sheriffs, there were Garland County deputy Whit Curl, Hot Spring County deputy Harper Leeper, and two United States deputy marshals, Young and Burns.[23] The officers parked their two Ford automobiles about three-fourths mile from where the

---

[20] Ibid., 18 November 1922.

[21] *Sentinel-Record*, 22 December 1921, p. 3. When money was being pledged to the schools, because of a shortage, the local Ku Klux Klan delivered $500 in cash to the School Fund chairman, Rev. C.E. Hickok. Because of the coincident that Rev. J. Ellsworth Coombs always seemed to be near Klan functions he was believed to be the "set-up man." The Klan had planned to build a two-story building across from the Market Street Garage, having bought a lot, but because of declining interest did not do so.

[22] *Sentinel-Record*, 24 November 1921.

[23] Ibid., 25 January 1919, p. 1.

still was suspposed to be. By three o'clock the officers had worked their way through the scrub brush to attack the camp. The heavily armed officers approached a large bonfire four men were using to illuminate the area in which they were working. As the six men came around a knoll they fanned out in a semi-circle and one of the lawmen commanded the busy men to surrender. There was a pause, then two of the men grabbed their pistols, "and opened fire on the officers." All six of the officers, who had taken cover behind trees, returned the fire. According to the inquest held later, two of the moonshiners got off five shots while the officers fired thirty. Almost instantly killed was Charles Burris with nine bullets in his body. Homer Cheeks was mortally wounded with two shots to the chest and one in the leg, and would die a couple of days later. Fletcher Efford was shot through the body and leg. He staggered some distance and fell after climbing a fence. He would recover. The fourth man, John "Pink" McInvale, who was unarmed, tried to crawl from the scene but was captured, uninjured. None of the lawmen were scratched although Federal Marshal Burns had a bullet hole through his overcoat sleeve.

Raiding a still in Garland County — ca. 1927
Dave Brown, John Harper, Marion Anderson, Garland Van Sickle, Jim Floyd, Will Lowe

Then there was the fatal shooting of Dr. J.H. Rogers, an alledged deputy U.S. Marshal, near Jessieville by James Carmody, as Rogers attempted to search Carmody's car on suspicion of transporting moonshine whiskey.[24] Rogers, perhaps overzealous, fired a shot into Carmody's car where his family was and Carmody shot Rogers three times, killing him, claiming self-defense. It was a most dangerous time to be a moonshiner and also, an enforcement officer..

The era of bathtub gin, moonshine whiskey and bootleggers would dominate the news for over a decade, and Hot Springs and Garland County was caught up in the middle of it. An enforcement official during this period, Major D. Keating, announced from his office in Little Rock, "Garland County is the worst in the state in whiskey stills," he said, proudly showing a large state map with colored pins in it, designating stills located, "In fact," he continued, "I'll go further and say it is the worst in the south." There were rumors, though never proven, that the amount of moonshine whiskey distilled in Garland County was so great, that the king of all bootleggers, Al Capone, was attracted to the area and bought up all he could get and shipped it to the ready markets around Chicago.[25]

---

[24] *Sentinel-Record*, 10 July 1920. A jury acquitted James Carmody on a manslaughter charge for the slaying of Dr. LaFayette Cummings who engaged in a fight over a "crap-shoot" in the rear of A.W. Jackson's Barber Shop. *Sentinel-Record*, 13 September 1923.

[25] Local reseacher of that era, Fred Mark Palmer, is convinced from his studies that Capone used Mountain Valley Water jugs to ship the illegal hootch out of the county.

Homeward Bound and Changes

The war had been over five months and Leo P. McLaughlin was still in France. His unit had been designated to be assigned to the Army of Occupation. This meant that Leo might be in Europe for another year or so and he was very anxious to go home. Through a petition sent by his mother through U.S. Senator Joe T. Robinson, expressing a need that Leo be returned home as soon as possible, he was detached from that unit and reassigned to a casual detachment, unassigned.[1] The casual companies were on stand-by, waiting orders to move toward the seaports and then home.

One morning in early April 1919, while waiting transport home, and while Leo was still at Yerres, France, he had a pleasant surprise. He was shaving at one of the make-shift bathing areas and was peering into a mirror affixed to a post. As he shaved one side of his face with the government issued razor he caught a glimpse of a soldier walking behind him who looked familiar. McLaughlin stopped and turned. The other young man also stopped, not certain at first who he was seeing. The two men stepped toward each other as recognition broke across their faces. Leo P. McLaughlin and Al Brooks warmly shook hands and the two men began "an old fashion Hot Springs reunion."[2]

Alfred Lee Brooks had been born five miles east of Hot Springs on the Malvern Road on Christmas day 1895. His family had moved to town while he was very young and he grew up on Lincoln Street. He had attended Central School and had graduated in 1914. When war broke out Brooks had not waited to be drafted but had enlisted in 1917 and volunteered for the Quartermaster Corps, the supply department of the army. He had arrived in France about the same time Leo McLaughlin had. He spent a major part of his leisure time in writing letters to his sweetheart in Hot Springs, Miss Dannie Cobb, whose father was a well known local attorney, M.S. Cobb. Dozens of letters kept her informed of Alfred's travels, sights and scenery he was seeing. For some unexplained reason the two young people broke up and their expected marriage failed to take place. After the warAlfred Lee Brooks met a newcomer to the Spa who had moved from Dickson, Tennessee, Lorena Lucille Gibbs and the two were married on Valentines Day 1920.[3]

Brooks had been in a unit that was destined to be assigned to the Army of Occupation, until his father became very ill. His mother made a plea through the governor of Arkansas that he be permitted to return home as quickly as

---

[1] VA File.

[2] Life & Times of Leo P. McLaughlin (LAT), oral interview of Al Brooks, 29 July 1980.

[3] *Sentinel-Record*, 17 February 1920.

possible, hence his assignment to a causual company waiting transport home.

Even though the two men had not been well-acquainted, McLaughlin was extremely glad to visit with someone from home. He told Al Brooks they needed to be assigned to the same company. When Brooks told Leo that he doubted that was possible McLaughlin went to the company headquarters and as a good attorney, presented his case. He pointed out that both he and Brooks were doing nothing important and only waiting transport home because of need by their families and that they were headed for the same destination, Hot Springs. Why, then, could they not be assigned to the same unit and could travel together? Brooks was surprised when Leo McLaughlin returned with papers transferring Brooks to McLaughlin's company.[4]

A few days later both men and their casual company of 1,200 men embarked for America on the U.S.S. Seattle, a heavy cruiser. The crew of the warship had been reduced to accommodate the troops. Hammocks were strung in every available space to provide the soldiers a place to sleep.

McLaughlin came up with another scheme involving Brooks. He had learned the ship was in need of additional personnel to feed the increased number of passengers. Leo could be very persuasive as Brooks discovered. "Look Al," McLaughlin said, "I've learned that as a member of the Quartermaster Corps, you hold the same rank as a ship's cook, and as a ship's cook you would be given privileges. You don't want to buck that chow-line all the way across the Atlantic, do you?" Brooks said he found himself volunteering to help in the mess hall, a move that surprised the naval officer in charge of that department, but who was glad to have his help.

"Leo and I had a special meeting place near one of the big gun turrets," Brooks said, "And I would bring Leo sandwiches and food all across the Atlantic. Leo never forgot my friendship."[5]

As the ship steamed toward home, Leo McLaughlin was having a miserable trip. It wasn't that he was seasick like some of the other men, he couldn't breathe. His hammock for sleeping was below deck and the ventilation in the area was poor. Leo had never been able to tolerate tobacco smoke as the membranes in his nose became inflamed when he was subjected. Because of this he had always abstained from the use of tobacco. It seemed that everyone else aboard ship smoked but him. Some evenings when the smoking lamp was on, a pall of smoke hung stagnant in his sleeping area, and the air return system removed only part of the smoke by the time taps sounded. He either couldn't sleep or awoke the next morning with a fierce headache and inflamed

---

[4] LAT, Al Brooks, 29 July 1980.

[5] Ibid. Brooks stated that after Leo became Mayor if he needed work done on the street near his home or a ditch cleaned out all he had to do was to call McLaughlin.

throat.[6] When the Seattle docked and his unit was sent to Mitchell Field, Long Island, New York for discharge, McLaughlin was given an order by the ship's medical officer to report to the base hospital for examination. He was admitted to the hospital April 25, and treated for "Rhinitis, acute, catarrhal."[7]

McLaughlin and Brooks were discharged two days later and provided with a voucher for the train fare home. The two men arrived in Hot Springs on the Iron Mountain at 9:30 in the morning.[8] Corporal Leo P. McLaughlin had been away from home almost eleven months, almost to the day, and he would never be away for over a few days at a time the remainder of his life.

The local newspapers were faithful in reporting the arrival of ships transporting troops from France and listing units containing local boys. Almost every week in the first five months of 1919 local servicemen arrived in the Spa via The Iron Mountain or The Rock Island (formerly Diamond Jo).

To express appreciation for the dedication and sacrifice of the returning servicemen, a large party and picnic was organized at Riverside Park with both Bess and Verne Ledgerwood serving on the organizational committee. Tributes were paid to those who had fallen on the fields of France and Belgium. The picnic at Riverside Park was followed with one of the biggest Fourth of July celebrations ever held at Whittington Park. Something was planned for every family member. There were band concerts, community sing-a-longs, patriotic speeches and fireworks. Prizes were awarded to winners of foot and bicycle races. A balloon ascension was held, as well as a battle royal where several pugilists slugged each other senseless until only one remained standing. As the fight ended, contestants suddenly imbued with renewed engery, scrambled about the ring to pick up nickles, dimes and quarters that were tossed by the onlookers. The merry-go-round and the leap-the-dip rides were busy all afternoon. And finally as the sun set behind West Mountain and the day cooled into night the dance pavilion opened to the strains of Strauss waltzes.[9]

The Hot Springs that the servicemen returned to at the end of the war was much the same in appearance as when they left, but it was beginning to look a bit different. In fact, Central Avenue had begun to change its appearance in 1911 with the construction of the Maurice Bathhouse, followed by the razing of the old Rammelsburg, the Magnesia and the Horseshoe. No longer did the Interior Department permit new bathhouses to be constructed on the west side of Central Avenue. Newer and more sanitary structures were being built

---

[6] McLaughlin brought home, as a souvenir, a French Army gas mask which he displayed on his office wall with a "No Smoking" sign beneath it.

[7] VA File.

[8] LAT, Brooks.

[9] *Sentinel-Record*, 28 June 1919.

under close supervison of the Interior Department, who had the authority to lease the land near the hot springs.[10] Three men were very instrumental in the movement to create a beautiful row of fabulous buildings that would become known worldwide as Hot Springs' Million Dollar Bathhouse Row--Samuel W. Fordyce, George Latta and W.B. "Billy" Maurice. The Fordyce Bathhouse opened in 1915, the Superior in 1916, both the Ozark and Ouapaw opened their doors in 1922, followed the next year by the Lamar. The old Hale would not be rebuilt until 1938.

As the ex-soldiers returned home and slipped back into their jobs other changes were just beginning. Automobiles were becoming more numerous and the need for better streets and roads was becoming a political topic and a plank in any politican's platform. There were only a few of the main streets in town which were paved. Even though the automobile was changing the face of America and towns were becoming linked with ribbons of concrete, there was not one paved road leading in to Hot Springs. Various civic organizations, including The Business Men's League, began to call for paved highways and efforts were made to have Hot Springs included in some of the national roads, which were in the planning stage, the Bankhead, Pershing Way, and a bit later the Albert Pike highways.[11] Several improvement districts were organized in the city with the intent of paving Prospect, Laurel, Grand, Hawthorne, Valley, Hazel and others. Two of the city Commissioners, W.W. Gentry and E.N. Roth, wanted the city to contribute to the paving. Mayor McClendon and commissioners Martin A. Eisele and Harry Jones were of the opinion that the city was in such poor financial condition, never having fully recovered from the disastrous fire of 1913, that no support was possible from the city.[12] This division between the commissioners was only one reason that citizens were beginning to regret the change of municipal goverment from the aldermanic to the commission form. The change back to the aldermanic form was closer than most folks believed.

Labor union organizers had never been welcome or successful in the Spa of enticing working groups to unite and organize into bargaining unions. In 1919, two men from Chicago appeared on the scene and were successful in persuading food handlers, cooks, waiters, waitresses, pastry and kitchen help to form a union. Promises by the organizers had been made and expectations ran high among the workers they could demand and receive better wages and benefits. They had been led to believe that any demands made of their

---

[10] Ibid., 16 September 1926. This was a report of a speech given to the Rotary Club by the described bathhouse "dean," pioneer and citizen, W.G. "Billy" Maurice, whose family first visited Hot Springs in 1870, and settled at the Spa three years later.

[11] Ibid., 3 February 1920, also 10 April 1920.

[12] Ibid., 20 February 1920.

employers would quickly be granted. The local workers had been misled by the union organizers as the tight-fisted business men of that day had no intention of acceeding to the demands of the new union.

In early February 1920, the young union tried to flex its muscle by making several demands of their employers. When the demands were rejected the union called a walkout of twenty-four restaurants, confectioneries and bakeries, including some of the better-known eating establishments. The properietors quickly organized and advertized for replacement employees with promises of "good wages, and fair treatment guaranteed." Protection from the strikers was also promised.[13] They continued to operate in the face of pickets in front of their businesses.

The union decided to raise the ante and on Sunday night February 8, several men and one woman strikers entered Frisby's Resturant, one of the town's finest eateries. Standing in the center of the dining room the leader addressed the seated patrons in a loud, circus tone voice, "La-di-es and gentle-men--" and that was all he got said as the resturant's owner, Jack Frisby, hit the striker with a right cross to the jaw. The man sagged to the floor unconscious. The others fled. Police arrested three of those who had hurriedly departed the cafe as well as the one with the sore jaw.

Perhaps the union had been lulled into a false sense of security as it was common knowledge about town that Municipal Judge Verne Ledgerwood was a bonafide card carrying member of the Musicians Union. As a young man he had played the drums, and sometimes the cymbals, in the Ledgerwood Brothers Band and had become a member of the union. Ledgerwood often joked and told the tale that while he was not really as musically inclined as others of his talented family, he had played in the band because it took trips and he was able to go along as a drummer. In the event the Food Handlers Union believed the Judge, because of his "union connection," would be indulgent in their recent activities they were sadly mistaken as he placed each of those arrested under $100 bond for disturbance of the peace.

He admonished the strikers as he said, "I am a member of a labor union myself - the Musicians Union, but I will not permit any interference with the rights of business people. You people have a right to quit but you have no right to enter a place (of business) and make a disturbance, and if you do, you may expect to get the full limit of the law when brought into this court."[14]

The Food Handlers strike was very short lived.

Labor activities led to a tragic result in 1929 and involved the Royal and Princess theatres and the American International Alliance of Theatrical Stage Employees and Moving Picture Operators union.As theatres changed from

---

[13] Ibid., 8 February 1920.
[14] Ibid., 10 February 1920.

silent movies to the talkies, fewer people were needed and movie houses over the country began to lay off surplus personnel. So did Sidney Nutt, owner and operator of the two local theatres. When that occurred he was notified by the union his theatres were included in what was referred to "as the national list of unfair practices employers." Nutt worked in trying to show he wasn't being "unfair" but merely was making needed business decisions. He received a telegram about the 25th of October advising him his explanation was acceptable and his theatres names were being removed from the "black-list." Apparently word of the union president's telegram failed to reach three union activists, namely Roy V. Pugh, age forty-six of Tulsa; W.W. Sikel, age forty of Seminole, Oklahoma; and Spencer Bryant, age forty, formerly of Fort Smith but who had been working as a painter and decorator at the Kingsway Hotel in Hot Springs. Both Pugh and Sikel had been arrested in the bombing of five theatres in the Tulsa area but because lack of evidence they were never convicted. Bryant, who was residing at the Dixie Hotel on Broadway in the Spa, had been suspected of setting off a stink bomb in the Princess Theatre a few weeks before.

The three men had just gassed up a Graham-Paige coupe at the Red Ball garage on Ouachita and at 1:10 in the morning were sitting in the car on Chapel Street one block from the Princess Theatre. Apparently the three had made a bomb using an ordinary alarm clock as a timing device and a quart can of nitro-glycerine and were checking the device when a terrible mistake was made--it exploded in the vehicle. The devastation was immense. One body was hurled through the roof of the car and came down seventy feet away and in the process broke telephone and light wires. Another was hurled over fifty feet and the third was outside the completely demolished car. The front porch of one of the homes on Chapel Street was wrecked. All windows in dwellings and rooming houses along the street were blown out with the Chapel Hotel having to replace over forty full windows. Doors of houses were blown off their hinges and front walls were covered with "clots of blood and pieces of flesh." Parts of the timing device was found on the top of Dr. H.L. Swan's home near the scene of the explosion. Both the national union headquarters and the local representative Henry Gillen, denied any union involvement and said,"There is now no misunderstanding beteen the motion picture house proprietors and the operators."[15] The issue ended there.

Civic changes were also underway. Several groups and organizations, including the Lions and Rotary clubs, began taking an interest in organizing a Y.M.C.A. to provide activities for the boys of the city. It was hoped that funds would be donated sufficently to provide a center and hire a leader. Many

---

[15] *New Era*, 29 October 1929. This is a very detailed and descriptive article of the explosion.

of the businessmen supported the project including, Sidney Nutt, Walter Dodson, Walter Gentry, Dr. G.S. Moffatt, Arthur Katz, Milton Nobles, Lynn Howlett, Ray Smith, George A. Callahan, S.E. Dillon, Dr. W.T. Wootton, Dr. C.E. Hickok and Allen Hotchkiss.[16]

A large parade involving each of the schools was organized. Stunts were planned by the boys from the various schools, each team trying to outdo the others. The community seemed to have come together on this worthwhile project.[17] The endeavor was termed "a success," but was doomed to fall by the wayside during the Depression years.

The three-story brick building at the corner of Benton (now Convention Blvd.) and Cottage Street serving as city hall had been constructed by convict labor and opened for business in 1904. It housed the municipal offices, including the mayor's, clerk's, city treasurer's, engineer's, city nurse's offices and municipal court room. In addition, the City Auditorium Theater, with its very large stage and wonderful acoustics was located immediately at the rear, and the central fire department equipment bays and living quarters were to the west. The city jail occupied the northwest corner of the city hall and the main entrance was down a long, narrow passage way, along the west side of the building, appropriately called Jail Alley. This was situated between the fire department and the building west of the alley occupied by the Business Men's League. Since the city hall had moved from Prospect and Exchange Streets, the new building had little maintenance and the facilities were showing much wear and were shabby in appearance. City Manager Belding undertook a remodeling of several areas of the building, but most particularly the municipal court space, which had at times been referred to as a "hooley-hooley hall," perhaps called that from the parade of gaily dressed prostitutes who came to pay their monthly fine, and who were sometimes loud and raucous. It had always been a bit drab and its design was very poor and did not impress many people brought before its bar of justice. What dignity it exuded was by the judical presence of his honor, Judge Vernal S. Ledgerwood.

After its remodeling it was called a court setting, "long on dignity." The judge's bench was a large, attractive, raised half-moon shaped bar of justice, flanked by two posts on which rested two globed lamps to illuminate the work area. A platform had wooden folding chairs for a jury, which was seldom used, on one side, and a witness chair on the other. The room, also served for council meetings.

Judge Ledgerwood was most pleased with the changes and announced that in the future attorneys would be seated at a table for them and they should not wander about the room or "converse in loud tones until their particular case

---

[16] *Sentinel-Record*, 29 March 1919.
[17] Ibid., 23 March 1919.

called."[18] One newspaper reported the new opening, "In other words this articular legal racket is going to be run according to Hoyle."
A new roof and a coat of paint spruced up the municipal building.
It seems from a study of the history of Hot Springs that the city is almost estined to go through some sort of sensational happening, scandal or disaster very few years. These happenings and disasters were highlighted by the fires f 1878, 1895, 1905 and 1913. The scandals certainly included the Flynns and ne Dorans using Central Avenue for their private firing range in the mid-880s, and most assuredly the dramatic gunfight between the police epartment and county sheriff's office which dispatched five souls into ternity,wounded others, and sent hundreds of visitors scurrying to the train ations. The city was greatly embarrassed by the con-men fleecing visitors and hich was broken up in 1913. The doctor "drumming" scandal extended over period of years and really did not reach a climax until 1916. Another incident as coming on stage in 1919. Hot Springs was about to experience its first car heft ring.
In the spring of that year Hot Springs Detective Oscar Sullivan received a elephone call from an acquaintance and fellow officer, Sgt. Thomas Pitcock, f the Little Rock Police Department. Pitcock wanted Sullivan to meet him at restaurant in Benton, Arkansas, on what Pitcock described as " a sensitive natter." Sullivan accommodated Pitcock meeting with him the following day.
The Little Rock officer revealed to Sullivan that since May, he and fellow fficers had been investigating a number of car thefts in the vicinity of the alace Theater in Little Rock. Several of the cars stolen had been owned by rominent people of Little Rock, such as E.O. Bagley, circulation manager of ne *Arkansas Gazette*, Leo Pfeifer, owner of Pfeifer's Department Store, Dr. ohn Dibbrell, Dr. Anderson, and Lewis Bull. The cars had included Fords, uicks, a Willys and a Hudson Super-Six.
After staking out the area several nights arrests had been made of two ouths--Horace Hays, and Clyde "Slobbers" Campbell. A search was being nade for a third suspect. Pitcock said Hays confessed to delivering eighteen tolen vehicles to Dr. Albert Housley, in Hot Springs. The young thief said Housley had told them they had nothing to worry about from the police in Hot Springs as he had "protection here."[19] Housley susposedly paid the boys ne hundred dollars for each car they delivered. Pitcock further advised ullivan his office was working on getting signed confessions from both car hieves before presenting the case to the prosecuting attorney.
Sullivan had a lot to think about on his way back to Hot Springs. He was not ware of any "crooked" officers on the force but decided to play it safe, and

---

[18] Ibid., 12 July 1919.
[19] *Sentinel-Record*, 18 July 1919, p. 1.

he went directly to City Manager George Belding and told him the entire story. Belding called in another officer to help Sullivan, Bert Hall, and told the two they should meet with Garland County Sheriff Brad O. Smith and apprise him of the facts and begin their investigation of the allegations, especially those against the police department. Belding told them to report to him and when the time was ripe they would inform the press.

The officers sprang into action and in a few days the trail led to a stolen Willys sedan stored in a barn on a farm owned by Dr. Albert Housley, local veterinarian. Housley "became very indignant, and declared that he would like to learn the name of the person who had put it there."[20] But it was too late for the twenty-seven year old vet--the cat was out of the bag.

The officers had already followed one lead to a garage owned by W.H. Gibson, a black man, at 114 Ivy Street, and found a dismantled Empire automobile which Gibson admitted he was storing for Housley. By this time Oscar Sullivan had been joined by officer Joe Wakelin, who had grown up in Hot Springs and worked earlier as a cobbler, his father's occupation, and for one of the bath houses, before joining the sheriff's office as a deputy. Between the two officers, they were able to persuade Gibson he should cooperate. The man knew he was in trouble and he sang as sweetly as a songbird on a bright sunny morning. He told the story of trying to buy a car from Housley and had actually paid him several hundred dollars for a Hudson, but all of the parts to the vehicle had not been delivered and it would not run. The vehicle was sitting behind Gibson's shop. He then confessed that he, Housley, and another man had burned several bodies of cars and kept the chassis. He took them to a site on Hot Springs Creek, near Hollywood cemetery and showed them several charred car bodies. He told the officers, with the help of the vet and the other man, they poured oil on the car bodies and set them on fire. He claimed he was unaware that the vehicles had been stolen. In an effort to clear himself, Gibson agreed to call Dr. Housley with Sheriff Brad Smith listening in. Gibson told Housley he would like to return the sedan to him and asked Housley to return his money which he had paid him for the car. Housley told Gibson he "should not talk so much and that everything would be all right."[21]

More leads surfaced and led the officers to former deputy sheriff Ben Murray. Murray had bought several of the cars from Dr. Housley, then resold them to individuals. Even though titles to automobiles were much simpler in those days, a faked title or bill of sale was presented to each buyer to allay suspicion. One vehicle was traced to well-known contractor Ed B. Mooney, who said he had stored the car for Murray.[22] The trail led on. First, to the Sims

---

[20] Ibid.

[21] *Sentinel-Record*, 18 October 1919.

[22] Ibid., 18 July 1919, p. 1.

Paint Shop on Summer Street where colors on cars had been changed, and then to Thrasher's Body and Paint Shop, where car bodies and tires were changed out to disguise the vehicle and make identification difficult. In each instance, the owners of the garages admitted the cars they had helped paint or change had been brought there by Albert H. Housley.

Both Murray and Ed B. Mooney were charged with receiving stolen property. The charges against Mooney were soon dropped.

Confessions from the young thieves at Little Rock seemed to have sealed Housley's fate. He was charged on several counts, including one of attempted bribery of Detectives Oscar Sullivan and Bert Hall. Hall alleged Housley offered him one hundred dollars to take the car he and Sullivan had removed from his barn and which had been stored behind the city hall and leave it at a location on Benton Street and park it. The car, as evidence, would disappear. He told Hall he would also "give Sullivan one hundred dollars so he wouldn't be after the car."

Sullivan claimed Housley offered him and Hall $150 a week, "if they would not interfere in his alledged traffic in automobiles."[23] Dr. Housley would later testify that he never seriously offered the officers any money, but admitted he had a way of joking with them and he really did not intend to try "to bribe them."[24] The veterinarian was further damaged as a third officer, John Young, came forward and testified at the trial that, he too, had been approached by Dr. Housley with a bribe of $200 to recover the Hudson automobile, which Sullivan and Wakelin had recovered from Gibson.[25]

When all the evidence was in, Housley and Murray were indicted by the Grand Jury in late July 1919, and trial was scheduled for October.[26]

Albert Housley was represented by attorney George Whittington and Murray was represented by M.S. Cobb. Cobb immediately filed a motion in Garland County Circuit Court for a change of venue. Even though a number of witnesses were introduced, each supporting a change of venue for Murray, Judge Scott Wood denied the application. Attorney Cobb spoke briefly on behalf of his client, referring to the fact that the witnesses had testified to "a long existing prejudice against Ben Murray, and that deep rooted prejudice was within the minds of the people."[27] Whittington, too, had filed a request for his client, but withdrew it before Judge Woods could rule on it. He had seen from the handling of Cobb's motion that Judge Woods was not going to be swayed into changing venue.

---

[23] Ibid., 20 July 1919, p. 1.
[24] *Sentinel-Record, 19* October 1919, pp. 1 and 3.
[25] Ibid.
[26] Ibid., 26 July 1919, p. 1.
[27] Ibid., 12 October 1919, p. 1.

The trial for Housley was set for October 15, and Murray's was scheduled for the last week of that month.

The results of the trial of Dr. A.H. Housley was almost a foregone conclusion as many of the incriminating pieces of evidence had been described in the press and talked about town. But people who knew of his defense attorney knew not to rule out George Whittington, who put up a spirited defense in behalf of his client. However, there were just too many witnesses and too much evidence to overcome which seemed to place Housley at the head of the car theft ring. Witness after witness testified they had bought cars from the veterinarian only to discover their bill of sale was worthless and that the car had been stolen. The two car thieves, from Little Rock admitted stealing the cars in Little Rock and delivering them to Hot Springs. "Slobbers" Campbell was more certain in his identification of Dr. Housley as being the man they had turned the vehicles over to than the other thief, Hays. When Hays wavered on his identification of Housley, Prosecuting Attorney Haskins pulled a slip of paper from his file on the counsel's table and turned back toward Horace Hays. "Mr. Hays," Haskins addressed the witness, "Are you acquainted with a Little Rock lawyer named George Hays? Perhaps I should say former Governor Hays." An objection by Whittington was overruled.

Nervously, the witness answered, "Yes sir, I know him, but not very well."

The Prosecuting Attorney shot back, "Isn't it a fact that you are related to former Governor Hays, and isn't it a fact that you signed a statement to the effect you delivered eighteen cars to Dr. Housley, cars you and Mr. Campbell had stolen, and isn't it also a fact that former Governor Hays visited you at the Walls where you were confined two weeks ago, and that until that visit you were positive in your identification of Dr. Housley as being the person who paid you to steal the cars?"

It was never revealed who had sent former Governor George Hays to the jail to visit with young Hays or how his testimoney was changed by that visit, but doubt must have been placed in the minds of several jurors as to its intent and purpose.

The young witness was stunned by the revelation that the prosecution was aware he had been coached while in jail into changing his testimony. Whittington was aware from this point on that he had a lost cause. He was not surprised that the jury was out only a few minutes and returned with a guilty verdict. Everyone was then surprised as the jury did a strange thing--it recommended minimum punishment for the local vet. A sentence of one year was assessed by the court.[28]

In a strange comparsion, the two young car thieves who had brought the automobiles to A.H. Housley were tried and sentenced in Pulaski County

---

[28] *Sentinel-Record*, 19 October 1919, p. 1.

Circuit Court to the penitentiary for twenty-four years each.

Why such a small sentence for Housley, who was obviously the head of the ring, as opposed to the sentences meted out to the young car thieves? The answer, of course, was the young men had actually committed the thefts while Housley was guilty of receiving stolen property. But, there was another reason the vet's sentence was so light--family. Albert Housley was from a well-known family. His father was Evander T. Housley, a partner in Housley Brother's Dry Goods, located at 314-316 Ouachita Avenue, who in his long tenure in the Spa had made hundreds of friends. The senior Housleys as well as their children all bore sterling reputations. One was Elza Housley, who was serving as County Treasurer and Tax Collector. Any person entering the courthouse and passed his door or went in received a friendly wave or a warm handshake. Another relative of Albert's was Floyd Housley, a cashier at the Arkansas Bank and Trust Company, a well liked young man, who years later would be elected mayor five terms. All during the trial the family had been seen about the halls of the court house or in attendance in the court room, supporters of Dr. Housley, regardless of the evidence and outcome.[29] The selection of the jury had been very difficult as the "long and honored career of Evander T. Housley, and the Housley family generally delayed the selection of a jury in some manner, for there were many good jurors who frankly admitted that they were biased in favor of the defendant because of their long friendship for Mr. Housley and his family."[30] Dr. Albert H. Housley benefited from this community regard and respect for his father.[31]

The jury listening to testimony in the Ben Murray trial, accused of receiving stolen property, could not reach a verdict and the judge ruled it to be a hung jury.

****

---

[29] Ibid. The paper pointed out Evander T. Housley was "one of the most honored men in this community for forty years."

[30] Ibid., 10 October 1919.

[31] Dr. Albert Housley would again embarrassed his family when he was indicted along with trainer Lavon E. McLellan, for the "doping of a race horse, Dashaway" at Oaklawn. This indictment was by the same Grand Jury that indicted Leo P. McLaughlin. *Arkansas Democrat*, 23 May 1947. "Doc" Housley also built and owned the Chicago Inn, a small roadhouse on the Little Rock highway near where Club Belvedere was built. In fact, part of the property encompassing the Belvedere Dairy and grounds were owned by Housley and purchased by Jacobs in 1927.

Bangtails, Railbirds and "Umbrella Bill"

The early history of horse racing, the sport of kings, at Hot Springs, was one reported to be fraught with difficulties, uncertainties, interruptions and mishaps. For a period of time in the late 1800s, the Spa had boasted of two small tracks which had lured hundreds of sporting and betting people to the city. Neither of these two tracks, Sportsman Park and Coombs Track, were destined to greatness and only scant records remain of their existence. It was apparent by 1895, the two racing ovals were in difficulty and were handcuffed by anti-gambling and anti-racing laws. In 1903 a bill was introduced in the State Legislature to repeal the anti-racing bills. One of the key supporters of the measure before the State House of Representatives was from the Garland County area and had a great deal to gain from the passage of the measure. He was "Umbrella Bill" McGuigan, a very controversial figure who carried an umbrella everywhere he went, and who lived and resided in a large home five miles east of Hot Springs in Sulphur Township at Lawrence Station on the Rock Island Railroad. It was almost a foregone conclusion that when "Umbrella Bill" became involved in a project that problems and controversy were not far behind. One individual who had uncertain dealings with McGuigan described him as, "You never know where he's jumping from or the direction he is headed, and then, when he is landed, why he is there?" It seems that McGuigan owned a large tract of level land lying on the east bank or Gulpha Creek near where it emptied into the Ouachita River. "Umbrella Bill" envisioned it to be an ideal place to construct a mile-long race course and had assembled some investors. Optimistically, the group began to build a racing plant initially named Camp Lawrence. McGuigan worked the halls of the State Capitol as a state representative from Garland County, the only session he served, and believed by many for this one and single purpose. Through his tenacity and persuasiveness he effectively lobbied the passage of what was known as the Whitthorne Bill, repealing the anti-racing laws.[2] While racing dates were being sought from the Western Jockey Club, the organization which controlled racing in Arkansas, trainloads of horses were already arriving at the new facility to be stabled in several large wooden barns with tin roofs situated adjacent to the railroad. The Western Jockey Club with Louis Cella, of St. Louis as its acting president, gave the "go-ahead."

A crowd of three thousand patrons and railbirds flocked to the new trac

---

[1] *Historical Report of the Secretary of State - 1986,* "Bill" McCuen, Secretary of State, 371.

[2] Peggy Maddox, *The Record - 1972,* "Horse Racing In Hot Springs 1891-191 Hereinafter cited as Maddox.

n opening day, 25 February 1904.[3] The fans were delighted to find a modern ıree-story grandstand of almost 24,000 square feet facing a racing oval of one ıile. The track's name was shortly changed to Essex Park. Even though it was even miles from town the distance seemed not to matter. The Rock Island n several trains daily, and other people would buggy out crossing Gulpha reek where the James-Younger Gang had robbed a stage coach of people ver twenty-five years before. Large trees, shaded paths and picnic tables gave ıe track a park setting, indeed. The meet was deemed a success and the wners of Essex Park declared a very nice profit.[4] The success of the infant ıce track had not gone unnoticed however, and storm clouds were rolling on ıe horizon.

Dan Stuart and Charles Dugan had come to Hot Springs from St. Louis in ıe early 1890s. They were referred to as business men, but probably the term sporting men" would have been more appropriate as they were definitely ıterested in the gambling future and prospects of the Spa. In 1893 the two ad opened a plush gambling club in downtown Hot Springs. It was named ıe Southern Club and was to endure into the 1960s. They followed that up ith a five-story hotel and professional office building, named after ıemselves, the Dugan-Stuart Building. The two had closely monitered the ıccess of fledgling Essex Park and before the end of the racing season had een completed they were conferring with contacts in St. Louis to develop a 40-acre tract of land they owned on Central Avenue, south of the city limits, ıto a racing plant. The contacts were Leo Mayer, John Condon and Louis ella, and a bit later his brother Charles Cella, owners of the Detroit Jockey lub, and Douglas Park in Kentucky. The group incorporated the Oaklawn ›ckey Club, empowered Henry Schrader and forty men to build "one of the nest tracks in the South," and subscribed a half million dollars to the roject.[5]

With two first-class racing plants in existence the importance of racing dates ecame primary. In this endeavor, Oaklawn Park easily had a decided dvantage as the owners of Oaklawn also controlled the Western Jockey Club hich organization assigned the racing dates.[6] To the dismay of Essex Park's ew president, W.T. Shannon, they were given very early dates of operation, hen the weather was most unfavorable. On 24 February 1905 Oaklawn

---

[3] Kathy Cranford, *The Bloodhorse*, "The Glory That Was Essex Park," 15 January 2000, 366. Hereinafter cited as Cranford.

[4] Maddox. The owners pocketed a profit of $20,000.

[5] *Oaklawn Racing, Mail-A way Guide, 1985*, a copyrighted article 1983. Hereinafter cited ; *Oaklawn Racing*.

[6] Maddox.

opened its door and a very successful season followed.[7]

Meanwhile, "Umbrella Bill" McGugian had sold his holdings in Essex Par to W.T. "Billy" Shannon, gambler and later owner of the Kentucky Club i Hot Springs, Simon Cooper, a local livery stable owner, and Sam Davis, a investor, all strong supporters of racing.[8] McGuigan had damaged hi reputation with horse owners, if that was possible, by inserting a "ringer" i a race and practically bankrupting several of the bookmakers. The story goe that McGuigan had a racehorse that was very slow and was known t everyone about the track. The horse had a large white marking on its sid making it easily identifiable. What was unknown to the racing crow McGuigan had purchased a very classy horse that was almost identical i contour and appearance to the slow one, minus the large white spot. He kep that horse in a large red barn about a quarter-of-a-mile from the track. Th fact that the horse did not have the large identifying spot presented little or n hinderance to either McGuigan's scrupples or artistic ability as he secret painted a mark on the "ringer" identical to the other one, and registered hi in a race at long odds. Not only did the horse run away with the race winnin the purse, but McGuigan cleaned out several of the bookmakers. Of cours everyone was suspicious and the story came out, but supposedly no one coul prove anything against "Umbrella" Bill.[9]

Apparently the new owners were either extremely optimistic of their abili and chance to secure favorable racing dates or they were completely naiv when they purchased the holdings of McGuigan as the wily "Umbrella Bil had inserted a reverter clause in the sales contract. The clause stipulated th in the event horse racing did not continue at the Spa for at least five years, th property, "known as Essex Park," would revert to McGuigan's ownershi How in the world did three susposedly worldly and astute business men g suckered into such a deal with an individual known to be tricky an controversial at best? Especially so since their competitor, Oaklawn Par greatly influenced the assigning of racing dates. It did not take long f McGuigan's plan to unfold to the consternation of his former friends, and th owners at Oaklawn, who he now perceived as his enemies.

---

[7] *1985 Oaklawn Throughbred*, "History of Oaklawn." A discrepancy as to the openi date of the track exists. Peggy Maddox"s "Horse Racing in Hot Springs, 1891-1919," states t Oaklawn season that year was February 15 to March 18. Mamie Ruth Abernathy, in *Histo People, Places & Events*, indicates Oaklawn Park "Was opened for horse racing on March 1, 1905 and Kathy Cranford's "The Glory That Was Essex Park," lists the opening date for Oaklav Park as being 25 February 1905, four different dates.

[8] Cranford.

[9] The story came from Ray Stanage whose family purchased 83 acres of the land th had been in the McGuigan Estate. Mr. Stanage permitted the writer to review the land abstra involving part of the McGuigan property.

Billy Shannon and his partners fought hard to get favorable racing dates for the 1906 season, but the best they could come up with was an overlapping schedule with Oaklawn Park. With hats in hands they approached John Condon and Dan Stuart and tried to persuade the two Oaklawn officials to share some of the better racing dates with Essex, but it was like crying into the wind--no one was sympathetic, and no one was listening. Dejectedly, the owners of Essex Park had to concede that it would be economically impractical to go "head to head" with Oaklawn which was only a short street car ride from downtown. The day before Essex was scheduled to open, the racing season was cancelled. It was only a matter of time until the track would be involved in bankruptcy proceedings. Many of the owners and trainers at Essex Park loaded up their horse and moved to Oaklawn.

Meanwhile, the cagey McGuigan was doing a 180 degree, complete turn-about, or a flip-flop from his previous position of supporting racing to one of declaring horse racing should be banned. Suddenly, McGuigan had decided racing was bad and evil. Had the cancellation of the season for Essex Park, and his turn against racing, have anything to do with the reverter clause in the sales contract to influence his thinking? It would certainly seem so, and his motives then, as now, did not appear crystal pure. He had pocketed the money he had been paid and in the event Oaklawn could be shut down his revenge would be complete and he stood a chance to regain Essex Park and its land for only attorney fees. He camped out in Little Rock and caught the attention of State Senator Walter S. Amis, representing the Sixteenth Senatorial District, composed of Lincoln, Cleveland and Dallas counties, who was sponsoring an "anti-pool hall" bill, which outlawed the operation of such establishments, making it a felony with fine and imprisonment of sixty days to six months. Influenced by "Umbrella Bill," Senator Amis attached an "anti-gambling" bill to the pool hall bill and it passed the senate 27-2 on the day the Oaklawn Park meeting started, 4 February 1907. The governor declared he would study the bill as he was not certain it was constitutional. Oaklawn continued to operate as the governor appeared to be in no hurry to sign the measure, possibly encouraged to delay by an evelope he had received from interested parties, marked, "Re-election fund." But, the track's time was running out.[10]

On March 4, the day the anti-gambling bill automatically became a law, Garland County Constable John Smith and deputies, encouraged by anti-gambling forces, raided the betting compound at Oaklawn and arrested several of the bookmakers. There were no para-mutual betting machines in those days and wagers were placed with individuals who offered odds on the horses as they saw fit. The bookmakers paid the track a daily commission, said to be

---

[10] Maddox. The Governor let the bill lie on his desk and it became law on March 4, unsigned.

$100, for the priviledge of booking bets. Each bettor was given a slip of paper reflecting the amount of the bet, the odds and the entry.[11]

Garland County Sheriff R.L. "Bob" Williams was charged with non-feasance by being at the track and permitting those engaged in accepting bets. Williams reasoned that even though the anti-gambling bill had been passed it had not been signed into law. He was represented at trial by Oaklawn Park attorneys who gained an acquittal after twenty-two days in court.[12]

Darkness descended on both Oaklawn and Essex Parks which would last nine years.

In 1916 the Spa was mired deep in the doctor-drumming controversy and the number of visitors had declined. Everywhere business was hurting and ways of stimulating commerce was sought. After a lengthy debate, at which time the discussion turned to gambling, the Hot Springs Businessmen's League decided to take a poll of its members to see "which way the wind blows," so far as horse racing was concerned. The only surprising thing about the vote was the lop-sideness as it was 387-13 for legalized racing.[13] A civic club voting in favor of legalized racing was one thing and influencing a legislature only sensitive to voters "back home," was another. But the Businessmen's League was undaunted and appointed a delegation to journey to Little Rock and lay out the need at Hot Springs. The men were not given much hope at first, then finally the legislature threw them a bone. They were told that a thirty day meet would be granted on a one time basis. But, there was a catch, there could be no wagering. Owners of the track told the civic club, "that was no problem." For appearances, there would be no open betting. The mechanics of the operation would just be changed. Money would still change hands, just in a more discreet fashion. Slips would be given the bettors, and the bets would be written on small chalk boards which could be quickly erased, should the long arm of the law suddenly appear. This certainly was good news to those who depended on visitors and the income they generated. Even though they had been told this was a "one-time only," they were pleased--next year could take care of itself, they reasoned.

March 1, of that year saw the gates open at Oaklawn and a large, excited crowd descended on the refurbished park. Mayor Jacob McClendon had requested the merchants to close their businesses for one-half day and support the races.[14] Fans were delighted at the renovated track and the newly-enclosed glass and steam-heated grandstand, advertized to be the only one in the

---

[11] Info as to this type of betting obtained by writer from Don Grisham, retired Senior Columnist for the *Daily Racing Form*, 24 April 2000.

[12] *Arkansas Gazette*, 20 June 1907, and 22 June 1907.

[13] Cranford, p. 382.

[14] Maddox.

country. By this time the original owners Dugan, Stuart and Condon were dead and the track was under the ownership of Louis and Charles Cella. It was considered a "great meet," and the Businessmen's Club began plans for the next year. In fact, they reasoned, why not try to obtain racing dates for both Oaklawn and Essex Parks? By this time Essex was owned by interests out of Texas, as the litigation first instituted by McGuigan, (who had died during the interim), then by his estate, had been settled. It was certainly welcome news that they might be able to race and began cleaning up the plant which had stood idle so long.

This time Essex had more favorable racing dates with the opening taking place March 30, with over 6,000 fans journeying out. A Kentucky Derby winner of 1914, Old Rosebud, won the large stakes race to the delight of the throng. Everything looked rosy for the jubilant owners, who no doubt, envisioned a bumper season lay before them and that their expenditures on refurbishing the track could be recouped.

Unfortunately, more bad luck was in the offering for the star-crossed track. That night the grandstand caught fire and burned to its foundation.[15] The newspapers reported the fire had originated in some trash on the second floor and even though it was quickly discovered, the fire could not be contained. It seems that the original owners had gone to the expense of building into the racing plant water mains and a sprinkler system just for such an occasion. Unfortunately, no one had ever checked the fire protection system or they would have discovered that it had never been hooked into the main water supply--the sprinkler lines were completely dry! For years there were many local people who refused to believe the fire at Essex Park had been accidential, but that was only idle speculation, as no actual proof has ever been discovered to support that view. From its very inception, little had gone well for the track or its owners. Perhaps the demise of the beautiful racing oval, started by the grandstand fire, was just as well. It would be only a little over ten years until the waters of a new lake would begin to lap at and finally cover the backstretch, and its unused barns and stables would fall to decay and rot, from non-use.

Oaklawn Park, which had just finished its season on 29 March 1917, generously invited and permitted Essex and its owners to move the remainder of its meet to their facilities. Thus, Essex's final season was finished by using its competitor's racing plant. In fourteen years, the "snake-bitten" track had been able to complete only two seasons, a bitter and dismal ending for such a beautiful facility. Ironically, Oaklawn's owners purchased the grounds of its old competitor and used the rich soil and turf to renew its own racing surface several times, so that one might say, Essex lives on in the sport of racing.

---

[15] *New Era*, 31 March 1917, p. 1.

Things may have appeared bright for Oaklawn Park in 1918 and 1919, but difficulties lay ahead. It had been increasingly difficult to obtain approval from the state to operate each year. Only through the efforts of the Businessmen's League had the track been permitted to run. It became an annual pilgrmage for a committee to journey to the capitol each session, hats in hands trying to convince the legislators of the great economic benefit the races were to Hot Springs. Each session of the legislature there were those solons who would rise in the marbled chambers of the state capitol and give forth their oratory and rail against racing, painting it in the most evil context they could. Their interviews with the press afterwards were further damaging. Some of these speeches may have been done in sincerity; others were known to be just posturing for the voters back home. For when the vote was taken they reluctantly conceded that since Hot Springs was in such dire straits it was their duty and they "just wanted to help," and would not stand in the way. Then, there were the little envelopes that were passed to some of the key floor managers to "help grease the bill," so that it would "slide through" smoothly. The envelopes, containing folding money was known as "expense money" and in some instances designated as "campaign funds." But no one wanted to acknowledge the existence of such payments. Hot Springs had become well aware of how the game was played.

But the state legislature was just one obstacle Oaklawn had to overcome. There were always individuals, groups and organizations who were opposed to the running of the bangtails. It was no different in 1919. Rev. C.F.J. Tate, pastor of a "suburban church," who was described as "having a palatial home within a stone's throw of the Oaklawn course," and Dr. W.H. Connell, caused "the introduction into the (state) senate of a measure through which the presence of a race track within three miles of a church or school house anywhere in the state would be prohibted."[16]

It was obvious that not only would the bill threaten the thirty-day proposed Oaklawn Park season, but every state and county fair in Arkansas where racing was sponsored would be affected. Robert A. Jones, President of the Businessmen's League and several members journeyed to Little Rock and spent several days in lobbying against passage of the bill.[17] The success or failure of a bill in state politics many times hinges on the old adage of "whose ox is getting gored." This time, it wasn't just Oaklawn who was affected and unexpected help from different areas of the state arrived and the measure failed, and Oaklawn Park was granted a thirty-day operating season. When news hit Hot Springs there was jublilation in most of the business community. Again, Mayor J.W. McClendon issued a proclamation, urging all businesses to

---

[16] *Sentinel-Record*, 23 January 1919, p. 1.
[17] Ibid.

leclare a half-holiday and support the races. The press reported, "the city has never been so filled with notables from all over the country." The feature of he day was named the Arlington Hotel Handicap.[18]

By the time the last race of the season had been run, called "Trails End," the Cella brothers were congratulating themselves on the best meet the track had ever had. What they could not foresee was that it was the trail's end for Oaklawn Park for over a decade and a half as the anti-racing forces were mounting a drive to outlaw all racing.

[18] *Sentinel-Record*, 15 March 1919, p. 1.

Orlando H. Sumpter was not always an easy man to like. He could be gracious at times and totally offensive at others. He could be confrontational one moment, agreeable and polite the next. He probably had inherited some of his argumentive traits from his father, John J. Sumpter, also an attorney. In fact, father and son had been in a couple of push and shove matches with citizens of the community and were commonly referred to as "the fighting Sumpters." The James Sumpter family were early settlers in the Spa and operated one of the more popular medium-sized hostelries, the Sumpter House, located on Exchange Street. Sometimes Orlando pushed too hard in his dealings with people and seemed to easily make enemies by letting his temper get out of hand. Because of this, as a politcian, Sumpter was a failure, but whatever one thought of him it had to be admitted he was one of the more efficient lawyers practicing in Hot Springs.

While some lawyers might have looked at the handling of the city attorney's duties during the absence of Leo P. McLaughlin as secondary to their regular practice, Sumpter took the job seriously and ably represented the City of Hot Springs. During this time he had even "taken on city hall," and won. He discovered that the City Commissioners had signed an agreement with a bonding company that the city would pay 12 percent interest on an extension of the city's indebtedness of $200,000. He renegotiated the agreement, over the objections of a couple of commissioners, to 8 percent and was working to further reduce the payment when the council, very pleased with his work, authorized him to conclude the deal. This saved the city $8,000 the first year.[1]

He had also been active in forcing some paving contractors to comply with the agreement they had made with the city over curb and guttering. Too, through his efforts the Water Works Company was pressed into completing an agreement to afford the city with ample fire protection.[2]

It would seem that with the results obtained by Sumpter, acting on behalf of the city and its interests, he would be greatly appreciated by the mayor and commissioners, however, this was not the case. He was just too abrasive in his conduct toward others and one might describe him as "a bull in a china shop." Therefore, the return of Leo McLaughlin, to the remainder of his term was welcomed by the city commissioners and even by Mayor McClendon, who had helped defeat Leo after the Sanitorium fiasco.

In the first month after his return, Leo McLaughlin approached the city attorney's job with renewed energy. He began research on an old case where voters had approved the extension of the city limits of Hot Springs, but which

---

[1] *Sentinel-Record*, 16 April 1919.

[2] Ibid.

had been set aside because a group resisted annexation. They were represented by attorney Tom K. Martin, who believed he had found a technicality in the law, and the City Commissioners caved in without following through on determining whether or not the vote was legal. When McLaughlin appealed the previous ruling to circuit court, Judge Scott Wood reviewed the case and held that "the affidavit which should have accompained the original motion to appeal was not in evidence." The vote had been during the term of city attorney Sam A. McConnell, and Judge Wood gave the city four days to prove one had been filed.[3] McLaughlin got in touch with McConnell, who was in the real estate business at Nashville, Arkansas. The former city attorney told him he was quite positive he had filed a proper affidavit "and notice of appeal." He agreed to come to the Spa the next Saturday morning for a hearing and testify.[4] The appeal was granted and finally the annexation vote was reported to be valid.

At this time with the number of automobiles greatly increasing, it was recognized that the city's traffic code was woefully inadequate. The commissioners appointed city attorney McLaughlin and city manager George Belding to draw up the needed rules governing autos. To the credit of both men they took a very open approach, by inviting the public to submit ideas and suggestions to be taken into account. McLaughlin told a reporter, "I was pleased to receive some very good suggestions from Charles Lemley, Tom Martin and others, and I believe that if the public in general and automobile owners in particular would also take an interest in this matter we can draw up a satisfactory code."[5] The city attorney and the city manager worked on the project several weeks and then presented it to the council for review.

An invitation was extended by the city commissioners for the public to attend the "second reading" of the new traffic ordinance, which contained thirty-six sections, although "some sections are brief."[6]

Municipal Judge Verne Ledgerwood addressed the commissioners and audience at the bidding of city manager Belding. Ledgerwood said, "That of the many visitors who had been brought before my court it was generally because Hot Springs' laws were not uniform with other cities and it was an 'honest' lack of knowledge as to what the traffic law was that caused their arrest."[7]

Always aware of the economic importance the Spa's many visitors had on the economic stability of the city, Ledgerwood encouraged the council to

---

[3] *Sentinel-Record*, 8 July 1919, p. 8.
[4] Ibid., 10 July 1919, p. 8.
[5] Ibid., p. 2.
[6] Ibid., 22 July 1919, p. 2.
[7] Ibid., 24 July 1919, p. 5.

adopt the code but to apply it to the many visitors in a courteous way. "When a visitor violates the law, save when he is speeding, which is inexcusable, the traffic officer should give a copy of this ordinance to the visitor, speak to him in a courteous manner and set him right. Keep the visitor out of court, if possible. But, we have got to make traffic provisions, else someone will be killed. When the Bankhead highway is built and other roads completed into Hot Springs, we will have 500,000 cars a year coming into this city, and we have got to do something to control such traffic. There are some who will complain. The doctors will yell, no doubt, because they cannot park (double park[8]) their cars as they now do, but we cannot help that. Let the ax fall where it will, for the issue that is facing us is immediate action and when that ordinance is passed and becomes effective I want you gentlemen to understand I stand ready to enforce its provisions."[9]

The ordinance passed and printed cards were handed out by the beat policemen and mailed to every auto owner in the city. Most of the ordinance was just common sense, such as, "Always kill [turn off] your engine when leaving your car;" "Have two headlights and two tail lights burning at night;" "Never pass street cars on the right side when they are receiving or discharging passengers;" "It is a violation to drive over fire hose."

Some of the regulations were limiting parking to certain areas. Former city commissioner, Hamp Williams, President of the Citizens Bank, at Central and Bridge Streets, was one of the first violators of the new code by parking his car on Bridge Street. Officer Bert Hall's "eagle eyes spotted the car improperly parked," and since the keys were in the vehicle drove it to the police station. This was before the "ticket age" began. When Williams emerged from his office he discovered his car was missing. Too late, he remembered the ordinance banning parking on Bridge Street. He walked over to the police station on Benton Street to recover his car. Instead of being angry or fuming over the incident, he paid his fine and commended the officer for having done his duty.[10]

Other issues faced the city government in 1919. Sanitation problems were beginning to raise its ugly head--again. The Spa, almost from its earliest days, had suffered with sanitation problems. In the early days, all the garbage and sewage had been dumped in Hot Springs Creek, causing a very ugly sight and unpleasant odor in the downtown area. Private contractors were used to remove the trash and garbage from the area. Many of these carried it to the

---

[8] There were complaints that many doctors would double park in the street if they could not find a space immediately in front of their office. Because of the street cars and the narrowness of Central Avenue with no parking on the east side, traffic jams could occur with just a few cars.

[9] *Sentinel-Record*, 24 July 1919.

[10] *New Era*, 19 August 1919.

outskirts of town and merely dumped it down hillsides where it remained for years, rotting, stinking and becoming the breeding ground for rats and mosquitos. The growth of the city toward those dumps soon revealed why this had been a bad idea. By the late teens the city had an agreement with independent contractor Robert Murray to handle the problem and for a short time all appeared well. Then the complaints recommenced--Murray's services were little better than his predecessor. The idea of burying garbage and debris, as is now the common practice, was completly foreign to the thinking of the hauler of that day. Then the city's board of health, composed of Dr. Leonard Ellis, president, and Dr. Cassidy, city physician, gave a report to the commissioners of the very unsanitary conditions of the dump being used by Murray, which was appropriately called "Tin-Can Hill," and pointed out the health hazards it posed to the entire city. Once again the sanitation issue became a "hot potato." One of the commissioners' meetings in November turned into a real legal hassel. Berry H. Randolph represented Robert Murray; Orlando Sumpter spoke on behalf of Bob Boswell, one of Murray's sub-contractors, who had been singled out for critical comments of his handling of trash and garbage; and Leo P. McLaughlin tried to reflect the city's official position on the matter. Before the evening was over the commissioners were inundated with legal opinions leaving every one in a confused state. After three and one-half hours, the subject was postponed. As one tired reporter bemoaned in an article next day, "In the meantime the garbage situation is just where it was last year, the year before and the year before that. Murray's still on the job."[11]

There are few people around today who remember when Hot Springs had a poor water system. The life-sustaining water that has flowed through the conduits and mains over the years has always been of a high quality. But there were times when the city simply outgrew the capacity of the water works. The system had been inadequate at the time of the fire of 1905 and it had completely failed when the pumping plant burned during the devastating fire of 1913. And, while the city had insisted the water system be improved since the "big fire," improvements had not kept up with the growth of the city. There were areas where people could get only a trickle of water from their faucets, and not even that at certain times of the day. It was frustrating for one to be taking a bath or shaving and after lathering up, the faucet refused to emit any further water. Complaints poured in to the city commissioners and some said they could not even sit down with their families and partake a simple meal without some irate citizen calling with a complaint of the lack of water. While Leo McLaughlin was in the army, acting city attorney Orlando Sumpter had pushed the water company into expanding the city's fire protection by the

---

[11] *Sentinel-Record*, 2 November 1919, p. 3.

installation of several new fire plugs, but the company had not installed a better pumping system. And too, there were just too many homes connected to some of the small feeder lines to be effective. Finally the patience of the city commissioners was exhausted and they authorized Leo McLaughlin to press the Hot Springs Water Company into "keeping its agreements and faith with the city."

A new avenue had been provided for the handling of grievances by municipalities with utility companies. State Senator Houston Emory had sponsored a bill, which had passed and created a body to hear complaints against utility firms, called The Arkansas Corporation Commission. While this was a new plan of pursuing grievances against supposedly "unhearing entities" it had already brought relief to one city, Marianna, in the eastern part of the state.

Emory was one of those men who had started a career in one field, became dissatisfied, then changed to another. He had first taught school at Bismarck, in Hot Spring County, and then studied law and began practicing as an attorney. He moved to Hot Springs and served as principal of Jones School. He then hung out his shingle and began a practice in law. He was elected to the Arkansas State Senate and seemed to be a young politician on his way up.

Because Emory was familiar "with every provision of the bill," he was hired by the city commissioners to assist city attorney Leo McLaughlin in the case against the Hot Springs Water Company.[12] The two men worked well together and assembled all the facts needed to appear before The Arkansas Corporation Commission to present the Spa's case against the water company. As the city attorney and his co-counsel began to play their cards, the officers of the utility realized they were holding a losing hand, folded their cards and tossed them on the table. McLaughlin and Emory got a concession from the utility to build a large reservoir and install larger mains in the southern part of the city. By enlarging and improving the water system citizens of the resort would benefit from reduced fire insurance rates, saving $75,000 per year in premiums.[13]

Leo P. McLaughlin was on a roll and he was helping the city win some needed issues, many of which had been pending for years. In less than a year following his discharge from the army, he had tried thirty-one law suits for the city and was "successful in all but one suit."[14] An enviable record, indeed, although political opponents would later claim "that every lawyer, and juryman knows he has never tried an important case without assistance."[15] There was

---

[12] *Sentinel-Record*, 20 August 1919.
[13] Ibid., 4 April 1920, p. 8.
[14] Ibid.
[15] *Sentinel-Record*, 6 April 1920.

some truth to this charge.

Admittedly, Leo McLaughlin generally associated a capable lawyer with him when presenting an important case to a jury. It was as if he just wasn't quite sure of himself, possibly realizing the deficiency in his legal education. However, the splendid record in court cases on behalf of the city somewhat helped repair his tarnished reputation caused by his part in the sanitarium debacle three years earlier.

McLaughlin had reopened his law office upon his army discharge, and again adjoined the office of his mentor, George Whittington, in the Arkansas National Bank Building. The publicity of his successful representation of the city's business, even with help, had assisted him in his private practice. The majority of his cases were still divorces and land spats. It appeared he was about to enter the field of becoming a defense lawyer by getting to represent, along with attorney Joe Alford, Mrs. John Cristie, who was accused of murdering George Tobrea, a Kansas City horse trader. The killing took place at the Loyd Wagon Yard, in December 1919, and alledgedly occurred when Mrs. Christie objected to her husband selling a horse she claimed belonged to her. She pointed a gun at her husband, John, and Tobrea, who tried to grab the pistol and was shot.[16]

McLaughlin appeared with Mrs. Christie before Judge Verne Ledgerwood in municipal court, and successfully obtained bail for his client. The defendant was bound over to the circuit court for trial. For reasons unknown, possibly on the advice of friends, Mrs. Christie discharged Leo McLaughlin as her attorney and hired the more experienced George Whittington to handle her case. Whittington was able to convince the jury the shooting had been an accident and Mrs. Christie was exonerated.

[16] Ibid., 27 December 1919, p.2.

The spring of 1920 turned out to be a wild one at Hot Springs. It seemed as though everyone was dissatisfied with everything. There were problems in almost every department in the city. The police were so short of personnel the men were required to work twelve hour shifts every day of the week. The fire department was also shorthanded with the day shift working ten hours and the night shift fourteen hours. The street department's equipment, what there was of it, was obsolete and worn out. Salaries were low and there was always the lack of proper equipment. The city coffers were bare and streets that were paved needed repairs and those that were dirt or gravel needed grading or paving. Morale was very low among the employees. The commission form of government was barely working and it was strangling because of the lack of funds. On almost any issue presented to the council the commissioners were divided, generally by a 3-2 vote. The mayor and city manager were at odds with each other. There were even questions as to whether the commission form of government was legal.

Disappointed and disillusioned, Mayor McClendon obtained the services of attorneys W.G. Bouic and Col. George W. Murphy and filed suit on behalf of the City of Hot Springs to remove all the commissioners from office on the basis that the original bill creating the commission form of municipal government was unconstitutional. The suit also named City Manager George Belding and Collector E. L. Howlett.[1] The suit alledged the special legislative act was designed only for Hot Springs, as no other city in the State would have qualified as having between 12,000 and 15,000 population.

Mayor McClendon explained, "I am causing this action to be brought without any spirit of animosity against anyone. I do not desire any friction whatever, and my sole purpose in taking the matter into the court is that I feel it my duty to determine once and for all whether or not the law creating our present form of government is constitutional."[2]

The commissioners, represented by Martin, Wootton and Martin and Murphy and Stalcup, answered back, "That regardless of the constitutionality of the act by which the city of Hot Springs was changed from an aldermanic plan of government to a commissionership, the present city government is not subject to attack from Mayor McClendon, who acquiesced under the change, became a candidate and was elected under it." The demurrer claimed that Mayor McClendon himself is not in a position to seek the relief, and that the "City of Hot Springs," was named in the cause as a plaintiff without the authority of the governing body of the city." The matter was to be in court for

---

[1] *Sentinel-Record*, 7 March 1920.
[2] Ibid.

several months, and both sides eagerly awaited the outcome.

The only office of the city up for election in 1920 was the position held by Leo P. McLaughlin. He was first to announce and was afforded a nice write-up in the local press. It read, "He gives careful attention to the small as well as the large municipal litigation, and is present in the city court promptly every morning to look after the affairs of the city."[3]

The following day another native son of Hot Springs, Sidney S. Taylor, announced for city attorney. Sidney was the son of Dr. and Mrs. R.H. Taylor. He had been educated in the local schools and had gone on to receive degrees in education and law at Vanderbilt and the University of Texas.[4] Sidney Taylor had sought the office of city attorney in 1908, and had been aided by Leo P. McLaughlin, who was a senior in high school. For some reason Taylor had withdrawn from the race before the election.[5]

For three weeks it appeared these two would be the only candidates vying for the elected office. Then a rift appeared in the relationship of Leo P. McLaughlin and an another native of Hot Springs, Orlando H. Sumpter.

McLaughlin had once hired Sumpter to represent him when the city was considering going from the aldermanic form to the commission type of government, and as it appeared at first that then city attorney, Sam McConnell, would be able to get "a free ride" of two years without running for office. Sumpter was able to force an election and McLaughlin defeated McConnell.[6] When Leo had entered the army in 1918 he had not paid Sumpter everything he owed him for the work he had performed. After coming out of the army he had paid some of the debt but was apparently slow in clearing the matter up and Sumpter decided to run for Leo's job, and filed on March 28, just a few days before the election.[7] It appeared to Leo that Orlando had entered the race merely to embarrass him about the money he owed him. He would not be forgiving toward Sumpter.

What had appeared to be a "ho-hum" low key election, suddenly heated up.

Taylor opened fire on both his opponents. Of McLaughlin he said, "Can you reconcile your conscience in casting your vote for him? He was a slacker during the war. Are you going to work and vote for him for that? Has he any professional attainments which warrant your voting for him? Has he inspired confidence by the way he has treated his clients?"

Taylor recognized that Leo McLaughlin was his main opponent and he dismissed Orlando H. Sumpter with few words, "Time is too precious and

---

[3] *Sentinel-Record*, 4 March 1920, p. 8.
[4] Ibid., 5 March 1920, p. 8.
[5] Ibid., 4 April 1920, p. 4.
[6] Ibid., 6 April 1920, p. 6.
[7] *Sentinel-Record*, 31 March 1920, p. 6.

newspaper space too valuable to attempt to try to add anything you already know."[8]

In the waning days of the campaign, Taylor erroneously perceived an alliance between Leo McLaughlin and Orlando Sumpter and openly referred to the agreement the two had made when Leo was drafted into the army and Sumpter had held his job for him until his return. Apparently he was uninformed that Sumpter was irritated with McLaughlin over money owed to him. Taylor asked the question in the press, "Is it true that if elected you intend to divide the office between you? If not, why not?" He accused McLaughlin of allowing Mayor McClendon to use his name and office in the suit against the commissioners and accused McLaughlin of not "dealing on the square with the commissioners." He ended his inquiry with, "Are you trying to 'tote' water on both shoulders?"[9]

When a small black weekly newspaper, *The Echo*, came out prematurely with an announcement by the mayor and city commissioners of their support for Leo P. McLaughlin, Sidney Taylor was indignant, stating, "McLaughlin is evidently in due distress as he has called for the open help and endorsement of the administration."[10]

It was true, the city administration had endorsed Leo P. McLaughlin for city attorney and in a large advertisement cited several of his accomplishments on behalf of the city since his return from military duty. The administration urged the city voters to reelect him.[11]

In the same issue of the paper as the mayor and commissioners endorsement, McLaughlin had an advertisement. It was clear he sensed victory and gave his customary, "I have conducted my campaign upon a clean basis," statement, and he had. For once in Leo's political life he seemed to take the high road and generously pointed out that Sumpter and Taylor, "have both always been my friends, and after this race is finished I hope that I will still be honored by their friendship."

The election was not even close. Leo P. McLaughlin steam-rollered his two opponents, receiving almost a two-to-one vote over both men combined. Sumpter received only 99 votes citywide; Taylor 301, and McLaughlin 776. Leo carried every ward in the city. Maybe, just maybe, he was learning "to 'tote' water on both shoulders."

While the city attorney's election settled the question of who was going to serve the city as its legal adviser for the next two years, it did not settle the dislike Orlando H. Sumpter had developed for Leo P. McLaughlin. The results

---

[8] Ibid., 28 March 1920, p. 3.
[9] Ibid., 1 April 1920, p. 8.
[10] *Sentinel-Record*, 6 April 1920, p. 6.
[11] Ibid., 4 April 1920, p. 8.

in McLaughlin's one-sided victory had been humilating for Sumpter's ego. He probably figured with no more friends than the vote results showed he had, he'd probably better start carrying a gun for protection. The loss continued to gnaw on Sumpter. He had again approached McLaughlin about the money he believed was owed to him, and McLaughlin had taken the attitude the debt was settled especially after Sumpter had opposed him in the city attorney's race. Leo told Sumpter to "get a judgement, if you can and it will be paid."[12]

Later that same day, Sumpter confronted Leo in front of the Great Northern Hotel at Malvern and Benton Streets. This time, he was accompained by Ernest Ellsworth, a local real estate broker. Sumpter told McLaughlin if he did not pay him the money Leo owed by Monday, he would "whip him or take a whipping" from McLaughlin every time they met. When Ellsworth was questioned by the city attorney as to why he was involved, Ellsworth stated, "I'm a friend of Orlando, and I will help him in the event he needs help."[13]

It was apparent Leo P. McLaughlin was not afraid of Orlando Sumpter, man-to-man. Leo was younger than Orlando and in far better physical condition, but if Sumpter was going to be after him with a "body-guard," that was a different matter. He decided to do something about Sumpter's threat and requested Judge Scott Wood to place Sumpter under a peace bond, and it was granted. But Sumpter would not let the controversy rest.

Two days later Sumpter saw Leo McLaughlin standing outside municipal court, talking with police detective William Brandenburg. He jostled hard into the city attorney, who recovering from almost being knocked down, told Sumpter he did not want any trouble from him. Orlando then made a mistake, he let his mouth over ride his brain as he accused the city attorney, "You're a coward, Leo, and a S.O.B." Almost instantly, McLaughlin struck out and staggered Sumpter with a straight right to the shoulder. Several by-standers separated the two, but Sumpter pulled away and pressed the issue, hitting Leo a glancing blow. A surprised reporter, watching the encounter wrote, "McLaughlin struck the former county judge with such force as to almost stand him on his head. Sumpter's eye was bruised and cut and he bled freely. McLaughlin was unhurt."[14] There seems to be no record that a rematch ever occurred.

Several weeks prior to the city election in April 1920, the town awoke one morning to learn there was no police department. The city commissioners and city manager had requested the resignations of "Chief Wheeler, Detective

---

[12] *New Era*, 15 May 1920, p. 1.

[13] Ibid., Also, *Sentinel-Record*, 15 May 1920, headlines reporting, "Attorneys Engage in an Open Fisticuffs."

[14] *New Era*, 17 May 1920, p. 1.

Oscar Sullivan, and Patrolmen Trammell, Houpt, Dillard, Young and Ellison."[15] The entire force had been dismissed and Commissioner Walter W. Gentry was placed in charge. But, in charge of what? There were no policemen left.

For sometime the low-paid policemen had been under criticism from different quarters of the city. Citizens were calling for a crack down on thieves, gunmen and pickpockets which infested the Spa. In spite of the small force, with only a chief and three men working days and three men working nights, and never a day off, some results were being shown. The Elks Club Minstrel, always a favorite and well attended affair, was plagued by those with swift hands and nimble fingers. Three of the pickpockets were arrested and Judge Vernal S. Ledgerwood fined them $100 each.[16] City Manager Belding complained that one local citizen was getting $500 for getting the thieves off, but declined to provide a name. Two other pickpockets were arrested after ripping off two men from Missouri who were leaving a ballgame at Whittington Park. The thieves successfully removed one man's billfold without him noticing, but dropped the second's on the floor of the crowded street car. Ledgerwood hit them with fines of $300 and ordered them out of town.[17] And these were only two incidents where the crooks were apprehended, whereas there were many cases where they were not.

While the gambling clubs were shut down there were places people could shoot dice, play poker and play other games of chance. Small time gamblers would float into town, rent rooms in some of the smaller hotels and set up a gambling operations. Word of the floating game would travel quickly by word of mouth and by greasing the palm of one of the bellboys with "a fiver or ten spot," and told "to spread the word." The operator knew once word reached local authorities, he had to be swift to leave. He was much like Longfellow described in his poem, *The Day is Done*: "Shall fold their tents, like the Arabs, And as silently steal away."

But it was the small-time local operator who could get away with such a setup much longer. He was generally an individual who had worked around the clubs before they were shut down, was known to be a pretty good fellow supporting a family and was known to the local authorities. It is reasonably certain that some of these type operations were uncovered or known to the police and if the officers were inclined to look the other way for a few days, their wives and children might suddenly be seen sporting new wardrobes.

But when something went badly amiss, the question quickly arose, "Where were the police and why didn't they know about it?" And things sometimes

---

[15] *Sentinel-Record*, 16 March 1920, p. 1.
[16] Ibid., 31 March 1920, p. 8.
[17] Ibid., 16 March 1920.

did go awry, as in the instance of the Howard House. The Howard House was a three-story, split-front, medium sized hotel located at 510 Central Avenue, across the street from lower bath house row. It was owned and operated by Sam Bowman. During the first of March 1920, Bowman rented two rooms to a man who was well-known about town, James Ray. Ray was known to have worked around several of the clubs, was fifty-five years-old, married, and he and his family lived on upper Whittington. The rooms rented were on the second floor at the rear of the hotel and Ray paid Bowman $100 for a month's rent, no questions asked, and Bowman kept no further tabs on what the rooms were being used for.[18] Ray was trying to carry on his occupation, even if it was illegal. A few days after Ray rented the room there were two large poker games going on with "at least a dozen players." Two men suddenly entered and both were armed with pistols, and ordered, "all hands up." The players were robbed of over $2,000. Since the games were illegal, no formal report was made to the local authorities. By the time the police became aware of the robbery every one who knew anything about the holdup had vanished.[19]

But the story does not end here, for the city awoke on March 11, to the headlines in the morning paper, "Gunmen Murder James Ray In Howard House Card Room." At the time the article was written it was believed the shooting was the result of an unsuccessful attempt to rob the "fifty players" in the rooms. That was in error, as bit by bit the police investigation began to show. The crowd that had been in the two rooms fled into the night. The black porter claimed he didn't know anything and told police he was downstairs. Then it was discovered two other men who had been in the room had been injured by gunfire. One had a bad wound to a knee, the other to the foot, and medical treatment had to be sought. The story began reluctantly to come out.

About an hour before the gunplay, one of the card players became embroiled with a large man, also in the game, accusing him of cheating. A fight ensued and Ray ejected the large man who threatened he would be back. The hotel was equipped with a bell system which was operated from the desk downstairs to announce to a particular room the arrival of guests. About an hour after the confrontation, the bell buzzed and Ray, thinking another player wanted admittance to the games in progress, opened the door. It was the man he had previously ejected. With only an oath, the man pulled a gun and fired several shots into Ray who slumped to the floor, fatally injured. The gunman cast his eyes around the room, now in complete panic, apparently looking for the individual who had accused him of cheating. With the assailant blocking the door it was like shooting fish in a rain barrel. The other player was already

---

[18] *Sentinel-Record*, 16 March 1920, p. 3.
[19] Ibid., 11 March 1920, p. 1.

getting to his feet and had pulled his own weapon and got off two shots wounding another gambler in the foot. The slayer of Ray fired two more shots, this time at his accuser, shattering the man's knee. He then backed out the door into the hall and was gone. The little hotel was probably jarred to its foundation as the fifty card players tried to exit the rooms. Spilling into the hallway, some hurled themselves down the narrow stairwell and exited through the rear door into the alley. Others went out a window on the second floor to the fire escape and dropped to the ground. When the police arrived a few minutes later only the porter was there with the dead body of James Ray.

Several arrests were made, but the police were shooting into the dark. No names and poor descriptions were all they could come up with. It was poor timing for the police failure as the grand jury was in session and already involved in investigating the local department and quickly scored "places where this element (thieves and gunmen) congregate to rob the unwary."[20]

In addressing Circuit Judge Scott Wood, the jury said, "We regret to report that certain classes of criminals whose sole business is to prey upon the visitors and the public in general are permitted to remain and operate their nefarious business in our city. We refer to professional gamblers who remain in Hot Springs at all times and systematically swindle the visitors who come to our city to secure the benefits of our healing waters and who are entitled to be protected from the operation of such criminals. The places which these professional criminals operate are in disreputable hotels and in the back end of some pool rooms, cigar stands and attract criminal classes of all kinds."[21] In the lengthy report the grand jury urged the "city commissioners and city manager to investigate the actions and all departments and especially the police department and officers who are required to uphold the law."

Even before the grand jury's report came out, it was leaked and there was a "knee-jerk reaction," at city hall. The commissioners and city manager trying to shift all the blame for the police inefficiency on the officers, swept the entire police force out of office and almost instantly regretted their hasty decision when a loud hue and cry went up by the friends of the discharged men. Businessmen expressed their fears there would be a great increase in robberies and burglaries as the crooks became aware of the city's lack of law enforcement officers.

After two days, the commissioners relented and put out another announcement that only Chief Henry Wheeler would be discharged at that time. Trying to put a humorous spin to the affair, the paper wrote, "the disposal of the six men of the whole police force will not be accomplished

---

[20] *Sentinel-Record*, 13 March 1920, p. 6.
[21] Ibid.

until April 1st, so that April Fool's Day may be properly celebrated."[22] The force would continue to be headed by Police Commissioner Walter W. Gentry.

A search for a chief began. There were news reports the $125 per month chief's job had been offered to "three or four citizens, and that each one had refused to accept the "honor."[23] Other reports were bandied about that the commissioners were interviewing men from out of town in consideration for the job, but all applicants had declined.[24] Several older residents were quick to remind city officials that years before authorities had imported a man from St. Louis named Shevlin, who had been touted to be the savior of the police department, and even before he could learn the names of his men, he was fired.[25] Finally, the uncertainty was over as City Manager George Belding, along with the city commissioners announced former city detective Oscar Sullivan would be appointed chief. It was a popular move with the citizens. Tom Ellison, a former chief of police, Charles Trammell, a former constable and Henry Houpt, veteran law enforcement officers, were relieved of duty. John Young, Andy Dillard, and Bert Hall, were retained. New hirees included patrolman O.L. Owen, Tom Temple and Monroe Green. William Brandenburg, a former officer, and H.M. Williams were appointed plain-clothes officers and Jack Fry, the first fingerprint man at the Spa, was named as police clerk. Thus the force was beefed-up from seven to ten officers.[26]

One incident involving the police during this time brought a chuckle or two for many in the city--but not for the city manager. During the turmoil at city hall, City Manager Belding, doing an audit on police accounts, discovered money missing from a particular fund. A couple of months before the upheaval, the public was made aware that the police lacked certain equipment. Two of the local civic clubs sponsored a boxing benefit to raise the needed money. A little over $500 was raised, and instead of turning the money into the city to be used for purchase of the needed equipment, the management of the auditorium turned the money directly over to the police. Oops! In short, the seven-man force took the proceeds literally as advertized, "a benefit for the police," and divided the money, each benefiting about $70 each, and as one story put it, the money "goes a long ways these high cost of living days, and they were getting along swimmingly until something happened." George Belding went looking for the money. He demanded the money's return, but it was like throwing straw into the wind and searching for the strands

---

[22] Ibid., 18 March 1920, p. 3.
[23] Ibid., 17 March 1920, p. 8.
[24] Ibid., 28 March 1920, p. 9.
[25] Ibid.
[26] *Sentinel-Record*, 2 April 1920, p. 7.

afterwards. The policemen, those left, had spent it.[27]

But better days were on the way for the battered police department. Under the energic leadership of Oscar Sullivan, the morale of the department steadily rose. By the end of the year the commissioners were so impressed they authorized the hiring of four additional policemen.

Before the end of the year,1920, other lesser problems faced the city. The telephone company was receiving many complaints from new businesses who were having difficulties in receiving proper service. It finally reached a point the matter was addressed by the city commissioners. City Attorney Leo McLaughlin suggested a meeting be held with representatives to ascertain the cause of the delays. Telephone officials were willing to meet, and explained they were aware of the need for better service and were planning on expanding service with the installation of additional cables.

A petition was presented the commissioners with sixteen names of "prominent merchants, requesting the commission prohibit three public auction houses," from operating. For many years these houses had operated along Central Avenue selling and auctioning their merchandise, exotic and foreign made objects. There were rugs from Persia and Iran, jade articles from China, and bamboo articles from Malasia. Each had barkers at the doors proclaiming an auction was to start in so many minutes and there were bargains galore--how could one resist? Sitting inside were several people, apparently waiting for the sale to begin. Many of the visitors were unaware that some of these were plants or shills placed there to keep the bidding high. If a person got caught up in the bidding frenzy, they could get stuck with an object, sometimes paying far more than it was worth. Complaints were bound to come up. The auction houses were represented by Attorney Tom Martin, who had gone to a number of the hotels and other businesses and obtained a petition "asking the commissioners not to prohibit the houses." After a two-hour debate, the commissioners wearily voted 3-1, not to prohibit the houses. Mayor McClendon called attention to the absence of Commissioner Gentry who reportedly was home ill. The mayor said he almost wished he had had a chill himself, to avoid a decision on the matter.[28]

Early in December 1920, City Manager George Belding had had enough. He was tired of juggling the city's finances, trying to decide which bills he could pay each month and which would need to wait. He was at odds with a couple of department heads, but had improved relations with the police department with the appointment of Oscar Sullivan. He had experienced periods of friction with a couple of the commissioners as well as Mayor Jacob McClendon. At times he felt like a cricket on a hot griddle. Feeling the

---

[27] Ibid., 23 March 1920, p. 6.

[28] *Sentinel-Record*, 17 December 1920.

ressure, Belding submitted his resignation. The commissioners came up with list of potential prospects for the job. But, there was a problem, there was "wide divergence of opinion," among the council. They reportedly were ooking for an individual who could "bring more harmony in the workings of ity affairs." Several names were brought up, but not over two commissioners vere in agreement on any individual, that is, until the name of Major John ordyce was mentioned. Suprisingly, all five were suddenly in agreement. But he question was, would Fordyce accept? When approached, Fordyce, leary of he turmoil at city hall, told the city officials, "I appreciate the compliment. I m not unmindful of the honor bestowed, but I cannot accept it,"[29]

Disappointed, the commissioners returned to their task and could not agree n any of the names. Finally in caucus on December 20, someone suggested A.G. Sullenberger to fill the job until at least the election in April, when two of the commissioners would rotate off and two others be elected. Sullenberger had served as Garland County circuit clerk and was presently filling the city clerk's job which had been left vacant by the leaving of the previous clerk. Contacted later that day, Abe Sullenberger agreed to accept the job.[30]

[29] Ibid., 18 December 1920.
[30] Ibid., 21 December 1920, p. 5.

The Passing of a Good Man and the End of a Bad One

It had been four years since the City of Hot Springs had voted in favor of the Commission form of government. Sentiments and opinions seemed to be changing. It wasn't that the citizens distrusted their elected commissioners there was just a lot of dissatisfaction with the way the present government was functioning. Sometimes it appeared to the citizens that it took too long for the council to solve even the most simple problems. The voters either had forgotten that under many of the previous mayor-aldermanic administrations there had been a multitude of complaints because of graft charges and the "patronage" meted out to friends, family or supporters, or else those complaining were unhappy because they had been removed and were no longer able to feast at the "pork barrel," themselves.[1] When the courts decreed and the legislature passed a special measure, allowing the Spa to again hold an election to determine its fate as either a mayor-commission or mayor-aldermanic operated municipality, there was sorrow in some sectors and joy in others.[2] Both sides hastily organized and began a campaign espousing the benefits favoring their views and down-playing those of their opponents.[3] In a fairly close vote of 904-860, the mayor-aldermanic form prevailed.[4]

Suddenly, the city awoke to the fact that all elected positions, except city attorney which had been held the previous year, were open for the taking. There was a mad dash to the clerk's office as candidates queued-up for filing.

Four individuals announced for the city clerk's position the first day of filing: J.C. Ault, Robert O. Carpenter, Phillip Sisney and Fred Fowler.[5] Sam Garrett and Vernal S. Ledgerwood filed for municipal court judge, but a few days later, Garrett pulled out of the race.

In an unusual move the five financial institutions tried to become more involved in the politics of the Spa by running a slate of bankers. Claude Marsh, cashier of Citizens National Bank filed for mayor. In all probability had the banks all put their support behind Marsh he very well may have been elected, but they did not stop there. Robert Neill of the Arkansas National Bank was encouraged to run for alderman in the first ward; Stanley Lee, of the Comc Trust, filed in the third ward; Dave Burgauer of the Arkansas Trust Company threw his hat in the ring in the fifth ward; and C.C. Sparks of the Security Bank in the sixth ward.[6]

The banks' intentions may have been completely innocent, lily-pure, and

---

[1] *Sentinel-Record*, 2 March 1921.
[2] Ibid., 16 March 1921.
[3] Ibid., 12 March, p. 6, and 2 March 1921, p. 3.
[4] Ibid., 16 March 1921.
[5] Ibid., 27 March 1921.
[6] *Sentinel-Record*, 19 March 1921.

even civic-minded, but they were not so perceived by the public as criticism was immediately forthcoming. This move appeared to be a power-play and reeked of collusion. As one individual commented of the "smelly" situation, "If it looks like a skunk and smells like a skunk, you'd best watch out. You've probably got a skunk on your hands." The brain trusts of the banking houses, stung by the public reaction, swallowed their pride and withdrew all of their candidates from the races.[7]

The withdrawal of the bank employess left no dearth of candidates as each ward had at least four men for the two positions. For about two weeks the candidates were running over and bumping each other in the neighborhoods, knocking on doors, passing out cards, giving out advertisements such as pasteboard nail files and "funeral" hand fans, all trimmed in the patriotic red, white and blue, and asking for the people's vote. It is extremely doubtful if there was ever more hand-shaking going on in the history of the Spa than during this election.

When Claude Marsh dropped from contention for mayor, it appeared the position was wide open for the taking. Abe Sullenberger, acting city manager, had been considering making the race for mayor. He had been encouraged by others that Dr. Jacob W. McClendon, who had served eight years, was in extremely poor health and probably would not run again. McClendon's health, plus the fact that he had never really recovered over the loss of his only son, even led many of his closest friends to believe he would not make the race again. Sullenberger hestitated too long in making up his mind, as exactly one week after Claude Marsh left the race, Mayor McClendon announced his intention to again seek the office.[8] Some of his close associates had appealed to his civic pride to enter the race and not wanting to disappoint them, he made the filing.

Abe Sullenberger almost did not enter the election, but many of his friends, probably those wanting "patronage" jobs and positions, convinced him he should go ahead and run for mayor, believing he could beat Jacob McClendon. He was an advocate of paving city streets through the organization of improvement districts. He believed the street department should be used to keep the streets clean and repair pot holes. He "shot himself in the foot," though when he publicly stated, "If curtailment of force in any department is made necessary by lack of funds, it is my judgement that at all events the street department should be favored."[9]

With the city always strapped for the lack of money, and layoffs were fairly

---

[7] Allbritton, Orval E., *The Record - 1998*, "The Fire at City Hall: Accident or Arson, p. 3."

[8] *Sentinel-Record*, 26 March 1921, p. 2.

[9] Ibid., 30 March 1921, p. 8.

frequent, Sullenberger, had in one fell swoop alienated the police, clerk's office and fire departments, their families and friends, and many of those citizens who still remembered the great fires of 1905 and 1913.

Chief of Police Oscar Sullivan, who was not really getting along very well with the city manager, picked up the gauntlet thrown down by Abe Sullenberger. Sullivan accused Sullenberger of interferring in the operation of the police department, even to the extent of not even consulting him on new men being hired. He told the press he had been completely unaware Sullenberger had hired one individual until he received a call one night at home informing him, "a man wearing a gun was representing himself as a police officer." Sullivan had gone downtown, located and arrested the man, only to learn that Sullenberger had hired him and put him on patrol downtown, without informing the chief.[10] If nothing else, this certainly indicated that Sullenberger's communication skills might need a little tune-up.

Hot Springs Police Department - 1920

Back row, left to right: City Clerk Fred Fowler, Chief Oscar Sullivan and first fingerprint clerk. Front row: center, in white hat is Assistant Chief W.S. Brandenburg; to his right, Henry "Red" Terry; to Brandenburg's left, Joe Scott

---

[10] Ibid., 2 April 1921.

As election day arrived many voters were undecided. An editorial by John Higgins in the *Sentinel-Record*, gave good counsel: "Today the people will gin over again under an aldermanic government. You might start right by ting for the best man for the various offices. That means the best qualified en to serve your interests. The public interest is yours. Every now and then u wake up and find that out. Today is the day of the voter. It is his portunity. And remember this; your public affairs are merely an echo of urselves. If you are dead from the neck up you will have political troubles. you are alert and alive to a demand for better government, you will surely t it. That's all there is to the whole situation. And the voter can not avoid e responsibility."

t was good that Dr. McClendon's friends were trying to assist in his election he was so ill he was confined to his bed at home. It was no secret that the y's chief executive officer was too ill to even make it to the polls. It made le difference, as Jacob W. McClendon was victorous in his race and was ected to his fifth term by a vote of 1,100-1,010.[11] Mayor McClendon had erated for many years on small majorities, but the victory was especially couraging to him. He announced while still in bed he was looking forward the swearing in ceremonies and the opening of his new administration.

His friends leaked the news that as soon as the new administration was arted on its way Mayor McClendon and his wife would entrain for Battle eek, Michigan, where he would seek medical treatment and try to improve s health.[12]

On April 11, Dr. McClendon advised he would be unable to attend the vearing in ceremonies for his administration and expressed his regrets. When otified, Judge Verne Ledgerwood hastened to the McClendon home at 308 easant Street and administered the oath of office to the sick mayor, propped by pillows. Because of his character, Dr. McClendon had never gone down defeat, but he was about to lose the biggest race of his life, for sadly, the day ter he had been sworn in for his fifth term, the Spa's beloved chief executive acefully passed on to his greater reward.

The public had been aware of his illness, but few imagined Dr. McClendon as to be removed from their midst so suddenly. The entire city went into a riod of mourning. City hall was draped with black bunting as a sign of spect. His body lay in state at the Business Men's League, next door to city ll, as lines of mourners passed by his bier and casket. As news of his death ached the outside world, the Western Union and Postal Telegraph offices ere inundated with wires from his many friends in the business and medical ofessions, expressing their regrets.

---

[11] *Sentinel-Record*, 6 April 1921.
[12] Ibid., 10 April 1921, p. 6.

An expression of sorrow was drafted by the leaders of Greek citizens of H
Springs, namely George Antonio and James Fotio, and sent to Mr
McClendon. So did the Rotary and Lion's clubs.

A touching tribute was paid the late mayor by members of the blac
community headed by Dr. C.M. Wade, J.M. Page, Thomas Myers and B.
Shaw: "In the passing of our distinguished and lamented Mayor Dr. J.
McClendon, we the colored citizens of Hot Springs wish to subscribe o
quota of grief and sorrow at this unexpected and ill timed departure of o
most distinguished citizen. We feel he is not only lost to his family and to t
city, but especially to the colored race of the city, for his kindly hand w
always spread in a beneficient attitude over them. He will ever be remember
by us for his many kind utterances and encouraging words to our people."

But of the many beautiful tributes paid to Dr. McClendon, one stood abo
all as Editor John Higgins of the *Sentinel-Record* wrote: "Mayor McClend
was honest. There is an axiom that 'An honest man is the noblest work
God.' Mayor McClendon's integrity has never been questioned by even h
bitterest enemies. In his administration of public affairs there might have bee
critics of his ability, but never one to challenge his rugged honesty. In h
home life, Mayor McClendon was a loving husband. No more fond fath
could ever be described than Mayor McClendon in his almost inconsolab
sorrow over the death of William McClendon, Jr., a few years ago, and fro
which grief he never fully recovered. Peace to the ashes of May
McClendon. There was much in his life in which to find emulation."[14]

The funeral services for the late mayor took place in the Central Methodi
Church. The sermon was given by an ex-pastor, Dr. Alonzo Monk. Followi
the service, a long line of cars and people followed the hearse to Hollywo
Cemetery. His casket was borne up the hillside by George P. Shepherd, D.
Parker, Vernal Ledgerwood, W.R. Downen, Oscar Sullivan and Leo
McLaughlin.[15]

As one put it, "Never breathed a truer friend to those whose loyalty
enjoyed."[16]

But of all those who were grieving over the passing of Jacob W. McClendo
none were more so than his faithful dog and companion, Blue. The two h
been inseparable for years. About the only place Blue did not accompany h
master was to church on Sunday. The dog would lay in the waiting room
Dr. McClendon's medical office and accompanied him to city hall, layi
under his desk until the mayor had completed his duties.

---

[13] *Sentinel-Record*, 13 April 1921, p.2.
[14] Ibid., p. 4.
[15] Ibid., p. 2.
[16] Ibid., p. 4.

For two or three days following Dr. McClendon's funeral no one noticed where Blue was. Then Mrs. McClendon began to search for the dog and when it was learned Blue was missing, word spread rapidly about town and a general search was made for the animal, but to no avail.

One day, several weeks later, Blue suddenly appeared at the Thompson Building where his former master's medical office had been located. Discovering it closed, Blue went to city hall where he was warmly welcomed by the firemen, who provided him with food and water. As they tried to pet the dog he emitted mournful whines and moans. The dog then ran up the stairs to the mayor's office, then occupied by Harry Jones, who recognized the animal and invited him in. He curled up under the mayor's desk for a few minutes and after resting a bit got up and next appeared at the McClendon home. Mrs. McClendon was overjoyed at the return of Blue. She saw the dog tiredly lay down in his bed on the backporch and wearily fall asleep. When she checked on him the following morning she discovered he had died during the night. No one ever came forth with an explanation as to where Blue had been the past several weeks. His sudden return to the places he had been familiar with led one to believe the grieving dog was making one last search to see if he might locate his kind, loving and gentle master, and failing to find him, the heart broken Blue gave up, lay down and died.

Over the years Garland County and the Spa had been visited by some of the most deadly and violent individuals in the country. Frank and Jesse James, Bob and Cole Younger, Wyatt Earp, Frank Flynn, S.A. Doran, Ed Spear, Coffee Williams and later Al Capone and Lucky Luciano, just to name a few. None though compared in toughness, cunning, skill with a gun and the will to use it, and none were more deadly than Tom "Curley" Slaughter, who left his mark on the community in 1920. Everyone seems to be in agreement Tom Slaughter and his twin brother were born on what in the Christian world is considered the most peaceful and holy day of the year, December 25, 1896. It is the location of his birth that has confused researchers for many years. In a story appearing in *Dynamic Detective Magazine,* October 1935, entitled "The Crimson Bandit," author Devergue Barber credits Slaughter's birthplace to be near Russellville, in Pope County, Arkansas. Writer Jerry Gibbons, "The Short Violent Life of Tom Slaughter, Con-man, Killer, Celebrity," *The Record - 1993,* indicates he was born either at Bernice, Louisiana or Dallas, Texas. However, the Bureau of Vital Statistics Death Certificate for the outlaw, which was filled out by his widow, Mrs. Myrtle Slaughter of El Dorado, places her husband Tom Slaughter's birth in Lee County, Arkansas.[17]

As a teenager, while living with an uncle near Russellville, Slaughter was to

[17] BVS - Death Records, 6716/2213, 3 June 1922.

register his first criminal offense by stealing a yearling and being sentenced to the then Reform School. Escaping the minimum security institution he was apprehended and returned to complete his sentence. Before he was twenty years-old he was arrested in Texas for several automobile thefts and sentenced to the state prison at Huntsville, Texas. There, he was introduced to every form of criminal from petty thieves to burglars, bank robbers and hardened killers. He learned the tricks of the trades of these outcasts of society and put that knowledge to use when released, organizing a gang that ran off a string of bank robberies, including a bank at Petty, Texas in July 1919, where over $24,000 was taken. Slaughter and his gang hit banks in Missouri, Oklahoma, Kentucky, Louisiana and even one at Beaver Falls, Pennsylvania, where he was accused of killing a bank cashier. Things were going well for the crooks until their luck ran out in July 1920, when they were apprehended near Athens, Texas, and Slaughter again found himself to be confined to jail at Huntsville. He stayed there only a short time, faking an illness and escaping from an isolation hospital his first night in the medical unit.

On the run, with police in a half-dozen states on their trail, the gang hid out in the Osage Hills of Oklahoma. Finally, with their money running low, the gang, consisting ot Tom Slaughter, Fulton "Kid" Green, Lee Jarrett, Albert O'Connor, the last two half-breed Indians, and nineteen year-old Paul Witters, left Oklahoma for Hot Springs. Accompanying the five men were nineteen year-old Nora Brooks, girl friend of Slaughter, and sixteen year-old Ruby Smith, a seemingly homeless waif. While in prison, "Curly" Slaughter had learned there was a "fat little bank at Hot Springs, just waiting to be cracked." The bank was later identified to be the Arkansas National Bank.[18] Slaughter had disposed of a couple of stolen cars at Hot Springs several years before and had been impressed with the gambling clubs in operation and thought that one of these might be a "soft touch." What he wasn't aware of, was this was a period of reform in the Spa and the clubs were not operating, at least not openly.

The gang did not want to appear conspicuous, was running low on funds and decided not to stay at a hotel. Coming in from the east from Lonsdale they camped out near Six Mile Bridge, a long wooden structure over the east fork of Gulpha Creek. Planning to hit the bank on Monday after the weekend receipts were deposited, the gang began to drink and party Saturday night. Even though the area was somewhat isolated, the noise of the revelers disturbed several families in the area. Two of those made calls to Deputy Constable J.W. Wilson, who in turn called Deputy Sheriff Row Brown and

---

[18] Barber, Devergne, *Dynamic Detective*, October 1935, "The Crimson Bandit," p. 3[illegible] (Hereinafter cited Barber)

Deputy Constable D. Adams for help.[19]

On Sunday morning the three officers drove to the campsite and interviewed three men and two women, who reported they were just in the area to "have fun." Slaughter and Green were not present and it was later learned they had driven into town in an attempt to see Ben Murray about selling him their dark green Buick, and to get some information of any gambling clubs that might be operating. Murray was not home and probably would not have been interested in the car as he had almost "been burned" in the Doc Housley automobile theft ring and had also had difficulty in disposing of two cars he had previously bought from Slaughter as they were stolen.

Convinced it was just a group of young people partying, the law enforcement officers got back in their car and started back to the main road. The car began to heat up and Brown, who was driving stopped to get some water for the radiator from the nearby creek. Before getting back underway they heard an approaching vehicle and saw that the car was occupied by two men. Row Brown stepped into the middle of the dirt road and held up his hand. The other vehicle was a dark green Buick touring car. As Brown advanced toward the car, the two occupants slid out the right door. Then as Adams would later say, "All hell broke loose."

Slaughter grabbed a Winchester automatic .351 rifle and aiming it at Brown and Wilson, who was a short ways behind Row, ordered the officers to drop their weapons. Brown began to back toward his car followed by Tom Slaughter again ordering the officers to drop their guns. Brown said, "Just put down that gun; there's no need for anybody to get hurt." Slaughter told Green to "Get their guns." Green, who was armed with a .45 automatic pistol started toward the officers. D. Adams, who had been seated in the rear of Brown's automobile, started to get out and was ordered to remain where he was.

Row Brown then made a sudden movement which set off the deadly chain of events, he grabbed for his gun. Slaughter did not hestitate, he fired twice and Brown was hit with two heavy slugs, one in the throat and hand. Wilson tried to take cover and fired once with the bullet passing through Tom Slaughter's wide brimmed hat. Both outlaws turned their fire on Wilson, who lost two fingers on one hand and one on the other, and was shot through the jaw, causing the loss of an eye. Brown, badly wounded, reached his car, pulled his rifle out of its scabbard, fell behind a small tree and tried to get off a shot at the bandits. Both turned their fire on him and he was shot through the

---

[19] Wirges, Joe, *Arkansas Gazette - 1952*, "Joe Wirges Recalls Infamous Arkansas Crimes." Wirges was the police reporter for the *Arkansas Gazette*, for many years. Hereinafter cited - Wirges. Row Brown was an experienced officer, having worked for Sheriff Webb and later Sheriff Brad Smith. He was raised at Dardanelle, had served in the Spanish-American War, had come to Hot Springs for the baths, and stayed.

chest.[20] Adams had only one cartridge in his weapon and was no factor in the shooting. Fulton Green approached Wilson, lying prostrate on the ground, and aimed his .45 at the injured man. "Please don't shoot me again," Wilson begged. Green, looking down at the shot-up man softened and replied, "Alright, I won't, but I need your spud [gun]." Slaughter and Green drove quickly to their camp and picked up the other three men, leaving the women. The gang came back through Hot Springs, turned south on Central Avenue and quickly disappeared from the area.

Fatally wounded, Row Brown was able to drive a mile or so up the road and was able to stop a young couple in a coupe. He told them he was dying and needed medical help. They placed Brown on the right seat and the woman rode the rear bumper, holding onto the spare tire, as her husband drove to St. Joseph's Hospital, where Brown died a few days later, but not before he gave a deposition to the prosecuting attorney, John Hoskins.

Hot Springs was outraged at the killing and quickly started a drive to raise a reward of $5,000, for the capture and return of Tom Slaughter and Fulton Green, "dead or alive," to be delivered to the Rock Island depot.

Following the shooting, Hot Springs officers decended on the campsite, finding it deserted. They learned the two molls were at a neighbor's home and they were quickly removed to the Garland County jail. The two women misled the officers as to where the gang had gone until they realized a couple of days later they had been abandoned and were left to face the charge of murder. Then, they began to sing as sweetly as choir girls at a musical festival. The lawmen learned the identity of the gang and that their base of operations was a saloon at Ponca City, Oklahoma, and they had a cabin in the Osage Hills they used as a hide-a-way.

Garland County Sheriff Brad Smith and Police Chief Oscar Sullivan immediately departed for Ponca City, Oklahoma, arriving there dressed as oil field workers and began hanging out at the saloon where they had been told Slaughter and his gang frequented. They were in town only a few days until they received word that Slaughter and Green had been captured in Kansas.[21]

The bandits had become so brazen they were trying to pull off two bank robberies at the same time, one in Sedan and the other in Cedar Vale, a few miles apart. The gang had stashed automobiles and horses for their expected getaway, and had provisioned a log cabin in the hills for their hideout, but things had gone very wrong as the entire gang was apprehended.

Smith and Sullivan headed for Topeka to gain audience with the governor about extraditing Slaughter and Green for the murder of Row Brown. The governor was polite, but cool to turning the fugitives over to the Arkansas

---

[20] Ibid.

[21] *Sentinel-Record*, 30 October 1920.

authorities who learned Slaughter and Green had retained two powerful lawyers to represent their interest, and who intended to fight any extradition attempt.[22] Temporarily thwarted, the two Arkansas law officers decided to try another approach to remove the wanted men to their custody, bypassing the governor's office--a risky move! Brad Smith called his Chief Deputy Whitney Curl and explained to him he needed the $5,000 reward money as soon as possible. They then went to Sedan, Kansas and contacted Chautauqua County Sheriff Ed Powers, whose men had apprehended Slaughter and Green. The two Garland County law enforcement officers were surprised to learn that the two felons had confessed to bank robberies at Allewee and Frederick, Oklahoma, and Slaughter and Green had pledged not to fight extradition to that state on those charges. This was an obvious ploy to avoid going back to Arkansas and facing a much more serious charge of murder. Sheriff Powers explained that as soon as the interested Oklahoma officials arrived he would be forced to turn his prisoners over to them. Smith saw a window of opportunity. He told the Kansas sheriff that Hot Springs had raised a reward of $5,000 and he would see that "Sheriff Powers and his men" received the reward if he could get Slaughter and Green delivered to South Coffeeville, Oklahoma. Further, he believed that the Oklahoma authorities just might be willing to let Arkansas try the killers on the murder charge, where they faced a far stiffer penalty than the ones on the bank robberies charges where the two men would be back robbing banks again in a short time. This was an appealing prospect to the Kansas county sheriff. Sheriff Powers studied a moment and told Brad Smith and Oscar Sullivan in the event the money arrived before the requisition from Oklahoma did, it was a deal.[23]

A hitch developed as Captain Gunning, a Dallas, Texas officer arrived wanting to take possession of the two bank robbers on charges from that state, including escape from the Texas penitentiary. When Gunning learned Hot Springs authorities were awaiting receipt of $5,000 reward money, it appeared the release of the two fugitives might turn into a bidding war between the two states as he told Sheriff Powers he was certain that he could raise a reward of $6,000 for the return of the two wanted men to Texas. Smith, again communicated the info of this latest development to Hot Springs.[24]

People had subscribed the reward money but all of it had not been collected. Fearing that a delay in payment of the reward might lose the killers to another

---

[22] Barber.

[23] *Sentinel-Record*, 30 October 1920.

[24] *Sentinel-Record*, 2 November 1920, p. 1. Not wanting to tip anyone off what the lawmen from Arkansas were up to, Sheriff Smith drove to Coffeyville, Kansas to send the wire, asking the reward be sent to him at the bank at Sedan as he told the Hot Springs Business Men's League, "The sheriff will not turn the men over to me without the money. He is afraid to start with them. He is afraid they will get away."

state, Sidney Nutt, Sam Watt, Robert Neill and Walter Dodson, "personally pledged the payment of the money. The reward was personally delivered to Kansas by City Commissioner Walter W. Gentry and Deputy Billy Cockrill. Sheriff Power, upon seeing the reward money became a very practical man. Believing "a bird in the hand is worth two in the bush," he decided not to wait on the Texas authorities to arrive with a promised larger reward and agreed to meet the Arkansas officers at South Coffeyville. He loaded Tom Slaughter and Fulton Green into his car and told them they were going on a "little ride." The two gunmen at first believed they were being removed to Topeka, "for safe keeping." When they realized they were not headed in the direction of the Kansas capital they became very nervous and upset and even more so when they were delivered into the hands of Sheriff Brad Smith, his deputy Billy Cockrill and Chief of Police Oscar Sullivan. Once safely in Oklahoma they transferred to a train bound for Little Rock. As soon as the train conductor discovered the identity of the lawmen and who they were escorting he moved all other passengers to another car for safety.[25]

Word reached Hot Springs that "Curly" Slaughter and "Kid" Green were being returned to Hot Springs. When it was learned which train they were coming on a large crowd, estimated to be three thousand people, hoping to get a glance of the famous robbers, assembled on the platform at the Rock Island Depot. The crowd was disappointed when the train backed in to the station and only visitors disembarked. Sheriff Smith and Chief Sullivan had anticipated there might be a crowd to meet them and in order to avoid any possible trouble had stopped the train at Price Station where a waiting deputy with a car, whisked them to the Garland County jail.[26]

Had the crime occurred in this day and age it probably would be a year or longer before a trial would be set. Delays of one kind or another, caused by lawyers filing briefs and pleadings, taking of lengthy depositions and the scheduling of pre-trial hearings, postponements and reschedulings, would eat up the calendar. That wasn't the norm in the nineteen twenties, however. Judge Scott Wood had already laid the groundwork, having assembled a grand jury after the murder of Row Brown and issued an indictment on the testimony of witnesses. As soon as the accused men reached Hot Springs, he announced that trial would commence Monday November 15, less than five weeks after the shooting had taken place.

Slaughter's reputation as an "escape artist," was taken seriously by Judge Wood. He even received a letter from a police official in Texas warning him of how crafty, resourceful and cunning Slaughter was and advising he should be watched at all time. Armed men were stationed inside the jail compound

---

[25] Wirges.

[26] Barber.

and in the halls. Judge Wood requested Governor Brough to provide some militia for security while the trial was underway. A detachment of sixteen men from the Pine Bluff Machine Gun Company arrived the day before the trial and took over the security of the Garland County Court House. Anyone entering the court house was stopped and searched. Armed sentries were stationed in the hallways. First come spectators were permitted in the court room, until all seats were taken and no others allowed. If a person left the court room for any reason, they were not readmitted. The militia made several searches of the cells of Tom Slaughter and Fulton Green as rumors circulated the two men intended to make a jail break. Susprisingly, they "found two table knives, one of the blades of which had been converted into a rather useful saw." Also, found in a separate search were three saw blades.[27]

Slaughter and Green were represented by the ablest defense attorney in Hot Springs, George Whittington, but the two accused murderers wanted a bigger name to assist their local counsel and sent for Judge W.L. Crawford, of Dallas, Texas. Judge Crawford arrived on the Iron Mountain Railroad November 16 and met with Whittington, and his two clients. According to the press, the meeting "did not last long as suitable pecuniary arrangements were not made to retain him." In other words, they had no money to pay the high-priced attorney. The Texas attorney may have been enticed to come to Arkansas by the many stories which abounded to the effect that Tom Slaughter had secreted away a treasure worth up to $200,000, none of which has ever materialized. Hearing the news the alledged bank robbers were broke, Crawford left town on the next train.[28]

As the trial began 116 talesmen were examined and from that group ten jurors were selected.[29] Judge Wood ordered the sheriff to call another twenty-five men so the jury might be completed.

For five days the trial went on. Eye witnesses--Deputy Constable J.W. Wilson, still wearing bandages of his wounds from the encounter; Deputy Constable D. Adams, who was only a few feet away when Deputy Sheriff Row Brown was shot down; Mr. and Mrs. J.F. Simpson and a Mrs. Brest, all of Little Rock, who had stopped near the bridge for a picnic; and Mr. and Mrs. John Daus, who were returning from Sunday School and stopped on the bridge and were horrified, watching the shooting--testified the occurrences from their various view points. George Whittington, a skilled defense attorney, in his cross examinations, was able to bring doubt as to who fired the first shot, Slaughter, Green or Wilson.

Slaughter and Green admitted they fired on the officers, who they said they

---

[27] *Sentinel-Record*, 18 November 1920, p. 1.
[28] Ibid., 16 November 1920.
[29] Ibid.

believed were men intending to rob them and both insisted Row Brown just ordered them to stop, never identifying himself as an officer of the law. Neither Wilson or Adams could confirm or deny this. The two bank robbers also testified that J.W. Wilson had fired the first shot which pierced Slaughter's hat, and they had returned fire in self defense.

In his summation, Whittington portrayed Slaughter and Green to the jury as wronged men and persecuted vacationers, who had merely come to the area for fun and frolic instead of intending to commit a robbery as their girl friends had testified.

After fifteen hours of deliberation by the jury the verdict was brought in and the foreman read, "We the jury, find the defendants guilty of murder in the first degree--and fix their punishment at life imprisonment." It was the penalty George Whittington had been battling for.

As the sentence was pronounced, Slaughter's face broke into a smile and he said, "We have had a square deal, Judge, from you." Fulton Green nodded in agreement.[30] They had narrowly escaped the electric chair.

While the two murderers were satisfied with the verdict, Sheriff Brad O. Smith was greatly disappointed and expressed his feelings that Slaughter and Green deserved the death penalty. Historically, Garland County juries have been very reluctant to hand down the death penalty, so great in fact, Judge Scott Wood once lectured the county in an article in 1917, calling attention that sometimes, crimes deserve the ultimate sentence, and juries were doing a disservice in meting out a lesser penalty.

Within an hour the two convicted murderers were on their way to the state penitentiary at Little Rock, located on the west side of Little Rock on Roosevelt Road. It was a large red brick facility with high walls and turreted guard towers. Not many escapes had been recorded, but it had not held many convicts with the cunning and ability of Tom "Curley" Slaughter, either.[31] While the connection of this bank robber and murderer should end at this point so far as the Spa is concerned, it is of interest to follow his brief career a bit further just to show what a desperate and determined man he was.

Even though Slaughter and Green had susposedly been removed as a threat to society, the two men quickly made contacts inside the "walls" at Little Rock, and within a month were organizing an escape attempt with two other convicts, Charlie Petty and Oscar Ford. The plot became known when a letter

---

[30] *Sentinel-Record*, 18 November 1920.

[31] Only four days after the trial came to a close, the sixteen year old girl, Ruby Smith who had accompanied the Slaughter gang to Hot Springs, died at the Leo N. Levi Hospital. A Mrs. W.T. Ross had felt compassion for the "frail little girl," who had been locked in a jail cell begged the authorities to release Ruby into her custody until the trial started. Ruby had contracted pneumonia in the cold jail cell and it got continually worse. She was another casualty from the affair. *Sentinel-Record*, 24 November 1920, p. 1.

from Petty to his wife giving her instructions to buy several guns and how to smuggle them in, was intercepted in the hands of a trusty trying to sneak it out to mail.[32] This attempt to escape came on the heels of one at the Tucker Farm unit, near Pine Bluff, a few days earlier, when several men fled into the swamps. Governor Brough, near the end of a "lame duck" term, and who had been highly criticized for various faults of the Arkansas penal system, increased the guard force. A few days later, December 28, 1920, a second plot involving Slaughter and Green to escape emerged and sent shivers through the entire prison system.[33] The fact that Slaughter had escaped from the Arkansas Reform School, the Dallas City jail twice, from officers transporting him at Greenville, Texas and the Texas State Penitentiary now made the Arkansas prison officials as nervous as a long- tailed cat in a room full of rocking chairs. Once again, Governor C.H. Brough ordered the Pine Bluff Machine Gun Company to establish security at the "walls." Slaughter and Green had been working in the prison's tailor shop, making uniforms for the convicts, Tom sewing on buttons and Fulton running a sewing machine. It was decided to separate the two and Slaughter was sent to Tucker Farm, where he found life much more harsh and difficult than at the "walls." He was shackled to long lines of convicts, slowly moving across the wide, flat fields, planting crops, hoeing weeds in the rows, and picking cotton until his fingers bled. At the "walls," he had worked in the tailor shop, sewing buttons on uniforms. At the "farm" he was always under the watchful eyes of trusties carrying shotguns and mounted guards equipped with Winchester rifles. The trusties had the duty to thwart any fleeing felon and who could expect their own sentence to be reduced or even receive a pardon if they prevented a prison escape. As an incentive to stop any escape, the trusty immediately lost his privileges if he allowed a breakout. Slaughter got off on the "wrong foot," with Warden Dee Horton, who punished Slaughter for any infraction of prison regulations by having him whipped with a leather whip, called the "big flog."[34] He would later state, "I have been cursed and lashed to the point where I would rather die than endure it any longer."[35] He even wrote a letter to the governor, protesting his treatment, however, it evoked no response.

Tom Slaughter, always the opportunist, had made friends with Hal A. Cooper, a convict sentenced from Crawford County, who had served eight months of a two-year term on charge of grand larceny. Cooper was paroled from Tucker Farm the last of July 1921. Later investigation led authorities to believe that through Cooper's connection in prison he had been able to

---

[32] *Sentinel-Record*, 28 December 1920.
[33] Ibid., 29 December 1920.
[34] *Sentinel-Record*, 20 September 1921, p. 1.
[35] Ibid., 21 September 1921, p. 1.

smuggle a 16 shot Winchester .32-.20 rifle and 100 cartridges in to the prison and hide it under a bath house. As facts showed, Slaughter knew exactly where the gun was hidden, and even though it shot only a 115-gram bullet, in compasion to his favored .351 calibre 171-gram bullet, it was a most lethal weapon in the hands of desperate Tom Slaughter.

On Sunday morning September 18, nearly 200 men were being marched to the bath house for their weekly bath. Some had already reached the facility and entered. As Slaughter arrived at the bath house he suddenly reached underneath the building standing on blocks and pulled a burlap sack out slipping the rifle from the bag. At a signal from him the convicts hit the ground leaving him standing and facing several guards who were stationed in a semi-circle. Shooting from the hip with the rifle, he shot trusty Bliss Adkisson, a draft resister from Cleburne County, through the heart, killing him instantly. Adkisson susposedly was one of the men who had used the "flog" on Tom. The next shot from his weapon critically wounded Jim Morris, a Mississippi County man serving a life sentence for murdering his wife. The rifle barked again and a Craighead County convict serving time for night riding, Dewitt Garrett, fell wounded. A convicted murderer from Pope County, Rube Russell, was next to catch Slaughter's attention, as he, too fell wounded. Finally, William Elliott, of Arkansas County, serving a sentence for grand larceny was shot as he tried to flee from Slaughter's accurate fire.[36]

Slaughter made a dash for a nearby bayou, but a hail of fire from guards drove him back and into the bath house, where he ran from window to window firing his rifle. The thin-walled building provided scant protection from the high-power rifle bullets fired by the guards outside, and the convicts inside lay prostrate on the floor expecting to be killed at any moment. Warden Horton, hearing the gunfire, hastened to the scene and Slaughter reportedly fired at him twice, but missed. Tom hollered to Horton telling him he would give up his gun if Horton would come get it. Dee Horton hadn't arrived in town on a turnip truck and knew Slaughter's hatred for him and declined the offer. Sam Payne, a trusty, and a "lifer" with three murders to his discredit was successful in getting the bank robber to throw down his weapon and surrender.[37]

The escape had failed and Jefferson County was quick to indict and try Slaughter. The outcome was predictable, the jury convicted him of killing Bliss Adkisson and sentenced him to death in the electric chair Friday December 16.[38] Judge W.B. Sorrells questioned Slaughter concerning the killing of a bank cashier at Beaver Falls, Pennsylvania, and as to robbing a bank at Athens,

---

[36] *Sentinel-Record*, 20 September 1921, p. 1, p. 8.

[37] Ibid.

[38] Ibid., 2 November 1921.

Texas, and the convicted killer denied both events. He was returned to the "walls" at Little Rock for safe keeping until the execution, which had been delayed an additional sixty days.

Warden Dempsey, not wanting to be embarassed by another of Slaughter's attempts to escape, had him locked in one of the death cells and stationed a guard outside the door, twenty-four hours a day. But in spite of all the precautions the master escape artist had one last hand to play. As it happened, the prison was playing host to a wounded bank robber, Orville Reese, whose injuries needed considerable attention. A registered nurse, Alta Cumbie, age 32, had been employed to look after the bandit's wounds on the night shift. This had not gone unnoticed by Tom Slaughter, who incorporated Miss Cumbie into his plans, even though she might be unwilling, but whose valuable help was needed. On the night of December 8, Slaughter put his plan into motion, first by feigning illness. The guard reported this to Warden Dempsey, who lived with his family on the prison grounds. The warden ordered another guard to take Nurse Cumbie to check on "Curley." A slight temperature was detected and she gave him a couple of aspirins and left. A short while later Slaughter was acting as if he was going into convulsions and the guard summoned the nurse once more. Checking him, Miss Cumbie, covered him with another blanket and left. As the guard started to leave the cell, Slaughter produced a cocked and ready to fire .45 automatic pistol and ordered both guards, a man named Brown, and Tony Coppersmith, who had been convicted on gambling charges from Garland County, into the cell.[39] Having disarmed the two guards he set free an inmate named Herman Vezollie and had him to stand guard. Slipping into the kitchen he surprised Nurse Cumbie who was heating some milk and told her if she would follow his commands she would not be hurt.

Almost reading like a Hollywood movie script, Slaughter, using Miss Cumbie as a shield, methodically began to take over the entire prison, including Warden Dempsey and his family. The family, possibly fearing harm, was reassured by Tom Slaughter as he locked them in the death cell he had occupied, "The captain has been too square with me to hurt him. I'm going to play fair with him."[40] He captured the four guard towers, one by one, never hurrying. He opened the cells of those wanting out. For five hours he was in command of the walled prison in Little Rock, described as being the safest in the state. Inviting as many of the convicts as would to join him, he disabled two vehicles that might be used in pursuit, and tore out some of the telephone

---

[39] It was never learned how Slaughter had gotten the weapon or who had smuggled it to him. He certainly always put a severe strain on the security system of any jail or prison in which he might be incarcerated.

[40] Wirges.

lines. Provisioning a large touring car with food, he and James C. Howard, a convicted forger of railroad time checks from Garland County, and five Negroes pulled through the large prison gates at 3:00 a.m. Shortly afterward, Warden Dempsey was released and discovered one telephone the escapees had failed to disable. His first call was to Saline County Sheriff Jehu Crow, advising him of the jail break. Hastily, the sheriff was able to reach one deputy and two deputy city marshals and set up a road block at Main and Sevier Streets in Benton. They had barely got into position when the fast moving car of escapees hove into sight. Tom Slaughter was driving and seeing the blockade swerved a hard right turn onto Carpenter Street as both the lawmen and bandits opened fire on each other. Slaughter was able to turn onto the new Benton-Hot Springs road, which was far from completion.[41]

A shot from one of the lawmen's rifles struck a pistol in the car and glanced, hitting and wounding one of the black men in the hip. Slaughter stopped several times and disabled telephone lines along side the road. When the escaped convicts arrived at the Alum Fork, they discovered the bridge to be washed out by large rains, and they could proceed no further. Tom Slaughter, cursing his luck, drove the car off the road as far as he could and the men carrying their provisions hiked to a clump of trees and made a fire.

Tom Slaughter, a man of limitless immagination and ingenuity, who had always been able to count on the loyalty of members of his gang and though now surrounded with convicts whom he had freed suddenly found himself alone. More than once he had compared himself to another famous robber and he once told a reporter, "Why I can put Jesse James in the shade," and urged the newspaperman to write of his life.[42] He was more prophetic than he knew. James' storied career, known to ever schoolboy, came to an end as he briefly turned his back to an acquaintance, Bob Ford. In a split second Ford fired shots into the head and back of Jesse James, killing him. Ford would never have dared to try to slay Jesse face to face. It was the same with Tom Slaughter as he tiredly stretched his feet toward the campfire and started to doze. J.C. Howard had taken the guns from the Negro convicts at Slaughter's orders, and the two were the only ones having any weapons. Slaughter had trusted the wrong person as Howard fired three shots from a .45 into the head of Tom Slaughter, killing him.[43] He, too, had feared to face the leader.

J.C. Howard and two of the other escapees turned themselves in to the Saline County authorities. At first, Howard was proclaimed a hero, but as more of the story was told it came out that Tom Slaughter was asleep when Howard had fired three shots into his head, a public outcry was great and

---

[41] *Benton Courier*, Benton, Arkansas, 15 December 1921, p. 1.

[42] Wirges.

[43] *Sentinel-Record*, 10 December 1921, p. 1.

murder charges were filed against Howard, but were later dropped. The remainder of his short sentence would be pardoned by Governor McRae, but Howard could not stay out of trouble and was soon back in the penitentiary.

Tom Slaughter was buried at Oakland Cemetery in Little Rock and the newspapers reported a crowd of on-lookers of over five thousand people.[44] It took several trucks to carry the many wreaths and sprays of flowers. His *modus operandum*, of bank robberies and fast getaways, was the pattern later used by Pretty Boy Floyd, John Dillinger, "Sonny" Lamb and Bonnie and Clyde Barrows in the 1930s. Slaughter's legacy in Garland County has been a long-lasting one: the bridge on State Highway 88, east of Hot Springs, where Row Brown was killed, has carried the name of Slaughter Bridge for the past eighty years.

[44] Barber.

The Roaring Twenties Fire Up

The era of 1920-1930, commonly referred to as the "Roaring Twenties," related to an unsettled time in our nation's history. It was a period that in retrospect was wild and adventuresome, with bath-tub gin, speakeasies, flappers, the Shimmy, Charleston and the Black Bottom, fast cars and loose living. Many hundreds of thousands of men, who previous to the world conflict in which they had just fought, who never traveled widely, had been given the opportunity of seeing new sights, and new methods of doing things and they were no longer ready to return to the sometimes "hum-drum" lifestyle they had lived. Changes were taking place. Automobile travel was possible and families who had never left the county in which they lived were able to journey to places they had only read about. The restriction of Prohibition had become a challenge to those who may have never even wanted a drink before, until they were told by the government it was illegal, and that just made them want it that much more. And changes were taking place in politics.

At Hot Springs, city politics were really in a mess following the death of Mayor Jacob W. McClendon, who had just been elected and had never even held one council meeting under the new government. Members of the council met in caucus and decided they needed to set up a new election date for the purpose of electing a mayor. They scheduled it for Tuesday May 3, 1921.[1]

Because there was so little time to conduct a democratic primary, plus the fact there was "no central committee in existence," none was attempted.[2]

Names of several men were advanced as possible candidates. Some businessmen urged Robert A. Jones to make the race, however he was reluctant. The names of Ed Bradley and Walter W. Little, both members of the newly elected city council were mentioned. Leo P. McLaughlin was "chomping at the bit," to run but was still fearful of mixing it up with the "heavy weights," knowing he still had the "sanitarium fiasco," around his neck. Also, it seemed that at this time he received no encouragement to enter the race. Former city manager, Abe Sullenberger, who had been defeated by Dr. McClendon said he was available, and had some support but not as much as he had expected. Charles Dodson, an insurance agent; Claude E. Marsh of the Citizens Bank, a member of the school board; Jesse Murphy; Seward Erickson; and several others considered their chances.

One name kept coming up who was well respected and liked by nearly

---

[1] *Sentinel-Record*, April 1921. This would mean three city elections in a little over six weeks. A paid announcement *Sentinel-Record*, by George P. Shepherd, Mayor Pro Tem, gave the election date as Wednesday 4 May 1921, however this appears in error.

[2] Ibid.

everyone, Harry A. Jones. Owner and operator of the Majestic Hotel, Jones had been a central figure in the business and political operations of the city for twenty years. He was serving as a city commissioner at the time of the change back to the aldermanic system, and had even served as a councilman before the commission form of government. When approached by friends urging him to run for mayor, Jones was at first, unwilling. He pointed out that a campaign might take so much of his time that it would not be worth it. His supporters continued to pressure him and as Jones weakened to the pleas and persuasions of his friends, they decided to contact some of the others who appeared to be inclined to run for the office of mayor. A compromise was worked out to prevent a general conflict that might keep Harry Jones out of the race.Several of those who were considering making the race, including the only three who had qualified, Jesse B. Murphy, Abe Sullenberger and Ed Bradley, said if he ran, they wouldn't. Jones relented and announced his candidacy.[3]

Jones, of course, was elected and assumed control of city affairs and quickly demonstrated his executive ability, appointing the various committees necessary for the city government to function.[4] During his tenure as mayor he donated his mayor's salary to charity, much as Dr. McClendon had done.

A number of good things came to pass during the administration of Harry A. Jones. Within a year of his election he was able to report that every department was working efficiently and that the city's income was exceeding its output.[5] He advised the council of his appointment of Cecil Ledgerwood as city plumbing inspector on the basis of recommendation of various plumbing firms operating in the city. The council approved the appointment and he served in this capacity for many years. The yearly number of visitors to the Spa increased from 130,968 in 1921 to 265,500 in 1925, bringing great financial benefit to the area. Five major paving projects were completed by his second term--Park, lower Central, Whittington Avenues and Market and Valley Streets. Paving districts involving Orange and Third Streets were organized. Contracts were let on paving Prospect, Cedar and Ouachita Avenues. Enlargement of the city's sewer system was undertaken. A large new Seagrave pumper truck was purchased for the fire department, a new washer truck for the street department.

As the decade of the 1920s got underway Verne Ledgerwood was solidly entrenched as municipal judge. He had turned away several challengers for the bench he occupied and his political influence was increasing. He ran a good court, disposing of the run-of-the-mill cases in a most propitious manner. He demonstrated he was in charge, not the defendants' lawyers, although he

---

[3] *Sentinel-Record*, 22 April 1921.
[4] Ibid., 7 May 1921.
[5] Ibid., 2 May 1922.

tolerated legal viewpoints to be presented as long as they were productive and informative in arriving at a just settlement to a matter being heard. Let an attorney make a caustic or flippant remark and he could expect a reprimand. A young attorney in the 1930s, Sid McMath, said sometimes Ledgerwood would take over the questioning of a case being heard and ignore the lawyers completely. He wanted to move the cases along. "What do you say about this matter?" he might ask a witness, and then turn to another and inquire, "And what is your story?"[6]

Verne Ledgerwood loved it when the docket could be cleaned up by noon. When that happened he would be fishing in his favorite hole on the river, and later the lakes, by early afternoon. At this time about the only thing that would delay his almost daily trip to the river would be a problem on the construction of a new apartment he and Bess were building on Ouachita Avenue across the street from the Moody Hotel or an extremely long docket. The couple had been living in the large house owned by J. J. Ledgerwood and his second wife.

Verne and Bess decided to erect a building and occupy one of the apartments. It was to be of two stories and cost $30,000, a sizeable sum in those days. It would have sixteen apartments, and was designed to have steam heat in the winter and cooled "by an elaborate system of cold air ducts in the summer." A laundry was to be installed in the basement for the convenience of the renters.[7] It was to be the forerunner of a number of apartment houses constructed in the early and mid-1920s. And it would bear the name, Ledgerwood Apartments, for many years.

But going fishing or checking on the construction of his new apartment building was not always possible as occasionally, the docket was so crowded Ledgerwood's afternoon plans had to be scrapped. When this occurred you could rest assured he was not pleased. One Monday morning he arrived at the municipal court room and promptly started court at 9:00 o'clock. There were forty-eight cases involving forty-seven different offenders. While the judge was delayed from his early afternoon activities, it was a most profitable session for the city's coffers as he assesed fines totalling $585, many of the cases being drunk and disorderly charges, as fourteen were fined for "imbibing too freely in the joy making juice." It also seemed as fighting had been a popular weekend sport as nine others were fined, some still sporting their cuts, bruises and bandages as evidence.[8]

A heavy docket could always be expected following a three-day holiday

---

[6] Taped interview of former Governor Sidney S. McMath, 11 September 1997, by Orval E. Allbritton of the Garland County Historical Society.

[7] *New Era*, 29 June 1921, p. 3.

[8] Ibid., 26 July 1921, p. 6.

weekend. Many of the cases were for drunk and disorderly charges and when the judge asked, "Guilty or innocent?" and the person responded "Guilty, your Honor," a ten dollar fine ended the case. But when someone was brought in who had made a practice of vagrancy, wife-beating or "coupled with the beating of women boarding house operators," the accused could not only expect a fine to be imposed upon him, but a sentence of "ninety days on the chain gang." One such habitual offender volunteered, "Judge, I'll leave town," but Ledgerwood responded, "You can leave town after you have done your sentence to the city."[9]

One dark-complexioned man charged with an assault, and who was no stranger to the municipal court was let off with a warning. As the man started to leave, he turned to Judge Ledgerwood and said, "As I don promised you before, I won't come back no mo, and when I does anything else, I'se going to leave here forever and ever before dey gits me."[10]

A young Negro boy, described as a "Tiny Highwayman," was brought in one morning, wide-eyed and peering up at the magistrate's bench. He had been charged with taking five dollars from a nine year-old white boy.

Ledgerwood, having some fun at the expense of the youngster, sternly addressed several police officers in the court. "Men, what shall we do with the prisoner?"

"Better take him out and hang him," one of the policemen replied.

That really got the attention of the frightened boy and he began his defense in earnest, "Fer Gawd's sake, Jedge, don't you all let 'em do that. I swear I'll never come back here no moah. Honest, I won't, and I'll see dat white boy gits his five dollars back, too, honest I will."

"Judge, we have the rope all ready. Shall we take him now?" inquired one of the teasing officers.

Needless to say, the young bandit escaped the hangman's noose and hopefully stayed out of further trouble.[11]

While the incident may have been humorous to those in court that morning, the young black boy believed he had cause to worry. He undoubtedly had heard stories of such incidents involving the blacks of that day being dragged out and lynched for some crime they were accused of having committed, and sometimes without even a trial. Hangings and lynchings were quite common in the South. Hot Springs, a much more liberal and cosmopolitan city, was seldomed subjected to such a problem but was not completely immune to such mob incidents. It was true the last one up until that time--1919--had occurred six years before. That event occurred when a young black boy

---

[9] *Sentinel-Record*, 4 January 1922, p. 4.
[10] Ibid.
[11] Ibid., 4 November 1919, p. 8.

allegedly raped and killed fourteen year-old Garland Huff, daughter of C. Floyd Huff, a prominent attorney. Quickly captured, the young man was hastily lynched in Como Square by a mob of men, his body riddled with bullets and burned. The community was horrified and shocked as it should have been. No one seemed proud of the deed and when it was mentioned it was in hushed tones. Nothing resembling that act occurred until August 1922.

That tragic incident involved Maurice Connelly, the nephew of County Judge Charles Davis. Connelly, age 26, was a well known man about town and was employed in the insurance department at the Arkansas Bank and Trust Company. He was single and lived at 433 Orange Street. Shortly after midnight August 1, Maurice returned home from a dance on the roof-top garden of the Como Hotel and as he walked down the hall of the boarding house he suddenly encountered a black man searching a room near the rear of the building. He and the man, who was armed with a pistol, grappled in the hallway, and the burglar got off two shots at Connelly with one seriously wounding him. The assailant, who was in his sock-feet fled into the night, down Orange and Woodbine Streets, but was seen by several people awakened by the gunfire. Connelly was taken to Park Hospital where several doctors tried to save his life. He died a few hours later.[12]

Police Chief Sullivan turned out the entire police force to search for the killer. A tip led Sullivan and Constable Bert Hall to the home of "Punk" Harris, a recently paroled black man, who had served four years in the penitentiary and who was a suspect in several recent home burglaries. Harris had been convicted of a burglary at the home of James Smith about five years before and was defended by attorney James L. Graham. On that case the jury remained out for an unusually long time leading Graham to believe he had raised a doubt as to the guilt of the accused. When the jury returned with a recommendation of four years each on two larceny counts, Graham made the remark "If the jury had stayed out any longer they might have hung Harris."[13]

When captured by Sullivan and Hall, Harris' socks were damp as if from the dew and his wife refused to alibi that he had been there all night. He was arrested and carried to the city jail where it was said he refused to confess to the killing although he was given the "third-degree." As word began to spread that Connelly had died early that mornng and that the police had arrested the alleged killer, a mob began to gather on Benton Street in front of city hall. Chief Oscar Sullivan was able to disperse the gathering, however, it soon reassembled. Mayor Harry A. Jones arrived at city hall and said to Verne Ledgerwood, "Surely they will listen to reason," to which Ledgerwood replied, "Mr. Mayor, I know those men, many of them are the sons of the pioneers

---

[12] *Sentinel-Record*, 1 August 1922, p. 1.
[13] Ibid., 2 August 1922, p. 8.

who settled this town and they mean business."

"But I've got to try to stop them," Jones said.[14]

Both Mayor Jones and former Circuit Judge Scott Wood talked to the crowd from the steps of city hall, urging them to "let the law take its course," but nobody left and the mob became more menacing and threatening.

This was an ideal time for some knot-hard marshal, portrayed in the movies by the likes of William S. Hart, John Wayne or Henry Fonda to have come striding onto the scene with a big silver star pinned to their vest and carrying a double-barreled sawed-off shotgun and in a loud and firm voice warning, "The first man that starts this way is going to get both barrels of this scattergun in his chest, and I hope none of the buckshot will spray you other fellows." In the movies that generally ended the desire to drag someone from the jail to attend a "neck-tie" party. Unfortunately, no hero showed up that day, and there was no one able to deter the unruly mob. Besides, the mob knew it was made up of men who paid the salaries of the police and elected officials.

As the police blocked the jail alley, some of the mob gained entrance to the city hall and sucessfully entered the jail from the second floor. They reportedly were armed and "covered Chief Sullivan and others with pistols."[15]

A final stand was made by Mayor Harry A. Jones, a one-armed man, who stood before the cell of "Punk" Harris. Jones pleaded with the mob not to take the prisoner, "but he was thrust aside."[16]

Dragging the hapless prisoner into the streets he was placed in the back of a truck to the shouts from the crowd of "Let's go to the woods." This was answered emphatically, "Como Square, that's the place." In five minutes Como Square was filled with the noisy mob and on-lookers who gathered.

Sitting on the curb in front of Woodcock and Lawson's Dry Goods Store watching the excitement was a young boy, T.G. Hopkins, who had accompanied his family to town from Glenwood. One man detached himself from the crowd, "Son," he addressed the boy, "I'll give you a quarter if you'll shinny up that pole and drape this rope over the top." Hopkins tucked the rope in his belt and climbed the pole and placed the rope as directed.[17]

Leaders of the mob placed a noose around the trembling black man's neck and asked if he still proclaimed his innocence? He did. It was not a customary type of hanging with a hangman's noose, a platform with a trapdoor to be sprung or blocks to be knocked out from under the accused's feet where he

---

[14] LAT, Ledgerwood.

[15] *Sentinel-Record*, 2 August 1922, p. 1.

[16] Ibid. Jones had lost his arm to bone cancer several years before.

[17] As told by T.G. Hopkins to the writer, Orval Allbritton, Victor H. Cox and lawyer Bill Green in 1963. Mr. Hopkins owned and operated a Rexall Drug Store on Albert Pike for many years.

would fall and break his neck. The accused was not even placed on a horse to be swatted from under him. There were no experts for this type of execution in the mob. The mob just wanted to kill him. And kill him they did. They simply pulled the rope until the helpless man was raised near the top of the pole and he strangled to death. After hanging from the pole for fifteen minutes police finally moved in and took possession of the body. By this time most of the crowd had dispersed.

An inquest was held, but of what use or value did it serve? The official inquest merely came to the conclusion that Harris "came to his death from the hands of a mob," which hundreds of citizens had witnessed.[18]

One of the Como Square lynchings

---

[18] *Sentinel-Record*, 2 August 1922, p. 8.

The community was ashamed and subdued. Visitors were shocked. Even those who had taken part were not prone or proud to boast of their deed and the police force had proven so ineffective it was almost as if they had been in sympathy with the mob. The *Sentinel-Record* made a half-hearted attempt of justifying the hanging and pointing out something good that might come from the act in an editorial by the usually fair-minded John A. Higgins. He wrote: "The lynching in this city yesterday morning of the negro Harris will put an end to the house robberies that has been prevalent here for sometime. Aside from avenging the murder of Maurice Connelly, the lynching will put the fear into that criminal class which invades the homes of the people - ."

In an attempt to salve the conscience of the community, Editor Higgins came to the conclusion, "There was not racial prejudice in that lynching of yesterday morning. Any other thief who would have killed a well-known and popular man in the act of robbery would have received the same treatment."[19]

Right! The only lynchings in the long history of Hot Springs just happened to involve two black men. The subject was an embarrassing one and was rarely mentioned in polite conversation from that dreadful day forth.

In the spring election of 1922, city attorney Leo P. McLaughlin had no opposition. In a council meeting, Mayor Harry A. Jones let it be known that the city attorney's services in securing refinancing of the city, by which means the interest on the debt was lowered, and the savings applied on the principal, had been most valuable.[20]

Later that year, two new faces appeared on the county political scene who would be around for a number of years, W.G. Bouic and Earl Witt.

William G. Bouic had been one of the leading attorneys of the local bar association for several years. He had served as an assistant prosecuting attorney and had been most instrumental in leading the successful fight against the practice of drumming and its evils. He announced for prosecuting attorney.

Earl Witt, a tall, lanky, Lincoln-like individual, of Montgomery County, announced his candidacy for circuit judge. He was from a family of lawyers. His father, Gibson Witt, Sr., had served as prosecuting attorney for Garland and Montgomery counties in 1912-1913. Earl Witt's brother Jerry, was a well-known lawyer practicing in Mt. Ida. Their younger brother, Gibson Witt, Jr. was beginning a law practice in Garland County and would later serve as prosecuting attorney.

In Earl Witt's announcement to run he told the voters, "I will not be the candidate of any clique or faction and will stand firm against any rule by *political cliques or clans*, but will be for justice to all, with a firm desire to uphold

---

[19] Ibid., p. 4.

[20] *Sentinel-Record*, 23 March 1922, p. 7.

Earl Witt and niece, Pat Witt [Wolf] – ca. 1940
Courtesy of Pat Wolf

the law and see that good order and decency are always the rule."

Undoubtedly, Earl Witt, as most young politically-aspiring candidates, truly meant what he promised. Unfortunately, he would forget his words and pledge as he and others were destined to establish one of the most powerful political "cliques" ever witnessed in the South.

Both Bouic and Witt would win their elections that year.

In 1923, the Spa was again host to, and suffered a couple of diasasters which ever so often seem to visit the Spa. The first of these involved one of the most popular hotels in America, the Arlington. Actually, this was the second hotel of that name. It had opened in 1893, and was commonly called the "red-brick" Arlington. It had been constructed to compete with the massive 500 room Eastman Hotel, which was referred to as the "Monarch of the Glen," and which had opened for business in 1890.

Shortly after noon on 5 April 1923, the Arlington's head waiter, W.M. Acree, discovered smoke coming from beneath floor tile in the spacious dining room. Not wanting to alarm any guests, Acree and a couple of maintenance employees, removed the tile and discovered more smoke, but no fire. No call was made to the fire department as the hotel employees continued to search for the source of the smoke. Many guests were unaware of the problem and remained in their rooms, others lounged in chairs on the wide veranda watching traffic on historic Central Avenue. As heavy smoke began to pour from various openings the management finally placed a call to the fire department--fifty-five minutes after discovering the smoke. By the time the fire trucks hove in sight the firemen could see dark billows of smoke spiraling upward and flames beginning to lick out windows and openings.

The hard-working firemen were at a decided disadvantage as the fire had so great a start before they arrived. The fire spread through the beautiful structure, racing up stairwells and elevator shafts, eating away at the waxed and polished paneling and ornamental posts. Carpets, draperies and linens fueled the hungry flames. Thousands of gallons of water, from multiple hoses, were poured onto and into the hotel to cool the inferno, but sadly to no avail.

The west side of Central Avenue was crowded by on-lookers as the entire city seemed to pause in its tracks and witness the destruction and death throes of one of its treasured landmarks. Even though several people had to be rescued from their rooms by ladders, and dozens of others were hurried down hallways and steps to safety it is remarkable, not one of the 405 registered guests were injured. The same could not be said for the fire department. Young George Ford, a rookie fireman, was killed by a falling wall. Two veteran firefighters, John Wood and Butler Brown were also injured.[21]

But the hotel, described by many as the most beautiful in America, lay in ruins. The general manager of the hotel, W.E. Chester, urged the stockholders to rebuild and through his leadership and the citizens of Hot Springs who invested thousand of dollars, a newer and more imposing building was planned, this time on land it owned across the street.[22]

The town was barely over the shock of losing the Arlington when it was struck a double blow of flood and fire. Flooding on the downtown streets could be expected every few years. After all, the business district had been built in a valley with a large watershed area coming from the hills and mountains draining their waters into Fountain, Park and Whittington Avenue. These then poured into Hot Springs Creek running under Central Avenue. Normally the large conduit contained the average rains without any trouble. It was that twenty-five or fifty-year deluge that caused problems. When that occurred the tunnel filled with water to capacity and Central would become a raging river with no place for the water to go but into the business houses. The water would begin to build around the entrances to the underground conduit on Park and Whittington and gain depth and strength at the intersection of Fountain Street. Up until 1923, the worst floodings recorded were in 1871, 1910 and 1913. Of course, the conduit for Hot Springs Creek was not even in existence during the 1871 flood. It was just an open stream spanned by wooden foot bridges. During the night of May 27, 1871, rain fell steadily for several hours, filling the creeks and streams. Then "a terrific storm raged here this afternoon, and rain fell in torrents, swelling the brook running

---

[21] Ibid., 6 April 1923.

[22] Ann L. Greene, "The Arlington Hotel: An Arkansas Institution, 1875 - 1945, *The Record - 1996*. Records reflect that Bridget McLaughlin, who had tried to avoid any investment in the Sanitorium project, bought $1,000 stock in the new hotel.

through the place to an extent never before known or dreamed of. The flood has already swept away three buildings - the Hale House, the California House and the office of Dr. Ellsworth and is still rising."[23] All but one of the foot bridges were washed away. People in the downtown area huddled on the mountain side, waiting on the creek, now a raging river, to subside.

In 1913, after weeks of almost constant rain, the ground was completely saturated. A sudden downpour provided the impetus for flooding on Central Avenue, reaching a depth of three feet in some stores. Hot Springs was cut off from rail traffic as both the Iron Mountain and Rock Island had track washed away and it took several days to repair.

But that was puny in comparison to the flood occurring on May 14, 1923. Apparently forgetting the terrible destruction and suffering caused by the great fires of 1905 and 1913, one paper reported, "Hot Springs today gazed upon the greatest scene of devastation she has ever witnessed in all of her long series of disasters - the aftermath of the combined horrors of flood and fire from which the city suffered yesterday in the most crucial hours of her history."[24]

The *Sentinel-Record*, in an Extra Edition that same day, was almost as forgetful of the Spa's past miseries: "Flood and fire yesterday brought devastation to Hot Springs in greater proportion than this city, acquainted with big disasters, ever had met before."

With the three large basins, north, east and west, emptying the heavy rainfall onto Central Avenue, reports of water reaching depths of six to nine feet were common. Large sheets of asphalt paving were torn loose from its footing, and in some instances shifted about and slammed into businesses and light posts. Automobiles were floated away from their parking space, some deposited far down Hot Springs Creek. Two cars were pulled into the underground conduit of Hot Springs Creek, coming from either Whittington or Park, and were washed through its length and deposited in the stream's rocky bed near the Iron Mountain Railway yards, nothing was left but twisted metal and they were almost unrecognizable. Other vehicles were stacked on top of each other like cord wood near Spencer's Corner.

Many acts of heroism, bravery and narrow escapes were recorded. Mrs. Hirschall Herman, standing in a Central Avenue music store, saw an automobile floating by with a scared three year-old girl. The woman quickly waded into the raging water and pulled the child to safety.

Sheriff W.R. Downen and two unidentified men rescued a Mrs. Christianson, who could not escape her car as her hair was caught in the steering wheel. She had already lost consciousness and appeared dead when the three men waded into the water trying to save her. Downen, using his

---

[24] *New Era*, 15 May 1923.

pocket knife, cut her hair free. She was taken to Gross Mortuary where they used a lung-motor on her and the woman revived, and was taken to a hospital, suffering a fractured skull and many wounds and lacerations.[25]

A young businessman, Hill Wheatley, was in his car when he was swept down Central Avenue by the flood. When the automobile was washed into a light standard near Spencer's Corner, where the water was said to be nine feet deep, Wheatley decided it was time to "abandon ship." He grasped the pole and climbed to the first light cluster, getting one leg over it and clinging perilously for over two hours awaiting rescue.[26]

From his perch of safety above the swirling waters, Hill Wheatley could see dozens of cars being swept down Central and Valley (later Broadway). Two fireplugs were sheared off by floating automobiles. These emptied the water mains and added to the growing torrent. Heavy rain, thunder and lightning continued to hammer the Spa. A bolt of lightning lit up the sky and apparently struck wiring to the Grand Rapids Furniture at the corner of Spring and Central. In a few moments flames could be seen coming from the furniture store. The fire fed southward, destroying the Barker service station, fronting onto Valley, then Oliver-Finnie grocery store, the American Express office, Rosenthal shoe store, the Dixie Cafe, and the Marquette Hotel, all went up in flames.[27] Only the Citizens Bank Building remained undamaged in that block. The fire department reponded to the alarm but discovered such low pressure in the water mains, caused by the two broken plugs, they just dropped their drafting hoses into the water in the street and pumped it onto the fire.

Captain John Lovett of the Hot Springs Fire Department rescued a woman from one of the burning buildings. Carrying the woman to safety, he then lost his footing in the swift water and the current swept him down Valley Street until he struck a pole and was knocked unconscious. Fortunately, he was pulled to safety by fellow fireman Sam Brown.[28]

The downtown area was a sad sight to greet the eyes of citizens and visitors when light first broke on Tuesday morning, the day following the flood. The devastation and loss was unbelievable. Meeting quickly with the council's emergency committee, Mayor Harry Jones announced the city was hiring all available men to clear the streets and clean up the tons of debris.

Road paving contractor, George Nichols, assembled his "entire working crew, and nine teams of mules, and began clean up at 5:30 a.m. His action was voluntary and without cost to the city."[29] Many other men came dressed for

---

[25] *Sentinel-Record* - Extra Edition, 15 May 1923.

[26] *New Era*, 15 May 1923.

[27] There was no insurance coverage for flood damage at that time. The business which burned did have fire insurance.

[28] *New Era*, 15 May 1923. Also, *Sentinel-Record*, of the same date.

[29] Ibid.

work and with no expectation of remuneration. The business community began to sweep out the mud and debris from the stores and in two days many were back in operation.

Few cities in the nation have the resiliency or the determination to meet any disaster as Hot Springs, Arkansas. It has always risen from its ruin and destruction caused by calamities, time after time, and on each occassion, it has became and even greater city. It is a tribute to the people who have lived and spent their lives here. One might say "they were tried by fire and flood and they prevailed."

George Whittington
Attorney George Whittington's advice and guidance was treasured by both Leo P. McLaughlin and Verne S. Ledgerwood.

The administration of Mayor Harry A. Jones was rolling along so smoothly he had only one opponent in 1923, Dr. J.B. Shaw. Shaw, of the sixth ward, was from a pioneer family of the Spa, and was a very well-known physician practicing with Dr. E.R. Browning in the Thompson Building. He had served a couple of years as coroner.

Normally the sixth ward in Hot Springs had been conservative in its politics. Historically, it has voted against "sin and corruption;" against "whiskey and gambling," although it did have residents and supporters of those "vices." Dr. Shaw's announcement and statement to run for mayor was veiled in rhetoric, but the curtain was raised enough that he seemed to be conveying the message he supported an "open town." In speaking of his platform he said, "I think the majority of the people favor an administration with such a slogan, which if *properly worked out* will give us a wonderful city such as we could place before the people of the world in *connection* with our God-given healing waters and invites them to come here with the reasonably certainty that their sojurn here would be one of *mutual pleasure and profit.*"[1] [Italics ours] But, it was not his words alone that leads researchers to come to the conclusion of Shaw's liberal tendencies as he freely and openly admitted these in his campaign ads.[2] It was his associates and supporters who were "tagged" with the name liberals and who favored an open-town versus a closed-town, namely Leo P. McLaughlin and George Whittington.[3]

Mayor Harry Jones did not do any campaigning, leaving that up to friends and supporters. His Publicity Committee Chairman, E.H. Wootton, did an outstanding job of letting the citizens know what an active mayor they had. In a large advertisement, Wootton asked, "Who Is This Man Harry Jones?" He then proceeded to outline Jones' career from the time he came to Hot Springs as a very young man about the turn of the century and took a very modest job as stock-boy at the Waverly Hotel and how by hard work and "earnest endeavor," won the respect and admiration of all his associates and how he was able to become manager, then owner of the Majestic Hotel and had always worked for the upbuilding of Hot Springs. Many of Jones' good deeds and charities were cited. He had once paid rent and furnished groceries for "twenty destitute familes for three weeks," who were traveling by wagons and were stranded at Hot Springs." Further, he provided insurance protection at his expense for his 147 employees, a rarity for employers in those days.[4]

---

[1] *Sentinel-Record*, 31 January 1923,
[2] Ibid., 1 April 1923, p. 8.
[3] Ibid., 10 March 1925, p. 8.
[4] Ibid., 1 April 1923, p. 3.

In another full-page advertisement, Wootton gave figures to prove that through Jones' administration, the city deficit had been turned around and in only a year a profit was shown.[5]

When Harry Jones had announced for a second term for mayor, he said, "I first want to impress upon those interested that my motives are not actuated by any desire for political prestige or to further selfish ambitions, or for personal gain, but prompted only by ambition to further serve the city, the welfare of which means everything to me."

He outlined the accomplishments of the city during the past two years; was complimentary of his opponent; and concluded that he was too busy with the city's business and his own to campaign and the voters could judge for themselves if he had been a good steward of their trust.[6]

Several weeks before the election in April, Harry Jones became very ill. He was unable to leave his rooms at the Majestic. Many wondered if his situation compared to the ill-fortune of his predecessor, Dr. Jacob W. McClendon, who lived to see his victory, but was denied, by death, to serve as mayor. Fortunately, Jones did live to serve as mayor again. In a fairly close race, Jones defeated Shaw 1274-1116 votes.[7] While Shaw's loss was disappointing to him and his followers, the race was close enough to encourage him to try again in 1925. That race, too, was against Harry A. Jones and Robert B. Sigman, alderman from the sixth ward.

Again, Harry Jones did little campaigning and left activities of this nature up to his friends. And again, Jones was victorious, winning his third term. In that race Leo P. McLaughlin and George Whittington openly supported Dr. Shaw.[8] Jones swept every ward except the sixth, where both opponents resided.[9]

In that same election Verne Ledgerwood defeated M.S. Cobb for municipal court judge. Cobb also carried the sixth ward while Ledgerwood took the other six.

Jones' administration continued to make progress. Improvements were made in many areas of the city. Encouragement was given to any area wanting to set up an improvement district. The fire department was brought up to its highest standard, as of that time. Morale of city employees was high and workers could expect their pay checks on time.

It thus came as a shock to the city council at its meeting of February 1, 1925, when Mayor Harry Jones asked the city clerk Fred Fowler to read a prepared statement. In that statement Jones resigned as mayor. There were shouts of

---

[5] Ibid., 3 April 1923, p. 3.
[6] Ibid., 25 February 1923.
[7] Ibid., 4 April 1923.
[8] Ibid., 10 March 1925, p. 2.
[9] Ibid., 11 March 1925, p. 1.

"No, no," and "We won't accept it."

Alderman Lynn Howlett finally got recognized and put the situation in perspective. "This has come as a bolt out of the blue sky," he said. "I am familiar with the administration of Mayor Jones. No one in this council feels more keenly the severing of official relations with him than I do, but I know the sacrifices he has made. I believe there is not another man in Hot Springs who would have gone as far as Harry A. Jones has for the city he loves. I know his situation and I know what his medical advisers have told him. There are certain limits beyond which no man can go. I am going to move that his resignation be accepted, and I hope that in so doing my motive will not be misconstrued. I don't believe it will. The parting comes with the deepest appreciation for what he has done for this city and with the most regret that it be necessary. I move that the resignation be accepted."

Reluctantly, the council accepted Jones' resignation and elected Lynn Howlett to act as interim mayor.[10] The complication of heart disease, from which he suffered from for years, would bring the death of Harry Jones in January 1929.[11]

George McLaughlin was never accused of over-working himself. On the contrary, McLaughlin was a master of doing nothing. When work was to be done, George was never to be found. He was never a candidate for membership in any of the civic clubs, for those organizations required their members to work in times of drives or for worthwhile purposes. His brother Will was somewhat inclined, but did take a great interest in running his hardware store at Church and Malvern. He would put up newly-received stock and wait on customers, but when that was done he enjoyed sitting in his cane-bottom rocker and visiting with his drop-by friends. Their brother Leo was more energetic than either of his brothers as he attended municipal court, city council meetings and met with clients at his office. But, when real work was required, Leo, too, always had "urgent" business elsewhere.

A wise man once said you could take the laziest man alive and if you could ascertain what his interests were and put him to work on those, he would no longer be lazy. That was the way it was with George McLaughlin. He loved the game of baseball. He had admired the great ball players who had wintered and trained in Hot Springs--Babe Ruth and Tris Speaker of the Red Sox and Honus Wagner of the Pirates, and later Al Simmons, Jimmie Foxx and George Earnshaw of the Athletics. He would have loved to have been a professional ball player and live their seemingly carefree life. Oh, George played the game and he was good; just not good enough to play professionally. He had played on the Spa teams before the World War and also afterward. He had broken an

[10] Ibid., 2 February 1926.
[11] Ibid., 8 January 1929.

ankle sliding into a bag before the war and the old injury continued to trouble him. After the war the local team playing under the name of the Hot Springs Athletics assembled a strong team of very fine players. Earl Smith, a catcher, had been born at Sheridan but moved to Hot Springs and was scouted by the major league teams and played several years for the New York Giants and the St. Louis Cardinals. Rock Banski and Roy Gillenwater were on the team and later played in the high levels of the minors.

George McLaughlin, serving as team captain, played first base and in some ways equalled Smith, Gillenwater and Banski. In 1920, playing fifteen games, McLaughlin was second to Roy Gillenwater in hitting an average of .449, an impressive figure.[12] And the quality of their opposition was quite good, playing teams from Pine Bluff, Little Rock, Ft. Smith and even the Missouri Pacific Railroad All-Stars from the Munsey League in St. Louis.[13] While George hit at a high average almost every year he played he was not considered a heavy hitter and had very little foot speed. Also, he was only a mediocre fielder, averaging an error every two games. Feeling their "oats," the locals challenged the Little Rock Travelers of the Southern Association to a game at the end of their season. Traveler manager "Kid" Elberfield declined the challenge. The Spa Athletics then challenged the Southern Association's team that was playing the last game of the season at Little Rock. That brought attention from both the *Arkansas Gazette* and *Arkansas Democrat*.[14] The Travelers quickly relented, but insisted on playing a double-header instead of a single game. That was just in case the local team lucked out and won.

In what was described as the largest crowd in years at Ban Johnson Field at Whittington Park, the fans were treated to two fine ballgames, both won by the Little Rock Travelers. The AA team felt fortunate to escape Hot Springs with wins of 2-0, and 5-4.

When George McLaughlin wasn't playing baseball he tended to hang out around some of the cigar stores and pool hall. Even though this was in the middle of Prohibition, drinks could be purchased if one was known, and everyone was acquainted with George. He was a beer drinker and not a very good pool player. In fact, he was not even a very good beer drinker as he did not hold his alcohol very well. At times he became belligerent and obnoxious after a few drinks and wanted to fight and he was not a very good fighter, either, perhaps more of the bluff and bully type. When he would refuse to leave a club or pool hall, the police would be summoned. All of the city officers knew George and were aware he was the city attorney's brother. Generally they put him in the squad car and patrons of the club would believe

---

[12] *Sentinel-Record*, 16 September 1920, p. 3.
[13] Ibid., 4 September 1921, p. 2.
[14] Ibid., 14 September, p. 3.

he was being hauled off to jail, when in fact they just carried him home with the officers knowing he probably would be more severely dealt with by Bridget McLaughlin, his mother, than if booked and docketed at city hall. There were occasions, however when George would want to fight with others or the officers and he would be taken down to the jail and booked.[15]

Sometimes George would get into difficulties which would cast reflections on him or his family by the associates he met at the places he frequented. One such character was Hubert Coates.

Coates and been raised in and around Hot Springs, at least part of his early life. His parents, Albert Doran Coates and Madaline Etchervane had been married at the Spa on 3 April 1892.[16] His father died when Hubert was small, forcing his mother to take whatever kind of work she could get. Hubert had attended a few grades at Ramble School, but because of the lack of home discipline, he was left pretty much on his own and began to cut classes and finally dropped out of school altogether. Madaline and her son moved to an apartment over E.R. Bradley's Drug Store at 141 Central Avenue. The landlords, Sol Godwin, a long-time deputy sheriff, and his wife also lived in the building. Young Coates quickly found a great fascination in hanging around several of the pool rooms in the vicinity of their apartment.[17]

Whatever one thought of Hubert Coates in later years, he would have to be accorded the fact that he was one of the great pool hustlers in the country. He had learned his trade so well that by the time he had reached his early twenties, about the only pool player who could consistently defeat him was the great "Minnesota Fats." But pool was not his only interest. He had become a card sharp and expert poker player. He also was quite a good golfer, good enough to "hustle" some unsuspecting amateurs, who were always led to believe they were playing with a beginner or "duffer." In later years he would sometimes "team-up" with the legendary all time con-man of the century, Clarence Thomas, alias "Titanic" Thompson, who used to drop by the Spa on one of his hustling forays.[18] Coates had left Hot Springs sometime during the war and had become well-known in gambling circles in Kansas City, St. Louis and Detroit.

---

[15] Hot Springs City Jail Docket, 1 February 1923 and others. Judge Ledgerwood would allow George McLaughlin to plead guilty and fine him the minimum for that offense.

[16] Garland County Marriage Records, Book 3, p. 120.

[17] This was about 1914 1915, and Hubert Coates would have been about fifteen years-old.

[18] "Titanic" Thompson once suckered two men into betting $300 that he could not throw a thin-shelled English walnut from the sidewalk in front of the Arlington Hotel across Central Avenue onto the top of the Southern Club. Thompson slight-of-hand exchanged the walnut for one loaded with lead and easily lobbed it on top of the club to the astonishment of the two "suckers."

His reputation as a "sporting man" followed him wherever he went and he would need to make a quick "score" before being invited by the local police to leave town. Coates would periodically show up at Hot Springs every year or so and could be counted on to become engaged in some type of mishief. It seemed as if many of his activities were a bit on the "shady side."

In March of 1921, he became a suspect in a holdup of seventeen men in an illegal gambling operation on Cedar Street.[19] As the men were playing high-stakes poker and shooting dice, they were suddenly surprised by "five masked men" who battered in the door. Each bandit was carrying a new .45 automatic. The gamblers had not even had time to hide any of their money and over $10,000 in cash and about that much in diamonds and jewelry were taken.[20]

For a time the identities of the gamblers were unknown. A lucky break delivered one of the gunmen, Jack Thompson, into the hands of the police. He was carrying a "grip" with five new Colt .45 automatics, the guns believed to have been used in the robbery. From the "grilling" of Thompson, several names began to come out. One of those was the name of Hubert Coates. The police learned Coates had been one of the players and was believed to be the "inside-man;" the individual who was to warn the other five if things were wrong for the heist. The police were unable to "pin" any charges against Coates and he disappeared from town as soon as he was released from the questioning.

A year later, he showed up in Hot Springs with the Pine Bluff police department hot on his trail. They had a warrant for his arrest in connection with a robbery very similar to the one that had occurred at Hot Springs the year before on Cedar Street. In the one in the river city, on 4 June 1922 following a boxing match, a prominent Pine Bluff cotton buyer and insurance agent, A.N. Bloom, had invited several men to his home for a "party," which included gambling.[21] There were a total of twenty-four men inside the Bloom home, including Hubert Coates, and J.E. Briggs, a former Garland County deputy sheriff, and then the manager of one of H.W. Campbell's United Shows, a small carnival. "About midnight," the papers reported, "three men one of them masked, broke into the room and commanded those present to throw up their hands." Over $6,200 in cash plus a quantity of diamonds and jewelry were taken.

Investigating officers became suspicious of Coates and Briggs as being the "inside-men." Detectives from Pine Bluff arrived in Hot Springs on 12 June with a warrant for the arrest of Hubert Coates. Coates' mother's old landlord deputy Sol Godwin, was on duty at the Garland County Sheriff's office and

---

[19] Ibid., 9 March 1921, p. 1.
[20] Ibid.
[21] *New Era*, 13 June 1922, p. 1.

said he believed he knew where Coates could be found. Godwin and deputy Jim Floyd quickly located Coates at the Palace Pool Hall on Central Avenue and he was arrested. The Pine Bluff officers took the prisoner to that city for interrogation, but again were unsuccessful in making any robbery charges stick. Judge S.A. Miller, at Pine Bluff held the "evidence insufficient," and Hubert Coates was freed.[22]

Hubert Coates had an apartment in the Thompson Building and "was known as a man of leisurely habits," and was reported to be "mixing in society."[23] After being a suspect in the Cedar Street and Pine Bluff robberies, he was paid a visit by Police Chief Oscar Sullivan. Sullivan warned Coates against becoming involved in any type of gambling, con or fleecing operations in Hot Springs and possibly may have implied it would be better if Coates pursued his activities elsewhere. Again, Coates was not seen about Hot Springs for some time.

In early 1924 he returned to the Spa. It was later learned he had been in Oklahoma for a number of months and while there had become embroiled in an argument with a man while gambling and Coates had shot and killed him.[24] He had initially been charged with murder, however his plea of self-defense had been successful and he had been exonerated.

Coates appeared to be a very successful young man even though he had no job. He wore expensive clothes and jewelry and drove a large late model Cadillac sedan. Several local officers stopped Coates for speeding his vehicle about town. Police Department Fingerprint Clerk Jack Fry stated that "the chief had learned that Coates had been doing some gambling here, and had given him orders if it happened again he would be run out of town."[25] Thus, the bad blood existing between Coates and Sullivan, began to heat up, and Hubert began to carry a gun.

George McLaughlin was drawn to Hubert Coates like a moth to a flame and the two men were seen every night about town. George was impressed with Coates' free and wild style of living, his clothes and especially his large and powerful automobile, and the fact that he always seemed to have plenty of money to spend. They knew the places, although illegal, where they could get a drink and they drank until the wee hours of the morning.

After midnight of 14 April 1924, Coates and McLaughlin were sitting in the Cadillac on Central Avenue. They were parked just north of the Arkansas National Bank when they noticed a small roadster driven by a young woman pass by several times. Coates, who was a handsome man, always had an eye for

---

[22] *New Era*, 14 June 1924, p. 1.
[23] Ibid., 13 June 1922, p. 1.
[24] *Sentinel-Record*, 14 April 1924, p. 1.
[25] Ibid.

the ladies and smiled at the driver and waved. After a couple of trips by their parked car, the woman began to flirt back at Coates and as she turned her car onto Broadway, Coates started his vehicle and followed. The woman, Margaret James of Little Rock, pulled her car to the curb and parked near the rear entrance to Paul's Cafe, owned and operated by Paul and Pearl John. Before Coates could say anything to her she disappeared into the restaurant, where she had an appointment--or was it a liaison due to the lateness of the hour--with Chief of Police Oscar Sullivan, and informed him two men were following her.

Sullivan emerged from the restaurant and upon spotting Hubert Coates and George McLaughlin, became very angry and irritated. With clenched fists he started toward the two men.

Oscar Sullivan was a large and powerful man. He had such confidence in his own physical strength he sometimes forgot to be careful and prudent when approaching people who might be dangerous. Sullivan had never been known to have even drawn his pistol when apprehending suspected criminals. Later, according to Coates and George McLaughlin, the chief began to "abuse and hit Coates." As McLaughlin tried to explain to Sullivan they had followed the woman because she had flirted with them, Sullivan turned toward George, who was known to be a bully, but never a fighter, and George took flight and ran north on Broadway.

Sullivan turned back toward Hubert Coates, who was carrying a .45 automatic he had borrowed from an acquaintance, Richard "Dick" Lawrence. Coates would later testify Sullivan had drawn his weapon, however witnesses would state it was still in the officer's scabbard when he fell. Coates pulled the gun and began firing. Chief Oscar Sullivan was struck by three bullets, either one of two of the bullets would have been fatal, and the chief grabbed his chest and slowly sank to the sidewalk dead.[26] Hubert Coates stood for a few seconds staring down at the prostrate chief of police, then quickly jumped in his car and sped off. It probably was Coates' thought to flee the city, but he may have been fearful of being found by members of the local police force who were loyal to Sullivan. He veered off the beaten path and called Deputy Sheriff Garland Van Sickle, an acquaintance, using a telephone at a warehouse and offered to surrender. Van Sickle met Coates, who turned himself and the murder weapon over to him.[27]

Realizing he was in a difficult position, Coates quickly hired the best defense lawyers in Hot Springs, George Whittington and the firm of A.J. Murphy and Scott Wood. Bond was arranged and not wanting to risk running into any of Oscar Sullivan's friends bent on revenge, Coates wisely decided to leave town

---

[26] *Arkansas Gazette*, 15 April 1924, p. 1.
[27] *Sentinel-Record* - Extra Edition, 14 April 1924.

until the trial.[28]

While at Hot Springs he had met and been dating a young lady, Lavina Ellis. She was from a very prominent Hot Springs family and her father was a well-known physician. She was a very headstrong young woman and over the objections of her family she journeyed to Tulsa, Oklahoma, where she and Hubert Coates were married.

The murder trial was set, reset, then reset again and finally was scheduled for Garland County Circuit Court for 23 April 1925. Prosecuting Attorney W.G. Bouic "made a hard plea for conviction on any of the minor degrees of murder," but was unsuccessful. As seen before, Garland County juries, especially in cases before 1950, were not inclined to assess the murder penalty, except in the most heinous crimes. This one, was no exception.

When the jury freed Hubert Coates on the charge of murder, "relatives and close friends of the late chief of police were plainly disappointed he had been acquitted.[29] The verdict of not guilty voided the life insurance policy on the life of Chief Sullivan, since George Whittington had been able to convince the jury he had been the aggressor in the dispute. The insurance contract carried the provision, "if the officer meets death in an encounter in which he is the aggressor and not in performace of duty, the insurance is not in force."[30]

Coates and his "young wife returned to Tulsa, Oklahoma, following the trial." Their marriage was doomed to failure.[31]

At the time of the slaying of Chief Sullivan, Mayor Harry Jones was at Rochester, Minnesota seeking medical attention. His friends on the city council, out of concern for his health, did not notify him of the chief's death until his return. Detective William Brandenburg was promoted to chief of police.

Irene Dorthy McLaughlin was born at Hot Springs 28 February 1896 to John Henry and Bridget Russell McLaughlin and was the next youngest of their eight children.[32] As had her brothers and sisters, she had attended school in Hot Springs and graduated from Hot Springs High School. She and her

---

[28] Ibid., 26 March 1925.

[29] Ibid.

[30] Ibid.

[31] In February of 1943, Lavinia Ellis Coates Reed, was residing with her parents, Dr. and Mrs. Leonard Ellis, when their two-story house located on the Malvern Road, caught fire about 2:00 o'clock in the morning. Lavinia and her small son were sleeping on the second floor when the fire broke out. The youngster fled safely down the stairs, but Lavinia was trapped in her room and fell from the second floor window and onto traffic officer J.V. Ross. Lavinia Reed suffered an injured spine. *New Era, 9 February 1943.*

[32] There is a discrepancy as to Irene's birth date. 1910 Census Records indicate she was born in 1892; however, the 1920 Census and the Caruth Funeral Records indicate 1896, and are believed to be correct.

sister Stella were seldom seen outside of the McLaughlin home with the exception of attending St. Mary's Church on Sundays or on special occasions.

In the early 1920s she and Stella began attending baseball games at Whittington Park as their brother George played for the Hot Springs Athletics. George was captain of the team and played first base. Whether the two ladies were more interested in baseball or used the outing for a diversion in their otherwise hum-drum life is debatable.

At one of the games brother George was approached by an acquaintance, "Dick" Lawrence, who wanted an introduction to his sister, Irene. George was accommodating and Dick and Irene sat together. Before the game was over he had asked her for a date to go to the movies and she agreed.

Richard "Dick" Lawrence was about fourteen years older than Irene. He had come to Hot Springs shortly after the turn of the century, having served as a very young man in the Spanish-American War in Cuba with the16th Indiana Volunteers. His first job in the Spa was as a bookkeeper for J.W. Millmine Plumbing Company on Malvern Avenue. He roomed at 819 Central Avenue for several years, but changed his residence to a boarding house on Reserve after getting a job as clerk for the Superintendent of the Government Reservation.[33] When the United States entered World War I, Lawrence enlisted and was given the rank of lieutenant and was initially assigned to Camp Pike training recruits. Later, he went to France and rose to the rank of captain.[34] Upon his return to the Spa, he was promoted to manager and superintendent of the government free bath house on Spring Street. Lawrence seemed to resist his loneliness by involving himself with several local business clubs, especially the Elks, the Veterans of Foreign Wars and American Legion Club.

Richard Lawrence probably believed that meeting Irene might be the turning point in his life. Having been around Hot Springs for several years, undoubtedly he was aware that trying to court any of the McLaughlin girls would be a major undertaking--that undertaking being named Bridget. But Richard Lawrence was determined and he saw Irene every chance he got. When her mother, Bridget, learned of the romance, she began her crusade to break up the couple. She probably tried to persuade Irene that Richard was beneath her social status and no doubt pointed out the large age difference between the two. Irene could have used the argument that there had been quite a difference in her father's and mother's ages, and may have mentioned the fact that because of her mother's attitude there surely wasn't a line of suitors beating the path to their door to see her and she wasn't getting any younger. The final argument was used by Bridget in pointing out the religiou

---

[33] *Polk's City Directories, Hot Springs*, 1910, 1912 and 1917.

[34] *New Era*, 23 May 1925, p. 8.

barrier, the McLaughlin's being Roman Catholic and Lawrence being a weak Episcopalian. It was a constant harangue as Bridget continued to pressure her daughter to end the relationship with Lawrence. There is no evidence to suggest that she received any support from her sisters and brothers, Elizabeth, Stella, Will, Leo and George. Irene finally gave in and informed Richard Lawrence that she would be unable to see him anymore. Lawrence persuaded her to have one last date and hoped that their relationship might be saved. The two drove out the Little Rock Road and near Arbordale Springs parked. It is not known if in their desperation the two made a lover's pact to end their lives. It may be that Richard Lawrence was so distraught at the thought of losing Irene he decided to kill her and end his life, also, is unknown. At any rate, about 11:00 p.m. Richard, using the .45 Colt automatic he had loaned Hubert Coates and which had been used to kill Chief of Police Sullivan, shot and killed Irene McLaughlin.[35] The jacket jammed on the gun and did not eject the spent shell and Lawrence could not clear the weapon. Frustrated, leaving the car parked where the killing had taken place, Lawrence walked back into town and to his room at the Milwaukee Hotel. He had a second gun in his quarters and used it to kill himself.

Irene Dorothy McLaughlin was buried in the family plot in Calvary Cemetery. Richard Lawrence rests across the street, buried in the American Legion plot of Greenwood Cemetery.[36]

Strangely, in life, the two--Irene and Richard--had been separated by Bridget and her obssession that her children not marry, and in death by Third Street. One can only wonder if Bridget McLaughlin ever had any self incriminating thoughts as to her part in causing Irene's and Richard's death? Probably not, but we, of course, shall never know.

---

[35] *Ibid.* It was reported that following the trial of Hubert Coates, for the killing of Oscar Sullivan, Lawrence had reclaimed the gun from the police. He had testified as to the loaning of the gun to Coates.

[36] When the writer researched this item we discovered a discrepancy as to the date of the murder-suicide. From *Garland County, Arkansas Tombstone Inscriptions*, by Inez Cline and Bobbie Jones McLane, Richard L. Lawrence's date of death is reflected as May 7, 1925. Caruth Funeral Home Records indicate Miss IreneMcLaughlin died May 13, 1925. The *Sentinel-Record*, 25 May 1925 reads, "a double tragedy occurred yesterday."

Following Mayor Harry A. Jones' resignation in February 1925, his good friend and colleague, Lynn Howlett, owner and operator of a laundry and cleaning firm, served as interim mayor until an election could be held. Friends of Robert A. Jones (no relation to Harry A. Jones), persuaded him to run for the office and he was elected.[1]

Robert A. Jones was a long time resident of the Spa. His father, A.C. Jones had been engaged in the ice business for many years and had been quite successful. Robert grew up in the family business, becoming manager in 1915, and eventually taking his father's position as President. This was in an age before the home refrigerator and the ice-making business flourished with several plants being scattered around Hot Springs. Almost every home was equipped with an icebox which was dependent upon ice being delivered to the home at least twice a week. It was about the only means of preserving and keeping meat, milk and butter fresh. Patrons seldom forgot to hang out their ice-card, a heavy paste board square with quadrants giving the amount of ice needed, 10, 15, 25 or 50 pounds. Ice wagons and later trucks could be seen on every street about Hot Springs up to about 1950, when most homes had self ice-making refrigerators.

Robert A. Jones and his wife Susie were prominent in Hot Springs society circles. He took the office of mayor with everyone knowing he was a republican serving in a democratic majority city. He was considered to be a progressive individul and had been quite instrumental in leading the "fight" to get the Little Rock highway paved. His tenure was rather low-key, making no changes in the department heads. Perhaps the benchmark of Robert Jones' administration was the installation of a complete new shift of sixteen firemen, raising the department's ranking with the Fire Underwriters Rating Bureau and reducing every property owner's insurance.[2]

The local democratic organization voted to hold a primary election for mayor in December 1926. The winner would face any opposition in April 1927. Winning the Democratic Primary without opposition was a young businessman, Sidney M. Nutt.[3] The *Sentinel-Record* wrote, "The tribute was one that came to Mr. Nutt because of recognized ability as a successful business man and leader in community work." And this was true, he really was a very successful business man.

---

[1] *Sentinel-Record*, 6 April 1926.

[2] The writer's father, Odus E. Allbritton, was one of the sixteen men who went to work on Jan 1, 1926. He died in 1993 and was the last of the men who went to work that day. He retired from the Hot Springs Fire Department in 1947 and served as Chief of the Malvern Fire Department for twenty-six years.

[3] *Sentinel-Record*, 8 December 1926.

Sidney M. Nutt
Businessman Sidney Nutt won the Democratic nomination for mayor in December 1926 and was opposed by Independent Leo P. McLaughlin in the April 1927 election. Nutt lost to McLaughlin in what was termed the "dirtiest" election in the Spa's history.

Nutt had been born at Fordyce, Arkansas, 7 March 1886. Only eighteen-ears old, he had graduated from the St. Louis College of Pharmacy in 1904. he following year he came to the Spa and bought an interest in the Jackson harmacy.

Sidney seemed uninterested in the drug and pharmacy business and roadened his business scope. He became involved in the movie industry, uilding the Central Theatre in 1910 and later the elaborate Princess Theatre n downtown Hot Springs.[4] He became enamored in the up and coming era f the automobile and opened agencies for Overland, Buick, Dodge, and ackard automobiles. For several years he was the franchise dealer for Goodyear tires and accessories. Nutt became involved in the banking business nd met and married Harriet Johnson, daughter of Ed Johnson, President of he Como Trust Co.[5]

When Sidney Nutt won the Democratic primary unopposed he had the

---

[4] The first Central Theatre was constructed at 618 Central Avenue and Sidney Nutt ater moved it to a location in the 1000 block of Central and it became the New Central Theatre. he old location became the Paramount Theatre, next door for many years to the S.H. Kr ess o.

[5] D.Y. Thomas, *Arkansas and Its People, Vol. IV*, New York, 1930, pp. 146-147.

support of most of the business community and really did not expec
opposition at the city election scheduled in April 1927. He believed the Apri
vote would be merely a confirmation or rubber-stamp approval of hi
democratic nomination.

But as usual, when things seem to be going well, difficulties seem to follov
or appear suddenly. There was no exception for Sidney M. Nutt.

Municipal Judge Verne Ledgerwood had a close personal acquaintance witl
Sidney Nutt and referred to him as "a fine gentleman" and had supported an
voted for him in the December primary.[6] But Ledgerwood had a concern an
that concern was Chief of Police William "Bill" Brandenburg. For som
reason, the two men did not get along very well. Ledgerwood was also awar
that City Attorney Leo P. McLaughlin and Brandenburg did not see eye-to-ey
on various problems involving the city. The municipal judge hoped Sidne
Nutt would appoint a new chief of police in April and approached him on th
matter. Much to his surprise Sidney Nutt told Ledgerwood it was his intentio
to reappoint William Brandenburg, telling Ledgerwood, "Verne, I think Bi
has done a credible job and morale seems to be high on the force."[7]

The judge asked Nutt to reconsider the appointment and told th
democratic nominee that in his opinion the police force needed a goo
cleaning. But Sidney Nutt was unyielding and said Brandenburg would be hi
appointee.[8]

Ledgerwood inquired, "Sidney, I'm afraid there will be a loud hue and cr
is that your final word?"

"It is," replied Nutt.

With that refusual, the course of Hot Springs, its business economics an
its political history would be changed forever. Municipal Judge Ledgerwoo
left the meeting intent on creating some opposition for Sidney Nutt an
already had the individual in mind.[9]

He met with George Whittington and explained the situation to him. Th
two agreed Leo P. McLaughlin might be willing to run against Sidney Nutt i
the city general election in April. The two met with McLaughlin and Georg
Whittington came right to the point. "Leo, we want you to run against Sidne
Nutt in April. We believe enough opposition can be generated against Sidne
Nutt that you can win."

Leo McLaughlin was not totally surprised by the request. For some time h
had wanted to run for mayor. Even on his return trip home, at the end of th

---

[6] LAT, Ledgerwood.

[7] Orval E. Allbritton, *The Record - 1998*, "The Fire at City Hall: Accident or Arson,
10.

[8] *Sentinel-Record*, 31 January 1927.

[9] LAT, Ledgerwood.

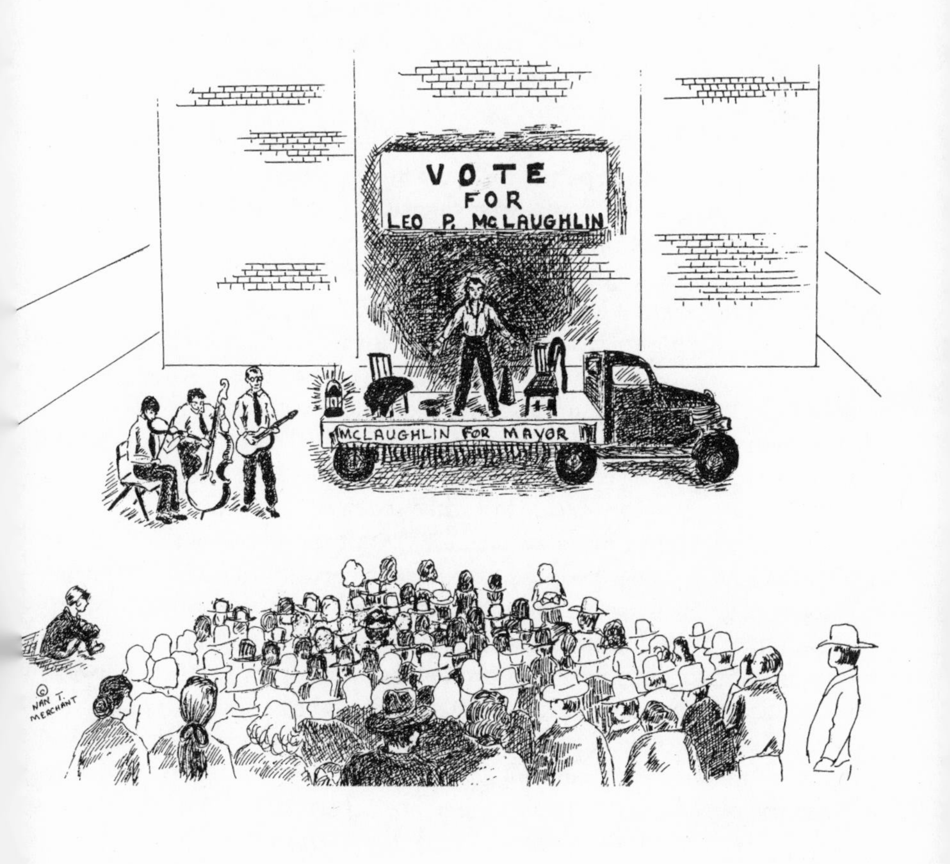

Leo P. McLaughlin was unmatched in local circles as a speaker. As he "heated up," off would come the coat and tie, then, rolling up his sleeves, he would "flail" his opponents.

war in France he had confided to Alfred Brooks his desire to run for mayor. He told Brooks he had some ideas for the City of Hot Springs he would like to try out. Others were aware of the fact that he coveted the office. However he had been hesitant and some doubt lingered in his mind as to whether the voters would approve him for the top municipal post. There were those around who still blamed him for the city losing its opportunity to gain the sanatorium project. Others looked on Leo as being a "slacker" in resisting the draft and his attempt to evade going to France.

And another doubt was bound to exist. Sidney Nutt, because of his business skills and success, was looked on as "the boy wonder" of his day.[10] Leo realized Nutt was supported by many of the pioneer families of the community. And certainly, Leo knew he would be unable to match up with Nutt in financing his campaign.

Leo expressed his concerns to Ledgerwood and Whittington. Whittington, sensing a hesitancy on the part of McLaughlin said, "Leo, we know you would like to run for mayor and now is your chance. If you want to run with the big dogs, you've got to get off the porch."

McLaughlin replied, "Just give me a couple of days to see what support I have, and in the event it looks possible, I agree to run."

To gain the support necessary for his race for mayor, Leo McLaughlin put out the word of a meeting at the Garland County court house. A considerable number of people showed up for the meeting--Leo's estimate was "more than 200." A substantial number of the group represented the community which was in favor of opening up the city. McLaughlin allowed "a free discussion of local conditions, and (he) decided to make the race."[11]

As usual, McLaughlin made the promise, "At the onset I want the people to understand that I do not propose to indulge in personalities or mud-slinging of any sort. If such tactics are pursued, it will be at the instance of the opposition."[12] Nutt followed suit promising to "take the high road" and refrain from mud slinging. The promises meant nothing. In just a few days both political camps began to hurl accusations toward each other.

Verne Ledgerwood told Leo P. McLaughlin, "I will write your ads and support you in any way I can. All I ask is that if you win I be permitted to appoint the police chief and select the police department."[13]

As soon as the announcement was made the *Sentinel-Record* saw its duty to

---

[10] "Life and Times of Leo McLaughlin," taped winterview with Jimmy Dowds, 24 July 1980. Hereinafter cited as LAT, Dowds. Jimmy Dowds was an accountant and at one time was a business partner in some of Sidney Nutt's ventures.

[11] *Sentinel-Record*, 27 February 1927, p. 10.

[12] Ibid.

[13] LAT, Ledgerwood.

support Sidney Nutt, the democrat nominee and pointed out "The administration of political affairs in Hot Springs within recent years has passed from the professional politician to the control of business men."

Further, it cited the state democratic governing body's rules and penalities for those running or voting outside the party's cloak of safety. "The State Democratic Central Committee a short time ago in session affirmed one of its rules, in effect that any person who had publicly supported or voted for any independent or republican candidate, as against a democratic **nominee**, would be prevented from voting in a primary election for two years."

Then the newspaper brought home the point, "Comes into the picture Leo Patrick McLaughlin, all of his adult years an office holder, much of the time through grace of democratic primaries, and declares himself a candidate for mayor as opposed to the regular nominee for mayor."[14]

Leo P. McLaughlin fired back and took to task the *Sentinel-Record* in a paid advertisment in the *New Era* entitled "Consistency Thou Art A Jewel." He called to attention an editorial published in the *Sentinel-Record* 3 October 1926, in which the newspaper excused the selection of Robert A. Jones, a republican, by the democratic committee to run for mayor and the newspaper had supported the committee's action on the basis, "The circumstances preclude that Robert A. Jones, present mayor **can be considered in the primary, because of the partisanship variance."**

But Leo apparently had forgotten his own appeal to the voters in 1916 as he stated when opposed by an independent candidate for the position of city attorney, "I was nominated by the Democratic Party at a fair primary and **it is the duty** of every democrat to support me unless he has evidence that I secured the nomination unfairly."[15]

At first, Sidney took only a cursory view of McLaughlin's entry into the mayoral race. Nutt felt secure in the knowledge he had won the democratic nomination without opposition, which was usually tantamount to election in Garland County. Why, Nutt even had the support and endorsement of the republican leaders in the city.[16] What in the world did Leo P. McLaughlin have in mind running against the democratic nominee? There had been very few candidates for political office who had run on the independent ticket who had been successful, and only Dr. J.W. McClendon had been elected to more than one term as an independent. McClendon, of course, had always been the exception!

However, it was only two or three weeks until Sidney Nutt and his close friends realized they were in for a "dog-fight." They began in earnest to

---

[14] Ibid.

[15] Ibid., 2 April 1916.

[16] Ibid., 3 April 1927, p. 3.

organize support for the nominee.

Within days the mayor's race had developed into the dirtiest political race in the city's entire history. The two sides mobilized, drew their lines into position, and began to bring their heavy artillery up and the entire City of Hot Springs became their battleground. The fight was carried from city hall to the court house; from downtown into the suburbs. Political posters were nailed to trees and telephone poles, handbills and pasteboard emory finger-nail files, hand-fans and combs urging the citizens to vote were passed out. No area was left untouched, no voter uncontacted.

The McLaughlin camp, initially consisting of Leo, Verne Ledgerwood, and George Whittington, knew they could count on the support of such stalwarts of the gambling community as Sam Watt and William S. Jacobs, owners and operators of the Southern Club and Jacob's partner in the Ohio Club, William P. Klothe. Louis Larsen, Gordon Henderson and George Pakis, owners and operators of the Blue Ribbon Club at 732 Central and Ben Harrison of the Citizens Club at 740 Central, and their employees were counted on for support. At that time these clubs were little more than speak-easies with backroom gambling. Ed B. Mooney, a large contractor, Fred Fowler, city clerk, Herbert "Dutch" Akers, who had a detective agency, and Joe Wakelin, who had worked at the Maurice Bath House and also as a private detective and a deputy sheriff at times, were counted in the McLaughlin fold.[17]

There were a few men who openly supported Leo McLaughlin who did not have the best of reputations. In fact, in some instances they were just downright shady. But, a vote was a vote!

Ben Murray, a former deputy sheriff had been involved, charged and tried, but not convicted, in the killing of Oscar Chitwood, a prisoner in the Garland County Court House in 1910.[18] Also, he had narrowly escaped charges when a couple of stolen automobiles had been traced to him in the Housley theft ring. It was also known that sometime prior to Tom Slaughter killing Deputy Row Brown, Slaughter had delivered two stolen vehicles to Ben Murray, who had difficulty in disposing of them.[19] Murray had also been involved in some bootlegging business and only by the skill of his attorney did he escape the penitentiary.

Then there was Melvin Lockett. In 1917 he had been charged and tried for enticing two fifteen year-old girls into his car and taking them outside the city for immoral purposes. After a trial, which the newspapers called "sensational,"

---

[17] Ibid.

[18] *Sentinel-Record*, 29 1910. Murray, a Chief Deputy, and temporary deputy appointee, John Rutherford, were charged in the killing, but were able to convince a jury they were not guilty. No others were ever tried for the crime.

[19] Ibid., 2 October 1917, 3 October 1917, and others.

Lockett was acquitted. That was in the day and age when the defense attorneys were permitted to badger and harass young witnesses and the two young girls wilted before the skillful attack of the lawyers. However, Lockett was not so fortunate in avoiding the penalty of the law when he was convicted of an assault on a young woman on West Mountain the following year. He appealed the guilty verdict to the Arkansas State Supreme Court and lost. He was sentenced to three years in the state penitentiary.[20] Lockett could not stay out of trouble and shortly after he emerged from his prison sentence he was suddenly arrested by Sheriff Brad Smith for operating a whiskey still on Cedar Brook in Union Township. It was called the "most complete 300 gallon capacity plant ever located in the state."[21]

It appeared at first, McLaughlin would be unable to match up with Sidney Nutt and his supporters. After all, Nutt had won the democratic primary and had the support of the party. He boasted of having the majority of business interests on his side. He had the endorsement of civic clubs, women's groups and educational leaders. Several union labor leaders had come out on his side, and many of the churches openly supported Sidney Nutt.[22]

Endorsements from the democratic office holders in the court house and members of the democratic committe were forthcoming. Circuit Judge Earl Witt; Prosecuting Attorney W.G. Bouic; County Judge Charles Davis; Garland County Sheriff Garland P. Vansickle; Chancellor William Duffie; Tax Collector George P. Leatherman; County Clerk Trager Freeman; State Senator G.D. Dillard; State Representative C.H. Dodson, and others took out large advertisements endorsing Sidney Nutt.[23] Hot Springs Mayor Robert A. Jones, a republican, came out openly in support of Nutt.[24] It seemed as if he would be a shoo-in for mayor.

The campaign moved from downtown to the neighborhoods. Large rallies were held at the end of the carlines of Park Avenue and at Hobson and Sixth Street. The Whittington Junction at Central Avenue saw both candidates speaking to hundreds of people. Broadway and Malvern and Malvern and Grand brought out a thousand or more citizens. Fagan Park on Ash Street was filled to capacity to hear Leo P. McLaughlin, most of these were from the second ward. The City Hall Auditorium was over flowing when Sidney Nutt spoke.

Both candidates used a flatbed trailer as a rostrum or platform when speaking to crowds outdoors. Sidney Nutt was only a mediocre speaker at

---

[20] Ibid., 6 November 1918, p. 8.
[21] Ibid., See 16 and 17 September 1920.
[22] Ibid., 3 April 1927.
[23] Ibid., 5 April 1927, p. 3.
[24] Ibid., 1 April 1927.

best. Nutt depended on some of his supporters who were better speakers than he to get his message across. One of the best in campaigning for Nutt was W.H. Martin, a well respected lawyer and former U.S. Attorney.

In campaigning, Leo McLaughlin was the best. He always seemed comfortable before a crowd, in fact he seemed to thrive on it. Both campaigns put on a show. Drawings were held for bags of groceries donated by various stores. A hand-crafted leather belt or certificate for a shirt or pair of shoes were given to encourage people to attend. Some music, generally by a small string-band, was provided to "warm-up" the crowd. Some evenings there would be a kerosene lantern burning brightly at one end of the platform, as the crowd arrived, but Leo never seemed to be aware of it.

When McLaughlin's turn came the crowd became attentive. Always dressed immaculately in a fresh-pressed tailored suit with a lapel handkerchief or flower, Leo strode from one end of the platform to the other, as if to give everyone a chance to see him. He would start off slowly, perhaps joking with some acquaintance in the crowd by telling him, "The woman with you tonight is much more attractive than the woman I saw you with last night." There would be loud laughs at the man's discomfort and the wife's always steeley glance at her husband, but she probably enjoyed the flattery and moment of attention. McLaughlin would start off slowly with hand gestures to emphasize the point he wanted to make, then gradually his voice and actions would increase until he was waving his arms. Off would come the coat. Then, symbolic that he was ready to go to work, he would roll up his shirt sleeves a turn or two. By this time many of his supporters were worked up to a fever pitch. Next he would hurl questions at his audience: "Do you want a mayor who will work for you?" The answer always came back as a chorus, "Yes, we do."

"Do you want more streets oiled, graded and paved, more water mains and sewer lines laid?" Again, only louder, "Yes, we do."

"Do you want someone as mayor who can operate the city on its present income?" "Yes, we do," came the answer.

"And who do you believe can do these things for you?"

And led by some of his staunchest supporters, the answer was thundered back, "Leo McLaughlin, Leo McLaughlin."

McLaughlin never came right out and said if he was elected that the gambling clubs would be reopened, he was too smart for that. He would tell the story that a few nights before, he had came out of the Arlington Hotel about 8:00 o'clock and noticed how everything was closed and how deserted the street was. He would hold his arms as if he was shooting a rifle and say,

"I could have emptied a Winchester down Central and not hit a soul."[25] He would go on and tell the crowd that the city had to provide more excitement and better entertainment for our visitors. He never spelled it out as to what kind of entertainment he had in mind--most of the crowd knew he was referring to gambling. As he reached this point in his speech, the lantern, left unnoticed, suddenly flickered its last rays and went out.[26] He would then turn toward the lantern and call attention to it. "Hot Springs is just like that lantern. As long as it has fuel it burns brightly, but let it run out of oil, the light goes out. Folks, if we don't provide the entertainment our visitors want and crave, the beacon light of our city which shines out inviting people to come and bathe in our mineral springs and partake of our pleasures will dim and go out. Without those visitors, jobs will become few and times will get more difficult."

Sidney Nutt's rallies held in the City Auditorium and at the large intersection of Broadway and Malvern Avenues brought out huge crowds of people. Several of his close friends, W.H. Martin, County Judge Charles H. Davies and Circuit Judge Earl Witt, each spoke for him and urged the voters to get out and go to the polls.

When McLaughlin turned his attack on some of Nutt's supporters instead of the nominee, the Nutt camp came back strong. They attacked McLaughlin's war record, calling him a "slacker" pointing out how he had tried to evade the draft and even after he had been inducted into the army he had tried to avoid going overseas by malingering in the base hospital. They even published an affidavit by Dr. Loyd Thompson attesting to the findings of the medical board at Camp Beauregard that Leo Patrick McLaughlin had been malingering.[27]

The McLaughlin camp responded by securing the support of eighteen Garland County men who had had some contact with McLaughlin, either in camp, or overseas during the war. The men placed an advertisement in the papers, stating: "We know that Leo P. McLaughlin made a good soldier and are proud of the opportunity given us to vote for him for mayor of Hot Springs."[28] It was signed by some good men including Joe M. Harmon, owner and operator of Palace Cleaners and Dyers; Cecil McClard, grocer and operator of a cotton gin in South Hot Springs; Everette Jones, manager of the Alhambra Bath House; Robert Larkin Allbritton, motorman for the Hot Spring Street Railway (author's uncle); Fred Mott, mechanic at Murphy Bros.,

---

[25] LAT, Dowds.

[26] Will McLaughlin devised the lantern trick for his brother, Leo. He trimmed the wick and timed the fuel so that it would burn out near the end of the speech. Leo apparently kept an eye on the flickering light and knew just when to bring the subject of the lantern into his talk. The writer's father advised McLaughlin had several ways to work this.

[27] *New Era*, 29 March 1927.

[28] *Sentinel-Record*, 13 April 1927, p. 2.

and others.

When McLaughlin began to "bend the truth" a little, the election really heated up. He attacked the friends and supporters of Sidney Nutt. He suggested to his followers Nutt had so many businesses and enterprises he planned to hire ex-city manager George Belding to run the city. Belding immediately denied the story saying he had never been offered such a proposition and were it true, he was not interested.[29] W.H. Martin, as an attorney representing the telephone company, was portrayed as wanting to raise all the telephone rates in the city. This, too, was denied.[30]

In a speech given in the second ward, Leo promised the black voters, "In the event of my election I will abolish the bloodhounds." This was a baseless promise as the city of Hot Springs did not own any tracking dogs and there were no records it ever had. This was pointed out by the *Sentinel-Record*.[31]

Probably Leo P. McLaughlin was hoping that an event he had been involved in five years before had been forgotten or overlooked. It wasn't, and was dragged out to "refresh the memories of the voters."

In 1922, an elderly and ill man, Thomas Cosgrove of Ellsworth, Kansas, had arrived in Hot Springs hoping his health might be improved and his life prolonged. Cosgrove had no friends or acquaintance here and needed help in handling his affairs. He sought advice from St. Mary's Church and the priest suggested Cosgrove contact Leo P. McLaughlin, an attorney and parishioner of the church. The ill man trustingly went to Leo McLaughlin and explained his need. McLaughlin learned Cosgrove, before leaving Kansas, had made a will leaving all his property, including $45,000 in liberty bonds to a Catholic orphanage at Abilene, Kansas. Cosgrove wanted McLaughlin to look after him in his last days and pay his bills. Whether he was cognizant of the contents of the agreement McLaughlin drew up and which Cosgrove susposedly signed, is quite debatable. The agreement stipulated the attorney would use Cosgrove's money for his welfare and care, and in exchange McLaughlin would receive any money or bonds left when the Kansan died. Cosgrove passed away a very short time later.

After Cosgrove's body was shipped to his home for burial, Leo produced his agreement and made claim for the remaining $42,500. When St. Joseph Orphans Home in Abilene learned of their benefactor's passing, "they came forward with the will." Leo P. McLaughlin refused to budge, perhaps thinking the distance between Abilene and Hot Springs might be a discouragement and determent to the Orphans Home and if it sought redress in the local chancery court they would be playing in McLaughlin's ballpark. The attorney

---

[29] Ibid., 2 April 1927.

[30] Ibid.

[31] Ibid., 1 April 1927.

representing the home was too clever to be pulled in to that situation-- he filed an action in Federal Court suing Leo P. McLaughlin. It is not known if this action came unexpectedly to Leo, but it appears he was uncertain what the legal outcome would be with his "agreement" versus the "will." Perhaps fearing the decision of the court, McLaughlin offered a compromise settlement to the home--each take half the money. The home and its attorney considered the proposal and decided to take McLaughlin's offer rather than spend a considerable sum of money trying to recover on a case with the outcome being unclear and uncertain.

There had been little publicity about the case, but word quickly spread and Leo came out appearing "greedy" and somewhat tarnished in taking money away from an orphanage sponsored by Leo's own church denomination.[32]

As a last shot, Sidney Nutt told his audience, "The campaign is nearing an end. There is a big stake involved for the professional politicians. Leo Patrick and Ledgerwood are betting the works for complete domination of the city hall. Business versus professional politics is in the balance and the people are the trial jury."[33]

One evening shortly before the election, Leo invited the crowd listening to him to attend a meeting at the auditorium the following night as he intended to "uncork something that'll rock the community to its foundation." The Nutt camp scrambled about to ascertain what McLaughlin's sensational revelation was to be. They quickly discovered the opponent's camp intended to have with them Wallace Fulton to alledge brutality on the part of the Hot Springs Police Department and possibly discredit Sidney Nutt in reappointing William Brandenburg as chief of police. Fulton and two other men had acquired the name of "The Blue Overall Gang," and had been arrested and charged for a series of highway robberies of the occupants of more than twenty cars in January and February, 1927. The robberies had been daring and had caused quite a lot of attention and had posses from Garland, Hot Spring and Clark counties scouring the hills around Bismarck for the bandits.[34] Through good police work of Prosecuting Attorney W.G. Bouic, Sheriff Garland P. Van Sickle and deputies Jim Floyd and Marion Anderson, two of the highewaymen, Wallace Fulton and Merle Moorehead, were apprehended. At first the two men denied their involvement even though items of jewelry taken from the victims were discovered in their possession. Under "stiff questioning," the two men confessed and several of the victim's identified the culprits. Because the crimes were committed in Hot Spring County, jurisdiction rested there and he

---

[32] *New Era*, 29 March 1927.

[33] *Sentinel-Record*, 1 April 1927.

[34] Ibid., 2 and 5 February 1927. For complete story see Orval E. Allbritton, "The Blue Overall Gang," *The Record - 1999.*

trial would be in Malvern. The prosecutor for that district was a young fledging lawyer, John L. McClellan, and he used the case as a stepping stone to the U.S. House of Representatives and later to the U.S. Senate. He was successful in obtaining a "guilty verdict," on both men. During the trial Wallace Fulton testified that he and Merle Moorehead had been subjected to "third-degree" treatment to gain their confessions by both the Garland County Sheriff's office and the Hot Springs Police Department.[35]

To counter the alledged beatings the State produced several witness who had been in attendance at the initial questioning, all of whom denied any brutal tactics as being used. These included W.G. Bouic, Prosecuting Attorney; Earl Witt, Garland County Circuit Judge; Jim Floyd, Chief Deputy Sheriff and Hot Spring County Sheriff Tom Fisher.[36]

When the Sidney Nutt camp learned of Fulton's connection to McLaughlin's boast he would "rock the community" with some startling news, they bought a large advertisement and entitled their rebuttal, "McLaughlin's Minnesota Bootlegger," informing the public what they had learned concerning Fulton. They set forth the fact Fulton's own physician, Dr. R.A. Simpson had examined Wallace Fulton following his arrest and interrogation and he "did not find any evidence that Fulton had been abused."[37]

Fulton, who was out of jail on bond waiting on an appeal before his imprisonment, was at the meeting, but Leo McLaughlin and his advisers decided not to use him as his story had been revealed and he had been somewhat discredited.

When that occurred, the Sentinel-Record scorched McLaughlin with the report: "Leo Patrick's great, sensational community-rocking expose' was a 'dud.' It didn't go off, for the very good reason he had nothing to shoot. He fooled his audience. He baited them and failed to make good. He told them nothing new whatever, and his entire speech was a defense of his conduct in taking the $45,000 in bonds that had been willed to an orphanage in Kansas of his own religious faith, of giving up half the bonds when sued in federal court; of his war record, when he failed to volunteer and fought the draft, and of his tirade against the community builders of the city who had rallied to the support of the democratic nominee, Sidney M. Nutt."[38]

The *Sentinel-Record*, believing it stood with the majority of the voters and on the side of the community-minded nominee, had spoken its piece and made

---

[35] *Malvern Daily Record*, 4 March 1927.

[36] *Malvern Times Journal*, 24 March 1927.

[37] *Sentinel-Record*, 3 April 1927. In June 1925 Wallace Fulton had been sentenced to two years for burning his neighbor's barn. While he was being searched for that arrest, the policeman quickly jerked his hand out of Fulton's pocket, where the accused kept a live, three-foot snake. He had also been involved in illegal bootlegging operations before coming to this area.

[38] Ibid., 5 April 1927.

its stand. It had come down hard on the insurgent independent, who was circumventing the rule of politics. The repercussions however, could not be forseen at that time, but the proud daily would be forced to bow before McLaughlin and his administration for twenty years.

In a city where many of its people had been brought up aware gambling had been a way of life for seventy-years, wagers between the supporters of the two candidates became inevitable. It became so widespread that finally the two camps came to an agreement and a system for handling the betting was established. They selected Claude Marsh of the Citizens Bank to keep the records and hold the bets. One man, not having cash at the time, mortaged his cotton gin for $700, and bet on Leo McLaughlin. By the time the election rolled around Marsh had been entrusted with bets totaling over $50,000.[39]

By election morning all the venom of both sides had been spewed out. Everyone was tired, but eager for the decision to be reached--who would serve Hot Springs as mayor for the next two years?

The issues were plain and simple. Sidney Nutt and his followers wanted to continue a business-like approach to the management of the city and keep the town in a steady, slow-growth mode. Leo P. McLaughlin intended, if he won, to open the town wide-open to gambling and all that it would bring. There were no political polls of the voters at that time, but everyone knew it would be a very close election.

Because there had been rumors afloat for days before the election that there would be attempts to "steal" the election, warnings were issued by both Circuit Judge Earl Witt and Prosecuting Attorney W.G. Bouic that violators would be prosecuted. Garland County was not new to the idea of "cheating a little-bit at the ballot box."

In 1906 there had been a political contest for Garland County sheriff between Gus Buchanan and the incumbent, Sheriff R.L. "Bob" Williams. Williams was declared winner in that race, but Buchanan contested the vote. When the ballot boxes were brought into court for a recount the ones from the Sixth ward and Hot Springs Township, where Buchanan was strongest, did not have ballots, only burlap bags. Williams continued to resist Buchanan's claim to the office but after eighteen months of legal hasseling, the Arkansas State Supreme Court awarded the office to Buchanan, who had only a few months left on his term to serve. It would forever be known as the "gunnysack election."[40]

In a more recent election, in 1920, voting improprieties were alledged, involving Sheriff W.R. Downen and two supporters. It seemed that Downen's

---

[39] LAT, Ledgerwood.

[40] *The Torrid Twenties*, published by the Hot Springs Junior Chamber of Commerce Auxiliary, 1951, p. 41.

two friends got carried away in purchasing poll taxes illegally for over sixty people with several of them voting in an election. In a trial lasting three days Downen was acquitted of wrong doing.[41] A previous companion trial found one of Downen's supporters guilty.[42]

On the day of the election, people were seen hurrying about and lining up at the polls to cast their votes. The mayor's race was the big item and there was only one other city office being strived for and that was one of the aldermanic positions.

Only a few untoward incidents occurred, mostly of minor significance. One though, may have had a large impact on the election. Sidney Nutt would later tell his business partner he had learned that on election day a train had backed into the Iron Mountain depot and about one hundred black men, reportedly from Malvern, Arkadelphia and Prescott, alighted and wanted directions to the "second ward polls?" Susposedly, each was carrying a poll-tax receipt, which was necessary in Arkansas to vote and there is no record they were denied the privilege of voting.[43]

The board of election commissioners was composed of Charles Goslee, Richard M. Ryan and Hamp Williams. They selected the Community Bank and Trust Company, located across Ouachita Avenue from the court house, as site for the tabulation of the vote. A large chalk board was set up for the recording of the vote and in order that the supporters of the candidates could keep track of the progress of their respective leaders. As the results would be chalked up on a newly-arrived box a cheer would go up from half of the watchers and a groan from the other side. The next box might cause the same cheers and groans just opposite from the previous result.

With only the Second and Fifth wards unreported, Nutt led by a mere four votes over his opponent. The Fifth ward boxes arrived and gave a big boost to Nutt with a plurality of 146 votes. In an election so close this seemed to be an unbeatable lead, but disaster was about to strike the Nutt camp.

The last reporting boxes were from McLaughlin's home ward--the Second. His "home precint broke all records at 331 votes." The count from these late arriving boxes gave Leo P. McLaughlin a victory by 122 votes. But where was

---

[41] *Sentinel-Record*, 10 October 1927.

[42] Ibid., 2 October 1920.

[43] LAT, Dowds. Dowds stated he had been in partnership with Sidney Nutt on several enterprises and Nutt always believed the election had been stolen from him. The writer discussed this situation with Roy Bosson, former Night Editor of the *Hot Springs New Era*, and later feature writer of the *Arkansas Democrat*, and we agreed that the 1927 election was the nearest to being honest of any of the following nine that Leo P. McLaughlin ran in. In that election McLaughlin and Ledgerwood did not have control of the election machinery they would have in two years. Also, illegal bettors could have "beefed-up" the vote in the Second Ward as the records indicate it had a record turn-out.

the victor? He had not been seen around the court house or the court house all night.

Mayor Leo P. McLaughlin
McLaughlin served ten terms (1927-1947), and after the first two elections had almost no active opposition.

When the last ballots had been posted and the results were made known, there was a loud cheer from the hundreds of McLaughlin supporters thronging the court house lawn and overflowing into the street. The backers of Sidney Nutt, discouraged and downcast, were understandably quiet and headed to their homes. But not Leo's supporters!

A wild celebration began. Shouting and singing, mingled with the ringing of cowbells and automobile horns peeled forth their victorious message. The large crowd made its way down Ouachita to Central and to Bridge Street. It appeared none of the joyous crowd was ready to go home for the night. It was "pay-day" for those having bets on Leo McLaughlin. Some had won hundreds of dollars. They crowded into the hallway and office of Verne Ledgerwood on the third floor of the Citizens Bank Building where the "paymaster" Claude Marsh counted out the winnings.

"Someone had a keg of moonshine and set it up in my office," said Verne Ledgerwood.[1] The crowd was getting noisy, some wanting to know where the new mayor was. "I always figured," Ledgerwood said, "that Leo was a bit uncertain and fearful of the outcome of the election and just stayed home."

As the party became more rowdy, Ledgerwood told Sonny Davies, his partner, "Let's try to get all these people down to the street and head them down Malvern Avenue to Leo's. He's the one they want to see." Within minutes the large boisterous crowd, some carrying torches, was moving slowly but noisily down the street. Someone had called the McLaughlin home, to warn what was on the way. Several hundred people crowded into the yard and intersection, as Leo McLaughlin, his mother Bridget, brother Will and two sisters, Elizabeth and Stella appeared on the porch with broad smiles and to loud cheers. For almost an hour Leo shook hands and received back-slaps and congratulatory praises.

Bridget McLaughlin spotted Verne Ledgerwood in the crowd and moved over to him. She said, "I just want to thank you for helping my son become mayor. I always wanted him to be, but I know without your help and encouragement he'd never have gone it alone."[2] It may have been the warmest moment to ever exist between the McLaughlin family and the citizens of the Spa.

McLaughlin and Ledgerwood met at the latter's office the next morning. McLaughlin, always of a revengeful nature, had been contemplating ways to get back at some of Nutt's supporters, especially those who occupied elected offices. "Verne, I think we need to get opposition for all those yahoos in the

---

[1] LAT- Ledgerwood.

[2] Ibid.

court house who opposed us. I believe you can beat Witt for circuit judge in the next election and we need to get opposition for Bouic and Van Sickle, too. They came out against us."

But Ledgerwood had something else in mind. "No, no, Leo, first of all I don't want anything else. I've got just what I always wanted. Besides if we handle this right we can win the court house crowd over to our way of thinking. We have an opportunity to band together and support each other and that will make each of us stronger. You and I need to go out to the court house tomorrow, invite them to a meeting and tell them what we have in mind. It's simple, we'll just tell them you scratch our backs and we'll scratch yours. They are smart men and will recognize the benefits of banding together. We can do the same thing with the city council. Hell, we can get control of the whole county."[3] It was this plan that was expanded into what became known as the McLaughlin machine, but it was Ledgerwood's idea.

Verne Ledgerwood was always the clearer thinker of the two men and he tried to look farther in to the future than McLaughlin. He realized that an opportunity presented itself which might never exist again. If the elected officials of the county could be persuaded to put away their differences and dislike for city hall, and vice versus, the entire group, city and county office holders could support each other and their tenures in office might be lengthened. Besides, if the town was to be opened up cooperation between city and county officials was a must.

Hearing Verne's reasoning, McLaughlin agreed.

It was on the selection of the chief of police that caused the first disagreement between McLaughlin and Ledgerwood. Leo had not promised Fred Fowler, current city clerk, he would be appointed chief of police, but Fowler believed Leo had agreed to his request for the job. Fowler had worked hard in the election and Leo knew it. He had never told Fowler he was not being considered. Actually McLaughlin had indicated his preference to be former sheriff W.R. Downen.[4] Downen had a certain following in the city and he had used his influence to steer those votes in to the McLaughlin column. For a few days following the election rumors abounded to the effect Downen could have the appointment if he so desired. Downen, who operated a furniture store on Whittington Avenue, realized he had quite a bit of opposition and finally made a statement he was not interested in the position and "would devote his time and attention to his furniture store."[5] The statement by Downen eased the pressure a bit on McLaughlin.

Verne Ledgerwood was not pleased to see Leo McLaughlin waffling on what

---

[3] *Ibid.*
[4] *Sentinel-Record,* 10 April 1927, p. 13.
[5] Ibid.

he had perceived as an agreement. He confronted McLaughlin. "Leo, I think you need to go ahead and clear the issue on the chief of police. You recall I told you the only thing I expected out of the election was to appoint the police department and that included Joe Wakelin as chief."[6]

Leo remembered, but seemed reluctant to go ahead with the appointment because of an incident which had occurred several years earlier involving Wakelin and a prizefighter's wife who was believed to have been mixed up in the robbery of gamblers on Cedar Street. The woman, Mrs. James L. Gates, who was residing at that time on Spring Street, was arrested by Deputy Sheriff Joe Wakelin on a "tip" he had received to the effect Mrs. Gates was in possession of money and jewelry taken in the Cedar Street holdup. She claimed she had some things fitting that description in a lock box in the American Bank of Commerce in Little Rock, but adamantly insisted these belonged to her and her husband who was up east fighting. Wakelin had gone to his brother-in-law Municipal Judge Verne Ledgerwood and secured a hand written warrant without a seal of the court. Mrs. Gates agreed to accompany Wakelin and the two drove to Little Rock.

Apparently the bank became suspicious of Joe Wakelin because as he and Mrs. Gates came out of the deposit box vault, they were suddenly stopped by Little Rock police officers and Wakelin was arrested.[7] Wakelin tried to explain he was a commissioned officer and showed the Little Rock officers the warrant, which because of the lack of an official seal made them even more suspicous. Wakelin and Mrs. Gates were taken to the Little Rock Police Department and the items taken from the lockbox were left in possession of the bank.[8]

It took several days for the matter to be straightened out and there was never any proof that the items in Mrs. Gates' possession were a part of any loot taken at Hot Springs. No Liberty Bonds had been reported as being stolen in the Cedar Street robbery and Mrs. Gates had over $5,000 in these and had proof she and her husband were well off and they had money in a Florida bank. Wakelin provided a statement of sorts to justify his rather furtive actions. But, as one newspaper reported, "The whole affair has been more or less shrouded in mystery-."[9]

When Leo McLaughlin mentioned his concern to Verne Ledgerwood, the judge rose to the defense of his brother-in-law, "Leo, you know Wakelin was trying to recover money and jewelry taken in that Cedar Street robbery and he'll be no more of an embarrassment than your brother George, who was

---

[6] LAT - Ledgerwood.

[7] *Sentinel-Record*, 29 March 1921.

[8] Ibid., 31 March 1921, p. 2.

[9] Ibid.

running around with Hubert Coates, when he killed Oscar Sullivan, and who you now want to appoint as police clerk. And you know W.R. Downen was charged and tried on election fraud charges and some of his accomplices were sent to the pen."

McLaughlin knew he had pressed the issue as far as he could and he knew Ledgerwood would not back down from what he had perceived to have been an agreement between the two.

"Alright Verne, we'll go with Joe. I know he's loyal and worked hard for us. I'll announce it in a day or two." Ledgerwood was satisfied.

The two men began to go over the list of personnel at the police department trying to decide if and who, if any, of the present force might be retained and those who would be fired. They had quite a task as 126 applications from men wanting jobs on the police force had been received.[10]

In an effort to soothe some hurt feelings the new mayor told the disappointed city clerk Fred Fowler, they were replacing Gene Files, the assistant clerk in Fowler's office with Clara, Fred's wife, and would also combine the police matron's job for her as Mrs. Emma Warrington, long-time matron, had quit.[11] Clara was overjoyed with her appointment and for a time Fred Fowler's ego seemed salved, but it was an agreement which Leo P. McLaughlin would soon regret.

One appointment suggested by McLaughlin certainly pleased Verne Ledgerwood. That was the appointing of Verne's law partner A.T. "Sonny" Davies as city attorney as Leo was having to resign that position in lieu of his becoming mayor.

Cleveland Smith had been city engineer for sixteen years and had been instrumental in laying out and paving many of the streets in recent years. Leo was comfortable with Smith, however, this was another appointment that would turn sour for him.

Fire Chief Lloyd Tate and Street Commissioner James Holland had been fixtures at city hall for many years and were generally low-key when it came to politics. Leo would stay with both men.

Cecil H. Ledgerwood had been the Plumbing Inspector for several years and as there was no question where his loyalty lay, he was reappointed.[12]

Leo P. McLaughlin and Verne Ledgerwood went to the court house a couple of days after the election. It was a bit awkward at first for Leo, but Verne soon had the office holders congratulating them on their victory. The two made each official aware they were calling a meeting the following morning in the city auditorium and hoped each would come. It was hinted, of

---

[10] Ibid., 10 April 1927, p. 13.

[11] *New Era*, 12 April 1927.

[12] Ibid.

course, the particular office holder Ledgerwood was inviting was special and would play a big part in the plans he and Leo had for revitalizing the town.

It is probably fair to suggest that not all of the county elected officials approached the meeting with Leo P. McLaughlin and Verne Ledgerwood with any degree of optimism, and perhaps a few with down-right skepticism. Some of these men had been quite sucecessful in their own right politically and may have believed nothing new could be shown which would encourage them to climb on the McLaughlin bandwagon.

Perhaps as McLaughlin and Ledgerwood unfolded their plan the following morning, some of those who were a bit skeptical began to listen more attentively and understand what the plan was about. It was basically simple as described by Verne Ledgerwood, "You scratch my back and I'll scratch yours."[13] It was a mutual pact, beneficial to both parties.

In essence, McLaughlin and Ledgerwood were saying, if all the heads of departments and their employees and the employees families bind to vote together for all county and city heads, who ascribe to the plan, the strength of each politician will have increased. A second step was to hire no one under them who was not loyal to the ticket. Third, every employee would be required to have a poll tax as well as one for their spouses and all adult members of their family and to make certain every one would be at the polls on every election day and cast their vote for the "selected" candidates. "It meant their job," said Ledgerwood.[14] Anyone disloyal to the administration or any of its "approved" candidates would not receive the administration's "blessing" or endorsement and be frozen out.

The plan further disclosed an attempt would be made to open the town and how this would benefit the city at large and even to some extent the office holders. Office holders approved by the administration would receive "donations" from club owners for their help in keeping them open.

By the time the meeting was over, the boys from city hall had won over the support of all the key positions in the courthouse.

The city council was next. McLaughlin asked members of the new city council to meet with him in caucus in the offices of Judge Ledgerwood. There is probably a very good reason the meeting was held in this location rather than in the municipal court space which doubled as the city council room. That was because Leo had some things he wanted to discuss with the council off the record and away from the ears of political opponents and the press.

Leo knew the council members personally and several were already supporters. Of the sixteen aldermen at that meeting there would be seven staunch McLaughlin men who would still be representing their wards the

---

[13] LAT - Ledgerwood.
[14] Ibid.

entire twenty years of the McLaughlin administration--a remarkable record. They were Samuel Smith and Frank Moody of the First Ward; Carl Wilson of the Second Ward; H.H. Blauhut of the Third; John Wolf of the Fourth; Fred Young of the Fifth; and Charles Lester of the Eighth Ward.[15] Of the remainder, a couple would die in office and others retire. And a few would be beaten by an opponent when the men failed to cooperate with the administration and their name was stricken from the "approved" list of candidates, a little pink-slip passed out to voters suggesting how to vote and please city hall. Filling the open positions would be such McLaughlin supporters as Frank Grant, Frank Tawney, Dave Dodd, W.R. Downen, Edgar Mowrey and Ed Vance.

It probably had not dawned on the council their role would not be so much of representing their own wards as the rubber-stamping and approving plans of Leo P. McLaughlin for the "advancement" of Hot Springs.

The carryover members of the council were well aware of the lack of money that always faced the city planners. Mayors and councilmen had worried with the financial plight of the city ever since the fire of 1913 caused a large endebtness. They were just glad to listen to someone with a new plan and Leo McLaughlin was optimistic he could lead the city out of its financial doldrums.

The first city council meeting was six days following the election. One newspaper reported the scene in the crowded council room as: "The new mayor was given an ovation when he entered the room. Among those who witnessed his induction into office was his mother, and he remarked to friends that her presence was 'the best part of the ceremony.'"[16]

Leo P. McLaughlin was sworn into office by his old school-mate, Judge Verne S. Ledgerwood. As he presented his appointments to the council for approval, he pointed out he was completely reorganizing the police department which would result in a saving to the city of $500 per month. He announced the only men being retained from the previous force were Owen Corrigan, patrolman; Henry Houpt, jailer; and night captain Bert Hall. New personell added were Joe Wakelin, Chief; Green Brown, chief of detectives; W.T. Pate, Detective; W.A. Young, patrolman; Will Turner, Henry "Red" Terry and John Baldwin, night patrolmen, and F.H. Tucker, jailer.[17]

Then came a moment which gave a great deal of satisfaction to Verne Ledgerwood--the swearing in as city attorney of his friend and law partner, A.T. "Sonny" Davies.

After all appointments were concluded, reports from the various department heads were heard. Then began the council's principal business during the

---

[15] *Polk's Hot Springs City Directories, 1928 - 1946.*

[16] *Sentinel-Record*, 12 April 1927.

[17] *New Era*, 12 April 1927.

McLaughlin years, approving new street lights and granting requests for ditches to be cleaned out. Leo would handle the important matters!

Leo P. McLaughlin was clearly in the driver's seat. He had a lot of plans in mind, but he didn't have one for the relinquishing the position of mayor.

W. S. Jacobs

Gambling czar W.S. Jacobs was installed to operate the local gambling in 1927. He was known in the industry as a fair and honest man. His word was "law."

Just how do you "open" up a town in the way Leo McLaughlin and Verne Ledgerwood had in mind? You couldn't just advertise, "Anyone who wants to open a dive or club with gambling or bookmaking, have at it." That would be an invitation to questionable elements and undesirables whose mere reputations would bring unfavorable publicity and attention on the town. People who had supported the administration to power would be turned off and become critical. There had to be some control and caution had to be exercised.

Some assurance was needed from the State Government, most importantly the Governor. The Spa needed the state's chief executive officer to say "Hot Springs can handle its own affairs and there will be no interference from state sources." Of course, no politician in his right mind would openly state that, but local authorities needed to know if the Governor was comfortable with the idea. The promise of political support, both donations for reelections, and voter support generally did the trick. If all else failed there would be the well filled envelope which would turn the governers' attention away from the "evils" at work in the Spa.

Gambling had gotten so out of control in 1913, the owners and operators of the clubs, paid little attention to Mayor W.W. Waters and Sheriff R.L. "Bob" Williams, when they ordered a close-down because of con-artists, who were using the clubs as their base of operation, and who were bringing unfavorable publicity on the city. Waters failed to understand that some members of his police force had made their own deals with the clubs, and were taking pay-offs and permitting them to remain open in spite of the mayor's orders to close. His inability to deal with the problen cost him reelection.

Sheriff Bob Williams marched to the beat of a different drummer and when he gave an order, whether it be for the peace of the county or to the gambling community he expected it to be obeyed. "I have been the friend of these men for thirty years," he said, "and have never before seen the day when they would not obey strict orders against gambling."[1] When Williams realized he could be prosecuted for malfeasance in office by permitting gambling to continue, he not only ordered the clubs to shut down he followed up with raids, even on his own brother's club, confiscating gambling equipment and under orders of Circuit Judge Calvin T. Cotham, burned the contraband on

---

[1] *Sentinel-Record*, 18 February 1913.

the courthouse lawn.[2] That kind of action the gamblers understood. Rather than have their equipment burned, they closed their doors.

McLaughlin and Ledgerwood knew a strong hand was needed to keep gambling under control. Neither of them knew the ins-and-outs of the gambling profession and both needed to disassociate themselves as far as possible from the actual operations to "avoid the appearance of evil." The two agreed that W.S. Jacobs, a well-known local gambler, just might be that individual. He was known to be straight and had access to individuals who might finance the resumption of gambling in the Spa under a controlled and protected environment.

William "Bill" Stokley Jacobs had been born in 1876, at Christana, Tennessee, a small hamlet located between Murfressboro and Shelbyville. Hardly out of his teens, he took a job with the old Illinois-Gulf Railroad. Not long after going to work for the railroad he suffered the loss of a leg in an unfortunate accident and was fitted with a wooden leg. He migrated west to Memphis and was successful in opening and operating the 317 Club, "one of the largest and most famous establishments of its kind in the south."[3] Flush with money from the sale of his club, he came to Hot Springs in 1907 and got involved in the movie business as owner of the old Lyric Theater on Central Avenue. However movies really did not hold Jacobs' interest, and it wasn't long until he became a partner with Coffee Williams in the Ohio Club and later with Sam Watt. He and Watt bought out the Southern Club. When the clubs were forced to close in 1913, and Prohibition followed, Jacobs operated the Ohio Club under the guise of it being a cigar, tobacco and pool hall. But, he continued to conduct some "backroom" gambling operations from it, paying a monthly fine before the police judge in order to keep operating.

Jacobs was generally known as a straight and honest gambler and most importantly from the standpoint of Leo McLaughlin and Verne Ledgerwood, he was trusted fully by the gambling community in Hot Springs. He was in Memphis at the time of the election, but undoubtedly was aware of who the winner was. When he received word McLaughlin and Ledgerwood desired to meet with him as quickly as possible, he took the next train to Hot Springs, probably concluding he was being offered the opportunity to help organize the gambling when it was opened. He may have been unaware he would be asked to limit the gambling so that it could be controlled, however, this would be an ideal setup for an ambitious gambler--protection of the local authorities. It would be similar to locking up a rat in a cheese factory or a kid in a candy

---

[2] Orval Allbritton, "Big Charlie, The Fixer and the Brass Kid," *The Record - 1997.* This article deals with the eradication of the con-artists from Hot Springs and shutting down of the gambling clubs.

[3] *Sentinel-Record,* 27 December 1927, p. 9.

store. Jacobs and the two elected city officials saw eye-to-eye on the fact it would be more advantagous and profitable if it could be kept locally owned and operated.

Under the plan, each club would have an obligation to the City of Hot Springs for the privilege of operating their business. This would encourage the support of local citizens as they became aware the fines imposed upon the gamblers to support the city meant their own taxes would be kept low. Because the operation of a house or club for gambling was strictly illegal and a misdemeanor under the laws governing the City of Hot Springs, it would be incumbent for the owners to be willing to subject themselves to a systematic fining system and on a regular basis. The penalty prescribed by law was a fine "in any sum not less than ten or more than twenty-five dollars."[4] The fine for gaming was considered by local authorities on the same level as that of breaking the Sabbath--both had equal fines.[5]

So that the patrons and visitors to these gambling places would not be subjected to arrest under Section 198, of the Laws & Ordinances of the city, the owners or operators would be required to be willing to voluntarily appear before the municipal court, where the presiding judge would administer a fine befitting the offense, or they would not be able to operate. It was just that simple.

When complaints came from local residents and church groups, and they could be expected, the only officials having authority to call for an investigation by a grand jury were the circuit judge and prosecuting attorney. Since both of these officials were "in the circle" it could be anticipated that the "good citizens" called to sit on the grand jury would be liberally inclined and generally in agreement with the policies of the current administration. In all the cases for twenty years this was the route taken and the "friendly" grand juries generally came back with a report that there was insufficient evidence for an indictment and the matter would quietly pass away.

How many clubs offering gambling of one form or another should be allowed to operate? Certainly it would be a mistake to saturate the town with too many. That would cause problems because fierce competition would develop into a "cut-throat" situation and either get out of hand or bring scrutiny from the State in Little Rock. It would not benefit the town or its visitors. A modest start would be practical for all. There were a number of

---

[4] *Digest of the Laws and Ordinances of the City of Hot Springs*, by E. W. Rector, Digester, Gazette Publishing Co., 1887, Misdemeanors, Section - Gaming, Section 195. A much later compilation was adopted April 18, 1955, and Sections renumbered, but wording is the same as the 1887 edition. Gambling was also a violation of state law but violations were easier controlled under the city ordinances.

[5] Ibid., Section 222 and 223.

local citizens wanting to get involved, some who had supported Leo P. McLaughlin in his quest for mayor. These would be favored over any others.

The keystone to the gambling would be the Southern Club. It had a long history involving gambling and was located in the heart of the city across the street from the Arlington Hotel. Of course, "Bill" Jacobs already owned a major share of the club, so there was no surprise there. A small grill to the club had been established in 1925 seating only fifteen people but this had been increased to seat 325, and was located on the ground level. It would be under the operation of Jimmy Phillips, and at this stage of Prohibition it would be a BYOB (Bring Your Own Bottle) Club, although for a price the waiter would produce a bottle of the finest liquor compliments of "Big Al" (Capone).[6] The casino was located on the second floor, up a set of wide carpeted stairs with bright brass handrails to assist the elderly and ladies wearing heels. Later, the first escalator in Hot Springs would be installed. This was a club room having all the modern gambling equipment, shiny roulette wheels, green felted blackjack and poker tables, elongated dice tables with stools for the patrons and the walls lined with slot machines. One area was for daytime operation only, the horsebook. It was Jacobs plan to expand the club but needed the city to deed an alley to enlarge the building. That presented no problem with Leo McLaughlin leading the way at city hall.[7] He knew the favor would be returned ten-fold.

The second club to be franchised was the Ohio, a small club located a block south of the Southern. It had a street level bar, which for a price dispensed illegal hootch, with gambling rooms on the second floor and was also equipped with a horsebook. Large lined blackboards hung along one wall with names across the top, "Arlington Park," " Narragansett" "Pimlico" and "Laurel", denoting racetracks from which results would be received during the day, by wire, and race by race posted. Maybe not so coincidental, W.S. Jacobs also had a large interest in the Ohio.

Another club having a long history in gambling in downtown Hot Springs was the Kentucky, located at 314 Central, between the Ohio and Southern Clubs. In its early days a very colorful couple, Mr. and Mrs. Tom Shannon had owned and operated it. In 1927 it was being run by a long time citizen of the Spa, Louis A. Blum.

Erb O. Wheatley would locate his franchise, The Ozark Sporting Club,

---

[6] *The New York Times*, 5 July 1931. Also, see Robert J. Schoenberg, *Mr. Capone*, Quill William Morrow, New York - 1992, p. 290. It reads: " Along with expansion, Capone also kep increasing his booze business, shipping as far east as New York, south to Tulsa and Ho Springs..."

[7] In the *Sentinel-Record* - Mail Away Edition, February 1938, it was reported ove 350,000 meals had been served by the grill and dining room at the Southern Club. It employe forty-five persons during the slow time of year and ninety during the season.

The Southern Club — early 1930s
before dark glass front and remodeling

upstairs and next to the Western Union Office across Central from the south end of bath house row. Primarily, the Ozark would be operated as a bookie joint.

Within two years of opening the town up, the above clubs would be followed by the Citizens Turf Club, owned by administration supporter Ben Harrison; the Blue Ribbon Club, owned and operated by Louis Larsen, Gordon Henderson and George Pakis. A short time later the White Front Bar would be opened as a bookie by Tony Karston and would be followed by the Reno and Central books, the last run by "Jockey" Ryan.

In later years the Avalon, a small dinner club and bar on the Malvern Road, would try to edge into the world of gambling. However, it was short-lived as it mysteriously caught fire one night and burned to the ground. Another, much later, was the Tower Club near the intersection of the old Little Rock Highway and Gorge Road.

Of course each club had its slot-machines, a favorite of small-time gamblers. Some of these were nickle slots and several scattered around town in bars were owned by individuals. The mayor's brother, George McLaughlin, regularly ran his like running a trot-line.

By 1929 Jacobs was so successful he opened up one of the most beautiful and widely known clubs in the south, Belvedere. It was built on the original tract of forty acres of land Jacobs had purchased three and one-half miles out of Hot Springs on the old Little Rock Highway.[8] An earlier road house, The Chicago Inn, a rowdy and bawdy place, owned by "Doc" Housley, had operated there following his release from prison. It had been raided and shut down by Sheriff Brad Smith and Constable Oscar Davis of Antioch township, for illegal gambling and its equipment burned.[9]

Jacobs would eventually surround his new club with several hundred acres of land he used as a dairy. He had envisioned the club to be one of splendor and sophistication in order to attract the many notables who visited the Spa each year and it lived up to his expectations. It was situated on a hill commanding a view of the winding road from the highway to the club. The club was surrounded by spacious and well manicured grounds. Initially there was an awning covered walkway from the parking lot to the double door entry which led into a large lobby. The awning would be replaced during remodeling a few years later with a large portico, all for the convenience of the club's treasured clientele.

The club had a large and tastefully decorated dining room which ran the length of the building. Beautiful velvet drapes adorned the eighteen large windows. Twelve elaborate chandeliers provided light for the dining room. A small stage generally featured Jimmy Capra and his dance orchestra, or perhaps an out-of-town artist. The entire room was carpeted in deep purple.

Dining at Belvedere was generally a pleasant experience. Well-known chefs prepared food for as many as six hundred people at a time. Large trays of deliciously prepared food were carried into the dining room by a small army of waiters and waitresses, all dressed in white uniforms trimmed in black. While many people went to Belvedere for dining, dancing and the music of the dance band, there were others who looked upon those features only as the preliminary event. They had come to try their luck on the gaming tables of the casino located just off the dining room. It was here the well heeled took their betting seriously and where fortunes were made and lost on the turn of the roulette wheel or the cast of the dice. For years Sam Watt was the floor boss of Belvedere overseeing the contingent of dealers, croupiers and cashiers.

There was no doubt who the boss of gambling was in Hot Springs during this period. "Bill" Jacobs was known throughout the world of gambling as a man of his word. There had been gamblers of importance over the years who had considerable influence in the Spa, but not even in the turbulent 1880s when Frank Flynn "ruled the roost," did anyone's authority in the "world of chance" equal that of W.S. Jacobs. One dishonest act by an employee meant he was gone if the "Old Man" heard of the misdeed. Yet he was perceived by

---

[8] For a good description of the life of the club see: Inez Cline's and Mark Palmer's article, "Belvedere," *The Record - 1992.*

[9] *Arkansas Gazette*, 21 February 1928.

Club Belvedere was called the "classiest" club between New York and California. It was known not only for its casino, but for its elegant dining.

the community as a fair and benevolent citizen as his purse was always ope
to a good cause. When he died it was discovered he had several I.O.U.s an
loans he had made to individuals, including police officers, who had neve
repaid him. There was no evidence he had ever attempted to collect th
debts.[10] His employees were loyal and refered to him fondly as "Old Man"
Jacobs. He was quite well-known in Hot Springs, especially by the firemen an
policemen who he employed as "heavy men" or guards on their nights off a
the Southern and Belvedere. These jobs were very sought after as the pay wa
greater and the job less tiring than their regular jobs.[11]

And Jacobs was loyal to Leo P. McLaughlin and Verne Ledgerwood
although he was not considered a "close friend" to either man. Theirs was
business arrangement! In fact, Jacob's closest friend was John H. Morris, wh
ate lunch with him every day except Sundays and holidays. Morris acted as hi
secretary for thirteen years, handling correspondence, preparing his tax return
and aided him with his sizeable property holdings.[12] Jacobs knew the salarie
of city employees were low and this included the mayor and municipal judge
He also was aware the two city officials were taking a big risk, not only thei
political careers but in almost open defiance of the laws of the State o
Arkansas. Though neither man would probably have admitted it at the time
but they were almost flirting with the penitentiary. He saw to it that a
envelope of money was delivered to the mayor's office every Monda
morning, generally by a "runner" Elmer Walters, whose name appeared on th
city's payroll records, but seemed to have no official duties but claimed to b
a "city fireman." The contribution was picked up from all of the clubs whic
were up and running. It was important to "Bill" Jacobs and the operators o
the clubs to keep McLaughlin and Ledgerwood happy and in office.

For thirteen years Jacobs was a steadying influence in a very unstead
environment.

Hot Springs was sometimes referred to by non-residents as "Sin City" o
"Hot Town" and these were not only referring to the hot mineral waters o
the gambling alone. It also was generally a reference to the rampan
prostitution which existed here. Called the oldest occupation, it had bee
around Hot Springs for many years. It was almost a constant between 187
and 1927, the time the McLaughlin administration went in to power.

There never seemed to be any effort by any of the city's administrations t
prohibit the practice, not even during the terms of Mayor Jacob McClendo

---

[10] Garland County Probate File, W.S. Jacobs, # 4552.

[11] 11 The author's father was being paid by the City of Hot Springs less than $3.00 f
a 24-hour shift on the fire department. Jacobs and later Otho Phillips and Otis McGraw we
paying $5.00 for sometimes less than an eight-hour shift at the club. During the Depression t
part-time employment meant a lot to the low-paid city employees.

[12] Probate file - Jacobs, # 4552.

Belvedere Crew — 1931-1932
***Seated:** Polly Phillips, Eddie Oreger. **Second row:** Earnest Gibbs, Mr. Jiles, Archie Ledgerwood, Freddie Price, Lloyd Lemons. **Back row:** Julius Reed Ibing, Arch Cooper, Bobby "Hughes" Vallow, P.O. Witt, Otho McCraw, Johnny "Brown" Mattinson, Buddy Wakelin, Billy Kirkham, Carl Hodges*

when gambling was driven to the backrooms and underground. For many years the city seemed not to try to control prostitution as much as regulate it. The town enacted ordinances making it a misdemeanor and placing a fine on anyone involved in operating a bawdy house of between five and twenty-five dollars. Few madams were jailed as that did not produce any money for the city's coffers. Inmates could be assessed a similar fine but seldom faced the maximum, generally being fined five dollars for each offense. For years the police judge and then the municipal judge had fined the madams and inmates monthly. This provided a steady cash flow to help with the city's budget.

No one woman tried to get control of all of the houses or brothels operating and each seemed to be satisfied in being allowed to go her own way. There were a few madams who stood out over the years and their names are emblazoned into the musty stored records of the city. The locations of some of those brothels are less known than the names of the madams. The old Arkansas Club, which stood for years on the southeast corner of Spring and Broadway Streets, was reported as a "gentlemen's sporting club," and to have had rooms to rent on an "hourly" basis, however the name of the madam is not known. Some have appeared in court trials and sensational stories which reached the press and who might be referred to as "Queen Bees."

One of the better known madams was Josie Belmont, who first began her operation as a three-woman brothel on Malvern Avenue. She appeared on the local scene in the late 1890s and lasted for twenty years, becoming the proprietress of the West End Club, a sporting house at the endof the car line on Whittington Avenue. She enlarged her operation by opening a second brothel on the second floor of a store building at 422 Malvern Avenue.[13]

Another long time operator was Cora Hutchinson who took Lotta Hager in as a partner after she kicked out a pimp by the name of Ray Lewis. Cora had thought of Ray as her personal boyfriend, but when she learned he was sampling the wares of the "house," old Ray was gone. She and Lotta ran a "rooming house" over a business at 804 Central Avenue. They sometimes had a stable of ten girls working for them and it was certainly one of the largest operations in Hot Springs history.

Millie Tolliver, a black woman operated a brothel at 336 Elm Street (Broadway) and generally had seven inmates working the cribs. Her house, located near the Iron Mountain Railroad yards, catered to the black railroad workers.

Collee Potter employed eight girls; so did Grace Woods; and long-time favorite on upper Central, Lottie Wagner, five. Susie Rogers, operating on Ouachita Avenue, had five girls working for her. Smaller operations, one or two hookers, worked from some of the many rooming houses on Market, Ouachita, Benton, Church and even for a short time on Ramble Streets. In the late 1930s and until the 1950s a Mrs. Coomer and Lillian Bahre operated the Piggly Wiggly Rooms at 809½ Central Avenue and always had several girls employed. The name, Piggly Wiggly Rooms, had nothing to do with the grocery chain, as suggested by one writer. Another well-known madam was Evelyn Anderson who operated a while from Central Avenue, and also on Ash Street, then moved on Benton Street.

Many of the girls probably came from farms, were not educationally equipped with office or secretarial skills and did not want a low-paying sales job, and drifted into the houses. They became caught up in a profession which aged them quickly and sapped their youth. Some possibly escaped, married and had families. Undoubtedly most took aliases in order to disguise their identities. The records abound with the names of Trixie, Belle, May, Lu, Fern, Billie, Blanche, Vera, Zetta, Flo and Katie.[14]

McLaughlin and Ledgerwood decided to let the houses continue to operate, but imposed a limit on the trade to five white houses and two black houses.[15] They insisted the police permit no solicitation of dates on the streets and each inmate had to have a health examination by a doctor each month.

---

[13] Docket of Police Judge of City of Hot Springs, Cases # 2645, 2915 and 3196.

[14] Ibid. Taken from 1911 - 1916.

[15] LAT - Ledgerwood. Judge Ledgerwood seemed impressed at the business abilities of the various madams and mentioned they seemed to be able to handle drunks and disorderly men very well.

A favored courtesan of the time was an auburn-haired beauty whose real name was Jewel Laverne Grayson, a twenty-two year old woman who arrived from New Orleans in 1928. Grayson had been born and raised at Paris, Texas but left home in her teens, traveling to New Orleans where she quickly learned the ropes of prostitution.[16] As with most girls, she changed her name to Grace Goldstein, and sometimes used the prefix of Mrs. in order to discourage some unwanted suitor. Through the good management of her money she was able to establish a small brothel of her own in the Crescent city. Other madams were jealous of the newcomer and her success and used their "pay-offs" to police to hassle Goldstein. She and two of her girls decided to move to Hot Springs. Having a good eye for location she leased the small Hatterie Hotel adjacent to the Arlington and just a block and a half from the Majestic.[17] The first floor of the hotel was occupied with a hat shop, owned and run by Hill and Elmer Wheatley. The second and third floors were occupied by Grace Goldstein and her girls. She seldom operated with over five girls and she was very discriminating, hiring only pretty and attractive girls. She recognized the fact if her house was to attract and cater to the wealthy and influential clients the girls needed to always be neat, well-dressed and present a healthy appearance. To achieve the latter, she would load her girls in her car and take them out near the lake and have them run several miles of roadwork three times a week. She would then bring them back to town and treat them to a big breakfast at Jim and George's Cafe.[18]

Grace also realized if her operation was to be tolerated by the local administration she and her girls, had to play the game by the rules. Monthly health checks were mandatory and on the 28th of every month she and her girls would go to municipal court and appear before Judge Ledgerwood. As a madam, she would be fined twenty dollars and her girls five dollars apiece. She required the girls to dress up for the event and with their beautiful clothes and traffic-stopping figures it was good advertising for her business. Verne Ledgerwood, remembering the event said, "Those girls were something to see. Why, every gay-blade in town was down to see them."[19]

Grace Goldstein's success led her to open a second and more discreet

---

[16] United States District Court Records, United States v. Grace Goldstein, Conspiracy and Harboring, National Archives, Ft. Worth, Texas.

[17] The Hatterie Hotel was formerly known as the Pendleton Rooming House and was purchased in 1919 by Eddie Schupp and his partner, Hillary A. (Hill) Wheatley, who operated a hat manufacturing business at 245 Central. The front of their building was painted a bright yellow and they installed a large electric sign atop of the new location advertising "The Hatterie." Later Hill Wheatley purchased the property from his partner and he and a brother ran a hat shop on the first floor. *Sentinel-Record*, 11 October 1919.

[18] LAT - Roy Bosson. He recounted Grace Goldstein would bring the girls back into town and treat them to breakfast at Jim and George's Cafe.

[19] LAT - Ledgerwood.

location in a two-story house on Palm Street. Taxi drivers and hotel clerks all knew its whereabouts. Anyone delivering a "John" or sending him to her places of business could expect a generous tip.

Generally Grace could handle any problems arising with inebriated or belligerent customers, but occasionally the "party" would get even too rough for her to handle. One night in 1931 three men became too demanding of Grace and one of her girls, Mary Cole, and a brouhaha developed. Pedestrians on Central Avenue were treated to the sounds of fighting, cursing, hollering and the breaking of glass and china. A call to police headquarters brought three officers who arrested the two women and three men.[20] Normally Grace was not bothered by the police as Chief Joe Wakelin was quite friendly with her.

But Grace was a "lightweight" when it came to fighting with drunks and "rowdies'" in comparsion to another "Queen Bee" who appeared in the Spa years later. Maxine Harris Jones, an imposing six-foot amazon, was probably the all time "champion" brawler, and was dubbed the "Blonde Bomber." Born Dora Maxine Temple in 1917 near Warren, Arkansas, she operated two houses of prostitution in Hot Springs and a "ranch" just outside the city limits in the county. She took over the lease of another madam, Mary Williams, who was renting the second floor of the J.H. McLaughlin Building at the corner of Central and Prospect. The landlord initially was none other than former mayor Leo P. McLaughlin, who owned the building. Maxine was successful and bought an old sandstone sixteen- room house at the corner of Benton and Palm Streets and promptly named it the "Mansion." It was a stately looking place and had been owned by a black doctor. Some of her clients were high state officials, even an attorney general. She did her own "bouncing." A male client once began to complain and berate one of Maxine's girls. When the man became threatening Maxine knocked him through a door and down some steps. But he wasn't to escape so easily. She followed the man into the yard and picking up a 2 x 4 piece of lumber began to beat the man who tried to get away by crawling under a porch and screaming at the top of his voice "Someone please call the police." Only the intervention of police officers prevented serious injuries from occurring to the "John."[21]

Maxine became too confrontational even for Hot Springs authorities, and she was always at odds with the circuit judge, P.E. Dobbs, who had represented her as her attorney when she first came to town. One night at the gate of her "ranch" she stopped the Garland County Sheriff from entering her premises with a shotgun. She was already in trouble with law enforcement authorities. This did nothing to change their opinion of Maxine. She had los

[20] Hot Springs City Jailers Docket, 22 August 1931, Case # 1997.
[21] Maxine Temple Jones, a biography, *Maxine - Call Me Madam*, Pioneer Press - 198

any support she ever had and her time in Hot Springs ran out. She was sentenced to the State Penitentiary on a drug charge which she claimed was a "frame."

The "Blonde Bomber" married three times and described two of her husbands as "tough dudes." Worth Gregory, whom she called a "Texas hit man," died in jail, and Edward Jones, who she claimed to be "the best safe (cracker) man in the country," also wound up dead in a Tulsa hotel room, neither apparently as tough as Maxine believed.[22]

But Maxine was not in Grace Goldstein's class when it came to associating with, "tough dudes," as she described in her book. Grace and her girls hosted a number of the Chicago mobsters including Al and Ralph "Bottles" Capone and Frank Nitti. She boarded and lived with the toughest of the toughs in 1935, Alvin "Creepy" Karpis, the number one wanted criminal in the country, big time kidnapper, bank and train robber, and his sidekick, gunman and killer, Fred Hunter, who had become enamored with one of Grace's girls, Connie Morris, and who would be apprehended by the FBI with Karpis and Hunter at New Orleans. Grace would later be convicted and sentenced to two years in a federal penitentiary for conspiracy and harboring.[23] The court learned that at a time when money was very scarce, Karpis had spent $20,000 on Grace and even purchased her a new Buick from local car dealer Raymond Clinton. During her trial she tried to convince Federal Judge Trimble she had been married to Alvin Karpis, and though invited by Trimble to prove it, Grace couldn't. But, that is another and separate chapter in the Spa's history.

By the mid-1970s the brothels in Hot Springs, as visitors and citizens had known them, became a thing of the past. It wasn't that prostitutes had given up on the city. It was just changing from houses to call girl operations.

---

[22] Ibid. Maxine was her own worst enemy. She became critical of nearly every official in Garland County. She was sent to the State Penitentiary and served several years. She came out a broken and foul-mouthed old woman who could not get along with the residents of the Levi Towers and had to eat her meals alone. She passed away in a nursing home at Warren, Arkansas April 15, 1997, at the age of 81.

[23] LAT - Ledgerwood. Ledgerwood said that Grace Goldstein had "a heart of gold" and gave generously to charities. He said he and his wife, Bess, were surprised one Christmas to receive two fine wool blankets from Grace Goldstein.

Leo P. McLaughlin, safely ensconced as mayor, now turned his attention to solving some of the ills which beset the city. He had promised the voters that if he was elected he would try to alleviate some of the flooding, which occurred on some of the city's main streets when rain and thunderstorms suddenly dumped several inches of rainfall on the watershed surrounding the town. On the recommendation of city engineer Cleveland Smith, McLaughlin set about to come up with money to institute a program on Central Avenue of enlarging a number of the storm drains. Large, heavy grilles and grates were installed in enlarged holes in the gutters which permitted a much larger amount of runoff to quickly flow into the underground drains. He had similar work performed on Park Avenue and the citizens of that area were so appreciative of his efforts they sent a letter expressing their thanks.[1]

The city hall needed a new roof, but the cost of $5,000 had not been budgeted because of the lack of funds. With the additional money beginning to come in from the increased fines for gambling, Leo was able to authorize the repairs. He also, was able to have all the exterior woodwork painted, and twenty-four cracked and broken window panes, replaced and windows puttied. McLaughlin was very frugal with the city's money and closely watched and inspected any repairs in progress. When a savings of $150 was made on the roof job, he turned around and had the women's jail cell replumbed and refurbished. Repairs were made to the steam boiler which heated the city auditorium. The mayor's office was repainted as was the health department office.

Few repairs had ever been made to the City Barn, the area designated for repairing and storing of city vehicles. The street department employees were surprised one morning to see a crew of men beginning to tear off an old leaky roof and install a new corrugated iron roof. Also, electric lights and natural gas was hooked up. New grading equipment was purchased and greatly improved the efficiency of the department as the street department began a systematic grading of the Spa's dirt and gravel streets and alleys. Paving had begun on several streets.

New roofs were installed on the two substations of the fire department, one on Whittington and Water Streets, the other in South Hot Springs on West Grand.[2]

Leo P. McLaughlin was beginning to come into demand as an "after-dinner" speaker. As mayor he was invited by the various conventions which came to town to give either a welcoming address or the after dinner type of talk. As

---

[1] *Sentinel-Record*, 12 August 1928, p. 7.
[2] Ibid., 4 January 1929.

groups began to realize Hot Springs was "wide-open," more companies, groups and organizations began scheduling their meetings and conventions in the Spa. The Businessmen's League, and later the Chamber of Commerce, were deluged by inquiries concerning what the city was able to offer in housing accomodations and entertainment.

Leo was always entertaining, "telling those Negro stories"[3] and ending his talk with, "You folks have a good time. Stay out as late as you want and spend your money. Keep out of trouble, but if you do get in trouble and you can't get out of jail, call me. I'll come down and get in with you."[4] That generally brought a chuckle or two. As time went on and he became more famous and well-known he became greatly in demand as a speaker.

McLaughlin had always been a good dresser since his high school days and that image did not change, although his appearance did experience a metamorphosis. If truth be known, McLaughlin may have secretly admired and wished to emulate the style of flamboyant New York mayor Jimmy Walker. Gentleman Jim Walker had a flair and strut about him that drew attention and was quite a snazzy dresser. As one reporter wrote, "Smith always looked as if he had just come directly from a bandbox." So did Leo!

McLaughlin was slender and wore his clothes well, whether it was business, sports or formal wear. Leo kept his wardrobe in excellent condition having his suits pressed and cleaned often and rotated them well through the seasons. His clothes were generally tailor made and he was seen quite often going into or comimg from V.G. Verneux's Tailor Shop at 607 Central Avenue or possibly ordering a new riding habit from the Arlington Toggery. A number of times he received a call or a note from an appreciative club owner to go by his tailor to be fitted for a new suit. Leo never considered this type of gift, or any other for that matter, to be improper or unethical for an official in his position. But there were three constant things concening his attire which always drew attention, his hat, his boutonniere and his crisp white lapel handkerchief. He nearly always had on a hat and it rested on his head at a rakish angle with part of the brim turned up and part down and a fresh flower

---

[3] LAT- Ledgerwood.

[4] Ibid.

adorning his lapel. It was his signature and he never changed.[5]

The first test of how well the McLaughlin machine would hang together was in the state-county democratic primary in August 1928. Of course, there were no city offices being contested, however there was one city official running for a county office, Fred Fowler. This was not supposed to happen, but it did. Leo P. McLaughlin and Verne Ledgerwood had convinced the city and county office holders if they supported each other all would be stronger and their jobs would be relatively safe. What then had gone wrong? Nothing had been said or agreed on specifically concerning one machine member running against another, however it was generally understood it wouldn't be done.

When Fred Fowler, city clerk of Hot Springs, announced suddenly for county collector against incumbent George Leatherman, Leo's phone began to ring. The calls were from various county officials wanting to know, "What's going on?" Leo and Verne were placed in an embarassing position. It turned out that Fred Fowler was still miffed about not getting the police chief's position and decided to run for a job which paid more than the clerk's job he was holding. McLaughlin and Ledgerwood conferring, decided on a course of action--they would do nothing but notify the voters that the administration was supporting Leatherman. Fowler was a duly elected city official and they had no authority to "order him" to resign from the race. And that's what they did, furnishing a "pink slip" to all city employees and each poll tax holder they had been able to sign up. The slip was a minature ballot indicating the administration's selection of the candidate for each office. The name of Fred Fowler had a big heavy black mark drawn through it. Fred had been "scratched," and left to "twist slowly in the wind."

Fowler had initially ran for city clerk in the spring of 1921. In a four-man race he had come in second to Phillip Sisney. Sisney was a well-known man about town and a decorated war veteran, but after entering the clerk's office had some questionable banking and bookeeping practices and was impeached following an audit by an accounting firm and was replaced by Seward Erickson.[6] Within two weeks, Erickson resigned taking employment in private business, and through the sponsorship of Leo McLaughlin and Verne Ledgerwood, Fred Fowler replaced him.[7]

By all accounts Fowler had made a good city clerk and was re-elected three

---

[5] LAT - Whittington.

[6] *Sentinel-Record*, 2 April 1922, 4 February 1923. Sisney appealed the impeachment to circuit court and Judge Scott Wood ruled the City Council was justified in the removal of the city clerk.

[7] Ibid., 27 May 1922.

times.[8] He had become quite popular and must have come to his own conclusion he did not need the administration's help in unseating Leatherman. Fowler apparently did not fear there would be any repercussions in making the race. Never was he more wrong.

Fred had always ran well politically and he saw no reason he would not do so again. What must have been an "eye-opening" experience, Fowler lost to George P. Leatherman by over a two-to-one margin. Out of thirty-seven boxes in the county, Fred Fowler had been able to carry only two, and one of those had less than a total of forty votes.[9] It was a convincing example to the county's office holders McLaughlin and Ledgerwood were able to deliver as promised.

Amazingly, Fred Fowler may have been one of the few people around city hall who did not understand what had occurred. He had observed that Garland County Sheriff Garland P. Van Sickle had barely defeated J.M. "Jim" Lowrey, squeezing by a margin of only forty-seven votes. Realizing the one man in the court house who had openly critized the city's administration, he believed McLaughlin might back him against Van Sickle in the next general election by running as an independent as McLaughlin had done. He first went to Verne Ledgerwood to ascertain if he might get some support to run. Ledgerwood referred him to McLaughlin.[10] Leo was not sympathetic with Fowler, and even though he had not gotten along with Van Sickle he told Fred Fowler the administration would not help him if he ran against the sheriff.

About this time another incident occurred to complicate things. McLaughlin received word of something supposedly said by Chief of Detectives Green Brown, criticizing the administration. Green Brown was an individual who did not fear man nor beast and no one could keep him from saying whatever was on his mind. His temper sometimes got the better of him, especially if he had too much to drink. About ten or twelve years before he had been in a partnership with a friend, Dave Young, as private detectives and bounty hunters. The two men had captured a criminal with a price on his head. When Brown and Young received the reward money they threw a party for their friends at a saloon. One man would buy a round of drinks, then the other man. They became confused over whose turn it was to buy the next round and an argument ensued. The next thing to occur had the patrons of the saloon diving under tables and crawling behind the bar as the two friends pulled their guns and started blazing away at each other. Green Brown was wounded, but

---

[8] Orval E. Allbritton, "The Fire At City Hall: Accident or Arson, *The Record - 1998,* pp. 1-46.

[9] *Sentinel-Record,* 16 August 1922.

[10] "The Fire at City Hall," Allbritton.

lived. Dave Young was fatally wounded and died a few days later.[11]

When word reached the ears of Leo McLaughlin that Green Brown was deriding the administration, he summarily discharged the officer. He ordered Herbert "Dutch" Akers as Brown's replacement as chief of detectives.

"Dutch" Akers had two previous tours of duty on the police department. He was more or less a controversial subject, having been suspected of some shady types of operations including working with a couple of car thieves. One story which circulated was an individual from Little Rock upon leaving the Arlington Hotel discovered his new Hudson automobile to be missing. He went back in the hotel and told the desk clerk of his missing car. The clerk raised his eyebrows at the story and suggested the owner go to the police station and ask for officer Akers and tell him the car was missing and put up a reward of fifty dollars for the return of the vehicle. In that instance, by the time the man got back to his hotel he discovered the car to be parked near where it had been stolen from. Other stories similar to this one, involving Akers, cropped up ever so often. Sometimes an individual wanting to buy a pistol was referred to the Chief of Detectives, and he generally had one to sell, possibly confiscated off some criminal. Prostitutes needing jewelry could depend on "Dutch" being able to provide what they wanted at a nominal cost. Where he had gotten the jewelry was a mystery.

[11] Taped interview with James Evelyn Young by Orval E. Allbritton, 4 March 1998. Ev Young is the nephew of Dave Young.

He had been arrested by federal authorities on a liquor violation charge while he was employed as a railroad detective.[12] He had been able to wriggle his way out of the charge with minimal damage to his reputation.

What ever one might say about Akers and his reputation, there is one certainty--he was a highly astute and skilled police officer and had an almost uncanny ability to spot a crook, even in a crowd of people. Because of his ability and expertise in spotting pickpockets, word spread widely in that criminal fraternity Hot Springs was not a safe place to practice their slight- of-hand profession. When Akers met a train at the depot, he scanned the face of each person alighting from the cars, and as a result of his memorizing the photographs from the wanted posters and flyers, was able to arrest numerous felons and crooks. When he spotted noted confidence men and small time crooks who were not wanted at the time, he told them. "It's nice to see you. For your information there's a train leaving in a couple of hours. Be sure and be on it."[13] The message to the visiting con-man was clearly understood, he was no longer welcome at Hot Springs. Akers, was also alert for descriptions of stolen automobiles and recovered a number, generally receiving a small reward for each as it was not considered at that time to be unethical. He cruised the streets of Hot Springs looking for wanted criminals while many other officers might have overlooked the same individual by having their attention diverted by the pretty girls from Kress and Newberrys 5 & 10 stores hurrying to and from lunch.

But Akers had another function, and that was to report things going on in town to Mayor McLaughlin. Leo wanted to know everything happening in town and what prominent and important people might be visiting Hot Springs, and especially if there were any vacationing mobsters or gang members.

McLaughlin had informants in every department of the city. Some were likened to the always present "tattle-tales" in elementary school, running to Leo and reporting the least remark which created an uneasy atmosphere around city hall. Akers was not one of these, but he told the mayor only certain things and kept others to himself.[14] But who kept watch on "Dutch" Akers? Why, George McLaughlin, the mayor's brother who was carried on the city's payroll for twenty years as police clerk but was never able to explain what he did. Nobody at city hall was able to tell what George's duties were, although all knew what function he played and behind his back was referred to as "the mayor's snitch." Policemen and firemen were cautious in their talk around George McLaughlin. If they were conversing and saw George

---

[12] *Sentinel-Record*, 12 March 1925, p. 4.

[13] LAT - Bosson.

[14] LAT - Earl J. Lane.

approaching they would switch subjects or if they wanted the mayor to hear something it was easy to allude to it while George was in earshot. They knew it would reach the mayor's ears before the next morning. Ledgerwood depended only on one informant, his brother-in-law, Police Chief Joe Wakelin.[15]

Word reached Leo that city engineer Cleveland Smith was getting ready to make a run against him for mayor in 1929. Swift action by McLaughlin relieved Smith of his duties before he had planned to resign to make the race.[16] Disloyalty in any degree to the administration was not tolerated.

Smith announced for mayor and Arthur Cobb, son of attorney M.S. Cobb, who had unsuccessfully run against Verne Ledgerwood six years before, announced for the municipal judge's position. When this occurred Clara Fowler, Fred's wife, who was working in the city clerk's office, urged her husband to support Smith and Cobb in their races. Fred was just beginning to understand how ruthless the mayor could be when he was opposed, and initially cautioned Clara from becoming too actively involved. The Fowler's were probably aware that Leo had a "plant" in their office in the form of W.H. Hall, a former alderman, who had been assigned to that office by the mayor. The race turned out to be another "barn-burner," as the rhetoric and campaigns heated up.

McLaughlin began to point out all he had accomplished as mayor in the past two years. And, he had made progress, had done a good job administratively, and was due a lot of credit. In fact, all sixteen alderman signed an endorsment for the mayor and urged his re-election. Unfortunately, Leo sometimes went too far in claiming credit for things which should have been given to others. It was a flaw in his character and he was never able to overcome it. For instance, he claimed he had enlarged the personnel on the fire department, whereas Mayor Robert Jones was in office when the shift of sixteen men had gone to work January 1, 1926, fifteen months before Leo P. McLaughlin won the mayor's race. He claimed great responsibility for rebuilding the arch under Central Avenue, whereas this was mainly a federally-funded and supervised project by the U.S. Corps of Engineers and the U.S. Department of Interior. Leo had added his "blessing" to the project, if that counted. But a lot of people continued to believe, "Mr. Leo got the arch rebuilt."

Cleveland Smith and Arthur Cobb tried to bring out an incident involving a very unhealthy war veteran who was jailed with another individual for supposedly "shaking down" a prominent Park Avenue woman who was never identified. While on the chain gang, Jerome Estey, described as "being an emaciated hunchback and almost bent double" man, received two pension

---

[15] LAT - Earl Lane.

[16] *Arkansas Democrat*, 23 April 1929.

checks. Estey alledged Chief Wakelin, Chief of Detectives Herbert Akers and Captain Arch Cooper had demanded he sign the checks over to them for part of his fine and he refused as that still would not pay his entire fine.[17] When that did not work, the officers apparently got Judge Ledgerwood to reduce the bond, hoping the man would sign the checks to get off the chain gang and leave the area. Estey still refused to endorse the checks over to the officers. Cleveland Smith and Arthur Cobb tried to convince the citizens of the Spa the whole thing had been a "shakedown" operation by the police who intended to pocket the proceeds from the pension checks.[18]

Mayor McLaughlin struck back in a large advertisement entitled, "Nailing the Lie," and defending his police department. He pointed out Estey had been released over two months before he brought charges alledging he had been mistreated and that it was a totally political ploy by enemies of the administration.

Realizing their campaign had bogged down and further proof was needed in the Estey affair, they persuaded Fred Fowler to provide them with an affidavit reflecting the original charge against Charles Hull and Ernest Estey of "Obtaining money by false pretense" was changed later to read "attempt to obtain money by false pretense," in order to "legally reduce Estey's bail."[19] This amounted to calling McLaughlin a liar and the mayor reportedly was furious.

If Fowler had ever believed he had any chance to advance his career by running for office in Garland County, he surely must have realized the affidavit had ended all hope. He was dead politically in the event Leo McLaughlin won re-election, and had no other recourse except to openly support Smith and Cobb.

The affidavit had little effect on the outcome of the election as McLaughlin ended the political career of Cleveland Smith by a vote of 3006 to 1145, and Verne Ledgerwood defeated Arthur Cobb 2875 to 1067 and was able to say he had beaten both Cobbs, M.S. and son.[20] They too, were finished politically.

If anyone was not convinced that things had not changed politically in Hot Springs in the two years of the McLaughlin administration, all they had to do was compare the statistics of the elections of 1927 and 1929. In McLaughlin's first race for mayor he had polled 318 votes in the second ward defeating Sidney Nutt by 251 votes in that precinct. In 1929 almost three times more blacks had poll taxes, thanks to Leo McLaughlin and his ward-heelers, Will and Pete Page, and Leo polled 728 votes out of 829 in the second. The

---

[17] *Sentinel-Record*, 31 March 1929.
[18] Ibid., 30 March 1929.
[19] Ibid., 31 March 1929, p. 13.
[20] Ibid., 4 April 1929.

machine was tightening its grip on Hot Springs.

Even the Democratic Committee and the Election Commissioners had new looks. John J. Ledgerwood and Walter W. Gentry now headed the Election Commissioners and it is easy to understand by a review of the judges selected by them as having a definite bias in favor of Leo and Verne. Many were good men but would be lifetime supporters of the administration: Carl Miles, Cecil Ledwidge, Carl Wilson, Ben Johnson, Barry Larcade, Jack McJunkin, Dave Dodd, L.L. Asbury, Sam Garratt, Cecil Brock, Roscoe Owens, J. Henry Reece, Joe Terry, J. Longinotti and Frank Head.

There appeared little Leo could do to Fowler until the next election, at which time he could supply Fowler some opposition, but until then, he could only hassle him with an audit of the clerk's books and proceeded to order one by a Memphis firm. Fowler had undergone several audits before and his books had always balanced and in fact he had been complimented by the auditors on the clarity of the records he kept. While Fred was protected somewhat as an elected official, Clara was not. McLaughlin fired her from her jobs as assistant city clerk, police matron and health nurse and there was nothing the Fowlers could do about it.

Then, in a series of bizarre and unusual incidents, Fred Fowler was delivered into the hands of Leo P. McLaughlin.

During the election campaign Clara Fowler had received some anonymous and annoying calls from an unidentified woman chiding her about supporting Smith and Cobb. The calls continued even after the election and through a friend at the telephone company, she had been able to trace the calls to a telephone at Connelly Press on Ouachita Avenue. Clara was acquainted with the owner, Jeannette Connelly, and knew the voice was not hers. Irritated and wanting to get to the bottom of the harassing calls she headed for the printing company. Upon arriving she took a small .25 automatic pistol from her purse and clasped her hand around it.[21] Entering the establishment she explained to the owner the annoying calls having come from the Connelly's telephone. Mrs. Connelly called the only woman employee in from the printing room, Mrs. Organ Terry, wife of Hot Springs police officer Henry "Red" Terry, a strong supporter of the administration. Clara Fowler went on the attack accusing Organ Terry of the calls and Mrs. Terry denying she had made any. Organ Terry suddenly shoved Clara out the door onto the sidewalk and locked the door. By this time, Clara, mad as the alligator when the creek went dry, raised her small pistol and fired through the glass door. The shot did not hit Organ Terry, however the bullet struck a wall, ricocheted, and struck Jeannette Connelly on the cheek. Clara Fowler was immediately repentant and offered

---

[21] *Arkansas Democrat*, 23 April 1929. For full story and details of the incident see Orval E. Allbritton's "Fire at City Hall," *The Record - 1998.*

to take her to Dr. Browning's office in the Thompson Building and Mrs. Connelly agreed. The two women had hardly got underway until Organ Terry was calling Captain Arch Cooper at police headquarters, and acquainting him with the details of the shooting. Cooper left for the Thompson Building and upon arriving, picked up "Red" Terry, Organ's husband who was on patrol on that part of Central Avenue. A policeman friendly to Fred Fowler called and apprised him of the situation and asked not to be identified as the caller. Fowler, too, headed for the Thompson Building, taking a .38 Colt automatic pistol with him. He arrived in front of the building just in time to see Cooper and Terry emerge, escorting Clara toward the parked police car. Neither officer saw Fred Fowler walk up behind Arch Cooper.

"Honey, you don't have to go with these fellows," Fowler said.[22]

Cooper glanced over his shoulder and growled, "Fred, you stay out of this."

The officer suddenly felt something hard jammed in his ribs and looking around saw a pistol in the hands of Fred Fowler. "What the hell?" Cooper said. "Do you know what you are doing, Fred?"

"Maybe not Arch, but you aren't taking Clara in the police car." Fowler removed the officer's gun from its scabbard. Terry, who was always known as a very low-key and not an excitable type of officer, had remained silent during the episode. "Arch, you and Red get in the car. I'll bring Clara to headquarters."[23]

An angry, unhappy and embarrassed police captain and officer "Red" Terry got in the police car, witnessed by several sidewalk pedestrians and drove away at a high speed. Fred and Clara Fowler realized they were in deep trouble. Not only had Clara tried to shoot Organ Terry, she had wounded Mrs. Connelly, by accident surely, but Fred had actually drawn a gun on two duly-commissioned officers and at gunpoint freed an arrested prisoner. And to top it off, Fred had taken the police captain's gun from him. They had been in difficulty with Mayor Leo P. McLaughlin, now they were in trouble with the police.

Changing their minds about giving themselves up at city hall, they solicited the help of Ed B. Mooney, a local contractor and friend who helped them surrender to Constable John Young, who escorted them to a bond hearing.[24] Afterwards, the two decided in view of the turmoil surrounding them to go to Little Rock for the night and seeing their names in the afternoon *Arkansas Democrat*, registered at the Lafayette Hotel under assumed names.[25] Fortunately, they had friends, a *Gazette* reporter and hotel employees, to confirm their

---

[22] *Arkansas Gazette*, 23 April 1929.
[23] *Sentinel-Record*, 23 April 1929.,
[24] *Arkansas Gazette*, 23 April 1929.
[25] Ibid., 24 April 1929, also *Sentinel-Record* 3 May 1929.

whereabouts, as a mysterious fire gutted the city clerk's office and damaged the city hall that very night.

Leo McLaughlin immediately began declaring the fire to be arson, even before it had cooled enough to be inspected. He wanted Fowler charged with arson. Judge Ledgerwood was more temperate in his attitude, realizing there were no witnesses to the fire and the Little Rock Police Department's investigation in that city, indicated the Fowlers to have been at the Lafayette Hotel at the time of the fire. Fire Chief Loyd Tate summoned the State Fire Marshal, however his report failed to reveal any accelerant had been used. With neither Tate or the fire marshal finding any conclusive evidence the fire to have been deliberate the strongest position they could take was that it was a suspicious fire.[26]

Upon returning to Hot Springs and learning of the fire, Fowler, desiring to see how badly damaged his office was, went to city hall and entered the clerk's office through one of the broken windows. He had hardly gotten inside when he heard a noise behind him and there stood Police Captain Arch Cooper, who had followed him in, and with a gun trained on him. "Fowler, hold it right there and get your hands up," the officer commanded.

Unseen by Cooper or Fowler, another party had come in one of the broken windows. It was former Chief of Detectives Green Brown, and he had a gun leveled at Cooper. "Arch, drop that gun and turn around slowly," he said.

Cooper froze, "What the --," he exclaimed, glancing around and saw Green Brown pointing a pistol at him. He let his gun drop into the ashes and debris on the floor.[27] Fred Fowler quickly picked his weapon up and also covered Cooper.

But the scenario had not been fully played out, for standing in one of the windows with gun drawn was Deputy Constable Charles Trammel. "Hold it right there you two," aiming his pistol at Brown and Fowler. Arch Cooper quickly recovered his gun and reentered the action. All four men stood with guns pointed at each other, frozen as each man was reluctant to make any kind of move that might trigger a blood bath in the burned out clerk's office.

One newspaper reported the incident: "The near tragedy that took place amid the ruins of the city clerk's office was witnessed from outside by many members of a large crowd that had assembled to view the damage done by the fire. When the spectators saw pistols being drawn there was a wild rush to safety."[28]

---

[26] "Fire Record, City of Hot Springs," by Loyd Tate, Chief. Alarm # 498, 23 April 1929, 2:45 A.M.

[27] *Sentinel-Record*, 25 April 1929.

[28] *Arkansas Gazette*, 24 April 1929. Also see Orval E. Allbritton's "Fire at City Hall," *The Record - 1998.*

Fred was arrested and jailed. He wasn't even allowed to see his attorney until the following day. When Clara went looking for Fred she, too, was arrested, but after several hours was permitted to make bond, but was not able to talk with her husband.[29] She tried to organize Fred's friends to get him out of jail on bond, but the city authorities blocked this move.[30] It was obvious, Fowler no longer carried any influence at city hall. The administration was playing "hardball." It was the following day before Fred was given a *habeas corpus* hearing and allowed to make bond.[31]

Leo McLaughlin made arrangements with County Judge Charles H. Davis for some temporary space in the court house until the city hall could be repaired. He, also, rented some space from Al Reynolds, owner of the Como Hotel. Damage to city hall was estimated to be about $35,000, a sizeable sum in those days, part of which was covered by insurance and work was authorized.

McLaughlin then turned his full attention toward Fred Fowler. He addressed a joint meeting of the city council members and members of the Board of Public Affairs as well as auditors Charles Case and Maurice Jones. The mayor stated, "The time and money already spent on the city audit were wasted."[32] Case and Jones were startled by this proclamation by the mayor as they had already been interviewed by reporters and had told them, "We have gone back into the (city's) records for three years and as far as we have worked the books appeared to be in fairly good shape, no shortage being apparent."[33] At the time of the fire the auditors were almost through and were tying up a few loose ends.

The mayor, however, had other ideas and was unsatisfied with the uncomplete audit. He ordered the auditors to complete their work and strongly urged them to taken another look into the records as he believed Fowler was guilty of something. He said in the event the auditing firm, Homer K. Jones and Company of Memphis, Tennessee, desired any further business from the City of Hot Springs, they needed to recheck their findings. The suggestion by the mayor was duly noted and they assured him they would check further into the cashbook, even though they had inspected the book several times.[34]

McLaughlin then went in to caucus with the council and asked that a special

---

[29] Ibid.

[30] *Sentinel-Record*, 26 April 1929 - "Twice A Week Edition."

[31] *Arkansas Gazette*, 24 April 1929.

[32] *Arkansas Gazette*, 24 April 1929.

[33] *Sentinel-Record*, 3 May 1929.

[34] Hot Springs City Proceedings, Demurrer Answer and Plea of Fred J. Fowler, 1 May 1929, p. 3.

meeting of the council be called for the purpose of impeaching Fred Fowler.[35] The principal charge would be for failing to protect the records, some of which were damaged or destroyed by the fire. Those were normally locked in a steel safe, but because Fred and Clara Fowler left town after Clara's involvement in the shooting, the books were left out and damaged by the fire.

There seemed some minor disagreement by two or three council members as the vote was not unanimous and the mayor called another meeting twenty hours prior to the impeachment procedure, this one closed to the press and the public. When the meeting broke up the council was 100 percent behind the mayor and only Fred Fowler's "scalping" remained. Had Leo twisted the arms of the aldermen who appeared reluctant to so easily "crucify" Fowler? Whatever persuasion he used, it worked!

Attorney A.J. Murphy, representing Fred Fowler pointed out to the council and public in attendance, "It is contrary to the fundamental principles of our Government for the mayor and council to act as accusers, prosecutors, judge and jury in this case." He appealed for an "impartial tribune" to hear the case, but to no avail.[36] The vote to impeach Fred Fowler was 15-0.

The vote must have pleased Leo P. McLaughlin. He asked the council to appoint his old acquaintance from the second ward and acting assistant city clerk, W.H. Hall, to replace Fowler. Again, the vote was 15-0, in favor.[37] Leo was in full control!

When it seemed as if nothing could get worse for Fred Fowler, it did. McLaughlin unveiled the auditor's report reflecting the clerk's office to be short $3,009.03.[38] On August 13, 1929, the grand jury indicted Fred Fowler on embezzlement charges to the satisfaction of Leo McLaughlin.[39]

Prosecuting Attorney William Bouic based his case against Fred Fowler almost solely on the auditors' report. When defense attorney A.J. Murphy cross-examined the auditor Charles Case, the spectators and jury quickly became aware how flimsy and how big the "holes" were in the prosecution's case. When the city car license fund was examined it was learned that Fred Fowler, at the instructions of Mayor McLaughlin, had given all city and county officials car tags, including Prosecuting Attorney Bouic and Circuit Judge Earl Witt, the court became as nervous as a long-tailed cat in a room full of rocking chairs. The jury required less than an hour to deliberate and came out with a "not guilty" verdict for Fowler.[40]

---

[35] *Arkansas Gazette*, 25 April 1929.
[36] Council Proceedings, 1 May 1929.
[37] Ibid., 26 April 1929.
[38] *Sentinel-Record*, 7 August 1929.
[39] Ibid., 14 August 1929.
[40] Garland County Criminal Court Records, Box 61, jury verdict signed by Lyn Dodson, foreman, 22 October 1929.

Fred Fowler had been exonerated of the embelezzment charges by a jury of his peers. He and Clara had also been charged with carrying a gun, however these charges were dropped. The Fowlers would leave the Spa, there was no place for them in a McLaughlin-controlled town.

Leo had been unable to successfully charge and prosecute Fowler, but he had taken his job and sullied his reputation. The charges against Fred and the firings of Green Brown, Cleveland Smith and Clara Fowler would serve as a reminder of what could happen to anyone not loyal to the McLaughlin administration. As Attorney A.J. Murphy contended, "The real grievance against him (Fowler) is that he is not in harmony with the city administration."[41] It was a time if an individual had a political thought contrary to the administration, it best be kept to oneself.

Grover Cleveland Smith
Smith was Mayor Leo P. McLaughlin's second opponent for the office. The election was a crushing defeat for Smith in 1929.

[41] Council Proceedings, 1 May 1929, p. 4.

Stella McLaughlin was thirty-six years-old and in love. Maybe she wouldn't be an old maid after all. Almost all of her friends from high school days and church had been married several years and had growing families. She did not relish a confrontation with her mother, Bridget, but if she was ever going to stand up to her mother it had to be now. Her sister Irene had been dead over a year and there did seem to be a loosening of Bridget's parental ties to her children. If Stella's stubborn nature was showing a bit, she had come by it naturally. She had inherited it from both her mother and father.

When Stella told her mother she had met a man at a dance at the Kingsway (Eastman) Hotel in whom she was interested and he in her, it opened a floodgate of questions from Bridget. Who was he? Where was he from? And, most important, what was his religous faith?

Stella had most of the answers, but rightly feared these would not totally satisfy her mother. His name was Charles Stanley Snyder and he was thirty-seven years-old. He preferred being called Stanley. He was from Miami Beach, Florida, a veteran of the World War, and drew a pension. He had a nice car and yes, he was a Catholic. And, most importantly, Stanley wanted to marry her. Stella was right, those answers did not satisfy her mother and her agitation still existed toward anyone in which she or her siblings indicated an interest.

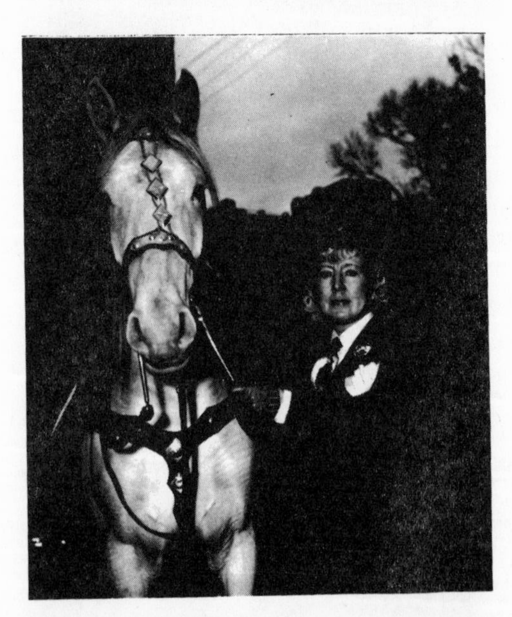

Stella McLaughlin Snyder, as an equestrian, was very good. She had one ill-fated marriage to Charles Stanley Snyder in 1926.

Will and Elizabeth McLaughlin remained neutral on the subject, but Leo and George, seeing how unhappy their mother was making Stella, sided with her. Bridget gave in but stopped short of giving her blessing.

Leo was quite well acquainted with Trager Freeman, Garland County Clerk, and on 25 July 1926, signed the marriage license as guarantor and security. It is interesting to note when Leo filled out the form, he listed Stella's age as twenty-nine. Had Stella misinformed her fiancee of her age, or had Leo just made the mistake? That same afternoon Stanley Snyder and Stella McLaughlin were married by Father William J. Carroll of St. Mary's.[1] The records are silent as to whether the private wedding was attended by the bride's mother, Bridget.

The newlyweds honeymooned in the mountains of eastern Tennessee. On the return trip, Stanley drove down to Chattanooga, and introduced his bride to his mother, Annie Snyder. Annie seemed pleased with her new daughter-in-law, and the two women immediately took a liking to each other and began a correspondence during the next several months with Stella sending her several small gifts and a dress of which her mother-in-law was appreciative.[2]

At least for a few weeks Stella seemed happy as she and Stanley moved to a small apartment on Pleasant Street and set up housekeeping. But all was not well within the Snyder abode. Stella began to notice how much alcohol Stanley consumed each day. She recalled on their trip to his mother's, Annie had asked her out of the hearing of Stanley if he was drinking "again"? At that time, Stella had told his mother that Stanley was not drinking to excess. However, the situation had drastically changed during the first few weeks of their marriage.

One night Stanley experienced a state of confusion and hallucinations. With the aid of friends Stella was able to get Stanley to a hospital. The attending physician explained that Stanley was having "delirium tremens," a condition arising sometimes in chronic alcoholics. Futher, the doctor said, "His condition is so serious his mind might be affected because of (his) excessive drinking."[3]

Stanley seemed to recover a bit, then one night when the couple attended a theater with friends he began to drink from a bottle he had brought along. Stella discreetly tried to stop him which resulted in Stanley becoming abusive of her and he cursed her loudly. With the help of her friends and a couple of ushers, they got Stanley in a taxi and home. He continued to drink, becoming more abusive and profane and needed hospitalization again.

Stella finally wrote Annie Snyder and told her how concerned she was for

---

[1] Garland County Marriage Records, p. 298, recorded 30 July 1926.

[2] Garland County Chancery Court Records; Box 337, Case # 9499, Stella Snyder v. Stanley Snyder. Several letters from Annie appear in file.

[3] Ibid. This was taken from an affidavit by Stella McLaughlin Snyder.

her husband's health and that he seemed to be getting worse. Annie Snyder replied to Stella in a letter of 20 February 1927, admitting she knew far more about Stanley's drinking problem than she had indicated before. She admitted having received a letter from one of his friends in Miami Beach who reported he was quite concerned over Stanley's alcohol problem, before leaving that city for Hot Springs. Mrs. Snyder urged Stella to try to get Stanley "to take the cure," but said the nearest good facility was in Atlanta.

When Stella suggested to Stanley that he needed medical treatment and "the cure" he became enraged and more difficult to deal with. She grew more desperate claiming her husband was abusing her and that while he was confined to St. Joseph's Hospital, had humilated her before friends and acquaintances, cursing her in a loud voice.[4]

She discussed the situation with her brother Leo and the two decided there was no reasonable course for Stella to take but to file for a divorce. One day, less than eight months after being married, Stella separated from Stanley Snyder and moved back into her mother's home on Malvern Avenue. Hopefully, Bridget showed some compassion and did not taunt Stella with, "See, I told you so." It would be Stella's only venture into the bonds of matrimony.[5]

Probably had someone been given the task of match-making all of the unmarried men and women in Hot Springs, it would have been astronomical odds that George J. McLaughlin and Fannie Benedict would ever have been paired. But, that is just what happened. Love sometimes takes unusual paths to achieve its goals and that was certainly true with this couple.

George McLaughlin was dull, coarse and a bore to some people. He was arrogant, uncouth and a bully to others. He kept company with unsavory characters who sometimes led him into trouble and he was not trusted by city employees who knew him to be the "mayor's spy" in their midst. But when Fannie indicated an interest in George, he was smitten by the attractive Jewish girl with the effervescent personality. She saw something in George McLaughlin that others failed to see. He could make her laugh and was on his best behavior whenever Fannie was around. They enjoyed each other's company and she brought out the best in George.

Fannie's parents, Louis "Ludwig" and Mary Elizabeth Benedict operated a popular bakery in their home at 508 East Grand, catering especially to the Jewish segment in the Spa. There were four Benedict sisters, Sarah "Sadie," Hannah Louise, Fannie Elizabeth and Helen Mae.

Fannie had a short-lived marriage to Shug Gwinn, who was killed in an

---

[4] Ibid. From the affidavit of Tobey Fincel, an employee of the hospital.

[5] A divorce was granted in June 1928, and Stanley Snyder disappeared from the scene.

George McLaughlin
McLaughlin was charged in the death of Fats Long, but was exonerated when six State witnesses suddenly disappeared without explanation.
Courtesy of Norwood Phillips, Jr.

ccident.[6] She had trained to become a registered nurse and utilized her raining in several jobs including Public Health Nurse and much later as upervisor and then Administrator at the Leo N. Levi Hospital where a wing s named in her honor. She was one of those rare individuals who treated veryone she met as special or a friend. The children who recieved their accination and other health shots loved her, and there were thousands over he years. She seemed to be fondly known by a majority of the Spa's populace.

George McLaughlin was ten years her senior, but the difference of years neant little in their relationship. To George's credit, there was never another voman in his life after he met Fannie. The two quietly slipped away and were narried in Benton, Arkansas by Justice of the Peace, E.F. Holiman, 23 July 1930.[7] And George had not solicited his mother's opinion or permission. Her

---

[6] Recorded interview of Maurice Norwood Phillips, Jr. by Orval E. Allbritton at El Dorado, Arkansas, 20 July 1998. His mother, Hannah Benedict Phillips was a sister to Fannie McLaughlin. Mr. Phillips is an attorney and senior partner in the Shackleford Law Firm at El Dorado. Hereinafter cited as Norwood Phillips.

[7] Saline County Marriage Records, Book U, page 302, recorded 23 July 1930.

answer would probably have been, "An Irish marrying a Jew. Never."

In spite of George's often drinking bouts, the marriage worked. Verne Ledgerwood once asked her, "Why do you put up with him Fannie?" Her reply to Ledgerwood was, "When he comes in that way, (drinking) I just put him to bed and take care of him. I guess I just love him."[8] George was a rascal, but he was Fannie's rascal.

Strange, but George and Fannie's marriage, as illogical as it seemed, was the only one of the McLaughlins to last--all others failed. George, the rascal, probably would have been the first to admit Fannie was the best thing to ever come in to his life. Everyone, who knew the two, agreed.

Sidney M. Frink and his wife, Lula, moved from the Kansas City, Missouri area about 1918. He was self-employed as an architect and one of his first jobs was designing the Central Garage for Sidney Nutt. For several years his office would also be located there. He would later draw up the plans for Nutt's New Central Theatre, adjacent to the garage.

The eldest of two daughters, a very pretty and pleasant girl, Mary Francis, was scheduled to be in the graduating class of 1924 at Hot Springs High School. Whether she dropped out of school or attended a finishing school elsewhere, is unknown. She had several clerical positions in the five-and-dime stores of that day. It is not known where or when Leo P. McLaughlin first laid eyes on Mary Francis Frink, but even though he was sixteen years her senior he managed until he made her acquaintance. She was probably quite enthralled at the thought that the handsome and well dressed mayor had noticed her. After keeping company for several months, Leo persuaded Mary Francis to accompany him to the Kentucky Derby at Louisville.

It seems the "wily" Leo did not have matrimony on his mind and was just wanting to have an attractive companion on his arm at the races, dances and balls during the festive week. Yet, there was one thing which concerned Leo. It was a federal law which had been sponsored by James Robert Mann, Congressman from Illinois and introduced into Congress in 1910, a bill often referred to as the White Slave Traffic Act. "The law forbade the interstate transportation of a woman for immoral purposes, "whether she was a 'slave' or not."[9] There had been quite a lot of publicity attending a trial, only a few years earlier, involving a governor of the State of Mississippi who had taken his mistress from Jackson, to Memphis, and was charged with the above federal statute. It had ruined the man's career. Leo did not want the same thing to happen to him.

So what was McLaughlin to do? He came up with a plan and got in touch with James C. Williams in the Garland County Clerk's office and explained to

---

[8] LAT - Ledgerwood.

[9] Don Whitehead, *The FBI Story*, Random House, New York, 1956, p. 28.

George McLaughlin and Fannie Benedict were married in Benton in July of 1930. Their marriage was the only one of the McLauglin offspring to last. They had no children.
Courtesy of Norwood Phillips, Jr.

Williams he was contemplating getting married, but was not positive at that time. Could he provide him with a license in "skeleton" form and if he and the young lady he had in mind decided to get married they would be able to do so? Oh, there was one other thing, Williams was asked to note across the top of the clerk's copy, "Please do not publish." Leo wanted no publicity. No one signed the license application as the Principal (either Leo McLaughlin and/or Mary Francis Frink) or a Security, as required.[10] The license could be used as evidence of Leo's "sterling" intentions should something go awry on the trip and he and his attractive traveling companion be discovered. Apparently Leo had said nothing to Mary Frances relative to the license. As the old adage goes, "Be sure your sins will find you out," proved true. While Leo was out of the couple's hotel room Mary Francis discovered the uncompleted license.[11] She may have been pleasantly surprised and may have presumed Leo intended to marry her. It is not known if she confronted Leo about the license upon his return to the room or not. It is known that upon their return to Hot Springs the secret was out. Mary Francis went up and down Central Avenue, buying new clothes and charging everything "to my husband, Mayor Leo P. McLaughlin." A quick check by reporters of the clerk's records revealed the partially completed marriage application. Leo had trapped himself and there

[10] Garland County Marriage Records, Book - 36, p. 37, 16 April 1931.
[11] LAT - David Whittington.

was little he could do about it. In the event he claimed they were not married he left himself open to a felony charge under the White Slave Traffic Act, for transporting a woman across interstate lines for immoral purposes. And he had many political enemies who would be glad to furnish federal authorities with the juicy details. The charge was much more serious in that day and age when even personal escapades, which this had started out to be, were looked on as a serious matter. He realized if his actions were made public his political reputation might be damaged. So, McLaughlin went along with the marriage ploy. As far as anyone knows, no actual marriage ceremony was ever performed. The certificate of marriage was never completed by the Garland County Clerk's office and no priest, preacher, justice of the peace or judge ever validated the certificate of marriage.[12]

Leo McLaughlin was not so naive as to believe he could take his new bride to live in the McLaughlin home on Malvern. While he held the status of "favorite son" with his mother, Bridget wasn't ready to accept a daughter-in-law into the home, and certainly not a Protestant. He quickly arranged accommodations for him and Mary Francis at the Kingsway Hotel.

For the first few days following the couple's return to the Spa, marital bliss seemed to reign. However, the "marriage" was to be short-lived. The McLaughlins had always been a gregarious family and Leo began to miss their company. The couple was invited to have supper at the McLaughlin home. Mary Francis would later say she was treated rather "cooly" from the beginning and she was never made to feel as a part of the family. Stella and Elizabeth were politely curt in their conversation with her, Bridget withdrawn. Within a few days of that visit Leo was insisting they visit his family every evening. As the visits became more frequent, Mary Frances became more uncomfortable, being left out of the conversation by the McLaughlin family. One night she protested in going with Leo to visit his family and she told him how she felt. According to her later testimony he became abusive and began to curse her.

Mary Francis stayed with Leo for about four months, during which time the conflicts between the two increased. When she told Leo she wanted a divorce he made no protest and helped her hire Attorney A.T. "Sonny" Davies, long time acquaintance of the mayor, which may not have been a good idea in view of his close ties with Leo. After several months of wrangling a negotiated settlement was arranged with Mary Francis receiving a total sum of $6,500.

This was a relatively large sum in that day and age, and probably the reason McLaughlin did not dispute the amount was he was willing to pay his wife to gain her silence, plus the fact McLaughlin suddenly got in a hurry. The decree making the divorce final was issued on 3 November 1931 and restored her

---

[12] Garland County Marriage Records.

maiden name, Mary Francis Frink.[13] Unbelievably, McLaughlin had another young woman waiting in the wings and the day following the divorce decree, they married. Leo had spent only a few weeks with his first wife, Juanita Gilliam, mostly while he was in a military hospital, and the marriage to Mary Francis had lasted only four months. Was he improving his people skills? One observer commented, "The McLaughlins did not seem to make good marriages."[14]

City Hall — built in 1904
Mayor's office on second floor, Municipal Court on third floor, entrance to City Auditorium on steps to right.
The building was damaged by a mysterious fire in April of 1929.

---

[13] Garland County Chancery Court Records, Box 399, Case 10795, When the uthor was researching this divorce as well as another with the assistance of one of the lerks, we were surprised to discover a "Receipt For Papers" charge out card signed by Leo . McLaughlin, 19 July 1934. In the other, Box 557, Case 13446, a cross complaint, Leo P. lcLaughlin vs. Florence McLaughlin, only the jacket remained. All affidavits and filings f both divorce files were missing. The assistant clerk commented, "Why that b-----d stole oth of those files." The writer agreed. It certainly appeared to be so.

[14] LAT - Jimmy Dowds. Mary Francis Frink moved back in with her parents and ey resided at 209 Hobson. In the early 1930s, she met and married Frank G. Flynn, a radio alesman, but the marriage was of short duration. She later married William Sealy and the ouple lived in Dallas, Texas. *Sentinel-Record,* 10 January 1955.

The Saga of "Blackjack" George McLaughlin[1]

As the year 1932 approached, the citizens of Hot Springs began to plan a giant centennial celebration. The year was to commerate the 100th birthday since it had been made "the first national park."[2]

A large parade and celebration was organized by a committee chaired by M.T. Relyea with Major Howell Brewer as grand marshal. Twenty-nine beautiful floats designed and prepared by various clubs and organizations took part. The floats depicted the different eras and stages of the history of Hot Springs. Mayor Leo P. McLaughlin headed the parade accompanied by his new and third wife, Florence Paul McLaughlin, who represented the Museum Committee. They were followed by the 154th Infantry band and a detachment from the Army and Navy General Hospital, several National Guard units and a number of college and high school bands.

Mrs. William J. Little, the oldest living native-born citizen of the community occupied a horse-drawn victorian carriage and was the honoree of the celebration.[3] The news media reported that a solid mass of people lined both sides of the parade route and thousands of others occupied upper stories of the buildings. "Never had such an event been so attended here."[4]
It was a nice pause in the life of the Spa as a terrible economic depression descended over the country.

Almost everyone in "the know" was aware that George McLaughlin was a "silent partner" with Frank L. Clark in the operation of a number of slot machines in 1933.[5] McLaughlin had invested some money in the purchasing of several slots and helped in the collection from the boxes. Clark, owner of a couple of rooming houses on Cedar Street, did not have the best reputation in the community, had need of George McLaughlin. He knew if George could obtain the "blessing" of his brother, Mayor McLaughlin, Frank and George could make some money. The mayor apparently approved of this "union" and unofficially authorized them to set up a number of the "one-armed bandits" around town, mainly in cigar stores, pool halls and back street dives. These

---

[1] The nickname of "Blackjack" George was given to McLaughlin by the tabloi[d] newspaper, *The Public Opinion*, published at Hot Springs, 13 October 1933, pp. 6 and 12.

[2] There has always been a disagreement as to whether Hot Springs or Yellowstone wa[s] the first National Park. President Andrew Jackson signed a special act of Congress setting asid[e] the area surrounding the Spa city as a government reservation in 1832. Yellowstone w[as] "established in 1872 and was the first National Park in the United States." It is the wording o[f] reservation and park that fuels the argument. *The World Book Encyclopedia*, 1960, Vol. 8, p. 33[?] and Vol. 19, p. 464.

[3] *Sentinel-Record*, 24 April 1932.

[4] Ibid.

[5] *Sentinel-Record*, 27 May 1933.

were the nickel and quarter machines and there was no conflict with those slots being operated by W.S. Jacobs at the Ohio, Southern and Belvedere Clubs. Jacobs catered to a very different clientele than Frank and George. Leo hoped that "giving George a little piece of the action" would keep him out of trouble. It was wishful thinking--it didn"t!

On 21 January 1933, George McLaughlin received a call from his partner Frank Clark. Clark informed him a cigar store proprietor had reported a local taxicab driver, Sidney B. "Fats" Long had hit a jackpot on a nickel slot machine owned by George and Frank, and carried away about eighteen dollars in coins. The "rub" was not that Long had won, it was he had been using lead slugs to operate the machines.

George McLaughlin was furious and went immediately to the slot-machine accounting office at the rear of the Waukesha Hotel. Entrance was gained by walking down a narrow alley between the Medical Arts building and the Waukesha. As McLaughlin arrived and began to discuss the matter with his partner, they were joined by another "shady and illusive" character, Dick Galatas, aka, Richard Tallman Galatas, Dick Gladdas, Richard Galatis, Prichard Sheridan, Dick Sheridan, etc.[6]

Dick Galatas was a "well known confidence man and fixer of officals" and a close and friendly acquaintance of Mayor McLaughlin.[7] His FBI "rap-sheet," reflected he had been arrested in Toledo, Ohio, Los Angeles, California, Columbus, Ohio, and Flint, Michigan, on charges of operating as a con-man, fugitive-bunco artist, etc. But, his most important criminal participation was still several weeks in the future--the setting up of the Kansas City Massacre.[8] In January of 1933, Galatas and his wife Elizabeth, were renting a house off Park Avenue and he was involved in the book at the White Front Club.

George McLaughlin called the Yellow Cab office, which was near the slot-machine office, and asked for "Fats" Long, the night supervisor. When told Long was not there but was expected at any time, McLaughlin left word he wanted to see him. Bryan Dismuke, an employee of the cab company informed Long of the message when he came in a little later. Long walked down the alley toward the slot-machine office with Robert Dugan, who was employed by Frank Clark and George McLaughlin.

As soon as Long entered the room George McLaughlin accused him of putting slugs in their machines and a physical confrontation followed.

Joe Meyer, a high school boy and clerk at the Medical Arts Drug Store was just leaving work and upon hearing a noise looked down the alley beside the

---

[6] Justice Department or Federal Bureau of Investigation, Identification Order, # 1201, 1 August 1933.

[7] *The Public Opinion*, 18 August 1933, p. 8.

[8] FBI, I. O. # 1201.

pharmacy and saw Sid Long being held by one arm by Dick Galatas and struggling to get away. He heard Galatas say, "Come on back here or I'll hit you myself." Meyer saw Long pull free of his coat and come down the alley to the taxicab office and enter. Meyer noticed one lens of Long's glasses was broken and his face had a large bruise. He retrieved Long's hat and coat and followed.

Long and Meyer had barely got inside the cab office when George McLaughlin, highly agitated, came in the door and was followed by Clark, Galatas, remaining outside.[9] Clyde Diggs, Bryan Dismuke and cab drivers John Haynes (an ex-policeman), Floyd Snooks and Robert Dugan, McLaughlin and Clark employee, all heard the mayor's brother threaten Long, "You ---- , I ought to kill you."

These witnesses indicated Long put up no resistance and McLaughlin suddenly pulled a long-barrel Colt pistol and struck the taxi employee "on the head with it, causing him to slump against the wall and sink to the floor." McLaughlin then struck Long several times with a blackjack and kicked him while he was still prostrate on the floor. He then turned out Long's pockets looking for money he said Long allegedly owed him. Dismuke said that during this time Long never resisted and tried only to shield himself from the blows, and had not been drinking.

Sidney Long, suffering cuts and bruises to his face and a deep laceration to his scalp, sought treatment from Dr. Howell Brewer, a physician at the Army Navy General Hospital. Two days later he went to Dr. W.M. Blackshare, physician for the Warren Townsend Post of the American Legion where Long was a member. Dr. Blackshare was concerned with Long's injury and believed he needed additional treatment. He recommended Long be admitted to the Army-Navy General hospital. Sidney Long died there on January 26 as a result of septicema--blood poisoning, which was "caused by an injury to the scalp."[10]

These events were indeed shocking. But only at Hot Springs in the 1930s and early 1940s, could the following underhanded and devious acts have been committed and so blatantly displayed. It reflected the depths of depravity the administration of Leo P. McLaughlin would sink to protect one of their own.

Word of the affair was out on the street for several days, but no details could be verified as reporters for the *Sentinel-Record*, *Arkansas Gazette* and *Arkansas Democrat*, scrambling about for information, were kept in the dark. No information could be obtained at the police department and the mayor was out of his office or would not talk with newsmen. The *Sentinel-Record*, after finally learning some details, complained, "Although it was known that (George) McLaughlin had an altercation with Long and that the maimed man

---

[9] *Sentinel-Record*, 27 January 1933.
[10] Ibid.

was in a serious condition,newspapermen were balked at every turn in attempting to ascertain the true circumstances regarding the case. There was an evident attempt to "hush-up" the affair, several witnesses having been instructed to divulge no information and no report of the affair being available at police headquarters."[11] (Underlining, ours!)

Had Long not died, it is doubtful if any record of the bludgeoning would have ever been recorded. What story did George tell his brother, Mayor McLaughlin? How did Leo take it? Rumors were that the mayor was stunned and indecisive and had no plan of action. Only after Long died and word of the fatal encounter begin to circulate throughout the community that several of the machine politicians, who were concerned for their own welfare, called a meeting. Leo said he did not want his brother indicted. While some of the city and county officials were sympathetic, they were of the opinion if something was not done quickly the administration would be severely damage once the public became aware of all facts of the crime. McLaughlin argued against indicting George and lost his composure, yelling at several of his comrades when they tried to explain their point of view. It was leaked out of the meeting that at one point Judge Ledgerwood, frustrated by McLaughlin's stubbornness, stood before the mayor and slapped him sharply, telling him they had a crisis on their hands and that it needed to be dealt with. Ledgerwood said, "Leo, I believe if it was me, I'd give the facts to the grand jury and let them indict George. He can claim self defense and probably win."[12] Incidently, not a slot machine could be found in Garland County the day after "Fats" Long died. But they would suddenly and miraculously reappear after the trial.

The mayor had tried to "stonewall" the facts getting out and it may have worked had Long not died. He realized that with the death of Long things had drastically changed. Leo called on some of the "team players," Prosecuting Attorney Houston Emory and Circuit Judge Earl Witt, and explained the "game plan." Witt immediately summoned the grand jury and a hearing was scheduled.[13] The foreman of the grand jury was Cecil Ledgerwood. Prosecuting Attorney Emory issued warrants for the arrests of George McLaughlin, Dick Galatas and Frank Clark.[14] The three were taken into custody by Sheriff Jim Floyd and bonds of $3,000 on each man was set and paid. It must have appeared to the general public that the city and county officials were sincere in their efforts to prosecute the indiscretions of the mayor's brother and that there would be no favoritism shown. As it turned

---

[11] Ibid. (Shades of Richard Nixon and the Watergate Affair)

[12] LAT - Ledgerwood.

[13] *New Era*, 1 February 1933.

[14] *Sentinel-Record*, 27 January 1933.

out, it was nothing but a sham!

After the grand jury heard several witnesses, George McLaughlin was indicted and charges against Galatas and Clark were dropped. Judge Earl Witt scheduled George McLaughlin's trial to be held Monday 29 May 1933.[15] Not surprising, George McLaughlin was represented bytwo of the most successful criminal lawyers in the Spa, George Whittington and Richard Ryan. Mayor Leo McLaughlin would also help with his brother's defense.[16] George's indictment was that he "did unlawfully, willfully and feloniously kill one Sidney B. Long by striking and beating him, the said Sidney B. Long, with a pistol and a blackjack then and there held in the hands of him, the said George McLaughlin, and from the effects of said striking and beating as aforesaid the said Sidney B. Long died on January 26."[17]

With the charge of voluntary manslaughter hanging over George McLaughlin and the number of people who were either eye or material witnesses to the encounter, one might wonder what kind of defense could be made. Would "Blackjack" George throw himself on the mercy of the court and plead guilty hoping for a light sentence? Of course, anyone acquainted with the craftiness of the administration knew that was not going to happen. Surely, though, justice would win out, but one should never underestimate the wily and resourceful barristers of that day. George and his "dream team" of lawyers had worked out a plan.

First, George would plead self-defense and maintain that he used only the "necessary force" to defend himself from a "frenzied attack" on his person by Sidney B. Long. He would claim Long violently seized one of George's fingers and almost bit it off. Of course, if that was to be a part of his testimony it would be necessary for George to stop telling everyone who inquired about his bandaged finger that he had slammed a car door on it. Just a little change in the story and Long had severly bitten the digit. And, the county coroner, Dr. Randolph could testify he saw the "managled digit." But what about the witnesses who saw what really had occurred?

Almost as unbelievable as a Hollywood grade "B" movie script, the *Sentinel-Record* reported on the eve of the trial in front page headlines, "Six Witnesses in McLaughlin Case Declared Missing." It was followed by "Six star witnesses in the trial of George McLaughlin, which is scheduled to come up in circuit court here Monday morning cannot be located at present and Prosecuting Attorney Houston Emory is doubtful of his chances to make a trial without the aid of at least one of them."[18] Emory was preparing the voters for the

---

[15] Ibid., 23 May 1933.
[16] Ibid., 30 May 1933.
[17] Ibid., 23 May 1933.
[18] Ibid., 27 May 1933, p. 1.

worst, and he did not want the voters to doubt his ability as a prosecutor. Unbelievable! Six missing witnesses--what audacity!

It seems just as soon as the witness subpoenas were issued at the court house, word "somehow" was leaked to the witnesses, and before they could be served a scramble occurred "to get out of Dodge." It was rumored that one man, a former officer, who had never owned an automobile but showed up at a used car lot with a pocket full of money, purchased a shiny little roadster and drove off in to the sunset with a big wave and a smile at his friends. Two of the taxi employees and Geneva Freeman, former girlfriend of "Fats" Long, left town for parts unknown on an unexpected "all expense paid," vacation. Robert Dugan, young employee of Clark and McLaughlin, was suddenly gifted with a paid trip to Kansas City and for company was escorted by Elmer Walters, the mayor's bagman and flunkie to entertain the young man. Interestingly, their return trip would conveniently coincide with the day following the end of the trial.[19] How's that for timing?

Leo McLaughlin and his two attorney cohorts had everything under control. But to make sure there was no slip-up, a couple of "ringers" were installed on the jury as a safety precaution and if things went awry. A hung jury was always better than a "guilty" verdict.

The Depression had been underway for a number of months and jobs were scarce. This was particularly true of the city. In fact, salaries of city employees, with the exception of the mayor, municipal judge and a couple of department heads, were sliced down the middle.[20] But, in those days it was still considered a good job. One widow, Mrs. Dode Crawford, who operated Crawford Apartments, an unattractive two-story stucco building at Malvern and Gould Streets, had an unemployed son, Roy. She had tried to get him a job with the city with no results because of a hiring freeze at city hall. Her name came up on the McLaughlin jury and she discovered the importance of her position had changed the situation at city hall, and it "might be possible her son could find employment there." Only five days after the trial was ended, Roy Crawford was hired on the "city fire department on the recommendation by the mayor."[21] When the jury was empanelled, eleven members had been seated

---

[19] *Public Opinion*, 2 June 1933, p. 1. The bulletin read, "News Flash," 31 May 1933. " Robert Dugan, missing witness in the George McLaughlin trial on Monday, arrives in city Wednesday, accompanied by Elmer Walter." Local resident James "Ev" Young, in a recorded interview by Orval E. Allbritton, said Dugan had confirmed the above to him while both were with the National Guard unit sent to Alaska in World War II. Dugan received a letter from Leo P. McLaughlin, inquiring how was he doing.

[20] The writer's father, employed on the Hot Springs Fire Department as a driver, was earning $120 per month and was told "Effective last pay day, all pay checks will be 50% less."

[21] *Public Opinion*, 9 June 1933, p. 8. Roy Crawford was fiercely loyal to the Mayor and administration. He was a burly young man with an extremely hot temper. Ray Smith, local businessman, stated Crawford had approached him about withholding an article in *Public Opinion*.

with the prosecution having exhausted all of its challenges. Judge Earl Witt instructed the sheriff to bring in one of the reserve jurors. When Second Ward Alderman Carl Wilson was quickly brought into the court room, Houston Emory immediately objected. Without a blink of an eye, Witt overruled the prosecuting attorney, reminding him he had exhausted all his challenges.

Wilson was a very close acquaintance and supporter of Leo P. McLaughlin and his brother George, the defendant, and was considered an important cog in the administration's political machinery. When Leo was out of town on council nights, Wilson filled his spot. In 1929, city clerk Fred Fowler had run afoul of McLaughlin over the mayor "secretly" putting Carl Wilson on the city's payroll for three months. No one questioned McLaughlin; however, Fowler paid the price.[22] Almost everybody in town was aware of Wilson's connection. If a juror ever had a conflict of interest, it was Carl Wilson. Judge Earl Witt, an experienced jurist, saw nothing wrong with seating the alderman. But nothing was too unethical or too embarrassing to shame this administration.

It was obvious the prosecution would be crippled without the six missing witnesses. Would Emory request a postponement, certainly a reasonable and legitimate request? But no such request was made, and speculation leads one to believe it would not have been granted, even if made!.

It seemed that a spirited attempt was made by the prosecution as the two young men, Bryan Dismukes and Joe Meyers, testified as to their eye witness observation of the crime. Whittington and Ryan, on cross examination, "tore" in to the young men, trying to destroy or discredit their testimony. The papers reported both young men appeared honest and certain in the facts of their testimony. When the state rested, the defense introduced Dick Galatas and Frank Clark as "honest and sterling" citizens of the community. Just how "sterling and honest" were these two testifying on behalf of the mayor's brother, George? In less than five months the FBI would be tracking Galatas across country for his participation in the Kansas City Massacre and Frank L Clark would be behind bars and indicted at Little Rock on the fleecing of a Dr W.S. Johnston of Roanoke, Virginia, out of $10,000.[23]

Not even strong administration supporters could stomach the story of th bludgeoning of Sidney Long as advanced by the defense. Galatas, Clark, an McLaughlin all gave sworn testimony and acted surprised when slot machine were mentioned. They knew nothing; they didn't own any and did not kno

---

Smith told him he did not entirely control the publication and could make no promises. A fe days later, after the article had been published, Crawford struck Smith "twice under the left ey leaving that optic very black." *Sentinel-Record* 10 June 1933, p. 3.

[22] Council Proceedings of the City of Hot Springs, 14 February 1929.

[23] *Arkansas Democrat*, 19 August 1933.

anyone who owned slot machines. Clark humbly admitted he had a few penny weigh machines scattered about town and used his office to count the coins and repair the scales, but slot machines? He appeared shocked just at the thought. Never!

The unholy trio--Galatas, Clark and McLaughlin--testified George never threatened "Fats" Long concerning putting slugs in a slot machine. George innocently said,"If Long had put lead slugs in slot machines, it would have been nothing to me." George said his sole occupation was his position as police clerk, from 9:00 in the morning until 5:00 in the afternoon.[24] Perjury seemed to be an unknown word and not feared at the defense table.

Well, if George was not involved with slot machines, as almost every man walking the streets of Hot Springs believed, what in heaven's name caused the altercation?

Then George, the masterful storyteller, nervously twisting his handkerchief, began to spin his tale. He claimed a check had been given by Geneva Freeman (one of the missing witnesses) to Lawton Miller and that it was no good. Lawton gave it to him for collection. Instead of contacting Mrs. Freeman, McLaughlin knowing Sidney Long to be her boyfriend, decided to contact him about the debt. George "innocently, humbly" and "politely" approached Long. Upon mentioning the check, Long, according to George, flew into a rage and attacked the defendant and had to be pulled off by Galatas. According to George McLaughlin, Long left the "scales" office and went to the Yellow Cab office. George, not generally known as a sensitive and caring individual, said he felt "badly" about the encounter and "decided he should go and apologize to him for mentioning Mrs. Freeman's check to him." He claimed when he entered the cab office, Long charged him and as he pushed "Fats" away, George's finger got caught in Long's mouth and he began biting it. He said he pulled his gun and struck Long only once.

George McLaughlin had to admit to have been carrying a pistol on the "peaceful mission" of collecting on the bad check. He said as a police clerk he was authorized to carry a gun, but admitted he never made arrests and that the Freeman check was the only one he had ever tried to collect.[25]

Ridiculous? You bet. But, the jury was convinced after Mayor McLaughlin made an "eloquent plea" and attacked the professional abilities of the doctors at the Army-Navy General Hospital.[26] He claimed their poor treatment of Long's injury caused his death, but produced no medical support for his allegation. This was a typical Leo P. McLaughlin smoke-screen. He had done it all his life--divert attention from the subject and always blame someone else.

---

[24] *Public Opinion*, 2 June 1933, p. 3.
[25] Ibid.
[26] *Sentinel-Record, 30 May 1933.*

It had always worked. Why change now?

The verdict was a foregone conclusion as the jury returned in only fifty-three minutes with an acquittal for "Blackjack" George McLaughlin. There were a number of people who had supported the administration because they, too believed in the "open town" policy, but the farce of the trial left a bad taste in their mouth. It made one wonder, just how far were the city and county officials willing to go in protecting their base? It appeared they were willing to do whatever was necessary.

Had George learned his lesson and would he control his temper in the future? Not hardly. He again made the headlines in a few months as he reportedly "pistol whipped" one Bill Grayson for "selling liquor and who wasn't paying the proper respect to the administration." Fortunately, Grayson was not seriously injured and George did not need the expert and "honest testimony of Frank Clark, who was locked up in jail, and Dick Galatas, who had the FBI hot on his trail.

The Welcome Mat was Out

In the 1920s and 1930s, the underworld had code names for the Spa. It was ometimes referred to as "The Springs," or "Hot Town." It changed to Bubbles" in the forties. The Spa during that time was known as one of three or four "safe-cities," a place where mob members or gangsters could retreat when they were being hunted or when they felt they needed to lay-low or drop out of sight for awhile. Others used it as a place for recreation and as a respite rom the gang wars they had temporarily left behind or the cold weather of ierce northern winters. Just as the Indian tribes had treated the area several hundred years before by laying aside their weapons and forgetting their hatreds, even for a short time, the mobsters in an unwritten code classified Hot Springs as a sanctuary. They were also encouraged to a great degree by the attitude of the administration of Leo P. McLaughlin in a "live and let live" policy. There was nothing written, but the word was out: the mobs were welcome to come, spend their money and enjoy the wonders and pleasures of the area--just as long as they didn't bother the locals and behaved themselves. And come, they did. Most notable in the beginning were the gangs from the Chicago area, the Northsiders and the Southsiders.

John Torrio, head mobster of the Southside Gang in Chicago, began using the Spa as a vacation spot shortly before 1920, bringing his family first, then introducing it to members of his gang. To quote one authority, "John Torrio was the thinking man's criminal."[1] When he left New York and moved to Chicago, he came under the tutelage of his uncle, "Big Jim" Colosimo, vice-lord of the windy city who was being threatened by a terroristic extortion gang called the Black Hand. Colosimo turned the problem over to Torrio, who immediately took over the negotiations with three of the Black Hand members. It didn't turn out the way the extortioners envisioned, as Torrio killed two immediately, the third dieing the next day in the hospital. One historian wrote, "The drama of three killed at one time immediately chilled the enthusiam of other free-lancers for this particular target."[2]

Torrio became entrenched in the Chicago rackets and in 1919 hired a young hood he had used as an underling in New York to "bolster his muscle," who quickly became his first lieutenant, Al Capone. No gang leader ever had a more dedicated or dangerous right arm as Alphonse "Scarface" Capone was to Torrio. Torrio introduced Capone to Hot Springs and "Big" Al was hooked on the beauty of the Spa. As he moved up in the hierarchy of the mob, he scheduled it as an annual event for a number of years.

---

[1] Robert J. Schoenberg, *Mr. Capone*, Quill-William Morrow, New York, 1992, p. 22. Hereinafter cited as *Mr. Capone*.

[2] Ibid.

Alphonse Capone,
alias Al Brown, boss of Chicago's Southside gang, loved to visit the Spa. After being asked to leave the Eastman Hotel, they made their headquarters on the fourth floor of the Arlington.

During the early years, the gang stayed at the Eastman Hotel, but after an unusually loud and raucous party one night they were politely invited to leave. They just moved their vacation headquarters on up the street to the new Arlington Hotel, where occasionaly they would take an entire floor. One particular suite, 442, became a favorite of Capone's. It overlooked Central Avenue and the Southern Club, where he spent a considerable amount of time gambling.

"Big Jim" Colosimo had been assassinated in 1920, and many believed Torrio and Capone had done the deed, but both had "air-tight" alibis.[3]

Up until the early 1920s, Torrio's gang derived most of their income from operating brothels and whorehouses in a Chicago area known as Levee, the protection rackets and running saloons and gambling joints south of Madison Avenue, the dividing and territorial line between the Northside and Southside gangs. Rivalry between the gangs grew in intensity as opportunties to cash in

---

[3] Marie J. MacNee, *The Crime Encyclopedia,* U-X-L, Detroit, et al. - 1998, p. 14. Hereinafter cited as *Crime Encyclopedia.*

on illegal bootlegging and whiskey running became commonplace and as Prohibition approached.

The Northside Gang was run by a fearless and somewhat unpredictable individual, Charles Dion O'Banion, who had a fairly difficult life growing up, selling papers. He became a member of a juvenile group called the Market Street gang and as he developed phyiscally, a bouncer.[4] As he rose in the ranks and gradually became the acknowledged head of the Northside gang, he surrounded himself by a number of hardened criminals and killers.

There was no one in Chicago more feared than Hymie Weise, a slender and hawkish looking man whose temperature could go from normal to boiling in only a few seconds. He manifested his loyalty to O'Banion in several gangland style killings.

Another dangerous confederate of O'Banion was George "Bugs" Moran, who was of Polish decent, but pretended to be Irish in order that he might be accepted in the Northside gang. Moran, with the two Gusenberg brothers, Pete and Frank made a dangerous trio of ruthless killers.[5]

But Torrio and Capone also had a number of deadly "heavies," each notorious in his own right. There was Frank Nitti, sometimes called the "Enforcer," a deadly gunman; "Little" Augie Pisano and Louis "Lugi" Morganno; Albert Anselimi and John Scalise, each a deadly killer and hit-man.[6] Capone learned of treachery on the part of three of his trusted henchmen--Joseph Gunita, John Scalise and Albert Anselmi--who planned to murder Al for $50,000 each. Capone struck first, having received a tip, and personally murdered all three, beating them almost senseless with a baseball bat, then firing numerous bullets into their bodies. Their beaten, tortured, and bullet-riddled bodies were found by police at Spooner Nook, Indiana. The violence was so great in these killings it caused one mobster to remark, "No one kills like Capone."

Both gangs seemed to thrive and grow in strength during the early 1920s by providing all the beer and booze the illegal speakeasies and thirsty Chicagoans could use. The vast amount of money they accumulated allowed them to bribe police officers, city officials, judges, "fix" entire juries and vacation and relax in the sun far away from the cold and violence of the streets of Cicero and Chicago.[7]

Then began a series of events that "drew the line in the sand": the hi-jacking of each others' beer and whiskey shipments, the beating up of bartenders and

---

[4] *Mr. Capone*, pp. 106-107.

[5] *The Crime Encyclopedia*, p. 443.

[6] Ibid., p. 13.

[7] Estimates of the Capone gang's income ran from fifty million dollars a year to three hundred million.

saloon owners who purchased their alcohol products from the rival gang. Their hidden and illegal breweries were subject to attack and bombings. Even when the killings of the others' "soldiers" started there would be periods of time when an unofficial time out or pause would come and members would journey to "The Springs" for rest and recreation. After O'Banion was slain in a flower shop he operated and the gang was taken over by Hymie Weiss and a bit later by "Bugs" Moran, they brought several of their top henchmen with them and checked into the Majestic Hotel. The Northsiders had been in the Spa only a day or two until they discovered Al Capone and a number of his boys were headquartered down the street at the Arlington Hotel.[8] Both gangs nervously kept an eye on the other.

That evening the two gangs attended the prize-fights at City Auditorium and uneasy police officers, in the style of the "Old West" invited the mobsters to "Check your guns, here." It was claimed one box was provided for the weapons of the Southside mob and another for the Northside. It may have been an unnecessary precaution, however any fight fans who were aware of the identity of the tough-looking men probably rested easier. No untoward incidents resulted, to the relief of everybody.

Once back in Chicago, however, they reverted to their baser nature. On 24 January 1925, John Torrio was gunned down and very seriously wounded. He

Al Capone, left, with Danny Stanton at Happy Hollow.
Stanton was a member of the Ragen Colts, a Southside gang.
Courtesy of Mark Palmer

[8] LAT - Roy Bosson. Also, from an undated *Arkansas Gazette* article, "Leo P. And the Tough Guys," by Doug Smith.

recovered, but had enough of Chicago and turned the Southside mob over to Capone.[9]

From that point the killings got worse and several times when a "hit" was made the leaders of one gang or another conveniently had an alibi of being in Florida or Hot Springs, enjoying the major league baseball teams in training, taking the baths, or bowling in the basement of the old Dugan-Stuart Building.

The Northside gang used ten automobiles and three times that many "shooters," each armed with a sub-machine gun or shotgun and blew apart the first floor of the Hawthorne Hotel, headquarters of the Southside mob, in retailation of the slaying of Dion O'Banion. A quick thinking bodyguard shoved Al Capone to the floor and he barely escaped the hail of gunfire as bullets sliced through the Hawthorne. Police later said over one thousand bullets had been fired into the hotel. Apparently the "gunners" were not the best of marksmen as they also hit thirty-five parked automobiles. Miraculously, no one was killed and only four people were injured.[10]

Capone quickly learned the shooting had been engineered by Hymie Weiss, who had taken O'Banion's place. Capone had some of his gunmen to set up a sniper's nest across the street from the deceased O'Banion's flower shop which still served as headquarters for the Northside mob. Three weeks after the Hawthorne Hotel had been used as a shooting gallery, Hymie Weiss and one of his bodyguards, Patrick Murray were gunned down in front of the flower shop. Weiss' attorney, who was with them, was painfully wounded, also.

Chief of Police Collins, philosophically noted, "I don't want to encourage the business, but if somebody has to be killed, it's a good thing the gangsters are murdering themselves off. It saves trouble for the police.[11]

Other attempts would be made on Capone's life, one at Hot Springs, by Vincent "Schemer" Drucci. Regarding that occasion, author John Kobler, wrote, "In March [1927] Capone took a short pleasure trip to Hot Springs, Arkansas. Drucci, who somehow got wind of it, followed him and there, fired a shotgun at him, but missed."[12] It was rumored that Capone was alone and driving toward Belvedere, when Drucci tried to ambush him[13]. Perhaps in

---

[9] *The Crime Encyclopedia*, p. 441.

[10] *Mr. Capone*, p 160. The Hawthorne incident occurred 20 September 1926.

[11] Ibid., p. 163.

[12] John Kobler, *Capone*, Fawcett Publications, Inc., 1971, p. 189. This writer has been unable to confirm this happening. However, unless it had occurred in a public place it is doubtful it would ever have been reported as the mob generally took care of problems like this. It is doubtful Capone would go anywhere by himself. See following text.

[13] Local historian Mark Palmer, who has devoted many years of studying the gamblers and gangsters who visited the Spa, advised that one story had the ambush near Belvedere, another on upper Park Avenue.

Drucci's twisted thoughts he believed if he shot Capone outside the city limits of the Spa he would not have been breaking the unwritten code protecting all gang members while here and he would not be held accountable for breaking the peace. It is interesting to note Vincent Drucci came to a quick end a few days later. On 5 April 1927, in a mysterious set of events involving a young police officer, Drucci was killed. Drucci's lawyer immediately screamed his client had been murdered, but the Chicago police claimed it was a justifiable killing. Hot Springs was so caught up in the "hot" city election campaigning between Leo P. McLaughlin and Sidney Nutt, little attention was drawn to the local affair.

It was estimated hundreds of gangland killings took place in Chicago during the 1920s. Most were directly related in trying to circumvent the Prohibition laws. Capone capped off the killings in grand style with the Saint Valentine's Day Massacre when seven men were murdered in cold blood. It was a Capone effort to get "Bugs" Moran, which failed but greatly weakened the Northside mob. Of course, Capone had an air-tight alibi as usual, he was basking in the warm sun in Flordia and entertaining a district attorney. He had imported members of the Purple Gang from Detroit, to do the dirty work. That gang, also was known to have vacationed in Hot Springs a time or two.

When the Chicago mobs were vacationing at "The Springs" they pretty much stayed to themselves. Some played the horse books and gambled at the tables at the Southern and Belvedere Clubs. They breakfasted at the Arlington, Majestic and Eastman. They dined at Stutes, a fine southern fried chicken resturant, and Belvedere for steaks. The mobsters were big spenders and generous tippers. From shoe-shine boys, to caddies, bellhops and maître-de's they were welcomed up and down Central Avenue. Some bought souveniers and sent post cards to their families and girl friends. Others purchased candy and sweets from the London Candy Shop, and showy items from the auction houses. Capone and five or six of his "heavies," could be seen strolling down bath house row on warm and sunny days. He loved to show any first-timers of his party to the Spa, Happy Hollow, where comic postcard pictures were made.[14] Grace Goldstein and the girls at the Hatterie Hotel, adjacent to the Arlington, always welcomed the boys from Chicago and sometimes they would "buy the house out," and throw a big party.

Capone played poker at the Southern Club and always occupied a chair from which he could view the entire gaming room. He generally carried a large roll of one-hundred dollar bills, but would many times play on his "marker" paying up at the end of his stay. Once, however, he had a streak of bad cards and angrily stalked out of the Southern Club, cursing and leaving a stack of unpaid

---

[14] At least two of those shots remain and are frequently published.

markers. W.S. Jacobs quickly complained to Chief of Police Wakelin, who got in touch with Al's brother, Ralph "Bottles" Capone and related Al's debt to him. Ralph supposedly told Al, "We'll never be able to come here again if we try to "stiff" them on this." Al relented and sent one of his men to Jacobs to pay the bill.[15]

Occasionally one of the gang members would get in trouble in some way and the leaders would try to work it out, drawing as little attention to themselves as possible. Once, a golf caddy at the Hot Springs Country Club, ill-advisely made a critical remark about the golf game of one of the hoodlums and was promptly thrashed for his candor. The young man made a report to the police and filed a complaint and the gangster was charged with assault and battery. He was required to appear before Municipal Judge Ledgerwood. When the case was called, Ledgerwood was told by the caddy, who seemed to be in an unusually good mood for a person who had been assaulted, "I was wrong in saying what I did and I'd like to drop the charges." Ledgerwood said, "It was obvious they had 'fixed' the boy or paid him off. Since there was no complaint I had to dismiss the case."[16]

One gang member got in a confrontation with a local officer on a petty matter. The officer knew what to do and instead of filing a charge against the mobster for "resisting arrest by an officer," marked the docket he was being arrested for "stealing chickens." The gangster blanched at the charge and asked how much it would cost to drop the entire matter. He willingly paid the fine assessed. There was no way he wanted to return to Chicago with a charge of "stealing chickens," on his record--the boys downtown would never let him live it down.

After Capone lost his battles with the Internal Revenue Service over the evasion of income taxes in 1931 and his banishment to the federal penitentiary--first at Atlanta, then to Alcatraz--he was really fighting another battle which he was also destined to lose, a battle against syphilis, which he no doubt had contracted in one of the "play pens" his organization operated, the visits from the mob members decreased.[17] That is, all but "Bottles." Ralph Capone and a few of the boys would come to the Spa every spring and vacation for a couple of weeks. They still spread the money around and "Bottles" enjoyed near celebrity status, but it just wasn't the same without the

---

[15] LAT - Ledgerwood. The markers were said to total $13,000. "Bottles" Capone was a much lower profile than his brother. Ledgerwood said that "Bottles" always acted like a gentleman. Even after Al Capone was sent to prison, Ralph continued to vacation in Hot Springs.

[16] LAT - Ledgerwood.

[17] *Mr. Capone*, pp. 348-349.

"big guy." It just wasn't as exciting.[18] Ralph enjoyed the attention he received at Hot Springs, but complained of his own lack of identity in other places in 1941, "It's tough being pointed out as Al Capone's brother," he said.[19]

Even though the visits to the Spa by the big mobs were unannounced, their presence was quite often known to the townspeople. The large black sedans, some armored like a battleship, stood out like a rooster in a hen house.[20] They required gasoline and oil and when stopped at a service station brought admiring glances from the attendants and anyone else present. Or when repairs were required the shop's owner proudly boasted, "I worked on Al Capone's car."

For years the Capone mob purchased several cars a year from the Denemark LaSalle-Cadillac dealership in Chicago. For a considerable time after racing resumed in the Spa in 1934, Emil Denemark and his wife brought a string of their fine thoroughbreds to race at Oaklawn Park. When Ralph Capone was in town he would visit with Mr. and Mrs. Emil Denemark and the trio would

Alfred "Gee" Raso
and one of the Capone brothers, possibly Ralph.
Arlington Park — 1933
Courtesy of Mark Palmer

---

[18] Ralph "Bottles" Capone continued to come to the Spa into the 1950s. "He was a perfect gentleman while he was here," Verne Ledgerwood once said.

[19] *Mr. Capone*, p. 361.

[20] Capone had three large armored limousines which were auctioned off after his death. One Park Avenue serviceman claimed it took two men to raise the heavy sheet metal hood.

go out to Stutes to dine. The association somehow started the rumor that Mrs. Jean Denemark was the sister of Al and Ralph Capone. Even as late as 1989, one of the *Arkansas Gazette* staff writers wrote that Mrs. Denemark's fine racing stable was partially due its success because of her brother, Al Capone.[21]

The writer inquired of Don Grisham, retired writer for the *Daily Racing Form*, if he had ever heard the story of the supposed relationship between Mrs. Denemark and the Capones. Grisham informed the writer that one racing correspondent had spent a considerable amount of time in tracking down the story and was disappointed to learn there was no truth to it. But, according to Grisham, the story crops up every few years. It seems the only connection was that the mob had bought a number of cars from the Denemark car agency and there was no kinship.

While the mid-western gangs of mobsters frequented the Spa, there were other notables of the underworld who visited from time to time. From the eastern syndicate two were "Bugsy" Siegel and Meyer Lansky, who in their early days ran the "Bug and Meyer" mob, a deadly "hit" gang which took contracts on people the syndicate wanted "rubbed-out." Siegel came to the Spa for fun and relaxation, Lansky for more somber reasons.

Meyer Lansky, sometimes called the Chairman of the Board (National Crime Syndicate) or the Godfather of the Godfathers, owned a myriad of gambling interests from New York to Cuba, had a young son, Buddy, who was born with cerebral palsy, and was crippled from birth. Lansky, who always liked to be in charge of everything in which he was involved, felt frustrated in not being able to get medical treatment which would cure his son. One doctor suggested taking the boy to Hot Springs for the thermal baths. Lansky, desperate, called an acquaintance and former gang leader in New York and at that time residing in Hot Springs, Owney Madden. Madden informed him there were numerous testimonies of people having been cured or at least relieved and their health improved by taking the baths. He assisted in making reservations and arrangements for Lansky and his son. In spite of their lengthy stay and subsquent visits the boy's basic health remained unchanged.[22]

Other notables from the eastern mob included Dutch Schultz, "Legs" Diamond, "Lucky" Luciano and Frank "Prime-Minister of the Underworld" Costello, each an interesting and dangerous character.

Owen Vincent Madden, most often just referred to as Owney or "The Duke," had been born at Leeds, England. While young he had immigrated to America and was raised by an aunt in New York City on the edge of the area

---

[21] *Arkansas Gazette*, "Hot Springs Cleanup Slower than Oaklawn Park's," by Kim Brazzel, 17 January 1989.

[22] Robert Lacy, *Little Man - Meyer Lansky and the Gangster Life*, Little Brown & Co., Boston, Toronto - London, 1991, pp. 85-86.

Owney Madden behind the bar at Happy Hollow jokingly holding a gun on friends.
Madden, former boss of one of New York's bootlegging gangs, was banished to Hot Springs by Thomas Dewey.

called "Hell's Kitchen." This was in a neighborhood so brutal that only the toughest survived, either by escaping to a better life or fighting one's way up in one of a number of juvenile gangs which existed there. Madden became head of the Gophers, a notorious street gang that was constantly in trouble with the law over muggings, robberies and even killings. His meteoric rise in the hierarchy of New York's underworld soon brought the attention of the local law enforcement authorities, and his career in crime was not without its conflicts and dangers. Owney Madden shot and killed William Henshaw, a man who tried to date one of his girl friends in 1910. He followed Henshaw onto a trolley car in Manhattan and shot him there. After terrified witesses refused to testify, Madden was set free.[23] He almost died from several bullet wounds incurred at a night club, The Arbors, in New York, compliments of The Hudson Dusters, a rival gang.[24] While Owney was recuperating from the wounds, his gang took retribution on the Hudson Dusters as six of his assailants were killed.[25]

There were other shootings and killings and Owney Madden served nine

---

[23] *The Crime Encyclopedia*, p. 428.

[24] *New York Sun*, Morning Edition, 6 November 1912.

[25] Graham Nown, *The English Godfather*, Hollen Street Press, Great Britain, 1987. See Chapter 4, p. 35. Nown writes the six men were killed "within a week - a week." Also, *The Crime Encyclopedia*, p. 438.

years of a twenty-year sentence in New York state's Sing-Sing Prison. That was for the murder of Patsy Doyle, a gangster who attempted to muscle in on Madden's territory.

His gang grew more powerful and influential in the underworld as the mob tied itself to the bootlegging industry. It invested in legitimate as well as illegal businesses. Madden was co-owner of the well known Harlem night spot, the Cotton Club, which catered to the elite of society who liked to rub elbows with underworld characters such as "Dutch" Schultz, "Legs" Diamond, Jimmy Hines and Charles "Lucky" Lucanio. Writers Damon Runyon and Walter Winchell regularly appeared at the Cotton Club and got much of their material from the characters who frequented the place. Madden had a deal with Winchell that he wouldn't write about Owney.

Madden was a silent partner in several operations including the Silver Slipper, Stork Club and various speakeasies run by colorful Texas Guinan. It was in the confines of the Cotton Club and speakeasies that jazz music got its big boost in the east. He helped advance the careers of George Raft and Mae West, with whom he reportedly had a torrid affair. Owney had more than a fifty-percent interest in the Broadway show, *Diamond Lil*, which established Mae West's legendary sultry image. At the cast party on opening night she reportedly said of Madden, "Hmmmm, so sweet--and so vicious."[26]

He also became an investor in several prize fighters of the era, most notably, Primo Carnera, reportedly "the champion of fixed boxing matches."[27]

When Owney Madden came under heat from the state district attorney's office for rackerteering and parole violations, he took a vacation to Hot Springs. It was here he met a woman with whom he would fall in love and marry.[28] Agnes Demby, in her thirties, was the daughter of James Demby, local postmaster. She operated and barely eked out a living with Agnes' Gift Shop and Tea Room at 314 Central Avenue. A courtship developed between the mobster and the local girl, and after Thomas E. Dewey, an ambitious district attorney and crime-fighter, had effectively placed restraints on Owney's activities and all but banished him from New York, Owney and Agnes were married.

Owney Madden's reputation preceded his moving to the Spa and he met with Mayor Leo P. McLaughlin and Municipal Judge Ledgerwood, whom Madden recognized as being the power brokers of the community. He was informed at that time he would encounter no resistence from the authorities

---

[26] *The Philadelphia Enquirer*, "A Cotton Club Story, Starring Mae West," by Kevin Thomas, 31 December 1984.

[27] *The Crime Encyclopedia*, p. 440.

[28] Owney Madden had been married once before and was divorced before World War I.

as long as he behaved himself. They made it clear to him he was to have no interest in any of the gambling clubs. "If it was known you had any interest in the clubs here," Ledgerwood told Madden, "We wouldn't be able to operate."[299] This policy toward Madden would change upon the death of the chief gambler, W.S. Jacobs, in 1940, and he would gradually be accepted as an investor in some of the clubs and also would control the wire service to the horse books.

Madden did become a good citizen of the Spa, making generous donations to worthy causes. The writer recalls, as a member of the Boy's Club in the 1940s, of being dispatched by the club's manager, "Moon" Mullins, to "meet Mr. Madden and help him." Owney and Agnes lived less than two blocks from the Boy's Club, and as the writer ran from the Armory Building, Owney Madden was seen struggling along the sidewalk carrying a large box with the handles of several baseball bats protruding from it. It was an excited bunch of kids who gathered round us when we got back to the club. There were baseballs, gloves, balls, bats, a football and basketball and a couple of pairs of boxing gloves. Owney had visited Stearns Hardware Store on Central Avenue and bought every item they had of sports gear. He just stood back and enjoyed watching the happy expressions on the faces of the youngsters. Madden, who had grown up on the edge of poverty, understood what the sporting equipment meant to a poorly equipped Boy's Club, and he wasn't looking for any plaudits for his generosity.

For years he remained the contact of the big gangsters when they came to town. His friends did not forget him and when they visited, he always picked up the tab. To show appreciation for Owney's help with his career, his old friend, George Raft, bought him a sleek, polished and waxed Chris-Craft inboard motor boat which he used on Lake Hamilton for pleasure.

Then there were those criminals who arrived in Hot Springs who were on the run and hiding from the law. One such, was Frank "Jelly" Nash, an escapee from the federal penitentiary at Ft. Leavenworth, Kansas in October 1930 with several other criminals. He had been a member of the Al Spencer gang of bank and train robbers. When he was apprehended at Sierra Blanca on the Mexican border, 9 September 1923, he had been sentenced to a term of twenty-five years for a train robbery in Oklahoma. About a year after his break in 1930, seven prisoners had made a bloody break for freedom, three of those being slain. Two of those had been members of the Al Spencer gang. Nash was blamed for smuggling guns to them.[30]

"Jelly" Nash knew he was being hunted for helping in the prison break and kept on the move, going to Minnesota, Illinois, Missouri and arrived in the Spa

---

[299] LAT - Ledgerwood.
[30] *Sentinel-Record*, 17 June 1933.

in April 1933, staying only a short time, but returned in June.

He had met a divorcee, Frances Luce, who had a small daughter. Frances was impressed with Nash as a "big spender," and believed him when he promised to marry her. He kept his promise as the two were married at Hot Springs on May25, 1933. Nash used the alias of George W. Miller.[31] The three stayed a short time at the Woodcock Apartments on Woodbine Street, then moved to the Oaklawn Tourist Courts on south Central Avenue, before finally alighting in an apartment in the Thompson Building. This was only a few doors from Mathew Picchi's White Front Cigar Store at 310 Central. The White Front had the reputation of being a contact for visiting members of the underworld, principally because of Richard "Dick" Galatas, who may have owned a small part of the horse book at the club. Nash, who was acquainted with Galatas, used the name, "Doc" Williams.

Galatas made "Doc" welcome, and as previously revealed in his relationship with George "Blackjack" McLaughlin, was in tight with the city authorities, including Chief of Police Wakelin and Chief of Detectives, Dutch Akers. In all probability, for a price, Akers agreed to tip Nash if anyone arrived in town looking for him as this seemed to be his usual procedure.

Being flush with money from two recent robberies, Nash began to entertain some of his new friends at a couple of the night clubs.[32] "Jelly" loved to sing and would "tip the orchestra as much as fifty dollars to play, a *Shanty in Old Shanty Town,"* his favorite.[33]

After arriving in Hot Springs Nash had some cosmetic surgery done to his nose, grew a moustache and began to wear a wig, presumably to alter his appearance. Thinking he was relatively safe, especially since his friend Galatas had introduced him to "Dutch" Akers as "a good guy," he began to drop his guard. This was a fatal mistake for Nash, for at that moment FBI Agents Joseph Lackey and Frank Smith, accompanied by Otto Reed, Chief of Police of McAllester, Oklahoma, were arriving in the Spa and registered at the Como Hotel. The two federal agents had been running down leads on Frank Nash, including one that Nash's automobile had been spotted near the White Front Club on Central Avenue. Since neither agent had ever seen Nash they had invited Reed to accompany them as he was acquainted with the fugitive and could identify him.

Agents of the FBI were taught to work with and solicit the aid and support of local law enforcement agencies when working in their territory. But in the case at Hot Springs, the FBI and agents of the federal government had come

---

[31] Garland County Marriage Records, Book 37, p. 335. The record reflects that Frances Mikulish Luce, 31, married George W. Miller, 42, on May 25, 1933.

[32] Ibid., 18 June 1933.

[33] Ibid.

Charles "Lucky" Luciano
was apprehended in the Spa while strolling the Promenade with Chief of Detectives Herbert "Dutch" Akers.

to mistrust the Hot Springs Police Department, and as it turned out, rightfully so. They had discovered on several occasions when they notified the local authorities of their suspicion that a wanted criminal was in the vicinity, the prey they were certain to have been at the Spa had been tipped off and flown the coop. The more they dealt with Dutch Akers and Joe Wakelin, the more they became convinced this was true. At any rate, the lawmen were taking extra precautions and did not notify the locals of their arrival.[34]

On Friday 16 June 1936, the lawmen pulled their Buick sedan into a parking place almost in front of the White Front Club. The motor was left running and one of the men stood near it. The other two entered the White Front and failing to see Nash they bought some smokes and stood chatting. The fugitive sauntered from a rear pool room and leisurely walked toward the front of the store. Almost to the front door he was suddenly flanked by Agent Lackey and McAllester Chief Otto Reed. He felt a gun jammed in his ribs and knew in an instance unless something quickly occurred, he was headed back to Leavenworth. In just a few seconds he was pushed into the lawmen's sedan and it pulled in to Central Avenue, headed south, circling the block, then headed north on Central to the Little Rock highway. The capture had gone so smoothly it was hardly noticed. However, Matt Picchi saw the two men flank Nash and hustle him to the waiting car. Others on the sidewalk observed Nash being shoved into the car.

Picchi immediately informed "Dick" Galatas, who appeared stunned by the

---

[34] Mack Hamblen, "How Frank Nash Became Famous," Part 3, *Greene County Historical & Genealogical Society Quarterly*, Vol. 10, Number 4, 1997, pp. 142-143. Mr. Hamblen had written a three part article on the life of Frank Nash. Hereinafter cited as Hamblen.

news. He was not certain if Nash had been arrested by some law enforcement agency or perhaps kidnapped by some gang with a grudge against "Jelly." Galatas hurriedly called his friend Dutch Akers. Akers was also puzzled by the turn of events as he had not been notified by any police department or agency they were in town seeking Nash. He sent a car in fast pursuit of the Buick sedan, but it had no chance of overtaking the speeding car. Chief of Detectives Akers telephoned the Benton Police Department as well as Little Rock and told them a man named "Doc" had been "kidnapped" off the street in Hot Springs.[35]

The officers transporting Nash were stopped at both Benton and Little Rock and the officers were satisfied with the agent's credentials. Calls were placed to Hot Springs and Akers was told that federal agents had taken an escapee into custody and they had "backed off" and let them continue.[36] Galatas had Akers inquire as to where the federal agents were taking their prisoner. They were told the officers were driving to Joplin, Missouri. It was obvious that Nash was being returned to prison.

"Back in Hot Springs," one author wrote, "Dick Galatas panicked. He considered the possibility that Frank's underworld friends might think that he had 'fingered' Nash to the FBI. He knew retribution would swiftly follow if the underworld even suspected that he was involved."[37] This was quite possibly true as Galatas occupied a precarious position, that of being a go-between of the underworld and the local police department. He tried to walk a tightrope between the two.

Galatas contacted Frances, Nash's live-in girlfriend, who told him Nash had instructed her if anything should happen to him, to contact an individual in Chicago. Susposedly, Doc Stacci, the contact, told Galatas he would notify Verne Miller, an ex-sheriff turned hoodlum, in Kansas City to determine if a rescue of Nash might be made.

Dick Galatas chartered an airplane to fly him, Frances and her eight year-old daughter, to Joplin.[38] This story would later be denied by John Stover, manager of the small municipal airport.[39]

The lawmen drove to Fort Smith and boarded a train to Kansas City. Word

---

[35] Ibid.

[36] *Sentinel-Record*, 17 June 1933.

[37] Hamblen, p. 144.

[38] Ibid.

[39] *Sentinel-Record*, 18 June 1933. It is to be noted that Stover did engage in charter flights for some very dangerous and wanted underworld gangsters. In fact, four years later he would be charged and tried on charges of harboring and aiding Alvin Karpis on a couple of his trips. Stover would be exonerated at trial. It is highly possible Stover may not have known the identity of his customer, but should have been suspicious. After all, it was during the Depression and cash-paying customers for chartered flights were few and far between.

was received by the Hot Springs Police Department that Nash had been transferred at Fort Smith to a Missouri-Pacific train which was scheduled to arrive in Kansas City the following morning at 7:15 a.m.[40] During this time, Verne Miller was arranging a "reception" with gangster "Pretty Boy" Floyd and his side-kick, Adam Richetti, for the federal agents and an attempt at rescuing Frank Nash.

The FBI arranged for Special Agent in Charge of the Kansas City office, Reed Vetterli, and agent Ray Caffrey, to meet the train as well as two Kansas City police detectives, Frank Hermanson and W.J. Graves.

As the federal agents and lawmen began to load Nash into the front seat of Caffrey's 1932 Chevrolet two-door sedan, Chief Otto Reed and two agents climbed into the rear seat. The two Kansas City officers and agent Vetterli were standing by the car as the three gunmen suddenly appeared, each armed with .45 calibre Thompson sub-machineguns. One of the outlaws commanded, "Up! Up!" And then, "Let 'em have it."[41]

The sudden attack was so swift and unexpected the lawmen were caught completely unaware. The first murderous barrage killed Detectives Groom and Hermanson, McAllester, Oklahoma Chief Otto Reed, and FBI Agent Raymon Caffery. A second blast wounded two other agents. And what about the object of the gunmen's rescue effort--Frank "Jelly" Nash? He was still in the front seat of the agent's car, slumped over "with a bullet in his brain, a bullet from the gun of one of his "liberators."[42]

Five men had been killed in just a few seconds! And, for what? The individual the criminals were hoping to liberate had been killed. Probably because of his changed appearance, the gunmen had failed to recognize him. All they had done was to awaken a slumbering giant--the FBI. Because of the senseless killings, Congress granted broad new powers to this investigative agency to use in its fight against crime. And use them, it did. A massive manhunt for the gunmen--Vernon Miller, Adam Richetti and "Pretty Boy" Floyd--began. They were too "hot" for the underworld to hide and were not welcomed in their old hangouts.

Miller's bullet-riddled body was located near Detroit, his friends apparently afraid he would lead federal agents to their doorstep. Adam Richetti was apprehended in Ohio, tried and convicted of murder charges and executed by the State of Missouri in 1938 after numerous appeals failed. Floyd was "run to ground" by agents of the FBI in Ohio and died in a hail of bullets on 22

---

[40] Hamblen.

[41] Don Whitehead, *The FBI Story*, Random House, New York, 1956, pp. 97-98. At the time of publication, this was considered the most definitive and accurate of all works on the FBI and was given the "blessing" of its director, J. Edgar Hoover, who contributed the Foreword

[42] Ibid.

October 1934.[43]

"Dick" Galatas and Frances, Nash's new wife, were at the rural home of Herb and Esther Farmer, underworld contacts, near Joplin, Missouri, when word was received of the massacre and that the attempt to free "Jelly" Nash had failed. Worse still, to Frances, was the news that Nash had been killed. Both Galatas and Frances were stunned. Frances was also very frightened and immediately left, telling no one her destination. She was traced by agents to a relative's home in Illinois and arrested. Her attorney made a deal for her to turn State's evidence and she agreed to cooperate with the United States Attorney's office in exchange for immunity.

Galatas realized he had just been promoted to the "hot-spot," so far as the federal government was concerned. To the FBI, he previously had been "small potatoes," and suddenly he had became the object of a nationwide manhunt as Director J. Edgar Hoover blamed him and the Hot Springs Police Department for the five deaths at Kansas City. The Bureau issued a wanted poster, called an Identification Order, Number 1201, for Richard "Dick" Tallman Galatas, which was distributed to post offices, law enforcement agencies, motels, bus and train stations and carried a fairly clear picture of the fugitive. It also set forth he was being wanted in connection with the five murders at Kansas City.

Galatas led the federal agents on a long chase, from one coast to the other, but flee as he might, he could not shake them off his trail. He was finally apprehended at New Orleans. Tried and convicted in Federal Court for conspiracy to obstruct justice, he was given the maximum sentence in prison of four years and fined $10,000.[44] He would serve his time at Alcatraz.[45]

Public Opinion, the little tabloid newspaper published at Hot Springs, had a field-day with the chase of Galatas by federal agents, reminding the citizens of the Spa what type of character some of "our city officials" were hanging out with. The publication of 18 August 1933, sported large headlines, "Star Witnesses of McLaughlin Defense in Dragnet."[46] Sub-headlines heralded, "Dick Galatas wanted by Department of Justice in Connection With Machine Gun Massacre at Kansas City."

---

[43] Ibid., pp. 333-334.

[44] Hamblen, p. 152. When Galatas was released from prison, he and his wife Elizabeth returned to Hot Springs and resided for awhile at 18 Dell Street. Just to show how closely Galatas was tied in with the local administration is the fact that it was learned he had bought a car from a dealer in Hot Springs and that none other than Mayor Leo P. McLaughlin and his brother George had signed his note. *Public Opinion*, 25 August 1933, p. 3.

[45] *NewEra*, 26 November 1936. Richard T. Galatas served 14 months of his sentence at Alcatraz, and was returned to Leavenworth penitentiary for release. He took a pauper's oath and served an extra month in prison as he could not pay the $10,000 fine imposed upon him. He and his wife later returned to Hot Springs where he was referred to as a "sportsman."

[46] This, of course, was in reference to the George McLaughlin trial.

The local police department, especially Chief of Police Wakelin and Chief of Detectives Dutch Akers, were strangely quiet when it was pointed out that Nash had been around town for months and had not been picked up or any attempt made to arrest him. In fact, word got out that Akers was being paid to tip Nash off should anyone inquire of him. It was not the first suggestion Akers was harboring and protecting criminals and it was not the last.

The Editor of the *Hot Springs Sentinel-Record* was so appalled at the event of the Kansas City Massacre that he penned the following: "Any officer coming in contact with a man known to be a bank robber or hijacker should shoot him down with as little compunction as the same type of criminals show the the officers. And, No quarter, however, should be shown known bank robbers and hijackers who rob by force of arms. Let the coroner instead of the judge handle their case."[47]

From this moment forward, Wakelin and Akers would be "marked men," and ranked high on J. Edgar Hoover's "black-list." Their obvious cooperation with the criminal element had cost the life of one agent, Raymond J. Caffery, the wounding and life disabling of another, F.J. Lackey, and the wounding of agent R. E. Vetterli.

Joe Wakelin

Verne Ledgerwood's brother-in-law, appointed Chief of Police in 1927. He was charged and convicted of harboring kidnapper and bank robber Alvin Karpis.

---

[47] *Sentinel-Record*, 20 June 1933, p. 4.

While Frank "Jelly" Nash, who had been nabbed in the Spa, may have been the catalyst to have caused the "Kansas City Massacre," he was a small fish in the big underworld pond in comparison to another gangster arrested here. That distinction belonged to Charles "Lucky" Luciano, vice-lord of the east coast. He was one of the new breed of criminals who owed much of their "success" from the era of prohibition and the expansion of the prostitution, protection and gambling rackets.[48] Luciano was of Sicilian birth and like so many of the gangsters of that era had arrived in the United States as a small child. He quickly found his way into the tough youth mobs and quickly graduated his way into the racket gangs. He was a contemporary of Owney Madden, Meyer Lansky, "Dutch" Schultz, and Frank Costello.

By 1933 the State of New York had begun an intense investigation of the gangs operating there and particularly the leaders. The spearhead of the investigation was a special appointed state prosecutor, Thomas E. Dewey, who would use his success as a stepping-stone to the governorship. The inquiries into the underworld went on for several years. Criminals fearing prosecution, conviction or revocation of their paroles made themselves scarce.

As 1936 rolled around, Dewey was zeroed in on the prostitution rings and one name seemed to stand out as being the leader of an extremely large ring and that was Lucanio's. When one of his underlings began to talk to save his own hide, Dewey sought indictments from a special called grand jury. Several of the key leaders were indicted and one was issued for Charles "Lucky" Luciano. "Lucky" was one jump ahead of the warrant servers and escaped from his apartment in the Waldorf Towers, where he was living under an alias, by fleeing down the rear stairs. Making his way to Philadelphia, then Cleveland, he decided to head to Hot Springs on advice of a couple of friends who informed him the Spa was a sanctuary for guys on the lam and who did not want to be found. His lieutenants promised to keep in daily telephone contact. He left his car and took the train.[49] On 1 April 1936, Dewey announced a warrant had been issued for Luciano's arrest and declared Charles "Lucky" Luciano to be "Public Enemy Number One."

Upon Luciano's arrival he checked into the Arlington Hotel, accompanied by girlfriend Gay Orlova. One of the first things Luciano did was to contact Owney Madden, former New York gang boss, now "retired" law abiding citizen and underworld contact. He was introduced around and became quite friendly with none other than Chief of Detectives Herbert "Dutch" Akers.

In fact, Luciano was strolling the bath house row promenade with Dutch

---

[48] Martin A. Gosch & Richard Hammer, *The Last Testament of Lucky Luciano*, Dell Publishing Co., Inc., New York, NY, 1975, p. 171. Hereinafter cited as *The Last Testament of Lucky Luciano*.

[49] Ibid., 195.

when they were spotted by a New York City officer, John J. Brennan, who was in Hot Springs on other business, but who was aware of the outstanding warrant for the mob-boss. Luciano was quickly arrested by Sheriff Marion Anderson and officer Brennan. He spent almost three hours in jail until his local attorney Richard Ryan filed a petition for a *writ of habeas corpus* and was taken before Chancellor Sam Garratt. Garratt affixed a bond of $5,000, which the vice-lord easily made.[50]

When news was flashed to New York that Luciano had been released on a $5,000 bond, Special Prosecutor Thomas E. Dewey went ballistic. He was critical of Judge Garratt to the New York press, as he was quoted, "I cannot understand how any judge could make such an order unless he was ignorant of the facts."[51]

Dewey must have been clued-in as to the situation in Hot Springs as he immediately contacted Arkansas Governor Marion Futrell and Attorney General Carl Bailey and apprised them of the fact Hot Springs authorities seemed bent on the notion they would prevent Luciano's return to New York to face charges there. He told them, "Luciano is regarded as the most important racketeer in New York, if not the country. And the case involves one of the largest rackets and one of the most loathsome types of crime."[52]

Futrell, a close friend and fishing buddy of Municipal Judge Verne Ledgerwood, normally preferred matters such as this to be handled locally, but feeling the pressure of all the publicity, called Hot Springs and ordered Sheriff Anderson to re-arrest Luciano and instructed that he be held until extradition papers could be received from the State of New York. Carl Bailey, a politically ambitious state attorney general, ordered the Arkansas State Rangers (forerunners to the State Police) to Hot Springs to take Luciano into custody. Before they could arrive, Sheriff Marion Anderson and New York officer John J. Brennen arrested and took "Lucky" into custody at his hotel and he was held for a second bond hearing. In a flurry of warrant and petition servings, one issued by a Pulaski County Court to remove Luciano to Little Rock for extradition hearings; one to "restrain any but Hot Springs officers from taking the New Yorker into custody" and one issued by Municipal Judge Verne S. Ledgerwood to arrest and hold him on the original fugitive warrant, certainly "muddied the legal waters." Chancellor Sam Garratt got back in to the act and issued an order that the mob boss be held on $200,000 bond. By this time, 3 April, Luciano was represented by three Hot Springs lawyers, city attorney A.T. "Sonny" Davies, state representative James R. Campbell and Richard Ryan. Not wanting to leave any stone unturned, Luciano summoned one of

---

[50] *Sentinel-Record*, 2 April 1936.
[51] Ibid.
[52] *The Last Testament of Lucky Luciano*, p. 195.

his New York attorneys to help.

Attorney General Carl Bailey moved to dismiss the original warrant. City Attorney Davies objected, telling the court, "It is being done for the purpose of getting Mr. Luciano out of Hot Springs." Co-defense counsel James R. Campbell went completely overboard informing the court, the prisoner, "Is a citizen of Garland County, an owner of property here and entitled to hearing in his home county."[53]

The attorney general had brought Edward McLean, New York assistant racket prosecutor to Hot Springs with the expectation of the case being transferred to Little Rock for an extradition hearing before Governor Futrell. The two lawyers fully expected they would be able to take the mob-boss back with them to the capital city and had brought several Arkansas Rangers and two Pulaski Deputy Sheriffs to escort the prisoner. It was their turn to be surprised.

Just as the two Pulaski County deputies, Charles Caple and David Raper, thought they were being given permission of the court to take Luciano into their custody and had moved beside him, defense attorney "Sonny" Davies, "motioned to Garland County Chief Deputy Roy Ermey, who took him and escorted the vice-lord to his cell in the county jail."[54] For a few minutes bedlam existed. Bailey was outraged and threated contempt action against the local officers. Seeing they were outnumbered and showing complete distrust for the Garland County officers, law enforcement officials and the entire local judicial system, the attorney general left two officers to watch the prisoner with orders to take him into custody in the event there was any attempt to release him on bond or otherwise.

While Attorney General Bailey and assistant prosecutor McLain fumed at the treatment they had received at Hot Springs, the former now threatened contempt charges against not only Deputy Roy Ermey, but city attorney and defense counsel A.T. "Sonny" Davies, as well. That evening, confined to the Garland County Jail, and tired of the bland food, Luciano made the best of it and treated all the prisoners to a special supper he had brought in from a local restaurant. But this scenario was not complete, for at 3:00 o'clock the following morning the night jailer heard rough footsteps coming down the hall of the court house and when he looked, saw twelve heavily armed State Rangers and two more Pulaski County deputy sheriffs. He quickly locked the door and placed a call to Chief Deputy Roy Ermey who responded with several deputies. The Rangers demanded the release of Luciano into their

---

[53] *Sentinel-Record*, 4 April 1936, p. 1. As far as we have been able to determine, Luciano never owned any property in the Spa. In his appeal to the court, Campbell did not specify what type of property Luciano supposedly owned other than his clothes.

[54] Ibid., p. 3.

custody. With the county force being almost under siege for several tense hours, the local defense attorneys for Luciano were notified of the happenings and finally at 8:00 a.m. the Garland County sheriff's office released the gang leader into their custody.[55]

True to his promise, Carl Bailey filed "contempt proceedings against A.T. Davies, one of Luciano's counsels and Chief Deputy Sheriff Roy Ermey."[56]

Bailey had gotten Luciano to Little Rock, but getting him on to New York was another thing. An extradition hearing was held 6 April in the State Capitol. Not taking any chances on an attempt to free the prisoner, the local press reported, "Arkansas State Rangers holding sub-machine guns stood outside the executive suite during the hearing. More than a dozen deputy sheriffs and special officers, who brought Luciano to the governor's office from Pulaski County jail, where he is held for $200,000 bail on the New York warrant were posted around the suite."[57]

Irritated by the resistance from Hot Springs lawyers, court and law enforcement officials the papers reported in bold headlines, "Bailey Assails Spa." He went on to say that Hot Springs was an asylum for criminals, and claimed he had been offered a $50,000 bribe, "to co-operate in a release of this prisoner. Every time a major criminal of this country wants an asylum" continued Bailey, "He heads for Hot Springs, Arkansas."[58]

While the governor was granting the extradition of Luciano to New York, his attorneys were busy trying to obtain a writ of *habeas corpus* from Federal U.S. District Judge John E. Martineau, "Asserting they anticipated an effort will be made to spirit Luciano out of Arkansas if the extradition is granted." Judge Martineau agreed to a hearing. The writ was served on the Pulaski County Sheriff, requiring him to produce Luciano in federal district court the following morning.

The three Hot Springs defense lawyers--Davies, Campbell and Ryan--would not have fought as hard if someone was trying to steal the Arlington Hotel or the Army-Navy Hospital. They acted as if Lucky Luciano might have been "Man of the Year," or the Spa's "favorite-son." Even though they were fighting hard for their client, Luciano may have believed his local attorneys were beginning to let the case slip away and fearing he would be extradited, authorized Little Rock lawyer, D.D. Panich to take the lead role in his defense, possibly a mistake.

At the hearing, Judge Martineau granted the defendant ten days to appeal to

---

[55] Ibid., 5 April 1936. Headlines proclaimed, "Luciano Is Held in Pulaski Jail," and "12 State Rangers Take New Yorker From Spa Jail."

[56] Ibid.

[57] Ibid., 7 April 1930.

[58] Ibid.

higher court and Attorney General Bailey and Assistant Special Prosecutor ЛcLean immediately left for Kansas City to request the appellate judge to decide immediately whether he will be granted the right of appeal from)istrict Federal Court."[59]

D.D. Panich wired Attorney General Bailey from Kansas City on 16 April, ıe would present several motions before Judge Martineau the following day ɔ ask the judge to vacate his order of April 7 denying Luciano a writ of *habeas ɔrpus*. A lightbulb flashed in Bailey's mind. Apparently he and Panich had not one to the same school of mathematics. The ten days granted by Judge Лartineau for filing an appeal would end that night at midnight and here was uciano's lawyer telling him he intended to file a bunch of motions eleven ays after the court's decree. Bailey made a quick decision and called the New 'ork officers who were waiting in Little Rock for permission to return Charles Lucky" Luciano for trial.

Without any fanfare or announcement, "Luciano was turned over to New 'ork authorities and spirited away by train."[60] The vice-lord's attorneys were umbstruck and in the final days of the judicial maze had been completely outnaneuvered by the headline-grabbing attorney general.

The day after Luciano's departure from Arkansas the mob boss had to share ıe headlines with the state attorney general as Carl Bailey announced his andidacy for governor.[61] This was not good news to the City of Hot Springs, nd there were rough days ahead, as Bailey would remember the treatment he ad received at the Spa and would act accordingly.

Hot Springs certainly had not been so lucky for "Lucky" Luciano, who was ıitially arrested in the Spa 1 April 1936. Exactly one month later, 1 May 1936, ewspapers all over the country reported the arrest of the Number One Vanted Criminal in America by the FBI, Alvin Karpis.[62] That arrest was made y the Director of the FBI, J. Edgar Hoover, in New Orleans. Karpis had led ıe FBI on a chase lasting several years. Karpis' name was quite well-known t the Spa where he and his cohorts, Fred Hunter, Sam Coker and Harry 'ampbell vacationed and hid out over a year.

---

[59] Ibid., 10 April 1936.

[60] *Sentinel-Record*, 17 April 1936. Bailey explained to the press the exchange had been ade at 12:05 a.m. A Missouri-Pacific train had delayed its departure ten minutes to commodate the New York detectives bringing Luciano to Little Rock's Union Station, *ntinel-Record*, 18 April. When the train arrived in St. Louis, to avoid the possibility of another Kansas City Massacre," it was met by fifteen heavily armed officers.

[61] Ibid., 18 April 1936.

[62] Thomas Dewey had proclaimed "Lucky" Luciano as the No. 1 wanted criminal, but ıat was Dewey's personal opinion as New York Prosecuting Attorney. Alvin Karpis had been ı the FBI's ten most wanted list for sometime and had been "promoted" to the official status No. 1.

Marion Anderson

Anderson became Garland County Sheriff in a controversial election in 1936. He served the county ten years.

Of all the underworld characters with whom the FBI came in contact, an there have been literally thousands, Alvin "Creepy" Karpis must be ranke near the top for intelligence. Several of his school teachers accorded him th fact that he was about the smartest boy they had ever taught. Those sam teachers would have quickly agreed that he had never fully applied himself t his studies and as a student he was incorrigible and would have termed him a anti-social and a "lone-wolf."[63] Karpis was Canadian by birth but had grow up near Topeka, Kansas and by the age of sixteen had dropped out of schoo He began a series of burglaries involving groceries, service stations and jewelry store. He was apprehended trying to sell some of the loot, trie convicted and served two years of a ten-year sentence in a state reformator and escaped.

In 1931 he met a criminal of some note, Arthur "Doc" Barker, wh introduced Karpis to an education of "big-time" crime. Barker was one of fou brothers, whose mother, Kate "Ma" Barker, was the leader and teacher c "how-to" in the world of muggings, robberies and later kidnapping. Alvi Karpis fit right in with the gang and became one of "Ma's" most willing an

---

[63] Quentin Reynolds, *The FBI*, Random House, New York, 1954, p. 57. Hereinaft cited as Reynolds - The FBI.

able students. In fact, she discovered Alvin had some ideas in pulling jobs she had never before considered and soon the gang members were looking up to him as a leader and "Ma's" right hand. It soon became known as the Barker-Karpis gang and then very quickly the Karpis-Barker gang.

Karpis quickly got his picture on a wanted poster as he and "Doc" Barker killed Sheriff C.R. Kelly of White Plains, Missouri, who tried to question them at a garage where their car was being repaired.[64] Escaping the state, the gang of twenty crooks set up "housekeeping" at St. Paul, Minnesota.

Changing their tactics from robbing stores and state banks, they turned to kidnapping, a federal offense, which brought the FBI into the search. The first of their kidnap victims was William A. Hamm, Jr., scion of a wealthy brewer.[65] Hamm was hid out in a farm house in Illinois. He was not injured and after a ransom of $100,000 was paid by his family he was released.

That job, the gang concluded, had gone so well they decided to pull another kidnapping, this time a banker. Edward G. Bremer, president of the Commercial State Bank of St. Paul was kidnapped by the gang on 17 January 1934 and he, too, was taken to Illinois and held for $200,000 ransom. Things did not move as smoothly as the previous crime, but after three weeks, a successful transfer of the money was made to the gang and Bremer was released. Bremer had used his time to listen for sounds, trucks on a highway in the distance, airplanes passing overhead at the same time each day. He counted the steps up to the porch and even though blindfolded, caught glimpses of the design on the wallpaper and was able to provide the FBI a wealth of clues. The FBI was able to build its case to the extent twenty-five of the gang were eventually convicted or killed trying to elude capture.[66]

But before that occurred, the gang divided the money and split up. Ma Barker and son Fred fled to Florida where they rented a cottage on Lake Weir, and were visited by Karpis and gang member Harry Campbell, the latter pair rooming in Miami. Meanwhile, "Doc" Barker was captured in Chicago and from his personal effects, agents of the FBI were able to ascertain the vicinity where Ma, Fred, Alvin and Harry were hiding. Good police work led them to Lake Weir and Ma and Fred were trapped in the two-story frame house they were renting. Rather than surrender the mother and son, who were armed with machine guns and rifles, elected to shoot it out with the federal agents. As expected, they lost. Ma, who had never been convicted of a crime, but who

---

[64] Ibid., p. 59.

[65] Interestingly, the reporting of the Hamm kidnapping appeared in the same edition of the Sentinel-Record, 17 June 1933, as the story about Frank Nash being picked up by FBI agents in Hot Springs.

[66] Editors of Look, *The Story of the FBI,* E. P. Dutton & Co., New York, 1947, p. 130. Of the twenty-five members of the gang convicted, there were six life sentences; three killed while resisting arrest; three were murdered by gang members.

was a suspect in hundreds of cases, died with her son in a hail of gunfire. Fortunately for Alvin Karpis and Harry Campbell, they had not gone to the lake to fish that day. Hearing of the shootout and sensing their whereabouts might be known, they lit out up the coastal highway to Atlantic City. The description of their vehicle had become known to the FBI, and this information was distributed to all law enforcement agencies. Their car was spotted in a garage near the Danmon Hotel in Atlantic City. From a description of Karpis and Campbell furnished to the desk clerk, he told the police what room the men were in. Believing they had the two criminals trapped, the police ordered the men from the room. The door opened but instead of having their hands up and meekly surrendering, they had guns blazing and forced the policemen to take cover. The two criminals escaped the police trap and stole a car downstairs and sped into the night. Knowing that the identity of that vehicle would be flashed all over the country, the two desperados kidnapped a doctor in Pennsylvania and forced him to drive them to Ohio. The doctor was released unharmed.

Picking up a third hoodlum, Sam Coker, Karpis successfully robbed a mail truck of $72,000 near Warren, Ohio.[67] His success attracted another individual to his gang, Fred Hunter. Establishing their base of operations at Hot Springs and using it as a "sanctuary" to hide out and lay low they began their plans for the next robbery. Keeping the law enforcement agencies guessing where they would strike next, Karpis pulled off an old-fashion train robbery near Garrettsville, Ohio and escaped with $34,000. Karpis had added a new wrinkle to the fast moving criminals of that day--the airplane. He would send one of the gang members back to Hot Springs with their machine-guns and ammunition by car, while the others would fly. They had enough money to lay low for awhile and enjoy themselves.[68]

Karpis and Hunter rented a cottage from Mrs. Al C. Dyer at Dyer's Landing on Lake Hamilton located just off the Burchwood Bay Road. It was an ideal hideout, slightly off the beaten-path, yet near the amenities of a small metropolitan city. Best of all for Karpis, it was on the lake and "Creepy" loved all kinds of fishing.

But much of Karpis' and Hunter's spare time was spent in partaking of the pleasures afforded at Grace Goldstein's Hatterie Hotel, Hot Springs' most famous house of ill-repute. This was in May 1935.[69] It seems at first Grace just considered the two as "big-spenders" and she planned to play them for

---

[67] Reynolds, *The FBI*, p. 78.

[68] *New Era*, 24 October 1938. This was the reporting of the conspiracy trial in federal court of Grace Goldstein, Joe Wakelin, Herbert Akers, Cecil Brock, Mrs. Al Dyer, Morris Loftis and John Stover.

[69] Ibid., 26 October 1938.

"suckers." Then, when she realized she had caught Karpis' eye, not only just as a one-night stand, but as a girlfriend, she, too became enamored by the gangster. Was it his boyish face and tousled hair or the fact Karpis, who at that time was known to her as Ed King, always carried a sizeable bank roll? After all, Grace was a practical woman. The arrangement, at first, was Karpis paid Grace Goldstein two hundred dollars a week for her company and to be exclusively with him. At times they lived at the Hatterie Hotel, other times at her house on Palm Street.[70] Cupid must have been working overtime at the Hatterie, as Karpis' side-kick, Fred Hunter fell for one of Grace's girls, Connie Morris. Their relationship was somewhat stormy, but they remained together until taken into custody by the law the following year.

It wasn't long until Grace was introducing Karpis around as Ed King or Ed Parker and telling her friends he was the owner of a night club in Ohio. When Karpis was using the alias of Parker, Fred Hunter became Harold King and occasionally to really confuse people the two acted as brothers, Ed and Harold King. Grace introduced both men to Chief of Police Wakelin, Chief of Detectives Akers and Lt. Cecil Brock.[71] It is remarkable that the "budding romance" between Grace and Alvin did not cause a major problem. It was known in the inner circles at city hall and at the Hatterie, that Dutch Akers had manifested an interest in the auburn-haired Grace Goldstein, as she testified later, but the Chief of Detectives had curbed his own romantic interest in deference to his superior, Chief Joe Wakelin. Wakelin was known around the Hatterie as "the old man," who would often summon Grace for a rendevous.[72] It seemed to be a case where Grace Goldstein was using Wakelin for the protection of her operation by providing him free samples of her charm.[73]

Another remarkable thing was that if Chief of Police Joe Wakelin and Chief of Detectives "Dutch" Akers were really operating on the up-and-up, as they later maintained, how did two experienced peace officers fail to recognize the most wanted and sought after criminal in the country? In their trial, numerous witnesses testified that a large wanted poster and photo of Karpis hung on the wall of the city police department. Akers, sometimes called the "super-sleuth," who had an almost photographic memory of crooks and stolen automobiles, met with these two men time after time and yet he went to his grave professing his innocence. Well, the jury didn't believe him and neither did

---

[70] Ibid.

[71] Ibid., 25 October 1938.

[72] Ibid., 22 October 1938. This is still reported testimony from the conspiracy trial.

[73] LAT - Ledgerwood. Verne Ledgerwood stated the policemen were unable to take the stand in their defense since "one of the boys was dating Grace Goldstein." That "boy" was none other than his brother-in-law, Joe Wakelin.

many of the people who knew him. Wakelin and Akers must have been very impressed at the importance of these two criminals or did greed have a hand in the events? The two officers realized Karpis, Hunter and some of the others had come into a lot of money and were willing to part with some of it for their protection and to tip them off if federal agents came looking for them. This was during the Depression and several hundred dollars sealed their lips. It was documented Wakelin and Akers were frequent visitors to the cottage at Dyer's Landing and later to a house at 124 Club Street, which was rented by Karpis and Grace Goldstein.

Both Mrs. Al Dyer and Mrs. Toby Fincel (David), owner of the dwelling on Club Street, would later testify they had seen Joe Wakelin and Dutch Akers visiting Ed Parker and Harold King.

Grace said she learned in October 1935 the true identity of Alvin Karpis, as one of her girls kept "bugging" her that her boyfriend was Alvin Karpis and showed her a picture from an out-of-town newspaper. The girl stated Grace "turned pale" when she saw the photo, but tried to dissuade her of that notion, insisting she was wrong.[74] When Grace confronted Karpis with this evidence he supposedly admitted his true identity and according to her she persuaded him to throw two of his sub-machine guns in Lake Hamilton.[75] If that was true, Karpis was really infatuated with Grace Goldstein. As Christmas of 1935 approached she hinted she needed a new car and Karpis took her to the Clinton Buick Company on Market Street and bought her a new dark green coupe.[76]

During the summer of 1935 and winter of 1936, some of Karpis' gang members, who had been hiding out in other parts of the country, showed up in the Spa and were entertained by him and Hunter. Hunter arranged a big-bash at the Howe Hotel with four of the gang members being present and Grace and three of her beauties–described as Jewel Greta Gilstrap, a blonde, Ginger Jefferies, a brunette and red-haired Gertrude Theresa Nichols--providing the entertainment. The latter reportedly disappeared for awhile after the wild party as did $2,000 of Sam Coker's money.[77] But Coker was in no position to fill out a theft report with the police, but did tell Akers.

---

[74] *NewEra*, 24 October 1938. From the testimony of Ginger Jefferies.

[75] LAT - Ledgerwood.

[76] *NewEra*, 24 October 1938. Also, LAT - Raymond Clinton. Clinton later testified he sold a red sedan to Alvin Karpis, both times for cash.

[77] Ibid., 25 October 1938. Also, *NewEra*, 22 October 1938. Miss Nichols' testimony brought a chuckle to the court room when she answered defense counsels' cross-examination question as to whether she had taken Coker's money or not. She answered, "Well, if I did, seeing you are bringing it up, is just because I happened to beat the Hot Springs laws (police) to it." The defense counsel shot back, "Then you did take it off of him?" Nichols calmly answered, "I said, if I did."

But while Alvin Karpis, Fred Hunter and some of the other gangsters were enjoying fishing the lakes around the Spa during the day, and cavorting with the girls at the Hatterie at night, the FBI was following clues they had picked up in Ohio. As a needle on a compass points to north, the clues the federal men uncovered pointed menacingly toward Hot Springs, Arkansas.

Trying to work with Dutch Akers, the FBI was nearly always a step behind Karpis and his gang. When a description and possible location of the wanted men was made available to Dutch, he falsified his report and said he had checked it out and the two were just visitors "from Illinois" and who had been coming to the Spa for several years.[78] Each time Akers became aware the federal agents were on the trail of the gangsters, they suddenly moved to another location about town, telling their old landlord they were leaving for California. As things would quieten down Karpis and Hunter confidently would become more active, fishing the lakes and taking side trips.

Alvin Karpis chartered several flights from Hot Springs, hiring airport manager John Stover to pilot them. They once hired Stover to fly them to the Joe Louis-Max Baer heavyweight championship fight. Karpis had to cancel because of some problem. Hunter hired Stover to fly him and Connie Morris to San Antonio.[79]

When Karpis gave Grace a new car, the two visited her mother near Blossom, Texas. Grace was having difficulties in getting her car licensed, so Chief Joe Wakelin took the plates off his wife's car and put them on Grace's Buick.[80] Grace's main reason for the trip to Texas was to pick up her niece and to install her in one of her houses of prostitution. In her conspiracy trial in 1938, the government also tacked on a charge and indictment of violating the Mann Act and she would be given five years for this little infringement.

The evasive answers the FBI agents were getting from Mrs. Dyer, Morris Loftis, John Stover, Dutch Akers and the girls at the Hatterie, did nothing to satisfy the curiosity of the federal agents and they intensified their investigation to the chagrin of Akers. Also, newspapers began publishing articles about the Karpis gang and putting pictures in them to alert the public and ask for their help. Several persons reported to the local police they believed they had spotted some of the criminals in Hot Springs. To counter the heat, Chief Wakelin in a *Sentinel-Record* article, 14 October 1935, was quoted as saying an investigation by his department had shown Karpis was not in Hot Springs. In spite of this assurance, several people made reports to

---

[78] Ibid. From testimony of Special Agent R. L. Shivers.

[79] Ibid., 26 October 1938. Goldstein testified John Stover was paid $1,200 for several flights to Ohio, also. Too, from the testimony of Ginger Jefferies, *New Era*, 24 October 1938, she stated Stover took his wife on one flight involving Karpis and Grace Goldstein, to Canton, Ohio. *New Era*, 25 October 1938.

[80] Ibid., 24 October 1938.

Wakelin, Akers, Brock and Jerry Watkins they were certain they had seen the gangster at Hot Springs. On each occasion the officers responded, "We'll check into it."

A Mrs. Nyberg tried to convince Joe Wakelin she knew where Alvin Karpis was hiding. Wakelin's response belittled the woman, saying, "You are silly, he is nowhere in the vicinity."[81]

Believing the federal agents might be getting close, Akers tipped off Karpis and Hunter, and urged them to move. With Grace's help, they located a house on the Malvern highway, about six miles east of town and rented it. The house was known as the Woodcock place.[82] The house sat high on the crest of a hill and was surrounded by heavy foliage and was almost obscured from view below. Grace Goldstein and Connie Morris moved in with the two gangsters and the four set up housekeeping. This was 10 February 1936. In spite of all their precautions the federal agents kept boring away with their investigation and were getting closer and even Dutch Akers was getting nervous at the "snooping" G-Men.

It all came to a head six weeks later in March 1936. Both FBI agents and Postal inspectors began to question each inmate of the Hatterie and to show them photographs of Karpis and Hunter.[83] Connie Morris, Hunter's current "squeeze," panicked and told Fred she was going to try and get away. Hunter beat her up and insisted she come with him and Karpis as they no longer felt it safe to stay at Hot Springs. Dutch had informed the gang something was "brewing" but he didn't know exactly what since they weren't including him with their findings. The federal men no longer felt comfortable letting the detective know their plans. What Dutch did not know was one of Karpis' gang, "Burrhead" Keady had been taken into custody at Tulsa and after intense interrogation had revealed Karpis' location. The trio--Karpis, Hunter and Morris--hurriedly left town in two cars. The day after the three had departed, Grace Goldstein carried her maid to the hideout to clean it up. Grace had her wipe down the furniture, cabinets and woodwork in an attempt to remove any fingerprints. Karpis, who had weird tastes in pets, had left two alligators he had bought at the Alligator Farm on Whittington. The two women, who were scared to death of the small reptiles, had trouble getting them into a box.[84]

Two days after Karpis and his companions had left, federal agents and members of the Kansas State Police surrounded the Woodcock house and

---

[81] Ibid., 25 October 1938.

[82] Frederick L. Collins, "Hell in Hot Springs, Part IV, Purge," *Colliers Magazine*, 12 August 1939, p. 97. Hereinafter cited as Collins - *Purge*.

[83] Postal Inspectors had become involved in the investigation because of the mai truck robbery in Ohio.

[84] *Purge* - Collins, p. 48.

ordered anyone inside to come out. Having no answer and remembering the shootout with Ma and Fred Barker in Florida, tear gas canisters were fired through the windows. Anticipating a fusillade of fire to be returned from the building, all law enforcement officers took cover. However, there was nothing but silence. They finally rushed the house and discovered the occupants had fled.[85]

Hearing of the raid on Karpis' hideout and wanting to find out what was going on, Chief Joe Wakelin and Chief of Detectives Herbert "Dutch" Akers burned the rubber down the Malvern Road as they rushed to the scene. Their pride must have been injured when they were not permitted to enter the house while a search for fingerprints was being made. The two local officers may have even feared their own prints might be discovered in the house as they had visited it on several occasions.[86]

Large newspaper headlines greeted the readers the following morning, "Karpis Makes Getaway Before Spectacular Raid," and "Federal Agents Besiege Country Home Near Here."[87]

Appearing almost embarrassed, Joe Wakelin had to admit to the local press he really did not know much about the raid and had not been alerted it was to have taken place. You could almost hear the glee in his voice as he told the reporters, "I know that the raid was unsuccessful, and a failure." He also had to confess, "I didn't even know any Kansas highway patrolmen had been in the state."[88]

Grace Goldstein sneaked out of town, telling no one where she was going, and met Karpis at the zoo in Audubon Park in New Orleans about ten days after the raid. Connie Morris was still with Hunter and Karpis and the four frolicked along the beaches of the Gulf coast from Biloxi to Panama City and back. They rented a charter boat and went deep sea fishing, Grace's first time. Karpis and Hunter left Connie Morris in New Orleans while they quietly returned Grace to Hot Springs. When they returned to New Orleans they had a rude surprise for waiting for them was FBI Director J. Edgar Hoover and a squad of his crack agents. There was no fight left in the two gangsters and they meekly surrendered in front of their apartment.[89]

Karpis was sentenced to a life time imprisonment, first in the Atlanta Federal Penitentiary, then to Alcatraz, and Hunter received a term of thirty

---

[85] Wakelin's defense attorney would later say the federal agents had "shot up the place." There were others who maintained this. *New Era*, Extra Edition, 29 October 1936.

[86] *Sentinel-Record*, 1 April 1936. The government agreed to pay the owner of the house for the damage done.

[87] Ibid., 31 March 1936.

[88] Ibid.

[89] *Purge* - Collins, p. 48.

years for his part in the mail robbery.[90] Because of her cooperation with the government prosecutors, Connie Morris was sentenced to only one year for her involvement.

The news of the apprehension of the long sought-after gangsters did not bode well for some Hot Springs residents. Hoover turned his wrath loose on the Spa, particularly the police department as Chief of Police Joe Wakelin, Chief of Detectives Herbert "Dutch" Akers and Lt. Cecil Brock were indicted for conspiracy to harbor Alvin Karpis. But the conspiracy net flung by the government agents was large as indictments rained down on Grace Goldstein, Mrs. Al C. Dyer, her employee Morris Loftis, and municipal airport manager and pilot John Stover.

Two years later the trial in Federal Court in Little Rock began and ended twelve days later. Over one hundred witnesses were summoned, eighty of those from the Spa. They included federal agents, business and professional men, newspaper reporters, inmates of two houses of prostitution and ordinary citizens who had information of the activities of those charged.[91] Several testified how they tried to get one or more of the police to listen to them as to the whereabouts of Karpis.

After hearing the witnesses it became apparent to Federal Judge T.C. Trimble the government's cases against Mrs. Dyer, Loftis and Stover were weaker than the others. He called the defense and prosecution counsel into his chambers and discussed the various issues. Upon returning to the bench he gave a directed acquittal in favor of the three defendants.[92]

The only one of the remaining four defendants who took the stand was Grace Goldstein. She had tried to portray herself as Alvin Karpis' wife, but of course in his trial at St. Paul for the kidnapping charges, there was nothing she could add. In her own trial, she had to admit she could not produce a marriage license and had only lived with him several months. She put on quite a show for the court and the reporters present. Grace was dressed in "flamboyant clothes and easily the most colorful figure at the trial."[93]

But during the trial her bond was suddenly revoked and she was jailed at night as it was reported to Judge Trimble, Grace had threatened and

[90] Alvin Karpis was transferred from Atlanta to Alcatraz when that prison opened. He would eventually be released under the agreement he would leave the country. As agreed, he went to Canada, then he immigrated to Portugal, then Spain and died at Torremolinos at age 71. *Sentinel-Record*, 3 September 1979. Hot Springs had been fascinated with the knowledge that gangsters had been living in its midst as evidenced by a benefit softball game which was organized and drew 1,000 people. The two teams were named The Karpis Gang, winner 9-8, and the other, the Dillinger Gang. *Sentinel-Record*, 23 July 1936.

[91] *Sentinel-Record*, 28 September 1938.

[92] *New Era*, Extra Edition, 26 October 1938.

[93] *Purge* - Collins, p. 48.

intimidated three of her own girls concerning their testimony. This had taken place in the Frederica Hotel, across Capitol Avenue from the Federal Building, where the witnesses were being housed.[94]

The jury found Wakelin, Akers, Brock and Goldstein "guilty of harboring Alvin Karpis," and gave each the maximum sentence of two years.[95] Wakelin and Brock were transferred within the week to commence their prison terms at Leavenworth, Kansas.[96]

Dutch Akers was convicted on a separate charge of harboring Thomas Nathan Norris, a member of the Alfred "Sonny" Lamb gang.[97]

In February 1939, Grace Goldstein had an additional five years added to her sentence for the charge under the Mann Act, of bringing her young niece to Hot Springs and installing her in one of her houses of prostitution. A sordid event, at least!

Owen Poe, a furniture salesman and owner of the house on Palm Street, said he was unaware his dwelling was being used by Grace Goldstein for immoral purposes and he said she always paid her rent on time. H.A. Wheatley, owner of the Hatterie Hotel and who had rented the second and third floors to Grace Goldstein for eight years expressed his outrage, surprise and shock, to learn such activities were going on in his building. He had his attorney, James R. Campbell, file suit in chancery court to break the lease claiming she had violated the agreement by operating "an unlawful and indecent business thereby violating provisions of the lease."[98] He, too, had to admit Grace had been a good tenant and paid the rent on time, which was a strong recommendation during the lean years of the Depression. To anyone knowing Hill Wheatley and how carefully he looked after his real estate holdings, it would be a stretch of the imagination to believe he was not aware of the activities taking place in any of his properties. Especially so, since the first floor was occupied by his brother's hat shop.

Alvin Karpis served thirty-three years in prison and was released in 1969. He wrote his memoirs and described his relationship with Grace Goldstein and how he used the Spa as a hideout from 1933 to 1936. He denied his association with Akers and Wakelin, even denying he had ever known them,

---

[94] *New Era*, 22 October 1938.

[95] Ibid., 29 October 1938.

[96] *Sentinel-Record*, 6 November 1938. Wakelin would later be moved to a federal prison hospital at Springfield, Missouri. He was released 6 June 1940. Wakelin served as a guard and night watchman around Club Belvedere, a job his brother-in-law Verne Ledgerwood secured for him. After serving his term, Cecil Brock founded a fast delivery service in Hot Springs. He was killed in a head-on accident in the early 1970s, at Allison curve on the Malvern Highway. Dutch Akers, was a model prisoner and learned a new trade. He became an electrician and lived out his life in a home east of Hot Springs on a road that bears his name.

[97] Ibid. 5 December 1941.

[98] *Sentinel-Record*, 3 June 1937, p. 8.

in spite of the numerous witnesses who had seen them together, and possibly to discredit the FBI, which he hated. He certainly was candid as he began his book, "My profession was robbing banks, knocking off payrolls and kidnapping rich men. I was good at it." No joke. He really was good at it!

But not all criminals were welcomed in the Spa by the powers that be. Those who had committed some heinous crime or those who might pose a danger to the citizenry were unwanted. And any who arrived in town and did not pay their "courtesy call" on the proper law enforcement officials and make their presence known were considered by the police to be "fair-game." This was especially true if the criminal was wanted somewhere and had a price on his head. The police of that era were not bound by any set of ethics or mind-set to prevent them from collecting a reward.

In early August 1938, Earl Young, a 28 year-old native of Lebanon, Pennsylvania, who was wanted in four states for murder, rape, kidnaping and robbery, arrived in the Spa unnoticed and checked into a room on the third floor of the Marquette Hotel. A $7,000 reward for the capture of Young, dead or alive, rested on his head for the attack and murder of a young girl near St. Charles, South Dakota, and for kidnaping, rape and attempted murder of another teen age female near Hutchinson, Kansas. At the time of those crimes he was also wanted in his home state for robbery, jail escape and for another kidnaping in Kentucky. His stay in Hot Springs was to be one of short duration.

Ben Rogers had been promoted to night captain on the Hot Springs Police Department following a big upheaval when seven officers, including both the day and night captains, were discharged by the mayor following charges a jail prisoner, John Dickson, had been beaten to death.

Even though Rogers was a one-armed man, he was hired by the mayor for some favors Rogers had done for the administration and the fact he had a large family in the city and county and represented a sizeable vote was all he needed to qualify for the job.

The police captain, making his rounds, was tipped by a bartender of Young's presence in Hot Springs and said he had recognized him by several tattoos. The police captain was aware Young was tattooed heavily on his upper body. Spotting the individual, Rogers was able to follow the man to his hotel and saw him return to his room. Instead of summoning officers who were on night duty and possibly having to share the reward with them he called the day captain, Jerry Watkins to help him.

The two officers knocked on the door and Rogers identified himself as a taxi cab driver. The fugitive reportedly opened the door about four inches and recognizing Rogers as a policeman fired three shots through the narrow opening. The muzzle blast of the outlaw's gun powder burned the face of oth officers.[99] Rogers fired his .45 automatic twice through the door panel nd he and Watkins took up positions down the hall from Young's room. 'hey told a housemaid to summon additional officers and tell them to bring ome machine guns.[100]

Young, realizing he was trapped and that additional police would be on the ay, suddenly burst from his room and started firing his weapon at the two fficers in the hall. Both Rogers and Watkins fired two shots each. Rogers hit 'oung in the left leg breaking the bone and Watkins shot the outlaw in the ose with the bullet lodging in his brain.[101] Young died three hours later at the eo N. Levi Memorial Hospital.[102]

The two officers were awarded Combat Crosses for bravery under fire by ne American Legion in Little Rock.[103] When it came time to divide the eward, officers Rogers and Watkins learned that a total of nine claims had een filed, including the bartender who had tipped Rogers and the night clerk t the hotel. The Marquette Hotel claimed damages to walls, doors and vindows.[104]

Alfred "Sonny" Lamb was another desperado who used the Hot Springs rea as a hideout. Lamb had been born in Quannah, Texas and was being ought for two murders at Houston, numerous robberies and a jail escape rom Tarrant County jail at Ft. Worth.[105]

While running from the law he organized a gang of twelve members, several f whom were wanted for various crimes, including murder. The gang errorized the southwestern United States for several months. During this time amb met an "attractive brunette," Lorene Feaster at Colorado, Texas in late uly 1936 and after a very short courtship, they were married at Walters, Oklahoma. The newly weds were almost constantly on the move, staying a ouple of weeks near Lorene's family in Colorado, Texas, then moving to San Angelo, Wichita Falls, Animas, Colorado and back into Oklahoma. The couple isited Sonny's mother, Polly Denny, at Berryville, Arkansas. Lamb would

---

[99] *New Era*, 5 August 1938.

[100] Ibid. The police departments of the 1930s seemed to "fall in love" with the nachine gun. When "Lucky" Luciano was given a hearing before the governor, all the State Rangers were armed with machine guns.

[101] Ibid. Radio Station KSOO of Sioux Falls, SD, who had put up part of the reward noney, flew a news crew to the Spa to make a special report and broadcast.

[102] A story floated about town for sometime to the effect that there had not been an xchange of shots as the two officers described. Instead, supposedly one of the officers had tood on a chair and shot through the transom over the door, killing the fugitive. Evidence upports the text version.

[103] *New Era*, 22 August 1938.

[104] Ibid., 13 August 1938.

[105] *Sentinel-Record*, 2 January 1938. This was from an article assessing the previous year t Hot Springs.

periodically leave his bride at her mother's or one of the other locations and would be gone a few days, not telling Lorene his business or destination. During these trips he would meet members of his gang to pull off a job and then split up until the next holdup or robbery. When it appeared the police were getting hot on their trail, the gang would lay low for awhile.

Lorene and Sonny Lamb arrived in Hot Springs about the middle of June 1936 and took a room on Arbor Street, then one on Ravine for a week or two. They then moved to the Van Sickle Apartments at 256 Cedar Street. Already rooming there were three members of Lamb's gang, Sam Stegall Haines, Grady Hairston and Thomas Nathan Norris, known to everyone as T.N.[106]

Sam Haines, age 24, had discovered a fun place of entertainment, Fountain Lake, located six miles east on the Little Rock Highway. It was the popular place for young people to go and hang out. It had places to picnic or a canteen where sandwiches and soft drinks could be purchased. A juke box provided music to dance by and a large fresh water pool in which to swim. But Sam had discovered something else that caught his eye, for working there was a pretty eighteen year-old named Betty Jo McNeil, who was from Benton. Betty was not used to dating men who had plenty of money to spend as it was in the midst of the Depression, and she was swept off her feet after only two weeks courtship and the two were married. They became close associates with Sonny and Lorene Lamb and the two couples began going out together.

During this time gang member T.N. Norris, who was using the alias of Miller, became a close acquaintance of Herbert "Dutch" Akers, chief of detectives. Receiving a tip, said later to be from Akers, the Hot Springs police department had been alerted to be on the lookout for various members of the Sonny Lamb gang, who were believed to be in the area. Norris and Grady Hairston fled to the hills of northwest Arkansas. Sam Haines and Sonny Lamb mulled the situation over and since their wives were enjoying Hot Springs so much they decided to stay in the area, but to seek other housing. The Haines settled on Ramble Street and Sonny and Lorene rented a cottage at 30 Pullman Avenue, from Mrs. Ada Gower, who owned and operated the Gower Apartments, next door.

On or about 12 August, Sonny and Lorene met Sam and Betty Jo at Fountain Lake, where they swam and danced. There was a large crowd on that steamy, humid evening. In the throng of people was one of the new state troopers and former Arkansas Ranger, Bill Armstrong, who was assigned to the Spa area. As the merry-makers whirled around the dance floor, Armstrong suddenly caught sight of a face he had seen on a wanted poster. It was Sonny Lamb. Realizing the danger of a confrontation with so many people present, Armstrong tried to station himself where he could make an arrest

[106] *New Era*, 18 August 1937.

Unfortunately, Lamb and his friends did not leave in the direction the state trooper had believed they'd go.[107] Not having seen a photograph of T.N. Norris, he failed to recognize him. It was two days later before trooper Armstrong was to ascertain where Lamb was living on Pullman.

On Sunday night Armstrong had assembled a sizeable force of men including four Arkansas State Rangers, Sheriff Marion Anderson, Chief Deputy Roy Ermey, Saline County Sheriff Virgil Rucker, Public Safety Commissioner Weldon Raspberry and night captain Ben Rogers.[108] Had Armstrong intentionally not included Dutch Akers in the group? In light of what occurred a few days later it certainly appears so. The ten men were armed with three submachine guns, several rifles and shotguns as well as the sidearms each man was carrying.

Rev. Paul M. Clanton, pastor of the Pullman Heights Methodist Church, had concluded his sermon that Sunday night. A couple of men assisted him in turning off the ceiling fans, lights and locking the church doors. As the men came out of the sanctuary they joined a group of church members standing on the porch and steps, laughing, talking and enjoying a bit of fellowship before heading to their homes. It being a very warm night, many of the homes along Pullman Avenue had their windows up for ventilation and radios could be heard. The serene evening was about to be interrupted.

Lorene Lamb was dozing on a couch in the living room. Sonny was dressed only in his shorts and was trying to adjust a radio sitting on a table by an open window. A movement in the yard caught his eye and he saw a couple of lawmen trying to take up positions behind a large shrub. He tried to rush to the bedroom where he had nine loaded rifles and shotguns as well as an automatic pistol. The lawmen saw him bolt toward the open bedroom door and without orders they did not hesitate. All three of the machine guns opened fire, two through the living room window and the third through one of the bedroom windows. Several shot guns sent a dozen or so rounds of buckshot into the house. Sonny Lamb did not have a chance and crumpled to the floor trying to reach his weapons hidden under the bed. He was struck by at least nine bullets, five just below the heart.[109] At the age of twenty-six, the career of Alfred "Sonny" Lamb came to an end on the linoleum bedroom floor of the little cottage on Pullman Avenue. A large crowd of people, many from the Pullman Heights Church, quickly assembled in the yard about the cottage and stayed until the sheet-draped body of Lamb was loaded into an ambulance.

That same afternoon, Sam Haines had been arrested at Benton at the home

---

[107] *Sentinel-Record*, 2 January 1938, p. 5.
[108] *New Era*, 16 August 1937, p. 8.
[109] Ibid.

of his new in-laws. He went quietly. Grady Hairston did not put up much of a fight when arrested near Rogers, Arkansas the next day. His sidekick, T.N. Norris did try to resist arrest and was rewarded by being wounded in both arms and a leg by machine gun bullets. But, at least he was alive.[110]

Norris, painfully wounded and in custody, "sang like a choir boy." He confessed to be one of five men who had robbed the Southern Club in downtown Hot Springs in March 1937.[111]

Strangely, Dutch Akers, immediately came out and stated, "It will take a lot more than I've read in the newspapers to convince me that Norris took part in that job." Akers said he believed "the robbery was staged by Chicago gamblers and the eight victims indicated to local police that they personally knew the robbers."

In the event Dutch was attempting to discredit Norris from giving damaging testimony about the chief of detectives, it didn't work. From information furnished by Norris it was learned he had been tipped off that police were on their trail while at Hot Springs, by none other than Chief of Detectives Herbert "Dutch" Akers.[112] Akers, of course, denied the allegation, however the evidence was mounting from the Karpis case and now Norris.

Leo P. McLaughlin could no longer ignore the complaints being registered against Dutch Akers. Even people who had supported the administration were beginning to question the wisdom of keeping an obviously tainted police officer. When it became obvious that indictments against the detective would be forthcoming, McLaughlin could wait no longer and forced Akers' resignation. The reason McLaughlin furnished to the newspapers, was "because of health problems." This was only two weeks after Norris had alleged Akers had helped him avoid arrest.[113] Dutch's stint in federal prison at Ft. Leavenworth, mellowed the old lawman as he had lost all power over his former neighbors and he had become more approachable, congenial and likable after serving the two sentences for conspiracy.

Another unwanted underworld figure in the form of Joe Saltis, age fifty, and his son, Joe Jr., arrived in the Spa in early 1938, with the plan of making it their home. Joe Saltis liked to be known as "Gentleman Joe," but many of his acquaintances around the stockyard area of Chicago would have laughed at the thought of that nickname. In the Windy City he was known as "Pollack Joe," and for a time had controlled the district known as "Back of the Yards." He was described as "a shambling, broad-shouldered, six-foot and two-hundred

---

[110] *Sentinel-Record*, 2 January 1938.

[111] *New Era*, 17 August 1937. The *Sentinel-Record* reported the loss to be $35,000, whereas the *New Era* gave the figure at $21,000, both sizeable sums in those days.

[112] *Sentinel-Record*, 5 December 1941.

[113] *New Era*, 31 August 1937.

pound, wrinkle-jowled, pasty-face mess."[114] Saltis had been born in Hungary, but had lived in this country since he was eleven years-old. He had been accused, but not convicted, with beating to death an elderly woman over a petty disagreement.[115] He owned and operated three small breweries during the mid-1920s, and tried to provide the saloons and the speakeasies in his district with the illegal brew to slake the thirst of the stockyard workers. These he operated for some time with the "blessing" of John Torrio, Al Capone's predecessor. Torrio assigned a notorious killer, Frank McEarlane, to help Saltis enforce his territory. McErlane was like a "loose-cannon," and had been accused of machine gunning a rival bar in 1926.[116] When Capone took over the mob, the Southside gangs were at war with each other. Trying to calm things down was not easy and he had to choose which one he would support and which he wouldn't. Capone had a strong dislike of Joe Saltis and his strongarm, Frank McErlane, who he suspected had slain two of his men.[117] It was never healthy to have Capone dislike you, as "Pollack Joe" Saltis learned.

During the summer of 1926, Saltis had brutally murdered a "beer pusher," Mittes Foley, by tripping him and leaping astride the man and discharging both barrels of a shotgun into the hapless man's chest. Two eye-witnesses to the murder resulted in Saltis' arrest. Knowing he could expect no help from Capone, Saltis sought an alliance with Hymie Weiss of the Northside gang, Capone's sworn enemy, and certainly not a manuever to gain Al's favor. Wiess, reportedly began spreading money around to help Saltis and when he was gunned down near his headquarters by Capone's trigger-men for other reasons, a list of jurors was found in his pocket. Had he gotten to the jury? It didn't make any difference as the newly-selected jury acquitted Saltis, even in the face of strong testimony from the two eye-witnesses. The Chicago juries of those days were leery of having to convict any of the gang members and the best way of staying alive was to set them free, a very compromising position.

By October of 1929, Joe Saltis' district had been gobbled up by the Capone machine. Joe had worked for awhile in some of the bars. The end of Prohibition ended any of Saltis' dreams of getting back into the rackets. By 1938, he had enough and decided to leave Chicago and his old enemies behind and start anew at Hot Springs.

Leasing the old Wilson Tavern on the Arkadelphia highway on Lake Hamilton, Saltis and son reopened it under the name of "Big Joe's." It quickly became the "bloody-bucket" night-spot of the county beer halls and dives. Some type of brawl could be expected almost every night. Fights, knifings and

---

[114] *Mr. Capone* - Schoenberg, p. 83.
[115] Ibid.
[116] Ibid., p. 144.
[117] Ibid., p. 145.

shootings, all occurred. A patron, Norman Rouse, was seriously stabbed there the first week in August.[118] Another suffered head injuries when struck by a chair tossed by some ticked-off drunk. It certainly was a tough place and customers needed to be alert for flying ash trays, bottles and beer mugs. Several bullet holes in the walls and ceiling were a reminder to customers they should be prepared to take cover under a table or behind the bar in the event a serious argument ensued.

As the incident reports and complaints poured into the Garland County Sheriff's office, Marion Anderson and Prosecuting Attorney Curtis Ridgway became concerned. When they heard that Saltis had been showing off a couple of machine guns to some of his customers, it really got their attention. But what really galvanized them into action was the word that Saltis was conducting some gambling on his premises and this without consent of the local Administration. The two county officials decided it was time to act and a raid was conducted on the night of August 4, 1938. The old gang leader was not too happy to see the law enforcement authorities and he was not pleased when they searched the attic of his business and discovered an arsenal of weapons. Those included rifles, pistols, sawed-off shotguns and magazines for Thompson machine guns and a sizeable quantity of ammunition.[119] Search as they might, no machine guns were found. Anderson and Ridgway realized from the type of weapons discovered that they were not dealing with two squirrel or bird hunters. The two Saltis men were charged with operating a disorderly house and unlawful possession of sawed-off shotguns. Judge Ledgerwood placed them under a $500 bond as the case was appealed to circuit court.[120] Then, the U.S. Government intervened.

U.S. Marshals Bradley and Purvis from Little Rock, took Joe Saltis into custody and after a hearing before U.S. Commissioner Julian Glover, he was placed under a $10,000 bond for possessing illegal firearms.[121] Other charges followed--selling intoxicants without a license and failing to obtain license plates on three vehicles. It was obvious, the authorities were "throwing the book" at Saltis.

Saltis learned quickly he was no longer in Chicago, where courts sometimes took years before cases were brought to trial and which might restrict the accused's operations. And his poor financial condition probably prevented him from trying to buy his way out of his predicament. Circuit Judge Earl Witt was unimpressed with Saltis' reputation as a former Chicag mobster and issued a permanent injunction enjoining Joe Saltis from operating any business in the

---

[118] *New Era*, 10 August 1938.
[119] Ibid., 5 August 1938.
[120] Ibid., 9, August 1938, p. 7.
[121] Ibid., 24 August 1938.

county "in which violations of the law are permitted." Witt explained so there would be no misunderstanding, Saltis could not permit the drinking of intoxicating liquors on his premises and could not allow anyone "under the influence of liquor in his establishment."[122] Saltis and his attorney, James R. Campbell were speechless--Witt's injunction had effectively put the old mob leader out of business as the poor quality of food provided by the tavern was not enough to attract customers.

Saltis returned to Chicago and worked for a short time as a bartender. One author wrote of his demise, "After a wrenching divorce in which he denied paternity of his oldest son, Joe Saltis, who had been living in flophouses, died broke and alone in county hospital in August 1947."[123]

There were other gangsters, holdup men and hoodlums who passed through the Spa, but did not stay long for one reason or another. Pretty Boy Floyd and some of his gang floated through, but behaved themselves and quickly left. Bonnie Parker and Clyde Barrow, Texas' contribution to the gangster era, stopped in the Spa for rest and relaxation for a couple of days, but quickly moved on, knowing the price on their head would draw the attention of some bounty hunter or police officer. Harvey Bailey and his gang of kidnappers planned some of their jobs in the Spa. Earl Joyner, a notorious gangster and murderer, and seven of his gang were arrested here after a jail break in Louisiana. Rather than return the gang to Louisiana where they faced murder charges, they were sent to Texas who wanted them on robbery charges and where a $500 reward was available.[124] But if the criminal had money and knew the right contacts at "Bubbles," arrangements could be made for an extended vacation. There was no light shining in the window, but the welcome mat was out.

---

[122] Ibid.
[123] *Mr. Capone* - Schoenberg, p. 358.
[124] *Public Opinion*, 29 September 1933.

The John Dickson Case and Resulting Probes

As suggested in the previous chapter, events occurring in Hot Springs involving the underworld and linking it to some members of the local police department, reached a peak in the years 1933-1937. Complaints began to filter to the press and be reported in widely circulated magazines such as *Liberty* and *Colliers* of the "goings-on."

Prior to the dismissal of Chief of Detectives Dutch Akers, he was accused by one visitor, Harry Yudin, of being part of a conspiracy of physically beating and robbing him of $20,000, his life savings, and dividing it with "the city officials of Hot Springs and that the brother of one of the officials was the man who gave him the blow on the head," to render him unconscious while his money was taken.[1] The "brother," to whom he referred, undoubtedly must have been none other than "Blackjack" George McLaughlin. In spite of local criticisms, Akers had a thick skin and refused to react to the charges, except to curse the individual to his friends. He would later be quoted as saying, "When I received a proposition to go with the Hot Springs Police Department, I decided to steal with the rest of them. I wasn't able to align myself for a 'cut-in' on the large money from the gamblers. So I made mine from various other sources."[2]

This was confirmed by one of the FBI agents testifying in the harboring trial later that year. The federal agent said Akers had told him, "I was totally honest when I went to work for the Hot Springs police force. I'm not the only officer in the United States to have gone crooked."[3] But, retribution was on the way, not only for Dutch, but for several of his fellow officers.

In a series of events which caused problems for the local police department and brought very unfavorable publicity to the city, a total of nine officers would be discharged or sent to the penitentiary.

The first of these events started with the burglary of the Blue Ribbon Club's safe at 732 Central Avenue, one night in 1936, and the attempted holdup of the Ohio Club a few days later. As *Liberty Magazine* writer Frederick Collins put it bluntly, "Let a safe in a gambling house be jimmied open, the whole police force would be in hot pursuit."

In this instance, Chief Joe Wakelin headed the investigative squad and got a break in the case when one Robert Demars was arrested on a stolen truck charge from Saline County. According to former judge Scott Wood, Demars was held in the Hot Springs city jail for sixty-three days, "beaten and tortured." During this time Demars supposedly implicated others involved in

---

[1] "Hell in Hot Springs," - Collins, *Liberty Magazine*, Part I, July 1939.

[2] Ibid.

[3] *New Era*, 26 October 1938. Testimony of Special Agent E.J. Connelley.

the burglaries and robberies, including one John Dickson, a known petty thief.

Once his name was mentioned, along with some of his relatives, John Dickson, age thirty-two, became the focus of their investigation and the officers became convinced he was their man. Dickson was known to have a small farm in Perry County. In those days the Hot Springs Police Department thought nothing about going into another jurisdiction and making an arrest, sometimes without even notifying the sheriff of that county of their intentions. In this particular case, Chief Wakelin, Lieutenant Cecil Brock and Detective Glenn Buchanan went directly to the Dickson farm.[4] It was a cold and raw day and John Dickson and his nephew Alfred "Pug" Dickson, who would later be indicted on the Blue Ribbon burglary charges, were inside warming beside a wood heater. When they heard a noise and looked out they saw the police officers coming through the yard gate and fled out the back door toward several small outbuildings and a barn. The officers, who by this time were on the front porch, heard them running on the frozen ground and gave chase. The three officers fanned out, trying to get a glimpse of their quarry. As Joe Wakelin, who was armed with a .351 rifle and two pistols, came around the corner of one of the small sheds, either John or "Pug" Dickson, swung a 2" x 4" piece of lumber striking Wakelin across the face and head.[5] The chief went down like a sack of feed being dropped. His weapons were quickly removed from him by his attacker and the suspects, uncle and nephew, disappeared into some thick woods nearby. The injured Wakelin was placed in the police car and had to endure a very rough one and one-half hour ride to Hot Springs where he was hospitalized with severe facial and head injuries.

The police department pulled out all stops looking for the two Dicksons. Every lead was vigorously pursued and their diligence was rewarded as they learned John Dickson was hid-out with a friend between Prescott and Hope, Arkansas. This time, Captain Arch Cooper got close enough to the fugitive to take all the fight out of him, rapping him sharply across the head with a shotgun and sending the fugitive to his knees. Dickson was booked into the Hot Springs city jail 14 December 1936 on charge of grand larceny and assault, the latter for the attack on Chief Wakelin, who was still recovering from his injuries.

Old Testament history reveals it was not considered a very good thing for anyone in Biblical times to fall into the hands of the Philistines, a vicious and cruel people as evidenced in putting out the eyes of the Nazarene judge, Samson. And it was certainly not a good thing in John Dickson's life of falling into the hands of the Hot Springs police department.

Not only was Dickson wanted for questioning about the Blue Ribbon and

---

[4] *Sentinel-Record*, 7 January 1937.

[5] 5 Ibid., 3 January 1937.

Ohio burglaries and some auto-theft charges in Saline County, but also concerning the assault on Chief Joe Wakelin who still had not returned to work. One or more of seven officers must have considered it to be "pay-back time," for the attack on their chief.

Dickson was first placed in one of the regular cells where other inmates of the jail were kept. Later that day, he was taken to a room out of the jail which adjoined the rear of the building and was called the "boiler-room," housing some of the equipment for the heating of the auditorium and city hall. There, Dickson went through a tortuous questioning. Various prisoners would later testify they could hear slashing sounds, possibly from a whip or rubber hose, and the thud of blows, groans and cries coming from the room where Dickson was being questioned.[6] The witnesses said this type of interrogation would go on for thirty to forty minutes at a time, stop for a short time, then recommence. A grocerman and former policeman who was in the station, testified he saw bruises on the prisoner's shirtless back and saw blood running out of the man's mouth, nose and on the seat of his trousers. Another saw one of the officers washing blood off a pair of leather gloves. One officer was seen swinging a large towel with what appeared to be a bar of P & G Soap tied in one end.

Apparently, the policemen conducting the questioning were not getting the answers they wanted and the mistreatment continued for some time. Finally, an unidentified officer called Chief Wakelin at home and "reported that Dickson was in very bad condition and needed a doctor immediately."[7] "And, even worse," the chief was told, "no confession or admission of guilt had come from the mouth of Dickson."

A call summoned Dr. J.P. Randolph, city physician, coroner and strong administration supporter, to the city jail to check Dickson. Randolph took one look at the prisoner and suggested he be taken to a hospital right away. Unbelievably, it was four days later and under the covering darkness of night before an ambulance, summoned from Paul Heady Funeral and Ambulance Service, backed up to the rear door of the jail and took Dickson to the New Park Sanitorium on Breeze Street, not considered one of the better medical facilities in town. Dickson lived only four days and passed from this world on Christmas Eve. Dr. Randolph documented his death as being from "pneumonia."[8]

Everything was quiet on Christmas and for two or three days after that. Then, a fire-storm quickly developed. There were just too many people that had some knowledge of the sordid death of John Dickson, petty criminal and

---

[6] Ibid., 12 May 1937.
[7] "Hell in Hot Springs," - Collins.
[8] *Sentinel-Record*, 10 May 1937.

car thief, to sweep it under the rug. Leaks developed around city hall and rumors began to appear on Central Avenue, first in whispers, then bolder. Jim Dickson, father of the deceased, had tried to visit his son while in jail and had been refused permission. He made inquiries of his son through Dr. Randolph, Mayor McLaughlin and Municipal Judge Ledgerwood and had received no satisfactory answers to his concern. When he finally saw his son's bruised and battered body, he demanded an investigation into his death. Jim Dickson hired former circuit judge Scott Wood to represent his son's interest. Wood was considered a bitter enemy of the administration and the announcement of his involvement in the matter automatically triggered problems on the horizon for the police department and political machine. As Wood called for an immediate and impartial inquest and autopsy, Dutch Akers, who had no part either in the capture or death of Dickson, began to lean on several individuals, such as the ambulance driver and nurses at the hospital, and several individuals who had been prisoners, in an attempt to influence and moderate their testimonies and to thwart a hearing. The state papers had gotten wind that a coverup was underway and reported on December 29, that it appeared the "political machine" at Hot Springs had successfully blocked an investigation into the death of Dickson.[9] It seemed a hole had appeared in the dam and it was beginning to leak.

Both Hot Springs dailies, now owned by C.E. Palmer, considered a strong administration supporter, but which would not condone such treatment of prisoners, called for a full investigation of the matter. An autopsy was ordered and Circuit Judge Earl Witt empaneled a special grand jury to probe into the case.

Dr. Randolph's death certificate reflecting the death of John Dickson had been caused by pneumonia suddenly appeared to the public as a flimsy attempt to cover up and protect the police department. It caused one to wonder if previous reports by Dr. Randolph had been slanted in favor of the police department and if they had revealed all the facts. One case immediately came to mind, the death of Thomas S. Davis, of Lubbock, Texas in 1933. Davis had been found dead in his cell. Randolph's report indicated the man had succumbed of "natural causes." However, a local mortuary attendant noted the man had a large "wound over the right eye." This had been quickly explained by officers and backed up by the physician, that the injury had been sustained when the prisoner fell from his bunk just before his death."[10] Maybe!

---

[9] *Arkansas Gazette*, 29 1936.

[10] *Sentinel-Record*, 29 April 1933. Dr. Jesse P. Randolph died in Hot Springs 20 March 1941 after practicing medicine in the Spa since 1906. He had been educated in Hot Springs schools, the University of Arkansas, where he played on its first football team, and the Medical School of St. Louis University. He served as Garland Coroner for thirty-two years.

Several physicians conducting or witnessing the autopsy on the body of John Dickson, including Dr. Euclid Smith, Dr. D.C. Lee, Dr. H. King Wade, and Dr. F.J. Burgess, concluded the "Wounds were certainly contributing factors in death." In an obvious attempt to protect one of their own, they added "pneumonia preceeded the wounds by several days" and could have caused the man's death.[11]

The injuries, according to the examining doctors, consisted of two broken ribs; a ruptured kidney; knot on head size of a hen's egg; cuts, bruises, and lacerations; bleeding from mouth and rectum; burn marks to lower body, some possibly made by a rope, etc. There were rumors that the infamous "Hot Springs telephone," a tortuous hand-operated generator, had been used on the hapless prisoner. Dr. Euclid Smith later testified, "The kidney injury alone would likely have caused Dickson's death."[12]

Mayor Leo P. McLaughlin had closely monitored the case from his first hearing of the matter and realized he had to act. When the results of the autopsy reached his eyes he hastily acted without consulting anyone. He announced four officers were suspended. Those included Chief Joe Wakelin, Captain Arch Cooper, Lieutenant Cecil Brock and Detective Glen Buchanan.[13] Leo had been making his own inquiries with considerable information being furnished to him by his brother, George. He gave a statement that he acted "So that the officers will not be clothed in any official capacity during the investigation." Further, he stated, "My policy has always been, as mayor of this city, that a man in custody should not be mistreated."[14]

Four days later the grand jury foreman, Charles Goslee, announced indictments had been issued for seven policemen, charging them with second degree murder in the jail death of John Dickson.[15]

Wakelin, of course, was not directly involved in the death of the prisoner in as much as he had been at home, still recuperating from the injury he had received in the raid on Dickson's Perry County home. However, the grand jury did criticize Wakelin as it said, "We believe that Chief Wakelin should have exercsed a more dominant control over the officers under him in such circumstances as these revealed in the Dickson case and other cases of alleged mistreatment of prisoners would not have existed."

McLaughlin was now acting as one being in total control. Prior to this he had consulted with Verne Ledgerwood, Sonny Davis and a few of his other cronies. While he had been totally indecisive when his brother George had

---

[11] Ibid., 3 January 1937.

[12] Ibid., 12 May 1937.

[13] Ibid., 3 January 1937.

[14] Ibid.

[15] Garland County Court Records, State of Arkansas v. Arch Cooper, et al., 1/6/37, Box 69, Case 7594. Also, *New Era* - Extra Edition, 6 January 1937.

been in trouble, he felt little pressure in announcing he was firing the seven officers indicted by the grand jury. He named them as Captain L.A. Arch Cooper, Captain Bob Moore, Lieutenant Cecil Brock, Detective Glen Buchanan, Patrolmen Pres Griffin, Joe Scott and Andy Irwin. While Joe Wakelin had been completely vindicated by the grand jury's report, so far as any actual involvement in Dickson's death, he had been scored heavily and McLaughlin announced Wakelin would not be reinstated.[16]

The mayor did tell the press, "Off the record, most of the men have denied Dickson was mistreated and several have expressed confidence that trials will result in speedy acquittals."[17] Regardless of McLaughlin's appearance to the reporters, there seems to be little doubt that he believed John Dickson had died as a result of the brutality he underwent as he never wavered toward permitting any of the men to return to the police force. As far as Leo was concerned, they were history.

Verne Ledgerwood, Joe Wakelin's brother-in-law, knew even he could not save him and besides that, Wakelin had been indicted on federal charges of harboring and obstructing justice in the Alvin Karpis case.

In an unusual move, but one obviously thought out by Leo P. McLaughlin, he named Wakelin's replacement and said, "I have placed Weldon Rasberry in full control of the Police Department. I thought it best to put some person in charge who is not now a member of the Police Department. Mr. Rasberry is a lieutenant on the Fire Department and I have full confidence in his ability to command the police department."[18]

Weldon Rasberry had been on the fire department for seventeen years and had no experience in handling a law enforcement agency. Even though the leadership of the police force had been greatly decimated by the firings, several of the remaining police officers resented his appointment, if for no other reason, then as an outsider. While there may have been considerable discussion as to any underlying reasons the mayor may have had, Rasberry was known to be loyal to the administration and that was something Leo valued highly. Less than a month later Fire Chief Loyd Tate died of a heart attack.[19] McLaughlin took advantage of the opportunity by placing Rasberry over both the police and fire department and bestowed upon him the title of Commissioner of Public Safety. Leo had saved the city money as Rasberry was paid only one salary. Now it was the firemen's turn to complain, as Rasberry, who had held the rank of lieutenant on the fire department, had suddenly been promoted over Assistant Chiefs and longtime firemen, Riley Brown and Ila

---

[16] Ibid., and *Sentinel-Record*, 7 January 1937.
[17] *Sentinel-Record*, 8 January 1937.
[18] Ibid., 3 January 1937.
[19] *New Era*, 2 February 1937.

Trammel and Captains W.A. "Babe" Akers, Butler Brown and Vander Adams. While there were grumblings, no one wanted to confront Mayor McLaughlin. Jobs were too scarce during the Depression years and there were hundreds of men clamoring for any type of work and he could fill a position in minutes with a telephone call.

Trial of the seven officers was set for May 1937.

Normally, squabbles at Hot Springs had been mostly ignored by the rest of the state. The Spa was the "whipping boy" for state politicans who needed an axe to grind. Many of those same people who would condemn and rail against the vices at the resort would take their vacations or long weekends there because that was where the "action" was.

It just so happened the Arkansas State Legislature had entered into session when the Garland County Grand Jury brought indictments against the seven policemen charging them with the death of John Dickson. On January 14, Representative William M. Thompson of Independence County rose to the floor and told the members of the legislature there was an evident breakdown in law enforcement in the city of Hot Springs and asked that body to pass a resolution authorizing an inquiry into the death of John Dickson and "to determine whether articles of impeachment should be filed against the circuit judge and others in Garland County and to investigate reported open gambling, slot machines and peace officers and the judiciary who appeared to be in alliance with the criminal elements. Further, that it should be determined if a political machine dominated elections through violations of the election laws."[20] Thompson charged Earl Witt, circuit judge, with active participation of "assisting machine candidates," in the election of 1936.[21]

A heated debate immediately occurred as Garland County Representative James R. Campbell, a member and supporter of the administration, sprang to his feet and vigorously opposed the resolution proposed by Representative Thompson, and defended the reputation of Judge Earl Witt. As the debate broadened and support for the resolution grew, Campbell tried to defuse the moment by having the resolution postponed. The substitute motion to delay, failed.

He said, "I never knew of a case being tried in our courts in Arkansas without giving the defendant time to make a proper investigation of the charges preferred against him." Campbell apparently had not arrived in Hot Springs or heard of the "sand-bagging" of City Clerk Fred Fowler, over the fire at city hall.

Campbell attempted to deflect the subject, charging there was open horse-race betting being conducted in Little Rock and inquiring why no investigation

---

[20] *Sentinel-Record*, 16 January 1937.
[21] Ibid., 15 January 1937.

of that activity was being pursued. He said Hot Springs was being singled out.

Representative Thompson said he had never heard of the Little Rock conditions being described by Campbell and said the only reason the Garland County representative was bringing the matter up was "The delay can only serve one purpose and that will be to give time to the Hot Springs gamblers to get their money to work." Did Thompson mean the gambling community might use their money to influence certain members of the State Legislature? You bet he did! It wouldn't be the first or the last time gambling money greased the palms of some state members and influenced their vote.

Representative Nichols of Logan County sided with Thompson, and referred to the recent death of John Dickson, Hot Springs jail prisoner and the indictment of the seven police officers. "I make the prediction that if the house doesn't get behind them, they will turn those men loose. I can prove it is the custom and habit of the officaldom of Hot Springs to torture men. When Charles Luciano was arrested, the whole gang down there tried to thwart investigation."[22] It was hard for Campbell to argue that point, especially since he had been one of Lucky Luciano's lawyers. He did declare the charges were "frivolous, unfounded, unjustified and inspired by our political enemies."[23] Those words sounded almost as if they had came out of the mouth of Mayor Leo P. McLaughlin.

The debate waxed hot all afternoon and despite the fervent defense put up by James R. Campbell, the resolution passed by a vote of 72-21. A front page editorial in the *Sentinel-Record* said, "Rumors were rife on the street last night that the resolution was sponsored by a long-time resident of Hot Springs." This undoubtedly was a jab at former circuit judge Scott Wood, always a thorn in the administration's side. The morning following the legislative debate and vote, several carloads of State Rangers rolled into the Spa armed with subpoenas and "flashlight" cameras. The visit by state authorities was in the nature of a fact-finding trip and none of the patrons or gambling personnel or equipment were disturbed.[24]

The committee appointed by the legislature began immediately to complain that "high pressure tatics" were being used to deter the investigation.[25] Stories began to circulate that funds from gamblers was being placed in the hands of some powerful state politicans to blunt the committee's report.

City and County officials were summoned, including Mayor Leo P. McLaughlin, Circuit Judge Earl Witt, and Sheriff Marion Anderson, just recently elected. W.S. Jacobs and Roscoe Johnson represented the Belvedere

---

[22] Ibid.
[23] *Arkansas Democrat*, 15 January 1937.
[24] *Sentinel-Record*, 16 January 1937.
[25] Ibid.

and Southern Clubs, and Tink Young, the Ohio. Each was interviewed closely by committee members. But while several club owners had responded to the subpoenas in person, only Tink Young had complied fully, bringing his records. The others were warned that if the requested records were not forthcoming the men would be cited with contempt charges.[26]

When Jimmy Phillips of the Southern Grill reported to the committee he had been unable to bring the records, which were in a safe, and the owner was out of town, the committee told Phillips to "Load that safe on a truck and bring it over here. We'll open it."[27] Luckily, he found the combination.

As the session opened the next day, club owners, gamblers and their helpers were struggling under boxes of payroll, income tax and business records.[28]

While considerable resistence to the legislature's probe into conditions existing at Hot Springs was being encountered, there were some locals who supported it. Dr. Clyde V. Hickerson, pastor of First Baptist Church, presented to his board of deacons a resolution adopted by the Arkansas State Baptist Convention supporting the investigation and it passed. The Rev. W.J. Hinsley, pastor of Second Baptist Church, also supported the State Convention's resolution and declared, "The situation [in Hot Springs] is worse than newspaper reports say."[29]

When the *Hot Springs Sentinel-Record* printed a front page editorial on January 24, addressed in part to the Rev. Clyde V. Hickerson, pastor of the First Baptist Church, and the Rev. W.J. Hinsley, pastor of the Second Baptist Church, insinuating "if the two ministers had any evidence there were any illegal activities taking place in the Spa," it was the duty of the two ministers to bring it to the attention of the grand jury.

If there were any illegal activities taking place in the Spa? Where in the world were the newspaper people living? Had the publisher, C.E. Palmer, and editor Charles Goslee, who had been foreman of the grand jury, never been cognizant of their surroundings? It was only necessary to stroll down Central Avenue on a warm afternoon, before air-conditioning, when windows were up and doors were standing wide open, to hear the various clubs' announcers calling the fifth race at Rockingham or the fourth at Saratoga Park and in the background could be heard the click of poker chips being raked from the table, or dice rolling from the cup. Palmer and Goslee must not have been reading their own newspaper, for on the very day of the editoral, January 24,

---

[26] *Arkansas Gazette*, 18 January 1937. Others appearing were Matt Picchi, White Front Club; Jimmy Phillips, Southern Grill; Roscoe Johnson, Southern Club; Norwood Phillips, Chicago Club; Ben Harrison, Citizens Club; Louie Larsen, Blue Ribbon Club; Otis McCraw, Club Belvedere; and Ed Spears, Tango Club.

[27] Ibid.

[28] *Arkansas Democrat & Arkansas Gazette*, 18 January 1937.

[29] *Sentinel-Record*, 21 January 1937.

an article appeared in the *Sentinel-Record* advising the "bookies," had agreed to "tone down the loud calling of races"-- bookmaking being an illegal activity! Why every school boy above the eighth grade could tell you where a half-dozen or more slot machines were located--all illegal. And any taxicab driver or hotel clerk could direct an inquiring visitor to a brothel, either black or white, cheap or expensive--also illegal. All of the bars, cigar stores, newsstands and many grocery stores had punchboards, in plain open view, a petty form of gambling, but also against state laws. All the bars, taverns and some restaurants had pinball machines on which participants were paid off with a winning score, also illegal! If there were any illegal activities taking place in the Spa? The Sentinel-Record had overreached in its criticism of the two pastors as the Hot Springs Ministerial Alliance came to the defense of their fellow ministers and urged their members to support the stand the Alliance was taking. The paper never said how many telephone calls had been received in opposition to the editorial but admitted it had received "several" and quietly retreated to a more neutral position in its editorial stance.

Perhaps Rev. Hickerson and Rev. Hinsley had little confidence in the grand juries appointed in Garland County and believed their appearance would be a waste of time. One only has to review the lists of grand jury appointments to understand there were always a large number of Administration supporters on each panel. This is certainly understandable, as much power for those appointments rested in the hands of the circuit judge, Earl Witt, in calling or impaneling a grand jury. Over the past several years a number of cases had been presented to the grand jury with the public expecting indictments, only to read in the newspapers that the suspect had been released with all charges dismissed.

Take for instance a case involving Ed Spear, the only living participant of the gunfight on Central Avenue in 1899 when five men were slain--the same Ed Spear who was convicted and sent to the federal penitentiary at Atlanta as being the head of the infamous con-games of 1913. Spear was charged with the second degree murder of Jerome "Jerry" Bates in Spencer's Cigar Store at Bridge and Central on September 18, 1936. Witnessing an argument between Bates and Spear were police Captain Arch Cooper, patrolman Ben Rogers, storeowner C.J. Spencer and Hughey Roberts.[30] As the argument between the two men turned into a heated cuss fight, one of the policemen moved over beside Spear and turning his body, made his weapon available. Ed pulled it from the officer's scabbard and shot Bates, fatally injuring him. It was never explained why the two policemen had not stopped the argument before the shooting occurred. Maybe that was too simple an answer in Hot Springs during the 1930s. A story went around that a "throw-away gun" was found on

[30] State of Arkansas v. Ed Spear, Garland County Criminal Box 68, Case # 7564.

Bates. Wonder who threw the gun down for Ed Spear? Upon hearing the testimony of Cooper, Rogers and Spencer, the grand jury dismissed the case on grounds of "self-defense."[31] Roberts' version of the affair was never revealed.

For days the Legislative Committee interviewed subpoenaed witnesses and poured over boxes and record books. Over 100 persons were called. In the background, squealing like pigs caught under a gate, were the representatives from the eighteenth judicial district, downplaying the investigation by the committee and reminding other state officials of the on-going cost of such a probe. When the committee chairman heard of this activity, he was quick to issue a statement, "We are informed that the rumor is being spread that the work of the committee will be valueless and that no real investigation is being done. On behalf of the committee, the chairman desires to state Hot Springs will be given a square deal, but no kind of pressure, political or otherwise, will deter the committee from doing its duty."[32] Chairman Thompson probably was unaware what stones would be turned or how much money the "wily" gamblers were willing to spend to get his committee off their backs.

A few days later, Chief Justice Griffin Smith, of the Arkansas Supreme Court sent revenue agents to Hot Springs. This time they came in trucks and vans and returned to the capital city with an estimated $25,000 in gambling paraphernalia which fueled a large bonfire.[33] It was rumored that much of the gambling equipment destroyed was old and obsolete and had intentionally been set up by the gambling community upon being tipped that the raiders "were coming."

On February 22, 1937, the House of Representatives sounded the death knell to the Hot Springs investigation by voting overwhelmingly to discontinue the probe. The State Senate harshly criticized the House of "political persecution" and shamed its members for even beginning the probe of the Spa. State Senator Walter Wheatley, noted for spiriting super con-artist J.H. Ward, alias the "Brass Kid," from under the noses of the Chicago Police Department and returning him to the Spa for trial in 1913, quietly orchestrated the Senate condemnation.

The Legislative Committee's majority report, endorsed by five of its seven members, did score the police brutality and death of John Dickson as it reported, "Prison records nowhere reveal a case that will compare with the Dickson case, no doubt without a parallel in the history of prison systems. Yet when it became apparent that this man was going to die, he was denied the privilege of seeing his father, his family and even a doctor not connected with

---

[31] Ibid. The dismissal is dated 28 September 1936.

[32] *Sentinel-Record*, 16 January 1937.

[33] Ibid., 2 January 1938, p. 5, a recap of the year 1937.

the city administration."[34]

Even the minority report seemed uncomfortable with the Dickson case and mainly confined the two members' remarks to the cost of the investigation and recommended that nothing further be done.[35]

Everyone connected or dependent on the gambling industry breathed easier in the Spa.

The second degree murder trial of the seven police officers began in Garland Circuit Court May 10, 1937. Judge Earl Witt had recused himself because of the criticism he had received from the State Legislature Committee's report. He had asked Judge Dexter Rush, of Texarkana to assume the bench.[36]

It had been learned several of the State's witnesses had been threatened not to testify. One, Willie Williams, received a letter warning him to leave the state before the trial started. His attorney turned the letter over to the *Arkansas Gazette*, and that paper printed it in a story. Eighteen months later, the witness met one of the former officers on a downtown street and was badly beaten for his having testified. Judge Verne Ledgerwood fined the former police captain fifty-dollars.[37]

It was most difficult for the court in selecting a jury to hear the officers' trial. Nearly everyone in the county was related, closely acquainted or at least cordially knew one or more of the seven charged. A total of 117 talismen were examined before twelve jurors were finally seated.

The trial lasted several days and there was a parade of witnesses testifying as to what each had seen or heard. Some of the atrocious behavior of the local officers was shocking or unbelievable. The local public was more than anxious to hear and learn what the seven police officers would say in their own defense, but their attorneys, James R. Campbell, Ed Thacker and Jay Rowland, declined to permit their clients to take the stand. By their silence, it was almost like the colonists who founded the country and fearing reprisals from the oppressive English, as they said, "We must all hang together or we most assuredly will all hang separately."

The State's case was being handled by Prosecuting Attorney Gibson Witt, Jr., who was suffering from arthritis, and by his assistant Curtis Ridgway. Witt told the jury, "Dickson was a country man, tough as a pine knot and yet the

---

[34] The report cited interviews with three underage girls who testified they were "sexually abused and mistreated" by Chief of Detectives Herbert "Dutch" Akers and Lt. Cecil Brock, after being taken to the city jail. It was rumored around town that the father and brother of one of the young girls surprised Dutch and badly beat him for the mistreatment.

[35] "Hell in Hot Springs," Collins.

[36] *Sentinel-Record*, 9 May 1937.

[37] Ibid., 6 November 1938. Former Captain Robert L. Moore would be killed in a drunken brawl four years later at the Black Cat Liquor Store.

defense will tell you that he was injured from a fall off his bed or from sleeping (before capture) in the hills."

Representative Nichols, of Logan County, had accurately predicted the outcome of the Dickson trial when he said, "I make the prediction that if the house doesn't get behind them they will turn those men loose." He had only erred in believing that the State Legislature could make any difference.

The jury's deliberation was not lengthy, only two hours. Jury Foreman Nick Lund, reading from a paper in response from Judge Dexter's question, "How does the Jury find the defendants," replied, "We find the defendants not guilty to the charge of murder in the second degree."[38]

"Not Guilty?" If none of the officers were guilty in some degree of Dickson's death, who was? The newspapers reported a murmur ran through the court room, probably from Dickson's relatives, then shouts of joy from the relatives of the officers.

If the incident had not been so tragic, it would have been humorous and reminiscent of a story of the boxer who was taking a beating from his opponent. As he returned to his corner, bloody and bruised after a devastating round, his trainer trying to encourage him said, "You're doing fine, he hasn't laid a glove on you." To which the battered fighter, looking up through swollen eyes responded, "Well, you'd better keep your eyes on that referee, as somebody is sure beating the hell out of me."

There were several reactions to the case. Of course, the relatives of the freed men rejoiced. Business leaders feared the effect it would have on the reputation of the city and as to how it might affect the tourist trade and business. Some wondered about the status of the laid-off officers. Would they be entitled to return to their jobs? One former policeman told reporters following the verdict, he and several of the other men would ask for their jobs back. That answer came quickly the morning following the verdict from Mayor Leo P. McLaughlin as large headlines decried, "Mayor Says Ex-Policemen Not to Be Reinstated."[39] The officers, in the eyes of a lot of the public were tainted and even Leo wanted no part.

Perhaps the statement of former judge Scott Wood put the event into perspective as he said, "In the opinion of many people, the Dickson case is merely a symptom of the disease which now afflicts us. The root of the disease which is in the general viciousness of the ruling powers which prompts them to oppress all who refuse to surrender to them."[40]

---

[38] Garland County Criminal Records, State of Arkansas v. Arch Cooper, et al., 13 May 1937, Case # 7594, Box 69.

[39] *Sentinel-Record*, 14 May 1937.

[40] Ibid., 21 January 1937.

Public Opinion and How to Steal an Election

After Leo P. McLaughlin's margin of victory over Cleveland Smith in the city election of 1929, it was little wonder that no one announced in opposition to him in 1931. It was the first time since the city was incorporated that an incumbent mayor was unopposed.[1]

The public was able to observe that a number of Leo P. McLaughlin's campaign promises had been kept and others were in the process. He was the first "full-time" mayor and had made quite a show about declining a salary raise, stating, "Don't you folks worry about me. Leo'll get his." And, it was obvious to the voters he meant he would be compensated by the gambling community. The public seemed to have no objection to this system. Streets were being paved and water mains were being extended. Mosquito breeding ponds were being sprayed or drained and a big orange and black street flusher kept Central Avenue as clean as a pin--all with no increase in taxes.

That is not to say the administration had absolutely no opposition for that wouldn't be true. In 1933 a group tried to get Hot Spring's most "influential citizen," Martin A. Eisele, to announce for mayor. When he refused, his friends generated a write-in campaign for Eisele and even though his name did not appear on the ballot, he polled 1,044 votes.[2] That reflected there were still families and business people who believed that the opening-up of the town was not the right thing to do. Then there was the city election in the spring of 1937 when former state representative Elmer Tacket announced his candidacy for mayor against Leo P. McLaughlin.

Tackett stated, "I have been drafted by a cross-section of the business, professional and laboring men of Hot Springs to make a race for mayor. From all indications, *the mass* of people apparently feel the future welfare of Hot Springs depends upon a change in the mayor's office at this time."[3]

Poor Tackett. The "mass" of people, who he believed supported him, did not show up at the polls. He had misread the political climate of the Spa and was unaware how completely dominated the local election machinery was. His hopes were dashed upon the rocks of false politics as the morning after the election the headlines read, "Mayor is Elected to Sixth Term by Huge Margin." The vote cast was 4,699 for McLaughlin and 211 for Elmer Tackett.[4]

The people were just not willing to do battle with city hall and most were unwilling to discuss their opposition in public. That is, all but one single entity.

---

[1] *The Sun*, Norwich, New York, 28 April 1931.
[2] *Sentinel-Record, 5 April 1933.*
[3] *New Era*, 8 March 1937.
[4] *Sentinel-Record*, 7 April 1937.

The little weekly tabloid, *Public Opinion*, constantly reminded the citizens of the Spa of the corruptness and underhandness of the Administration. While the paper did report other news, probably 80 percent of its space, or more, was used to "flog" the Administration. Its ownership was never clearly revealed, however it was quite well known that some of its financial backing came from two anti-McLaughlin businessmen. They were Ray S. Smith, a realtor, and W.C. Brown, a wealthy timber broker and investor. Smith also contributed some of the editorials which appeared in the publication, some signed, others not. Some speciality articles were penned and signed by former circuit judge, Scott Wood, another Administration baiter. There were other contributors of articles such as W.T. Wootten.

The business manager and editor was a young woman, Gladys Wilson, who was raising two small children. Wilson not only performed much of the work associated with the operation of the paper, she did much of the writing. She was fiesty and sharp to the point in her articles directed toward the Administration. Because Leo P. McLaughlin so often referred to himself in his speeches and seldom gave credit to his associates, Gladys nicknamed him the "Big I." Also, Leo had once mentioned his cohorts at city hall and the court house as being "one big happy family." *Public Opinion* jumped on that like a bird on a June bug. A column was dedicated to "The Happenings in One Big Happy Family," under a pseudo by-line of "Burnham Crisp," and covered everybody in the city hall and the court house, many times unflattering and informing the readers of shady, if not illegal, shenanigans going-on by the city and county officals. The mayor, reportedly would seethe, rant and rave over Glady's accusations, which were generally well- founded from her investigations. Leo, when faced with something which displeased him generally went right to the source of his vexation and confronted that person with a personal call.[5] Generally a sharp attack from the mayor was enough to send most businessmen who had courted his displeasure into hiding.

But, with Gladys, Leo had met his match for stubbornness. She seemed unruffled and unfazed by his blustering threats. Once, while talking with some people in her office, the Mayor called, demanding she cease printing untruths about him and telling her how he intended to retaliate if she did not cease. Gladys merely extended the phone at arms length where the others in the room could hear the highly-irritated chief executive and she loudly said, "This is His Honor, the Mayor, threatening me, listen." There was a pause of silence and then the party on the other end of the line slammed the phone down

[5] LAT - Raymond Clinton. Clinton once received a call from Mayor McLaughlin threatening to "put me out of business." Clinton said he was able to weather Leo's wrath, but his business was damaged.

hard.[6]

The little newspaper, which had a larger circulation and wider readership than admitted by the mayor, was always overly optimistic about some underdog candidate's chance in running against some member of the political machine. It also misinterpreted the sudden increase in the number of poll tax receipts being purchased, believing it was a sign the citizens were up in arms and were demanding a change, whereas it was just the mayor urging city employees and gambling houses to get their lists and required quotas turned in. Some citizens refused to spend the one-dollar cost to buy a poll tax, believing it was a waste of time and money trying to oppose city hall and the court house.

When E.R. Boll, owner of a lumber yard in South Hot Springs, announced his intention to run against Leo P. McLaughlin for mayor in 1933, *Public Opinion* became highly excited and predicted "the handwriting was on the wall," and the demise of the political machine was not far off. The tabloid was optimistic that some new election officials recently installed, would ensure an honest election, whereas it was just the machine purging individuals who were no longer enthralled with McLaughlin and replacing them with ones considered more loyal. Boll told the press he favored a "New Deal" for citizens and his platform included lower utilities, telephone rates and a reduction in taxes, something everyone was interested in, but which no one seemed able to accomplish.[7]

When candidate Boll announced before the election date he was withdrawing from the mayoralty race, *Public Opinion* took him to task, indicating his excuse as "flimsy" and that the financial distress Boll described he was suffering was shared by others during those Depression days.[8] The editor was apparently unaware that E.R. Boll's business depended on three major contractors and builders and the Garland County Road Department. After his initial announcement for mayor, two of the builders informed him they were sorry but they could no longer buy lumber and building products from him. Then, he was notified by the county judge he was cancelling a large order for bridge timbers. In only a few short weeks, E.R. Boll was broke and he and his family moved to Pine Bluff where he took a low-paying night watchman's job to feed his family.[9]

After the election, *Public Opinion* printed large headlines, "Will The Grand Jury Investigate the Election?"[10] An anonymous juror responded and replied

---

[6] Interview of Ev Young.
[7] *New Era*, 2 March 1933.
[8] *Public Opinion*, 17 March 1933.
[9] LAT - Raymond Clinton.
[10] *Public Opinion*, 28 April 1933.

that individual grand jury members have little power to commence an investigation. He said, "I have never known of a single instance when the grand jury took up a major investigation entirely on its own initiative and against the wishes of the *judge* or *prosecuting attorney*."[11] And therein lay the problem. Why would the circuit judge or prosecuting attorney want to investigate, damage or impair the hand that was feeding them? After all, they were a part of the system.

When delegates from the Ministerial Alliance met with Circuit Judge Witt, imploring him to call a grand jury to investigate gambling or fraud of some type, the lankly jurist would wring his hands in despair, seemingly in agreement with the delegation. He would lower his voice and in a confidential tone explain, "The last two grand juries were instructed to look into those problems and after a thorough investigation, reported they could find no infractions on which to indict anyone." Amazing!

And each time Judge Witt would send the pastors back to report to their churches that, "Our Circuit Judge advises he is aware of the problem and we can be assured he is keeping his eye on the matter and if further evidence comes to him he will act." "Earl, is on the job," the tabloid sarcastically printed.

The front-page cartoons, though sometimes crudely-drawn, clearly depicted some situation with which the readers quickly identified. One showed a large, cigar smoking politician, identified as "One Big Family," with a protective arm draped around a sleazy-looking individual, labeled "Crooks" and underneath, "Starboarder."[12] Another reflected a shaky man labeled, "Voter," trying to mark a ballot with a huge menancing man looking over his shoulder, marked, "Present Power."[13]

Agreeing with the tabloid's political views could prove dangerous and unwise as one dentist learned. He had just left his office in the Medical Arts Building and instead of using a nearby crosswalk, started across Central Avenue in the middle of the block. He was stopped by a policeman who spotted a copy of *Public Opinion* protruding from the dentist's coat pocket. Instead of giving him a warning or a ticket for jaywalking he was hauled to the city jail and confined for several hours before being released and no charge being made. This was referred to "as hassling the opposition."

The paper was loudly vocal in its support for Cooper Land and Walter Hebert when they ran for prosecuting attorney and W.R. Downen in his race for sheriff in 1934.[14] *Public Opinion* pointed out, "Downen knows the ropes of

---

[11] Ibid., 28 July 1933.
[12] Ibid.
[13] Ibid., 28 April 1933.
[14] Ibid., 22 June 1934 and 2 February 1934.

he present gang and can lead the people from a continuation of the last year." ɦe should have, as a former sheriff he had been a strong supporter of the Administration a few years earlier, and had been considered at one time by Mayor McLaughlin for chief of police. What had gone wrong to disappoint him? It would be 1946 before Downen would be back in the graces of the McLaughlin machine, at which time they "threw him a bone," and supported him for alderman of the fifth ward. The tabloid had bubbled over with optimism when Houston Emory first ran for prosecuting attorney, then railed against him when Emory sided with the Administration over various matters and when he had been so ineffective in prosecuting George McLaughlin over Sid Long's death.[15] Nothing could have pleased the paper more than when Jay Rowland announced he was going to run against Circuit Judge Earl Witt.[16] The paper's editorial staff was naive enough to believe Rowland stood a chance against one of the most powerful men in the county. It tried to help Rowland by discrediting Witt and revealed that the judge frequently "imbibed too freely," and once had entered a sanitorium for "the cure" and he had been seen brandishing a lot of $100 bills about.[17] The paper wondered, "Where did all that money come from?" Many people could have answered that one. Gambling simply could not exist without the cooperation, support and understanding of the circuit judge. And one thing the gambling community tried to do was keep the judge happy.

Not one of the challengers sponsored or supported by *Public Opinion* would win the election they were vying for. It was a total washout. Had the editor of the paper been able to look in a crystal ball and see the future, she would have been disappointed to learn that the political machine would last another ten or twelve years. Also, she would have probably decided that some of those the paper had supported had not been worth the trouble. Jay Rowland had later joined the gang at city hall as city attorney after the illness and retirement of Sonny Davies, and quickly got into trouble, facing a penitentiary term for becoming involved in a city bond kick-back scheme which cost the city thousands of dollars.

The paper continued publication for a little over two years, finally succumbing to the hard times and losing some of its main advertisers. It finally had to go out of town to get a printer as pressure on local print shops was so great they refused to publish the paper. Probably none were happier to see the demise of the tabloid than the "Big I." Whatever one thought of *Public Opinion*, and the handful of citizens who ran it, all would have to acclaim, it was a "scrapper," and did much to turn attention to some of "The Happenings in

---

[15] Ibid., 5 January 1934.
[16] Ibid., 18 May 1934.
[17] Ibid., 28 April 1933.

One Big Happy Family."

The old saying, "Politics makes strange bedfellows," was never more true than at Hot Springs in the mid-1930s. It was necessary for the local machine to "court" the state politicians and bid for their support to maintain an open-town policy. The Spa needed an understanding at the state level that Garland County and Hot Springs would be permitted to deal with any problems which gambling and prostitution might create. The Spa was willing and able to support any candidate who would ascribe to these premises. Especially was this true of the gubernatorial candidates. In 1936, the Lucky Luciano fiasco had left Hot Springs with "egg on its face." Lawyers, including the city attorney, state representatives and officials such as the municipal judge and chancery judge, had unsuccessfully maneuvered to prevent Luciano being removed from the "protective custody" of the city and county by the state's attorney general and Arkansas Rangers, in order that he might be extradited to the State of New York. The attorney general, of course, was Carl Bailey who immediately announced his intention to run for governor. The local political machine immediately recognized it was faced with a major problem in the event Bailey was elected governor. Not only had the city and county officials tried to thwart the efforts of the attorney general when he was trying to take Luciano from their custody, they had been downright rude. The Administration had willingly supported Governor J.M. Futrell, who had turned his back from illegal activities taking place in the Spa and had even signed a bill legalizing para-mutual thoroughbred horse racing at Oaklawn Park. Futrell and Bailey were just like gunpowder and fire --they didn't mix!

Futrell was a close friend and fishing companion of Municipal Judge Verne S. Ledgerwood. They had fished the lakes and streams of Arkansas and hunted geese in the Mississippi Delta. Their wives had grown quite friendly with each other. Ledgerwood and Mayor Leo McLaughlin called on Futrell and tried to persuade him to run for a third term. Futrell told them he was appreciative of their support but that he would not run again. He said, "I don't believe that would be a good idea, as I've appointed too many of my relatives to state jobs and they haven't been earning their money." Ledgerwood later said, "He probably was kidding somewhat, but that was how honest he was with the situation."[18]

The Administration quickly looked at the eight announced candidates for governor--three of which would withdraw before the election--and tried to decide which one they could work with best and which one might defeat Carl Bailey, who was still unhappy with Garland County. Governor Futrell initially had confided to McLaughlin and Ledgerwood he intended to support R.A. "Bob" Cook, and told them he believed Cook was the kind of candidate they

---

[18] LAT - Ledgerwood.

Verne Ledgerwood, center, "engineered" a fishing contest between Arkansas Governor Futrell, left, and Louisiana Governor Allen. The match was called a "draw."

were looking for. They took his advice, and when Futrell changed his support from Cook to Ed F. McDonald, they followed suit. The Governor had promised voters that he intended to stay out of the election and not get involved, however only a few days after that statement he jumped into the middle of the race with both feet, lamblasting Carl Bailey and praising Ed McDonald[19]. It turned out that McLaughlin and his administration had made a poor choice of candidates.

Ed F. McDonald, age 49, a former school teacher and sheriff from Grant County, and at that time Secretary of State, had been successful in generating a lot of state-wide support and indicated to Hot Springs authorities that he understood their situation and promised they could depend on him to use the State Rangers as they should be used, looking for highway traffic violators rather than making customers nervous by raiding local gambling spots. McDonald was their kind of "folks" and sounded like the man they were seeking to support. Unfortunately for local Garland County supporters of the Secretary of State office holder, Ed F. McDonald, now running for governor, was a flawed candidate and was suddenly exposed for graft. It seemed he had made some very shady deals for roofing and plumbing repairs at the capitol. It was alleged he had paid out enough money to roof the state capitol

---

[19] *Sentinel-Record*, 7 August 1936.

buildings of five neighboring states, but got only the Arkansas state capitol covered. But it was his purchasing of soap and detergent which brought him the greatest criticism. When an inventory of the state capitol building revealed the basement, janitorial closets and various storage rooms to be filled with barrels of soap, a hue and cry rose up calling for an investigation.[20] The probe revealed he had bought $13,000 worth of soap at one time and had made a number of illegal purchases. Horrors! It appeared that the Arkansas Secretary of State had been taking kick-back money while in office. As a result of this little fiasco, the former secretary of state forever became known as "Soapy" McDonald. McDonald was quickly indicted for improper purchasing practices. A Pulaski County grand jury returned more indictments charging the former secretary of state with "obtaining money under false pretenses."[21] In the trial it was learned McDonald had also, bought an additional $29,000 in janitoral supplies from a firm in Memphis, which had also made substantial contributions to the politican's election fund.[22] While much of the state was appalled at the antics revealed about "Soapy" McDonald's past, this was just the sort of candidate the local Administration could identify with, they understood one another--they were of kindred spirits.

The 1936 state and county election in Garland County must stand in history as the prime example how a political machine can manipulate, control and accurately predict the outcome. And--oh yes--steal the election. To historical researchers, even sixty-five years later, the violations and infractions of the law remain astounding. It is a textbook example of how an election could be stolen.

Like generals planning a military campaign, McLaughlin and Ledgerwood worked to cover all the bases. Several meetings were held. First, all city employees met with the mayor who encouraged them to complete their poll tax lists, turn them in, and to prepare to get their families and friends and turnout and vote on election day. And by the way, they would be given slips indicating the Administration-supported candidates.

A second meeting was held and the business community was invited to attend. Leo explained the importance to Hot Springs and reasons that Ed F. McDonald should be elected because of his commitment in keeping the Spa open and free from state raids. Also, the mayor carefully explained, the campaign was going to cost money, a lot of money. Leo called it "the cost of doing business." He told them, "I'm sure few of you are prepared to make a donation today, but get your money ready. We'll send some boys by in a few

---

[20] Ibid, 6 August 1936, p. 5.

[21] Ibid., 8 January 1937, p. 8. The modern reader might be reminded of the "flag flap" by Secretary of State Bill McCuen in the 1990s.

[22] Ibid., 6 May 1936.

ays to pick it up." Several "collectors," including Elmer Walters, Guy IcClure and several of the police, were busy a few days later going from usiness to business, picking up the money and marking their lists. Only a few efused to participate and they were duly noted and reported to the mayor.

Another important meeting took place when McLaughlin called the Garland County Democratic Central Committee together. It was at this meeting that eo got complete control of the election machinery of the county.[23] As IcLaughlin unfolded his plan to create a majority within the minority a rift eveloped within the membership. The Administration forces were too owerful and five well known men, all from the minority, resigned from the ommittee. This aided Leo's plans even further as he replaced them with his upporters, George Collier, Cecil Ledgerwood, T.E. "Curly" Evans, Dan Haley nd Jim Holland.[24]

Another disagreement within the party occurred when Leo P. McLaughlin ould not release the names of the judges and clerks for the election. After everal days, "considerable criticism had resulted from the committee's action withholding the list from publication," and it gave in and turned some of e names over to the papers.[25] Withholding names of election officials from e public, though illegal, was not new in the county. In fact, in the last city lection the exact same thing occurred, causing "mild opposition within the arty leadership." Secretary L.V. "Rip" Freeman carefully explained the delay, hat some changes probably would be necessary."

It later leaked out that Leo McLaughlin had read a list of names of men to eet with him in the council chambers after the meeting. These were told at at time they were going to serve as the judges and clerks and "there can be o excuse for not serving except death."[26] It no doubt was a bit embarassing some of the committee, and some of the Administration supporters as the st of judges and clerks clearly revealed the men had been carefully hand-icked and heavily-weighted with McLaughlin people. No less "than thirty-two f the poll workers were employed by nine of the gambling houses" in the city nd county. The Belvedere, Chicago and White Front Clubs each had five mployees working as officials at the polls. These included owners, cashiers,

---

[23] LAT - Bosson. Bosson was a reporter for the *Sentinel-Record* & *New Era* and in fact, as selected to serve as one of the election officials.

[24] *Sentinel-Record*, 6 May 1936.

[25] Ibid., p. 7. Also, see *Sentinel-Record*, 5 August 1936.

[26] From Complaint filed in Garland County Circuit Court, George S. Mattar and Cecil alley v. Ernest Maner and James R. Campbell, p. 13. This suit is similar to one described in ote 22.

telephone operators, sheet writers, board markers, guards and dealers.[27] Thi in itself, would make the election illegal as those judges and clerks who we employed by businesses which were felonies and were operating against th laws of the State of Arkansas. Of those from Belvedere, one, Buddy Wakeli was the son of the chief of police, another had been employed as a policema and one was a supervisor with the city's street department. Jack McJunki Thad Rogers and Vander Retherford, represented the fire department.

Another major point of contention was the drawing for position on th ballot. It has long been believed that the most favorable place to have one name on a ballot is the top or first name for that particular office, the theo being that some people will mark the first name in the event they are n committed to any candidate. Candidates eagerly hope for the favored positic and usually attend the drawing for position. Not so in this election. Th drawing was held the third week in July 1936, without the candidates or the representatives and was held by the executive committee of the Garlan County Democratic Central Committe with none other that May McLaughlin watching the proceeding. Robert Ripley, of *Ripley's Believe It or N* undoubtedly would have been in attendance had he known the outcome. what must have been the most illogical and mathematically impossible "lu of the draw," that ever happened occurred that day! The names of all locall backed candidates "pulled from the hat" won the first or top positio Amazing! How lucky can one be?[28] That included the Justice of Peace ra where a total of twenty-eight names appeared running for ten offices--the te supported by the Administration all occupied the top positions. One of th local papers was too kind in its remarks as it reported,

"In the various county races the names of candidates reported to have th backing of the city administration appeared on top in many instances." In fa in all instances.

After the election another violation of state law came to light. The secreta of the County Central Committee was charged with having the official ballo printed, however it was learned this job was delegated to His Honor th Mayor.[29] How's that for setting the fox to look after the hen house? Wond where the extra ballots wound up?

A mysterious full page ad appeared in the papers advising that former circu

---

[27] Ibid., 6 August 1937, p. 7. Also, from copy of a complaint filed in the Garla Circuit Court, Clyde Wilson v. Marion Anderson. The complaint is a twenty-page docume dated 21 August 1936, and the copy given to the writer by attorney Richard Hobbs, whose l partner, William S. Bouic, was accused by Leo P. McLaughlin as having a hand in drafting t document. The attorneys of record were listed as Murphy and Wood.

[28] *Sentinel-Record*, 22 July 1936. Also, Wilson v. Anderson, p. 7.

[29] George S. Mattar and Cecil Talley v. James R. Campbell and Ernest Maner a Clyde Wilson v. Marion Anderson.

dge Scott Wood had a falling out with Governor Futrell and that Wood "Is ;ainst Ed F. McDonald," who was being supported by Futrell. The lvertisement continued, "The voters of Garland County must not vote for ıy man supported by Scott Wood." It was signed by "Committee of Business ıterests," but neither the Chamber of Commerce nor any businessmen :knowledged knowing anything about it.

Scott Wood responded in an article entitled, "To The Vaporings of an ısane Mind." Wood said McLaughlin had blamed him for all political pposition against him and that he "had not urged any man to offer (himself) ›r public office and have taken no active interest in any county or district ffice." Further, Wood wrote, "The Author of the fake advertisement signed Committee of Business Interests,' went crazy once before in a crisis, and the ıvings in yesterday's *New Era* is ample evidence that he has suffered a relapse ı the present crisis."[30]

August 11, 1936, found Leo P. McLaughlin as busy as a cat on a hot tin ›of. Even though it was a violation of the state's electoral laws, which stated ıe judges and clerks at polling places are charged with the responsibility or rohibiting the presence of any person except voters, Leo McLaughlin visited very polling place in town. He came and went as he pleased, laughing and ılking with voters, judges and clerks without being challenged by a single poll fficial. So did policemen and other workers for the Administration andidates. Their presence may have intimidated timid voters, as later claimed.

The most hotly-contested race was the one for Garland County Sheriff. After three terms, Jim Floyd stepped down and threw his support to a young leputy, Marion Anderson. Anderson had arrived in Hot Springs in the mid-wenties on the back of a Harley-Davidson motorcycle, which he had ridden ıp from Bastrop, Louisiana. Anderson had worked a short while on the Hot Springs police department and also, as a state highway patrolman. He started ıs a deputy under Sheriff Garland Van Sickle and stayed with Sheriff Floyd. He had the backing of Mayor McLaughlin. He drew two opponents in the 1936 race for sheriff, Monroe Young and Clyde Wilson.

Young was from a family of law enforcement officers, in fact one relative, ohn Young, was the Administration candidate for the office of constable. In general, they were better law enforcement men than they were politicans, ılthough one served years as a constable and another as sheriff.

Clyde Wilson had been born and raised in Hot Springs and was a self-employed businessman, owning a large furniture store at the corner of Hobson and Sixth Streets in South Hot Springs. He was well-known and well-thought of. Wilson wanted to get involved in politics, but received no encouragement from Administration sources. Not discouraged, he realized his

---

[30] *Sentinel-Record*, 11 August 1936, p. 9.

best opportunity lay in the fact that Jim Floyd was stepping down as sheriff and that he was better-known in Hot Springs than Marion Anderson. Wilson had married Hettie Wheatley, daughter of long-time State Senator Walter Wheatley, an Administration-backed candidate. Whether the father-in-law and son-in-law had any discussion about being on different sides is unknown, however, there were no hard feelings or animosity to damage the relationship of the two men.[31]

Wilson campaigned hard, getting out posters and advertisements, passing out literature and having spot radio announcements. He wired large signs to the sides of his delivery truck and drove through all the neighborhoods. To the erring eye of the public it appeared he had a big lead in the sheriff's race.

It therefore was a great disappointment to Clyde Wilson and his supporters when the vote was recorded: Anderson 4,878, Wilson 1,644 and Young 245. Bold headlines proclaimed, "Administration Candidates Triumph in Election." Every one of the Administration-backed candidates won by similar majorities.[32] Even in the governor's race the margin was similar: Ed "Soapy" McDonald had 4,442 and Carl Bailey 1,601. However, statewide, Bailey was the winner and Hot Springs was in big trouble.

In less than two weeks Clyde Wilson had filed suit against Marion Anderson, alleging he had received more legal votes in the election than his opponent. Wilson charged that about 4,000 illegal poll tax receipts had been purchased by the local political machine and they had been cast for the defendant, Marion Anderson, and that in some cases "more than one vote was cast for the defendant on each receipt."[33]

The poll tax receipt, which cost $1.00 and was necessary to vote, was alleged in the complaint and later by the returning G.I.s from World War II, had been used "to vote petty criminals, prostitutes, dead men, and hotel guests who hadn't been in the city for years."[34] Years later it would be proven that many transients who had worked at Oaklawn Park Race Track during the short 30-day racing period had lent their names and which appeared on poll tax receipts and used to vote in the 1936 election, though they were far away. Even names of deceased persons appeared on the voting rolls.

The Wilson law suit had no sooner hit the court clerk's office than Leo P. McLaughlin was notified. As always, McLaughlin began to place blame against others and divert attention from the matter at hand. He said, "When one reads

---

[31] From two discussions between the writer and "Shug" Wilson, son of Clyde Wilson and grandson of Senator Walter Wheatley, 16 January and 12 May 2001. Shug advised the two men always got along well and enjoyed each other's company.

[32] *Sentinel-Record*, 16 August 1936.

[33] Ibid., 23 August 1936.

[34] *Pic, The Magazine for Young Men*, July 1947, an article by Ed Cunningham, "New Bath For Hot Springs."

the complaint, one can readily recognize the authors, Scott Wood and W.G. Bouic. During the campaign I made the statement that Scott Wood was supporting Clyde Wilson. The latter received 1,644 votes. Marion Anderson received 4,878, which is conclusive proof that the people will not vote for any candidate who has the support of Scott Wood, and also further proves that the great majority of the people of Hot Springs are almost unanimously behind the city administration."[35] Notice, Leo never addressed the alleged violations cited in the complaint; as always he tried to turn attention away from the faults of the Administration and himself.

Marion Anderson, only thirty-five years-old and reported to be "the youngest sheriff in the state," was represented in the suit by A.T. "Sonny" Davies, city attorney, Gibson Witt, Jr., prosecuting attorney, James R. Campbell, state representative and Leo P. McLaughlin, mayor of Hot Springs.[36] This was a very important issue for the Administration: it could afford no mistakes or slip-ups and the leadership was there to steer it through the difficult judicial waters and channels the suit might be routed. They need not have feared, "Earl (Witt) was on the job."

Anderson's "dream team" of lawyers moved for dismissal on the grounds that Wilson was not a qualified elector and "that his complaint was faulty" because it did not make the third candidate, Monroe Young, a party to the suit even though he had polled a distant third with 245 votes. Without going into one issue or hearing one witness, Circuit Judge Earl Witt dismissed the case on the grounds the complaint was defective and that Wilson was not an elector.

Wilson's attorneys, still believing they had a strong case and a multitude of evidence to prove fraud had existed in the election, appealed the case to the Arkansas Supreme Court. Another disappointment lay in store for the independent candidate and his lawyers as the highest judicial body in the state, too, refused to look into the allegations and only at the style of the case, affirming Witt's ruling. Wilson was a loser on a "technicality."[37] It would appear Wilson's lawyers, one a retired circuit judge and the other a former prosecuting attorney, had blown any chance Wilson might have had.

Oh, the Administration crowed over that victory! Their braying could be heard up and down Central Avenue. It seemed as if they were invincible, and they were, at least in Garland County. It was on the state level that they had become vulnerable and a large question loomed before them. What would Governor elect Carl Bailey do once he was in office? Would he forget the Luciano embarrassment the local politicians had caused him and would he let

---

[35] *Sentinel-Record*, 23 August 1936.
[36] Ibid., 1 January 1937.
[37] *New Era*, 15 March 1937.

by-gones be by-gones over the support for his opponent, Ed "Soapy" McDonald? And would he forgive the way they had trashed him during the campaign? And was Bailey still sore about his challenge of Garland County election officials when he and Elmer Tackett, a candidate for prosecuting attorney, had prepared a *mandamus* action against the Garland County Democratic Central Committee, alleging fraud over the appointment of the biased election judges and clerks, and were unable to get a hearing before Judge Earl Witt as he could not be found, which they believed to be on purpose?[38] And, oh yes, Governor Bailey might just be a little out-of-sorts over a little known incident which occurred at the Belvedere Club several months before. It seems as if then-Attorney General Bailey and some friends had some type of complaint and were rudely and roughly treated and escorted to their car. Yes, it did appear the local Administration might have a problem.

McLaughlin, Ledgerwood, W.S. Jacobs and Davies put their heads together in an effort to come up with a plan to approach Bailey to determine if amends might be made. It was decided State Senator Walter Wheatley would be the one to contact the Bailey forces to ascertain the governor's temperament toward Hot Springs. Wheatley accepted the assignment and returned from Little Rock saying only, he was politely received but was given no assurance the governor was "willing to work with Hot Springs authorities."

The Administration and gambling community was as nervous as a long-tailed cat in a room full of rocking chairs waiting to learn what the new governor planned to do about gambling in Hot Springs. They even stationed a man out near Crow's Station on the Benton Highway, as a lookout to alert them in the event he observed any state police cars headed for the Spa. The answer was on the way, but apparently the watchman had quit for the day as late on the evening of January 29, 1937, four squads of state law enforcement officers rolloed into Hot Springs, bringing with them two large vans.

The first squad quickly entered the Belvedere Club and presented the manager Otis McGraw with a search, seize and burn *writ* for all gaming paraphernalia found on the premise. The *writ* perscribed that any such equipment pertaining to gambling, be burned within twenty-four hours.[39]

Simultaneous raids were being conducted at the Kentucky, the Ohio, The Blue Ribbon and the Citizen Clubs, and Millsap and Millers cigar stores and sporting results.

The *Sentinel-Record* reported," News of the raids swept over the town like wildfire. The downtown side walks were soon milling with curious pedestrians and crowds gathered in front of the bookmaking and gambling establishments.

[38] *Sentinel-Record*, 9 August 1936. Judge Witt later commented he didn't know why they couldn't find him for the hearing, he'd been "around town."

[39] Ibid., 30 January 1937, p. 8.

Central Avenue became jammed with automobile traffic. There were several minor collisions when drivers' attention was diverted in their eagerness to follow the movement of the state officers." It was much like running a trot-line as the two large vans, brought from Little Rock, moved from club to club picking up the confiscated equipment.

The state officers, who had only search, seize and destroy warrants, informed the gambling house operators, "We have no arrest warrants. You can use your own judgement about opening up tomorrow."[40] Governor Bailey knew how to get their attention--destroy the equipment!

What worried the club owners was much of the equipment was new as they had let some old paraphernalia be confiscated and destroyed when the legislature was doing its probe a short time before. The equipment had an estimated value of $15,000, and they did not want it destroyed. Quickly, W.S. Jacobs and some of the other owners employed "a prominent attorney," in Little Rock in an effort to prevent destruction of the gambling devices. All to no avail. A large crowd assembled at the state capitol to watch a bonfire eat away at the green-felt gaming tables and highly-polished roulette wheels. The message to the political machine at Hot Springs was clear, Governor Bailey was playing hard-ball. It only took two more raids until the Administration was ready to holler, "uncle."

How to approach the governor became the big question. During the Luciano scenario, someone, according to Bailey, had offered him $50,000 to keep Luciano safe in Arkansas, and he had reported this to the press. In fact, he had been complimented by Special Prosecutor Thomas Dewey of New York for his honesty.[41] Would he again make it public if he was approached by a small delegation from Hot Springs? A feeler was sent out in the form of State Representative Ernest Maner, who had a close acquaintance with one of the governor's aides. The word was more hopeful this time, Bailey was ready to listen. Perhaps he still had some outstanding campaign expenses that were pressing and saw a way to rid himself of these debts.

Because of the incident involving Bailey at Belvedere, W.S. Jacobs ruled himself out as one of the delegation. Also, because of the incident at the Garland County Court House which had occurred when Sonny Davies had kept Carl Bailey from taking Luciano back to Little Rock, he would not be welcomed by the Governor. That left Leo and Verne and they had supported Bailey's opponent in the last election. With hats in hands and appearing repentant, they journeyed to Little Rock for an audience with the governor.

After what must have been several uncomfortable moments McLaughlin

---

[40] Ibid.

[41] It was believed the offer from Luciano's gang had been delivered by Owney Madden or someone working with him.

and Ledgerwood carefully explained the unique situation the Spa was in having an almost complete dependence upon the tourist trade, the baths anc they had used a "controlled gambling" system to provide entertainment for the visitors and to help the city pay its bills. Ledgerwood, sensing Bailey was politically ambitious, said, "Governor, you may want to run for higher office someday, and we can help you. Our friends in the gambling industry are willing to provide campaign support for a candidate who is friendly to Hot Springs."

McLaughlin, seeing the governor appeared interested, chimed in "And we can guarantee delivering the vote in Garland County in your next election. You wouldn't want to throw that away." Bailey was impressed and the mayor anc municipal judge came away with an understanding Hot Springs could continue operation as it had under Governor Futrell.[42]

Roy Bosson, former *New Era* reporter and night editor and former reporter for *The Arkansas Democrat*, wrote, "A standard contribution to a 'friendly governor back in those days was $50,000, big money in that era. Casinos bookies and various 'houses' all contributed amounts generally related by their volume of business."[43]

So there would be no direct money trail tracing a monetary gift or donation from gambling sources to the governor, McLaughlin and Ledgerwood were briefed by an aide to leave any "gift" in a small closet or storage room near the governor's office and were given the room number. An envelope was left in the room several times, however the two city officals never observed who retrieved the envelopes or its contents.[44]

It was good news to the gambling community when McLaughlin anc Ledgerwood came back with an agreement with the governor. It was only a day or two until the bookies and clubs were running wide open. By the first of May, a group of citizens had noticed the increase in activity by the gamblers and not being aware that an "agreement" had been reached between the governor, city administration and club owners, they sent a delegation to Little Rock to apprise Bailey of this new effrontery. Not realizing the local machine had already reached the governor they requested their identities not be made

[42] LAT - Ledgerwood.

[43] *Arkansas Democrat, - 1969*, the third in a series of articles by Roy Bosson, entitled "McLaughlin's Power Grew With Hot Springs." This writer had also heard several people say an incumbent governor or a supported candidate could expect at least $50,000 for campaign expenses, if he was in sympathy with the local "open town" policy. In Roy Reed's fine work on the life of Orval Faubus, the former long-time governor never would admit receiving over $6,000. One state police officer once confided with the writer Faubus had dispatched a state police offical to Hot Springs to "escort" a sizeable donation back to Little Rock when he wa in a hot and expensive campaign for governor.

[44] Recorded interview with Dora Jane Ledgerwood Ellis and her husband, Trice Ellis

public as they "feared reprisals," against them would result.[45] They told him the "bookies are running wide open and are operating in the same establishments they had been when shut down by state law enforcement officers several weeks prior." Also, the slot machines had reappeared. The delegation quickly became aware the governor no longer exhibited any interest in the gambling at Hot Springs as he told them if they had problems along this line, "You should appeal to your local courts."[46] Appeal to the local courts? The delegation from Hot Springs realized that Bailey had "crossed over," and was now in cahoots with The Administration.

It turned out that Governor Bailey needed the Hot Springs political machine sooner than he had imagined. That event was caused by the death of U.S. Senator Joe T. Robinson, Senate Majority Leader. A special election was called to elect a replacement for the four years remaining on Robinson's term and Carl Bailey, seeing an opportunity, announced his candidacy. This was done at a meeting of the state Democratic party rather than as a bi-party movement to provide Senator Robinson's successor. In fact, Leo P. McLaughlin, to demonstrate he was now fully on the governor's side, made the motion that Carl E. Bailey be nominated without opposition. The motion passed and therefore excluded any other democrats who vied for the office. That included John E. Miller, U.S. Congressman from the 2nd Congressional District, who had specifically expressed an interest in the office. Because of Leo's and the party's action, Miller had to run as an independent, though he was a democrat. Other members of Arkansas' delegation to Washington condemned the action of McLaughlin and the Democratic Party and supported Congressman Miller's bid. Congressman John McClellan actively campaigned for Miller and in a "rousing speech" at Pine Bluff on October 11, said, "The nomination of Governor Carl E. Bailey by the state democratic committee to suceed the late Senator Joe T. Robinson was entirely illegal." McClellan would learn that legality many times meant little to Mayor Leo P. McLaughlin and his cronies. As promised, the McLaughlin machine threw its support to Governor Bailey.

Mayor Leo P. McLaughlin was invited to open the Southwest Arkansas Fair and to crown the fair queen which was scheduled for Oaklawn Park. Instead of just performing his duties as invited, he used the opportunity as a political platform and appealed to the "civic-pride" of the local citizens. He assailed Congressman Miller over remarks he had made relative to Carl Bailey's having let gambling reopen in the Spa after promising voters during the gubernatorial race, that if elected, he would close gambling. McLaughlin referred to Bailey as "the real democratic candidate," and Miller as an "independent" connotating that as a dirty word, when he had caused the problem to begin with.

---

[45] *Sentinel-Record*, 5 May 1937.

[46] Ibid.

Again, McLaughlin would divert attention from the issue at hand, namely, Bailey versus Miller. He said, "Hot Springs has been held up to the scorn of the world in the campaign. Politics in Arkansas have reached a new low level when they jump on a city like this instead of confining themselves to the national qualifications of the candidates."[47]

With the help of the local political machine, Bailey polled 1,230 votes to 580 for Miller, but Miller won the statewide election over his opponent.[48] Leo had again "saddled the wrong horse."

While the defeat did not loom so large to the local politicians at the time, as Carl E. Bailey was still governor, it would prove damaging in the long run. Leo had just "shot himself in the foot" and would not realize it for nine years. At that time a group of determined war veterans had returned from the war and were trying to rid the Spa of the powerful and corrupt political machine. They had just filed suit in federal court to remove hundreds of illegal poll taxes from the Garland County voting rolls.

Leo didn't even attend the hearing as he normally did in all legal matters relative to the city or his administration. He knew who the U.S. District judge was for the Western District of Arkansas and that he did not stand in the judge's best graces after having bad-mouthed him in the special election of 1937. The Administration's attorneys were A.L. Barber and E.A. Henry of Little Rock, and Jay Rowland of Hot Springs, and looking down from the bench to rule on the case was none other than Federal Judge John E. Miller.[49] The McLaughlin machine was about to be dealt a severe blow!

---

[47] *Sentinel-Record,* 12 October 1937.
[48] Ibid., 19 October 1937.
[49] *Arkansas Democrat,* 8 July 1946.

Hobbies and Another Plunge into the Waters of Matrimony

During the mayoralty campaign of 1927, Leo P. McLaughlin had convinced the voters "Hot Springs is dead," and revealed his plan to revive it.[1] And when elected, revive it, he did. Hot Springs had operated for years as a one industry town, but after the election of Leo McLaughlin it became a two-industry town, bathing and gambling. As one writer put it, "Most tourists try to parlay them [bathing and gambling]. In the end, everybody gets cleaned."[2]

Large conventions began to descend on the town where their delegates or members could conduct business during the day and partake of the lively night life the Spa afforded. Leo was generally invited by the conventions or functions to give a welcoming address or be the featured speaker. He exuded charm and personality and was Hot Springs' goodwill ambassador. He basked in the limelight, which his cronies were willing to allow. The word spread throughout the country, by word-of-mouth, newspapers and magazines, Hot Springs was the fun place to go. As he became better-known he received many invitations to give speeches throughout the Midwest and North. Leo and his sister Stella regularly attended horse shows at Chicago, St. Louis, Memphis and Houston.

Since Leo was being well-cared for by the gambling interests at Hot Springs, he began improving his own stable of horses.

Many people can still recall the beautiful matched team of horses that McLaughlin used to pull a snazzy little sulky down Central Avenue to the delight of the locals. Visitors would crowd onto the portico of the Arlington Hotel as word came, "The Mayor is on his way up Central." He would many times stop at the curb and visit a few minutes with some of the visitors. Leo cut a dashing figure in his snappy riding habit with turned up hat brim and bright red carnation in his lapel. The well-trained team, Scotch and Soda, were known to almost every citizen in town and remembered by many of the visitors. But few people remember the names of some of his other beautiful show horses. He and his sisters were partial to bestowing their mounts with Irish names, sometimes even changing the names of steeds they bought. There were *Killaro Kate*, *Kolarum Shammrock*, and *Irish Champion*. Stella McLaughlin was particularly fond of one mount she named, *Mercy Me*. Leo was invited to speak to the National Horse Show held at St. Louis in October 1937, and while there purchased a handsome six-year old black gelding described as being a five-gaited horse, he renamed *Timperary*. These were all riding horses.

---

[1] *Arkansas Democrat, 1989*, "McLaughlin's Power Grew with Hot Springs," a series of articles by Roy Bosson.

[2] *New York World Telegram*, 23 January 1946, "How Hot Springs Gets Away With Illegal Gambling," by Joe Williams.

Scotch and Soda were high-steppers and drew attention wherever they appeared with their highly visible master. Whenever a parade was scheduled in Hot Springs, Leo and sometimes Stella led the way in their flashy little sulky and the harness of shiny black leather with bright brass fittings. Nearly every article appearing in the northern or eastern press concerning the Spa covered the flamboyant mayor and his two beautiful horses. Few people know where he got the horses or how he came to have them. It is an interesting story, now faded into the past, but perhaps worth telling.

Leo P. McLaughlin met Ed Ballard of French Lick, Indiana in the 1920s. Ballard was well-acquainted in Hot Springs, having been in a partnership with Selim and "Meek" Mattar. The three men had built the Kentucky Club in 1912.[3] Ballard, a gambler by heart, remained in the Spa until Sheriff Bob Williams closed down the gambling the following year.

Ballard went on to invest into a myriad of businesses, owning several circuses and operating them under the name of the American Circus Corporation and a casino he and Robert Alexander operated on Palm Island, Florida. In addition, he had large land holdings in Indiana and once gave the Jesuit Order of Monks the West Baden Hotel for their use. It was estimated he had a wealth in excess of $20,000,000. Sources in his home town of French Lick claimed it was more like $100,000,000.[4] And, he had a beautiful horse ranch where he raised blooded stock.

He was an annual visitor to the Spa and he and Leo P. McLaughlin had become close acquaintances and enjoyed one another's company. In 1935 Leo went to the Kentucky Derby and ran into Ballard. Ballard invited him to his horse ranch and there presented him with two blooded horses, Leo renamed *Scotch* and *Soda,* and kept the beautiful team for over fifteen years.

In 1936, Ed Ballard, age sixty-two, had undergone some type of surgery in New York and was having difficulty in getting over it. In late September he came to Hot Springs, hoping the hot baths might help in his recovery. He had a suite at the Arlington Hotel for about six weeks. During that time he and Leo had lunch a couple of times.

Information later developed during the Legislative Probe into conditions at the Spa, revealed a curious note concerning Ed Ballard and Archie Ledgerwood, older brother of Judge Verne Ledgerwood. It seems that Archie Ledgerwood had developed tuberculosis in the early 1920s. Physicians at Hot Springs advised him to move to a drier climate in an effort to improve his health. This he did, moving to El Paso, Texas about 1922. With his health improved, Archie returned to the Spa in 1931 and went to work for W.S.

---

[3] *New Era,* 7 November 1936, p. 6.
[4] Ibid.

Jacobs at the Belvedere Club at a salary of fifty dollars a week.[5]

Jacobs liked Archie Ledgerwood and realized he was an important key to the local political machine because of his brother, Municipal Judge Ledgerwood. Jacobs offered to sell Archie 25 percent interest in the Belvedere and Southern clubs for a price of $15,000, considered a bargain. Ledgerwood did not have the money at the time, however Jacobs introduced him to Ed Ballard, a friendly acquaintance of Jacobs and on his recommendation, Ballard loaned Archie the money. Ledgerwood promised to repay "the money in October 1936, with 10 percent interest and a bonus of 25 percent of his part of the net earnings of the two clubs and books."[6]

Thus, Ballard's trip to Hot Springs in the fall of 1936 had a dual purpose for Ballard--his health and also for the purpose of collecting on his note from Archie Ledgerwood.

According to Archie Ledgerwood's testimony and also that of Sam Watt, to the investigators of the state legislature, he paid Ballard a total of $20,500 and stated he paid the sum in cash, since he, like so many others, no longer trusted banks. He told them he burned the note from Ballard and took no receipt.[7] Two days later, Ballard and a former partner, Robert Alexander, 65, were both killed in Ballard's hotel suite at the Arlington.[8]

Trying to piece together the events leading up to the double killing is most difficult at this late date. Many facts have been obscured and even suppressed by Chief of Detectives Herbert "Dutch" Akers and Coroner Dr. J.P. Randolph, who asserted, "No inquest was necessary,"[9] and "No investigation is needed."[10]

Dutch Akers told the press he had come to the conclusion that Alexander had an old grudge against Ballard and at one time he had filed suit against his former associate for $250,000, alleging breach of contract. Akers believed Alexander had learned the whereabouts of Ballard and came to Hot Springs to confront the Indianan. The two men were seen together and had seemed to be getting along well, with acquaintances saying they "had met in Ballard's suite for a business conference."[11]

Occupying a room next to Ballard's suite was Pat Pieper, radio announcer for the Chicago Cubs baseball team who was vacationing in the Spa. He told

---

[5] *Liberty Magazine*, "Hell in Hot Springs," - Collins, Part II, p. 17. This includes some of the testimony of Sam Watt at the legislature hearing. Watt had a 15 percent interest in Belvedere and Southern Clubs.

[6] Ibid.

[7] Ibid.

[8] *New Era*, 7 November 1936, p. 1.

[9] Ibid.

[10] *Liberty Magazine*, "Hell in Hot Springs," - Collins, p. 17.

[11] *New Era*, 7 November 1936.

investigating officers he had heard no loud or angry voices from the adjoining suite but clearly heard five pistol shots, one bullet of which came through the wall into his room. He notified the front desk and hotel employees forced the door and found Ballard dead, having been shot three times. Alexander was still alive but had two wounds caused from bullets piercing his lungs. Two guns were found in the room.

In only a matter of minutes a full police crew arrived with the ambulance. In attendence were officer "Curly" Evans, Chiefs Joe Wakelin and Akers, Detective Cecil Brock, Night Captain Bob Moore, who were accompanied by Ballard's old friend, Mayor Leo P. McLaughlin, who had been at the station when the call came in.

Robert Alexander died without confirming what had transpired in the hotel room. Akers and Randolph ruled it a killing and a suicide. Both men had multiple wounds, each which might have proved fatal.[12] As far as it is known no ballistics tests were conducted.

The money that Archie Ledgerwood said he had paid Ballard was not mentioned as being in the room or the hotel safe in any of the police or newspaper accounts. Only speculation remains as to what could have happened to it. Strange?

The papers reported the mayor was quite upset over the loss of his friend and the one who had given him two of his most beautiful horses.

All through Leo's career as mayor the one thing that would entice him out of town were the championship horse shows. He used the shows to further his acquaintances and make new friends, but most importantly he always kept his eyes open for that special colt or filly he might buy. About the middle of 1931 while attending a Houston horse show he spotted the filly of his dreams. Not the-four legged kind, but the two. She was Florence Paul, described as a young Houston society girl and from a "pioneer Texas family." Leo managed an introduction and Florence was impressed with McLaughlin, who could be quite charming when he wanted. In what might be described as a whirlwind courtship Leo swept the young socialite off her feet and when he proposed, she said, "yes."

However, there was a slight problem. Leo was still married to Mary Francis Frink McLaughlin, although they were separated and she had filed for divorce. Leo had been in no hurry to conclude the settlement as he probably believed Mary Francis would lessen her demands the longer he waited. Perhaps his new love interest encouraged the settlement to proceed. At least, the settlement seemed to benefit Mary Francis as she and Leo were divorced 3 November 1931. In what some might have considered a "hurry" Leo P. McLaughlin and

---

[12] Ibid., p. 6.

Florence Paul were married the following day.[13]

Leo proudly brought his new bride to Hot Springs and they took up residence at the Kingsway (Eastman) Hotel where Leo and Mary Francis had resided. No doubt, Florence was impressed with the beauty of the Spa and the important office her husband held. She was cordially received by his acquaintances and business associates. She was called "charming" and reported to have "all the social graces," and was a graduate of Fairmont Seminary in Washington, D.C.[14] It seemed as if Leo had finally found a "keeper." W.S. Jacobs, boss gambler, arranged a large and sumptous dinner party at Belvedere in honor of the newlyweds.[15] Even though Florence had been in Hot Springs only a few months she was accepted into the social circles and appointed by Mrs. J.H. Chestnutt, chairman, to the Centennial Museum Committee.[16] She and Leo were featured in the Centennial Ball at the Arlington and she wore a beautiful and dainty antebellum "calico frock."[17]

Mayor McLauglin presents Huey P. Long and his wife key to the City. Florence McLaughlin, at right.

---

[13] Pulaski Chancery Court Records, cases # 53799 and 56066, Complaint in Equity, filed 26 July 1937. In our research we were unable to determine where the wedding took place. Garland and adjoining counties, including Pulaski were contacted. The Harris County Clerk's office at Houston, Texas had no record. In the divorce proceedings, both parties stipulated to the court that the marriage took place 4 November 1931.

[14] *Arkansas Gazette*, 25 April 1932.

[15] LAT - Ledgerwood.

[16] *Sentinel-Record*, 24 April 1932.

[17] Ibid.

As the "first-lady" of Hot Springs, Florence seemed to take her role seriously and made several appearances with her husband at various functions representing the city. When Huey P. Long and his wife came to the Spa on vacation, she presented Mrs. Long with a basket of flowers while her husband, Mayor McLaughlin gave the "Kingfish," a large key to the city. The flamboyant senator from the bayou country of Louisiana, always alert for publicity opportunities, told the press he and his wife had been married for twenty-one years and were just getting to take their first honeymoon.[18] In the presence of the newsmen Huey Long handed his bodyguard some money and instructed him to go out and buy two axes and a crosscut saw and inquired of those in the room where the nearest woodyard is located? When told, he invited the reporters to be in the lobby of the Arlington the next morning at 7:30 and challenged them to accompany him to the woodyard for a "workout."

Maybe this marriage lasted longer than Leo's first two because Florence was not subjected to the close scrutiny from his mother and sisters, at least as early as Mary Francis had been. As Leo began to drift back into the pattern of having dinner with the McLaughlin family every night, Florence discovered his attitude was changing toward her. About a year after their marriage as they were returning to the Kingsway after dining at the McLaughlins, Leo suddenly "told her that he did not love her, despised her and wished she was dead."[19] Florence was crushed by this revelation and learned Leo's mother and sisters had been making false accusations telling Leo, "she hated him and had talked about him to everybody in town."[20] She offered to prove to Leo that those accusations were false and offered to prove to him she was telling the truth and that his family was causing their problems. But, Leo was always going to take the side of his family, right or wrong, and he would not listen. Florence said Leo began to drink and cursed her, treating her with contempt. After months of this type treatment she finally decided she could no longer live with him and told him this.

That same night McLaughlin went down to the hotel garage and drove Florence's car to the city hall and locked it in a storage area. When the couple had first married, Leo had been so infatuated and in love with his new bride he gave her a new, powder-blue Super Flight Packard sedan and had her initials, "*F.M.*" painted in gold on the front doors.[21] Florence had been proud of the vehicle and everyone recognized her as the Mayor's wife as she drove about the city.

---

[18] *Arkansas Gazette*, 22 November 1934.

[19] Pulaski County Chancery Court Records, Box 2023 Case # 53799, and Box 2048 Case # 56066.

[20] Ibid.

[21] Ibid.

The following morning, 24 April 1936, after Leo left the hotel, Florence packed and moved to Little Rock. Once settled and establishing a residency in the capitol city, she hired Charles B. Thweatt, who conducted quite an investigation of his own into the allegations of his client. While Thweatt did most of the "leg-work," he associated himself with R.A. Lasley, a well- known divorce attorney.

1936
Standing, left to right: Loraine Horner, Ida Bell Disheroon, Bettie Dodson. Seated, Ardeth Annen, Florence McLaughlin, Mrs. William Turner Wootton.

When Florence's story became known it caused quite a sensation in the Spa. According to her, Leo had told her that "he was in league with the gambling and lawless elements in Hot Springs." She said she had discovered after they had been married some time her husband had known such criminals as "Pretty Boy" Floyd and Alvin Karpis and that they had stayed and lived around Hot Springs.[22] Florence said Leo had once showed her a fountain pen, which he kept in a lock box and he said Al Capone had given it to him on one of his trips to the Spa. She and her attorney believed Leo "earns an average of about $5,000 a month and has an estate, unincumbered of about $500,000, consisting principally of cash and government bonds."[23]

Florence would later testify that when she and Leo planned a shopping trip to Little Rock, he would not spend his own money but always made a call and when they started to leave town he would stop in front of the Southern Club and some individual would run out to their car and hand the mayor an envelope which contained money.

When the divorce was filed Leo was extremely upset, not because Florence was seeking a divorce, but because it had been filed in Pulaski County where he had little influence. He quickly filed his own action in Garland County seeking to remove Florence's suit to this county.[24] Chancellor Frank Dodge of Little Rock and Garland County Chancery Judge Sam Garrett fought over jurisdiction of the case like two dogs over a bone. The struggle and hassle went on for over a year. During this time, McLaughlin was paying Florence $150.00 per month maintenance.

When Leo learned Florence's attorney, Charles Thweatt, had conducted an investigation at Hot Springs, he was irate, demanding copies of his papers. The court did not allow this as the documents were considered by the court as "priviledged." Thweatt did testify that he took several "statements of various persons as to illegal income alleged to be derived by the defendant (Mayor McLaughlin) from gamblings operations in Hot Springs, statements of dectectives and other persons as to large amounts of money and bonds alleged to be concealed by the defendant."[25]

As expected, McLaughlin lashed back, telling the press, "Neither I nor any other Hot Springs city official has ever received any revenue from gambling or any other illicit or unlawful sources."[26] Had Leo just told a falsehood? Many people remember when McLaughlin had turned down a raise on his salary as

---

[22] Pulaski Chancery Court Records, Florence McLaughlin v. Leo Patrick McLaughlin Case # 53799m, Response To Motion to Make Complaint More Definite and Certain.

[23] Ibid., taken from the Complaint in Equity.

[24] Garland County Chancery Court Records, Leo P. McLaughlin v. Florence McLaughlin, Box 557, Case # 13441.

[25] *New Era*, 8 July 1937.

[26] Ibid.

he said, "Don't worry about me. Leo'll get his." They, of course, had believed Leo was suggesting he would be paid by the gambling element.

Florence received a settlement, but a very modest one. She got only $3,500 plus approximately $1,800 in paid temporary monthly benefits and her attorney fees.[27] Much to Florence's chagrin, Leo got to keep the Packard sedan he had given her. He had again escaped relatively unscathed.

It was apparent that the "Jimmy Walker of the Ozarks," as one writer called him, was able to keep his horses much longer than he did his wives. Leo might have been compared to the neighborhood dog who chased cars and could not be broken. McLaughlin did not chase cars, but he did women, all his adult life. Like the dog, the chase was the important thing to him, as after he caught them he quickly lost interest!

One might conclude from Leo McLaughlin's actions his hobbies were collecting horses and beautiful young women, but perhaps not necessarily in that order.[28] Verne Ledgerwood's hobbies were not as spectacular perhaps as the mayor's, but did gain him considerable publicity. They were hunting and fishing. Everyone in the Spa recognized him as being the number one sportsman in the area, if not in the state. Whenever the Business Men's League and later its successor, the Chamber of Commerce, planned a sporting event, such as a fishing tournament, Verne Ledgerwood was always asked to be on the planning committee because of his expertise. Because many of the lawyers, doctors, bankers and businessmen of the Spa were invited to participate in these sports, Ledgerwood became a strong link between the Administration and the professional community.[29]

Verne Ledgerwood truly loved to hunt and fish. It wasn't just a matter of him getting in a boat, casting a line and lure into the water and waiting for the fish to strike. He studied the sport. He knew where the best fishing spots were located, the right type of plug or lure and the best times of day to fish. He did not have the modern electronic fish locators that are available today, but relied on his own experience and studies he had made. Verne kept a lengthy and detailed journal written in his clear and legible style, recording such data as the date and time of his trip, the kind, number and weight of the fish he caught.[30]

---

[27] Pulaski Chancery Court Records, cases # 53799 and # 56,066, taken from the Decree 30 September 1936.

[28] LAT - David Whittington. Whittington, who had a first hand acquaintance and whose father had been Leo P. McLaughlin's mentor, said he preferred younger women. When asked by the interviewer, "How young?" He replied, "Young, just out of high school."

[29] A number of people interviewed in the Life and Times of Leo P. McLaughlin project acknowledged the importance of Ledgerwood's tie-in with the professional community with his fishing and hunting trips and his and Bess's Christmas eggnog parties. One of these was Earl Lane.

[30] This journal is in possession of his niece, Dora Jane Ledgerwood Ellis.

Verne S. Ledgerwood, considered the Spa's Number One Sportsman
Courtesy of Dora Jane Ledgerwood Ellis

Few people are aware that Verne Ledgerwood had a small, but helpful part in getting the Remmel Dam and Lake Catherine project started. Once in the early 1920s, Ledgerwood was at a luncheon with Harvey Couch, the head of a small group of power companies destined to become the Arkansas Power and Light Company. Couch advised him of his dream of building two hydroelectric dams on the Ouachita River and had been seeking financing up east to fund the project. He said an old riverboat captain, Flave Carpenter, had encouraged him to look at the Ouachita River for a possible power source. Couch told Ledgerwood that the surveying of the river basin was needed to help convince bankers to finance the building of the first dam, but his company did not have the money at that time for the survey.

Ledgerwood told him, "I believe I can help you with that item." He then related to Couch that several years before he and some friends had been fishing on the Ouachita one day and had set up camp on a sandbar and were cleaning and beginning to fry the big catch they had made when a boat with three men pulled up. They learned the men were a survey crew from the U.S. Corps of Engineers stationed at Vicksburg, Mississippi. The men were invited to partake of a fish supper with Ledgerwood's party. During the evening, the visitors told them they had been commissioned to survey the entire Ouachita

River basin and had already spent several weeks on that project.

Ledgerwood suggested to Harvey Couch that he contact U.S. Senator Joe T. Robinson and ask him to use his influence with the Corps of Engineers to obtain permission to use the survey documents. Shortly afterwards, Couch announced their intention to build a dam on the river.[31] Sometime later, Couch told Ledgerwood that being able to get the plats of the survey had not only saved his company many months of work, but thousands of dollars in survey costs.

The power company, under Harvey Couch's leadership, completed the first dam in 1924, and named it after Harmon L. Remmel, who had been instrumental in obtaining permits from the government. Attending the dedication services were friends of Remmel, Secretary of Commerce Herbert Hoover and Secretary of Interior Hubert D. Work.[32] In 1929, another power project was completed and Carpenter Dam created Lake Hamilton, five times the size of Lake Catherine.

Probably no one used the two beautiful lakes, Catherine and Hamilton, more in those early days than Verne Ledgerwood and his brother Cecil. He and Bess moved to a house on Lake Hamilton and they fished every day they could.

But Verne Ledgerwood did not restrict his hobbies to Garland County. "At the end of every season," he said, explaining that after the races were over, "my friends and I went to Florida to fish. We chartered a boat and fished for sailfish and tarpons."[33] Some of his fishing companions were his two brothers, Cecil and Archie, Frank Moody, owner of the Moody Hotel, Al Reynolds, owner and operator of the Como Hotel, and Earl Ricks, partner in the Ricks-Clinton Buick Agency.

Ledgerwood became acquainted throughout much of the state as a result of his hobbies. He hunted squirrels in the Saline River bottoms; quail in Montgomery County; ducks in Arkansas County, near Stuttgart where he had an interest in a duck camp; and fished in Lake Chicot near Lake Village. He and his friend Governor Marion Futrell hunted geese in the lower delta of the Mississippi and deer in the wet lands of Louisiana. Once, he and Bess accompanied a noted sports writer to Montana where they camped and fished for trout at Glacier National Park.

Allen Ellender, a former classmate of Ledgerwood's at Tulane, called him in 1935. Ellender told him that Louisiana Governor O.K. Allen was making a trip to Hot Springs and planned to stay a few days. He told Verne that Allen loved to fish and suggested he arrange a trip of some kind. Ledgerwood then called his friend, Governor Futrell and suggested the governor challenge the

---

[31] LAT - Ledgerwood.

[32] *Sentinel-Record*, 31 December 1924.

[33] LAT - Ledgerwood.

Louisiana governor to a fishing match on Lake Hamilton. Futrell thought it was a fine idea and did so. Ledgerwood then tipped-off the Chamber of Commerce, the *Sentinel-Record* and *New Era*. The publicity generated by the event was astounding. Write-ups and photographs appeared in the St. Louis *Globe*, Chicago *Sun Times*, Memphis *Commercial Appeal*, New Orleans *Picayune*, *Arkansas Democrat* and *Arkansas Gazette*, as well as the two local papers, the *Sentinel-Record* and *New Era*. Verne was to be the guide and judge and he decreed no reporters could follow them or bother the two men while they were hotly engaged in the contest. The three men departed from his boat dock on Lake Hamilton and after fishing several hours returned to be met by several reporters and photographers. Both governors exhibited a string of ten large black bass each. Ledgerwood ruled the match was a draw.[34]

While Verne Ledgerwood was generally recognized by those in the know as being equal in power to that of Leo P. McLaughlin, he was entirely comfortable with letting McLaughlin be the "front man," and the spokesman for the Administration. It was acknowledged that he was more even- tempered and level-headed than Leo and could differ with an individual without losing his friendship. This, McLaughlin could not and would not do. Oppose him and you had an enemy for life.

The leadership between Leo P. McLaughlin and Verne Ledgerwood of the Administration was generally shared, at least for the first ten years of its existence. After the dismissal of most of the police force over the Dickson death and Karpis harboring cases, McLaughlin began to become more dictatorial. At times things became intense between the two old schoolmates.

Ledgerwood went about doing his job for thirty-five years, first as police judge, then as municipal judge, and very seldom was opposed for election. Roy Bosson, who covered the municipal court hearings as a *New Era* reporter and attorneys Sid McMath and Earl Lane, all indicated Ledgerwood was a good municipal court judge. He handled a big case load in those days, some complicated cases and others, run-of-the-mill. On days the prostitutes and gamblers appeared to pay their fines, Ledgerwood ran his court like an assembly line. From the bench, he was in control of the court.

It is amusing to look back on the municipal court records of the late-1920s and the 1930s. There was a deliberate attempt to disguise the names of those charged with gaming or gambling. Gambling, by state law was a misdemeanor, but after three appearances for the same charge it became a felony and was subject to being remanded to circuit court where the punishment became much harsher. Therefore, the police clerk, constable or municipal court clerk, (sometimes the city clerk) entered the names on the docket of those appearing to pay the regular fines of the clubs they represented. At first names were

---

[34] Ibid. Also, *Arkansas Democrat*, 2 November 1935.

changed about, variations added, wrong initials inserted and nicknames used. After years of this they were running out of aliases.

Then a plan evolved--use different categories as automobiles: Henry Austin, Joe Ford, Bill Chandler, Jim Plymouth, Abner Star, Ernest Desoto, Jack Chrysler, Walter Lincoln, and Pete Packard.[35] And what about colors: Joe Black, Ed Green, Jim Gray, Arthur White and Pete Brown?[36]

As time went on they became more inventive as they charged the gamblers under names such as Gus Polk, D.V. Clark, V.T. Grant, Jim Perry, J.B. Garland, and V. Montgomery--all names of counties.[37]

Then it became crops and pasture grasses: Dutch Millett, Mack Barley, Allen Wheat, Sol Rye, Everett Oats and Will Cotton.[38]

The possibilities were endless. They used names of months, trees, fish and birds. All this effort was to protect the gamblers who were quite willing to appear in municipal court twice each month under an alias and go through the motions of a hearing, knowing they would pay a fine for the privilege of operating his or his employer's club with the blessing and protection of city hall. This protection would assure them there would be no raids, at least from local sources.

But were aliases used for others? Rarely. Most citizens who were arrested with an expired license would be charged and docketed under his real name. So would those who were arrested for being drunk, double parking, disturbing the peace or violating some city ordinance. Even prostitutes were charged under the name under which they were working. In other words there were two standards of justice in Hot Springs--one for those connected with gambling and the other for everyone else. By today's standards such actions would be totally illegal and unethical. It was back then, too. The Administration just didn't let such things as the law and ethics interfere with its agenda!

---

[35] Constable's Municipal Record, Case # 14865, 8 January 1936. All of these were automobiles in that period.

[36] Ibid., 7 September 1935, p. 98, Case # 13798.

[37] Municipal Court City Jailers Docket, Case 12528, 22 March 1935.

[38] Ibid., p. 68, Case 17094, 26 October 1936.

The Hard and Difficult Years

As the Depression caused mainly by the stock market crash of 1929 deepened and began to descend and cast its gloom over the entire country, Hot Springs was having one of its best years and was running wide open. The gambling clubs and casinos had capacity crowds at night and the bookies during the day. Bathhouses had a steady stream of visitors who were arriving daily on the Rock Island and Missouri-Pacific railroads. The influx of tourists and visitors provided work for the bath attendants, hotels and staffs and the downtown restaurants and merchants. Yes, business was good in the Spa. The financial problems in the North and East seemed far remote for the citizens of Hot Springs. But there was a "bump-in-the-road," a big bump, and only a few could see it coming. As in the prophetic words of Rev. R.G. Lee, the famous minister of Bellview Baptist Church in Memphis, who preached one sermon hundreds of times, "Pay Day, Someday," hard times began to make its visit to Hot Springs. It was "pay-day." The visitors and bathers to the Spa began to rapidly decline and money seemed to "dry-up." Only the clubs and casinos seemed immune as the wealthy continued to visit the Spa, but even they were affected.

Many cities throughout the country experienced "runs" on their banks and failures of what had been believed to be strong financial institutes. Hot Springs was not to be left out.

For several years the Spa had boasted of having six banking houses. In those days there was no "safety-net" for depositors, no FDIC guaranteeing accounts up to a certain limit, and people placing their money in a bank did so based on the trust they had for the board of directors and staff of that business. No less than four of the local banks had failures of one kind or another and closed their doors with the depositors losing thousands of dollars of their savings. The Citizens Bank and Trust and the Como Trust, where E.N. Roth, a well-respected individual was president, closed their doors. The Security Bank, located on the southwest corner of Central and Reserve, had enjoyed a good reputation in the community and was headed by its president John B. Foote, always known as a conservative banker. A rumor got out one afternoon in 1930, that the bank was having financial difficulties. When its employees arrived the following morning there was a long line of customers waiting. Mr. Foote and his vice-president tried to assure the crowd that the bank was sound and all loans were secured and that the only difficulty was in a "short-supply of money." The two men tried to convince the depositors to withdraw only the amount of money for which they had an immediate need. Panic prevailed with the people demanding their accounts be closed out and the full amount of their deposits be paid. The first ones paid, took their money and walked across the street to the Arkansas National Bank and opened up accounts. Fred Rix, president of the Arkansas National, knew Foote's bank was sound and that he just did not have the cash on hand to satisfy all its depositors. The story was told how Rix and his bank, in an effort to save its neighbor, kept taking the deposits in the front door and rushing the money out the back door and over to the Security Bank to pay off more of its depositors. But the Security was doomed and closed its doors never to open again.

Less than a year later, 30 November 1931, the Community Bank, where Hamp Williams served as president, closed its doors. Its assets were listed at $807,486.96.[1] When it was announced that A.T. "Sonny" Davies, city attorney, had been appointed to liquidate the bank's assets, some eyebrows were raised and the little tabloid, *Public Opinion*, predicted dire consequences and doubts of the investors and depositors ever receiving much of their money. After the liquidation process had been under way thirty-two months, the paper printed a balance sheet to demonstrate how little money was being returned to the depositors' hands. It pointed out that Davies was paying himself a handsome salary of $350.00 per month to liquidate the bank while he was receiving a salary from the City of Hot Springs as its attorney as well as taking on clients at his law office. Three sources of income when so many men were out of work and their families hungry? Davies, according to the tabloid, really wasn't needed as he had had hired a young experienced banker from Waldron, Tom Stone, who was doing most of the actual liquidation, and the city attorney was only the figurehead, drawing what was a large salary in those days.[2] Former customers received about forty-cents on the dollar when it was over. After the purge of local financial institutions and the national banking system was re-organized, only the Arkansas National and the Arkansas Trust were left to serve the citizens of the Spa for many years.

By no means were the banks the only businesses that were forced to close. Several mills had to shut down their operations as home construction almost came to a standstill. At the beginning of the depression Hot Springs had 123 grocery stores of varying sizes, ranging from the large downtown stores to the little neighborhood groceries operated by families known as "Mom and Pop" stores. The numbers decreased to 90 stores by 1938. For several years there was a rivalry between two local grocery chains. By 1938 Jett Brothers, operated by Elmer and Andrew Jett, were running ten of the stores, each building-front painted orange and black. The other chain was Stueart's, under ownership of Henry Stueart and managed by Millard Stueart. The nine stores it had at that time were very distinctive in color, also, being painted white and black.[3]

Each week school boys scurried throughout the various neighborhoods

---

[1] *Public Opinion*, 4 August 1933, p. 1 and 8.

[2] Ibid.

[3] *Hot Springs City Directory - 1938.*

sticking a sales paper in the screen door of each house, announcing the bargains of the week as the two chains competed for customers. Sometimes the competition was so great that merchants were making only one or two cents on an item. During this time a loaf of bread was generally ten cents, but got as low as eight cents. Milk sold in glass returnable bottles could be bought for ten cents a quart. Stueart's advertised a can of pork and beans at only four cents a can, ten pounds of "fine white cane sugar" for forty-one cents, veal stew at five cents per pound, ham for nine cents per pound and bacon at a nickel a pound.[4]

A competitor, Piggly Wiggly at 116 Central Avenue, managed by Jim Midkiff, offered "thick roast, tender and juicy" at twelve cents per pound and "Wig Wam" maple syrup for fifteen cents a can.[5] Clothing was another item that was inexpensive, but still very difficult to obtain when the home provider was out of a job. S.S. Caldwell and Son, had operated a dry-goods store on Central Avenue in the Oaklawn area for years. With stock not moving because of the Depression, the store advertised "Our entire stock of ladies dresses at reduced prices." These sold from thirty-nine cents each all the way up to eighty-nine cents. And, men's hickory striped trousers were priced at ninety-five cents as were Big Smith bib overalls.[6]

When the Depression struck the country the Hot Springs area was filled with new car agencies and repair shops. Strange names, by today's standards--LaSalle, Hudson, Essex, Franklin and Graham-Paige--appeared in the newspapers, and directories. When the manufacturers of those automobiles shut their doors forever, so did the dealerships throughout the country. Some people got rid of their cars and relied on the street cars for transportation--it cost only seven cents to get almost anywhere in town. And many people were not too proud to walk--shoe leather was cheap.

Prices were low eveywhere, it was just the short supply of jobs and money that troubled people. It didn't make any difference how low prices were: unless a person had a job, the prices were still out of reach.

The hotels remained relatively unchanged, except maybe having to reduce their work forces. The Arlington, Kingsway (Eastman), Majestic, Desoto, Marquette, Park, Great Northern, Moody and Como, continued as favorites of those tourists still able to afford a visit to the Spa. Resturants changed little, although one long-time downtown favorite, Frisby's, closed forever as a new cafeteria, Franke's, opened a few doors down the street.[7] Frisby's had featured dinner music by a pianist, small stringed orchestra or a Hawaiian Song and

---

[4] As advertised in *Public Opinion*, 16 March 1933, p. 8.
[5] Ibid., 2 February 1934.
[6] Ibid., 28 July 1933, p. 3.
[7] *Hot Springs City Directories - 1926-1938.*

Dance group.[8] Greek resturants seemed to thrive as they employed almost every member of the household, cutting down on labor costs. Some were Jim and George's, Peter Skirvanos, George Gabriel, and the four Pappas brothers--Angelo, John, Peter and William.

The popularity of some of these restaurants was demonstrated at noon during the school year when those children who had not brought their lunch to school descended on Central and Ouachita Avenues. They filled the Green Castle for hamburgers; Skirvanos for sloppy-joes and chili dogs; and Pappas Brothers for three-ways and ham sandwiches. So many people ate at Pappas' over the years that the marble-slab step-plate at the front door wore half in-two.

Visitors on a budget and locals found several places economical to eat. Robert Callahan, a one-armed man, operated the Square Deal Cafe at 242 Ouachita Avenue until hard times and long hours--5:00 a.m. to midnight--overtook him in 1935 and forced his retirement. A person could eat three meals a day there for less than a dollar. Ham and eggs for breakfast was only twenty-five cents and that included coffee. A hamburger steak with Spanish sauce, with three side dishes, desert and coffee, tea or milk was another twenty-five cents and a special chicken dinner with homemade dumplings ran another thirty-five cents.[9] That still left fifteen cents for a tip.

Another low-cost restaurant was located next door to the Square Deal, the Baby Elephant Cafe. The space it occupied was so narrow it had only a counter and stools and served hot coffee and donuts or a good breakfast and reasonable lunch. It was operated for years by Leroy Hall.

Martin Westover opened a billard parlor and cigar store at 831 Central Avenue in the 1920s and sold soft drinks and candy. After Prohibition had been repealed he sold beer on one side and installed a lunch counter on the other. Little did Westover realize he had started a tradition that was to last many years in the Spa. It was operated on an honor system. There was no ticket. Just tell the waiter what you wanted and when you left informed the cashier what you had, paid for it and that was all. Martin's turned out plate lunches by the hundreds. They also served ham and hot roast beef sandwiches, soup and the best chili (no beans) in town. That was the fare--the menu and prices seldom changed. The resturant fed the city and county jail inmates for years. All customers sat on stools--there were no booths. They did have three or four tables, however those were generally occupied by domino players who slammed the pieces onto the table with gusto and loud laughter. Governors, senators, representatives and the rich and famous came, but they were not

---

[8] Taken from various advertisements, including a program of the Auditorium Theatre, season 1922-1923.

[9] Taken from a menu of the Square Deal Cafe, in possession of the GCHS.

treated any better than a store clerk or the dirty, tired and hungry brick layer or carpenter. Everyone had equal status at Martin's. It was a common place to meet for a quick and enjoyable lunch and the expression, "Meet you at Martin's," needed no other instruction but the appointed time. After lunch, friends could work off a bit of energy with a game of rotation, snooker or eight-ball pool. The more serious-minded and "pool sharks" could go up the street to Ferd Mazzia's pool hall. Martin's was a "rumor-mill" as an innocent remark that was incorrectly overheard and misunderstood became a fact and the person repeating what he thought had been said, proudly proclaimed it as gospel truth. "I heard it at Martin's," seemed to give it authenticity. After the races returned to Oaklawn, it became a beehive of so-called "racing information" and a half-dozen persons every day claimed to have inside information on a sure bet. A tip on almost any horse in any race could be heard at Martin's. Even though ownership of Martin's changed, the name never did and it lasted until the early 1990s.

One inexpensive place of entertainment was the movie theatres. They allowed a person, at a nominal cost, to get a glimpse into a more comfortable world, one of the glitter of Hollywood, of beautifully gowned and coiffured women and tall, handsome well-dressed men. It was a world of make-believe where none of the movie stars ever seemed to have a job but were able to have large and beautiful homes, servants and automobiles and where the star could always find a parking spot immediately in front of his apartment building though the streets were choked with traffic. It was a world that young boys and girls in the Depression era could only dream about. The movie theatre was a place to go and forget your troubles, and become engrossed in a fantasy world, at least for two or three hours. And it generally cost between ten and thirty-five cents. The films changed in most theatres three times a week and the previews claimed every one to be the best picture ever made. As the "talkies" made their way onto the silver screen, one of Hot Springs' most visible theatres, the Lyric, owned by Sidney Nutt, located in the 400 block of Central, near the Palace Hotel and the Ohio Club, caught fire in 1928 and was totally destroyed--a common peril for early movie houses.[10] Nutt also owned the Central, then at 616 Cental Avenue, and the Princess Theatre at 817. He moved the Central Threatre to a building he built at 1008. The old location became the new Paramount, a classy movie house for its time, equipped with a daylight screen to prevent "red-eyes," the first in the Spa. The Princess was a favorite of local people as on Saturday night it featured amateur programs, sometimes instrumentals, tap-dancing and singing. It also sponsored boxing and two local lads, Sid McMath and James Dowds, used to flail each other as patrons would throw coins into the ring in appreciation for their tenacity. The

[10] The Palace Hotel and Ohio Club were heavily damaged by fire 11 July 2001.

Princess, too, succumbed to flames and was totally destroyed by fire late on Christmas Eve, 1935. As the rear wall collapsed, it fell on a small hotel at the rear facing Broadway and several persons lost their lives.

Another downtown theatre in the 1930s was the State located in the 700-block of Central on the spot where the Royal had stood . The State, too, was destroyed by fire in the 1940s. Other theatres were the Spa, later replaced by the Victory on Ouachita, whose screen was at the front of the theatre, and the Strand, owned and operated by Mrs. Jessie Howe. After it had been remodeled in the 1940s, it sported two balconies. All the movie houses had at least one balcony designated for "Colored" as this was long before integration. In South Hot Springs there was a small movie house, The Best, on Hobson Avenue, and it lasted only a short while and was destroyed by fire. After its demise, The Roxy was opened across the street and operated a number of years until it also went up in flames.

The author, like so many other youngsters, had a "misspent youth," by attending so many Saturday matinees at the old Roxy. For only a dime a western featuring Buck Jones, Tom Mix, Tim McCoy or Hopalong Cassidy, a Boston Blackie or Dick Tracy detective film or a Laurel and Hardy or Marx brothers comedy, whiled away the hours. That was only a start. There were the weekly serials that always left movie-goers wondering how the hero could survive his fall off a high cliff or a plunge from a skyscraper, but survive, he always did! There was always a Pluto, Mickey Mouse or Three Stooges cartoon or comedy as young movie fans howled with delight and filled the theatre with laughter. Short subjects and Movietone News from around the globe kept us in touch with the rest of the world. For most of us that was our only contact with seeing the twin World's Fairs, one in New York and the other in San Francisco. And, last, the previews of coming attractions gave just a glimpse why it was so important to see next week's fare. You just couldn't miss it! The popcorn bag, when empty, could be blown up and exploded with a loud "bang" when the stars were about to embrace or kiss and added a little excitement and humor when the movie began to get dull. This, of course, was frowned on by the management and the advent of pasteboard boxes got rid of that problem, but created another, the box could be thrown into a row of girls just to hear them scream. That generally brought an usher to see what the commotion was. Of course, when the film broke and the house lights came up while the film was being spliced, the air was some times filled with a flight of home-made paper airplanes fashioned from the multi-colored movie advanced news of coming attractions. The old Roxy wasn't air-conditioned, but it was cooled somewhat by two large exhaust fans on either side of the screen and kept the air moving. Once when a squeaking bearing on the fan drowned out the movie sound the film was stopped while an usher climbed up on a step ladder with a small can of oil to soothe the stressed parts, all amid a salvo of popcorn box missiles. It was a hoot!

There were certain nights during the week some of the theatres used a gimmick to get people there. There were different names for the ploy--"The Big Drawing" or "Bank Night" or "Giveaway Night." Each person entering that night had a ticket stub placed in a circular wire cage that could be spun around and someone from the audience would be selected to make the drawing. The winner sometimes walked away carrying a $20 bill or toting a bag of groceries they had won. There were lesser prizes to encourage people to turn out. A few patrons each night could be seen leaving the theatre carrying a carton of Coca-Colas or Pepsi-Colas, which at that time only cost a quarter for a six-pack, but it didn't make any difference--they were winners.

For many years the Auditorium Theatre had movies as well as live shows. It had opened in 1904, and an aging opera queen, Adelina Patti, performed to rave reviews. It was her last performace.[11] Newspapers reported that when Miss Patti sang "Home Sweet Home" as an encore, "there wasn't a dry eye in the place." The theatre management showed hundreds of silent films, accompanied by an organist and sometimes by an entire orchestra, to dramatize the events. It was a time of audience participation, cheering the hero and hissing the villain. Frank Head, manager, scheduled hundreds of wrestling and boxing matches.[12] Once during a battle-royal, where several pugilists were in the ring at a time, Lucky Luciano's body guards heated quarters and half-dollars with a lighter and threw them into the ring just to see the combatants scramble and try to pick up the hot money.[13]

In 1924 the great John Phillip Sousa and the Sousa Band thrilled a packed Auditorium crowd with a rousing concert. From the time the great maestro tapped his baton to begin until the last bars of "Stars and Stripes" ended, "the audience was riveted to its seats." Miss Nora Fairchild, soloist, was loudly applauded for her encore of "Dixie," as was Meredith Wilson, with a flute solo.[14]

The Auditorium's stage was large enough to accommodate traveling road shows, even *Ben Hur*, which had a live chariot race. The great picture, *Birth of a Nation*," ran for a week. There were traveling minstrels; grand operas as *Carmen* and light opera hits such as *The Chocolate Soldier*. Elks Club Minstrels were annual occurences and sometimes high school plays. For awhile radio station KTHS sponsored a "Barn-dance," party on Saturday night as amateur performers were invited to share their talents for the listening audience. There was a lot of "pickin' and grinnin'" as it was patterned after Nashville's "Grand Ole Opry." In 1931, Will Rogers, Broadway star, humorist, lecturer and most

---

[11] *Hot Springs News*, 28 September 1967.
[12] *The Record - 1974*. Mary Hudgins.
[13] LAT - Roy Bosson.
[14] *New Era*, 10 February 1924.

nportantly, an Oklahoma cowboy, came to the Auditorium as a benefit for nose who were unemployed and in dire need. Over 1,200 persons sat and ood to hear Rogers make fun of the U.S. Congress while twirling a rope and ssoing unsuspecting stage hands. "When Congress passes a law," he drawled, :t is generally a joke. And unfortunately, when they tell a joke, it becomes w." His appearance raised over $2,500 in relief funds.[15]

People with money could find entertainment at the formal dances at the rlington and Eastman hotels and over the gaming tables at the Southern and elvedere clubs. Those less fortunate, which was by far the majority, looked orward to an occasional evening out at the Princess, Central or one of the ther theatres.

In spite of the depressed economy the Spa did not just sit still and wait oping for better times. The business community of the resort had always een alert to opportunities and the active Business Men's League and later the hamber of Commerce exhibited an energy toward utilizing every means at s disposal in bringing in new business. However, there was also help coming om another direction.

Years before, through the joint efforts of Dr. S.A. Garnett, Sam Fordyce nd General "Blackjack" Logan, they had interested the federal government 1 establishing a hospital to serve those veterans suffering from old wounds nd inflammatory ailments. The cornerstone of the first military hospital was iid in 1883 and an imposing structure was erected overlooking downtown Iot Springs. Service buildings, shops and officers quarters sprang up around ne hospital until it was quite a large complex. After serving the military forces or forty years it had become obsolete. With the large number of soldiers from ne Spanish-American and World War I needing treatment, a large modern rick and steel nine-story building was planned and erected. It had a bed apacity of 600. The construction of the new hospital afforded many raftsmen in the area with jobs at a time they were so scarce. The hospital, The rmy and Navy General Hospital would have been a handsome addition to ny city.[16]

But perhaps the greatest single impact on the city's economy was the return f thoroughbred horse racing in 1934.

For five years Leo P. McLaughlin had gone to Charles Cella, owner of)aklawn Park racetrack, trying to persuade him to reopen the track for a pring race meet. Leo had assured him the local Administration, including the olice, sheriff's office and courts would be quite sympathetic toward its eopening and that the prospect of the legislature legalizing throughbred horse

---

[15] *New Era*, 11 February 1931.

[16] "Sixty Years of Service," 1943, a dedicatory brochure prepared by the staff of the rmy and Navy General Hospital.

racing was improving in view of the state's need for additional taxes. Each time, Charles Cella turned the mayor down. Cella's pessimism proved accurate as three straight legislatures--1929, 1931, and 1933--had racing bills introduced and two of the three times were voted down. The bill submitted in 1929 did pass both houses by a small margin, however it was doomed for failure as Governor Harvey Parnell vetoed it.[17]

The 1933 racing bill had called for a twenty-five cent tax on each admittance and was to be designated for the State Hospital, Confederate pensions and schools. In a "turbulent night session lasting until 1:20 o'clock in the morning," it was voted down in the House 60-16.[18] It was a bitter defeat and Charles Cella could not be faulted for being less than optimistic when Leo McLaughlin approached him, once again. Undoubtedly Cella recalled when he and his brother Louis and their partner, John Condon, Sr., tried to defy the state with the backing of Garland County Sheriff R.L. Williams. That was in 1907 and they had refused to shut down, even in the face of various threats, when the Amis pool hall and anti-racing bill had been passed that spring by the state legislature. Oaklawn had even hired armed guards to quell any attempt to halt the racing season. When Constable Ben "Boss" Golden of Hale township appeared at the head of "several hundred citizens of the county," whom he had deputized and were armed with Winchester rifles, "the operators had changed their minds and ran up a white flag." The season had ended suddenly and abruptly.[19]

A glimmer of hope existed late in 1933 and early 1934 as there had been a change in governors. Governor Marion Futrell was a close friend and ally of Verne Ledgerwood. Both were sportsmen and loved to hunt and fish. Futrell had confided to Ledgerwood that if a racing bill could be passed and it reached his desk he would sign it into law.[20] The municipal judge immediatel passed this information along and Mayor Leo P. McLaughlin and Fred Rix President of the Arkansas National Bank went to St. Louis and met wit Charles Cella. They informed him that the political climate was changing fas in Arkansas and that a group of Hot Springs citizens were organizing the Ho Springs Business Men's Racing Association to support an effort to legaliz horse racing in Hot Springs. They told Cella how much the return of racin would mean to the Spa which was really suffering from the Depressior Several things in favor of a meet being held at that time were pointed ou first, the legislature would not meet in a regular session until 1935 and if successful season could be had the solons, who were hard pressed to rais

---

[17] *Sentinel-Record*, 7 March 1933.

[18] *Arkansas Gazette*, 7 March 1933. Also, *New Era*.

[19] *Arkansas Democrat*, 11 February 1934.

[20] LAT - Ledgerwood.

taxes, could be shown an avenue which could provide a large source of revenue and which could be used for various state projects. Second, a sympathetic sitting governor was in office who was willing to sign a racing bill, if passed, and who could delay taking any measures to close the track if pressured by activist groups. Third, with a short season planned, it would be over with before strong opposition could be generated. Cella agreed to run a twenty-one day season providing enough local support could be enlisted. Buoyed by their success, McLaughlin and Rix brought the news back to the Spa.

On 26 January 1934, a mass meeting of the business community and citizens of Hot Springs was held and sponsored by the newly formed Business Men's Racing Association, (HSBMRA). Appearing in the newspapers that day were full page announcements of the formation of the organization and apprising the citizens of the Spa of the intention of the group to return racing to the area. It pointed out the many vacant stores in downtown Hot Springs and the large number of unemployed and appealed to the citizenry for its support. It skillfully skirted any mention of gambling being associated with the endeavor.[21] Also, nothing was mentioned about it being totally against the law, but everybody already knew that! Hot Springs was desperate and defiant.

It was estimated between 1,500 and 2,000 persons crowded into the Auditorium. The crowd was informed that a season would begin March 1, 1934, and again no mention was made that the season would be illegally held. John G. Higgins, Chairman of the Board of the Arkansas National Bank and former publisher of the *Sentinel-Record*, presided over the meeting and introduced various responsible individuals who were involved in the planning. E.L. Howlett, president of the Chamber of Commerce, Fred Rix, president of the Arkansas National Bank, Mayor Leo P. McLaughlin, and George R. Belding, former city manager, made speeches. Loud applause followed each speaker's appearance. A telegram from Charles Cella was read at the end of the meeting, accepting the invitation to have racing once again in the Spa. Again, not one word was uttered from the speakers as to whether wagering would be permitted, however it was generally understood it would be.

Charles Cella, seeing a window of opportunity, seized the moment and promptly dispatched Joe Martin to Hot Springs to act as general manager of Oaklawn Park.[22] That was followed by an announcement that Henry Schrader, who had initially built the track, was ordered to get the racing surface and plant into service.[23] The newly-formed racing association began a subscription campaign to raise $10,000 to be used to advertise the reopening of the track

---

[21] *New Era*, 26 January 1934.
[22] *Sentinel-Record*, 27 January 1934.
[23] *The Chicago Daily News*, 27 January 1934.

throughout the country.

But everybody was not happy with the resurrection of racing at Hot Springs Governor Futrell, whose personal opinion regarding the legalizing of racin was not well-known, was immediately deluged with requests from variou religious groups throughout Arkansas that he use the state militia to ensur horse racing was not allowed a rebirth. A request was made of the states' attorney general for a ruling as to whether or not the governor was actuall empowered to use the militia in such a manner. Arkansas State Attorne General Hal Norwood promptly responded, informing the governor, and th press, "I do not think it was ever contemplated that the military forces of th state should be used to prevent the commission of misdemeanors and for th prosecution of persons guilty of petty offenses where no violence is used an there is no injury to person or property."[24]

That was the answer Futrell needed. He could refer any complainants to th local Hot Springs Police Department or Garland County Sheriff's Office an if any arrests were made the charged would be held to the municipal court fo a hearing. Does anyone doubt how such a situation as that would end?

Local ministers were appalled. W.J. Hinsley, pastor of Second Baptis Church, the largest in the Spa, appealed to the Ministerial Alliance for its help but found little support.

Reverend L.D. Summers, pastor of Park Place Baptist Church and forme President of Jonesboro Bible College, preached so vehemently against th reopening of the races some of his own members objected. The pastor aske for a vote of confidence from the membership and got it. But the issue di not stop there. Summers received a hate letter threatening him and his church It read, "Your church will be burned and you'll be among the missing." I strongly suggested he leave town immediately. Summers turned the letter ove to "Federal Authorities."[25] A guard was hired to watch the church's property But the threats to Rev. Summers, his family and his church had its effect. No desiring to rupture the harmony or fellowship of the church and perhaps a bi fearful for his family's safety, he met with his Board of Deacons an submitted his resignation.[26]

As news of the Spa's intention to sponsor racing filtered out to the heavily populated areas, large detailed articles appeared in prominent newspapers Grantland Rice, the legendary sportswriter, wrote an article on the "greates backfield" that ever played, "the Four Horsemen of Notre Dame," and share

---

[24] *Sentinel-Record*, 1 March 1934.

[25] *New Era*, 4 April 1934.

[26] *Arkansas Gazette*, 18 April 1934. Rev. L.D. Summers later made headlines, exposin the communist teachings at Commonwealth College, near Mena.

pace in *The Chicago Daily News* of Oaklawn Park's scheduled opening.[27] Local vriter Walter Ebel wrote "Thoroughbreds Will Gallop Again at Hot Springs," vhich was printed in several large dailies.[28]

An Associated Press article appearing in *The St. Louis Daily Globe- Democrat,* ad large headlines, "Hot Springs Plans First Race Meet In 15 Years." It was oyly pointed out, "There was no reference to any form of betting which is rohibited by state law."[29] People who had visited the Spa before probably elieved the locals would find a way to circumvent that little roadblock.

The Arkansas Gazette remained opposed to any renewal of racing at the Spa. *The Arkansas Democrat* was more temperate, explaining, "The plans for 1934 ome as a measure to beat the Depression, which has settled on Hot Springs long with the remainder of the country."

Sports writer Allen Tilden titillated racing fans with his feature article in the *Arkansas Democrat* recalling Oaklawn's past glory: "The glamorous racing days of 1919 will be revived at the Spa next month. Old Rosebud thundering down he stretch with the hopes of rabid race fans riding on his nose. Eternal winging into the final turn showing a clean pair of heels to a field of horoughbreds. Red Red Rose fighting for the rail position in a spirited drive lown the back stretch while fans in the stands on the opposite side of the rack scream and shout encouragement."

"All the thrills of Hot Springs' last race meet held in the spring of 1919, will e reinacted at the Arkansas resort city next month when old Oaklawn Jockey Club opens its gates to race horses and race horse men after 15 years of dleness."[30]

Leo P. McLaughlin, who had orchestrated the re-opening of the track, was lated. Most of the town was excited and two days before the opening, flags nd red, white and blue bunting adorned many of the businesses downtown. A full section in the *New Era* was devoted to racing.[31] Bold headlines nnounced the event: "Stage is Set For Revival of Horse Racing at Oaklawn." pecial trains from St. Louis, Chicago, Memphis, Tulsa and Little Rock were rranged by the Association's Transportation Committee, composed of John Fowler, Leon Numainville and J. H. Butterfield.[32]

The Mayor declared Thursday March 1, a half-holiday and urged the itizenship to cease business activities at noon to welcome the opening day of he race meet.[33] *Public Opinion* was critical of Leo P. McLaughlin and called

[27] *The Chicago Daily News,* 27 February 1934.
[28] *The Memphis Commercial Appeal,* 26 January 1934.
[29] *The St. Louis Daily Globe-Democrat,* 27 January 1934.
[30] *Arkansas Democrat,* 11 February 1934.
[31] *New Era,* 28 February 1934.
[32] Ibid., 26 January 1934 and various other papers.
[33] Ibid., 27 February 1934.

attention to the number of "I's" in his Proclamation--nine personal references in three paragraphs--and even suggested McLaughlin had tried to block the races from coming to Hot Springs and had printed that Leo had tried to turn the organizational gathering into a "political meeting."[34] This was totally incorrect and unfair to the mayor. Anyone acquainted with Leo P. McLaughlin was aware of his feelings about horse racing and his desire that Oaklawn Park should reopen. Even the management of Oaklawn was aware of the support he had rendered and retained him as their lawyer for many years. The track also provided him a box on the finish line which he occupied almost daily when the races were in progress. As a final gesture of the track's regard for Leo, they named a race after him, The Leo P. McLaughlin Inaugural, which was run for years.

Oaklawn officials have always manifested a certain nervousness about the opening day of their meet. Because the track has generally had an early starting date they always hope for good weather and have often been disappointed when a severe wet or cold front comes through causing decreased attendance. Thursday morning March 1, 1934 was miserable, by even the stoutest racing enthusiast's standard. Heavy cold rain blanketed the area and turned the racing surface into a sea of mud. In spite of the dismal day, more than 5,000 fans thronged the enclosed and toasty warm grandstand and paddock by post time. One look at the condition of the track sent fans perusing their *Daily Racing Forms*, in search of horses who were at home in sloppy conditions. Those who spotted twelve year-old Come Along were rewarded with a payoff of $17.40 for a $2.00 win ticket, as the gallant old veteran splashed his way to the finish line to the delight of lucky ticket holders.

As the weather improved, so did the attendance. On Little Rock Day a large delegation arrived with fifty people being the guests of Governor Futrell's daughters, Mrs. Grady McCall and Mrs. Ernie Maddox. Since the race meet was really illegal, Governor Futrell thought it best not to add his personal endorsement by attending. Races were named in honor of prominent Little Rock residents who attended including Roy L. Thompson, president of the Chamber of Commerce, former mayor Ben Brickhouse, department store tycoon Alfred Kahn, and hotel owner and race horse owner, Grady Manning.[35]

Day after day large crowds poured through the turnstiles breaking previous records. Over 12,000 people crowded into the park on a "colorful St. Patrick's Day," including Harvey Couch, director of Reconstruction Finance Corporation. Former Governor Harvey Parnell--who would not sign the racing bill of 1929 after it passed both houses of the legislature--and his wife now hypocritically, were enjoying watching illegal horse racing. So did former

---

[34] *Public Opinion*, 2 February 1934.

[35] *New Era*, 3 March 1934.

Oaklawn Park's re-opening in 1934 gave the Spa an economic boost

governor Charles Hillman Brough.[36] Leo P. McLaughlin and his wife Florence were regaled in green, commemorating the occasion and holding court from their private box.

The attendance and reception was so good for the planned 21-day meet, the Business Men's Racing Committee requested the track's owner to operate an additional six days, which Charles Cella was quite willing to do.[37] The fans had not been disappointed as there was wagering on all seven races daily. It was a system using "certificates" or ticket betting. Pari-mutuel machines would be installed the following season.

The final day of the meet saw a record crowd of over 15,000 fans jammed into the track and witnessed Lynx Eye win the Au Revoir Handicap, the classiest race of the year, there being no Arkansas Derby as yet.[38] The next morning's paper reported: "It became apparent early in the afternoon that Hot Springs was to be host to probably the largest crowd ever to attend a sporting event in Arkansas."

The large crowd pointed out several problems that would plague the Spa for years. The lack of parking around the track was manifested as motorists

---

[36] *Sentinel-Record*, 18 March 1934.
[37] *New Era*, 16 March 1934.
[38] *Sentinel-Record*, 23 November 1934.

sought a place to leave their cars. The side streets and yards of homes were filled with automobiles. S.E. Dillon of the Public Utilities had a count of cars in the area made and 2,640 were reported, with 388 of those bearing out-of-state license plates. The Street Railway system carried 4,665 persons to the track and had put on its largest trolleys and enlisted every driver it employed--even those on the extra-board.[39] Special street cars, making no stop south of Orange Street, helped transport the crowd and discharged them on passenger platforms inside the track. Fares were ten cents one way or twenty cents for a round-trip on the express cars. Additional trolleys making all the stops could be ridden at a cost of seven cents one way or four tokens for a quarter.

For two hours after the final race concluded Central Avenue was jammed from end to end with automobiles and street cars.[40] Most of the traffic had to go through the downtown area, going and coming. All of the Little Rock bound cars had to traverse this route and out Park Avenue to the only fully paved highway coming in to the Spa. Many of those headed to Little Rock elected to stop and dine at Belvedere and, if they had any money left, try their luck at the gaming tables. This allowed the traffic to clear some before heading home. The downtown traffic problem was just in its infancy, but like a hungry adolescent, it was growing rapidly.

Massive traffic jams occurred after the return of racing

---

[39] Ibid., 3 April 1934.
[40] Ibid., 1 April 1934.

It had been an exciting and most beneficial season, business wise and the HSBMRA received many calls "and letters thanking them and acknowledging that Hot Springs had just had the best winter season since 1928.[41]

The tail lights of the last car had barely faded into the night until the HSBMRA was beginning a plan to legalize horse racing at the Spa.[42] Douglas Hotchkiss, secretary of the body announced, "The work of the executive committee in connection with plans for the future is just begun. We very much desire to have racing legislation in Arkansas. If the state of Arkansas will give us legislation, the state will profit, and through an honest racing commission, we would have the authority to regulate the sport in a strict manner, and we believe that the legalizing of racing in Arkansas would bring unmeasured and continued prosperity to Hot Springs."

The racing committee began a search about the state to determine who might be available in the state legislature to help push a racing bill through the 1935 session. One unsolicited legislator was newly elected Dr. J.A. Christian, from Yell County. He had studied the problem and after canvassing members of both the House and Senate, predicted a bill he had drawn up would pass.[43]

Much credit for apprising every member of the legislature about Hot Springs' intentions were toward seeking legalized racing and laying out the benefits the entire state would receive was due Douglas Hotchkiss, secretary of the HSBMRA and also of the Chamber of Commerce.[44] It was estimated the taxes derived from attendance and mutuel handle would benefit the state of well over $100,000.[45]

By the first of the year, Representatives James R. Campbell and Ernest Maner and State Senator Walter Wheatley had made personal contacts with most of the state's governing body and discovered many to be "friendly" toward legalizing thoroughbred horse racing at Hot Springs. They predicted the bill they would submit would quickly pass. Perhaps they were a bit overly optimistic as the bill got "bogged-down" in the usual "red-tape," and it did not come up for a vote until well into the session. The bill had been revised and was finally introduced by Representative Eugene Hampton of Lee County. The gallery was full of citizens from Hot Springs when it was at last voted on. When it was announced the House had passed the racing bill, loud cheers rang throughout the building. An emergency clause was adopted which would put the measure in force immediately, "after it was signed by Governor Futrell."[46] It had cleared the Senate by a vote of 23-12, but the passage had its

---

[41] *New Era*, 16 March 1934.
[42] *Sentinel-Record*, 1 April 1934.
[43] *New Era*, 22 November 1934.
[44] *Sentinel-Record*, 1 January 1935.
[45] The first year of legal racing sent over $114,000 to the state coffers.
[46] *El Dorado Daily News*, 16 February 1935.

opposition. Senator Gilbert termed pari-mutuel betting "a damnable thing,"
and launched "into a bitter attack on the moral effect of the bill anc
announced he would oppose liquor bills and all other measures that seek tc
license evils and vices."

Rep. Cowart, Baxter County, stiffly opposed the bill in the House stating
"Every dollar of revenue you say this bill will bring in, smells of the brimstone
of Hades." Strong words? You bet! A co-legislator from Benton
Representative Bucklew also made a Biblical reference as he said, "The 344
passage of the bill would amount to the State of Arkansas selling its soul foi
a mess of potage."[47]

The Arkansas State Baptist Convention, meeting in Pine Bluff and led by
Rev. W. J. Hinsley of Hot Springs, tried to block passage of the bill and sent
eight delegates before a committee of the House urging its defeat, but to nc
avail.[48] By then, the bill was under a full head of steam!

The bill called for the appointment of a committee to oversee and regulate
racing. Governor Futrell lost no time in signing the bill and announcing his
appointments to the new Racing Committee. Chairman, of the select group
was H.W. Highfill of Blytheville. Members were J.H. Graves, Judsonia; Tom

Leo P. McLaughlin served over twenty years as attorney for Oaklawn Park Racetrack and had a box named in his honor. Here, Leo and his wife Florence (front right) entertain another couple, ca. 1934.

---

[47] *Sentinel-Record*, 12 February 1935.
[48] Ibid., 25 January 1935.

Compton, Prescott; Ed Gordon, Morrilton; C.F. Armistead, Fayetteville; P.H. Phillips, Ashdown; and Douglas Hotchkiss of Hot Springs, who had worked so hard getting the measure passed.[49] It is interesting to note that no politicians were appointed to the committee, giving it stronger credibility among the citizenry of the state.

As expected, when the news of the signing of the bill reached Hot Springs, rejoicing and celebrations took place up and down Central Avenue. Business men envisioned other good seasons would follow.[50] To the unemployed the opening of the track signaled the availability of jobs.

With the initial race named for the president of the Business Men's Racing Association, John G. Higgins, Oaklawn Park launched out into the world of legalized racing history. Records, both attendance and mutuel handle as well as tax revenue, would be set almost every season for the next fifty years. The track would be guided by Charles Cella until 1940, the time of his death. He would be succeeded by his son, John Cella, who would pilot Oaklawn until, he too, passed away. John's young son, Charles J. Cella would take over the helm in 1968 and the track would have a meteoric rise in the world of racing under his direction. The two previous owners were content to have Oaklawn Jockey Club known as the "best little track in the country." Not so, Charles J. Cella. He envisioned Oaklawn as being the best big track, and that was his aim. It was to become the fifth ranking track in the nation, being exceeded in attendance and average daily mutuel handle by only Belemont and Acqueduct in the east and San Anita and Hollywood Parks in the west, all located in large population centers.

Cella brought into being the single biggest week in the thoroughbred sport in 1974, by instituting The Racing Festival of the South, a stakes race every day. He made racing exciting!

The Arkansas Derby, which was birthed in 1936 with a purse of $5,000, grew to one of the premier races in the country, with a purse of over $500,000 by 1986. The winner of the first Derby was Holl Image, owned and trained by Jack Carter. There was the Fantasy, for three year-old fillies; The Bachelor Stakes, three year-olds, colts and geldings; The Prima Donna, three year-old fillies; The Count Fleet Sprint Handicap, four year-old and up; and the Apple Blossom Handicap, for fillies and mares, four year-old and up. And then there was The Oaklawn Handicap, a race for older horses which has been run since 1946 and has drawn some of racing's brightest stars. The first horse to run at Oaklawn that had won over a million dollars in his career was Royal Glint, owned by Dan Lassister and trained by David Vance, ran in this race. The

---

[49] *A History of Oaklawn - 1998 Media Guide*, by Don Grisham. Also, *Sentinel-Record*, 17 February 1935.

[50] *Sentinel-Record*, 16 February 1935.

gelding hooked up in the Oaklawn Handicap with Master Derby, a very tough competitor, and the two horses ran neck and neck the entire distance, thrilling the excited fans, with the latter horse nosing out the former. And who could ever forget the 1979 encounter between the great Alydar, who had ran second in all three of the Triple Crown races to Affirmed, but alas, had yet another second place finish, this time to San Juan Hill, a lightly-raced horse. That race was on a Friday and the largest week-day attendance ever--over 50,000 fans--crowded into Oaklawn Park to witness the event. The size of the crowd that day surprised even the track officials as they had to quickly reorder programs twice during the afternoon as the turnstiles continued to spin, as the crowd continued to swell. And then there were Best Pal, and Unbridled, who between then won over ten million dollars in their careers. And, of course who could forget the amazing Snow Chief, who blistered the mile-and-one-eighth race at 1:46.3 on April 17, 1987. And last, but certainly not least, was the great Cigar, who arrived at Oaklawn Park with earnings of nearly $800,000 but after winning the Grade I Stakes and his first place share of the $750,000 guaranteed purse, left Hot Springs a millionaire and went on to earn over ten million dollars.

Famous racing stables began to regularly schedule Oaklawn on their circuit as the purses were increased almost yearly. In 1935 the daily purse distribution was $3,248, and sixty years later had reached an amazing plateau of over $200,000 per day. Charles J. Cella practically rebuilt the entire racing plant with large new additions to the grandstand and new fire-proof barns on the backstretch. He opened the infield where college students picnicked on Saturdays and at Spring Break, and constructed large parking areas.

Well-known trainers and owners brought strings of horses to the Spa. The list read like a "Who's, Who in Racing" --Mr. and Mrs. Emil Denemark, D. Wayne Lukus, Ron McAnnally, William Hal Bishop, Jack Van Berg, Woody Stephens, Laz Barrera, Bob Holthus, Lynn Whiting and old-timer Ben Jones of Calumet Farms, and famous race car driver, A J. Foyt. Henry Forrest, called "one of turfdon's finest trainers," won a total of eleven training titles at Oaklawn. Arkansas' own John Ed Anthony, a Hall of Famer, and his Loblolly Stables brought horses named after people and places in his timberland areas-Van Landingham, Cox's Ridge, Pine Bluff, and Temperance Hill were just a few carrying the Anthony silks into the winner's circle.[51]

Some of the greatest jockeys in the history of racing rode at Oaklawn. The great Johnny Longden was the top rider one year. Legendary jockey Willie Shoemaker flew in to ride Miss Musket to the winner's circle in the 197[illegible] Fantasy Stakes. The names of top jockeys are liberally sprinkled throughout

---

[51] John Ed Anthony was elected and inducted into the Arkansas Sports Hall of Fame in 2001.

the records of Oaklawn, Eddie Delahoussaye, Eddie Maple, Jerry Bailey, Gary Stevens, Chris McCarron, and Jorge Velsquez are only a few. For years the track had a jockey colony with such dependable riders as Larry Snyder, who won over 6,000 races in his career; Sam Maple; John Liveley; the Whited and Fires brothers; and the all-time Oaklawn riding champion, Pat Day. Don Grisham once said, "Day could get on a mount that had morning line odds listed at 5-2, and because Day was the rider, the odds would go down to 7-5." Day won more riding titles at Oaklawn than any other jockey. There was probably a big sigh of relief in the jockey quarters when the Colorado native announced he was moving his base of operations to Kentucky.

The success at Oaklawn was so great and well-known that the management staffs of other tracks over the country began to try to find out what Cella and his 1,200 employees were doing. Charles J. Cella accommodated them by setting out six guidelines he believed in. Those included, "abhorrence of gimmick wagering," and an "unyielding adherence to the philosopy that any pre-race medication is foreign to the best interest of our sport."[52] Trying to save his track because of a decline in racing in general throughout the country and the advent of casino gambling in neighboring states, Cella was forced to abandon some of his own ideals and beliefs, instituting Exacta Wagering, Trifecta, Classix, Pick-Three, and adding races and a second Daily-Double. He begin to permit the use of certain medications on the thoroughbreds. He asked for Sunday racing and got it. He requested tax relief and the State of Arkansas granted it. Oaklawn came up with a plan for extending its regular season called the Simulcast or Satellite Season. It had no live racing but brought races in on television from tracks all over the country. As one patron described it, "Oaklawn's become the biggest bookie-joint in the country." When Oaklawn came up with a plan to permit certain areas in the state to have casino type gambling, including Oaklawn, the state's voters emphatically said, "No." Oaklawn's resourceful General Manager, Eric Jackson, came up with a device he called a pari-mutuel machine which closely resembles the slot machines of Las Vegas and Atlantic City but received the blessing of the local prosecuting attorney even though many people are not convinced of their legality. Some of these measures are helping the track survive.

But in 1934 and 1935, the re-opening of Oaklawn was certainly important to the economy of the Spa. Only a few minutes after the last race had ended each day the pink-sheets hit the streets. This was a publication of *The Hot Springs New Era*, giving the results of the day's races and the probable starting line-up for the next day. Newsboys hurried up and down the streets crying "Pink sheets, get your pink-sheets here." And the paper was really pink in

---

[52] A statement by Oaklawn Park owner, Charles J. Cella, *Oaklawn Jockey Club Historical Synopsis - 1974*, p. 21.

color and carried the mast-head of *The New Era*, as well as a few of the more important news articles of the day. For years this was almost a tradition in Hot Springs.

Another was the taking of the money from the Arkansas National Bank to the racetrack and the return later that day. Sheriff Marion Anderson and his deputies each morning would load several bags of money, to be used as change, into two or three sheriff's cars. This was done on Reserve next to the bank. Then with sirens screaming the parade would start. Citizens and visitors alike would see vehicles with heavily armed officers, shotguns and rifles pointed up and out the windows speed down Central Avenue and return the same way after the races were over. It was showmanship at its best; locals and visitors alike, loved it. The very visible security and show of force must have worked--they were never robbed. This type of armed escort has been replaced by the armored car. Louis Cella once said of his early racing days at Hot Springs, that he sometimes was able to carry the receipts of the day to his room in one small sack. Now it takes an armored van!

One other tradition that should be mentioned is that of the Clydesdales at Oaklawn. These were large, beautiful draft horses whose job it was to move the starting gate from one post to another. For years the Cellas had been friends with the Busch family of St. Louis, who bred the famous Budweiser Clydesdales, and bought the track horses from them. Fans enjoyed watching the huge horses pull the heavy starting gate about the track, seemingly effortlessly. But Clydesdales eat a lot of feed and hay every day of the year, and the upkeep can be quite expensive, while a tractor can be parked in a barn with little or no maintenance, even until the next season. Track officials said their replacement was a matter of economics. When the big gentle horses left Oaklawn, so did some of the allure and excitement and so did some of the fans. It just wasn't quite the same.

Some arrived by automobiles or bus. A few hitch-hiked their way and a large number came by train--the Chicago Rock Island Railroad ran a special car for twenty-five of them from the Chicago-Cicero area. Two walked--one from Leola, Arkansas, and the other from Hermitage--and amazingly, Harold Biggerstaff rode a bicycle all the way from Vancouver, Washington.[533] There were 250 of the excited and expectant young men, some carrying satchels and suitcases, most wearing baseball caps. They had come to the Spa to attend the Ray Doan Baseball School and the George Barr School for umpires. Each entrant had the aspiration he would make it to the major leagues, however few did.

Doan, a former major league player who lived at Muscatine, Iowa, organized his first baseball school in 1933. He had received such cooperation from the

---

[533] *Arkansas Gazette*, 26 February 1938.

Hot Springs Chamber of Commerce this became its home, even after selling the school to the great Rogers Hornsby after operating it for six years. When Doan announced the faculty for his school in 1934 the numbers increased. Boys from twenty-six states attended the baseball school in 1940, anxious to receive instructions from great and former great baseball players. Who was better qualified to teach hitting than Rogers "The Rajah" Hornsby whose life time batting average was a lofty .358? And young men who aspired to be pitchers had some of the best to show them the "ins-and-outs," Dizzy Dean and Lon Warneke. Even "Old Cy Young" came to town to teach. He had won more games than any other pitcher in major league history. When he arrived to teach in the 1938 class, over 2,000 fans crowded onto the Rock Island platform and blocked Benton Street. Mayor Leo P. McLaughlin presented him the keys to the city and the two headed a parade up Central Avenue to the Whittington Junction with the Trojan Band playing "Take Me Out To The Ballgame."[54] Catchers were taught by Yankee great, Bill Dickey and Detroit's Mickey Owens.

After Hornsby bought Doan out and operated into the 1950s, he always scheduled the school to run concurrently with the opening of Oaklawn Park. "The Rajah" and several of the faculty liked to wager a bit on the ponies and the school's hours, 9:30 in the morning to 2:30 in the afternoon, afforded adequate time to get to the track and watch the "bangtails" run a few races.

The Spa had always had a large segment of rabid, faithful and dedicated fans and the major league players who trained here and the schools held by great players whetted their appetite for baseball.

Hot Springs had not been a member of a professional baseball league since 1909 when it had a club in the short-lived Arkansas State League. Due to the expenses associated with traveling the league was forced to disband.[55]

After the major league teams stopped coming to the Spa for spring training it was pretty lean pickings for baseball fans. They had to be content with watching a few of the major league players who came to Hot Springs to get in shape for spring training and drying out.[56] Some of these were the greatest and destined for the Baseball Hall of Fame at Cooperstown, New York. They included Carl "King of the Screwball" Hubbell; the pride and joy of Waldo, Arkansas, and great third-baseman of the New York Giants, Travis Jackson; Tris Speaker; Babe Ruth; Rogers Hornsby; Grover Cleveland Alexander; George Sisler; Al Simmons; Jimmie Foxx; Mt. Ida's favorite son, "The

---

[54] *New Era*, 24 February 1938.

[55] *Sentinel-Record*, 20 April 1938, a commentary about the resumption of baseball in the Spa, written by Robert S. Dean.

[56] A good article to read about the early players coming to the Spa can be found in *The Record - 1998*, "Boiling Out at the Spa," by Don Duren.

Arkansas Hummingbird," Lon Warneke, who later became Garland County Judge; Honus "Hans" Wagner, who along with Branch Rickey taught a group of boys, including Verne Ledgerwood and Leo P. McLaughlin, to play basketball; and the great pitchers of Connie Mack's Philadelphia Athletics championship teams, Orval "Lefty" Grove and George Earnshaw, the latter who fell in love with Leo P. McLaughlin's longtime secretary, Hazel "Bobbie" Marsh, and married her.[57]

Several major league players had gotten their start in baseball playing on the local sandlots. Bill Dickey of the New York Yankees, who had been born at Bastrop, Louisiana, but played at Hot Springs before going pro, was one. So did Earl Smith, Jim Vaughn and Larry Doyle.[58]

In 1932, during the depth of the Depression, a group of citizens attempted to organize a professional baseball team to compete in the Class C Cotton States League, which had franchises in Arkansas, Mississippi and Louisiana. The local group was composed of Chamber of Commerce President William Anderson, Marion Riggs, S.E. Dillon, Porter Austeel, Charles Goslee, Frank M. Moody, Roy Gillenwater, County Judge Charles H. Davis, Al Reynolds and Van Lyle, all influential men. They invited Bob Tarleton, manager of the Dallas club in the Texas League, to meet with them and advise them what might be expected in such a venture. Tarleton was frank with the men and told them of the expenses they could anticipate in entering a team in a professional league and cited the overall cost.[59]

After having several meetings to drum up support for the project the group sadly decided it was beyond their capabilities at that time. But, the interest never died. That interest in baseball could easily be seen by observing the crowd of men around Spencer's Cigar Store, watching the results of the World Series being posted from a ticker-tape machine onto a blackboard and those listening to a radio at Ferd Mazzia's pool hall or around the pharmacy counter at Schnecks' Drug Store.

Then, late in 1937, a break occurred--or really two breaks--one bad for Vicksburg, Mississippi and the other good for the Spa. It seems that Douglas Hotchkiss, Secretary-Manager of the Chamber of Commerce, was contacted by J. Walter Morris of Monroe, Louisiana, president of the Cotton States League, inquiring if Hot Springs was interested and able to field a baseball team for the 1938 season. The Vicksburg club had extreme financial difficulties during the 1937 season and had given up its franchise.[60] Morris

---

[57] *Sentinel-Record*, 1 March 1959, by Maurice Moore.

[58] Ibid., 25 February 1940, "Famous Players Got Start on Local Sandlots," by Roy Bosson.

[59] *New Era*, 23 March 1932.

[60] *Sentinel-Record*, 11 November 1937.

advised the Pine Bluff, El Dorado and Helena teams "had expressed hope that Hot Springs would take the franchise."

Hotchkiss invited the Cotton States League prexy to come to Hot Springs for a meeting at the Chamber of Commerce Building. Morris, agreed. S.A. Kemp, Chamber president, appointed Roy Gillenwater as chairman of the meeting.[61] From this meeting a movement began to raise the necessary capital to field a team and the franchise was applied for and granted by the league. Hotchkiss called a meeting of other influential leaders.[62]

In what was described as "one of the most enthusiastic meetings" President J. Walter Morris of the Cotton States League had ever attended, local businessman Lloyd Adams was elected president of the local group; Van M. Lyle, Dr. King Wade, I. Moscowitz, H.H. Jefferies, Roy Gillenwater, S.H. Allman and Warren Banks were elected directors.

Willis Hudlin, a pitcher for the Cleveland Indians, arrived at the meeting late. He and his wife operated several tourist cabins on the Lake Hamilton and there were always several ballplayers there during the spring. As Hudlin entered the meeting he said, "I heard they were going to try and organize a ball club here tonight, so I had to come along, too."

"Brother, may I ask if you have subscribed for any stock in the new club?" inquired St. Louis Cardinal pitcher Lon Warneke.

"No one has asked me," replied Hudlin.

"Well consider yourself invited," declared Warneke as he handed the Cleveland hurler a subscription blank.[63]

But where were they to get players to field a team and where were they to play? Ban Johnson Field at Whittington Park had been built about the turn of the century and had been used by some of the major league teams who had used the Spa for spring training. It had a wooden grandstand with corrugated metal roofing and wooden bleachers along the first and third base lines. The field was encompassed by a ten-foot wooden fence, but because the distance to right field was so short a high screen rested atop the regular wooden structure. The playing surface was adequate, however the field had no lights as did the other ballparks in the Cotton States League. The lights were a must as most week games in the league were played at night for several good reasons. People who could afford to pay to see a ball game worked during the day and their support was definitely needed. Also, the league was in a hot area of the country and players and fans were more comfortable at night games.

---

[61] Roy Gillenwater was Garland County Tax Assessor and had played in the high levels of minor league ball. The writer was a player on one of the American Legion teams managed by Gillenwater in the mid-1940s.

[62] Letter from Douglas Hotchkiss, Secretary-Manager of the Chamber of Commerce to business leaders announcing plans for an organizational meeting, 19 November 1937.

[63] *Arkansas Gazette*, 29 November 1937.

Whittington Park, including Ban Johnson Field, was owned by the Hot Springs Railway Company. The entire complex--skating rink, dance pavilion, concessions and ball field-- were leased to Charles W. and Margaret Lester for operations, except from April 15 to October 15, which permitted the Railway Company to contract with the newly-formed group the use of the field at no cost.[64] The Railway Company could promise no improvement of the facilities and stressed to President Lloyd Adams and Board Member S.H. Allman, the company was financially unable to assist in building more bleachers or for providing funds for lighting the park.[65] It wasn't that the company was being uncooperative, but had recently been dealt a severe financial blow when the City of Hot Springs had ordered it to disband its street cars and replace them with motor buses, a very large expenditure.

When the matter of providing lighting came up, it was discovered that the overhead electrical street lines were not of sufficient size to carry the voltage up Whittington Avenue to Ban Johnson Field. A new line would be required, and the question was, who would pay? An agreement was worked out with the power company whereby the Association would make an initial payment of $1,000, and the Electric Company would "refund the sum at the rate of 30% per monthly bill."[66] But, the Baseball Association would have to foot the bill for the field equipment and installation. Seventy-foot poles were installed and a total of eight lamps of 1500 watts each lighted the field. All of the work was completed by April 5, and were tried out that night with a practice. The payment of $3,752.00 for the lighting system had knocked a big dent in the club's finances.[67]

While the community was proud to have a professional baseball team and a lighted field to play on, the facts were the lights were really not all that good and as time revealed, neither was the team. Players complained for years about the lighting. Andy Reece, a local sportswriter, wrote, "The hot tempered boss of the Greenville Bucks" loudly protested about the poor lights at Ban Johnson Field. Another writer, Roy Bosson, who had been appointed the official scorer for the Bathers, pointed out during a "recent series the lights on the field were so dim that players complained that a tiny 100 watt bulb in the press box was blinding them."[68]

In the Bathers' first year in the league the team had no true affiliation to provide them with young players, certainly not a major league tie-in. The club made some beneficial connections with Beaumont of the Texas League and

---

[64] A copy of the contract is on file at the Garland County Historical Society Archives.

[65] Memo of S.H. Dillon, 30 November 1937, on file at GCHS.

[66] Copy of letter of Electrical Company, 2 April 1938, to Federal Light and Traction Co. Of New York, on file at GCHS.

[67] *New Era*, 8 April 1938.

[68] Ibid., 26 June 1940.

an "acknowledgment," but no working agreement, from Detroit of the American League. Neither made any definite promises as to how much help they would provide. Three players were loaned to the local team. The club spent a little money buying players like first baseman Hal Grant from Pine Bluff, and signing a couple of players from Ray Doan's Baseball School that had been held in the Spa earlier in the year, and getting a few from a try-out camp sponsored by the team. The infield was completed with a key-stone combination of brothers Otis and George Brannon and John Hoagg, third baseman.

Mike "Spike" Hunter, a local product with a baseball background was appointed manager of the team.[69] Hunter was still in pretty decent condition and appointed himself to open the season against the visiting Pine Bluff Judges. Hunter did not disappoint the fans as he pitched a five-hit game and won 5-2 before a noisy crowd of 3,500 fans, including the 62-piece Trojan Band. In the pre-game festivities, Mayor Leo P. McLaughlin tossed up the first pitch to former major league catcher Earl Smith. The batter was Dr. H. King Wade and the umpire was Circuit Judge Earl Witt. "Doc" Wade "slammed a hard grounder between shortstop and third base for a clear hit."[70] After an absence of thirty years, baseball had returned to the Spa, but the way would not be easy.

For a short while the fan support remained good, but as the Bathers began to lose and drop to the cellar of the league the attendance dwindled. The club's Board had initially decided to operate the concessions inside the ballpark, but relented and "for his official help,"Mayor McLaughlin awarded that item to Jack McJunkin as he had done at Rix Field, home of the Hot Springs High School Trojan football team. What percentage of "the take" the mayor expected is unknown. McJunkin was always at the mayor's beck and call, even to the extent of being summoned from his duties as a city fireman sometimes to drive Leo's sisters and mother to Little Rock or just on an outing.

McJunkin liked kids, never having any of his own, and he realized a number of boys did not have money to get in to see the Bathers play. He prevailed upon the Board to permit him to organize a "Knot-Hole-Gang," and sell them a season's card or pass for a total of fifteen cents. Jack passed out dozens of those cards, paying the small fee himself. It was the only way many got in to see the ballgames--including the writer. McJunkin also collected any of the club's baseballs that had broken seams or cuts and bats that had cracks and

---

[69] *Sentinel-Record*, 16 January 1938. Hunter had played with Muskogee of the Wester n League, Little Rock of the Southern Association, Newark of the International and Bridgeport of the Eastern League. He had even grown a beard once and tossed for the House of David, a traveling bearded baseball team.

[70] Ibid., 21 April 1938.

would pass them out to appreciative youngsters. Youngsters chasing a foul ball up the mountainside behind the stands or retrieving a ball hit over the fence and returning it, were admitted to the game free.

The concession stand sold the usual peanuts and popcorn and little vanilla ice cream bars coated with chocolate which McJunkin got from Arthur Cook's in South Hot Springs. Sometimes the ice cream was sold in a small round paper cup with a pasteboard lid and small wooden paddle for a spoon. The underside of the lid was a collectible, each having a movie star's picture on it, and these were traded much like baseball cards today. Jack loudly and proudly advertised his hamburgers as "a pound of meat on a loaf of bread" for a dime.[71] While the hamburgers fell a bit short of McJunkin's claim, they were good and he sold hundreds. Everybody knew Jack and Jack knew everybody.

The low-paid players received a dollar a day meal allowance and many ate at Oscar and Lura Finch's Cafe across Hobson from Stell and Adam's store.[72] As an incentive for playing well several merchants offered prizes such as a shirt for hitting a home run or a haircut for a double. Once during the playoffs Dave Lockwood's Mens Store gave a suit to a player who hit a homerun with the bases loaded. Also, it was not uncommon if a player pitched a very good game Jack McJunkin or one of his helpers would "pass-the hat" by going through the crowd with a water bucket and fans would pitch in dimes, quarters, halves and an occasional dollar bill. The "take" was never very large, but at least it let the player know he was appreciated. Beginning in 1939, while the team was on the road fans could keep up by listening to a broadcast over radio station KWFC. The account was not live, taken from a ticker tape, but the announcer, Frank Rough, (pronounced Rau) with some sound effects made it seem to the listeners they were there.[73] He kept fans apprised of the batting averages of their favorite players and as to any injuries on the club. He would even tip-off the single and unattached ladies who listened as to which of the ballplayers were single and might be available. This sometimes helped attendance at the home games.

The Hot Springs Bathers operated from 1938 through the 1941 season, but the club was constantly struggling to meet its bills. A number of fund raisers were organized when it appeared the ball team was floundering and would be unable to pay its bills, but these were never enough. When club president Lloyd Adams announced at a director's meeting in May 1940, they were facing

---

[71] "Information About Hot Springs Bathers," an interview of Stell Adams, son of Lloyd Adams, President of the Bathers, by Mamie Ruth (Stranburg) Abernathy, Secretary to Lloyd Adams, 4 February 1985. Available at the GCHS Archives.

[72] Ibid.

[73] From two conversations with Shug Wilson, 25 August 2001. Shug's father, Clyde Wilson, was owner of KWFC. In fact, the stations' call letter stood for Klyde Wilson Furniture Company.

"grave financial difficulties which must be settled within the next few days," Mayor Leo P. McLaughlin urged local citizens to meet with him "to consider the ways and means of keeping the Bathers in the Cotton States League."[74] Leo was not considered "charitable" himself, but he was willing to help organize a fund raiser and "prod" others into giving. A mass meeting was held at the Auditorium and a plan was set forth to go into the community and sell 2,000 tickets at $1.00 each to be used at any remaining game. Over 300 were sold at the meeting.[75] The endeavor was successful to the point the team was assured of being able to finish the scheduled season. But, there were other problems, too. A ruling by Baseball Commissioner Kensaw Mountain Landis affected all of the minor leagues when he declared certain category of players to be "free-agents." The ruling swept the Bather's entire roster clean with the exception of Conrad Fisher, manager, and he quit to take a defense job.[76] The club was forced to recruit an entire new team.

Discouraged, Adams announced in December of 1940 he would not serve as club president any longer. The stockholders elected young W. Clyde Smith, to serve as president. Smith managed the two Malco Corporation theaters in the Spa.

Even though a working agreement was signed with the Nashville Vols of the Southern Association, the trials and tribulations of the Hot Springs franchise and the Cotton States League would continue. The Bathers had by far the best of the pre-war teams in 1941, but financial difficulties continued to beset the club. While the club was on a six-day road trip, heavy rains inundated the area. A large concrete arch covering a creek running under right field at Ban Johnson Field collapsed leaving a sizeable hole.[77] The repairs exhausted the club's meager reserve and funds had to be sought to continue the season. But financial woes were not limited to the Spa team. Others in the league were suffering. Two teams, due to financial difficulties, abandoned their franchises in mid-season. Another played its games the last two months in an adjacent town as its fan support had evaporated. In spite of all the difficulties, the 1941 season was exciting for the local fans and the Bathers won the pennant and playoff with the Monroe White Sox.

Roy Bosson, wrote, "What happened to some of the other clubs is a story which Edgar Allen Poe couldn't have done justice to in his most morbid

---

[74] *Sentinel-Record*, 14 May 1940.

[75] Ibid., 15 May 1940.

[76] Ibid., 18 February 1940.

[77] *New Era*, 16 June 1941. In 1944-1945, Ban Johnson Field served a fast-pitch softball league with teams from the Alcoa Aluminum plant at Jones Mill and the Army-Navy Hospital. A large section of centerfield caved in. It was roped off and when a ball was hit into the hole it was ruled a ground rule single.

moments."[78] There was a big question as to whether the league would be able to operate the following year. That question was settled by the Japanese, on December 7, at a place few had heard of before, Pearl Harbor. W. Clyde Smith advised the press that he had talked with officials of the league teams and all were in agreement many of their players would be called into the armed services and others would be able to earn more in defense work than they could make by playing baseball.[79] The league was abandoned for the duration of the war.

Almost all the quality baseball Hot Springs got to see during the war were a few games played at Ban Johnson Field and Sam Guinn Field, the black ball park on Ash Street, by some of the professional Negro teams. The Baltimore Elites and the Black Yankees of New York competed. So did the Kansas City Monarchs and the Memphis Red Sox.[80] There was a lot of showmanship, bragging and bantering going on, but there were some superb athletes on the field and it was a chance to see such stars as Josh Gibson and Leroy "Satchelfoot" Paige.

During the war the Army-Navy General Hospital fielded a team. A Firestone-sponsored team had such local talent as W.D. Roddenberry, Baldwin, "Red" Parsons, supplemented by some of the Boys' Club players as brothers Dewey and George Thompson, Jimmy Hill, "Shug" Wilson, Harold Wadsworth, Wayne LuPlace and the writer. That team played other independents from Pine Bluff, El Dorado and the strong mill team from Forester, Arkansas.

As soon as the war was over a clamor arose to reorganize the Cotton States League. The goal was to attract eight teams. However, several teams that participated in the league before the war declined in the interest of economy. Hot Springs was one of the six teams awarded a franchise, but again the club and league were beset with money problems. Since preparing old Ban Johnson for play would take a ton of money, a new facility called Jaycee Park was built on the site of old Dean Field, where Rogers Hornsby had held his baseball school. While the fences were shorter in height than at Ban Johnson, the foul lines were more equitable. However, it never had quite the "friendly" feel that the old park on Whittington had.

Between 1947, the first year of operation, and 1955, the team passed through a number of owners. H.M. Britt, who owned and operated the Goddard Hotel, and his brother Garrett Britt, were in partnership with local druggist, Gabe Crawford. Crawford sold his interest in the club to Lewis Goltz, a jeweler and later operator of the Southern Grill. Crawford was so glad

---

[78] *Sentinel-Record*, 29 October 1941.

[79] *New Era*, 15 December 1941.

[80] *Sentinel-Record*, 23 March 1944.

to get rid of his financial obligation, he practically gave Goltz his share. These three owners, after attendance figures remained disappointing, unloaded their shares of stock to former major league pitcher, Paul Dean, the "Daffy" in "Dizzy and Daffy."[81] Dean had big ambitions for the club and served as both general and field manager, but lack of quality players and low attendance continued to dog the club.[82]

Paul Dean finally gave up after operating the club for six months. He told the Board of Directors someone had to buy the club or he would be forced to move it to another city. To save the franchise, used car dealer Charlie Williamson announced on June 9, 1954 he had bought Dean's stock and appointed catcher Jack Bales as acting manager.[83] Both Williamson and Bales had their work cut out for them. Prior to Williamson's taking over the club there had been a fundraiser and Dean had used the proceeds trying to salvage the season. Williamson was placed in the very poor position of asking for another fundraiser to save baseball in Hot Springs. Also, Williamson discovered that the money received from advertisers for fence signs had already been spent. After being at the helm of the Bathers only five weeks, Williamson notified Emmet Harty, President of the Cotton States League he "would be unable to continue operations."[84] Again, low attendance and a nine game losing streak had put the club in a perilous condition. Other band-aid measures were tried--another fund raiser and business to business ticket sales. The Bathers, trying to increase attendance and strengthen the team, got caught up in a major controversy with the league by being the first member of the Cotton States League to break the color line, by signing two black brothers, Jim and Leander Turgerson.[85] This brought a fire-storm of protests from other clubs.

The Cotton States League, at that time, was only one of two leagues in the United States that did not allow black players, but in a Jim Crow type of election, the Bathers were voted out of the league. Hot Springs appealed to higher baseball authority and a ruling by the President of Minor League Baseball, stated the Cotton States League had overstepped its authority and ordered the Bathers reinstated. The following year revealed other teams fielding black players in the league.

Sadly, the Cotton States League folded as did so many others after the 1955 season. Television and air-conditioning were major factors in the demise of a sport that afforded thousands of people over the country many enjoyable

---

[81] Ibid., 30 November 1953. Also, an article by Jay Jennings, "The Black Bathers," *The Arkansas Times*, July 1991, p. 52.

[82] *New Era*, 9 June 1954.

[83] Ibid.

[84] Ibid., 23 July 1954.

[85] *Arkansas Times*, "Black Bathers."

hours. The few totally faithful Bather supporters could almost sympathize with those fans of the mythical town Mudville, in the classic poem, "Casey at Bat," as it ended:

Oh, somewhere in this favored land
The sun is shining bright,
The band is playing and somewhere
Hearts are gay and light,
And somewhere men are laughing
And somewhere children shout,
But there is no joy in Mudville
Mighty Casey has struck out!

For the Spa and the Cotton States League, they had "struck out" and the game was over. It had been a special and memorable time in the life of the community, just too short.

One of the most notable occurrences in Hot Springs' history happened in June 1936. The State of Arkansas was scheduled to celebrate its 100th birthday as a member of the Union that year. A Centennial Celebration was planned. Through the efforts of United States Senator Joe T. Robinson, majority leader of the Senate, and Harvey Couch, President of the Arkansas Power and Light Company and Chairman of the Centennial Committee, President Franklin Roosevelt was invited to open the ceremonies on June 10, at Hot Springs. Roosevelt was completing his first four-year term and intended to run for re-election and was getting out in the country and assuming a high visibility. He accepted the invitation.

Much planning and preparation went into the expected arrival of the chief executive. The city of Hot Springs was spruced-up, windows washed, yards raked, sidewalks swept and cleaned. The two street washers flushed the magnolia leaves along bath house row into the underground drains. Flags were draped from every building--it was a virtual sea of red, white and blue. When the President's itinerary became known it was discovered he planned to lunch at Couchwood, the lake home of his friend Harvey Couch, and from there he would motor to Malvern where he planned to attend a brief religious ceremony at Rockport Methodist Church, one of the oldest churches west of the Mississippi. The highway between Hot Springs and Malvern was a very rough and rocky road, and at its best, very dusty. All the local and state leaders looked upon the highway as an extreme embarrassment for the chief executive to have to travel. Governor J.M. Futrell, one of the hosts for the presidential visit, ordered the entire Arkansas Highway Department to pave the road from the Dam Fork service station, just east of the Hot Springs Country Club, to Malvern, a distance of approximately twenty miles. Generally a project of that magnitude required months of planning, surveys, preparations of road bed--allowing time for it to settle--then more months of paving. The Governor wanted no excuses: "Get the job done and quickly." There were no frills in the project, no new bridges--the ones over Gulpha Creek and Tiger Bay were one-lane steel framed and wooden-floored structures. Due to the lack of time, these would have to do. Very little enhancement of the road bed was made: no curves straightened, little banking of curves, and no shoulders prepared--just a smooth, hard-surfaced, dustless road was strived for. The project was one that ordinarily would have taken a year or longer, but was completed in a record of five weeks.

Whitewash and paint were made available to those persons living along the right-of-way and dozens of barns and houses were treated to paint or whitewash, many for the first time. Fences and gates were repaired and old junked car bodies had been hauled away. Hot Springs and Garland County put on their best face.

The Roosevelts arrived in Hot Springs early Wednesday June 10, 1936, via the Missouri Pacific Railroad. When the train backed into the station on Broadway there were already several thousand people assembled. Mayor McLaughlin in his proclamation setting that day as a "half-holiday," had ordered "No cars will be allowed on Broadway from the Missouri Pacific Station to the Great Northern hotel; on Benton Street, from Great Northern hotel to Cottage Street, on Cottage Street from Benton Street to Army Navy hospital gates. No cars will be permitted to park on any part of Fountain Street, (Happy Hollow); on Central Avenue from Arlington hotel to Prospect Avenue; on Prospect from Central Avenue to Curve Street, (entrance to West Mountain Drive) on Violet Street to Grand Avenue and from Grand Avenue to Malvern Avenue." This was the designated parade route within the city proper. All traffic arrangements had been under the direction of Chief of Detectives Herbert "Dutch" Akers. He had "borrowed" several dozen police officers from Little Rock and several Arkansas Rangers to supplement the local officers to control traffic. An officer was assigned at every intersection of the planned parade route.[86]

Mrs. Roosevelt was the first to leave the train. She was picked up in a Rolls Royce sedan loaned for the occasion by Colonel T.H. Barton, President of the Lion Oil Company. The first lady was taken to a breakfast with the Democratic Women of Arkansas at the Arlington Hotel.[87] She was ushered in to the meeting of 500 women by Mrs. J.M. Futrell, the governor's wife, and Mrs. Hattie Caraway, the junior U.S. Senator from Arkansas.

The President breakfasted aboard his private railroad car with friends.[88] When the large crowd of people first glimpsed President Roosevelt being assisted onto the rear observation platform by two secret service men, it broke

---

[86] *New Era*, 10 June 1936.
[87] *Arkansas Democrat*, 10 June 1936.
[88] *New Era*, 10 June 1936.

into loud cheers and applause. There he was joined by Mayor Leo P. McLaughlin, Senator Joe T. Robinson, Governor J.M. Futrell and Centennial Chairman Harvey Couch. The group posed for photographs before entering automobiles for a procession to the new Army-Navy General Hospital, led by the Hot Springs Trojan band. After winding through the streets of the hospital complex the cars stopped and Colonel William H. Moncrief, commander of the hospital, introduced a number of his aides, doctors and nurses to the President sitting in his automobile. The Colonel joined the group which proceeded along the Reservation Mountain Drive from the hospital coming out on Fountain Street at Happy Hollow.[89] It was only a long block to the Arlington to pick up Mrs. Roosevelt, who, having finished her breakfast, had been shaking hands in the lobby of the hotel.

The west side of Central Avenue was a sea of people as thousands tried to get a glimpse of the popular chief executive. They had been patiently waiting for the President's arrival and had been entertained with over an hour's concert by the seventy-five member U.S. Marine band as well as high school bands from Hot Springs and Magnolia.

The procession paused for a few minutes at Arlington Park as the Marine Band played "Hail to the Chief," and the President watched a short presentation of a pageant, "Arkansas Through the Years," performed by 250 school children from Ramble and Jones schools, directed by Superintendent Harvey H. Haley.[90]

Then the thirty-five car procession made its way down the wide bath house promenade, stopping at the Fordyce Bathhouse, where the President alighted from his touring car for the only time on his brief visit to Hot Springs. He was given a fifteen-minute tour of the bathing facilities.[91] Because of his own physical condition, he was very interested in the treatments afforded at the Spa.

They then traveled south on Central between throngs of excited and waving people to Prospect Avenue, turning west through neighborhoods choked with people applauding and waving flags. The tour turned up West Mountain Drive which had been widened and beautified by the work of one of Roosevelt's pet projects, the Civilian Conservation Corps. The president admired handsome rock work, embankments, drains and pull-out vistas which had been built by CCC boys.

The caravan made its way around the top of the mountain, stopping briefly for the presidential party to view the city below. Then back down the mountain to Violet and Grand Avenue. The writer, an eight year-old boy at

---

[89] *Sentinel-Record*, 10 June 1936.
[90] *New Era*, 10 June 1936.
[91] *Arkansas Democrat*, 10 June 1936.

the time, recalls standing on the corner at Fifth and Grand Avenue as the caravan swept by and the President and First Lady waving to the thousands of people lining the parade route.

The President's car stopped for a few moments in front of Our Lady of Charity Convent (Good Shepherd's Home) and a few minutes later at Lakeside School where a new building was being erected with the aid of WPA money, another federally-sponsored project.[92] The newspapers reported there were approximately 200 people on the school ground waiting to see the President.

It was only a few minutes drive from Lakeside School to Couchwood where a barbecue luncheon awaited the motorcade. The dignitaries ate in the dining room of Harvey Couch's home. The four photographers and thirty reporters accompanying the president had lunch on the lawn overlooking the lake. After resting a bit, the party moved on to Rockport for a brief stop and caught the train at Malvern to take FDR to Little Rock where he spoke that evening at Fair Park.

The President's visit to Hot Springs had been only a brief moment in the Spa's history, however it meant a great deal to the local citizens. They had gone through a terrible Depression, and in fact, some were still suffering from the lack of jobs and scarcity of money. But everyone knew Franklin Roosevelt was trying to pull the country back onto the road to recovery with the various programs he had been able to institute, and they appreciated his efforts. Also, his Fireside Chats seemed warm, personal and sincere and the thousands welcomed his visit as an old friend coming to visit. Thousands at the Spa would long remember FDR's short but historic visit.

---

[92] Ibid.

Street Cars, Parking Meters, Estates, and Homer

When D.A. Butterfield arrived in Hot Springs in 1874, one of the first things he noticed was the number of crippled and lame people struggling to walk the unpaved streets or the rough wooden sidewalks along Central (then Valley Street) Avenue. Seizing the opportunity the situation offered, Butterfield organized and established the Hot Springs Street Railway System (HSSRC). He and Colonel Sam Fordyce formed a partnership, and two years later the city awarded them a franchise for seventy-five years. Steel rails were laid on Central Avenue from the junction of Central, Park and Whittington along the mair thoroughfare to Spring Street and a short spur up Park Avenue to the car barn.[1] Small mule-drawn cars were used and became highly popular. An extension of the route later connected Happy Hollow Springs to the little railway. As the town grew so did the railway system--tracks were extended farther up Park and Whittington Avenue to a park that was owned and developed by the railway company. After a conversion to electricity in 1893 further expansion saw the tracks extended out Malvern, Ouachita and south on Central to Oaklawn Park. The Spa was only the second city in Arkansas to have electrically-powered trolley cars.[2]

When there was a public clamor that the trolleys stirred up dust in unmeasurable quantities, the HSSRC put on a car equipped with a large water tank for sprinkling down the right-of-ways. This did somewhat quieten the loudest complainants.

The street car system provided dependable and cheap transportation from the suburbs to downtown Hot Springs. As the automobile traffic increased the street cars were roundly criticized by autoists and businessmen alike. On part of Central Avenue the two sets of trolley tracks were in the center of the street and parking was on the sides, which caused a traffic jam behind the street cars. Along Bath House Row, the tracks were closer to the east curb where there was no parking and traffic traveling south moved fairly quickly but vehicles traveling north did so at a snail's pace. Several accidents occurred between the trolleys and automobiles, sometimes driven by inexperienced or intoxicated drivers.[3] Complaints continued to mount even though the HSSRC tried to be accommodating to the public. When special events were planned that ran late at night, the trolley car company would assign an "Owl Car" so that people had a way home. Or it would run a special car for school and church groups who would fill up an entire car and sing songs as the coach

---

[1] *Sentinel-Record,* 3 July 1976. Maurice Moore, "Spa Transit System Dates Back to 1974."

[2] Ibid.

[3] Ibid., 19 April 1933.

would roll through all areas of the city.[4] It was a great and inexpensive way to party.

A short-time experimental program was instituted in 1925 when two buses were put on special runs up Cedar, Prospect and Quapaw avenues. The advertisement for this addition to the trolley system was, "Beautiful inside, comfortable, pleated leather seats, cleanliness and refinement are appreciated by the women who make up a large share of our patronage." The fare--ten cents.[5] This program was abandoned a short time later because of the low volume of riders.

In 1937 an announcement by the Arkansas Utilities Commission it had ruled that the removal of street cars be done by May 1 placed the HSSRC in an awkward position.[6] The small transit company advised it could comply with the ruling, but because of the $37,000 estimated expense it would take to remove the tracks, it was financially unable to comply. Mayor Leo P. McLaughlin called on several business leaders to study the problem. He also explored the possibility of obtaining a federal works project.[7]

With some assurance the problem would be worked out a franchise was granted to the HSSRC. The company proceeded to order eight 21-passenger Yellow Coach street buses and on Sunday 16 October 1938, the first of these rolled from the old car barn on Park Avenue onto the streets of Hot Springs--a new era in local transportation had arrived.[8]

The problems caused by conversion of trolleys to buses were small in comparison to those occurring when the city installed parking meters. As the number of automobiles increased, so did the traffic in downtown Hot Springs. Many merchants insisted on parking their own vehicle all day, as close to the front of their business as they could get and paying nothing for this privilege. This selfish attitude resulted in decreased parking spots for customers which already were limited because of no parking on the east side of Central avenue along Bath House Row from Reserve to Fountain Street. There were just not enough spaces to go around. Also, Mayor McLaughlin had instructed the police department to "get tough with motorists and businesses who insisted in double-parking." Another "fly in the ointment," was when the street cars were discontinued and the safety island loading zones were removed, special bus stops were needed. These were created at the end of each block by

---

[4] Ibid., 3 May 1959, "Electric Trolley Gone But Not Forgotten."

[5] From a handbill published by the Hot Springs Street Railway Co., now on file at the GCHS.

[6] *Sentinel-Record*, 12 April 1937.

[7] A fine article on the history of the trolleys in the City of Hot Springs appears in *The Record - 1978*, The Hot Springs Street Railway," by Jim Hale.

[8] *The Yellow Coach News*, Vol. 9, May 1943. In four years the eight coaches had operated a total of 2,062,753 miles or "an average of 257,844 per coach."

eliminating two parking places so the buses could pull in and out and load o
unload passengers. This, of course, took away badly-needed parking spots.

McLaughlin, having visited other cities and talked with other officials, hac
come to the belief Hot Springs could control much of its traffic problem b
installing parking meters. He was also astute enough to realize the meters nc
only would pay for themselves but would provide additional funds for the city
which was always starved for money.

Leo just assumed everyone would be agreeable to his plan, as they alway
had been, and that there would be little or no opposition and proceeded witl
plans for the installation of the machines. Boy, had he figured that one wrong
When word got out, grumblings turned into loud complaints and the hom
telephones of the aldermen began to ring. Several of the councilmen, prodde
and awakened by their constituents, even had the nerve to broach the matte
to the mayor. They discovered in a hurry he had become quite testy on th
subject. He finally did tell them he would think about the matter. Som
citizens did not become aware of the project until the *Sentinel-Record*, comin
to the mayor's defense, printed a front page editorial entitled, "All Shoul
Cooperate," and explained the mayor's plan "where every citizen will benefit."
An accompanying article revealed, "Workers were busy last night installing th
meters." Even though McLaughlin went forward with his plans for installin
the meters, the furor did not die. When Guinn Massey, businessman anc
chairman of the retail merchants committee of the Chamber of Commerce
showed up at city hall with a petition signed by fifty-six others voicing thei
opposition to the meters it really ignited Leo's fuse.[10] He told th
representative the large number of absent signees indicated to him they mus
not be very interested in opposing the matter. Further, he said he did no
believe that many had signed the petition--the same as calling the man a liar
When he sent his own representatives to talk with some of the businessmer
who had signed the form, some became "weak-kneed" and backed down fron
their opposition.[11]

Two days after the installation, meter violators were failing "to appear in cit
court," and McLaughlin began to try to "strong arm" the disagreeing citizen
and gave police lists of names of those failing to pay their fines. The pape
reported only one violator out of thirty had appeared to pay the fine. Judg
Ledgerwood ordered warrants to be issued: "We are not going to start the nev
system by letting people off. They must pay their fines."[12]

Leo P. McLaughlin was stung by the number of complaints coming fron

---

[9] *Sentinel-Record*, 3 June 1937.
[10] *New Era*, 12 March 1937.
[11] *Sentinel-Record*, 10 November 1937.
[12] Ibid., 5 June 1937.

the business sector as well as citizens. Hazel Marsh, his secretary, spent much of her time screening calls about the meters. Reluctantly, the mayor agreed to remove the meters for a thirty-day trial period.[13]

The January 1938 council meeting was well-attended but only two persons, Guinn Massey of the Massey Department store and Mrs. G. Sigler Henderson of Jennings Drug store, had nerve to speak against the meters. The opposition to the meters had melted under the heat of the Administration and even some of the businessmen admitted the meters had helped control the parking problem. Leo had won, as usual, and re-installation of the meters began.[14]

From that point forward there was a rift between some of the members of the Chamber of Commerce and Mayor McLaughlin, and it would widen even further over the airport issue. Things would never be the same. It was an abuse of power on the mayor's part, but he left it clear --he was the boss of Hot Springs, whether they liked it or not.[15]

As the turbulent decade of the 1930s prepared to slip into the 1940s, the economy of the Spa was only slightly better than when the Depression first hit. The resort still had little industry other than the baths and associated needs, hotels, restaurants and some better paying jobs, although illegal and uncertain, around the bookies and casinos.

Many citizens of the Spa had been embarrassed by the scandals associated with the police department's involvement in the beating to death of an inmate and the harboring of known and wanted criminals. And there were other things no one was proud of: two high-profile murders-- one solved, the other unsolved.

The first was a heinous crime planned and committed by five persons in the robbery and murder of Eldon Cooley, 26 year-old son-in-law of M.L. Stueart. Cooley and his father-in-law co-operated the Stueart chain of grocery stores in the area. Cooley was selected as the victim by the five robbers because of his job in making the round of stores each night to pick up the day's receipts. The robbery took place as Cooley came out of the Stueart store at Grand and Grove Streets on September 8, 1938. As Eldon Cooley started to get in his car he was approached by two of the robbers, both armed, and he was ordered into the front passenger's seat. One robber, identified as Alfred "Pug" Dickson, slid in the car and took the driver's seat, and the other, Bill Anderson, got in the rear of the vehicle. The duo ordered Cooley not to look at them and by their later testimony, Cooley said only a few words, none defiant. Dickson drove the car out Spring Street then onto Mill Creek Road

---

[13] Ibid., 2 December 1937.

[14] *New Era*, 2 1938.

[15] For further information see Roy Bosson's Special to the *Arkansas Democrat - 1989*, "McLaughlin's Power Grew With Hot Springs."

and came to a stop in a very isolated area. There they were met by an individual, Bill Johnson, who had met Anderson when they were both serving a prison term. Johnson and Anderson's wives were accomplices in the planning but were not actually present when the robbery and murder took place.

Cooley was ordered from the car, marched up a ravine and ordered to undress. Supposedly Dickson then emptied his gun into the victim who had given the robbers no resistance.

Helen Cooley, Eldon's wife, became alarmed when her husband failed to return home that night and notified the police and a search began.[16] Cooley's automobile was located off Mill Creek Road and further searching of the area discovered his body several hundred feet from the car. When news of this horrible crime reached Hot Springs, the citizens, many who were not even acquainted with the likable Cooley, were greatly upset.

A tip from a sixth individual who almost became implicated in the robbery but who had backed out, became frightened when he heard of the murder and called the sheriff's office. He agreed to turn state's evidence. The law enforcement officers began a quick round-up of the gang members.

Indicted for first degree murder was Alfred "Pug" Dickson and Joe Anderson. Dickson was the nephew of John Dickson, who had been beaten to death in the city jail eighteen months before. Pug Dickson had been tried in Saline County for auto-theft and convicted.[17] Governor Bailey granted him a furlough on recommendation of the State Parole Board, after Dickson had served six-months of a year's sentence.[18]

The police developed a good case and when the trial was held the jury wasn't apologetic when it brought in a verdict of "guilty" and sentenced Dickson and Anderson to "death in the electric chair." The others received stiff, but lesser sentences.

The death sentences may have surprised some as Garland County juries seldom imposed the maximum sentence. Not even when Tom Slaughter had been guilty of gunning down deputy sheriff Row Brown did they render such a verdict and sentenced Slaughter to life imprisonment. But the vicious circumstances of the Cooley killing had so stirred up the community the verdict was almost expected, and Dickson and Anderson were required to pay with their lives for the violent deed.[19]

The second killing involved victim Brad O. Smith, age 58, former sheriff of Garland County and Hot Springs businessman. Smith was a partner with his

---

[16] *Sentinel-Record, Extra Edition* - 11 September 1938.
[17] *New Era*, 4 March 1937.
[18] *Sentinel-Record*, 7 October 1937.
[19] *New Era, Extra Edition*, 5 October 1938.

brother, Cleveland, in Smith Brothers Construction Company. Brad was also the builder and owner of the *Queen Mary*, a steel-hulled, two-decked pleasure and excursion boat he operated on Lake Hamilton. Ever since the lake had come into being Smith had dreamed of having such a craft on its waters. When he constructed the 54' x 22' vessel he hired Carlton K. Sturms, an experienced and licensed river boat captain, to oversee the management of the vessel and secured the services of Mr. and Mrs Harry Foley, known night club operators, to plan the evening buffet, menu, as well as schedule night cruises and dances.[20]

Brad and Cleveland Smith were known political enemies of Leo McLaughlin and his administration. It was no secret about town there was no love lost between the Smith brothers and the Administration, part of which feelings had emanated from the large and decisive victory McLaughlin had over Cleveland Smith in the mayoralty race of 1929. Both of the Smiths were members of the small minority of businessmen who believed the "open-town" policy for the city was wrong. Brad Smith had been vocally critical of the Administration at times. And as a reward for their open opposition against the Administration their construction company, one of the best in the county, was seldom recipient of any county or city jobs.

Because of the poor relationship existing between the Smiths and the Administration, there was no doubt that the local politicians hoped it could be proven quickly that the wound had been self-inflicted, or if murder, that the crime could be quickly solved. They knew there would be some in the community who would suspect foul play on their part. However, the evidence wasn't all that clear and the newspapers reported there "were two theories offered."

State Trooper William Armstrong made a paraffin test of Smith's hand to determine if he had recently fired a weapon and which might indicate it was a case of suicide. Armstrong had a big audience when he took the test as there was "the presence of a half-dozen city and county officials," as well as former judge Scott Wood, who had been hired by the family to observe. According to Armstrong's test there was a powder residue on Smith's hand indicating possible suicide. Strangely, Coroner J.P. Randolph, disagreed. He had learned the gun found on the seat under Smith was a .380 calibre, and did not belong to Brad Smith.[21] Also, according to Randolph, Smith had been wearing a hat and the angle of the head wound under the brim was awkward and did not indicate it to be self-inflicted.

---

[20] *Sentinel-Record*, 22 May 1937.

[21] Several close friends of Brad Smith, as well as his brother, Cleveland, advised they had never seen Brad use any pistol other than a .45 calibre, and had never known him to own a .380.

A coroner's jury was assembled and a number of witnesses were called.[22] I was deemed by that body that the evidence presented confirmed that "Smit came to his death at the hands of parties to this jury unknown."[23]

Based on the findings of the coroner's jury, Judge Earl Witt referred the cas to the Garland County Grand Jury and more witnesses were summoned a well as those who had testified at the coroner's hearing. The last two person known to have been with Brad Smith were held for a short time and release As witnesses were questioned by Prosecuting Attorney Ridgway, the cas became more confusing. No charges were ever made and gradually the crim faded into history without having been solved. There was considerabl speculation for a while that member of the Administration had somehow bee involved, but no evidence was ever produced pointing in that direction.

The little world of gambling at Hot Springs was stunned to learn W.S Jacobs had passed away on Christmas day 1940.[24] Jacobs, the gambling cza was referred to almost reverently around the clubs as "Old Man Jacobs, although he wasn't really all that ancient, having just turned sixty-four year old the day before his death. He was known by most of his employees as "M Jake," and as "Bill," to his close friends and acquaintances.

Jacobs had been involved in an automobile accident near Little Rock in th fall of that year and had suffered a number of injuries from which he ha never fully recovered. But his death at his home at 116 Cedar Street caught th local gambling fraternity as well as the local Administration by surprise.

William Stokley Jacobs had been an important and contributing citizen o the Spa for many years and the most important figure on the local gamblin scene, being the adhesive that bound it together. When he first arrived on th local scene about 1907, he had engaged in a partnership with Harry Hale i operating the old Lyric theater.[25] But running a silent movie theater wasn' Jacobs' "cup of tea." He'd always been a gambler and that was his interest. H went into partnership with Harold Beall in the Ohio cigar store and he an Sam Watt joined forces in buying out the Southern Club. John "Coffey Williams, Sheriff Bob Williams' brother, and Jacobs were in partnership fo a short while at the Ohio Club, but the gambling faction fell on hard times i 1913 when Sheriff Williams, later supported by Judge Scott Wood, closed th clubs and drove the gamblers to the backrooms.

Jacobs had stayed around Hot Springs conducting backroom gambling an running a pool hall until Leo P. McLaughlin and Verne Ledgerwood opene the town in 1927. From that point, Jacobs' fortune had changed and throug

---

[22] *Sentinel-Record*, 25 September 1938.
[23] Ibid., 29 September 1938.
[24] *Sentinel-Record*, 26 December 1940.
[25] Ibid.

his interest in six of the clubs, had made a tremendous amount of money and this had benefitted not only himself but those who had furnished protection for his operation. Jacobs jealously guarded his hold and his partners' interest, in the gambling operations at the Spa. There is absolutely no evidence that has come to light to suggest outside interests--financial or criminal--had a piece or part in the local operation until after his death.

His successes encouraged him to buy the building the Southern Club occupied. The building was still owned by Mrs. Katherine Dugan, widow of Charles Dugan, one of the founders of the club. Jacobs paid Mrs. Dugan $65,000 for the property and immediately launched into an enlargement and refurbishing of the facilities. Jacobs had installed a ten and one-half foot wide marble staircase which led into an enlarged casino area 60' X 80', which adjoined West Mountain behind the club.[26] He sheathed the front of the club in a rich, dark Pittsburg decorative glass that has lasted to this day.

Because of Jacobs' interest in five of the downtown clubs--the Kentucky, Ohio, Ozark, Southern, White Front, as well as his pride, Belvedere--"462 persons were numbered on his payroll."[27] That meant approximately 1,500 persons, directly or indirectly, depended on the Jacobs' interest for their livelihood. Therefore, it was of great concern what would happen to his holdings.

Services were held at the Paul Heady Funeral Home on Ouachita Avenue and the crowd was large, but only two hundred persons could get inside. Many stood on the sidewalk outside or waited in their automobiles to avoid a chilling rain.[28] Probably 150 friends of Jacobs from the Memphis area attended and joined the 300-car procession to his final resting place. All policemen were called for traffic duty.[29]

Reverend R.S. Woodson, pastor of the First Presbytertan Church, said Jacobs was "widely known for his good deeds and philanthropics." Rev. Woodson quoted from an editorial appearing in the local newspapers saying, "In the final analysis, the full measure and worth of a man is not by the yardstick of real estate holdings, financial ratings or political influence, but by his good deeds, kindness and grace."

William Stokely Jacobs was laid to rest in Greenwood Cemetery, carried by his pallbearers who were either the managers of his clubs or close confidants--Roscoe Johnson, Otis McGraw, Cleveland "Tink" Young, Loyd Lemon, James Phillips, John Morris, Fred Price and Harry Bledsoe. All clubs were closed that

---

[26] *New Era*, 22 October 1938.
[27] *Sentinel-Record*, 26 December 1940.
[28] Ibid., 28 December 1940.
[29] Ibid., 27 December 1940.

day.[30]

The last spade of dirt had hardly been shoveled onto the grave until a power struggle developed for control of Jacobs' property and gambling empire. In an end run, Leo P. McLaughlin placed himself in the "driver's seat." Just as soon as Jacobs' funeral was over, Chancellor Sam W. Garrett announced he had appointed Mayor McLaughlin as administrator of "the late W.S. Jacobs' Estate." This was only two days after the gambling czar had expired.[31] If Jacobs had prepared a will, no one admitted having any knowledge of its existence. Some of those closest to Jacobs reported, "he left no will," an unusual situation for a businessman with such large holdings.[32]

W.S. Jacobs had never married but had two very close lady friends at different times, Margaret Face and Lila Mize. Neither of these were in the "picture" at the time. He was survived by a brother, Oscar L. Jacobs of Hedley, Texas, a nephew, Wade Jacobs and a niece, Katherine Jacobs Stiece (sp.?), both of Hot Springs.[33] Wade Jacobs had been employed by his uncle in a low-key position as manager of the dairy and farming operation at Belvedere.

Leo McLaughlin really wasn't prepared to handle such a large and complicated estate claim. He would never have admitted it but he was neither legally educated or had the time to devote to such a large undertaking. But few lawyers would turn down such an opportunity, especially if the attorney was a little bit on the "shady side." And logically, Leo was the only man who had the power necessary to control and keep Jacobs' gambling enterprises operating. Years before he would have called on his mentor, George Whittington, for help, but Whittington had died years before. In recent years when needing a bit of legal help, he had relied on Richard M. Ryan for assistance. Theirs was an unusual relationship, Leo being a democrat and Ryan a staunch republican.[34] However, Ryan was a supporter of McLaughlin's "open-town" policy and Leo recognized Richard's professional expertise and ability as a lawyer. He would use Ryan when needed.

It seemed as if McLaughlin was destined to have problems every time he became involved in an estate case. There had been that time in 1920 in handling the Cosgrove estate, where he had "penned" an agreement makin himself the beneficiary of Cosgrove's money, whereas his client had alread willed it to an orphan's home in Kansas. There was no evidence Cosgrove ha ever changed his will and after being sued in Federal Court, Leo compromise the matter.

---

[30] Ibid.
[31] Ibid., p. 8.
[32] Ibid., 29 December 1940.
[33] Ibid., 27 December 1940, p. 9.
[34] *New Era*, 20 February 1957.

Then there had been a bit of scandal when Fred Rix, former president of the Arkansas National Bank, had died under mysterious circumstances in 1937 and Leo P. McLaughlin had been appointed administrator of the estate by County Judge Elza Housley.[35]

Rix had been in ill health since 1934 when he had been wounded in an accidental shooting.[36] He had become addicted to some medication and had even been arrested at Little Rock trying to forge a doctor's name on a prescription.[37] Rix had been discovered by his maid lying face down, his face buried in a soft pillow. Coroner J.P. Randolph gave as his findings death occurred by "accidental suffocation."[38]

Unlike the Jacobs case, there had been a will in the Rix case leaving one-dollar to an adopted eight year-old boy, Howard Rix, and the remainder to his wife, Fern, who was ill at that time in New York state. Before this estate was settled three law suits had been filed by Rix's half-brother Bertram Pike, his mother Mrs. Mamie Pearson Rix Pike, and his wife Fern Rix, all asking the court to remove Leo P. McLaughlin from the case. It seems as if Leo was not wanted in determining how the estate, exceeding $300,000, would be distributed.[39]

The court did remove McLaughlin briefly from the estate proceeding, then reappointed him after hearings by Judge Housley and Circuit Judge Earl Witt.[40] The final settlement left $30,000 to the adopted son and the remainder of the estate, less attorney's fees, to Rix's widow, Fern, with Tom Stone of the Arkansas National Bank being appointed permanent administrator, a wise choice.[41]

When sizeable amounts of money were involved Leo McLaughlin was much like the camel in the old Arab admonishment, "What ever you do, don't let the camel get his nose into the tent," meaning before anyone could remove the beast the tent would be wrecked and torn down. In the Jacobs estate, Leo had his "nose in the tent" and he intended to keep it there in spite of petitions filed by relatives of Jacobs to remove him as administrator. The local courts lent a "deaf ear" to the petitioners.

Many estates can be settled within a year or so, but not so in that of Jacobs. First, it was a sizable and complicated estate. It was tangled with scattered real estate holdings as well as voluminous personal property and both oral and

---

[35] Ibid., 22 November 1937.

[36] *Sentinel-Record*, 24 October 1937.

[37] *New Era*, 31 August 1937, p. 3.

[38] *Sentinel-Record*, 24 October 1937.

[39] *New Era*, 15 December 1937

[40] Ibid., 24 December 1937. When suit was filed to remove Leo P. McLaughlin as Administrator, he employed Attorney Richard Ryan to represent him.

[41] *Sentinel-Record*, 3 September 1938.

unwritten agreements involving illegal interests and numbers of people, partners, both known and unknown. Appraisals had to be made. Property needed to be inventoried and advertised and sold. Mysteriously, some of Jacobs' expensive jewelry, gold watches, diamond rings and necklaces collection, he had taken in on gambling debts, or bought to help someone, and of which many people were aware of, never made it to the inventory sheet and simply disappeared, but nothing was ever said about the missing articles. Several of the items turned up in the hands of some of his former partners, possibly keepsakes! In the meantime, though, it was the desire of the Administration that the clubs should continue to operate. Some attorneys could make a career out of handling such a case, except the law provided it be settled within five years. Leo McLaughlin squeezed it for its full length and even exceeded the prescribed time allowed for the inheritance tax to be paid and the State of Arkansas imposed a penalty of $2,979.61 on top of the $10,182.27 tax paid.[42]

For five years Leo P. McLaughlin used the Jacobs estate as his own. When Belvedere was not operating he hired former Chief of Police Joe Wakelin, who had been paroled from prison, and J.K. Hardister, as nightwatchmen, and Wakelin's Pump Service when work needed to be done around the dairy. Of course, it was expected that all supplies and materials be purchased from the McLaughlin Hardware store on Malvern.[43] It was only natural to do business with "the family." Other close acquaintances were favored in this manner.

It was learned that Jacobs had owned two-thirds interest in the Ohio Club; all the real and personal property of the Southern Club and the Belvedere Club and dairy, which took five legal, single-spaced typed sheets just to describe it. Even when some of the loot from a safe burglary at the Ozark Club occurred in 1941, McLaughlin filed suit on behalf of the Jacob's Estate, maintaining a part of the recovery belonged to the estate.[44] His other property was scattered throughout town and county. This included an apartment house at 174 Cedar Street; three lots on Hobson; two lots on Spring; twenty-five acres on the Malvern Road as well as lots on Malvern Avenue. He owned lots and business buildings on Ouachita; three lots at Sixth and South Streets and several lots in the Sims addition on Grand Avenue.

All of the empty lots were sold to local people like builder George Nickels; grocerman and later sheriff Duffie Searcy and businessman Robert S

[42] Garland County Probate File # 4552, State of Arkansas Commissioner of Revenues Otho A. Cook vs. Estate of W.S. Jacobs, Court Order, 14 May 1946. (Hereinafter cited a Probate File # 4552.)

[43] Probate File # 4552. From Third Annual Account, 5/10/45 - 5/9/46.

[44] *Sentinel-Record*, 11 June 1941.

appraisal value."

From an estate believed to have been worth well over a half million dollars, McLaughlin filed a report reflecting a total value of personal property of $62,807.17 and real estate of $208,150.00, making a total value of $270,957.17, an amount much less than most knowledgeable people believed. But, of course, from that sum Leo deducted various claims and expenses of $139,040.96, leaving the relatives of W.S. Jacobs $131,976.21. To say that the heirs were disappointed is to put it mildly, but they probably were lucky that McLaughlin did not have longer to settle the estate lest they might have wound up with far less.

While Leo P. McLaughlin was well paid for his administration of the Jacobs' estate he probably was most amply rewarded in meting out the "franchises" of the deceased's gambling interests in the six clubs in which he was involved. Without Jacobs' influence, McLaughlin was almost the sole boss. At that time Leo's scheme was, "if you don't pay, you don't play."

In an attempt to continue the operation of Club Belvedere and the Southern Club and to keep the two as an entity, six men formed a company. They were all local and well known to the mayor, and most were already involved in the gambling operation in one way or another: Archie Ledgerwood, Sam C. Watt, Roscoe Johnson, Loyd Lemon, William "Captain" Smith and Julius Reed Ibing. All of these understood the politics of the time and what was necessary to do to comply with the wishes of the local Administration. Unfortunately, there were disagreements and jealousy between the partners and after only nine months they decided to dissolve the partnership.[46]

But it wasn't just the inner turmoil and bickering of the partners that plagued the clubs' operation. At this time they were not making the amount of money they had anticipated as a return on their investment. And, it was mainly the fault of a fellow by the name of Homer--Governor Homer Adkins, that is!

W.S. Jacobs had realized several months before his death that the gambling interests at the Spa had a serious issue at hand. Carl Bailey would complete his second term as governor at the end of 1940. Since a bit of a rough start in January 1937, Bailey and the local gambling fraternity had developed a cozy, friendly and profitable working relationship. Therefore, since no friendly face was on the political scene, Jacobs, McLaughlin and Ledgerwood took it upon themselves to encourage Carl Bailey to seek a third term. Bailey was agreeable and threw his hat into the ring. So did a native of Pulaski County, Homer M. Adkins who was serving as Collector of Internal Revenues. He had served four years as sheriff of Pulaski County, 1923-1926, and he and his family were

---

[46] Dissolution of Partnership, petition filed Garland Chancery Court 10/10/41 and signed by Judge Samuel Garratt 18 December 1941.

staunch members of the Methodist Church.[47] There was no love lost between Bailey and Adkins and they were already political enemies. Like two junk-yard dogs, they took after each other.

Perhaps Jacobs, McLaughlin and Ledgerwood were a bit hasty in latching onto Carl Bailey without first discussing the matter with other Garland County leaders, but Leo had "jumped the gun" giving out a statement to the press, "I believe the people of Hot Springs will stick by Governor Bailey in his race for governor."[48]

Citizens of the Spa were not surprised to see police cars, fire trucks and street department equipment parading through the neighborhoods with political signs endorsing Carl Bailey for governor. This had been done before. It was when Marion Anderson, sheriff of Garland County unfurled a large banner from the courthouse endorsing Homer Adkins as governor that was puzzling to the public.[49] It was quite apparent there was some disagreement between the moguls of city hall and the denizens of the court house--very unusual for that period. Normally, they voted from the same "pink-slip."

The mayor may have been surprised to learn that not only Sheriff Anderson was friendly with Homer Adkins, but Circuit Judge Earl Witt was also. Instead of meeting with the county leaders in an attempt to work things out McLaughlin quickly "circled the wagons," gathering his forces and at the very next council meeting read a statement to that body advising of all the things the governor had done for Hot Springs, like paving some of the highways entering town and loaning the city a large truck to haul its steam shovel from one location to another. Left unsaid was the fact that The Governor had become very cooperative in allowing the clubs and casinos to reopen after he had closed them down. In fact, the political and gambling climate had never been better than during Carl Bailey's last three years in office. The clubs had run wide-open and with few hindrances. The aldermen were convinced and on the mayor's recommendation issued a resolution of "appreciation" for the favors bestowed on the City of Hot Springs and "endorsing his candidacy."[50]

In those days before the election there was a note of panic in the Bailey camp. Speaking at Jordan Stadium in Pine Bluff, the Governor told a crowd his opposition was "more brutal than Hitler," a strong accusation.[51] But he failed to mention any names or refer to any specific instances." He claimed his opponent was engaged in a whisper campaign. Bailey and McLaughlin were

---

[47] Nancy Williams, Editor, *Arkansas Biography*, "A Collection of Notable Lives." The University Press, Fayetteville, 2000. Hereinafter cited, *Arkansas Biography*.

[48] *Sentinel-Record*, 24 July 1940.

[49] Ibid., 26 July 1940.

[50] Ibid., 2 August 1940.

[51] Ibid., 25 July 1940.

kindred spirits!

Both United States Senators, Hattie Caraway and John Miller, who Leo McLaughlin had tried to "sabotage," announced their support for Homer Adkins. The local press was filled with advertisements pro and con for both major candidates, some being signed only as "Hot Springs Friends of Homer Adkins[52] or the mysterious group which never identified themselves and always claimed to be the "Business Interests of Hot Springs."[53] And, then as always, was the pre-election prediction of dire consequences if the Administration candidate was not elected--this from the mayor.[54]

Once again, Leo P. McLaughlin had picked the losing candidate. Oh, he was able to carry the county for the incumbent but not by the 2,800 vote margin it rolled up for Bailey in his last election. This time the margin was by 700, Bailey carried every city ward but the First and lost all but one precinct in the county.

The morning after the election, the *Sentinel-Record* pointed out that the city and county had been divided and that the county factions were claiming "there had been irregularities."[55] Horrors! Did that mean part of the local political machine was suggesting the other part had tried to *cheat*? Maybe not in so many words but Sheriff Marion Anderson and his deputies had arrested several men who were trying to vote more than once in the election.[56] What gall!

Adkins' statewide victory was sizeable and his election did not bode well for the City Administration. It was apparent that he did not care for Mayor McLaughlin and as far as Leo was concerned, the feeling was mutual.

Shortly after the runoff election in October, a local citizens group calling themselves the Arkansas Better Government League organized and headed by the pastor of the First Christian Church, Rev. Claude L. Jones, believed a "window of opportunity" existed to rid the county of illegal gambling completely. The group had noted the local political machine was sharply divided in its support for the gubernatorial candidates. Realizing in the past other organized groups had approached Circuit Judge Witt and he had patiently listened to their complaints and seemed sympathetic to their causes but claimed his hands were "tied". The newly organized group requested a meeting with him, Prosecuting Attorney Curtis Ridgway and Sheriff Marion Anderson, "for a general discussion of the gambling situation."[57] The three county officials agreed.

---

[52] Ibid., 11 August 1940.
[53] Ibid., 13 August 1940.
[54] Ibid.
[55] Ibid., 14 August 1940.
[56] Ibid.
[57] Ibid., 20 October 1940.

Rev. Jones addressed them, "This is the beginning of a job that shall have no end until open defiance of the gambling laws in Hot Springs has been ended."

As usual Judge Witt told the group of the many grand juries he had called over the years to address that same complaint. He told them, "The previous grand juries knew the history of the city and probably considered that bookmaking as now operated is *preferable* to conditions formerly obtained since the city and county derive revenues from it."[58] Witt was, of course, referring to the plan of assessing "fines" against bookmakers in municipal court. The circuit judge really had no intent to change the situation.

Earl Witt informed the committee that if they intended to pursue the matter further they should solicit the state legislature's help to change the violation of illegal bookmaking from a charge of misdemeanor to a felony. That of course, would mean involving State Representatives Campbell and Wheatley and State Senator Maner, all part of the local political machine, and which would lead only to a dead-end. Undoubtedly Rev. Jones and his friends left the meeting disappointed and frustrated as no definite help appeared to be forthcoming from the three county officials who could have made a difference, had they wanted to.

The committee had really misinterpreted the rift between city and county officials, as one side being for gambling and the other against, whereas, both were for the "open-town" policy. The two factions had disagreed over political candidates, not gambling.

In fact, Judge Earl Witt was somewhat a gambler himself, having frequented the Southern and Belvedere clubs on several occasions. He seemed to have no fear that he would be criticized and really was guilty of misfeasance inasmuch as he was aware illegal gambling was being conducted and as an elected official did nothing to stop it. On more than one occasion he had clearly instructed grand juries "to the best of my knowledge there is no record of any bookmaking conviction in Arkansas under a felony statute."[59]

Witnesses from the local citizens organization gave testimony to the next grand jury, even providing the location and addresses of local clubs, but nothing was done. *The Arkansas Democrat* and *Arkansas Gazette* printed the "Grand Jury reported it found no evidence to justify further action and was discharged."[60] So much for Earl Witt's help.

What may really have influenced members of the Grand Jury was Leo P. McLaughlin's appearance before it, telling them in the period April 10, 1927 through June 30, 1941, a total of $250,365 in gambling fines were assessed and

---

[58] Ibid.

[59] Ibid., 28 March 1944.

[60] *Arkansas Democrat,* 14 September 1941.

Witt Family in front of family home at 1535 Central, ca. 1920s
Adults, left to right: Lessie Witt (Plemmons), Thomas C. Witt, Gibson Witt, Jr., Madge Witt, Earl Witt, Florine Howell Witt, Gibson Witt, Sr., Jerry Witt. In front, Rena Virginia and Mary Frances Plemmons. The Witt home at 1535 Central no longer exists.
Courtesy of Pat Wolf

paid to the city's coffers--enough to run the city's street department.[61] As Leo coyly pointed out, "That was money you fellows did not have to pay in taxes."

But in Governor Homer Adkins the county officials, by their support, had helped create a "monster" so far as gambling was concerned. Delegations from Phillips and Garland counties quickly called on him to halt gambling. *The Arkansas Gazette* had conducted a survey and discovered "slot machines running openly at road houses" in Garland, Phillips and Pulaski counties.[62] At least the profits from the slot machines in Phillips County had been designated to charities and worthwhile purposes. In Garland County the profits went into the pockets of George McLaughlin and the club owners.

---

[61] *New Era*, 18 October 1941.
[62] *Arkansas Gazette*, 29 October 1940.

The Hot Springs Ministerial Alliance adopted and presented a resolution to Governor Adkins to "come to our aid with such authority and power you possess and to deal justly with this (gambling) matter."[63]

Only two weeks before Adkins had responded to a similar petition from the Citizens Committee of St. Francis County by sending State Police units to close down a couple of gambling houses.

Adkins issued a statement to the effect that open gambling "must end." He said he expected local officers "to exercise the duties incumbent upon them." The Governor continued, "If these local forces are not utilized to correct violations, such as slot machines, bookmaking (on horse races) and other forms of open gambling, I shall make lawful use of such forces as are at my command to secure proper respect for the laws of the state and rights of its citizens."

Homer Adkins was roundly applauded for his stand by the Arkansas Congress of Parents and Teachers and adopted a resolution supporting the governor. It read, "There prevails in many sections of the state an 'easy' attitude toward gambling which fosters corruption of officials and elections, destroys moral standards and is a definite hazard to the best character development of youth."[64]

It was understood that Governor Adkins was directing his remarks principally toward the gambling situation in Garland County. He had easily closed down small spots of gaming in other parts of the state but the clubs in Hot Springs continued to ignore him and go along their merry way. Other governor's had postulated similar statements and nothing ever happened. The difference--other governors had agreed to some type of "working" agreement with the Spa's gambling fraternity, they had none with Governor Adkins. And further more since none of the Spa's city officials were very welcome at the State Capitol because of their previous support for Carl Bailey, it appeared a stalemate existed. It wasn't from a lack of trying as Representatives Campbell and Wheatley and Senator Ernest Maner had tried to arrange a meeting with the governor, but all offers were turned down.

The owners of the local clubs were as nervous as a barefooted man in a dark room full of spilled thumb tacks. For two weeks after the governor's statement, the gambling community had staked a "watch-out" at Crow's Station on the Little Rock highway so they could be warned in the event state police cars were spotted.

Rumors were rampant on Central Avenue that October 15 had been set as the "deadline" for compliance in closing the clubs. Governor Adkins declined to comment about his threat to use force to close the clubs other than telling

---

[63] Ibid., 14 September 1941.

[64] Ibid., 3 October 1941.

reporters, "Just wait and see."[65] Some clubs while running, kept their doors closed and discontinued the "calls" or loud speaker announcements of the races in progress.[66]

On October 14 the State Police did visit Hot Springs, but not on a raid. Superintendent Gray Albright and Captain Lindsey Hatchett drove over to visit Garland County Sheriff Marion Anderson.[67] The exact nature of the visit was never disclosed, however it was believed because of Anderson's support in Adkin's race the previous year he was being paid a courtesy visit possibly to determine if Sheriff Anderson wanted to close the clubs down before the state acted. Anderson was caught in the middle. Much of his support had come from the gambling community. Should he take the lead in closing down the clubs much of his voter and financial support would vanish. He would permit the state officers "to do the dirty work" and get the credit. No doubt, the sheriff was reminded Governor Adkins was very serious about his statement and he did not intend to tolerate open gambling.[68]

The following day John L. Fletcher, Staff Correspondent of the *Arkansas Gazette*, came to the Spa to be on hand if the expected raids by the State Police materialized. Fletcher learned Mayor McLaughlin was in Little Rock "conferring with somebody." Likely, Leo was with Senator Ernest Maner and representatives from Garland County attempting to come up with a plan as to how they might approach the governor and get him "off of the Spa's back."

Fletcher walked Central Avenue and reported the clubs from the Citizens to the White Front were running "wide open" and every club was filled to capacity. The *Gazette* correspondent reported "Belvedere, the outstanding night club in this section, was as usual a bedlam of dice, blackjack, big-six and roulette tonight."[69]

Leo McLaughlin returned from Little Rock and admitted to the owners of the Belvedere and Southern clubs he and his contacts had been unable to secure an arrangement with Governor Adkins whereby the clubs could remain open.

On October 17, the clubs opened for business as usual, then "the word went the rounds that this is the day," and the bookmaking establishments began to voluntarily close.[70] Over one hundred employees left their jobs not knowing if or when the bookies would be allowed to reopen. It was only the second time in twelve years they had been shut down, the first being after Governor

---

[65] *Sentinel-Record*, 14 October 1941.
[66] *Arkansas Gazette*, 14 October 1941.
[67] *Sentinel-Record*, 15 October 1941.
[68] *Arkansas Gazette*, 16 October 1941.
[69] Ibid.
[70] *Sentinel-Record*, 18 October 1941.

Carl Bailey first took office.[71] The newspapers reported the "Death Knell" of open gambling in the Spa had sounded and printed "Sporting men dazed."[72] One paper carried a large photo of the vacant horse book room and empty chairs at the Southern Club and entitled it, "Empty Saddles in the Old Corral."[73] The publication's humor was lost on the beleaguered local gambling establishment.

It was a very unsettling time for the gamblers and bookmakers and it is understandable why the six partners in the Belvedere and Southern Clubs finally decided to dissolve their partnership.[74] Besides their own internal problems they were suddenly faced with a shut-down order by the state.

When word came from the governor's office that he might ask the state police to look also for other sources of gambling besides bookmaking, some pay-off pin-ball machines owned by Phil Marks, a local juke-box and pin-ball machine operator, were suddenly quietly picked-up and punch boards began to disappear under the counters at cigar-stands, beer parlors and pool halls.[75] Many of the locals became convinced Governor Adkins "had gone to meddlin."

Several of the bookies began to make their own interpretation of the governor's ultimatum as to "open gambling," by moving their operations into back rooms and letting in only preferred and known customers. This situation was quickly brought to the chief executive's attention by the Arkansas Better Government League. A call to the local sheriff's office brought Marion Anderson personally to visit "all local bookmaking establishments," and an admission he "had found indications that some of them might have been operating." Anderson ordered all of the gambling establishments to close in view of the governor's edict.[76] Reluctantly, the betting shops closed their operations.

However, it was not long until a few began to discreetly open up for business, but were not utilizing a wire service and were paying bets on the results of races published in the newspapers the following day.[77] This, of course, was a very unsatisfactory arrangement, both for the bettor and the bookie. One bookie years before had expressed his opinion of doing business

---

[71] *New Era*, 18 October 1941.

[72] *Sentinel-Record*, 19 October 1941.

[73] *Hot Springs Post*, 19 October 1941. This was a short-lived newspaper published at Hot Springs. It had a pleasing format, but the odd three-times a week issue and delivery had little subscriber appeal and it closed. It once offered a trophy to the horsebook which would remain closed the longest, however there were no claimers.

[74] Dissolution of Partnership Petition, filed Garland County Chancery Court, 18 December 1941.

[75] *Arkansas Gazette*, 21 October 1941.

[76] *Sentinel-Record*, 23 October 1941.

[77] *Arkansas Gazette*, 2 November 1941.

in this fashion.

"If we have to operate by paying off the next day, it will materially reduce the amount of business. The service (live announcements of races) enabled players to almost see the horses, and gave them the very latest information on each race. To play the horses without that will be just like drinking 'near beer' during prohibition days. The kick is out."[78]

As the holiday season approached in 1941, there was a lessening of threats coming from Governor Adkins' office and six of the horsebooks began to quietly reopen. Perhaps the governor's attention was drawn to the fact America was suddenly plunged into war by the treacherous attack on Pearl Harbor and was being pressured by the federal government to allow the imprisonment of thousands of Japanese at Rohwer, Arkansas, over Adkins objection. Whether Homer Adkins was involved with other state business or if he just felt benevolent toward the unemployed bookmakers and their employees is not known. But there was a period of inactivity of the governor's office toward gambling in the Spa.

The old saying of "give an inch, take a mile," was certainly true in the cases of the gamblers at Hot Springs. By the middle of January 1942 they had become as brazen and bold as ever and were running wide-open. It caught them completely by surprise when Governor Adkins cracked his whip and instead of issuing another ultimatum, which he generally followed with several warnings to the gamblers, sent several cars loaded with state police and revenue agents. It caught the horse books by total surprise. Why hadn't their lookout at Crow's Station alerted them of the coming raid? It was because the caravan of officers had "slipped in the back way," coming through Malvern and Magnet Cove. It was a concerted raid with officers hitting all the gambling establishments simultaneously and without warning.[79]

"Telephones were torn loose from the walls, loud-speaking equipment was dismantled, wall charts, form books and similar accessories were loaded into the rear of state police cars, and roulette wheels and dice tables were destroyed on the spot."[80] Some of this was new equipment.

The patrons of the clubs were ordered to leave while the owners and operators were detained. State Police Supt. Albright made his way to all six of the establishments and informed each of the gamblers "This raid is being made at the instance of Governor Adkins. The search and seizure warrants were issued by Justice Griffin Smith. We have not made any arrests, but will in the event any place is reopened."

The patron of one of the clubs stood on the sidewalk outside of the closed

---

[78] Ibid., 16 November 1939.
[79] Ibid., 25 January 1942.
[80] *Sentinel-Record*, 25 January 1942.

bookie and lamented, "This is the first time in three weeks that I've had a winner and I can't collect."

But in the 1930s and 1940s, there was no one with more "brass" than a Hot Springs bookie. It was in their blood and they had openly defied the laws for years and had basked and been nurtured in the warmth and the protection afforded by the McLaughlin political machine. Even though Leo P. McLaughlin had been unable to influence the State Administration to permit open gambling they were willing to take the risk of operating in defiance of the governor's warnings. They threw down the gauntlet and Governor Homer Adkins picked it up.

Several of the horse books "secretly" moved from their long time and commodious locations to lesser known places. These were much smaller then their original quarters and were called "bookie shops." They tried to be resourceful. One, Ben Harrison, rented a "back room" in the American Legion hall at 212½ Broadway. Several Legionnaires expressed shock and surprise their quarters were being used in such a way. A former city alderman, George Pakis, opened a betting room, renting from Dane Harris and his mother, over the Black Cat Liquor store at Central and Spring. Harris would later be elevated to become one of the top gambling figures at the Spa. Just north of that location, F.C. Nichols set up shop. Those three places were shut down by some of the Spa's most regular visitors, State Police officers from Little Rock.[81] Visits by officers to several of the known clubs, White Front, Blue Ribbon, Southern and Ohio, revealed nothing was going on.

Apparently Governor Adkins was reminded by some of the Garland county officials a large part of the governor's support in the last election had come from part of the local political machine. Adkins quickly responded and appeared unappreciative, saying, "The support the Hot Springs political organization gave me was wholly unsolicited on my part."[82]

Adkins continued raids throughout the summer of 1942. For awhile the closing down of the clubs and gambling shops and the confiscation or destruction of gambling paraphernalia was the extent of the raids. Then the operators and employees were arrested and taken to the police station, charged and docketed using their real identification. When the names of thirty-two "well known Hot Springs residents appeared on the Municipal Court docket, Municipal Judge V.S. Ledgerwood continued the cases indefinitely without explanation."[83] Ledgerwood was sympathetic with the plight of some of his friends and his handling went unchallenged.

As the state hammered away at the Spa trying to rid it forever of the "evils"

---

[81] Ibid., 11 March 1942.
[82] *New Era*, 17 August 1942.
[83] Ibid., 17 November 1942.

of horse books and other methods of gambling there were those in the city who tried to point out that the resort was not the only city in the state to have book making as a problem. It was like the "pot calling the kettle black" as the capital city, Little Rock, had its own secrets not well told.

The Arkansas Gazette had for years used Hot Springs as its "whipping-boy," and had quickly pointed out things amiss in the Spa while ignoring those which were wrong in Little Rock or other areas of the state. When horse racing recommenced, the *Gazette* had refused to print the daily results for a while.

The *Gazette* did have one reporter who had a knack for setting the record straight if only with tongue-in-cheek. His name was Hardy "Spider" Rowland who used a satyrical style and vocabulary all his own. He wrote concerning the bookie situation: "The office stooge came forward with an interesting question the other night. 'Why,' quoth he, 'do the State Police go way over to Hot Springs to raid the bookies? What's the matter with Little Rock joints; are they poison?'"

"Quite a few of Greater Little Rock's citizens have voiced that same question repeatedly, but evidently that is the $64 question and law enforcement officers would rather forget about it."

"Of course, if they really wanted to ease the minds of the anti-gambling element, they could stage some raids at just a few of the open book making establishments. They might raid the large one between Second and Third streets on Main street or they could even send a couple of policemen into the little joint off of Main street on West Third street. If they really wanted to make a spectacular scene, they could walk in on the crap shooters and horse race gamblers at 110 E. Washington avenue, North Little Rock."

"Evidently bookmaking, the kind that has to do with horses, football games and such, is essential to the war effort. At least that would be the conclusion of the casual observer who happens to notice that one of Greater Little Rock's most noted operator of "bookie" joints still is driving his oversized Cadillac around town with a "B" mileage ration sticker on the front windshield."[84]

Perhaps "Spider" Rowland was only trying to bring attention to the fact that the Spa wasn't so bad after all if compared fairly to Little Rock and other places. At least there was another side to the story. But not to Governor Homer Adkins, he still had it in for Hot Springs. However it appeared for a while the good Governor had slipped up and made a couple of mistakes. It seems he had sent the State Police on several raiding forays without arming them with search warrants.[85] Local gamblers and their attorneys jumped on that and won a victory in the local courts and a temporary reprieve. A victory

---

[84] *Arkansas Gazette*, 27 December 1942.
[85] *Arkansas Biography*, Adkins, p. 5.

came for Adkins on appeal from the State Supreme Court, nullifying the decisions of the lower courts.[86] The Supreme Court was sending a message that the lower courts had tried to rule "the places of chance virtually are immune to interference by state authorities," was totally unacceptable and state agencies armed with proper warrants still had a right of search and seizure. But the point was, the state officers *were not armed with proper warrants.*

After being criticized for failing to obtain warrants Governor Adkins made it easy for the State Police to obtain such documents to search and seize by appointing local Hot Springs resident Rev. Floyd Hurst, justice of the peace.[87] Hurst took his job seriously and stood ready day and night to supply search and seizure warrants to the raiding officers.

A "cat and mouse" game developed. The state police would raid the bookmaking establishments, who were warned ahead of time quite often, either by their watchout on the highway or from a friendly source at Little Rock. The gamblers would be back in business fifteen minutes after the raiders had left. Some, in fact had someone stationed on the sidewalks taking bets while the raid was being conducted inside and never missed a beat.[88] They were resourceful!

Frustrated, Governor Adkins tried another approach by sending a letter to Garland County Prosecuting Attorney Curtis Ridgway, with copies to various newspapers, "demanding" he take legal action against gambling establishments, "and to abate these nuisances by enjoining them from future operation." In other words, he wanted the clubs padlocked and closed as nuisances. Adkins even provided names and addresses and number of times each operator had been arrested by state officers during the past two years. He cited "Tony Karston who operates the White Front Club, 310 Central avenue, and who has been arrested nine times in 1943 and one time in 1944." And, "Louis Longinotti, who operates the Citizen's Club, 744½ Central avenue, and who has been arrested six times in 1943 and three times in 1944." The Governor pointed out that "Erb Wheatley owner of the Reno Club at 721½ Central avenue had been arrested three times in 1943 and three times in 1944." The list went on naming George Pakis, operator of the Blue Ribbon Club; Roscoe Johnson, the Southern Club; and a newcomer to the scene, Jack McJunkin The Tower Club.[89]

What was Prosecuting Attorney Curtis Ridgway to do? The highest ranking executive official in the state had gone on record requesting him to file charges that the gambling clubs be padlocked as being nuisances? These were some of

---

[86] *Sentinel-Record,* 16 November 1943.
[87] Ibid.
[88] Ibid., 18 June 1943.
[89] *Arkansas Gazette,* 12 March 1944.

the same people who had supported and elected him. Ridgeway was aware the Garland County Grand Jury was meeting at that time and it would be prudent for them to make the ruling on this situation and he could not be blamed for failing to comply with the Governor's request. Also, Circuit Judge Earl Witt had already instructed the grand jury with one of his patented speeches giving them the information, "It had been the general rule to prosecute those charged with bookmaking as misdemeanor cases."[90]

As could have been predicted, the sixteen-man grand jury remanded the gambling cases to municipal court. Judge Ledgerwood dismissed some of the cases and imposed $100 fines on others. It was merely business as usual.

Governor Homer Adkins was furious at the situation in Hot Springs. He made a request of State Attorney General Guy E. Williams "to seek injunctions in the Garland County Chancery Court for the closing of the establishments." Williams was less than enthused with the request advising the governor he would comply but candidly said "it is extremely doubtful whether the Attorney General's office has any authority to intervene in this way." He did suggest that the legislature could by statute authorize the attorney general to bring actions in the name of the state in the lower courts "in specified matters."[91]

For three and one-half years Homer Adkins had given his best shot to close down open gambling in Arkansas. He had succeeded somewhat in Phillips and St. Francis counties and had made inroads to at least driving the bookies underground in Pulaski County. It was Garland County that was the stone in his shoe. He had tried hardest in that county, but he had been frustrated because of his inability to get any cooperation from the local law enforcement agencies or courts. He had been able to close the gambling establishments but almost by the time the state police had reached the city limits on their way out of town, the bookies were up and running. His officers had arrested many of the gamblers, only to have the local court postpone the hearings indefinitely or assess minor fines.

By summer of 1944 Governor Adkins' mind was on other matters than bookmakers and gamblers in Garland County. He had entered a race for the United States Senate and his opponent was J. William Fulbright, who had served as President of the University of Arkansas until Governor Adkins had fired him. Fulbright would have his revenge.[92] Homer Adkins hardly campaigned in Garland County--he knew there remained little support for him in the business community.

---

[90] *Sentinel-Record*, 28 March 1944.

[91] *Arkansas Gazette*, 9 June 1944.

[92] *Arkansas Biography*, p. 6.

People around the nation were glued to their radios in early September 1939, as threats of war hung over the European continent. It was unthinkable that in only twenty short years Germany had risen from its ruins after the World War and was again threatening the peace of the world. But that was exactly what was happening. Surely, people thought, the United States would not be pulled into another European conflict. Then as the world listened and watched, Adolph Hitler bluffed his way into the Rhineland and Czechlosovokia, then when France and Britain stood idly-by and watched, he invaded Poland and World War II had begun.

As the United States gradually awakened from its lethargy and began to rebuild its military forces there was still a nationwide hope the country could remain neutral and not be drawn into the fray. What was the warning of George Washington about keeping this nation free of foreign entanglements? It appeared President Franklin D. Roosevelt was trying to avoid such a conflict and in one of his "fire-side speeches," he broached the news that the United States would be known as "The Great Arsenal of Democracy," and would furnish its friends war implements under a new program called Lend Lease. It all sounded good, but of course, it didn't keep the country out of war.

Less than a year after the war had started in Europe the President signed the National Selective Service Act, requiring all men between the ages of 21 and 35 to register.[1] Draft Boards were set up in every county and parish in the country. Doctors and dentists were ordered to give preliminary examinations of any of the draftees.[2]

Other legislation preparing the country for war, if it should come, followed The Office of Price Stabilization was designed to prevent "price gouging." The Production and Allocation Act, (later setting up the OPA) passed in May 1941 and was just a fancy name for "war rationing." Local citizens manned the Ration Board with the first one composed of L.V. Freeman, Clyde E. Wilson and Warren W. Wilson.[3] And a Civilian Defense program was instituted with the Fire and Police Chiefs heading the local program and a resident of each block designated as neighborhood warden. On dates appointed as "Air-raid drills," everyone was supposed to douse or dim their lights and cover their windows with shades or blinds. The local wardens walked around the block

---

[1] FDR signed the bill 16 September 1940 and became the first peace time conscription in history.

[2] After Pearl Harbor, a second registration was called for and men 18 to 65 were required to register.

[3] Francis J. Scully, M.D., *Hot Springs, Arkansas and Hot Springs National Park,* p. 34?

and notified anyone who was not totally blacked-out. Fortunately, after the initial war scare following Pearl Harbor, the drills were discontinued.

But long before Pearl Harbor and America's entry into the war the Spa was contributing with National Guard units, which had been in training, and were federalized and stationed in strategic areas of the hemisphere. Hot Springs had active guard units for several years going back to 1922 when Hospital Company 216 was organized by Major Howell Brewer. Need for services of that company came the following year, 1923, when severe flooding in the downtown area occurred. The mayor and sheriff requested that the local unit take over guard duty of the downtown area to prevent looting.[4]

The old units had met and trained for a period in the loft over the old Strand Theater, then moved to the Red Ball Garage on Ouachita Avenue. The first move to build the National Guard a building of its own was started in 1931, with a meeting being held in Mayor McLaughlin's office and included County Judge Charles Davis, Municipal Judge Verne Ledgerwood, Garnett Eisele, and various leaders of the Chamber of Commerce, Veterans of Foreign Wars, American Legion and state representatives.[5] Admittedly, the funding for the project was the big problem as the city was in the depths of the Depression and the effort failed. Finally an opportunity came to the Spa in the form of an offer by the Federal Government. As one of the last WPA projects approved before the war the government was willing to build a modern armory for the National Guard if the state would contribute $3,000 and the city $6,000.

Both newspapers had the warmest endorsement for an armory.[6] An editorial advised, "A Committee headed by Martin A. Eisele, veteran enthusiast for everything for the advancement and progress of Hot Springs heads the local committee for the armory." Even the members of the Guard got out and solicited funds. Major boosts were received from the Chamber of Commerce and the Civitan Club, plus the generosity of several of the hotels and businesses and the goal was met.[7]

The armory construction was begun in August 1937.[8] It was located on Woodbine Street, behind the Garland County Court House, and in less than a year the guard units began to move into their new quarters.[9]

At the beginning of 1940 there were two units of the National Guard training at Hot Springs, the Medical Detachment of the 153 Infantry and the

---

[4] *New Era*, 23 February 1941. This was a newspaper summary advising the activities in which the guard unit had been involved.

[5] *Sentinel-Record*, 7 January 1931.

[6] Ibid., 12 April 1937.

[7] *New Era*, 10 May 1937.

[8] Ibid., 23 August 1937.

[9] *Sentinel-Record*, 28 July 1938.

206 Coast Guard Artillery Anti-aircraft battery. The two units had a total of seven officers and 156 enlisted men.[10] Each man was paid one-dollar for each drill night.[11]

The 206th was mobilized 6 January 1941, and sent to Fort Bliss, near El Paso for further training and assignment.[12] One hundred thirty-four enlisted men and four officers marched from the Armory to the Southern Grill for breakfast and with full packs and equipment paraded down Central Avenue and to the Rock Island station on Benton Street. All motorized equipment, under command of Lt. Richard L. Craigo had left several days before enroute to their new assignment.[13]

For six months this group trained in the desert in and around West Texas in sand and severe heat. Would it be assigned to some hot and humid zone like the Philippines or the Panama Canal Zone? Of course not. Anyone acquainted with the army method of thinking would soon come to the conclusion this group of men had been acclimated for a duty zone in some frigid place--say the Aleutian Islands, west of the Alaskan Peninsula or near the Arctic Circle at Fairbanks. Pvt. Victor H. Cox, a Norman, Arkansas boy, who later moved to Hot Springs, would have agreed with this assessment of army logic as he crawled through the steamy jungles of the South Pacific, wondering what "military genius" had concluded his training with the ski troops in snowy Colorado, had fitted him for fighting in New Guinea. At least the men were now being paid better, $21.00 per month, or was it? It only came to about seventy-five cents a day.

Half of the men of the 206th were assigned to Unalaska and Dutch Harbor, the other half to Ladd Field at Fairbanks. Many of the accommodations for the troops were unfinished and it was necessary for some of the men to be housed in a large airplane hanger at the airport. The initial plan had been to house the men in tents until U. S. Senator Brewster, (R.-ME) happened by on a defense inspection trip and realizing how inadequate the preparations were, immediately criticized the military program in Alaska.[14] When he returned to Washington he complained loudly to the War Department that a "requirement of law exists that adequate housing be provided for troops above the Mason-Dixon line and that tents in an Alaskan winter will not answer that

---

°10 *Ibid.*, 23 February 1940.

¹11 Info from James E. "Ev" Young, 13 November 2001. Young was a member of the 206th Artillery, Battery H.

²12 "History of The 206th Artillery, Battery H In World War II," author unknown, a short concised paper on file at the GCHS Archives.

³13 *New Era*, 7 January 1941.

⁴14 *Arkansas Democrat*, 5 September 1941,

lescription."[15]

Brewster further reported there were several thousand men at Dutch Harbor o "defend one Navy Commander and two yeomen," the naval base being ınfinished at that time. The Navy took the hint and began to "beef-up" its ersonnel there.

Brewster's help was most welcomed by the army units in the area, but the enator was unaware how resourceful a bunch of GIs can be. The boys from Iot Springs had begun to "up-grade" their quarters almost from the time of heir arrival. Some took sheets of plywood from an army construction site and sed the material to floor their own tents and quarters. They didn't look on it s stealing--it all belonged to the Government--they were just transferring the ıaterial to a place that had an immediate need.

The islands and camps were remote--so remote bears were drawn in by the ood odors emanating from the mess hall. Pvt. James E. "Ev" Young wrote letter to his parents, Mr. and Mrs. W.A. Young, and told them of his new girl-friend, Josephine,"and then explained "Josephine was neither a dizzy, azzling blonde," or almond-eyed Eskino, but just a bear he had taken quite fancy to." "Ev" Young enclosed a photo of himself and the bear. His folks ıowed the picture around and it and the story appeared in the local paper.[16]

The 206th came under attack while at Dutch Harbor as the Japanese ombed the base and harbor for several days straight. After weathering two itter winters the 206th was transferred back to the States with some units eing shipped out to Europe for duty in that war zone.

The folks at home were hungry for news from their sons, brothers, usbands and friends. Mothers shared letters, each hoping to learn more of ıeir loved ones and the living conditions they had in Alaska and other areas. Vhen some soldier got leave to come home he spent a lot of his time calling ıe parents of his friends and assuring them their son was all right.

The local papers were always receptive about publishing news of our ghting men. In fact, the Arkansas units in Alaska generally assigned someone) write the happenings and activities. Cpl. Leonard Brown, "With Spa oldiers in Alaska," wrote of the cold and the winter clothes each man was sued. Carl Deaton, with the 153 Medical Detachment sent in a column ıtitled, "Written from a Ridge in Middle Tennessee," describing that unit's ail from Camp Robinson to Tennessee for war games, and from there to ort Lewis, Washington and then on to Alaska. He told how the unit actually ɔt in a "fist-fight" when boys from a Michigan unit made a move on the 53rd's food. He said the "Arkansas boys defended themselves and their operty quite well." Another local young man, Jack W. Riley gave first-hand

---

[15] Ibid.

[16] *Sentinel-Record*, 30 November 1941.

descriptions of the voyage from Seattle to the "last frontier," Alaska, as being quite rough and how nauseated the men became from the heaving of the ship and the bucking of the sea." Riley said the "nausea was accompained by a great loss of equilibrium and an undying wish we would never see the ocean or a ship again." M.C. Lewis, Jr. wrote of the Hot Springs boys in training at Camp Roberts, California and those assigned to the 51st Field Artillery Battalion.[17]

Some news articles were humorous like "Ev" Young and his bear, or about a moose attacking a Ford Model A car and almost demolishing it. Others were sad and unhappy news that the community shared with the agony of families being advised that a son was killed or missing in action in the line of duty.

Only a month after Pearl Harbor, Garland County received word of its first casualty. Sgt. William McCoy Hansford, who had attended Lakeside High School, was killed at Corregidor in the Philippines.[18] Memorial services were held for Hansford in his home church. In March 1942 word was received that Seaman James Obed Harper, son of Mr. and Mrs. Jewell Harper, was missing in action when the light cruiser Pillsbury was sunk in one of the early naval battles in the Java Sea. Jewell Harper was the last postman in Hot Springs to deliver mail on his route out of a buggy pulled by a horse. Sadly, news of other casualties would follow.

Every few days groups of pictures of the soldiers, sailors, aviators and marines appeared in local publications. The short lived *Hot Springs Post* specialized in writing about the servicemen, knowing it not only was the news of the day but encouraged the public to subscribe to its publication. Imogene Barnes was the staff writer assigned to this job and she encouraged parents to let *The Post* know of any news relating to their son or daughter and when that occurred she would have a nice write up along with a photo to accompany the article.

Families were proud to display Blue Star banners in their windows as notice to the world that one or more of their family was in the service of their country. Mr. and Mrs. Frank M. Ridgeway, proudly displayed a flag with four stars representing offsprings, Pvt. Jack E. Ridgeway with the U. S. Army at Camp Hann, California; Sgt. David P., and Sgt. Billy, both with the Coast Artillery in Alaska and daughter, Margaret with the Motor Corps, Red Cross unit.[19] Even that was not a Garland County record as the Frank Rapley family who resided on Mill Creek Road, had five members serving their country: Geraldine Rapley, Women's Motor Corps of the American Red Cross; John H., with the U. S. Marine Corps at Camp Elliott, California; Frank A., U.S.

---

[17] All of these stories are from undated clippings in a scrapbook entitled, "Fighting Men of Garland County in WW II," located at GCHS Archives.

[18] *Sentinel-Record*, 11 January 1942.

[19] Ibid., 24 January 1942.

Army Air Force, Shepherd Field, Texas; James J., 4th U. S. Cavalry, Ft. Mead, S. Dakota; and David R., in training with the U. S. Marines, San Diego, California.[20]

Long before the war ended the Spa would have sons and daughters serving in almost every theater of the war and in every branch of the service. While Sid McMath was winning the Silver Star medal for his actions at Cape Torokina, Bougainville and the Distinguished Service Medal at the battle of Piva Forks, Dennis Lindsey, another Hot Springs boy, took part in the invasion of the island of Sicily, writing his pastor, "By the grace of God I am still alive to tell about it," and received several commendations.[21] Commander Frederick Julian Becton, captain of the destroyer U.S. Laffey, another son of the Spa, saw thirty-one of his crew killed by six Japanese suicide planes, but brought his badly damaged vessel back to port[22]. Pvt. Wayne Allen, had his own adventures in the war having the distinction of capturing German General Walter Steinmueller, Commandant of the 70th Infantry Division.[23]

People at home sacrificed, too! There was rationing of almost every commodity. Each member of a family was issued ration books with tear-out stamps or coupons. Each month the newspapers published which coupons were good for bacon, five pounds of sugar or a sack of flour. Special stamps were used to purchase leather goods. Young ladies accustomed to buying a dozen pairs of shoes each year learned that they were limited to four or five pairs. Other rationing books related to automobiles, the purchase of gasoline, tires and batteries. Joyriding was prohibited and each vehicle was issued a sticker of its own indicating what priority rights that automobile or truck had. There were A, B, C, stickers designating whether the automobile or truck was for personal use, or transportation to a defense job or used in connection with a business. There were scarcities of chocolate bars and nylons. Word of the arrival of either would have people clamoring and lining up to buy their share.

Few automobiles were produced for civilian use during the war and to purchase one an individual had to have a good reason and a special permit which was a bit difficult to obtain. The Kingsway Garage, an agency for Pontiac automobiles, had five new ones on hand at the beginning of the war and because of the strict requirements had a difficult time selling them.

To reduce travel a share-the-ride plan was organized with one individual driving for a week and one of his passengers the following week. Transportation was necessary to get to one's work. In town a person could walk or ride one of the city buses. To get all the employees from Hot Springs

---

[20] *Hot Springs Post*, 11 January 1942.

[21] Undated Central Baptist Church Bulletin, GCHS Archives.

[22] *Arkansas Democrat*, 25 May 1945.

[3] From documents on "U. S. Servicemen in WW II," on file at GCHS Archives.

and Malvern to Jones Mill special buses were operated for the workers and scheduled for the shift changes. Others could ride and did take advantage of it, costing only fifteen cents each way. This plant had been erected by the Aluminum Company of America in 1942 to produce metal for the war effort.[24] It offered employment to hundreds of people at better wages than were being paid by the business sector in the Spa. Because of this many workers were enticed from local jobs and caused some minor friction in the business community. It turned out to be a major boost for the area's economy for many years.

There were many ways the community helped in the war effort. There were Bond Drives to raise money for the war effort. Even the schools participated with stamps sales. Each student was given a small booklet with spaces for gluing ten or twenty-five cent stamps. When the amount totaled $18.75 the booklet could be exchanged for a baby-war bond with a maturity value of twenty-five dollars. Of course, that was ten-years down the line, however it gave the purchaser the feeling that he or she was supporting the war effort. One teacher at Hot Springs, Mrs. Johnnie Mae Mackey, took the lead and pushed students to participate in the savings stamps sales, thus also teaching them to save. During this time if Mrs. Mackey was at an assembly she personally led the Pledge of Allegiance--no doubt hundreds of times. J.B. Johns, commercial teacher and superintendent at Lakeside, did the same thing, just not as enthusiasticly as Mrs. Mackey. Young women and girls volunteered and manned the canteens and USO centers, located in downtown Hot Springs and attended dances there and at Vet's Haven, on Lake Catherine. This was a state park and the army used it for the rehabilitation of American soldiers and also had a camp for the confinement of captured German soldiers.

The Boy Scouts in Garland County worked in paper and scrap drives, going from house to house and piling donated metal, old tires and bundles of papers along the curbs. These were then picked-up by city and county dump trucks and shipped to plants to be re-smeltered or processed. This writer was in a troop from Second Baptist Church where the Scoutmaster, Ralph Poda, was working a full-time job, taking flight lessons from Johnny Stover and leading the troop in the gathering of scrap metal. Many others were doing similar things.

Housewives were urged by First Lady Eleanor Roosevelt to save their bacon grease, telling the women of the nation grease was the source of glycerine, the base for high explosives. They were told to pour the grease into a clean coffee can and to turn it in to designated centers. Other ladies organized clubs to make Afghans and lap-robes to be sent to hospitals for wounded soldiers. All citizens were urged to participate in "meatless Tuesdays" and "fish on

---

[24] *Arkansas Gazette*, 4 August 1942.

Fridays," in an effort to help the fighting forces have adequate beef and pork supplies. It made us feel we were helping in the war-effort. The Government urged people to plant Victory gardens, small plots of land, and to grow vegetables for the family's use. It was estimated that one year these hundreds of thousands "backyard" gardens had produced nearly forty-percent of the vegetables grown in the country.

Each night people huddled around their radios to listen to Gabriel Heater, John Kaltenborn, or one of the other commentators on the progress of the war overseas. During the early days after America's entry into the war, there seemed to be only bad news, as American forces in the Philippines were pushed from Manila and down the island and finally onto Corregidor where the forces surrendered. News of the surrender of Wake Island and other places had residents scanning their maps to see how close the fighting might be to some loved one. Sometimes the loss of a capital ship would be kept from the American public until it could be tempered with some better news. In some cases the notification that some kin was missing in action or had been killed was the first announcement of a possible tragedy, the sinking of a large warship. News of a U.S. victory sent spirits soaring.

And to their credit, neither Milton Nobles, manager of the Western Union or D.A. Mooney, manager of the Postal Telegraph, would dispatch their young bicycle delivery boys to deliver one of the black-border "death" or "missing-in-action" messages to the parents of some unfortunate serviceman. The managers personally delivered the bad news and in several cases picked up a known friend, clergyman, neighbor or acquaintance to help break the woeful news.

When it became apparent an invasion of Europe was imminent the membership of several churches organized a telephone campaign and when news of the Normandy landings came, scores of people headed for their worship centers and prayers were made petitioning a merciful God for the protection and safety of their loved ones.

As the war went on the streets of Hot Springs filled with servicemen, some as out-patients at the Army Navy General Hospital, others on Rest and Recreation leave and still others being rehabilitated from wounds and injuries. Hordes of servicemen, some with wives or girl friends on their arms, filled Schneck's and Walgreen's fountains and downtown restaurants. Others having received back-pay patronized some of the bookies and casinos. Their presence enlivened business. Sometimes a bit too much, as evidenced in a fight between several servicemen and police officers. Troops were involved in maneuvers in Southwest Arkansas and while on leave they visited the Spa. The fray took place at Spencer's corner at Central and Bridge where the servicemen were waiting on a bus and became a little too boisterous. Officers Roy Dillard, John Portlock and Captain Jerry Watkins attempted to quiet the group and words were hurled between the GIs and law enforcement officers. As the dialogue heated up, and the officers threatened to run them in, one of the soldiers reportedly said, "Let's take 'em," and the fight was on. Officer Dillard suffered a split lip and badly bruised hand; Portlock lost a tooth "and various and sundry bruises from being bounced on the sidewalk and complained of having a cigar crushed in his face."[25] Four of the servicemen were arrested and appeared in municipal court. Judge Ledgerwood turned the soldiers over to military authorities. The army immediately assigned additional Military Police to patrol the city and they became a common sight in the Spa for the remainder of the war.

Another incident occurred that brought unfavorable publicity on Mayor Leo P. McLaughlin during this time. Officers at the Army Navy General Hospital saw the opportunity of organizing an officer's club which local and visiting military officers could enjoy. The leaders visualized the possibility of the club making a little extra money by installing five slot machines, believing they would provide entertainment for the men and seeing nothing wrong with it in view of the local attitude toward such things. Word of the slots reached Mayor McLaughlin's brother, George, who had an interest in many of the "one-armed bandits" in town and wasn't getting his cut out of the officer club's machines. George complained loudly to big brother, Leo. Without even thinking of the consequences, the mayor despatched police officers to raid the newly formed officer's club and confiscated the machines informing the stunned military personnel, "Slot machines were illegal."[26] Indeed they were. Again, it was just the idea of "Whose ox is getting gored." Police Commissioner, Weldon Raspberry and Sheriff Marion Anderson would only "parrot" the mayor, "The slots were illegal." Mayor McLaughlin refused to comment about the matter.[27]

As the number of soldiers grew and additional space needed, the government first purchased the 500-room Eastman Hotel in 1942 and converted the space into hospital rooms. Since the hotel was across Reserve Avenue from the hospital, a walkway over the street was constructed connecting the two buildings.[28] In 1944 the large number of returning servicemen required additional space and the government took over four of the Spa's major hotels, The Arlington, Majestic, DeSoto and Park.[29] The servicemen who where in town for R-&-R were treated to luxury accommodations most had never dreamed of. To furnish needed labor in the kitchens of the hotels a number of German POWs imprisoned on the south

---

[25] *Sentinel-Record*, 13 August 1941.

[26] *Saturday Evening Post*, 20 July 1946, an article by Collie Small, "The Town Without a Lid," p. 23.

[27] Ibid.

[28] Francis J. Scully, *Hot Springs Arkansas and Hot Springs National Park*, p. 305.

[29] *Sentinel-Record*, 15 August 1941.

side of Lake Catherine, were trucked in daily to fill the labor gap.

Television news commentator Tom Brokaw wrote of this time in his book, *The Greatest Generation*. Surviving the worst Depression in history and fighting a world-wide war would be a difficult argument to suggest that it wasn't the greatest generation in history. It humbles those who were a part of it or even on its fringe. It left indelible impressions on all of us.

The war forever changed the outlook of citizens of the Spa. A new generation of leaders would be coming home at the war's end and with new ideas and different views of what was good and bad for the Spa. And, they were tough as boot leather from hard combat. They had faced the best the Axis forces could throw at them head-on and had prevailed. They no longer feared or would be intimidated by a corrupt local political machine.

THE AIRPORT AND LUCILLE, A LADY SCORN'D

There were two things in the first half of the 1940s that would affect and dominate the life of Leo P. McLaughlin. One was an airport, the other, as might be expected, was a woman. Both afforded him pleasure and both would become a source of anguish.

In 1941 a joint committee from the Junior Chamber of Commerce and the Chamber of Commerce appeared before a special called meeting of the city council. Joe McRae, Hot Springs businessman, spoke for the combined committee and outlined a plan that would enable the Spa to get federal funds to build a Class III airport. Up until this time a small dirt-runway field located west of town had served as the only airport near the city. It really consisted only of a small hanger and two short runways or landing strips. Initially it was known as Marsh Field, after the owners of the property, but was more recently referred to as Stover Field, after Johnnie Stover who was a pioneer in aviation in the Spa area.

Johnnie Stover was born at England, Arkansas in 1902, and had been involved in aviation since 1922. He had purchased a World War surplus Jenny bi-plane, and had rebuilt it. At the time he had never flown and prevailed on an early aviator, K.E. "Doc" Yoder, of Stuttgart, Arkansas for flying lessons. He was a quick-study as after only three hours flying time, he soloed.[1]

He had come to the Spa and organized a small flying service and during WW II, taught flying lessons to young men before they headed off to war.

McRae's committee urged the council to accept the sponsorship of this project, citing the city would not be obligated financially "but would only have to sponsor the construction of the flying field as required by WPA and CAA provisions."[2] It also would have to acquire additional land adjoining the present landing field and a bond issue could finance that expense. The government was to construct the airport with a design already approved and consisting of two concrete-runways, each 6,000 feet long and 150 feet wide. The estimated cost was $2,000,000.[3] The council approved the resolution and agreed to lease the property to the Junior and Senior Chambers of Commerce for 20 years.[4]

At the beginning of the airport project, Mayor Leo P. McLaughlin remained low-key and almost uninterested. He didn't push the project, but he didn't oppose it either. Leo wasn't into flying. In fact during his entire life he never

---

[1] *The Record*, "John Henry Stover, Airport Manager," by Lewis Stephens, p. 113.
[2] *Sentinel-Record*, 5 March 1941.
[3] Ibid., 20 February 1941.
[4] Ibid., 5 March 1941.

ook flight in an aircraft.[5] Within a year, however, his attitude and enthusiasm oward the airport was to change and he was "to put his shoulder to the wheel," becoming its greatest backer to made sure it reached completion.

Leo's change of attitude came in June 1942, when he arrived at a city-council meeting, unaware that senior councilman, and long-time friend and supporter, Frank N. Moody had called a special meeting early without notifying His Honor, the Mayor. McLaughlin was informed the council, on basis of Moody's recommendation, had voted unanimously and without debate, to name the new airfield, McLaughlin Field.[6] In elementary school this type of behavior on the part of students would be referred to as "apple polishing," or trying to please or curry favoritism of the teacher. In adult circles it was referred to in more vulgar terms. With teachers, sometimes it worked and sometimes it didn't. In this case, it worked.

Leo was more than pleased, even flattered, at the thought he'd always be remembered by the airport bearing his name. "He was the proudest man I ever saw," said Municipal Judge Ledgerwood, "but I believed at the time he was making a mistake in letting the council do that."[7]

The reaction to the council's precipitous resolution when the news came out was loud and swift. So loud it came as a surprise not only to the Mayor but to the councilmen. As the *Arkansas Gazette* reported, "A storm of protest arose."

Several petitions began to circulate. Appeals by various citizens of the Spa were made to U.S. Senators John McClellan and William Fulbright and to Congressman W.F. Norrell, but to no avail. The Washington politicians, all Democrats, needed the support the Garland County machine could furnish and were not inclined to affront the powerful mayor by intervening. They merely passed the buck by referring the matter to the CAA and leaving the decision squarely up to that agency. The CAA refused to become the "whipping-boy" of the controversy and issued a statement to the effect it did not matter to them what name was given the airport.[8] As far as Leo was concerned that was final.

The mayor was blinded by the prospect of the honor and instead of trying to avoid a political pitfall, failed to consider withdrawing his name from the project, believing the outcry would die down. Again the *Gazette* reported the continuing dissension, "Friends told him he had made a mistake," but Leo's ego refused to allow him to listen. And the furor did die down as predicted by

---

[5] *Arkansas Gazette*, 20 April 1947.

[6] *New Era*, 12 June 1942. Also, *Arkansas Gazette*, 20 1947.

[7] LAT - Ledgerwood. Verne Ledgerwood further commented that he believed if Leo P. McLaughlin had taken the lead by refusing to allow his name on the field and had suggested it be named in honor of the fighting men, the city possibly would have "raised a statute in his honor." Quite possibly!

[8] *Arkansas Gazette*, 20 April 1947.

McLaughlin, but it continued to fester like an untreated wound.

McLaughlin took an active part in overseeing the airport project. When any problem developed to slow down the work he was quick to find out the source of the trouble and try to correct it. For two years during the construction of the airport little was said about the name, McLaughlin Field but as work neared completion and like an unwanted relative, the old issue returned. By this time hundreds of service men had returned home and more were arriving daily. They became caught up in the controversy over the name of the field.

Even before the field was dedicated, the Army Transport began landing large hospital planes bringing patients to the Army-Navy General Hospital for treatment. A special equipped fire truck was assigned to the field but having no quarters there, was housed in an old building at Albert Pike and Summer Streets, and would be notified of the arrival of each plane and be on hand when it landed.[9]

Dedication of the airport was scheduled for 20 November 1946. Alderman Frank N. Moody, who had started the controversy in naming the airport prematurely, was appointed the over-all chairman of the event by Mayor McLaughlin. Because the celebration and dedication services were so large it was broken down into five separate sections, each having a sub-chairman. There were the events leading up to the parade, the parade itself, the dedication, an air show and closing out were parties and dances planned at the Arlington.[10] A distinguished flyer, Earl Ricks was placed in charge of the dedication service. In a way this was unusual, inasmuch as Earl Ricks was in partnership with Raymond Clinton, an out-spoken critic of the mayor. Ricks was quite well-known and had flown the Japanese officials to the World War II surrender and signing on board the battleship Missouri.

A contest was held to select a queen for the event and the daughter of Mr and Mrs. Clyde Wilson, Hettie Lou, a junior at Hot Springs High School, won. The number of speakers and celebrities invited for the event was impressive. Outstanding speakers included Governor Ben Laney, Senator John McClellan and Congressman W.F. Norrell. Several movie stars had been invited, Lum and Abner and Dick Powell, but failed to attend. Officials with Delta Airlines and their number-one stewardess, Miss Frances Galbo, crowned "Miss American Aviation of 1946," were scheduled to fly in for the festivities, but failed to arrive as their plane was grounded at Memphis because of low cloud cover.

By proclamation Mayor McLaughlin set November 20 to be a full holiday for Hot Springs, even the schools were included, which Leo generally forgot

---

[9] *Sentinel-Record - New Era*, Mail-It-Away Edition, February 1942.
[10] Ibid., 20 November 1946.

hen proclaiming a holiday. Oh, the plans were for a grand day.

But all was not serene and happy in McLaughlin's "kingdom." As the date or the dedication neared, a sudden movement in the form of petitions was made asking the name of McLaughlin Field be changed to Hot Springs Memorial Airport in memory of those from the county who had given their ves in World War II.[11] The spokesman for the petition takers was automobile ealer, Raymond Clinton, who said at that time more than 2,100 residents of he area had signed the forms.

Clinton was quoted, "We have no intention of trying to handicap or mar the edication, but the people had no voice in naming our airport. It was done by McLaughlin controlled city council.

"The Hot Springs Chamber of Commerce and Junior Chamber of Commerce are responsible for the airport and not Leo McLaughlin. The city ouncil merely paved the way for an election to vote a bond issue for purchase of the site. This has been one civic campaign that has needed no pressure whatsoever. People have been coming to sign the petitions and also elephoning asking where they could get one to sign."[12]

As expected by everyone who was acquainted with Leo P. McLaughlin, a eply was forthcoming--and how! Leo said, "The first petition had not been n circulation fifteen minutes until friends telephoned me about it. Other riends called at my office to personally inform me."[13]

He then went on the attack, "The man who has been the instigator of these petitions is Raymond Clinton. He is *my most bitter political enemy."* This condemnation placed Raymond Clinton in a select group of well-known men. Judge Scott Wood, had once been portrayed by Leo McLaughlin, as "my most bitter political enemy." For years when things went awry Leo would blame it on Scott Wood. He had also accorded the distinction of "my most bitter enemy," to Orlando Sumpter and Sidney Nutt and Cleveland Smith and Richard Craigo. He would later bestow this "honor" upon Sidney McMath.

But in his bitterness toward Clinton he appeared to rise above the controversy, appealing to the public, "So let's keep it (the airport) out of politics. No one is more sincere than I am in favoring a lasting testimonial to those men of Garland county who made the supreme sacrifice in World War II."

Imagine the most political person in Garland County pleading to keep the airport out of politics. In his statement he downplayed the participation of the Chamber of Commerce and the Junior Chamber of Commerce and bragged on the part of the city Administration, meaning himself, had in the project.

---

[11] *New Era*, 11 November 1946.
[12] *Sentinel-Record*, 11 November 1946.
[13] *Sentinel-Record*, 12 November 1946.

And then forgetting *Public Opinion's* label of him, the "Big I Am," he began "I am proud that I personally, day and night for several days, played a important and persistent part in getting the government to begin constructic of the airport. Fortunately, my good friend President Truman, then Unite States Senator, was here in Hot Springs at that time. I saw him and he glad agreed to help us. I also personally contacted Congressman W.F. Norre Senator John McClellan and senators from other states who I know, togeth with other Washington officials and very influential friends in private life, an they all agreed to aid us, and did so."[14] There you have it--Leo's explanatic for why the name of McLaughlin Field should not be renamed in memory c those from Garland County who had died in the war. And shabbily, n mention of the participation of the two organizations who really got th project off the ground to begin with, the Chamber of Commerce and Junic Chamber Of Commerce. He had been of considerable help, but not the enti show.

But Leo had a solution to the controversy. Just leave the name unchange and create a "larger beautiful monument to cost not less than $25,000, and would like to see and would personally welcome the placing of such monument at the airport." He then personally challenged Raymond Clinto to "circulate new petitions and raise $20,000, and I will personally guarante the remaining $5,000."[15]

In the event the readers have difficulty in believing Leo's suggestion did nc bring a "storm of protest," we suggest that they read the letters to the edite of the local and state papers for the few days following his statement. Or started, "Dear Sir: Big hearted old Mayor Leo. He really wants t commemorate our local boys who gave their lives in World War II. To prov it, he has made a very generous proposition--one which will honor these me and at the same time pay homage to the man who says he alone is responsib for the prosperity of Hot Springs and for the realization of our $2,000,00 airport, namely himself."

The writer of that letter had her own counter proposal, "That we name th $2,000,000 airport for our war dead. Then, if Leo will raise $20,000, let th citizens donate an additional $5,000, and erect a monument to him, not at th airport, but either in front of one of the local gambling establishments, c before the municipal auditorium whose construction he has blocked." Mar agreed.

Another person wrote that since race horses and a race had been named i honor of Leo P. McLaughlin why not change the name of the City of Hc

[14] Ibid.
[15] Ibid.

prings to "McLaughlintown," or "McLaughlinville."[16]

Raymond Clinton's response to the mayor was swift in coming as he told eporters, "Leo McLaughlin issued a typical harangue to the press last night. requires little comment.

"No one but a Leo P. McLaughlin could step on that field and dedicate the irport to himself. He takes credit for causing it to be built, but the Hot prings Chamber of Commerce and the Junior Chambers of Commerce carted the project and the United States government built it on government ioney and hundreds of our boys died so that it would remain American. Our itizens know this."[17]

More people came by the Clinton Buick Agency to sign the petitions.

Five days before the dedication was to take place, a large advertisement ppeared in the *Sentinel-Record.* It was from Raymond Clinton, "Chairman of usiness Committee to Change Name of Airport."

In large black print the notice read, **OVER 5,000 CITIZENS DEMAND 'HAT LEO McLAUGHLIN CALL A SPECIAL MEETING TO)ETERMINE THE WISHES OF THE PEOPLE IN RE-NAMING 'HE HOT SPRINGS MUNICIPAL AIRPORT. WHAT ARE YOU ;OING TO DO LEO?**[18]

Citizens of the Spa eagerly scanned their morning and evening papers to earn what the mayor's reaction might be to the demand. But alas, city hall was s quiet as a graveyard at midnight. Rumors slipping out and afloat in the ommunity indicated the mayor was using some very descriptive and nflattering remarks, liberally sprinkled with four letter words, as to Raymond Clinton's ancestry.

Leo probably was fearful that some disturbance might mar his "big-day," but verything went smoothly and after the parade, ceremonies and air-show he ndoubtedly breathed easier. McLaughlin Field had been dedicated and Leo's ame was cemented into the building and the marble floor in the large lobby. The work had been done by marble craftsman Harry Crumbaugh. Crumbaugh xpected the design to be permanently implanted and had worked toward that nd. Or was it permanent? Only six months later Crumbaugh would be vishing he hadn't done such a good job as he slowly chiseled the name and lesign from solid concrete, as we shall see.

McLaughlin was about ready for another serious relationship. He was at an ge where he no longer attracted young women as he once had. Since his

---

[16] *Sentinel-Record,* 15 November 1946, "From the People," column. The remark oncerning the construction of the city auditorium referred to a proposed bond issue several of he civic clubs tried to sponsor. McLaughlin said he was not opposed to it, but worked behind he scene until the backers got disgusted and discouraged and quit.

[17] *New Era,* 12 November 1946.

[18] *Sentinel-Record,* 15 November 1946.

divorce from Florence he had been seen only occasionally in the company
some young woman and then for only one or two dates. His past reputatic
had labeled him as a "womanizer," and most were not willing to risk being
his company. He had reached a point that he began hanging out with Edd
Cockburn, a teller at the Arkansas Trust Company. Cockburn was the son
the late Thomas Cockburn and his widow, Zeulian, who had owned ar
operated the Ostrich Farm on Whittington. Eddie was quite a bit younger th
Leo, and still resided with his mother as did McLaughlin.

Cockburn probably would never have run for alderman from the Fifth Wa
without the assurance from Leo P. McLaughlin that he could be elected.
vacancy had occurred and a word from the Mayor saw the local politic
machine throw its support to Cockburn and he won handily.

But in August 1941 Leo found himself in love again. He had just got
glimpse of his dream girl. She had been walking on Central Avenue ne
Knox's Pharmacy in the 500 block. Leo always had an eye for beauty and
had spotted the young lady twice before and both times in that vicinity and
had been on the prowl trying to find out who she was and where she worke
As he saw her start down the sidewalk he hastened his pace--she wouldn't g
away this time.

The young woman was 25-year-old Verna Lucille Griffith. Mo
acquaintances called her Lucille, but a few of her closest friends referred to h
as "Susie." She had been born in Oklahoma and had lived there until Augu
1941, when she was transferred by the Rosenthall-Ackerman Company
manager of the millinery department at Kempner Shoe Store at 420 Centr
Avenue in Hot Springs.[19]

Lucille was a "head turner," or as the "boys" around the police statio
referring to the Mayor's girl friend would say, she's a "looker." She was ta
slender, and carried herself well. She had brown shoulder-length hair, da
eyes and full lips.

She had been married once to Robert E. Lee Jones in Oklahoma, howev
the marriage lasted only a few months and she reclaimed her maiden name.

When she arrived in Hot Springs, she had lived for awhile with Herbert ar
Thelma Day on Hagen Street. Herbert Day was manager of Kempner's ar
his wife Thelma sometimes worked in the store. Later Lucille had a
apartment at 904 Quapaw Avenue.

---

[19] Lucille Griffith, Plaintiff, v. Leo McLaughlin, Defendant, Civil Action File # 28
District Court of the United States, Western District of Arkansas, Hot Springs Divisio
Hereinafter cited as Griffith vs. McLaughlin. This is a very voluminous file having copies of n
only the filings but complete transcript and testimony of the Plaintiff, Defendant and Witne
Thanks to the local district court clerk's office, the file was located in the National Archiv
Depository at Fort Worth, Texas. It is a treasure trove of information.

[20] Ibid. From the testimony of Lucille Griffith, p. 48.

Lucille Griffith

When the mayor saw Lucille Griffith turn into Kempner's Shoe Store and disappear behind a curtain in the rear he knew he had located her place of employment. McLaughlin occasionally bought men's hose and Florsheim shoes there and was slightly acquainted with Herbert Day and his wife. When he entered the store that morning he saw Day near the front conversing with a customer. Seeing no one else, but hearing typing coming from beyond the curtain he strode toward the rear and pulled the cloth aside--what line would he use if the girl of his dreams was behind the curtain?

Lucille Griffith was seated in front of a typewriter when Leo pulled the curtain open and for the first time she laid eyes on His Honor the Mayor, Leo P. McLaughlin.

"Pardon me," Leo said, "but I have told at least 25 people that you have the most gorgeous hair of any girl in America."[21]

Corny? Perhaps. But it worked. McLaughlin invited the woman out to lunch and she accepted. A courtship developed between the 55-year-old mayor and the 25-year-old woman. Leo would pick up Lucille in his little black 1936 Chevrolet coupe or the blue Powerflite Packard he had purchased for his third wife Florence and which he had refused to give up. They took drives and were seen that fall at several Trojan football games. They dined at Belvedere and the Southern Club. McLaughlin showed Lucille off at two fashionable New Years dances at the Arlington Hotel.[22] In the spring he gave Lucille passes to

---

[21] *Arkansas Democrat*, 14 July 1946.

[22] *NewEra*, 1 January 1943. Also, Griffith v. McLaughlin, Case # 280, from testimony of both Griffith and McLaughlin.

Oaklawn and she met him there for the races. She accompanied him to the American Legion Club where he delivered a speech and to some function at the Armory, where he gave another address.

Lucille would later testify that Leo came by her apartment almost every night of the week. McLaughlin's memory was that it was only "one or two times a week, or possibly three."[23]

Lucille would recall Leo brought liquor to her apartment and both drank. Leo would deny he drank anything but Mountain Valley Water. She said as their relationship became more serious Leo gave her a nice cedar chest, "To put my trousseau in." He began to give her presents of money "for my birthday and my Christmas."[24] He gave her chocolates and sent flowers and corsages, dish towels and blankets. The only thing Leo denied about this was he had never said the cedar chest was for her "trousseau." And, he gave her more money, "a lot of money," Lucille said, an unMcLaughlin trait, as Leo was known to be tight, however he admitted doing this. He could not recall the largest amount he gave her at any one time, but said the smallest gift was "at least $25 or $30." Lucille began depositing the money into a passbook savings account establishing a record of the times he gave her gifts.

And the mayor presented the young woman three pictures of himself, one inscribed, "From Leo, with Love." She later testified McLaughlin called her at work several times during the day and when he was out of town on business or attending horse shows in Memphis, St. Louis and Chicago, he telephoned her.[25] Leo never denied this.

According to Lucille Griffith she believed Leo McLaughlin to be a wealthy man. He had once driven her about town, pointing out business buildings and property he owned. He confided he had once invested $35,000 in the 7-Up Company in St. Louis and received dividends from his investment. He claimed to "Have money in lock boxes all over the country."

She admitted having accompanied the mayor to several gambling houses and actually seeing gamblers come up to, and without explanation, hand Leo P. McLaughlin folded money on several occasions. This, of course, confirmed what two of his previous wives had said. McLaughlin would deny he ever received money from the gambling community. But Leo was known to bend the truth a bit at his convenience. She related being with McLaughlin when he stopped in front of the Southern Club and a man came out who was introduced to her as "Owney Madden." She said this happened often.

In trying to impress Lucille, Leo showed her a fountain pen with a little watch on the end of it which he kept in his lock box. He told her Al Capone

---

[23] Griffith v. McLaughlin, Case # 280.

[24] Ibid.

[25] Ibid. From testimony of Lucille Griffith, p. 29-32.

ad given him the pen. This, too, was another confirmation of what Florence ad testified to several years before.

Also, he told her he had known Alvin Karpis who had hid out in Hot prings from federal agents. Leo, of course, would later deny he had said this.

For almost three years Leo McLaughlin and Lucille Griffith kept company o some degree, based on who was telling the story. McLaughlin downplayed ow much time he spent with Lucille. She, on the other hand was able to lescribe numerous dates and outings and had kept newspaper clippings and nenus of the places they went. She said she was led to believe Leo wanted and ntended to marry her. She and Leo had agreed they would be married by October 1, 1944, but the year had not been very good to McLaughlin. There vere delays.

First, Leo's mother, Bridget Russell McLaughlin, passed away on 8 July 1944, only ten days shy of her ninety-fifth birthday. This was a definite blow o the mayor. He had been extremely close to his Mother and had valued her opinion on various matters.[26]

Then on December 1, Leo lost his elder brother, John William, who was 68 years old.[27] It would later be proven in court that Lucille had sent flowers to both funerals.

Leo had been in this relationship longer than he had ever had with any other women except his mother and sisters. He was not enjoying the pressure that was beginning to build up as Lucille pressed him for a date on marriage and he tried to cool it. Lucille, on the other hand was "humiliated," and "embarrassed," at friends and customers "always asking me when we were going to get married." She gave McLaughlin an ultimatum. She told him she had to take a transfer to handle a larger department and when he got ready to marry her he could come after her.[28]

The date came and went without any sign McLaughlin intended to marry Lucille. She went home for the holidays and stayed longer than Leo had anticipated. He suddenly became frantic, calling her and "crying and told her he had found out she was not returning to Hot Springs and that they were 'through.'"

She did return to Hot Springs about January 1, 1945 and continued to work at Kempner's. McLaughlin now remained aloof, sometimes refusing to return her calls. On February 22, Lucille received a very vile and unsigned letter which unnerved her. She suspected the anonymous letter to have been written by the Mayor's sister, Stella. She came to that conclusion by comparing the handwriting on the letter to two "Thank You" notes she had received for

---

[26] LAT-Ledgerwood.

[27] *Caruth Funeral Home Records*, p. 104.

[28] Griffith v. McLaughlin, U.S. District Court, Case # 280, p. 42.

sending flowers to Bridget's and Will's funerals. Stella had the reputation about town of being very protective of her brother, Leo, and when she learned someone had voted against him there were cases when she had called the voter up and let them know of "their transgression" and informed them the Administration was aware of it and would be watching. Over the years she had become known locally as the "Enforcer."[29] But as we have observed in the past, Stella had been a trouble-maker when it came to Leo and his wives or girlfriends.She was always going to interfere. So, Lucille probably was right on target when she believed Stella had written the unsigned letter.[30]

Lucille wanted to confront Leo McLaughlin with the evidence and did reach him by phone, however he refused to meet her and permit her to show him the letter. At this point in their relationship Leo was not going to allow Lucille the opportunity of accusing his family of anything. He was always protective of all members of the McLaughlin clan. And, Lucille was about to make a mistake--a big mistake!

Determined to show the letter to Leo, she called for a taxi. She told the driver, Emory Denton, to drive by "Jack McJunkin's place" the Tower Club. When she saw that Leo's car was not there she directed the driver down Central Avenue past several clubs and still not locating the mayor or his car she instructed the driver to take her to the McLaughlin home at Malvern and Grand.[31]

Lucille never expected to gain entrance inside the mayor's home even if he was there. She had gone with him over three years and had been in the house only once and that was the kitchen. She had gone there with Herbert and Thelma Day at Leo's invitation to view his horses in the stables at the rear of the house. Afterwards, McLaughlin invited them to step inside the kitchen and have a Coca-Cola. But that was as far as they got. The McLaughlin family simply did not entertain--anyone.

It was between 8:30 and 9:00 p.m. when the cab Lucille was in stopped in front of the McLaughlin home near the driveway. She saw Hot Springs Police Officer W.D. Stephens up the mayor's driveway and got out. Stephens had an unusual job on the police force. He was assigned to guard the mayor's property or act as a night watchman even though he was on duty for the city and drawing a salary from the Hot Springs Police Department. When questioned on the witness stand later he had to admit he spent most of his

---

[29] LAT-Jimmy Dowds, and other sources.

[30] And there were times Stella had caused Leo problems. She was said to be a kleptomaniac, taking small things from stores without paying for them. Leo had an agreement with most store managers in town that in the event she took anything not to confront her but call him and he would pay for the item. Kress and Woolworth had a policy of assigning an employee to watch her once she entered their stores.

[31] Griffith v. McLaughlin, pp. 86-87.

luty shift around the mayor's property although his assigned beat was the Malvern Avenue area, but admitted he was unaware of any other officers being ssigned to other neighborhoods.

Lucille asked Stephens if the mayor was home. He told her he wasn't and he said she would wait for him. The officer did not encourage her to wait, aying, "He don't want nobody to bother him up here because he has told me o."[32]

She was sitting in the cab when Leo McLaughlin drove in his driveway. Lucille jumped out of the car and "hollered at him," and when he saw her he lrove off.[33] Leo went straight to the city hall and called a fireman over and nstructed what he should tell the police. The fireman stepped back to the police department and told them, "The Mayor says a cab is blocking his lriveway and to move it." Commissioner Weldon Raspberry dispatched officers W.A. "Bill" Abbott and O.D. Griffin. After they had left, Raspberry lso decided he had better go out that way.

According to officer Abbott, when they arrived, Lucille was sitting in the cab vaiting for Leo to come home. The other officer testified she was "standing n the driveway, reeling around like she might be kinda intoxicated or omething." Abbott said they took Lucille out of the taxi; Griffin said he tried o get her "in the police car and she didn't want to go."

While the officers, and later Raspberry, would all remember and testify the voman began to curse them, they were divided in their opinion where Lucille vas when they arrived. None of the officers would say they smelled alcohol on her breath but all indicated she "acted as if she was drunk." She denied cursing the officers or that she had been drinking, although she admitted having had a glass of wine with her evening meal several hours earlier.

The officers took Lucille to the station and according to Abbott, Griffin and Raspberry, she gave them "a good cussing." They all testified they believed she vas drunk and they all testified she said she was going to "kill that Leo McLaughlin."[34]

The attorney later representing Lucille could not understand Hot Springs ustice as he later questioned the officers, "So after all that brawl and lrunkeness and a threat against the mayor you took her home."[35] The attorney pointed out that the cab driver was in control of the taxi and allegedly had parked his vehicle blocking the mayor's driveway and the officers made no offer to arrest him for "committing a misdemeanor." The reason given by one

---

[32] Ibid. Testimony of W.D. Stephens, p. 158.
[33] Ibid., p. 97.
[34] Ibid., p. 171.
[35] Ibid., p. 173.

of the officers was, "We didn't have any orders to arrest *him*"[36] Whose orders? Who had "ordered" the arrest of Lucille Griffith, but not the cab driver? Raspberry said he just ordered the car blocking the driveway to be moved.

Strange! It was just as if the mayor had said, "Scare her as I don't want anything more to do with her." And scare her, they did. Lucille realized she could not win in Hot Springs and returned to Oklahoma where she had a nervous breakdown requiring medical treatment and was unable to work for a while. It would take her a year to re-establish her residence in Oklahoma.

It appeared as if Leo McLaughlin had once again escaped scot-free from one of his escapades. He had had his fun and had got rid of someone who was beginning to be a problem for him. Like the thief, he'd stolen the milk, but had not bought the cow. But, he apparently had never read William Congreve's *The Mourning Bride*, and an excerpt relating to his situation:

"Heav'n has no rage, like love to hatred turn'd,
Nor Hell a fury, like a woman scorn'd"

And Lucille believed she had been scorned.

As the months passed other problems required Leo's attention, the construction and naming of the airport and returning G.I.s who believed changes were in order and who questioned the legality of the voting system as interpreted by the McLaughlin political machine. Leo's thoughts were as far from Lucille Griffith as possible as he tried to save his nineteen-year-old regime as the G.I. reform movement petitioned the federal court to throw out hundreds of poll tax receipts illegally obtained.

Leo McLaughlin had just received the bad news, for him, that the United States District Court had just thrown out 1,607 poll tax receipts or 24 percent of the largest vote ever recorded in Garland County when he received a call from the night editor of the *New Era*, Roy Bosson.

"Mayor," Bosson asked, "Are you aware you are being sued for breach-of-promise by Lucille Griffith in the sum of $200,000?"

McLaughlin had not heard of the suit and in typical McLaughlin fashion began blaming and castigating everyone but himself.

"This suit is purely blackmail and politics. The plaintiff in the suit left Hot Springs over a year and a half ago, and I have not seen her since. I cannot see where the filing of the suit at this time will convince the voters that the reform candidates are qualified to hold public office."[37]

The Mayor continued his tirade and insisted the paper print his statement. Bosson was afraid if he published everything McLaughlin was saying, especially concerning Lucille's attorneys, and it being "a frivolous lawsuit and political blackmail," his newspaper might be sued for libel. He called his

---

[36] Ibid., testimony of W.A. Abbott, p. 174.
[37] *Sentinel-Record*, 12 July 1946.

ublisher, C.E. Palmer and informed him what had occurred. Clyde Palmer, who was generally supportive of the McLaughlin Administration, thought a ew moments and told Bosson. "Make up a statement as to what the Mayor vants to say and have him sign it. Print it, and then lock it in the office safe." Bosson complied with those instructions and carried the statement to Leo McLaughlin, who signed it. The Night Editor safely locked away the tatement. Two nights later, while he and his wife were at the movies their ouse was broken into and ransacked. Bosson said that every drawer had been ntered and various papers were strewn about, but nothing was taken. He said e believed someone was there trying to recover the statement Leo McLaughlin had signed.[38]

Leo had blustered that the breach-of-promise suit was nothing but political moke and that as soon as the elections were over it would be dropped. It vasn't.

He predicted then that the same attorneys which had taken the Administration into Federal Court over the poll tax controversy would be the ame ones to try the breach-of-promise suit.[39] Wrong again! Frank Crouch, Frank Eagin and Rutherford Brett, a reputable firm of attorneys from Oklahoma represented Lucille Griffith and appeared with her in court.[40]

Lucille would have her day in court and she would cause Leo P. McLaughlin ome anxious and uncomfortable moments, but the deck was stacked against er. She never had a chance. Talk about being "snake-bit."

First, her lead attorney, Frank Crouch had a severe stroke and was ncapacitated and unable to attend the trial. He had done most of the ground vork or preparation and had to turn the file over to Eagin and Brett.[41]

Next, as Frank Eagin was traveling to the trial aboard the "Rocket" when the rain derailed in a very bad accident near Dardanelle and several persons were eriously injured. Eagin was slightly injured but very "shaken" by the xperience." His cohort, Rutherford Brett, had elected to travel to the trial by utomobile. When he reached Russellville he learned of the train's mishap and vas given erroneous information that the injured had been taken to hospitals n Fort Smith. He retraced that seventy miles only to learn that Brett had been aken to Little Rock. Setting off once again, his car broke down and repairs vere required and he got to the trial late. That should have been all the

---

[38] LAT-Bosson. He also told this writer he had no doubt that his home had been urglarized in an attempt to get back the libelous statement and thought he knew who the man vas, his initials, "E.W."

[39] *Sentinel-Record*, 12 July 1946.

[40] *Arkansas Democrat*, 12 July 1946.

[41] Lucille Griffith v. Leo McLaughlin. Application For Continuance, 2 April 1947. The ourt denied the continuance, 9 April 1947. It is interesting to note that the defense had equested a continuance several months earlier and it had been granted.

misadventures of those trying to assist Lucille Griffith in her trial, however, it was only the beginning.

Only a few days before the trial the defendants had wanted to take the deposition of Johnny Clements, a cab driver who Lucille believed to be totally on her side. Her attorneys had agreed and stipulated it would not be necessary for them to make the long trip--a mistake. They permitted Leo McLaughlin's attorneys, Grover Owens and Richard Ryan, to take the sworn statement without anyone being there to represent Lucille's interest. Clement was incapacitated and unable to be in court and his deposition, not surprising to anyone perhaps but Lucille, turned out to be totally pro-McLaughlin. Even if Clements had wanted to help Lucille, he was not in a position to do so. All businesses, especially taxicab companies, were regulated by the city and had to obtain special permits for assigned loading areas and locations on Central Avenue and around the depots. Clements just could not afford to have Leo McLaughlin unhappy with him. To top it off the recording secretary was none other than Hazel Marsh, loyal and faithful secretary to His Honor the Mayor.[42] Lucille's attorneys acceded to this as "no objection."

Those people who had been acquainted with the George McLaughlin trial fifteen years earlier and who were aware how the witnesses in that trial suddenly and quickly disappeared probably suffered a flashback as the breach-of-promise trial started. It seems that the two people, Herbert and Thelma Day, Lucille had most counted on to support her "had suddenly been called out of town on a family illness." Even the U.S. Marshal's office was unable to locate them for the trial.[43]

And that was not all that went awry for Lucille and her attorneys. They had subpoenaed the mayor's sister, Stella McLaughlin (Snyder) to question her concerning the anonymous letter Lucille had received, and when her name was called to take the witness stand the court learned, "Stella is confined to her bed under the doctor's care." The subpoena had been served on her and she had taken ill and gone to bed. McLaughlin's defense attorneys had a handwritten statement, indicating Stella was in no condition to testify, written on plain paper, no letterhead, signed by Dr. Alex Benedict.[44]

"Isn't Dr. Benedict the defendant's cousin?" asked one of Lucille's lawyers. Wrong question!

"No, he isn't." Truthfully answered Leo's attorney, Grover Owens. Of course Benedict wasn't Leo's cousin. He was closely related to Leo's sister-in-law, Fannie Benedict McLaughlin! Was the old adage, "Blood is thicker than

---

[42] Ibid. Transcript of Clements Deposition and "Certificate." 23 April 1946. The trial began the next day.

[43] Ibid. Statement of Attorney Frank Eagin, entered into the court record, p. 117-118

[44] Ibid. p. 124.

water," applicable here? We leave that to the reader's opinion.

The court accepted the doctor's certificate and Lucille lost another witness.

Then to cap it off, the jury was seated without a single woman on the panel. Twelve married men composed the jury. Even back then women served on juries, but they were carefully screened off of that one--there would be no sympathy for Lucille from that quarter.

Despite the uphill fight a good effort was made by Lucille's attorneys. They introduced such character witnesses as Bill Seiz, Jr. and Dr. E.A. Purdum, both well-known and reputable men, and who testified having seen Lucille at various public functions and that "she had always conducted herself as a lady." The point was however, Lucille had no one as a witness that heard her and Leo McLaughlin discussing plans for marriage. That is not all that unusual as few men are going to propose to a woman with people in the room and most wedding plans are made discreetly between the expectant bride and groom. The jury found Leo P. McLaughlin not guilty of breach-of-promise.[45]

Lucille Griffith's attorneys filed a "Motion For a New Trial," objecting to the verdict as being "contrary to the evidence" and that the "Court erred in refusing to admit competent and material evidence," and preventing the "plaintiff from having a fair and impartial trial." The Court overruled the motion and denied a new trial.[46]

Leo's luck had still held and he was a free man, although many people about town did not doubt he had led Lucille Griffith "down the prim-rose path," and in to believing he intended to marry her. That was just Leo's way.

---

[45] Ibid. Verdict filed 24 April 1947 by Truss Russell, clerk.

[46] Ibid. Order filed 5 May 1947.

THE THRILL OF VICTORY AND THE AGONY OF DEFEAT

V-J Day at Hot Springs was repeated thousands of times throughout the country. People were ecstatic, relieved and overjoyed the war was over. They rushed onto their porches and into the yards waving and talking excitedly to their neighbors. With the ending of hostilities the need to conserve the gasoline in the old car did not seem important any longer and people piled into their vehicles and began driving up and down the streets blowing their horns and waving to friends. The streets filled up quickly with people on foot and in automobiles. Soldiers on leave and those who were ambulatory flooded down the hill from the Army & Navy General Hospital to join the celebration. Some of the soldiers were wildly waving fifths of whiskey, stopping cars and offering the occupants a drink. It was August 14, 1945 and schools had not reopened from the summer vacations and many of us who were in high school took sandwiches, chips and soft drinks to the parks and on the mountains and picnicked. From the observation shed on West Mountain we could plainly hear the horns of cars downtown and the pealing of the bells from St. John's. They said the celebration in Times Square in New York went on for four days. It was over! The war had ended and those of us who were approaching draft age could relax and change the direction of our plans from entering the military service to continuing our education. With the birthing of the atomic bomb and the ending of the war, the world would never be the same.

Late in 1945 and early in 1946 a steady flow of returning war veterans was welcomed home to the Spa. Some had been gone only a year or two and had to wait a little longer as those who had been in four or five years and who had accumulated more service points were priority special and discharged early.

Changes had occurred during their absence. No town stands still. Each individual city is much like a living organism, growing, changing in size and shape and even dying. Sights, sounds and even smells change, too. It was no different in Hot Springs.

No longer was heard the clanging of the trolley's bell or the rumbling of its steel wheels on steel rails. It had been replaced by the roar of the gasoline powered engines of the city's new busses which left clouds of burnt fuel and fumes in its wake up and down the thoroughfares of the Spa. Another sound that would shortly disappear was the boom-boom of the Salvation Army's bass drum and the brass tones of its trumpet, trombone and the tinkling of its kettle bells and tambourines as its volunteers assembled just outside of Schneck's Drug store one night each week.

Over at the Rock Island and Missouri Pacific depots the once coal burning train engines were being replaced by diesel burning locomotives. The smell of coal smoke, once breathed-in by residents for blocks was replaced by fumes from the diesels.

There are probably few students of that era who attended Central Junior

High or Hot Springs High School, who do not recall those cool fall days when they were dismissed into the fresh air only to have their lungs filled with the odor of roasting coffee beans emanating from Cephus Edwards' Hot Springs Coffee Mill located on Market Street. The memory is still strong as were those roasting beans. And many may remember the pleasant odor of frying hamburgers, at noon at Ouachita and Central, coming from the Busy Bee Cafe where the cook stood in the window slicing onions and turning the beef patties for all to see.

But smells and odors were not confined to the downtown area--even the outlying neighborhoods had their own. In South Hot Springs, especially in the fall and winter, the sweet fragrance of cotton seed and its oil being extracted from loads of cotton arose from the T.J. Cook and Son, and McClard's cotton gins on Albert Pike. Because of the decline of cotton farming in Garland County and as fewer loads of cotton were received, these smells were being replaced by the tantalizing smell of burning hardwood and barbeque as the McClard family opened a family restaurant, situated between the two gins, which was destined to become a legend in the state. Others may recall the scent of fresh cut lumber and sawdust which sent their own distinctive odors from the sawmills on Valley Street and on the east side of town. Or the fresh peeled white-oak staves at Gibbs' keg and barrel mill on Malvern Avenue. And, out Oaklawn there were periods when it was difficult to ignore there was a racetrack and stables adjacent to Central Avenue, but generally they kept their property in a clean condition.

There were some constants, though. In the summer time, especially if there had been no rain for a long time, the pungent and sometimes offensive odor of Hot Springs Creek, wafting on the warm breeze would discourage people from sitting on their porches and enjoy visiting with their neighbors. Early morning downtown shoppers' nostrils were treated to daily bakery odors of fresh baked pies and donuts floating on gentle breezes from Oscar's or City's bakeries.

While Central Avenue had changed very little during the first half of the 1940s, there were noticeable differences the returning GIs noticed. In the old Gaines building was a new, all-night restaurant named the Steak & Shake. You couldn't miss it as it was totally decorated in black and white with bright flashing lights running around its large sign. Up on Ouachita, Woodcock and Lawson, a long-time favorite mercantile store had succumbed to "father time," and had been replaced by Baim's Department store, a small chain operation out of Pine Bluff.

Changes were taking place up on Park Avenue. As the soldiers were leaving early in the war a new restaurant had just opened, Phillips Drive-In. Its Willow Room was constructed around a large, beautiful willow tree, and the restaurant and dance floor quickly became a favorite eatery of the soldiers during the war. Vance's Bar-B-Q, located near the car barn, changed to Lewis' Drive-In. At the end of the old car line, Vance Bryan, opened a new five-story hotel, Jack Tar Court Hotel and the Jack Tar Resturant with its gaily decorated Rainbow Room.

Down at Grand and Central, the log building housing Clay Watt's rustic Pioneer Tavern had changed hands and was reopened as Coy's Steak House, named after its founder, Coy Theobalt. It was to become one of the classiest steak houses in the state.

There were other changes, too. Some of these were not readily noticeable and one had to be aware of the pre-war conditions as it pertained to the gambling community. It appears that following the death of W.S. Jacobs almost complete control of gambling fell into the hands of Mayor Leo P. McLaughlin and he no longer had the guidance and wisdom of the old "Boss Gambler," to advise him as to who should be permitted in the circle and who should not be. He was approached by various individuals wanting to open their own gaming establishment or horse book operation while Jacobs had never let over seven clubs to operate. It seems as if Leo was generally agreeable to grant these requests--for a fee, that is. If you wanted to play, you had to pay. McLaughlin was not as discriminating as Jacobs had been in doling out gaming permits. Several small black clubs located on Malvern Avenue were opened with Leo's blessing.

Walter Weldon had been a minor player in the Administration, doing odd jobs, filling up poll tax lists or acting as a runner for some of the clubs. He had operated poker and dice games at the Lone Star Bar and a horse book at the Milwaukee Bar. But, he wanted more and believing he had ingratiated himself in various ways approached McLaughlin with enough money which allowed him to open the Tulsa Club, a tavern and horse book at 421 Benton Street.[1]

Erb O. Wheatley, who had operated the Ozark Club at 514½ Central Avenue until Governor Homer Adkins' club-raiding caused him to close his doors, opened the Reno Club at 721½ Central.[2]

Also, Harry Foley, who had operated Club Avalon as a dinner restaurant and never had anything but a few slot machines in an alcove near the restrooms, got permission to open a horse book.[3]

The ownership and operation of the Southern Club had changed, too. After the "crackdown" of Governor Adkins ended those involved in the Southern were Otis McCraw, his brother Otho McCraw, Jimmy Phillips, Jack McJunkin, Owney Madden, George McLaughlin and Otis McCraw's son."[4] That club, as

---

[1] Grand Jury Report, "Receipts - Gambling Clubs - Year 1946." This report indicates that the 12-month period inspected saw The Tulsa Club gross $642,434.55.

[2] Ibid. The twelve-month gross for the Reno Club was $2,019,424.10.

[3] Ibid. In only three months of gambling, Avalon grossed $48,472.00 on the horse book and $4,000.00 on the slots. This club mysteriously burned one night.

[4] *Sentinel-Record*, 9 October 1947.

well as several others had instituted the game of Bingo, with large monetary prizes and which brought a lot of the "locals" out to play.

About the only change at city hall was the stepping down because of illness of City Attorney A.T. "Sonny" Davies, who had held that position since 1927.[5] He was succeeded by Jay M. Rowland who had no opposition and was machine backed in 1944.[6] Rowland, who had once opposed the City Administration, had apparently decided, "If you can't beat them, join them." It didn't take Rowland long to fit in with the "gang" and found himself hip-deep in trouble.

The workings of the political machine was another constant. For a city employee to hold his job or club owner to operate they were required to turn in lists of names for poll tax receipts. "It was essential," one club owner said.[7] That same gambler would also admit under oath, that a number of people's names appeared on the list who were not residents of Hot Springs. But why the big deal? Everyone knew how the system had operated ever since Leo McLaughlin had been elected mayor in 1927.

And Leo Patrick McLaughlin was a constant. If the Mayor had changed, he perhaps had become more arrogant and dictatorial with each passing year. He had reached a point by 1946 where he no longer believed he needed to consult the advice of stalwarts such as Verne Ledgerwood, A.T. "Sonny" Davies, W.E. Chester and Earl Witt, when special problems arose and sometimes found himself in difficulty. His ego blinded him to the fact that the ultimate power of his position, though corruptly used, actually lay in the hands of the voters, discounting the hundreds of illegal votes the Administration controlled. In an interview with an Eastern reporter he wrote, McLaughlin, "openly admitted his administration was morally and legally wrong and justified his policies, or tried to, on the basis that he was running a sporting town and the town must have gambling to exist."[8] McLaughlin probably did not recognize it at the time, but he had just set himself up for a fall–a big fall!

Sidney McMath had been born in Columbia County, near Magnolia, in south Arkansas, and had resided a short time near Smackover before his father, Hal, decided farming and oilfield work was not for him. The elder McMath moved his family to Hot Springs and took up a new career, barbering.

Sidney had attended local schools and had served as president of his freshman, sophomore, junior and senior classes. He had hoped to attend the

---

[5] A.T. "Sonny" Davies was born in 1888 and died 9 July 1956. His home was located on a small island in Lake Hamilton reached by a foot bridge. In later years it became known as Anthony Island and a motel was constructed on it.

[6] *Arkansas Gazette*, "The Weary Go-Round," April 1946, by Hardy "Spider" Rowland.

[7] Ibid., 21 November 1947. Taken from the court testimony of Lloyd Lemmon, who had an interest in the casinos at the Southern and Belvedere clubs.

[8] *New York World Telegram*, two articles by Joe Williams 21-22 January 1946.

Naval Academy, and in fact had received an appointment through U.S. Congressman D.D. Glover, however found he was weak in mathematics.[9] He first entered Henderson State Teachers College at Arkadelphia, then the University of Arkansas and graduated as principal honor student of the University ROTC program and received the school's only commission in the Marine Corps that year.

While at the University of Arkansas, he and another Spa student, Clyde Brown, became close friends and had long talks of their growing up in Hot Springs and the negative effects the political machine in power had on the Spa. Clyde was the son of Riley Brown, a city fireman and thus had somewhat of a knowledge of the functioning of the McLaughlin political machine and what a city employee was required to do to keep his job. Brown was also an expert with firearms and won two national rifle marksman titles.

McMath tried to practice law in Hot Springs after graduating but those were lean years for him, as well as other young lawyers, and he joined the Marines before the United States became involved in World War II. He returned from the conflict having seen some "hot-action" in the South Pacific and carrying the rank of Lieutenant Colonel and a chest full of decorations.

One of the first people Sid McMath talked with upon returning home was Raymond Clinton who brought him up to date on the local political climate. Clinton told McMath it was so bad that no one had opposed an incumbent at city hall or the court house since 1934, a period of twelve years. The two began compiling a list of the names of those who might be interested in a change of government at Hot Springs.

Several meetings took place at Clinton's Buick dealership, but the one that really was decisive was held in late February 1946, at Hammonds Oyster Bar on Central Avenue. Hammonds was an all-night restaurant and had a large circular booth in the corner with room for about eight or nine, crowding into it. "We must have drunk ten gallons of coffee that night," said David Whittington. "We were trying to figure out the weakness of the McLaughlin machine, and who might be interested in running," McMath said.[10]

Besides McMath and Clyde Brown, another individual who was to become part of the core of the movement was Nathan Schoenfeld. Schoenfeld had also grown up at Hot Springs. His father had died when he was but four years old. Nathan won an athletic scholarship to Syracuse University and did so well there in his studies he was awarded an academic scholarship to Harvard, where he studied law. He entered military service as a private and his recognized intelligence earned him the right to attend Officer's Candidate School. He

---

[9] Taped interview of former Governor Sidney McMath at Little Rock, 11 September 1997 by Orval Allbritton. Hereinafter cited as Sid McMath.

[10] Ibid.

served thirty-four months overseas in the Army Air Force Intelligence Section and was discharged at the end of the war with a rank of major. While several of the G.I.s were attorneys they admittedly agreed Schoenfeld was the legal brains behind their strategic planning. Probably Schoenfeld got less credit for the success of the group because he worked from the background and preferred it that way. As "Spider" Rowland wrote in the *Arkansas Gazette*, "Schoenfield is farther away from the public eye than a dollar seat in Madison Square Garden." He was unselfish, but completely supportive of Sidney McMath. Schoenfield, Clyde Brown and Sid McMath would compose the "core" of the "G.I. Revolt," the others would be the inner circle.[11]

One of the last-mentioned group that night was J.O. Campbell, native Garland countian. Campbell was a tall-lanky, soft-spoken, laid-back kind of a guy, and perhaps some people were fooled when meeting him the first time, for J.O. Campbell was highly intelligent, a deep thinker and turned out to be invaluable to the G.I.s planning.[12]

Another of the G.I's was David Whittington, son of the late George Whittington. The elder Whittington had been a close friend, supporter and defender of the Administration when it was in trouble. Whittington had little regard or respect for the political machine which his father had manifested, and was devoted to the return of the government to the people. He, too, was a lawyer having attended boarding schools in Arizona and New Mexico prior to graduating from the University of Arkansas in 1939. He had military service in the European theater and was assigned to the staff of General Omar Bradley. Bradley sent Whittington to be liaison officer on the staff of Field Marshal Bernard Montgomery. Whittington could be eloquent in his writings but a bit brusque in his speeches.

Another G.I. who was invited to attend the meeting was Q. Byrum Hurst, who had been born in South Hot Springs to Reverend and Mrs. Leroy Hurst. Byrum attended Oaklawn Elementary School and graduated from Hot Springs High School and LaSalle Correspondence School of Law. He had served in the Army Separation Center at Ft. Chaffee, near Fort Smith.[13]

An important member of the group was I.G. Brown, whose father, Green Brown served for a time as Chief of Detectives on the Hot Springs Police

---

[11] The three--Brown, McMath and Schoenfield--had a short-lived partnership in a law firm whose offices was on the third floor of the Arkansas National Building. It dissolved after McMath's election to the governorship.

[12] When the writer was transferred back to Hot Springs as manager of an insurance adjustment branch office, J.O. Campbell was one of the adjusters in that office. We became close friends and had a number of discussions about the difficulties and "road-blocks" the G.I.s had to overcome in up-ending the McLaughlin political machine.

[13] Taped interview of Q. Byrum Hurst by Orval E. Allbritton, 23 March 1998. Hereinafter cited as Q. Byrum Hurst.

Department. I.G. graduated from Hot Springs High School in 1935. He had served in several theaters during the war and was awarded the Legion of Merit, Distinguished Service Medal, European-African-Middle Eastern Campaign Medal, The Bronze Star and other meritorious commendations.[14]

Several others would be important to the movement and involved in running for elective office. They were W. J. "Billy Joe" Wilkins; Ray Owen; Tommy Freeman; and one who had no military experience but supported the "revolt," Leonard Ellis and who was "chomping at-the-bit" to run for office.

A number of others would work in the campaign, some aiding in legal research such as Julian Glover, Richard "Dick" Hobbs, and Leo McLaughlin's "bitterest enemy" Scott Wood and those that canvassed voters like "Birdie" Fulton and Oliver Livingston.

That night, working from a legal pad, Sid McMath outlined to the group some of his ideas. He proposed to attack the McLaughlin political machine by opposing every elective office in the court house in the Democratic primary, which was scheduled for July 30. The offices of prosecuting attorney, circuit judge and sheriff were most critical to the machine and which offices had the "muscle" to clean up the county. Any others would be a bonus. McMath wanted to know who was willing to run and make the sacrifice needed to get out and work for the people.

And, oh yes, they had to come up with a plan to off set the Administration's big edge at the ballot box in illegal poll tax receipts. They needed to counteract the lethargic and hopeless feelings many citizens had developed concerning opposing administration backed candidates. The G.I.s agreed that every voter in the county had to be reached and assured their vote would count and that it would not be reviewed by any workers of the political machine. The need to enlist the aid of the recently returned veterans numbering to over 1,200 was cited and all should be encouraged to quickly purchase poll taxes to enable them to vote in the Democratic primary in July. The men divided up some initial assignments.

"Go home," McMath told the group as sounds of the city awakening could be heard, "Discuss with your wives and family what is at stake and we will have another meeting at Raymond's [Clinton] in a few days. Be thinking about if you are willing to put your name on the ticket and run for some office. And," he emphasized, "let's keep what we discussed between us until we are ready to announce our intentions. You know the score."

Keeping that all night meeting confidential was not something which was going to happen in Hot Springs in 1946. Customers and waitresses had noted

---

[14] After serving as Garland County Sheriff, I.G. Brown returned to active service and rose to the position as Director of the Air National Guard and reached the rank of Major General. He died in 1978.

Standing: Leonard Ellis, Earl Ricks, David Whittington, Raymond Clinton. In front of car, Sid McMath and I.G. Brown.

the prolonged meeting and serious discussion going on in the large corner booth. Mayor McLaughlin had several people waiting to see him when he arrived at his office that morning and his secretary Hazel Marsh had received several calls from individuals wanting to alert Leo, "Something was going on." McLaughlin had "stoolies" all up and down Central. But none were able to inform him exactly what the meeting was about or the strategy the group intended to follow. There was considerable speculation, but no clear answers as to what the group's plans were. It wasn't long before word was spreading all over town that the young war veteran, Sid McMath, intended to enter the race for prosecuting attorney and by the time word reached the mayor, McLaughlin realized it was time to try to defuse the situation.

Sid McMath never said publicly who it was that contacted him and informed him, "he could have the nomination for prosecuting attorney without opposition if he was willing to go along with the McLaughlin Administration."[15] It appeared the Administration was willing to "dump"

---

[15] *New Era*, 30 July 1946.

Ridgway or encourage him to run for another position, possibly state legislator. In a speech Sid McMath admitted having been contacted by the opposition and related, "Recently he (the mayor) has been challenging my qualifications for the office of prosecuting attorney, but my qualifications were not questioned when that proposition was made."[16] He kept everyone guessing for several weeks as to whether he was really serious or not concerning his running for prosecuting attorney. All doubts were dispelled late in April when he appeared at the State Capitol office of Secretary of State C.G. Hall and filed for the office.[17]

The veterans group came out with almost a full slate on the county and district offices. McMath announced his candidacy for prosecuting attorney of the eighteenth judicial district against incumbent Curtis Ridgway, who had filed early. I.G. Brown faced off against Sheriff Marion Anderson and Byrum Hurst took on longtime county judge, Elza T. Housley. E. M. "Buddy" Houpt filed for county clerk held by another long time court house resident, Roy Raef. Another Administration-backed incumbent was Mack Wilson in the tax collector's office and he was opposed by G.I. candidate, Ray Owen. Leonard Ellis opposed John E. Jones, who had been in the court house so long most people believed he had been there forever. J.O. Campbell threw his hat in the ring against tax assessor incumbent, Roy Gillenwater. Former welterweight boxing champion of the world, Tommy Freeman, filed for Hot Springs Township Constable against Monroe Young, a very popular and long-time resident.

The one office that seemed uncertain and surrounded by mystery was that of circuit judge, which position had been held by Earl Witt since the early 1920s. Witt was reportedly "unbeatable." Shortly before the filing deadline, Clyde Brown, announced his candidacy opposing the formidable Witt.[18] The judge's only comment was, "The voters ought to have a choice of candidates." Thus all county offices had opposition for the primary with the exception of the office of county treasurer held by Henry Murphy.

There was increased activity on the part of the G.I. faction and which was duly scrutinized and noted by the Administration. On May 1 they opened a small campaign office on the third floor of the Arkansas National Bank Building adjacent to the offices of Brown, McMath and Schoenfield. This was the same floor on which Leo McLaughlin maintained a law office, therefore it could not escape his attention as to the activity going on down the hall involving the G.I.s.

---

[16] Ibid.

[17] *Arkansas Democrat* and *New Era*, 24 April 1946.

[18] Jim Lester, *A Man for Arkansas, Sid McMath and the Southern Reform Tradition* (Little Rock: Rose Publishing, 1976). Hereinafter cited as Lester.

Out at the court house J. O. Campbell and two helpers appeared one morning and asked Tax Collector Mack Wilson for copies of the poll tax book. When told that there were no extra copies Campbell and his assistants began copying names and addresses from those at the office as Wilson nervously watched.[19] The lists of Campbell's groups were given to others to go out in the suburbs and county and to contact each voter with the questions, "Did you purchase your own poll tax? If not, who did? Did you authorize someone else to purchase it? And did you pay for it or someone else? If someone else, was the poll-tax receipt returned to you in five days as the law requires.?"

Shortly before the filing deadline, McLaughlin called a meeting of the political machine. He had already "leaned-on" the gambling community for contributions on what was obviously becoming an expensive election campaign. He advised those office holders who were opposed that they should strongly consider enlisting someone to be a third candidate in the race. It was even suggested that if some returning serviceman, who was favorable to the Administration could be found it might siphon off a considerable number of opposing votes. At least it would dilute the vote and weaken the major opposition G.I. candidate, and prevent a run-off. The downside was, explained the mayor, each office holder was expected to bear the expenses for the third candidate. All of the political machine candidates complied with the suggestion, except one, Roy Gillenwater, the county tax assessor.

Gillenwater had been wrestling with his conscience for sometime. He had been known to be a fair and just man and he and his family were church attending people. He was acquainted with a number of the G.I. candidates and knew most of their families. He had tried to perform his job at the court house in a professional manner, but he did not like the chicanery and underhandedness sometimes associated with Administration politics. He suddenly disappeared from Hot Springs right in the middle of the campaign and for three weeks his whereabouts were known only to his family. He had been turning over in his mind that he wanted to get out of politics and when an offer was made to him for a job in Alaska with the Aluminum Company of America, he quietly slipped out of town. At Grand Junction, Colorado on May 23, he mailed a letter to Sid McMath, wishing the G.I.s well and enclosing a letter of resignation he requested be delivered to Governor Laney.

Instead of delivering the resignation letter to the governor immediately, McMath made an announcement late one evening he had received the correspondence. It read: "Dear Governor: At the present time I am tax assessor of and for Garland county. I was first elected to that office in 1936. Personal business reasons now require that I change my residence to a

---

[19] Ibid., 29 April 1946.

location outside of Arkansas. Therefore, I wish to submit to you my resignation, effective as of June 1, 1946. I am pleased to know that a well qualified veteran, who has so recently served his country on the field of battle, will now be nominated in the primaries without opposition. I would forever be thankful to you if you would appoint F.W. Rowles, my chief deputy, to serve my unexpired term. I am certain he would be acceptable to the people of Garland county.

Very truly yours
Roy Gillenwater"[20]

It was reported when word of Gillenwater's "defection" and "sympathy" for the G.I. candidates reached the ears of Mayor Leo P. McLaughlin, he went into a rage and was as angry as a disturbed grizzly in the midst of his hibernation. The deadline for filing for office had passed and there was nothing he could do about the tax assessor's position--G.I. candidate, J.O. Campbell had a clear ride, at least to the general election in November. But, Leo figured, there might be something he could do about the appointment of Gillenwater's replacement. McLaughlin probably had nothing against R.W. Rowles, who had served in various offices in the court house as a deputy for years, but just the thought he had been made deputy by Roy Gillenwater, and was now being recommended for a temporary appointment prejudiced Leo's thinking. He called Sheriff Marion Anderson and told him the situation. The two drove to Little Rock early the following morning hoping to beat Sid McMath to the governor's office. They learned, what McMath may have already known, that Governor Laney was out of town and J.L. Shaver was acting governor. Shaver probably believed the appointment could wait for the governor to return, however the papers reported, "Acting Governor Shaver, on the demand of Mayor Leo P. McLaughlin, head of the Garland county political machine, appointed Harry Lewis to the position of Assessor."[21] No doubt Leo gloated over this small, but hollow victory as Lewis' term would be for only a few months.

At the deadline for filing for office several men who were not all that well known had entered the races. Probably the two most widely known in Garland county were Charles H. "Stuffy" Dugan and H.A. Tucker.

Dugan was an ex-Trojan football star and had distinguished himself as a flyer in World War II. He had returned home and was attending college at Henderson State Teachers College under the G.I. Bill. His friends never really understood why Dugan would enter the race for sheriff against two totally

---

[20] *Arkansas Gazette*, 26 May 1946

[21] *Arkansas Democrat*, date on article appears to be 6 October 1946, a reprint of the happening.

serious candidates for the office, unless he was talked into entering the race to "split" the vote.[22] His campaign slogan came from his football days, "Let "Stuffy Carry The Ball." In most of his campaigning he seemed to criticize his "fellow G.I.s" and was non-committal on the Administration candidate leading most people to believe he was a "placed" entrant.

Tucker, a local "criminal" lawyer, who had moved to Hot Springs late in the 1930s filed in the prosecuting attorneys race against the incumbent Curtis Ridgway and Sidney McMath.

Another ex-G.I., Ralph Smith, though not affiliated with the McMath group, filed against Administration supported State Senator Ernest Maner. It had been believed for awhile that Maner's opposition would be Clyde Brown, who opted on the last day to run for circuit judge.

Others placed in the political arena by the Administration backed office holders or those who aspired for office were Joe King, described as a "merchant policeman and a beer parlor employee," who filed for constable; Barney Roark, operator of Barney's Place, a beer tavern on Lake Catherine, for county judge; Morris Hecht, a little known lawyer who maintained a desk in the office of Administration city attorney; Jay Rowland cast his name into the circuit judge's race; J.T. "Dear-Brother" Turner, owner and operator of the Delmar Hotel on Market Street and co-owner of the Victory Cab Co., and noted Administration supporter, dropped his name in the county collector's race.

Tucker and some of the other third candidates referred to themselves as "middle of the road" candidates.[23] It was difficult to understand where some of those individuals stood. They announced they "did not plan a big cleanup of Hot Springs gambling," but insisted they knew "how to enforce the law,"[24] whatever that meant since gambling was illegal? As it turned out none of the third person candidates did much campaigning, none won, none had much effect on the outcome of any of the races and all seemed to drift into obscurity after the election.

The opening "salvo" of the political battle was fired by the G.I. forces the morning of 4 July 1946. The citizens of the small town of Lonsdale in eastern Garland county were just finishing breakfast and getting ready to face the holiday when they heard the engine of a very low flying airplane. Many rushed onto their porches and into the yards. As they looked skyward they saw hundreds of circulars fluttering down. These had come from a plane being piloted by I.G. Brown, who continued to circle the small community and throw bundles of the circulars into the air. The circulars were invitations to

---

[22] *New Era*, 30 April 1946.
[23] *Arkansas Democrat*, 29 April 1946.
[24] *Sentinel-Record*, 30 April 1946.

"Rogue's" Gallery

★ of ★

Past and Present
PERFORMANCES

★ of ★

"LEO" and Company

★ *In A Glamorous Conception Of*

DICTATORSHIP & MACHINE-RULE

Compliments of

the following qualified G.I. candidates

SIDNEY S. McMATH
for Prosecuting Attorney

Q. BYRUN HURST
for County Judge

E. M. "BUDDY" HOUPT
for County Clerk

J. O. CAMPBELL
for County Assessor

CLYDE H. BROWN
for Circuit Judge

LEONARD R. ELLIS
for Circuit Clerk

I. G. BROWN
for Sheriff

TOMMY FREEMAN
for Constable

Room 308 ARKANSAS NATIONAL BANK BUILDING
Hot Springs, Arkansas

 3

TROTTIN' TRACK FOR MAYOR'S HORSES—
WHY NOT PLAYGROUND FOR KIDS?

BOOKIES
LEO P.
MONTGOMERY COUNTY
SCHOOLS
ELECTION MACHINERY
COURTS
GAMBLING CLUBS
BUSINESS

"The Hot Springs Municipal Airport Dedication"

"WE WILL WIN BY 2,500 VOTES," McLaughlin!

"WE WILL WIN BY 2,500 VOTES," McLaughlin!

attend a political meeting that evening and had several cartoons of a political nature. The one on the front of the circular depicted Leo McLaughlin riding a horse and giving the Nazi salute while an officer stopped all traffic.Later, the G.I.s would drop cartoon folders on Hot Springs with seven panels depicting the McLaughlin machine in a "bad-light." One of the little drawings was a large octopus sprawled over a city with the tentacles labeled, "Bookies, schools, courts, business, gambling clubs, election machinery and Montgomery county." Oh, yes, the octopus was wearing a hat at a rakish angle and written across its neck was "Leo P." It didn't take a person with a high I.Q. to understand who the G.I.s were focusing on even if he wasn't due for election himself until April of 1947. They were going right to the top with the theory of "kill the head and the body will die."

The meeting was scheduled at the Colony House, which would seat several hundred people, and was located in Lonsdale. This was a large, all-purpose tile and concrete building which had been constructed by Johnny G. Lonsdale, Jr., son of the late and wealthy John Lonsdale Sr., who owned the majority of stock in one of the largest banks in St. Louis, served as President of the American Banker's Association and once as Chairman of the Board of the Missouri Pacific Railroad, and for whom the town of Lonsdale was named.[25]

Young Lonsdale was more or less a "play boy," never really having to work or having a job and living on money from a trust fund his late father had left and also from funds doled out by his mother who resided on Quapaw Avenue in Hot Springs. Johnny had envisioned the Colony House as being a gambling casino but could never obtain the necessary permission of county authorities to operate a sporting house and over the objection of his neighbors in the small town. Lonsdale then announced he would run it as a movie theater, then a roller-rink and basketball gym, where Rural Dale School could play its games. Each of these ideas surged with interest, at first, then when attendance decreased he moved on to the next project and tried to turn it into a beer tavern and dance hall, all over the objections of his neighbors.

The G.I.s opened their campaign before a crowd of over eight hundred persons. It appeared the entire community of Lonsdale had turned out and a large number of people had driven out from the Spa. The veterans all wore their dress uniforms and appeared resplendent, each with a chest full of ribbons and medals. Each gave a short talk on "freedom and values," with the key-note address being given by the eloquent Sid McMath who had been honing his speaking skills by making patriotic talks before various school

---

[25] John G. Lonsdale's wealth had once been estimated as between $200 and $300 million, a staggering amount. He had grown up in Hot Springs and attended Jones School. He was active in local real estate sales until he moved his family. He maintained a retreat at Lonsdale. His son built a very rustic cabin in the valley and appropriately named it "Lazybones."

groups sponsored by the American Legion.[26]

He told the crowd that the Administration was already starting rumors against him and his friends. He said they were criticizing him as being against labor, which he said was untrue. He said his opponent had failed in his job to immediately investigate major crimes which had been committed in the Spa. He charged that he and the other candidates and their supporters had uncovered 4,000 illegal poll tax receipts, all in the hands of Mayor McLaughlin. "I object to any one man casting that many votes in one election," he said.[27]

McMath said because of his objection to the handling and issuing of fraudulent poll tax receipts he had been labeled a "reformer." "I am," he said forcefully, "also opposed to licensed murder." He then read to his audience headlines from local newspapers of recent murders in gangland fashion and the undue delays and laxity in prosecuting criminal cases.[28]

The large political rally had not gone unnoticed, for while McMath and his cohorts were stirring up the crowd, unknown persons were seeding the parking area around the Colony House with roofing tacks. There were a number of deflated tires before the crowd left that evening. Some of the G.I.s good naturally helped people change their flat tires.[29] While that situation never occurred again it was because the veterans posted guards at other rallys. It did signal the beginning of "dirtytricks."

As the G.I.s began their campaign they scheduled rallies at Jessieville, Sunshine School, the Labor Hall, Fountain Lake, and Hobson and Third Streets. The attendance at their meetings increased to such an extent they requested permission of the Hot Springs School Board to use Rix Field which had seating. When the request was denied they rescheduled a large rally at Dean Field which had very limited seating. J.O. Campbell explained the situation to the large crowd and apologizing to the throng, "You must remember that city attorney Jay Rowland is a member of the school board and it seems that the G.I. candidates are not welcome on any public property."[30]

As the races heated up, stories and rumors were quickly taken to Mayor McLaughlin who was fighting to keep his political machine intact. One such rumor was related to him as being something Assistant Fire Chief Riley Brown was supposed to have said and which suggested to the mayor that Brown was not loyal to the Administration because his son was one of the G.I. candidates. McLaughlin ordered Commissioner Weldon Raspberry to demote Brown from Assistant Chief to hoseman, a large decrease in salary and which would

---

[26] *Arkansas Gazette*, 5 July 1946.

[27] *Arkansas Democrat*, 5 July 1946.

[28] Ibid.

[29] Jim Lester, *A Man for Arkansas: Sid McMath and the Southern Reform Tradition* (Little Rock: Rose Publishing, 1976).

[30] *New Era*, 30 July 146.

greatly effect the fireman's pension benefits, which were based on the salary an employee was drawing at the time of his retirement. Brown, a thirty-five year veteran of the fire department heard of the planned move and went immediately to see Rasberry and confronted him with what he had heard of the planned demotion. "I heard I am to be demoted to hoseman and if that is true, I turn my resignation in now." Raspberry merely nodded, probably feeling embarrassment as he had worked under Brown and knew him to be a good man. To his credit, Rasberry approached the mayor and urged him to reconsider and meet with Riley Brown. Leo agreed. When Brown went in to see the mayor, McLaughlin told him that they had been friends a longtime and he wanted to clear up the misunderstanding. The mayor said he had checked the basis of the story that had been brought to him and he was convinced it was untrue. Brown told the mayor concerning his son, Clyde, "That boy is 36 years old. Do you think I can tell him what to do?"[31]

Another similar incident to the foregoing involved Police Captain Jerry Watkins. Watkins had initially been employed on the police department in 1933. He had avoided much of the troubles which beset the department during that time and was considered a good officer. He had spent two years in the Navy during World War II. He had been credited with solving several major crimes in the Spa including a robbery of the Esskay Art Gallery and that one took only five hours.[32] On another occasion, he and Captain Ben Rogers had shot it out and killed rapist and murderer Earl Young in the Marquette Hotel, and both received citations for bravery. Watkins, also was one of only eight city police officers in the United States who were selected by the FBI in guarding the delegates to the World Peace Conference in San Francisco.[33]

Watkins had been called in by the mayor before the Democratic Primary and informed the officer he had heard Watkins was "for the G.I.s." Watkins neither confirmed or denied the accusation, merely saying, "You can hear anything around here."[34] The truth of the matter was, Jerry Watkins was very friendly with both Sid McMath and Clyde Brown. Later in the year three officers were dismissed from the force by Commissioner Raspberry, including Captain Jerry Watkins. When asked, Raspberry advised the dismissals were "On the orders of Mayor Leo P. McLaughlin."[35] After Sid McMath won the prosecuting attorney's job, he appointed Jerry Watkins as a "special investigator" for his office.[36] One of the other two officers who were

---

[31] From an undated news article found in one of two scrapbooks of Nathan Schoenfield on page 5. The scrapbooks are now in custody of the GCHS.

[32] *Arkansas Gazette*, 28 December 1946.

[33] *Sentinel-Record*, 28 December 1946.

[34] Ibid.

[35] *Arkansas Gazette*, 28 December 1946.

[36] *Sentinel-Record*, 30 December 1946.

dismissed was Patrolman O.D. Griffin. His name may appear familiar to the reader as he was one of the policemen dispatched to the mayor's home when Lucille Griffith came out and a brouhaha developed. Not surprisingly, when Leo McLaughlin realized he would need Griffin's testimony against Lucille Griffith's breach of promise suit for $200,000, the officer was rehired on the police department.

Then there were several attempts made by various Administration officials or their supporters, to persuade some of the G.I. candidates to resign from the race by saying they would "pay what expenses you have been out and a little for your trouble." When that didn't work several threats were made. The first of these was made to Q. Byrum Hurst, who was opposing County Judge Elza T. Housley. Hurst refused to withdraw. When that occurred both Hurst and his wife received calls threatening harm to their young daughter. Hurst went on the radio the night of the calls and "charged McLaughlin followers of trying to force him to withdraw from the race." He disclosed the name of the individual who had called him making threats against his family as one "Garnett Tucker, former chairman of the Garland County Board of Equilization." Hurst told that Tucker "Had been arrested on numerous occasions on book making charges along with his partner Ed Spear." Further, he advised the radio audience that night that he had given a "sworn affidavit and turned it over to the FBI."[37]

The dirty tricks continued and became rougher. Earl "Birdie" Fulton and Oliver Livingston, two of the G.I.s who were checking poll tax lists and securing affidavits from voters who indicated they had never authorized anyone to purchase one for them or never received a receipt, had been working in the Second Ward. They were on the porch of a house at 119 Jefferson Street when they were accosted by two armed men who took the briefcases they were carrying and drove off.[38] Fulton and Livingston immediately contacted McMath and apprised him of the details of the robbery. The following morning Mayor McLaughlin was opening his mail when McMath, Clyde Brown and Nathan Schoenfield breezed by the mayor's secretary and entered his office. The trio of hardened combat veterans had grim faces and before Leo could say anything he was informed that two of their workers had been held up at gun-point and their briefcases and contents had been taken. Further, they informed him that he had until noon to return the briefcases and contents and that there had better be no further "gunplay"

---

[37] From several newspaper articles in scrapbook of Nathan Schoenfield, pages 7 & 8. Also Q. Byrum Hurst, interview. After Hurst had become county judge, he commissioned Garnett Tucker as "deputy constable," proving the old adage, "Politics makes for strange bedfellows." *Sentinel-Record*, 25 February 1948.

[38] *Arkansas Democrat*, 2 July 1946, also, *Arkansas Gazette*, same date.

because if the Administration wanted to get rough, they were ready to clean house and "We'll start at the top."[39] Leo, must have got the message as the briefcases were promptly returned with all of the contents intact.[40]

The G.I.s let the word out that "Leo had caved in to their demand." McLaughlin, trying to "save face,"called a press conference and tried to "discredit the charges." He expressed doubt the charges the veterans had made about the robbery were true and said he did not approve of such methods. "Anyway," he casually said, "I *dismissed* the entire matter, because I had known that sooner or later the practice of ringing door bells would become objectionable."[41] Leo's explanation would probably have sounded better to the citizens had he said, "I don't approve of such tactics and I've ordered the police to investigate the matter," instead of trying to blame someone else.

Those working for the reform effort at the court house ran into a "roadblock" in their research at the tax collector's office. When they requested permission to view the list of authorizations that people supposedly had made to purchase their poll tax, the G.I.s were told by deputies J. M. Elliott and J.W. Lowrey, they "couldn't find the authorization." When they asked to see Mack Wilson, Tax Collector, they were informed "He had left Hot Springs two weeks before," and had not returned. McMath said he was told Mr. Wilson, the collector, had taken the lists with him.[42]

There was even a case later when a city alderman was actually charged with attempting to bribe a witness in a trial involving George McLaughlin[43].

Perhaps not all the "tricks" were instigated by the Administration and its followers. When the breach-of-promise suit was filed by Lucille Griffith against Leo P. McLaughlin, the mayor screamed "blackmail and politics," as being its origin. He told reporters, "I have been reliably informed that one of the reform candidates returned recently from Oklahoma City, where the plaintiff resides."[44]

Sid McMath's response to Leo's allegation was, "I didn't know a thing about

---

[39] *Saturday Evening Post*, "He Wants to Make Something of Arkansas," by Joe Alex Morris, p. 115, February 1950. Also, *Arkansas Gazette*, 1 July 1946.

[40] Taped interviews of Sidney McMath, 11 September 1997, and Q. Byrum Hurst, 2. March 1998.

[41] *Arkansas Democrat*, 2 July 1946.

[42] *Arkansas Gazette*, 19 June 1946. Wilson later said the authorizations had been locked in his safe and he had told McMath that before he left town.

[43] *Sentinel-Record*, 15 November 1947, and *Arkansas Democrat*, same date. Sid McMath, prosecuting attorney at that time was trying George McLaughlin, when juror Daniel Rainwater reported an attempted bribery by Sixth Ward Alderman W. B. Timberlake. McMath charged the alderman, but after two hung jury trials of Leo P. McLaughlin, dropped the charges against Timberlake.

[44] Ibid., 12 July 1946, pp. 1, 12.

Seated: Clyde H. Brown, Sid McMath, I.G. Brown. Standing: Leonard Ellis, Ray Owen, Buddy Houpt, J.O. Campbell, Q. Byrum Hurst — 1946.

it until it was filed this morning in federal court. It certainly has no political connection with our campaign."[45] He later told this author, "I wish we had thought of it." There were those who believed the timing of the suit may have been encouraged by some of the G.I. faction.

The G.I.s were known to have "spread the word," especially in the black wards, that the election would be closely monitored by federal agents. They were also accused by the Administration that some of their workers identified themselves as U.S. Marshals in their canvassing for poll tax violations. This was also denied by the G.I.s.

Another incident occurred during the election campaign which the Administration tried to credit to the G.I.s. That was an article appearing in the July issue of the *Saturday Evening Post,* entitled, "The Town Without a Lid." Collie Small, the author, wrote of how wide-open the City of Hot Springs was at that time and how illegal gambling had been condoned since the 1920s. He wrote of the reign of Leo P. McLaughlin as almost a "king," stating "he

[45] *Sentinel-Record,* 12 July 1946.

presides over Hot Springs' delinquencies with a sharp eye and wondrous dignity."

It wasn't the pointing out of the city's wide-open stance on illegal gambling or the iron-fisted ruling of the entire county by McLaughlin that caught Leo's eye. He latched onto the ending quote of a physician at the Army and Navy General Hospital who commented on the curative powers of the hot thermal waters by saying, "Since I have been at the hospital we have been giving mineral baths to all our patients and I can truthfully say that in all that time we have *not had one case of smelly feet*."[46]

Oops! Small had just given Leo McLaughlin something he could use to "rally the troops." Realizing the pride which citizens had in the hot thermal baths, the source of much of the city's income, McLaughlin replied with righteous indignation, telling reporters, "I have read the vicious attack upon Hot Springs in the *Saturday Evening Post*. The personal attack upon me is of no consequence as far as I am concerned because I have been talked about before. But when such an attack as this has been made upon the curative value of our hot water then it is time to fight back."[47] The mayor was aware that all 1,400 copies of the *Post*, which had been allotted to news stands in the Spa had been "gobbled-up" in less than three hours. Did Leo blame the *Saturday Evening Post* for the "damage" done to the image of Hot Springs? He did not. The mayor placed "full blame on Sidney McMath." He suggested that Collie Small had been "invited" to come to Hot Springs to write such an article. And who was responsible? McLaughlin shared this information with the press. "Last Tuesday night," he said, " In a speech at Mountain Pine, Sidney McMath told the people to be sure to buy the next issue of the *Saturday Evening Post*. Naturally, he knew the exact contents of the article by Collie Small and was rejoicing and cared not that it might ruin the City of Hot Springs. That article was inspired and made possible by the opposition to the Administration." The newspapers reported his 25-minute "tirade" ended by McLaughlin saying "Political opposition that is bereft of decency and loyalty deserves and will receive a crushing defeat."[48] That was vintage McLaughlin, at his best.

A few persons were initially upset by the *Post's* reference to the "sacred" mineral waters which had made the Spa famous, but a number of people recognized the article for what it was intended as an exposé of conditions existing in the city and not an attack upon the Spa.

One well-known physician and president of the Hot Springs-Garland County Medical Society, Dr. Driver Rowland, when asked his opinion replied "I chose to ignore it." Bill Seiz, Jr., president of the Chamber of Commerce

---

[46] *Saturday Evening Post*, "The Town Without a Lid," by Collie Small, 20 July 1946.
[47] *New Era*, 22 July 1946.
[48] *Sentinel-Record*, 21 July 1946.

refused to enter the controversy but did drop a letter to C. E. Palmer, publisher of the *Sentinel-Record* and *New Era*, and suggested that getting in an "argument with the *Post* over the article might be unwise."[49]

The *Arkansas Gazette* columnist, Hardy "Spider" Rowland, observing the political races from Little Rock commented on Leo McLaughlin's political maneuverings, "In one way or another he arranges it so his political enemies feel more uncomfortable in Hot Springs than a catfish in a bird cage."

As the political wars heated up, working almost unseen in the background was Nathan Schoenfeld. He had come up with an idea, grabbed a package of legal pads, and headed off into the hills of northwest Arkansas. For several days Schoenfeld researched the University of Arkansas Law Library looking for anything that might help to level the playing field between the G.I.s and the McLaughlin political machine. Shoenfeld recognized the biggest hurdle for the reform candidates was to overcome or neutralize the thousands of illegal poll tax receipts controlled by the Administration. Workers were at that time frantically chasing down every receipt possible to determine which ones were legitimate and which ones were bogus or fraudulent. Nathan and his legal assistants knew it would be a waste of time and effort to file suit to throw out the illegal receipts if the filing had to be done in the local courts. Clyde Wilson, the unsuccessful candidate for sheriff in 1936 had tried to use the local courts and discovered that venue to be totally unsympathetic and unfriendly for anyone trying to overthrow the system.

Schoenfeld had come up with two precedents in law attesting to the right of voters for an "honest election" that might allow non-machine candidates a chance to win. By "piecing" these two cases, both Supreme Court decisions, one involving a "political machine" situation in New Jersey and the other guaranteeing "the right to vote is a civil right provided by the Constitution," Schoenfeld hoped to even the odds.[50] .

Prevailing upon a friend, Patrick H. Mullis, an ex-service man who lived at Dumas, Arkansas, to enter his name as a "write-in" candidate for the United States Congress, it might make it possible to get their case heard in federal court. The incumbent congressman from this district was W.F. Norrell, who was unopposed until the write-in candidancy of Mullis materialized. This particular incident was little noted and probably was not even noticed at first by leaders of the Administration.

When suit was filed in federal court by the G.I.s charging "fraud and unnumerable discrepancies" in so-called block purchases of poll tax receipts, "the cat was out of the bag." The suit sought to "invalidate 3,825 of the

---

[49] *New Era*, 22 July 1946.

[50] *PIC The Young Man's Magazine*, "New Bath for Hot Springs," by Ed Cunningham, July 1948, p. 98.

county's 10,797 poll taxes, good for voting in the Democratic primary elections in July and August 1946."[51]

Interestingly, four affidavits were attached to the suit alleging various election "irregularities in previous elections." One individual, R.H. Ball, swore he and six other men had in the 1940 election been picked up and transported by gambling club owner Jack McJunkin to "every ward in the city," where each of the men had voted with a different poll tax receipt furnished by McJunkin. Ball further stated he had voted for fourteen years and had never bought a single poll tax. Former constable John W. Spiva advised of serving as an election official, "about 12 years ago," and how several election irregularities were allowed and in fact occurred "with Mayor McLaughlin and Circuit Judge Earl Witt condoning such practices." Both Joe Scott, a former city policeman, and John T. Kilgore swore how they had helped "cover" alleged ballot stuffing tactics in the 1936 election.[52]

When suit was filed, Leo P. McLaughlin tried to put his best "spin" on the event, blaming his long time nemesis, former circuit judge Scott Wood. The mayor stated, "We knew this suit would be filed. It did not come as a surprise. It simply brings out into the light for all men to see the *little man* who always contests what the Administration does--Scott Wood. Heretofore, he has always contested elections after the ballots were cast.

"We have known all along that the *little man*, who hasn't been a factor in Garland County's official circles for many years, has been burning the midnight oil, probing deep into law books and working himself up into a condition of seeming civic virtue. Now he is out in the open and the people, who have in the past repudiated his opposition, identify him as the brains, the inspiration, and the 'pappy' of our opposition."

When Judge Wood heard of McLaughlin's attack upon him he answered "hotly," "He (the mayor) is just having another one of his spells. He has had them ever since the First World War. He'll get over it, I guess. He always has.

"I didn't have anything to do with the law suit. There are a lot of fine lawyers among the G.I.s. They are the ones that prepared the suit."[53]

Plaintiffs in the suit were Brad O. Smith, Jr., John T. Kilgore, Oliver Livingston, Leonard Ellis, I.G. Brown, et al.

There were nineteen defendants named, including Will Page, a noted Negro political leader, several gambling club owners, Jack McJunkin, George Pakis, Erb Wheatley, and A.J. Karston; city employees, Bill Abbott, Ben Rogers,

---

[51] *Arkansas Democrat*, 11 June 1946.

[52] Ibid.

[53] Ibid. It was apparent the Mayor was just guessing at who had prepared the law suit and not knowing of Schoenfeld's work, just assumed his "old enemy" was involved. Leo was prone to jump before knowing all the facts.

Rufus Manning and Fannie McLaughlin; machine "runners," Elmer Walters and Walter Weldon; and Mack Wilson, county collector; Roy C. Raef, county clerk; and three county election commissioners, Carl Miles, Richard Ryan and Ed Vance.[54]

The charges listed in the suit were almost unbelievable anywhere in the country except Hot Springs, Arkansas in 1946. The suit charged the defendants "are conspiring to control the 1946 primary elections," and challenged in effect the legality of 3,825 poll tax receipts. In fact, as Dick Allen reported in the *Memphis Commercial Appeal*, "The McLaughlin administration were conspiring to stuff the ballot boxes with fictitious and fraudulent ballots at this summer's primaries."[55] Further, a charge was made that many of the poll tax receipts had been purchased under the block system sometimes by one individual, including 2,199 by Will Page. Others purchasing large numbers were Jack McJunkin, 269; Walter Weldon, 153; Fannie McLaughlin, 75, and A.J. Karston, 71. The others ranged from 22 to 39.

The plaintiffs asked the court for a temporary court order restraining County Collector Mack Wilson from interfering with the rights of the plaintiffs to view the lists of authorization which had been denied them.[56] The Judge promptly ordered Wilson to permit the McMath forces to photostat any of the authorizations they needed to complete their investigation.

That news was followed by the announcement that United States District Judge J.E. Miller, of the Western District of Arkansas, would be hearing the case.[57] Yes, this was the same John E. Miller who had been so rudely treated by Leo McLaughlin when Miller sought the senatorial seat vacated by the death of Joe T. Robinson several years before. Miller had served the unexpired term as U.S. Senator and President Franklin Roosevelt had appointed him as a Federal Judge.

The Administration's attorneys filed motions attempting to remove the suit to local courts, but Miller proclaimed he was certain "This court has jurisdiction over wrongs done citizens by persons serving under color of the law." Judge Miller, also did not "buy" the plea by the defendants that Patrick H. Mullis was not a legitimate "write-in" candidate in the Sixth District Congressional election. He set trial at Hot Springs for July 8, scarcely three weeks before the first primary. The initial hearing turned out to be the first victory for the G.I. candidates.

As court opened, Judge Miller was informed by Attorney McMath that efforts of the G.I.s to examine the authorization lists held by Collector Mack

---

[54] Ibid.

[55] *Memphis Commercial Appeal*, 11 June 1946.

[56] *Arkansas Democrat*, 11 June 1946.

[57] *Arkansas Gazette*, 11 June 1946.

Wilson had come to naught and much of the evidence they had hoped to introduce had been surpressed. Miller was not particularly pleased to hear this and immediately ordered Tax Collector Wilson to furnish this information, "without delay," to the plaintiffs. Veteran J.O. Campbell and "about twenty volunteers worked two days and nights," going over the records.

In the meanwhile, a parade of witnesses were introduced by the plaintiffs who testified they had given "no authorizations to purchase of poll tax," in their names.[58]

Will Page, 76, the black ward-healer for Leo McLaughlin, accused of purchasing 2,199 poll taxes, took the stand and appeared as nervous as a maiden on her wedding day, and reportedly by one writer that he, "perspired profusely," to the tough questioning. Page could not explain why he had bought poll taxes for a lady who had died two years before or another who had been dead over five years, as death certificates were introduced. Several names of people appeared on his lists who the G.I.s could find no record of their ever having lived in Hot Springs. Some names appeared with addresses of vacant lots with utility records confirming they had never lived there. Judge Miller kept reminding Page to speak up and to "Stop being evasive." Page also tried to deny he had brought in authorizations for 2,199 poll tax receipts, saying "the figure was more like between 100 and 150."[59] He admitted he

Hazel "Bobbie" Marsh, Leo P. McLaughlin's loyal secretary.
She married George Earnshaw, baseball pitcher for the Philadelphia Athletics.

---

[58] *Sentinel-Record*, 9 July 1946.
[59] Ibid.

"obtained the authorization blanks from the secretary in the office of Mayor Leo P. McLaughlin," and only took "six or seven at a time," to County Collector Mack Wilson's office.[60] When Page was shown 107 pages of authorizations provided by the tax collector's office with 70 to 100 names each, he had to admit he had bought more than he had remembered. By the time the seventy-six year-old black was excused from the stand he was almost a nervous wreck and needed help in getting down.

When veteran J.O. Campbell, candidate for tax assessor, took the stand the suit probably hung in the balance. Campbell and Sid McMath's wife, Anne, had broken "the code," the night before and were able to establish a "definite pattern of 'skip or miss' on issuance of the majority of the tax receipts." He was able to demonstrate by the numbered stubs of the poll tax receipts that every third voter was a Negro and the next two were white. This went on page after page.

Tax Collector Wilson tried to defend his system, however the damage had been done--everyone, including Judge John Miller, could see the manipulation involved and the implausibility of that sequence occurring page after page.

The plaintiffs introduced W.H. Quackenbush of Lawrence, Kansas, a handwriting expert for thirty years and at that time employed by the Kansas Bureau of Investigation. Things really began to look bad for the Administration as Quackenbush began to testify how many of the poll tax authorization signatures had been signed by the same individual. When he started to go into detail, he was interrupted by Judge Miller, "Anybody can tell about those signatures," Miller declared, "I don't think there is any argument but that many of them were written by the same hand."[61]

Judge Miller struck a blow to the Garland County political machine from which it would never recover as he voided 1,607 poll taxes and ordered the names purged from the voter rolls. Over seven hundred of those were stricken from the Second Ward where Leo P. McLaughlin got his strength. The machine was not dead, but it had been sorely wounded.[62]

At the close of the trial Judge Miller passed along some advice as he said, "I think the Democratic party, if it hopes to maintain control of the party, must revamp its entire machinery."

As Leo McLaughlin and some of his cohorts were mulling over their defeat that evening, he received the second blow of the day when *New Era* Night Editor Roy Bosson called him with the news Lucille Griffith had just filed her $200,000 breach of promise suit against him. It appeared that it was going to be a long hot summer for Leo.

---

[60] *Arkansas Democrat*, 10 July 1946.
[61] *Sentinel-Record*, 9 July 1946.
[62] *New Era*, 11 July 1946.

Did Leo McLaughlin accept United States District Judge John Miller's decision to void 1,607 Garland county poll tax receipts? Of course he didn't. He had said immediately following the handing down of the decision, "In compliance with the court's decision, there will be no attempt to vote any of the invalidated poll taxes."[63] But after thinking about it and talking with his lawyers he changed his mind. As chairman of the Garland County Democratic Central Committee, he called a meeting and announced the court decision had nothing to do with the primary or runoff election, but only the general election in November, because that was the only election in which names of the congressional candidates appeared.

Secretary of the committee, L.V. "Rip" Freeman, backed McLaughlin, confirming he had elicited an opinion of the court decree from the law firm of Barber, Henry and Thurman, of Little Rock, and they advised the Judge's "decree did not apply to next Tuesday's primary."[64] Both State Senator Ernest Maner and Prosecuting Attorney incumbent Curtis Ridgway, rose to support this action of the Democratic Central Committee.[65]

Sid McMath immediately gained the floor and with scathing words attacked the two office holders as he said, "Curtis Ridgway and Ernest Maner have sworn solemn oaths to uphold the laws of Arkansas. Had they done their duty in the first place, it would not have been necessary for us to come home from the wars to bring a suit in federal court to protect the rights of the people of this county. "Ridgway and Maner are totally derelict in their sworn duty and they have the effrontery to argue in favor of possible future violations of Arkansas laws they have sworn to uphold."[66]

With time running out before the Democratic primary scheduled for July 30, the G.I.s filed suit in the 18th Judicial Court to remove Leo P. McLaughlin as chairman of the Garland County Democratic Central Committee. McMath and Clyde Brown held no illusions on what the outcome might be and admitted they "didn't stand a snowball's chance in hell," by it being in Earl Witt's court. They may have been disappointed, but not surprised as Witt ruled in favor of the Administration.[67] McLaughlin would remain as chairman.

But perhaps their effort had not been in vain. The mere fact they had openly opposed and challenged the political machine, they had suddenly gained the respect of a lot of doubting voters. The crowds at the political rallys for the veterans groups seemed to increase by leaps and bounds. On July 29, the eve of the primary election, over 6,000 people crowded onto Dean Field

---

[63] *Arkansas Democrat*, 12 July 1946.
[64] Ibid., 25 July 1946.
[65] Ibid.
[66] Ibid. Also, *New Era*, 25 July 1946.
[67] *New Era*, 15 July 1946.

to listen to last minute speeches and promises of the G.I. candidates that the voters' ballots would be kept confidential, something that had not occurred in many years. That same evening the Administration supported candidates spoke to a crowd of several hundred voters in the City Auditorium.

Three days before the election the G.I. faction took out a full page advertisement in the *Sentinel-Record* in the form of "An Open Letter to Henry Murphy Garland County Treasurer." The letter charged Murphy , under law of being the custodian of the Duplicate Ballot boxes after the up-coming election. It cited the statutes of law imposing the duty and trust on the county treasurer to maintain the secrecy of each citizen's vote and the penalty for breaking of that trust. The advertisement was not only designed to remind the county official of his obligation under the law but to instill confidence in the voters that their ballot would be protected and remain confidential.[68] Murphy acted wounded over the advertisement as he said, "Those kids kind of touched me off when they put that ad in."[69] But citizens of that day had a reason to be concerned and did not trust the system of keeping the ballots secret. When young Jacob King, an accountant, had applied for a job in the court house the county official interviewing him, told him to wait a few minutes. When the office holder returned he informed King, "I was just checking your ballot to see if you voted the *right way*."[70] While King was incensed that his vote could be examined by anyone in the courthouse it demonstrated how little the voter was protected during this period.

Another ad placed by the veterans read, "Your Vote Will be Secret, Leo P., Lizzie, George, Lumpy Ed and all the rest of them will be excluded from the polls when you vote."[71]

Election morning, Tuesday, 30 July 1946, broke with an uneasiness and nervousness existing throughout the town. No one knew what to expect. Both political camps were preparing for trouble and both seemed bent on prevailing at all costs. Stories circulated that there were squads of men who were heavily armed, riding around in cars.[72] The G.I.s stationed men at each poll, not only to watch but to be available in the event trouble occurred. One group was kept in reserve at the Ricks-Clinton Buick Company on Market Street, equipped and ready to roll to any precinct in the city or county should trouble develop.[73] Others had home-movie cameras and took pictures of voters in line. Frank "Red" Carpenter, a G.I. supporter, carrying a large aerial camera, snapped his camera at all voters in the Second ward poll with the result many individuals

---

[68] *Sentinel-Record*, 27 July 1946.
[69] Ibid., 28 July 1946.
[70] Taped interview of Jacob L. King by Orval E. Allbritton, 8 April 1998.
[71] *Arkansas Democrat*, 30 July 1946.
[72] Ibid. Also, McMath interview.
[73] McMath interview.

declined to enter the polling place, probably fearful of being accused of some voting fraud. What those people did not know was Carpenter had no film for his camera.[74]

Leo McLaughlin was out bright and early as he always was on election day. He had always been used to going to each poll and putting in an appearance, not that he was needed, but for almost twenty years he had been an intimidating force. When he arrived at the Sixth Ward that morning he had a surprise. He was not permitted to enter, being reminded he lived in the Second Ward and that was where he was supposed to vote. He informed the young man that he was "Chairman of the Democratic Central Committee" and he had always been allowed to enter the polls, "and check on how things were going." To McLaughlin's chagrin the poll watcher and guard was not impressed with his credentials and politely refused his entrance. The mayor seemed ruffled and indecisive, even to the extent he shook the young man's hand twice, but made no further attempt to enter and departed the scene.[75]

All day voters lined up and waited their turn to get in and cast their ballot. Quite often during the day, the phrase, "I challenge that vote," rang out, especially in the Second and Fifth wards. Generally these were some of the 1,607 poll taxes voided by the federal court. Fortunately no gunplay or untoward incidents took place. The counting process at each poll took several hours.

Richard Ryan, a strong supporter of the McLaughlin political machine, was standing on the Rock Island railroad platform observing the lines of people waiting to vote and was overheard to say, "Sometimes I'm glad I'm a Republican."[76]

From the returns reported at the Garland County Court House it appeared that all of the G.I. candidates had gone down to defeat. The Administration incumbents "murdered" their opponents in the two predominately black wards, the Second and the Fifth, while the G.I.s had done quite well in the Third, Fourth and Seventh wards. Late that evening, Sid McMath placed a call to Mt. Ida and learned he had overwhelmed his opponent in Montgomery county to such an extent he had overcome the deficit in Garland county. He had defeated Curtis Ridgway, the Administration candidate for prosecuting attorney. This was the first defeat of an Administration candidate since 1927. Surprisingly, Clyde Brown had beaten Judge Earl Witt in Witt's home county, but because of the heavy vote in Garland county the incumbent had held on, winning, but by only 224 votes. *The New Era* reported, **Litigation Looms Over Second Ward;** and **Montgomery County Voted Against its Native**

---

[74] Ibid.

[75] *Arkansas Gazette*, 1 August 1946.

[76] *Arkansas Democrat*, 30 July 1946.

son, Circuit Judge Earl Witt in Yesterday's Election.[77]

None of the third candidates entered in the various races were a factor and no run-off was necessary. Morris Hecht, in the circuit judge's race drew only 72 votes. Hiram Tucker, who opposed McMath and Ridgway, garnered only 69 votes. Out of the nearly 6,000 votes cast in the sheriff's race, Barney Roark, a native of the county, received only 118. It was the same story for the others.

Keeping their word to the voters, Sid McMath and some of the other G.I.s stayed all night at the court house and did not leave until all duplicate ballot boxes were locked in County Clerk Roy Raef's vault for safekeeping.[78]

It was expected that charges of election fraud would be made in view of the fact that many of the voided 1,607 poll tax receipts had been used for voting in the Second and Fifth wards. A member of the State Democratic Committee had tried to warn Garland County officials telling them, "I would go pretty slow about voting those receipts. You might find yourself in contempt of federal court."[79] But Garland county politicians were not prone in those days to take advice from other sections of the state, generally informing those who freely gave their counsel, "You folks paddle your boat and we'll paddle ours."

It was a bit of a surprise when Curtis Ridgway filed a petition with the Montgomery County Democratic Committee asking for a recount of eight of the county's twenty-one precincts.[80] He then challenged 960 voters in the Sixth and Seventh wards as not "personally assessing" their property and purchasing poll taxes for the year 1944, which qualified them to vote. It is interesting to note he challenged only five votes, all white, in the Second and eight in the Fifth wards. The G.I.s printed all names and requested voters to verify this with George Callahan at the G.I. campaign headquarters. Not totally unexpectedly, Ridgway did not get a great deal of help from the political machine. It was somewhat satisfied to come out of the election losing only two offices, the prosecuting attorney to Sid McMath and tax assessor's to J.O. Campbell, that one by default.

Following the primary, the G.I. group had four courses they could take. First, they could accept the victories of McMath and Campbell, and the defeats of the other candidates and go on with their lives. Sid McMath and J.O. Campbell knew if that happened they would get no cooperation from the Administration and they would be "one-termers" in office.

Second, they could go into court and challenge the improprieties of the voting in the Second and Fifth wards, or third, they could violate their pledge to the Democratic party by denouncing the election methods and enter the

---

[77] *New Era*, 31 July 1946.
[78] Ibid.
[79] *Arkansas Democrat*, 26 July 1946.
[80] *Arkansas Gazette*, 6 August 1946.

general election scheduled in November as independent candidates.

The second choice of going in to local court would mean another travesty of justice with the results predictable and the only recourse would be appealing their case to the State Supreme Court, a time consuming matter, with only a few weeks left until the general election.

The choice of running as independents bore its penalty also, as the opposition could legitimately claim the G.I.s had violated their oath to support the winning democratic candidates in the general election.

After much "soul searching," a compromise between the second and third choices was made. They would file suit challenging only 350 votes as being illegal and to present a slate of independent candidates for the election in November. In a speech at Lonsdale on October 17, Sid McMath declared their "party pledges did not bind them to support Democratic nominees elected by fraudulent and corrupt methods." Clyde Brown, knowing the Administration was sending "spies" to all their rallies, had opened the meeting, "Citizens of Lonsdale, visitors, *a few stooges for McLaughlin*--and friends."[81]

Since the suit was filed in the local circuit court, Judge Earl Witt, realizing he was working on a very small margin of votes from the primary with Clyde Brown breathing down his neck, and not wanting to offend any voters, decided not to risk hearing the case. He recused himself and changed circuits with Judge Lawrence S. Auten, of Little Rock. The transfer seemed not to matter and did not bode well for the G.I.s as Judge Auten threw the veterans out of court on a "technicality." His decision read, "Frank "Red" Carpenter, who notarized the affidavits, (submitted by the G.I.s) was unqualified for the office and therefore that the affidavits were not in legal order as required by law."[82]

But Ridgway could have saved his money, as he, too, was unable to get the vote overturned in his favor. Because of the close scrutiny of both Administration and G.I. poll watchers, there had been little error in the actual counting of votes. And any attempt to go back into the poll tax receipt mess would "just be opening another can of worms." Appeals and other filings were made to the Arkansas Supreme Court, but would not be heard until after the general election.[83]

It was a strange situation. Leo P. McLaughlin was not running for any office yet he was the target of almost every G.I. candidate. Instead of helping, he was becoming more like a millstone about the necks of the court house incumbents because of their involvement in the political machine which he headed. The Mayor's misdeeds were highlighted for the public to see and

---

[81] Ibid., 18 October 1946.

[82] *New Era*, 17 August 1946.

[83] *Arkansas Democrat*, 28 October 1946.

some were just coming to realize what a "strangle-hold" Leo had on the Spa. McLaughlin's own term for mayor would run through March 1947, yet the main focus in the campaigns of 1946, was against the man who was serving his tenth term as the city's chief executive and who wasn't even a candidate in the up-and-coming election. He was being "pot-shot" from all sides as he struggled to save his political machine from crashing onto the rocks of defeat. Strangely silent in this campaign was Verne Ledgerwood whose sound advice McLaughlin no longer leaned on. Ledgerwood's term as municipal judge still had almost two years to run and he could have stayed on the side lines and never entered the game, but he had friends at the court house who needed help and he appeared at some of their rallies. He no longer prepared the campaign literature as McLaughlin insisted on doing that, sometimes going a bit far in his claims.[84]

McLaughlin was by far the most effective speaker on the Administration side and always was the lead speaker at the rallies. He could still generate fervor and excitement in the audiences as he tore off his coat, loosened his tie, and rolled up his sleeves. Then stalking up and down the stage or platform, waving his arms he would began his attack on his "bitter enemies." However, his old charisma seemed duller and perhaps a bit tarnished, even to his most ardent supporters.

Several of the large newspapers sent reporters to cover the entire fall election campaign at Hot Springs. Most of them took a favorable view of activities by the veterans' group and most wrote negatively of Mayor McLaughlin. The *Sentinel-Record* and *New Era*, long Administration supporters, seemed to sense a change might be underway, taking more of a neutral stand, accepting paid advertisements from both sides and printing fair accounts of their rallies.

Dick Allen, reporter for the *Memphis Commercial Appeal*, spent most of the late summer and fall here and wrote how, "Garland county citizens resented high-handed-policies of the long-entrenched machine." The mayor fumed.

John Scudder, a former resident of the Spa and Staff Writer for the *Arkansas Democrat*, had numerous front page articles of the political activities underway and wrote of the literal disregard the Administration had toward the law against gambling. And Leo fussed.

But it was the *Arkansas Gazette* McLaughlin disdained the most and even cursed their Day Editor, John L. Fletcher, who seldom had a nice thing to say about Leo or his cohorts. Leo Patrick was open in his criticism of the state's oldest newspaper. Speaking at a rally in the county one night he told the crowd, "If any of you boys get a skunk under your house, just throw a *Gazette*

---

[84] Bosson, taped interview. Roy Bosson said the papers would set the ads up, but were required to let Leo P. McLaughlin review them before printing.

under there to drive him out."

The sides quickly lined up prior to the deadline to enter the general election, and that ballot looked like this:

For Circuit Judge, Clyde Brown, Independent, versus Democratic incumbent Earl Witt.

For Prosecuting Attorney, Democratic nominee Sid McMath. It appeared for a time that Hot Springs City Attorney Jay Rowland would run against McMath as a "write-in" candidate. He was encouraged by Mayor McLaughlin to make the race and the rumor about town was that it was a "done-deal," however shortly before the election date, Rowland withdrew his name from contention.[85]

For State Senator, David Whittington, Independent, opposed Democratic incumbent Ernest Maner and a Benton resident J. H. Hutchingson.[86]

For Sheriff, Incumbent and Democratic nominee Marion Anderson opposed by Independent I. G. Brown.

For County Judge, Elza T. Housley, Democratic incumbent versus Independent Q. Byrum Hurst.

For County Clerk, Democratic incumbent John E. Jones, opposed by Independent Leonard Ellis.

For Circuit Clerk, Incumbent Roy C. Raef, opposed by G.I. Independent E.M. "Buddy" Houpt.

For County Treasurer, Democratic incumbent Henry Murphy, opposed by G.I. Independent "Billy Joe" Wilkins.

For Tax Collector, Mack Wilson, incumbent, opposed by G.I. sponsored Independent Ray Owen.

For Tax Assessor, Democratic nominee J. O. Campbell, unopposed. Like McMath, it appeared for awhile that he would be opposed in the general election, either by another independent or a write-in candidate. In fact the State Board of Election Commissioners announced Filmore Bledsoe, would oppose Campbell as an Independent Democratic candidate for tax assessor.[87] While Bledsoe had served his country in World War II, his allegiance, upon returning home, had been with the Administration and he had been appointed as a deputy in the Tax Assessor's office when Roy Gillenwater had resigned and Leo McLaughlin had secured the appointment of Harry Lewis to fill his unexpired term. Therefore it was believed by many that Bledsoe was being sponsored by the Administration, then it was learned that Leo P. McLaughlin

---

[85] *New Era*, 27 October 1946. Also, *Arkansas Gazette*, same date, and *Arkansas Democrat*, 28 October 1946.

[86] It is to be noted that the State Senatorial District included Garland and Saline counties, whereas the 18th Judicial District was composed of Garland and Montgomery counties. Maner was very strong in Saline county having many relatives living there.

[87] *Arkansas Democrat*, 18 October 1946.

was displeased with Filmore's entry into the race. Had he failed to ask Leo's blessing? Apparenty so, as Bledsoe told the press, "I am running the race on my own merits and qualifications."[88] Just as quickly as he had came into the race, without filing he withdrew, leaving the office open to Campbell.[89]

For Constable, Monore Young, Democratic incumbent, was opposed by G.I. sponsored Tommy Freeman.

One other race should be noted--that for the Sixth U.S. Congressional seat. Incumbent and Democratic nominee, W.F. Norrel, had defeated Patrick Mullis in the democratic primary. A "token" candidate, who was unsponsored, entered the race from Hot Springs. That was Dr. Marshal O. Evans, a chiropractor, who had run against State Senator Walter Wheatley in 1938, and after losing had filed a court action attempting to deny Wheatley from being seated. The Arkansas Supreme Court had ruled against him.[90]

Election day approached amid a deluge of accusations and counter-accusations. Every night the air waves of radio stations KWFC and KTHS crackled forth with candidates of both factions attempting to convince voters to get out and vote and especially to vote for them. Local and state newspapers had feature articles daily describing the intense campaign underway in the Spa. Both the *Sentinel-Record* and *NewEra* benefitted from the selling of advertising space as full page political notices appeared daily.

In the heat of the political battle, hard and hurtful statements were hurled at each side. Circuit Judge Earl Witt said, "Clyde H. Brown represents all the viciousness of a defeated, disgruntled candidate--his campaign is based on hate --nothing indicative of fitness or ability."

Brown responded by citing his own educational, military and public service records which compared most favorably with those of his opponents, and lashed back at Witt pointing out, "Who has been conducting a campaign of hate? Who shows a lack of fitness for the high office of Circuit Judge."[91]

When Ernest Maner made the statement he was "running his own race on his own money," his G.I. opponent David Whittington took him to task. He printed a copy of the "pink-slip," the McLaughlin machine had prepared and given out for the election of 1942, setting forth "Administration Recommended Candidates," and appearing thereon was the name of Ernest Maner.[92]

The Administration supported candidates had a full page political advertisement on the Sunday before the general election attempting to

---

[88] Ibid., 19 October 1946.
[89] Ibid., 15 October 1946.
[90] *Sentinel-Record*, 17 October 1946.
[91] Ibid., 3 November 1946.
[92] Ibid.

convince voters that Hot Springs had never enjoyed "greater prosperity," than at that time and asking "Why Should You Change? Why Trade Peace for Chaos? Why Substitute Qualified and Experienced Officials For Those Not Qualified and Totally Lacking Experience?"

But what grabbed the attention of a lot of readers, especially after the Federal Court voided over 1,600 illegal poll tax receipts, and learning poll tax receipts for dead people had been voted in previous elections and ballot boxes stuffed, was the statement on this ad, "A Progressive, Prosperous City is Proof of the *Honesty and A bility* of its Officials!"[93] Aw, come on, guys--it was one thing to claim "experience" as most of them had been in the court house for ages, but to boast of honesty in office was something else. These were "home-folks" they were trying to convince, and who had known them for years and the company they kept. It was like preaching to the choir. The office holders were *all* were members of the local political machine. They each had benefitted bythe lack of opposition and support of the organization. They had supported the machine by their actions and deeds, even to the extent of issuing large blocks of dubious poll tax receipts from lists of names written by the same hand. The circuit judge had been in sympathy with the gamblers and the open town policy and had appointed only sympathetic people to grand juries investigating the local situation. The sheriff was cognizant of illegal gambling taking place in the county, but did little to control it unless prodded by the governor or state attorney general. And by their silence, the office holders had condoned a policy that violated state law.

One surprising element in the election was the stance taken by labor. Until World War II, Garland county had never had much of an organized labor base. Little effort had ever been made to solicit mills or manufacturing plants. Leo P. McLaughlin had many times proclaimed that Hot Springs should be known as a "sporting town." But the arrival of the large aluminum plant and its high wages had changed that. In a strange move, the union, "claiming to have 1,000 votes in Garland County, joined the McLaughlin machine against Sid McMath and his G.I. slate."[94]

On the date of the election, November 5, the G.I.s pointed out in an advertisement, "McLaughlin has always refused to work with any organization, religious or secular, that he could not dominate." The "hostility" of the mayor toward the Chamber of Commerce was spotlighted, "because he didn't like its leaders, E.H. Wootton, Bill Seiz, H. King Wade, T.K. Martin and W.E. Chester."

They further commented, "All men who refuse to approach him in the

---

[93] Ibid., p 17.

[94] *Arkansas Democrat,* undated article found on page 89 of Nathan Schoenfeld's scrap book at GCHS. Date probably Sunday 3 November 1946.

attitude of fawning stooges are classed as enemies, and McLaughlin has published to the world, "We just don't do favors for our enemies."[95]

With the campaigning winding down and the date of the election rapidly approaching, tempers were rising on both sides. It was recognized by the leaderships that bloodshed was quite possible. Superintendent of the Arkansas State Police, Jack Porter, received a request from Circuit Judge Earl Witt to send police protection covering the election. On that same date, Governor Ben Laney received a similar request from Sidney S. McMath.[96] Porter assigned twenty members of the State Police to Hot Springs, "to maintain order."

Election eve rallies were heavily attended. Leo McLaughlin, speaking for his cronies at the courthouse and addressing some former servicemen at the City Auditorium lashed away at the the G.I.s. "Why don't they go to work like the rest of you boys did when you came back from the war, instead of wanting us to turn over the courthouse to them?" he asked. "The only thing they've found wrong with our political machine is that we're not supporting them," McLaughlin inaccurately stated. He promised the crowd, "I've been mayor a long time and I'm going to run again for office next April."

In response to the thousand copies of campaign cartoons, entitled, *Rogue's Gallery of Past and Present Performance of* "Leo" *and Company*, he said, "I am not a dictator. I have always looked after the little fellow and the little fellow has always looked after me." Perhaps that had been true at one time, but no longer. A lot of "the little fellows" no longer believed it and had crossed in support to the other side.

Election day, November 5, 1946, was a cold, rainy and damp day, which normally would mean a decrease in the expected voter turnout. Unbelievably, long lines of people with overcoats and umbrellas braved the elements and began to queue up at the polls by the time they opened. There were armed state police guards at all the city precincts, a sign of possible trouble. Fortunately, only minor problems occurred.

By daylight and even before the polls opened, Mayor Leo P. McLaughlin visited every polling place in town talking with the Administration supporters and shaking hands with people waiting to vote. But it was not the usual confident, dapper-dressed mayor the public was used to seeing. Appearing in the *Memphis Commercial Appeal* the day after the election, was a photograph of McLaughlin emerging from his voting precinct that caused people who knew him to stop and scrutinize the picture. Somber and almost gaunt was a tired looking man, wearing no tie, an open-throated shirt with an uncharacteristic

---

[95] *Sentinel-Record*, 5 November 1946.

[96] *Arkansas Gazette*, 31 October 1946.

canvas jacket, sporting no lapel flower or neatly folded handkerchief.[97] The fire and defiance which had always burned in his eyes when opposed or confronted seemed very dim that morning and surely from observing the large turnout of voters, Leo must have suspected what was in store for his courthouse friends later that day. Verne Ledgerwood read the mood of the people correctly, "They wanted a change."[98] And a change they got. The largest voter response in Garland county history took place that day as almost 11,000 people stood in line in the rain and cold to cast their vote.

Circuit Judge Earl Witt, a veteran of the courthouse for over twenty-three years, who had never tasted defeat and had nosed out Clyde Brown by 224 votes in the primary, was the first to concede to his opponent.[99] Not only had Brown doubled the vote over Witt in his home territory of Montgomery county, but he had beaten him by over 1,400 votes in Garland county. Witt conceded the victory with some class as he added his wishes "for success to all the new officials."

One by one the courthouse "crowd went down to defeat. Sheriff Marion Anderson lost to I.G. Brown; County Judge Elza Housley lost to Q. Byrum Hurst (in fact, Hurst defeated Housley in the Second Ward); Treasurer Henry Murphy was defeated by W.J. "Billy Joe" Wilkins; Tax Collector Mack Wilson lost to Ray Owen; County Clerk Roy Raef was defeated by E.M. "Buddy" Houpt; and Circuit and Chancery Clerk John E. Jones was defeated by Leonard Ellis. The only bright spots for the Administration were Constable Monroe Young held on to defeat Tommy Freeman, and Ernest Maner defeated David Whittington for State Senator.[100]

In one fell-swoop, the courthouse was swept clean. A total of 176 years experience had been voted out of office.[101] A new day had dawned on the Spa but would it prove to be any better?

---

[97] *Memphis Commercial Appeal*, 6 November 1946.

[98] Ledgerwood.

[99] *Sentinel-Record*, 7 November 1946.

[100] Ibid. Also, *Arkansas Gazette* and *Arkansas Democrat*, 7 November 1946.

[101] *Arkansas Gazette*, 31 December 1946. This included such long term "occupants" as Elza T. Housley, 34 years as county judge and county treasurer; Circuit Judge Earl Witt, 24 years; Circuit Clerk John E. Jones, 24 years; Prosecuting Attorney Curtis Ridgway, County Clerk Roy C. Raef, and County Assessor Harry Lewis, each with 16 years experience as office holders or deputies, etc.

TO THE VICTOR BELONGS THE SPOILS

The election victory by the G.I.s was proclaimed throughout the nation and many newspapers carried full accounts of the happenings. One publication in a neighboring state summed it up in an editorial: "The victory of the young war hero, Sidney S. McMath, for prosecuting attorney and friends in the two-county district including Hot Springs, Arkansas, carries touches of national signifiance because of the probability that it sounds an eventual death-knell for the 20-year rule of one of the most notorious gambling political machines in all 48-states - the machine headed by Mayor Leo P. McLaughlin under which Hot Springs has become an infamous mecca for seekers and operators of all forms of vice."[1]

The editorial further pointed out the McLaughlin machine's "control was so strong that often there was no opposition to its candidates at primary time." The editor of that paper certainly had the correct slant on Garland County politics.

Late in December 1946, Carl Bell of the Associated Press, announced that the biggest news story of the year in Arkansas, was the overthrow of "old-line" county political machines by the returning war veterans.[2] The victory had pleased many people, disappointed others and confused some.

There were a number of citizens who believed the county had merely traded one political machine for another. "Not so," said the leader of the G.I. group, Sid McMath. He was quoted that he and his friends, "have no intention of attempting to organize a political machine to replace the one headed by Mayor Leo P. McLaughlin." The Ex-Marine explained, "Our first objective is to repair the breaks in the election machinery in Garland county which have denied the people fair and honest elections."[3]

It was true, there would be no threat of a political machine arising from the ashes of the old one. First of all, the old office holders had held on tightly to the jobs they had and none seemed to want to run for a higher or state office. That was not the case with the young G.I.s. They had been places and on the move for years. Ambition burned within some of them to the extent they would not remain at Hot Springs for long as they sought other ventures. Some would enter private business and make their mark there. There seemed to be no desire or leadership who was interested in setting up a political machine. A couple, Leonard Ellis and Ray Owen, would "bounce" from one office in

---

[1] *The Shreveport Times*, Editoral entitled, "Emancipation For Hot Springs," 25 November 1946.

[2] *Arkansas Democrat*, 20 December 1946. The only other "top-ten" news story from the Spa that year was the destruction, by fire, of the Great Northern Hotel, a landmark since before the turn of the century.

[3] *Arkansas Gazette*, 8 November 1946.

the court house to another for several years. One of the G.I. office holders would even be impeached from office and another would be sent to the penitentiary. But before anything else took place the newly elected G.I.s had a job to finish. They had deposed the county half of the political machine in the November election, now they needed to concentrate on the city election scheduled for April 1947.

McMath had served warning to Mayor McLaughlin, two days after the election, "If he [McLaughlin] endeavors to maintain a city machine, we will use the weapons we have available."[4]

The mayor was not dense and understood exactly what McMath was alluding to as he was now the duly elected prosecuting attorney and was backed up by the Garland County Sheriff's office and the powerful circuit judge's office--all the legal machinery needed to effect anything legally in the county. Neither the political machine or the gambling community could operate or exist without the support and cooperation of those county officials. Verne Ledgerwood had figured out the system a long time before and Leo P. McLaughlin had honed it to perfection and even as it sagged under its own corruptness it had lasted nearly twenty years.

There was a definite concern in the gambling clubs throughout the city as to whether they would be allowed to continue operation following the swearing in of the newly elected officials. During the campaign, the G.I.s had carefully hidden any preconceived opinions concerning gambling, although it was known that some in the G.I. camp approved of gambling while others did not. A couple of the G.I.s were in favor of letting the system continue operating illegally with gamblers paying periodic fines. Some of the others were in favor of trying to "legalize" it.[5]

Shortly after the general election the newly-elected sheriff, I.G. Brown, was queried on the question but refused to be drawn in to commenting on the status, saying, "I am still a private citizen and will not become a law enforcement officer until January 1, therefore I don't feel it would be proper for me to comment." Other G.I.s took a similar stance.

Before the election, the *Sentinel-Record* had come out with an article and asked, "What will the G.I.s do about gambling? The item pointed out, "Hot Springs was filled with businessmen who considered gambling as something necessary to attract "the spending class" of tourist trade and where gambling is considered more or less a reputable business."[6]

Others were troubled by the prospect that gambling houses might be forced to close. Emmett Jackson, long-time city clerk, furnished figures reflecting that

---

[4] *Memphis Commercial Appeal*, 8 November 1946.
[5] *Sentinel-Record*, 10 November 1946.
[6] Ibid.

over $31,600 in fines had come from the gambling community in 1946. All of that had come from the seven clubs in operation. It was believed, should that revenue be lost to the city, it would become necessary to raise the occupation and real estate taxes, always an unpopular move.[7] For years Mayor McLaughlin had boasted he had operated the city's entire street department from fines gamblers had paid.

With the "swearing-in" date rapidly approaching, the gambling house owners became almost frantic in trying to ascertain what the newly-elected court house politicans planned. They were suddenly leaderless. Leo P. McLaughlin had assumed the oversight and direction of the clubs following the death of W.S. Jacobs late in 1940. But with the election of the G.I.s, and because of the bitterness of the campaign which had just taken place, McLaughlin knew he was without credit with the victorious veterans. Several individual owners began to try and "feel-out" what the G.I. position would be, but to no avail.

The clubs began preparations to close operations, packing and crating some of their more valuable pieces of equipment, roulette wheels, dice tables and slot machines. Some of these were taken to little known and safe storage facilities in the county. It was reported that several club owners were preparing to take "extended vacations."[8] The last day of operation, December 28, John L. Fletcher of the *Arkansas Gazette* reported that horse players, "ran over each other trying to put down heavy money on horses that wouldn't come in. Their farewell contributions to the Garland county pot must have been cheering to the boys who split it."[9]

Another news source reported Sid McMath was out of town and "The word had been passed if they were operating the next week he would run them out of business."[10]

From Jack McJunkin and the McGraw brothers' Southern Club on upper Central to Erb Wheatley's Reno Club near Bridge Street and across Central Avenue to Longinotti's, situated over Jim's and George's Cafe, down to the leading black Cameo Club operated by "Bubba" Page and Leslie "Fresh Out" Norris, the lights went out at 5:15 p.m.[11]

Some of the club owners headed to Dallas and the Cotton Bowl where the Arkansas Razorbacks would take on the Louisiana State University Tigers on New Years Day. Two local football stars were a part of that University of Arkansas team, Alton Baldwin and Bud Canada. If those gambling house

---

[7] Ibid. Undated article found in Nathan Schoenfeld's scrapbook, page 45.
[8] Ibid., 29 December 1946.
[9] *Arkansas Gazette*, 29 December 1946.
[10] *Memphis Commercial Appeal*, 28 December 1946.
[11] *Arkansas Gazette*, 29 December 1946.

owners thought the climate at Hot Springs was cool to them, it was nothing compared to the frozen weather conditions in which the game was played that day, ending up in a tied score, 0-0. Several thousand fans were marooned in Texas for several days. Leo McLaughlin and his party stayed at the Adolphus Hotel and did not venture in to the frigid stands but listened to the game on the radio. The next week he tried to get Bud Canada to refund him for his unused tickets. Bud tried to explain to the mayor that refunds were not due on unused tickets. Leo was not happy at this news.[12] The new year did appear interesting, if not promising.

A few minutes after midnight on New Years Day, January 1, 1947, nominee Clyde Brown stood behind the judge's bench in the circuit court room at the Garland County courthouse, and in front of long time Chancellor Sam Garratt. "I, Clyde H. Brown," he repeated, "do solemnly swear, that I will faithfully discharge the duties of the office of Circuit Judge in and for the 18th Judicial Circuit."

Chancellor Garratt replied, "You are now the circuit judge, and I congratulate you."[13] These words were completed at 12:10 a.m. and spotlighted a watershed moment in the history of Garland county. Not only was a new year beginning, but it marked a new era in the political life of the county.

A few minutes later the new judge swore in I.G. Brown as county sheriff. The other seven, Sidney McMath, Q. Byrum Hurst, Leonard Ellis, Ray Owen, Billy J. Wilkins, J.O. Campbell and E.M. Houpt were sworn in that afternoon with family and friends overflowing the court room witnessing the ceremony.

The new office holders had been "miffed" by a childish act by some of the outgoing officials who had set the court house flag at half-mast, in a state of mourning, to denote their "passing."[14] But most shocking to several of the newly sworn in county officials were the condition of their offices and lack of furniture and equipment.

New Prosecuting Attorney Sidney McMath discovered his office equipped only with one "cuspidor, a table, chairs and no desk, or phone." County Judge Q. Byrum Hurst was informed by Roscoe Owens, newly-appointed road overseer, that only one of four of the county road graders would operate and it needed repairs. Only two of the five county pick-up trucks were usable. All tools, which had been owned by a former maintenance supervisor had been taken.

---

[12] Bud Canada - interview. Canada said what really "galled" him was that he knew McLaughlin had not paid for the tickets which had been bought by Jack McJunkin.

[13] *Sentinel-Record*, 1 January 1947.

[14] *Arkansas Democrat*, 2 January 1947. A picture of the flag at half-mast accompanied the article.

The most unwelcomed surprise probably was reserved for Sheriff I.G. Brown. As he inspected the jail facilities he was appalled at the filth that had been allowed to collect in the cells, probably since the election. Old newspapers, dirt, cans and bottles littered the floors. An uncovered garbage can over ran with whiskey bottles--and this was inside the jail area. Exposed and bare electric wires were hazardous, the plumbing was in a deplorable condition and the "stench was almost unbearable." Two old stoves had faulty connections and endangered the lives of the inmates. In retaliation, Brown invited newspaper reporters and photographers to tour and view the facilities. He ordered the incarcerated men to work, sweeping, mopping and painting the interior of the jail, and then had a plumber and electrician to make the area safe.

Sheriff Brown also discovered there were no shotguns, rifles or machine guns available and initially assumed the previous sheriff and deputies had "cleaned-out" the place. This idea was quickly corrected when it was learned that all of those guns had been the personal collection of former sheriff Marion Anderson who had sold the guns to the Hot Springs Police Department.

When it was learned how little furniture had been left in the court house, many private citizens donated items of furniture for use Former county clerk, Roy C. Raef, came to the defense of the former county officials. He told an *Arkansas Democrat* reporter that much of the furniture reported missing from the offices of ex-Prosecuting Attorney Curtis Ridgway, ex-Circuit Judge Earl Witt, and ex-Sheriff Marion Anderson was the personal property of those individuals. He explained that County Judge Housley "was too economical to spend money on office furniture for county officials."[15] That helped explain the missing furniture situation, but not the condition of the county jail.

But not all the county offices were in that condition. The only thing that Judge Witt took was his large desk chair which he had purchased. Ray Owen reported that all furniture and equipment was in the tax collector's office when he took it over. To his predecessor's credit, former collector Mack Wilson had invited Owen to meet with him and go over the duties of the office and to acquaint him with the record system. Owen said he was appreciative of this overture.

The former officials had the opportunity to be "good sports" about the losses of the offices, which they had held so long, however the bitterness of the past campaign would not let them.

Even though Leo P. McLaughlin had "weathered" the election he realized his political machine had been badly buffeted by the adverse vote. The only bright spot for the mayor, before the end of the year, was the planned

[15] Ibid.

celebrations around the dedication services and naming of the new airport for him, McLaughlin Field. And even that was becoming a worry to the haggard McLaughlin. A few years earlier no one would have dared openly oppose him or complain, but now, groups were organizing to oppose the naming of the airport after him. Leo was determined to go through with it and a weak-kneed city council was still afraid of him and were not prone to oppose his will. He had said he intended to run for the office of mayor again in April 1947, and from all evidence the council seemed to believe he was as strong politically as he ever was. The sixteen councilmen were sadly ignorant of how the political climate in the Spa had changed and how the Mayor had been weakened by the November election.

In his run for circuit judge, Clyde H. Brown had promised the voters in a campaign speech on October 3, if elected, he would call a special grand jury to investigate Leo P. McLaughlin and his contact and control in the Spa's gambling. When he took office he discovered a grand jury already assembled by the previous circuit judge, Earl Witt. Brown dismissed that jury in February and convened another.[16]

From the 4th of March to the 24th of that month, Hot Springs was treated to a classic example of the far-reaching power and depths a grand jury might probe into a community and its activities. A searching inquiry into the affairs of the city and county was made. Inspection of volumes of city and county records was undertaken. The summoning, subpoenaing and interviewing of 162 witnesses was conducted. Many of these were city and county employees, businessmen and gambling club owners and employees, and the grand jury's probing questions sent tremors throughout the community. The gambling community became quite concerned and apprehensive as subpoenas were issued requiring the books of the clubs be opened for inspection by an accountant on the grand jury, Jacob King.[17] Even though some of the books may have been "cooked," they provided a lot of information and revealed clues for further investigations.

There were nightly meetings of some of the gamblers and members of the Administration for the purpose of comparing notes on what sort of questions the Grand Jury was asking. The operators and employees of these club

---

[16] *Sentinel-Record,* 1 April 1947. Leo P. McLaughlin would later claim Judge Brown in dismissing the old grand jury, 21 February 1947, "Without cause," and that the newly summoned jury was composed of 16 men, "all of whom are members of the G.I. political organization or are ardent supporters thereof, who openly and publicy declared themselves to be political and personal enemies---" had violated his Constitutional rights. Leo was probably more right than wrong in this allegation. The grand jury was weighted heavily with G.I. supporters. Of course, McLaughlin didn't mention the fact that his machine had been doing the same thing for 20 years.

[17] Jacob King.

wanted to each tell the same story in order to protect all, but in doing so their testimony was so similar it was noticeable. "There has been an organized effort to withhold evidence from this Grand Jury," the report read, "To the extent much of the testimony is identical."[18]

Even before the final report was printed indictments began to "rain forth."

One of the first was for the arrest of the old gunfighter from the Central Avenue shootout in 1899, and the leader of the con-artists and games of 1913, "The Fixer," Ed Spear. Until the first of the year, Spear had been serving as a deputy constable and a special tax assessor for Harry Lewis, the replacement appointed for Roy Gillenwater, who had resigned. Spear became aggressively active during the recent political campaign, and even more so in trying to "prevent a witness from testifying before the Grand Jury," with threats of force.[19]

The Mayor's likeable and even-tempered secretary, Hazel Marsh, was charged with perjury as she walked a "tight-rope" trying to present her boss in a favorable light and was very vague in her answers, which did not impress the sixteen jurymen.

Samuel Kirsch, Sr., operator of Esskay's Art Gallery, was also charged with perjury.

Elmer Walters, known as the Mayor's "bag-man" and "messenger" and who had no offical title at city hall, was indicted with "accepting city funds illegally."

Then, the Mayor's brother, George McLaughlin, who had drawn a check from the city for twenty years, but seemed to have no duties to perform was charged with accepting city funds illegally.

The only court house official to be indicted was former county collector, Mack Wilson, who was charged with being "as an accessory to illegal voting."[20]

The sheriff and Grand Jury announced the two gunmen who had robbed Earl "Birdie" Fulton and Oliver Livingston of affidavits during the campaign had been identified, apprehended, and charged. The two were taxi driver, T. G. Hightower and truck driver Fred Wilson. The men pled "guilty," but would only admit each "had been paid $15.00 per day to watch the activities of the G.I. investigators and that the affidavits they had taken from Fulton and Livingston had been delivered to a 'prominent politician' in the city hall."[21]

Hot Springs City Attorney Jay Rowland was charged with bribery in connection with transactions involving the sale of the Hot Springs Water Company.

---

[18] *Arkansas Gazette*, 23 March 1947, direct from the Grand Jury's report.
[19] Ibid.
[20] *Arkansas Democrat*, 23 March 1947.
[21] *Arkansas Gazette*, 23 March 1947.

But all these seemed anti-climatic to the charges leveled at Mayor Leo Patrick McLaughlin. A total of thirty-seven charges were made by the Grand Jury, and included in sixteen indictments against the city's chief executive officer "ranging from accepting bribes to being indirectly interested in the operation of gambling houses."[22] These charges of his included accepting bribes, being an accessory to illegal voting and misuse of public funds.

When the first nine indictments were issued it was well into the evening and Leo was home with his family, when the officers arrived for his arrest. Sisters Stella and Elizabeth accompanied him to the court house and were permitted to sign his bond. It is to be noted that when the booking took place there were a number of reporters and photographers present. Leo would blame I.G. Brown and his deputies with having "set him up," by notifying the press in an attempt to humiliate him. The summons for the last seven indictments were personally delivered by Sheriff Brown and Deputy Sheriff Walt McLavey who located the Mayor and his sister, Stella in their box at Oaklawn Park "just as the third race was completed." It must have been like the taking of a king from his citadel or sanctuary. Was nothing sacred to these G.I.s?

McLaughlin was surprised to learn that his sisters would not be permitted to sign any further bail and surely it must have been demeaning to the proud Mayor to have to ask two of his supporters, John Wolfe and Ed B. Mooney to be his guarantors. After booking, Leo was taken to the city jail, just a short distance from his office in the city hall, where he was "mugged" and fingerprinted."[23] No doubt, it was terribly embarrassing to McLaughlin. And in hindsight, perhaps the G.I.s were rubbing it in a bit much. Many detractors of Leo believed he was at last getting what was coming to him, but it was abhorrent to the many McLaughlin supporters to believe anything so degrading would ever befall the Mayor who had been a symbol of strength and defiance for two decades. The mighty had indeed fallen.

But more revealing and unpleasant news was to come. Over the past years the general public had developed a sort of ho-hum attitude toward reports from grand juries. The findings never criticized city or county officials and were generally used to hear evidence against criminals for indictment. Not this one, however. When the lengthy final report of the Special Grand Jury was released it burst over the Spa like a mighty fourth of July skyrocket. It surprised even the most calloused citizens and shocked those around the state who were not acquainted with the "shady aspects" of politics in Garland County. The *Arkansas Gazette's* headlines bespoke the Spa's miseries, **Jurors Charge Shocking Graft in Hot Springs**, and **Deplore Conditions under Rule of McLaughlin.** Well, Leo had always said John Fletcher of the *Gazette*

---

[22] Ibid. One of the indictments was later dropped, leaving the Mayor to face fifteen
[23] *Arkansas Democrat*, 23 March 1947.

Mayor McLaughlin was arrested at Oaklawn Park and taken to the Garland County Sheriff's Office to make bond. Pictured here are Sheriff I.G. Brown, deputy Walter McLovey, Mayor McLaughlin and his sister, Stella.

was out to get him, but were the other papers more forgiving? It didn't appear so in the *St. Louis Post Dispatch*, or the Memphis *Commercial Appeal* as both carried full-length stories of the Grand Jury's findings. The *Arkansas Democrat* filled its pages with, **McLaughlin Controlled $30,000,000 Gambling Syndicate, Jury Charges.** That paper's reporter, George Douthit wrote," The Special Garland County Grand Jury Yesterday linked Mayor Leo P. McLaughlin's Administration with a $30,000,000 a year gambling syndicate, controlled and operated under direction of the city hall."[24]

Many Sunday readers that March 23 came to realize just how morally corrupt their city and county governments had been as they commenced to read the Grand Jury's full report and its tone of outrage, as it began:

"Our investigation has revealed a shocking series of crimes; bribery, attempted bribery, malfeasance, misfeasance, non-feasance in office, graft, misuse of city funds, and other crimes and misdemeanors committed by officials of the City of Hot Springs and others. Those crimes against the

[24] *Arkansas Democrat*, 23 March 1947.

people of Hot Springs, Garland County and the State of Arkansas have permeated the city administration. They have gone from the highest officials to employees performing minor public jobs.

"The extent of graft and corruption in this city is unbelievable. Its effect has directly or indirectly touched our school system, our social, religious and business lives.

"It is certain that there has been gross negligence on the part of former county officials, the circuit judge (Earl Witt), the prosecuting attorney (Curtis Ridgway), and the sheriff (Marion Anderson). No effort was made to enforce criminal statutes of this state.

"These officers knowingly permitted violation of election laws in order to insure their re-election. They thereby made possible the continuance of a gambling syndicate of immense proportions. There was a co-ordinated effort to encourage disobedience of the laws, to encourage a disregard of the rights of the citizens. The county officials submitted themselves and their offices to the will of the Mayor of Hot Springs."[25]

The report then became more direct. It alleged the following against Leo P. McLaughlin: (1) That he accepted bribes of $25 a month from each of four wholesale beer distributors, the Falstaff Distributing Co., C.J. Spencer and Co., L.D. Cooper and G.L. Merritt and Son. (2) That he was an accessory to illegal voting, influencing thirteen followers, including several gamblers, to obtain lists of persons to whom poll tax receipts could be issued under the bloc system. (3) That he was indirectly interested in conducting gambling houses. While he was acting as the Administrator of the estate of the late W.S. Jacobs he "corruptly rented the gambling houses known as Club Belvedere and the Southern Club to Otis McCraw, Otho McCraw, J.O. McCraw, Jack McJunkin and George McLaughlin. Mayor McLaughlin sold gambling paraphernalia at the clubs to the new operators and received a commission from the rent and sales and charged that the clubs were openly operated illegally under his protection."

Many "irregularities" were noted concerning the conduct of officials of Hot Springs though no indictments were issued, either because the statute of limitation had expired or the offense was minuscule in comparison to other infractions. Some, however, were spelled out: (1) The city engineer, L.R. Plemmons, had engaged in private business and secured contracts from the city for work without competitive bidding. He secured employment as engineer on paving projects by virtue of his office. He used city employees, trucks and equipment for his personal benefit and the benefit of other city officials. (Plemmons would later deny some of these allegations) (2) Mayor

[25] *New Era*, *Arkansas Gazette*, 23 March 1947. Direct quotation from Grand Jury report.

McLaughlin used city employees and equipment for his personal gain. City employees and trucks were used to haul materials for buildings on his private property. City employees and equipment were used to build the major portion of the private horse trotting grounds constructed on private property on Malvern Avenue. (3) City books indicate gross extravagances at the municipal airport. The city paid Alderman Moody $200 a month while the airport was being built --. (4) Hundreds of thousands of dollars worth of equipment was bought without proper presentation to the City Council. Most of this equipment was purchased from one individual.[26] (5) City property has been sold without proper notice and advertisement. Five city trucks were sold, without public bids, for $50 each to the mayor of Hot Springs, the city street commissioner, an alderman, Mr. Timberlake, E.J. May and Drew Adams, city employees.

The report pointed out that when private gravel haulers complained that city employees and street equipment had been used on private jobs and that it took away their livelihood, they were penalized and denied access to the city gravel pits, "their principal source of supply."

The Grand Jury discovered that Aldermen Frank Grant and Carl Wilson, both elected officials, were occupying paid positions on the city payroll, a violation of state law. Grant was drawing a salary as "deputy city collector" as well as his $30 monthly salary. Carl Wilson was drawing a salary as "superintendent of the city disposal plant," in addition to his alderman's pay.[27] There were a number of other areas of the Grand Jury's investigation which appeared suspect, but the lack of time precluded further inspection. It was recommended a closer look be made.

And what was the reaction to the Grand Jury's report from Leo P. McLaughlin? As expected, the Mayor replied, "I am not guilty of *any of the charges* that have been made against me, and I do not in the least fear the outcome of any of them."[28] Leo must have forgotten that on several occasions when being interviewed by out-of-town reporters or article writers he had almost bragged at opening the town up, permitting illegal gambling and that he fined the gamblers on a regular basis to off-set the city's operating expenses.

Publicly, McLaughlin may have sounded bold and defiant, but to his close

---

[26] Percy Hinton, a salesman for the *American LaFrance* fire trucks and related equipment company, was very close to Mayor McLaughlin and all the fire equipment purchased after 1927, was through Hinton, generally without bids being offered. It is to be noted that the equipment was of the highest quality and there were no complaints on that quarter. It can only be speculated as to whether or not there was a "kick-back" to the Mayor, if so, it would not be an isolated incident.

[27] *Arkansas Gazette, Arkansas Democrat, New Era*, all 23 March 1947.

[28] *Arkansas Gazette*, 23 March 1947.

associates, Leo was shaken. His political machine had undergone a sever mauling in losing the November election. Then the city-half of the machin had been decimated by the Special Grand Jury report.

McLaughlin had already announced his intention to run for mayor a unprecedented eleventh term.[29] Things had changed and to his supporter surprise, Leo withdrew his name as a candidate!

To the public, the giant had been slain and David had cut off Goliath's hea --the McLaughlin political machine was dead. An era had passed away.

It would be a week from the time of the city election until the induction o the new mayor and council members. Leo McLaughlin lost no time in callin a special council meeting and made certain that all of the city's bills were paid- leaving the city debt free and with "sufficient money in the City Treasury" t carry on the City's business.[30]

On the evening of April 7, Leo P. McLaughlin addressed the citizens of th Spa by radio. McLaughlin was a bit melancholic as he reminisced that he ha been sworn in as the city's mayor exactly twenty years to the day. He reflecte that when he first went in office the "affairs of the City were in a deplorabl condition." In fact, the city was so broke he was forced to borrow mone from the County Collector to meet the pay roll and pay the monthly bills o the City. He said there were outstanding bills of $80,000, which did no include utility bills of $110,000 and the city had a bonded indebtedness o $300,000.[31]

As Hot Springs' first full-time mayor, McLaughlin introduced a plan whic included "establishing a financial program so that the operating expenses o the City could be kept within its income and at the same time, a sinking fun was created for the retirement of all unpaid bills and outstandin indebtedness."[32]

Leo McLaughlin reviewed the improvements that had taken place in the cit since he had assumed leadership, the numerous streets which had been pave the partial solving of the downtown flood problem; the improvements whic had been made in the water and sewage departments and the modernizatio of those agencies, especially the building of a new disposal plant. Several majo pieces of fire fighting equipment had been purchased. The police departmen had been modernized with new cars and a two-way radio system, only th second in the state.

---

[29] The local papers announced McLaughlin's intention to run for Mayor on 2 February 1947, however he had indicated prior to that date he was going to be a candidate.

[30] *New Era*, 8 April 1947.

[31] *Sentinel-Record*, 8 April 1947. Also, LAT-Jimmy Dowds. Dowds, an accountant, sai McLaughlin was a shrewd negotiator on behalf of the City and worked with the utilit companies until the debt was paid off.

[32] Ibid.

The outgoing mayor described the enlargement of the City's street department, the City's water supply and the health department.

McLaughlin could rightfully be proud of some of his accomplishments. The Spa was a more beautiful place because of the many new paved streets which were kept free of litter and a street flusher kept Central Avenue neat and clean. He had placed the city's affairs on a solvent basis and had been a good administrator, carefully planning improvements while staying within the city's limited budget. In his speech he acknowledged that no new parks had been built, but said he was for them.

It probably seemed to the listening public that the Mayor had taken the "high-road" in his speech and had left personal issues and politics out. Then, he commented on his part in securing "the magnificent $2,000,000 airport that bears my name," and "Because I had taken such an active part in getting it built, members of the City Council honored me by giving the field my name."

Leo just couldn't let it go, and in an almost whining tone continued, "Until recent political campaigns, the airport has been kept free of political contamination. It now is in politics." Anyone acquainted with Leo P. McLaughlin realized that anything the mayor had a hand in was always *political*, one way or another. And to so stubbornly resist the petitions of thousands of the public to name the airfield after the many dead soldiers, sailors, marines and airmen who had lost their lives in defense of their country, was nothing short of selfishness on his part. In fact, he had refused to accept the petitions when presented at a council meeting. He had completely lost sight of the fact that the mayor's job was a patronage position permitted by the voters and even though he had controlled the local election process for many years, the ultimate power still lay in the hands of the public.

Before concluding his talk, McLaughlin added, almost threateningly, "Let me state in all sincerity that if those who are to direct the affairs of the City for the two ensuing years wish to chisel out the words, "McLaughlin Field" on the Administration Building, or if they wish to gratify their personal animosity to me by removing the stone having that designation, that will be all right with me. But it must be remembered the United States Government has an equity in this building."[33] Politicians in Washington wanted no part of this "hot-potato" and had no intention of antagonizing several thousand voters over a "lame-duck" local mayor's ego. Leo P. McLaughlin was "whistling in the dark." No longer was the general public afraid of him or his political fangs, and certainly not the new Mayor, Earl Ricks and seven newly elected councilmen, who had been sworn into office by Circuit Judge Clyde H. Brown.

During the second council meeting presided over by Mayor Ricks, petitions

---

[33] Ibid.

containing over 7,000 names of citizens, were presented, "asking that the airport's name be changed."[34]

Mayor Ricks commented, "This is distasteful to me, however, I do not know of an airport anywhere in the United States that has been named for a man who has never been in an airplane." McLaughlin's aversion to air travel was quite well known.[35]

The newly elected alderman from Ward One, J.B. Johns, introduced a resolution to change the airport's name from McLaughlin Field to Memorial Field. The resolution passed 10-4, with only McLaughlin holdovers, Moody, Downen, Blahut and Miles casting the dissenting votes.[36] Three of those four would lose their seats in the next election, the other would not be up for reelection for two years.

Two contracting firms volunteered their services, without charge, to remove Mcaughlin's name from the airport. Rededication plans were made with Walter Schrader being appointed chairman on charge of the festivities.[37]

A "low-key" rededication of the airport was held May 30, 1947, on Memorial Day. Appropriately, Sidney S. McMath, who had started the upheaval of the Garland County political machine, gave the dedicatory speech. Honored during the ceremonies were sixteen men who had given their lives in World War I, and163 who had made the ultimate sacrifice in World War II.

Lon Chessey and his Arlington Hotel Concert Orchestra played and was accompanied by "Miss Dora Jane Ledgerwood, one of Hot Springs' outstanding young vocalists," who sang "The Lord's Prayer," and "My Buddy."

Leo McLaughlin made no public comment on the changing of the airport's name, but it must have been a "bitter pill" and a blow to his ego. His friends had "told him he had made a mistake" in letting his name be placed on the airport in the face of such severe opposition, however in typical McLaughlin fashion, he was hearing only what he wanted to hear.[38]

The transition of the City's government went much better than expected, although there was considerable tension among the several hundred people attending the opening ceremonies. The old council, met briefly without going Mayor McLaughlin and concluded one item of unfinished business. McLaughlin then adjourned the meeting and with hardly a glance or word to anyone walked slowly out of the room, thus ending his long and flamboyant political career.

---

[34] *New Era*, 19 April 1947.
[35] *Arkansas Gazette*, 20 April 1947.
[36] *Ibid.*
[37] *Sentinel-Record*, 14 May 1947.
[38] *Arkansas Gazette*, 20 April 1947.

Circuit Judge Clyde H. Brown then swore in Ricks as Mayor and seven new ouncil members.[39]

The week before the new officers were sworn in, L.R. Plemmons, city ngineer for the past fourteen years had submitted his resignation.[40] So had 'arl Wilson, alderman and superintendent of the sewage disposal plant.[41]

Most noticeable, was the swearing in of James R. Long, replacing Vernal nell Ledgerwood, Police and Municipal Judge for the past thirty-four years.

Ledgerwood had quite a struggle in reaching the decision to resign his osition as he still had a year to go on his term. As he saw his friends resigning heir positions, one by one, and Leo McLaughlin withdrawing from the nayoralty race he decided to go. He wrote a letter of resignation to Governor 'en Laney, setting the day of his departure as 7 April 1947.

Word of Ledgerwood's resignation spread rapidly and when the Judge ntered the third floor municipal court room for the last time he was surprised t the size of the crowd. *Sentinel-Record* reporter Edna Lee Howe covered the urist's last day. "Persons from all walks of life, representing both races, many f them with tear filled eyes, Monday said good-bye to Judge Verne edgerwood, who completed 34 years service as Hot Springs' only municipal udge. This quiet-mannered, soft-spoken jurist wrote 'finis' to a long, colorful areer in the city hall his father helped build in 1904, as he disposed of the inal case on Monday's docket. He has heard more than 200,000 such cases ince taking office."[42] He told the packed courtroom he was leaving with ertain regrets, but added, "I am getting a great load off my shoulders."[43]

A few moments were then taken as tributes were paid to the retiring nunicipal judge. The Garland County Bar Association expressed its regrets f Ledgerwood's resignation and Attorney Richard Ryan reviewed his long ssociation and friendship with the jurist. A new gavel, of seven different inds of wood, made by Otis Young, was presented to the retiring judge on ehalf of the "Young family."[44] It was estimated that Verne Ledgerwood had scended and descended the three flights of stairs in the city hall over 20,400 mes, a distance of over 309 miles.

---

[39] *Sentinel-Record*, 8 April 1947.

[40] Ibid., 3 April 1947.

[41] Ibid., p. 10.

[42] Ibid., 8 April 1947. Longtime Hot Springs Attorney Earl Lane, said had Verne edgerwood wanted to stay on the bench that there was nobody in the county would have been nable to unseat him as he was popular in the business and professional community.

[43] LAT-Ledgerwood. He said that while he enjoyed being in the "center of verything", he had begun to feel the daily pressures. He never said outright he and Leo IcLaughlin were having difficulties, however, he did indicate they no longer saw "eye-to-eye."

[44] The gavel which Ledgerwood had used for so many years had been given to him y a resident of the Panama Canal Zone and "was fashioned from a mahogany cross-tie used y the French in building a railroad in the canal zone."

State Representative James R. Campbell added a little humor to the solemn occasion as he said, "One angle, which is not meant facetiously, and which I think [Robert] Ripley [Believe It Or Not] should be informed of is that you have never found a man not guilty."[45]

The change-over of administrations was moving rapidly. Mayor Ricks began his appointments of various offices within city hall. He announced he would not reappoint Cecil Ledgerwood as city plumbing inspector, who had held that position for over twenty years. He had no criticism of Cecil, but saying, "He's had the office long enough."

The Mayor named Dr. R.F. Smallwood as head of the City-County Health Department on April 25. The following day it was announced the firing of Fannie McLaughlin and her sister Helen Mahaffery from that unit.[46]

The popular Fannie McLaughlin had headed the health unit for over twenty years and her sister had worked there for eleven years. The only reason given to Fannie by Smallwood, of her dismissal was, "You know why you've been discharged," --suggesting politics. Even Mayor Ricks said he had never heard anything against Mrs. McLaughlin's service with the Health Department. But he said it had always been his policy to back his department heads.

But Fannie McLaughlin would not be without a job for long. She walked up the hill on Prospect and was hired by Leo N. Levi Memorial Hospital as superintendent of nurses. A few years later, when Regina Kaplan retired after thirty-five years as administrator of the hospital, Fannie would be elevated to that post.[47]

Weldon Rasberry, the only man to ever hold the title of Safety Commissioner for the City of Hot Springs, submitted his resignation, which was accepted by the new city council.[48] When Mayor Ricks announced he was appointing George L. Callahan to fill the police chief's job, all kinds of problems developed. Callahan, who was short on experience, having served only as a deputy sheriff for four years, was immediately resented by ranking officers in the department, including Captain Milford Sanders, who had been serving as acting chief.[49]

Members of the police department hired State Senator Ernest Maner to represent their interests. Maner alleged the appointment of Callahan was

---

[45] *Sentinel-Record*, 8 April 1947.

[46] Ibid., 26 April 1947.

[47] Ibid., 31 December 1950.

[48] To Rasberry's credit there was never much controversy involving his leadership of the police and fire departments, although he was resented by higher ranking and more experienced officers in both departments. He later served four years as a deputy sheriff. He died in 1963.

[49] *New Era*, 27 February 1948. Also, *Sentinel-Record*, 11 February 1948, *Arkansas Democrat*, 12 February 1948, etc.

invalid since the offices of Police and Fire chiefs came under authority of the Civil Service Committee, which had been created in 1933. Maner, of course, never once mentioned that from the year a Civil Service Committee was appointed in the Spa, until 1947, when Leo P. McLaughlin withdrew from the mayoralty race, the commission had not been convened to select the head of any of the city's department, including the firing of Joe Wakelin from the Police Department or replacing Loyd Tate, Fire Chief, who died in office. Or, for that matter, to hold competitive tests for promotions inside the departments. All of that had been handled by "His Honor, Leo P." No one, including Ernest Maner, attorney for the Arkansas Municipal Police Association, had dared to object. Now the officers within the police department were crying "foul" as Ricks tried to appoint the man of his choice, a well-known G.I. supporter.

Local officers told the press they would not obey orders from Callahan. Then the Civil Service Committee, emboldened by the sudden publicity, gave forth a statement. Chairman Leland Leatherman issued a directive that orders from Callahan "must be obeyed," at least until a court decision was rendered.[50] One state paper's headlines reported, **Virtual Revolt Begun By Police in Hot Springs.**[51]

Then a "volley ball" legal battle developed. Chancellor Sam Garratt signed an order "enjoining" George Callahan from serving as "chief" but allowed him to hold the office as Commissioner of Public Safety.[52] Maner then filed a petition to "enjoin" Callahan from holding the Commissioner's position as that would still put him in charge of the police department as well as the fire department. The Arkansas Municipal Police Association, which had been backing the local officers in their fight, announced that organization had "solely" been interested in the case from a civil service point-of-view, and wanted no further part in the Spa's "messy" struggle.[53] Even the Arkansas Supreme Court tried to pitch the "hot-potato" back to the Spa by ruling "authority was vested entirely in the Civil Service Commission."

The CSC met and ruled that Callahan had been hired under the "emergency clause" of its regulations, as there were no qualified applicants in the department ranks, and not based on "experience." Tests were offered and only one officer applied and was turned down as the Commission said his spelling and writing skills were very poor as well as other deficiencies. This set off another round of suits. Again Judge Garratt became involved and this time his

---

[50] *Sentinel-Record*, 26 February 1948. Other CSC members beside Leatherman, were Cleveland Smith and Herbert Brenner.

[51] *Arkansas Gazette*, 26 February 1948.

[52] *New Era*, 26 February 1948.

[53] *Sentinel-Record*, 27 February 1948.

ruling upheld Callahan's appointment.[54] Then the Supreme Court would overturn Garratt's last ruling.

That was only one of the problems Mayor Earl Ricks had to deal with his first year. There were others, almost as perplexing. In trying to overhaul the garbage and trash pickup, the garbage haulers were upset and went on strike. Then a hot dry summer caused a severe water shortage, even to the extent of the city having to ban the watering lawns, washing of cars and limiting of bathing was imposed until emergency pipe lines were laid to the lakes to alleviate the water shortage.

After only one term as mayor, Ricks had had enough and accepted an air adjutants' appointment from then Governor Sidney S. McMath.

Sidney McMath used the Prosecuting Attorney's office as a stepping stone to run successfully for Governor.
Here he stands behind a table of items, all manufactured in the State of Arkansas.

[54] Ibid., 16 May.

JUDGEMENT DAY FOR SOME

From mid-summer 1947 until the end of 1948, citizens of Garland and Montgomery counties were treated to daily dosages of political maneuvering as Prosecuting Attorney Sidney McMath and his two deputies, Nathan Schoenfeld and David Whittington, prepared their cases against those indicted by the grand jury.

It was obvious that Leo P. McLaughlin's two lead attorneys, Henry Donham, of Little Rock and C. Floyd "Babe" Huff, had adopted a strategy of delay and stall. If trial could be abated for a while, the prosecutors and people might grow tired of the entire process. Too, the longer the delay the dimmer the memories of witnesses become. And the papers were filled with former Mayor McLaughlin's moanings about how his "constitutional rights," were being violated and "how it was a shame," that he could not get a fair trial "in the county I was born in." Then his attorneys filed a writ, seeking "to block further action here."[1] A petition was submitted to the Arkansas Supreme Court claiming that the special grand jury, which had indicted Leo McLaughlin and his cronies, had been convened "illegally." That court's decision was brief and to the point as it stated, "Writ Denied."

Even when Circuit Judge Clyde H. Brown disqualified himself from trying the cases and agreed to exchange circuits with Judge Maupin Cummings whose court had jurisdiction over Washington and Madison counties, the defense was unhappy.[2] It wanted the privilege of choosing who would have judgement over the defendants. The prisons are full of people who would have enjoyed that privilege. The Supreme Court rejected that request, too.[3]

Wiggling and squirming like a pig caught under a gate, McLaughlin's two attorneys came up with what they called, "a better solution." Let the Garland County Bar Association choose who would hear McLaughlin's case. Yeah! Right! Doubtfully, there was not a single attorney in town who did not favor either the G.I.s or the McLaughlinites. They struck out again.

Attorneys Huff and Donham then petitioned Federal Judge Miller of the Western District Federal Court of Arkansas to remand the case from local to Federal jurisdiction. Miller ruled this was not something of a federal nature and ordered the case to be tried on the local level. Huff and Donham, grabbing for straws, appealed Miller's decision to the Eighth District Court of Appeals at St. Paul Minnesota, even though no procedural precedence existed.

When Federal Judge John B. Sanborn asked Attorney Huff, "Do you really believe that an order to remand is appealable?" Huff's weak reply was, "This

---

[1] *Sentinel-Record*, 23 April 1947.
[2] *The Arkansas Handbook, Fifty-Second General Assembly*, pp. 83-84.
[3] *New Era*, 28 September 1947.

involves the civil rights and constitutional rights of my client. We think this is a *little* different than the ordinary case."

Nathan Schoenfeld, representing the Prosecuting Attorney's office, calmly contended, "There are no cases on record that allow an appeal from an order to remand. "This move is purely and simply an attempt to delay the scheduled trial. The attempt to bring the matter before this court is frivolous. The law is very clear."[4]

Upset by the preparedness of Schoenfeld, Huff offered to go to trial "in the federal courts starting September 17th, to prove there has been no effort to delay the case." To which, Schoenfeld remarked, "We are willing, too, but the federal courts do not want jurisdiction."

The three-judge appeals court agreed with the deputy prosecutor's assessment and ordered the case returned to the local courts in Arkansas.[5] Other efforts were made to delay the trial, for some real or contrived reasons.[6]

Sid McMath and deputies, eager to begin trying some of the ex-administration defendants, and thwarted from getting a trial date for Leo McLaughlin, changed their tactics and requested Judge Maupin Cummings to schedule trial for City Attorney Jay Rowland, charged with bribery. Cummings agreed.

The Rowland family had moved to Hot Springs in the early 1920s. Rowland had entered a law practice during the Depression and because of the lack of business, had run for public office, hoping to get a regular salary to help feed his family of six. He was unsuccessful in that race and he had learned quickly that if you ran for political office in Garland County you needed the blessing and backing of Leo P. McLaughlin. Rowland was a quick learner however, and curried McLaughlin's favor offering to do "little" favors for him. When A.T. "Sonny" Davies fell ill Rowland volunteered to fill his place as city attorney. His offer was accepted. With Davies gravely ill, Leo McLaughlin had Rowland appointed "acting city attorney." Then when Davies passed away Rowland was easily elected to that post, "unopposed" and with the full support of the Administration. Also, Rowland, with McLaughlin's nod, was successful in winning a position on the Hot Springs School Board. He was called a "leader" and "pillar" in his church.[7] Thus, he had worked himself into a powerful position and had become an important cog in the administration's political machinery.

When charges of bribery were filed against the city attorney, many believed

---

[4] *Arkansas Democrat*, 31 August 1947.

[5] *Arkansas Gazette*, 31 August 1947.

[6] See *Sentinel-Record*, 27 September; *New Era*, 28 September; *Arkansas Democrat, 15;* all 1947 and *Sentinel-Record*, 18 February 1948, and others.

[7] Jay Rowland held the office of President of the Board of Trustees of the Orange Street Presbyterian Church.

it was politics that was "paddling the boat." By the time the trial ended, they weren't so sure.

The two attorneys representing Rowland, Henry Donham, and C. Floyd "Babe" Huff, were very meticulous in examining the prospective jurors. They excused all veterans, save one, from jury service. "They asked elderly veniremen whether their sons or other close relatives were veterans." McMath and his assistants were equally discriminating and "wanted no juror who had worked for the city or who had been remotely associated with Mr. McLaughlin."[8]

As the trial opened, Prosecuting Attorney McMath informed the jury the State was prepared to prove that Mr. Rowland had accepted $50.00 a month from Otis and Otho McCraw, operators of a hand book at the Southern Club, in return for promising that the law against gambling would not be enforced. Also, that the city attorney received the money "for the benefit of himself and Leo P. McLaughlin."[9] It was also stated that it would be proven that Rowland accepted like sums from other gambling houses.

Further, the State contended, it would prove "Rowland with accepting $200 a month for 20 months from the Associated Art Galleries, an unincorporated group of auction houses, in return for his promise that he would use his influence in "emergencies."[10]

There was a third indictment against Rowland for accepting $500 from taxicab owner "W.O. 'Tiny' Bredwell, and others to influence him in preparing an ordinance "giving them special privileges." Judge Cummings ruled that the indictment did not charge violation of the law and dismissed that part of the case.[11]

It was obvious to the crowded court room that the first men subpoenaed by the state were reluctant witnesses. They were referred to as ex-gamblers since gambling in Hot Springs had been shut down. Otis McCraw, representing the Southern Club, Fred Nichols, former operator of the Main Cigar store "book," and Walter Weldon, "formerly" operator of poker and dice games at the Lone Star and Milwaukee bars and a horse book at the Tulsa Club, took the stand.[12]

---

[8] *Arkansas Gazette*, 7 October 1947.

[9] Ibid.

[10] Ibid. At that particular time some of the auction houses along Central Avenue had customer's complaining against them, "switching merchandize" or misrepresenting the "quality of jewelry" sold. There were instances where police officers accompanied complaining customers to the store and being ordered to return the money. When Rowland commenced representing them, officers quit bringing complainants to the houses. Those were the "emergencies."

[11] *New Era*, 6 October 1947.

[12] Ibid., 7 October 1947.

Each of the three witnesses admitted that for two years they had paid Jay Rowland monthly for "legal services," although it was very vague what those "services" were. The bookies admitted to having delivered the "monthly fees," at times to Hazel Marsh, the mayor's secretary, and once or twice, cash was given in person to Leo McLaughlin, "to give Jay Rowland," but they claimed it was never their intention that the money was a "bribe." They finally agreed that the money given to Rowland was "to protect them in the event they were arrested."[13] In spite of vigorous efforts by Rowland's defense counsel, they were unable to prove to the jury Jay Rowland had ever performed any services to the gamblers.

When the city attorney took the stand, he was quite willing to confirm the gambler's stories that he had not accepted the monthly fees as bribes, but as he described them as "retainer fees," a lawyer's term.

What really became most damaging to Rowland was the revealing of his involvement in his part of the "shady" sale of the Hot Springs Water Company's municipal bonds. The bonds were for the purchase of the water company by the City of Hot Springs from its owners, a New York Corporation. The sale of the bonds had been placed in the hands of the City Council's Water Committee and City Attorney.

The testimony of witnesses regarding this matter was quite a revelation to the citizens of the Spa and equivalent and as pleasing as opening a can of worms. After listening to only two witnesses, it became evident that not only was Jay Rowland representing the interests of the City of Hot Springs as its attorney, but that he also was in the employment of the Villereal Bonding Company. Lewis Cherry, investment broker for the Villereal Company explained his company's reason for employing the city attorney was "We wanted an attorney who was close to the administration."[14] And who was closer to the administration than the city attorney? Oh, yes, Cherry admitted his company did have its own attorneys to assist. You bet they did!

As Judas Iscariot delivered Jesus Christ into the hands of the Pharisees, Jay Rowland delivered the Hot Springs bonds into the hands of the bonding company. But Rowland was paid much better than Judas, who received a few pieces of silver. Rowland received $50,000.[15] Of course, $15,000 of that sum was called a "finders fee."

A "finders fee?" The sale of the bonds had been left in the hands of the Council's Water Committee, Frank Moody, Sam Smith and City Attorney Rowland. Like Little Bo Peep's lost sheep, were the city's water bonds lost and needed someone to find them? The people's trust, supposedly rested with its

---

[13] *Arkansas Gazette*, 9 October 1947.

[14] Ibid., 8 October 8 1947.

[15] Ibid., 9 October 1947.

elected officials, seemed misplaced.

Lewis Cherry testified that a day or so after he had mailed Jay Rowland his "finders fee" check of $15,000, Rowland appeared at his office in Little Rock and asked Cherry to cash the check as "he didn't want the people of Hot Springs to know about the fee."[16] Why not? Rowland said he was afraid the voters "wouldn't understand." Of course they wouldn't understand. Any first semester law student could have pointed out there was a strong conflict of interest in Rowland attempting to represent everyone. As Prosecutor McMath told the jury, "He was City Attorney, for the people of Hot Springs, attorneys for the gamblers, auctioneers, and bond brokers. What Master was he going to serve?"[17]

But wait, there's more! After the bonds cleared and Rowland received another $35,000, he generously shared $11,500 each to the two aldermen on the city council who had helped deliver the bonds to the Little Rock firm, council members Sam Smith and Frank Moody.[18] When Frank Moody told the court, "Mr. Rowland said the money he gave us was a "finders fee," the court room was rocked with laughter."[19] However, it did not appear humorous to Rowland and his defense counsel.

While hindsight indicates Rowland was guilty of accepting bribes, it wasn't so clear to the jurymen over fifty years ago. In fact, the jury asked Judge Maupin Cummings for clearer instructions on what constituted "bribery?"

Cummings summoned the attorneys for both sides into his office in an attempt to agree on a simple set of instructions for the jury. That was a mistake as a "heated argument" took place between the two sets of lawyers. After an hour of this wrangling, Judge Cummings asked the attorneys to return to the court room. He told them, "I appreciate your interest, but I am not going to have another morning like I have had today. I am going to write my own definition. Just let your nerves cool off. I am not going to put anything over on either side and you may see a copy of my definition before I read it to the jury."[20]

But the new instructions did little to clarify the problem as after nine hours of deliberation, the jury was hopelessly deadlocked, 6-6.[21] At 11:00 a.m. Judge Cummings dismissed the jury. An onlooker, Leo P. McLaughlin, smiled broadly, as did City Attorney Jay Rowland.[22]

---

[16] This is a direct quote from the court transcript and can be found in *Arkansas Gazette*, 8 October 1947.

[17] *New Era*, 9 October 1947.

[18] *Arkansas Democrat*, 8 October 1947.

[19] *Arkansas Gazette*, 8 October 1947.

[20] *Sentinel-Record*, 8 October 1947.

[21] *Arkansas Democrat*, 9 October 1947.

[22] *New Era*, 9 October 1947.

Their glee did not last long however, as Prosecuting Attorney McMath requested Judge Cummings for an "immediate retrial" of Jay Rowland. Defense attorneys, surprised at McMath's request, stormed to their feet, objecting. Cummings overruled the objection and granted McMath's request for an "immediate new trial."

"At least," pleaded the stunned Henry Donham, "Let us have a recess until tomorrow morning to get our wits together." Cummings agreed.[23]

Both sides quickly issued new subpoenas and had the constable's office begin serving them. Try as the constable would, the two city ex-councilmen, members of the Water Committee, Frank Moody and Sam Smith, could not be found. They had quickly disappeared after the first trial and did not reappear in the Spa until after the second Rowland trial had ended. This time their testimony was not needed as City Attorney Jay Rowland was found "guilty."[24] He was sentenced to a year in prison and a fine of $750.[25] It was announced that the city of Hot Springs was filing suit in chancery court against former aldermen Moody and Smith to recover the $11,500 "finders" fee they had accepted.[26] What a reversal--it sent shock waves through those indicted on other charges.[27]

The verdict and sentencing of Jay Rowland had occurred on a Sunday morning. Prosecuting Attorney Sidney McMath, announced plans to begin the trial of Ed Spear the following day. Spear had reportedly been ill the last days of the Rowland case and a daily report of his condition was furnished the court by Attorney C. Floyd Huff. Then on the last day of the trial, Spear's physican, Dr. Lon E. Reed said Spear's "health would permit his appearance."[28]

As it turned out, there was not much of a trial for Ed Spear as his "plea of guilty," not only stunned the court but "took his own counsel by surprise."[29]

---

[23] Ibid. Also, *Memphis Commercial Appeal*, 10 October 1947.

[24] *Arkansas Gazette*, 11 and 13 October 1947.

[25] *Memphis Commercial Appeal*, 13 October 1947.

[26] *Arkansas Gazette*, 16 October 1947.

[27] *Arkansas Democrat*, 18 October 1947. Rowland's attorneys immediately filed for a new trial, which was denied at the circuit level, then later sustained by the Arkansas State Supreme Court. Several efforts were made at Hot Springs, by friends of Jay Rowland ,to keep him from going to the penitentiary and to free him after he went. Three sets of petitions were presented to Governor Sidney McMath to pardon him, however McMath refused. Then in what appeared a "concocted" scheme, the Governor traveled to Washington, D.C. and Lt. Nathan Gordon was also out-of-state, which made Ellis Fagan, pro-tem of the senate acting governor. Fagan, too, left the state making James R. Campbell, speaker of the house, acting governor. Campbell had papers ready for such a situation, signed them, and filed the forms with the Secretary of State restoring Jay Rowland's civil rights. *Sentinel-Record*, 9 July 1951.

[28] *Sentinel-Record*, 14 October 1947.

[29] *New Era*, 10 October 1947.

The *Arkansas Democrat*'s headline told the story, **Spear's Dramatic Action Sock to Own Attorneys.**

Prosecuting Attorney McMath advised the court that several days before he had been requested by Spear and his wife to come talk with them. Prosecutor McMath informed the court, "I went out and talked with his (Ed Spear's) family. He wanted to plead guilty and asked me what my recommendations would be in the case."[30] McMath said he had made no promises to Spear nor did Spear promise to testify against any of the others indicted.

After the judge called a ten minute recess to "ponder" the situation he returned to the court room and summoned the defendant to stand before him. Ed Spear, known as "The Fixer," and "McLaughlin's Handy Man," stood meekly and attentive, as Judge Cummings addressed him.

"Such procedure of pleading guilty without informing your counsel of what you intended to do, is most unusual and embarrassing."

Judge Cummings then passed sentence on the crusty old gunfighter and con-man and gave him a three-year suspended sentence.

Then the court rendered an unusual sentence. "The conditions under which I give you this suspended sentence are, that you shall go to the church of your own choice regularly and behave yourself. You haven't gone to church much and it will be good for you. You are 75 years old. You may live for another 10 years and you may not live another 30 minutes. It is time for you to settle down and make the rest of your life clean and good."[31]

"You won't have any more trouble with me," Spear told the jurist. "I am going to live the right kind of life the rest of my life." Spear was overheard in a low tone to say as he was leaving the court room, "Hell, I just about as soon go to the pen as have to go to church."

George McLaughlin's trial was next. The ex-mayor's brother was charged with "having accepted $21,612 in city funds which he did not earn."[32] The indictment charging the ex-mayor's brother, stated his name had been on the city's payroll for twenty years and "that his job was never authorized by the City Council."

City Clerk Emmett Jackson told the court he had come to work for the city in 1934 and that George McLauhlin's name was on the payroll. "What exactly did he do?" asked Sid McMath.

"He appeared in my office every morning and went with us up to Municipal Court. He came down after court to the Mayor's office or to the fire department. That was the usual procedure."

"What did he do in court?" Jackson was asked.

---

[30] *Arkansas Democrat*, 14 October 1947.

[31] Ibid.

[32] *Arkansas Gazette*, 17 October 1947.

"He would stand behind the judge's desk."

"What did he do besides stand?"

The witness paused, then answered, "That was all. He never had any specific or general duties as far as I know."[33]

Former Safety Commissioner Weldon Raspberry told the court, "George McLaughlin was around the city hall every morning and was on the payroll as long as I was there. The police department did not have a police clerk. I do not know what George McLaughlin's duties were."[34]

Former Municipal Judge Verne S. Ledgerwood testified, "George McLaughlin performed no duties in my court. I didn't know he was on the city's payroll until six months before I retired."[35] When Verne Ledgerwood said he didn't know George McLaughlin was on the payroll, until he read it in the papers, "the crowded court room laughed aloud."

Roy Bosson, correspondent for the *Arkansas Democrat* and a former reporter and night editor for the *Hot Springs New Era*, testified he had "covered the city hall for years," but knew of no assigned duties for George McLaughlin.[36] George, according to Bosson, came and went as he pleased.

As the *Arkansas Gazette* wrote, George McLaughlin was the mystery man of the Adminstration.

Probably at this point in the trial had a vote of the jury been taken, George McLaughlin would have been convicted. But the defense was just coming up to bat.

Aldermen Dewell Jackson, Edgar Mowery, W.R. Downen and Ed Vance and former alderman W.B. Timberlake, all testified they were aware that George McLaughlin had been on the city payroll but no one could describe what his job was or what he was being paid to do.[37] They weren't much help to the defense.

It therefore appeared that the only thing that might keep George out of the cotton fields of the state penitentiary would be the testimony of his brother, former mayor Leo P. McLaughlin. Leo had been looking out for George's interests for many years. He had helped extricate him from his involvement in the death of police chief Sullivan, who was gunned down by Hubert Coates, George's companion. Leo had most certainly helped to produce a "farce" of a trial of George over George's killing of "Fats" Long. Leo had helped George secure an interest in the Southern Club and permitted him to do some things he would not allow others to do. But what could Leo say to sway at least part

---

[33] *Sentinel-Record, 17 October 1947*

[34] *New Era*, 16 October 1947.

[35] *Arkansas Gazette*, 17 October 1947.

[36] Ibid.

[37] *Sentinel-Record*, 17 October 1947.

of the jury?

"I hired George as an *undercover man* in 1937," Leo dropped on the surprised court room. "He reported to no one except me. I *didn't* even tell Chief Rasberry."[38]

John Fletcher with the *Arkansas Gazette* seemed skeptical as he wrote, "The McLaughlin brothers kept their secret so well that the police chief, city clerk, municipal judge and aldermen didn't learn of it for 10 years. The latter officials testified today, seven months after the McLaughlins left office, that they still didn't know it."[39]

When Leo McLaughlin said, "All law violations *ceased* in Hot Springs after George became a crime investigator," the court room was rocked by raucous laughter as most people in the Spa viewed the ex-mayor's brother as a bumbler, not as a "super-sleuth." Judge Cummings pounded his gavel for order.[40] It took several minutes until the spectators had quit their snickering.

The general public in the Spa speculated, "Would George McLaughlin take the stand in his own defense? The smart-money was that he would not. George, they reasoned, would be "cannon-fodder" for the ambitious Prosecutor Sid McMath and his tenacious deputy Nathan Schoenfeld. Defense attorneys Donham and Huff realized the danger of letting George face the two ex-G.I.s, and they kept him seated and silent throughout the trial.

After deliberating two hours, the jury reported to Judge Cummins it was deadlocked 8-4. Cummings ordered the twelve jurors to "resume deliberations."[41] After two more hours of deliberations, and with the hour late, the jury reported there had been no change in the vote and "we are hopelessly deadlocked."[42] The weary Judge Cummings discharged the jury.[43]

There was no joy or elation on the part of the defense or state. George McLaughlin, sullen-faced, refused to permit photographers to take his picture.[44]

The defense attorneys were slow to move from their table, perhaps expecting Prosecuting Attorney McMath to request that a second trial begin immediately as he had done in the Rowland trial. But, there was no such request, as the prosecutor's team was as tired and worn out as the defense.

---

[38] *Arkansas Gazette,* 17 October 1947.

[39] Ibid.

[40] *Sentinel-Record,* 17 October 1947.

[41] *Arkansas Gazette,* 17 October 1947.

[42] *New Era,* 17 October 1947.

[43] *Sentinel-Record,* 17 October 1947. It was later reported that the 8-4 vote had been for conviction.

[44] A photographer with the Tyron Co. had snapped a picture of George McLaughlin without his permission, and reportedly was "blessed-out" by the defendant. *Memphis Commercial Appeal,* 17 October 1947.

The mistrial brought various comments from around the state, but J.G. Coughlin of West Memphis put the situation into prespective: "For countenancing this degrading racket (gambling) the city government of Hot Springs collected in the form of "fines" less than one-tenth of one percent of the gambler's take and even this meager financial benefit was wasted in such obvious misappropriations as "salary" payments to the Mayor's brother George who, after twenty years on the payroll, could find not a soul, save his own brother, who would testify that he'd ever done a lick of work."[45]

Or how about this one? "While not the first man in Arkansas to be charged of drawing down a municipal or government salary without working for such, (George) McLaughlin was accused of holding the record - for two decades Mayor McLaughlin was in office."[46]

Ex-mayor Leo P. McLaughlin was the fourth member of his administration to be scheduled for trial. Efforts to have the case tried in federal court had failed as had the defense's efforts to prevent Judge Maupin Cummings presiding over it.

Defense attorneys Henry Donham and C. Floyd Huff petitioned the eighteenth judicial circuit for a change of venue to remove the trial from Garland County to Mt. Ida in Montgomery County.[47] McLaughlin added his voice to the plea, telling the press, "Every officer of Garland County and the Garland County Circuit (Court) is hostile toward me."[48]

A total of 164 witnesses were summoned by the defense for the change of venue hearing alone.[49] It appeared that it would be a long and arduous hearing, but in a surprise move Prosecuting Attorney Sidney McMath told the court "the State will not contest the defendant's motion for a change in venue, and even further joins the defendant in his request that the cases be transferred to Montgomery county."[50] The young prosecutor added, "The case already has become a classic in legalistic delay."[51]

When the court concurred in the change of venue to Mt. Ida there was a flurry of activity to reserve rooms at the four small tourist courts in the Montgomery County seat. While the expectation of businessmen in Mt. Ida was that there would be a big surge in business, the Mayor J.I. Brakefield, operator of an auto parts company and garage, was not enthused. Bemoaning the lack of communication to the outside world he commented, "We're just

---

[45] *West Memphis News*, 28 October 1947.
[46] *Arkansas Democrat*, 26 October 1947.
[47] *New Era*, 12 November 1947.
[48] *Memphis Commercial Appeal*, 13 November 1947.
[49] *Sentinel-Record*, 13 November 1947.
[50] *New Era*, 13 November 1947.
[51] *Sentinel-Record*, 14 November 1947.

to small to cuss very loud and we're too big to cry."[52]

At that time Mt. Ida was ten miles from the nearest railroad and had no telegraph and only one telephone line. The owner of the single telephone line, H.D. Straughn of Glenwood, promised to quickly "string two additional lines." Western Union quickly leased one of the new lines and with the expectation of a lot of news wire reports to be sent and assigned an operator.[53]

Fortunately, the court room, where the trial was to be held was large and occupied almost the entire second floor of the stone courthouse which had been constructed in 1923.

For several days preceding the trial there were a rift of rumors afloat that some on the jury panel had been "contacted" by parties interested in the case and that "bribes" had been offered. Assistant Prosecutor David Whittington later acknowledged that some juries in Montgomery County had been "approachable."[54]

One rumor that was making the rounds was that a gambler from Hot Springs, who was very close to the ex-mayor, had made a sizeable donation to the Mt. Ida band "to buy new uniforms." This turned out not to be just a rumor, but fact. Jack McJunkin, part owner and operator of the Southern, Belvedere and Tower clubs, admitted to having bought several tickets from the Mt. Ida Band Mothers Auxiliary. McJunkin susposedly returned the tickets to the members, telling them, "My only request is that if I get in jail over here, I want the band to come and play for me."[55]

Another story indicated that several livestock farmers, who just happened to be on the jury panel, had sold some cattle to outsiders for very handsome profits in hopes of influencing them.

Apparently Judge Cummings became aware of the possibility that the jury panel might be "contaminated" and he decided to do something about it. He announced at the beginning of the trial that he was "disqualifying the entire panel."[56]

"What?" screamed out defense attorney Donham. "Can't we have a conference on this? I don't know that the defendant (Leo P. McLaughlin) is requesting that the panel be disqualified and I don't think that the court has the power to do it, unless the defendant requests it."[57]

Seemingly disorganized, Donham pleaded, "We will need time to confer and ask that you give us 30 minutes. You're doing things so fast we need a little

---

[52] *Arkansas Democrat*, 16 November 1947.
[53] Ibid.
[54] LAT - Whittington.
[55] *Sentinel-Record*, 21 November 1947.
[56] *Arkansas Democrat*, 18 November 1947.
[57] Ibid

Just why wasn't defendant McLaughlin willing for the jury to be changed? He had requested his case be changed from local to federal jurisdiction. He had requested that a judge other than Maupin Cummings be assigned to hear his case. And, he'd asked that venue be changed from Hot Springs to Mt. Ida. Was the fix already in on this jury? Cummings wasn't taking a chance.

Judge Cummings was firm as he told the defense counsel, "I am disqualifying the jurors anyway. It is the only fair thing to do in the matter."[59] The only reason advanced by the jurist was, "The motion for a change of venue from Garland to Montgomery county set up as the principal reason for a change the *bitterness* and *intensive* feeling that existed between Judge Clyde Brown and the defendant and as far as I am concerned I want the defendant to get as fair and impartial trial as is humanly possible to give."

Judge Cummings went on to point out that the defense attorneys had alleged that McLaughlin's request for a change of venue was because Judge Clyde Brown had appointed the jury commissioners in Garland County, to which the defense had objected. Cummings reasoned, Judge Brown had also appointed the jury commissioners in Montgomery County. Donham's own arguments were being used against him and the defense sat silenced as Judge Cummings ordered Montgomery Sheriff Bill Black to summon another set of jurors.[60] "I want men of high character, above reproach. I want a few women. I want some jurors from the towns in the county and some from the rural sections. I want them not of one religious faith and not involved in politics in this matter."[61]

Sheriff Black realized he had a big job to do and he had no deputies to assist him. That evening and night he rounded up twenty-nine of the thirty-six required prospective jurors. He had driven over 300 miles on rain-slicked dirt and gravel roads. He had not slept all night and was about to report to Judge Cummings that he needed more time when he got a break. As he started to park on the courthouse square, Black spied a sizeable crowd of people on the sidewalk in front of a store. The Merchants Association was having a drawing for a prize of $100 and they were gathered for that. Like a hawk swooping down on a flock of unsuspecting chickens, Black cornered the group and came up with the remaining seven jurors.[62]

All thirty-six of the jurors were examined before twelve were finally selected. The jury was composed of eight farmers, two clerks, one barber and one merchant. Their ages ranged from 25 to 65 years. In spite of the caution by the

---

[59] *Sentinel-Record*, 18 November 1947.

[60] *New Era*, 18 November 1947.

[61] Ibid.

[62] *Sentinel-Record*, 20 November 1947. Also, Sheriff Bill Black provided an interview tape in the Life and Times of Leo P. McLaughlin project, 3 April 1986, the interviewer being Dick Whittington.

circuit judge in selecting the jurors, there were several who had been bird-hunting partners of former Municipal Judge Verne Ledgerwood, who attended every day of the trial.[63] "I'd hunted with some of those boys for years, and just thought my presence there might help."[64] It probably did.

McLaughlin was being tried on the first of twenty counts, namely on the charge of bribery. Specifically, that the gift to the former mayor by Jack McJunkin of a list of the names of 269 persons from whom McJunkin had obtained authorization to purchase poll tax receipts and represented a bribe.[65] It was alleged by the State that the bribe of lists of poll tax receipts was in return for McLaughlin's political influence as mayor of Hot Springs in allowing McJunkin to continue operation of a gambling house.

It had been Prosecuting Attorney Sidney McMath's intention to call as his first witness the black owner and operator of the Pastime Club, Will Page, Jr., but as so often occurred in the past of trials in Hot Springs, the witness had suddenly disappeared. Page, and his father, who had admitted at an earlier hearing of obtaining over 2,000 names on poll tax lists, many of which were fraudulent or even dead, had evaded a subpoena and set off for parts unknown. Some of his closer friends suggested "he might be in St. Louis, but they did not know his whereabouts."[66] The suggestion that Page might be in St. Louis was an obvious attempt to mislead the authorities. Midway through the trial word leaked out that he was hiding in North Little Rock. Prosecutor McMath dispatched an officer to help him find his way to the trial.[67]

The trial opened with Prosecuting Attorney McMath trying to build his case on the poll tax lists which had been gathered by various gamblers and which had been presented to the mayor to curry his favor.

McJunkin took the stand and Jack admitted he had assembled a list of 269 persons for whom he purchased 1944 poll tax. He "denied emphatically" that his compilation of his list was connected in any way with his operation of a gambling house.[68] He said he was just interested in politics. The courtroom was rocked with laughter and Judge Cummings rapped for order.

He also testified he had never talked with Leo McLaughlin about poll taxes or gambling. He did admit he had purchased a twenty-five percent interest in the building housing the Southern Club from the Jacobs Estate, administrated by Leo McLaughlin, but of course, he said, Leo was not aware it was to be used for gambling as had been going on in the building for nearly fifty years. Again, loud laughter rang out. McJunkin claimed he delivered the poll tax lists

---

[63] LAT - Ledgerwood.

[64] Ibid.

[65] *Memphis Commercial Appeal*, 18 November 1947.

[66] *Sentinel-Record*, 20 November 1947.

[67] Ibid., 21 November 1947.

[68] *New Era*, 20 November 1947.

to Miss Hazel Marsh, the mayor's secretary.[69]

McMath pointed out to McJunkin, "You did testify before the grand jury that you got up the lists to stay in the gambling business, did you not?"

McJunkin's memory suddenly failed him and said, "I do not remember what they asked me."[70]

Jack McJunkin, loyal to the end, claimed he had never talked to the mayor about poll tax lists or gambling houses and denied they had a pact to help each other. McMath told the court, "The State is surprised at the inconsistency of the testimony of Jack McJunkin."

Three Hot Springs firemen, including Fire Chief Thad Rogers, took the stand and testified they had "reluctantly" compiled lists of poll tax lists on orders of former Mayor Leo P. McLaughlin. Rogers and firemen George Sanders and Joe Houpt each testified they had secured tax authorization lists from the mayor's secretary, Miss Hazel Marsh, and when completed, returned the lists to her. They said they had received instructions on filling out the lists at meetings in the city hall presided over by Leo McLaughlin.

Further, McLaughlin had told the group of city employees "that if they did not want to get names on the lists they could turn in their own names to Miss Marsh and *we will get some one who will.*"[71] Chief Rogers said he and the other firemen understood what the mayor was saying as being, "If we did not want to get the authorizations lists filled out we would lose our jobs."

Lloyd Lemon, gambler, testified that Leo McLaughlin had called on him and other gamblers to help get poll tax receipts. He testified he and 25-30 others were expected to get the authorizations.[72] Lemon told the court many of the names appearing on the lists were of people who did not live in Hot Springs--some having only visited here.

After a parade of witnesses, ex-mayor Leo P. McLaughlin took the stand. From the very beginning Leo "denied" everything. He denied he "ever received one penny out of gambling." That must have come as news to the citizens of the Spa as Leo had always told the city council when they proposed to give him a raise, "Don't worry about Leo. He'll get his," and from appearances, he had. McLaughlin denied knowing gambling was going on in Hot Springs--this from the man who had run for office on an "open town policy," and from the man who was the administrator for the "Boss Gambler's" estate, with him making certain the property and equipment remained in the hands of the gambling community, even to the point of selling or giving an interest in the Southern Club to his brother, George McLaughlin

---

[69] Ibid.

[70] Ibid.

[71] *New Era*, 21 November 1947.

[72] *Arkansas Gazette*, 21 November 1947.

And he denied that he was aware gamblers and city employees were getting poll tax receipts to support him and Administration candidates running for office, even though he had presided over meetings where he stressed the importance of getting the authorization lists completed and even used veiled threats against the city workers if they did not get their expected quota.

He told the court he was "shocked" when he heard the three firemen testify they had obtained the authorization lists at his office and that they returned the completed forms to his secretary. McLaughlin said, "Those firemen are good boys, but they are scared of their jobs. They are brow-beaten by those G.I.s at the city hall."[73]

The man who prided himself on "having his ear to the ground" and knowing everything going on in the Spa and who had claimed he used his brother George as an undercover detective and informant, told the court he was unaware that Jack McJunkin was involved in gambling and had never discussed gambling or poll-tax receipts with him.[74] Had brother George, the undercover agent, failed to mention to Leo that Jack McJunkin was "hip-deep" in illegal gambling in the Spa and that he was one of Jack's partners in the Southern Club? This, in spite of McLaughlin having helped McJunkin get options on the concessions at Rix Stadium and Ban Johnson Field, and who had backed McJunkin's meteoric rise in the gambling community.

A lot of people knew Leo P. McLaughlin was not being truthful when he testified he had not called a meeting of gamblers, businessmen and city employees since 1942. There had even been a newspaper reporter present when he had a large meeting in 1946. Her name was Edna Lee Howe and she said she had gained entrance with the help of Safety Commissioner Weldon Rasberry.

The jury composed of Montgomery county citizens may have believed McLaughlin when he said he did not know his secretary Hazel Marsh was keeping lists of the poll tax authorizations in her office, but there were few people in Garland County who believed the Mayor had not known such records were being maintained.

When the Prosecuting Attorney asked the defendant, "Did you tell Mr. Williams (Joe Williams, sport columnist for Scripps-Howard newspapers) "Hell, we violate the laws down here every day in the year except Sunday," McLaughlin disparaged the newspaper man in his usual manner, and took a shot at McMath. "Joe Williams," the ex-mayor said, "came in my office full of Scotch whiskey which he said you gave him."

"For your information," Sid McMath replied grinning, "I wasn't in Hot Springs when Mr. Williams was in town. Did you tell him you regulated

---

[73] Ibid., 22 November 1947.

[74] Ibid.

gambling here so only nice people can run it?"

Almost losing his composure, McLaughlin fired back, "These screwball writers don't write what you tell them; they write stories so they can sell newspapers, just like John Fletcher."[75] (*Arkansas Gazette*)

Sidney McMath and his two assistants believed they had produced enough witnesses and evidence to substantiate the charge against former mayor McLaughlin. The Montgomery County jury viewed it differently. The state, according to the jury, had not proven McLaughlin's guilt "beyond a shadow of a doubt and after deliberating only a little over an hour returned an acquittal. It seemed that Leo McLaughlin's luck of the Irish had returned.

The G.I. faction had been in office less than a year when signs of dissension began to be seen. As previously mentioned, the ones taking office on January 1, 1947, had banded together in a mutual cause to oust the McLaughlin Administration, but had been divided over the issue of a "closed" or "open" town. By September, rumors of the rift began to circulate enough to draw the attention of George Douthit, staff and investigative reporter for the *Arkansas Democrat.*

Douthit reported a schism existed. "There is an open political break between the Garland county G.I. organization and two of its members--County Judge Byrum Hurst and Tax Collector Ray Owen. The breach is common knowledge in Hot Springs where the city itself is almost evenly divided over the issue of an "open" or "closed" town."[76]

McMath claimed, "Hurst and Owen have gone over the the McLaughlin faction." Hurst denied he had even talked with McLaughlin.[77]

It became evident that Sidney McMath was entertaining thoughts about

---

[75] Ibid. Leo P. McLaughlin had loved all forms of publicity until he got in trouble. He had come to dislike the adverse publicity relative to his indictments and especially disliked John Fletcher of the *Arkansas Gazette.* He went so far at his trial as to wait beside the court room door and hand a subpoena to each reporter assigned. He did this so he could "envoke the rule" by having them excluded from the courtroom as "material witnesses." The reporters appealed to McLaughlin's attorney C. Floyd Huff, who promised them they could remain in the court room, however, Leo had his way and five were sent to the witness room, but none were called to testify. Therefore, they missed the proceedings of the trial. There was one cub reporter, Maurice Moore, *Sentinel-Record,* who was unknown to McLaughlin, and Moore covered the trial for the five "banished" reporters. LAT - Roy Bosson.

[76] *Arkansas Democrat,* 28 September 1947.

[77] Ibid.

running for higher office--possibly governor. And, why not? He had high name recognition state wide as a result of his leadership in breaking the strangle-hold of a powerful political machine. McMath was articulate and an excellent speaker and was in great demand at civic club luncheons, American Legion and VFW banquets. He was seen at the "lavish barbecue" sponsored by the Pugh brothers of Lake Village, a "must" gathering for political hopefuls of Arkansas politics in that era.[78]

McMath in making two speeches on the same day at Camden, the first a luncheon meeting before the Lion's Club and the second a night meeting of the Methodist Men's Club "ruffled the feathers" of some of the folks back home. The Garland County Prosecuting Attorney told the groups there was a new "liberal" party being organized in the Spa dedicated to the purpose of returning the town to an "open" policy.

"When an open town with commercial gambling," he said, "is operated, it isn't long until your law enforcement officials are in league with the gamblers."[79] He went on to tell his listeners of the effort being made by a group at Hot Springs to re-open the town.[80] He was referring to a meeting hosted by County Judge Q. Byrum Hurst and Tax Collector Ray Owen, who had invited 250 business and civic leaders held in the Willow Room at Phillips Drive In. It was described as a "non-political" stag party.[81]

The group unanimously adopted a resolution opposing any return to wide-open gambling, but did propose "a small number of high class clubs operating under strict supervision" to provide entertainment for visitors "within the limits of liberal morality," whatever that meant. The group, to gain wider recognition, offered its support for a newly-proposed boys club and said it was in favor of the development of parks and a band shell--all worthwhile projects designed to cover the real purpose for its organization, gambling.

A steering committee of fifteen members was appointed with a further meeting scheduled to be held at the DeSoto Hotel the following week.

Perhaps McMath's statement was ill-advised or misstated concerning the new Hot Springs group as being "composed of business men who went out of business January 1, 1947," and that it was "sponsored" by professional gamblers." His statement brought an immediate and "heated" reply.

Alderman, tavern operator and former coach of the Hot Springs Trojan football team, Milan Creighton, chairman of the recently organized Progressive Business Men's Association (PBA) took issue. He was quoted as saying, "Mr. McMath has definitely shown his hand in condemning one of the

---

[78] *Arkansas Gazette*, 7 August 1947.
[79] *Arkansas Democrat*, 22 January 1948.
[80] *New Era*, 22 January 1948.
[81] Ibid., 20 January 1948.

finest groups of business men that could be assembled together in any city in the state, and that group is the Progressive Business Men's Association of Hot Springs."[82]

Since it was obvious that the newly-formed group was proposing a plan of "illegal" gambling, Prosecuting Attorney Sidney McMath, who had higher political aspirations, did not want to tie his future to an organization advocating something contrary to state law.

There had been a few signs that gambling in Garland County was not quite dead. A surprise raid by city police of a meat market at 325 Malvern Avenue had interrupted a book making establishment.[83] Another raid seized eight slot machines from "Phil Marks, who was reputed to have held the slot machine concession for Garland county during the McLaughlin regime."[84] Raids on several small taverns and "bust-out" joints seized another eleven machines.[85] But, the large clubs remained darkened.

The PBA claimed that sidewalk and alley gambling was flourishing and was beyond "suppression." Creighton, perhaps went a bit far as he stated, "Such gambling is entirely out of control," and that "such gambling is taking place in full view of the school children of our city."[86] Now, he'd done it!

Unlike former circuit judge, Earl Witt, who would have paid the remarks with scant notice, Judge Clyde H. Brown, upon learning of the PBA's remarks concerning "gambling out of control," and it being conducted "in full view of the school children of our city," lost no time in convening the Garland County Grand Jury. He charged the jury, "Statements which have been made may be loose and unfounded, made with ulterior motives in mind. On the other hand they may be based on actual knowledge of law violations. The citizens of this county have the right and you have the duty to determine the truth or falsity of the existence of such conditions."[87]

It had not been chairman Creighton's intention to stir the circuit judge into convening the grand jury, but only to gain the public's attention. He would get his opportunity to tell his story before that body and he was immediately summoned. Others, also invited to appear before the Grand Jury were County Judge Q. Byrum Hurst; K.W. Douglas, and Arthur Welcher, all officers in the PBA, Tax Collector Ray Owen; Police Chief George L. Callahan; Sheriff I. G. Brown; Prosecuting Attorney Sidney McMath, and

---

[82] *Sentinel-Record*, 23 January 1948.

[83] Ibid., 12 September 1947.

[84] *Arkansas Gazette*, 21 January 1948. Because the search warrant was served without the signature of a justice of the peace, a requirement of State law, the case against Marks was dropped. *New Era*, 24 January 1948.

[85] New Era, 5 August 1947.

[86] *Memphis Commercial Appeal*, 20 January 1948.

[87] *Sentinel-Record*, 30 January 1948.

others. An invitation was extended to "any volunteer witnesses who cared to testify as to knowledge of open gambling in Hot Springs."[88] That was a refreshing change from the court's position of a few years back.

After hearing various witnesses and "studying the plan of the liberals" the Grand Jury issued a detailed statement appearing in the newspapers: "A so called 'liberal' movement in Hot Springs has received a sharp rebuff from the Garland County Grand Jury, which reported that 'no one has presented a plan whereby gambling can be presented under present laws.'"[89]

It further reported their investigation found no evidence to substantiate allegations that "sidewalk and back alley gambling" was prevalent in the presence of school children in the Spa.[90]

Statements by some of the PBA members that visitors to the Spa had sharply declined was not borne out by the records of the National Park Service. In fact, this agency advised that in January of 1946, while Mayor Leo P. McLaughlin was still in office and "open" gambling was taking place, the city had a total of 18,497 visitors. For the same month in 1947, with the town closed, 18,626 people registered in the Spa, an increase of 129. There was a slight decline in the number of thermal baths given for the same periods.

The "liberal" element in Hot Springs was even more desperate than before the Grand Jury's report. Almost 400 people had lost their jobs because of the shut down of the gambling in Garland County. The only way, reasoned the PBA, to reopen the town was to regain some of the key offices in the court house and city hall and which office holders would permit gambling, at least on a "controlled" basis.

There was some good news for those who were longing to return to a "wide-open" town policy, as a "thorn" in their side was about to be removed.. It had become obvious early in 1948 that Prosecuting Attorney Sidney McMath had no intention of seeking reelection as he was being urged by supporters over the state to run for the office of governor. In fact, by May, McMath had already opened a State Campaign Headquarters on the second floor of the New Capitol Hotel in Little Rock.[91] Q. Byrum Hurst, county judge, who had "switched camps" and who was being supported by the PBA, decided to "toss his hat into the ring," and announced for the prosecutor's job. So did R. Julian Glover, who reportedly had the support of the "fractured" G.I. organization, and Walter Hebert, who claimed he was being supported "independently." Since the circuit judge's position, held by Clyde

---

[88] Ibid.

[89] *Arkansas Democrat*,, 30 January 1948.

[90] *Arkansas Gazette*, 30 January 1948. The *Sentinel-Record*, 30 January 1948, printed the full test of the G.I.'s report.

[91] *West Memphis News*, 5 May 1948.

H. Brown, was not up for reelection for another two years, the other key county office was sheriff, presently held by I. G. Brown. Milan Creighton of the PBA announced to oppose Brown, Jerry Watkins, policeman and a former deputy, John Ermey.

With the prospect of another "heated" political race looming in Garland county, several national newspapers and wire-services dispatched reporters to the Spa to report the expected struggle. One reported a possible revival of the old political machine: "Meanwhile, members of the McLaughlin organization, or elements of the old group are stirring themselves and seeking to form a new alliance under a "liberal" banner. (PBA) One of the leaders in the move is former Municipal Judge Verne Ledgerwood, often credited with being the "brains" of the McLaughlin regime."[92]

Another political group formed, calling themselves, Government Improvement League (GIL). It seemed to be composed by some of the original GI organization and some independents. This group, in general, did not favor the return to an "open" town policy. Some of the leaders of this movement were H.D. Bennett, Jacob King and M.C. Lewis.[93] Then to confuse the voters there were others, such as Walter Hebert, who claimed to be independent democrats.

As might be expected, Sid McMath's preparation to run for governor required him to spend much of his time out of Garland County making speeches and drumming up support through the young Democrats organization. McMath had intended to try Leo P. McLaughlin on the second charge in February 1948. A trial of this multitude before the summer's elections would certainly have been beneficial in publicity and increased McMath's name recognition throughout the state and magnified his image as a "political machine buster." However, that was not to be, for first one reason, then another. One of McLaughlin's lead attorneys, Henry Donham, was incapacitated for several weeks because of illness. McMath pled that the former mayor still had four other lawyers working on his case, but to no avail as the trial judge pushed the schedule down the calendar to November.[94]

While Sidney McMath campaigned for governor, his aides, David Whittington, Nathan Schoenfeld and Richard Hobbs tried to prepare for McLaughlin's trial. By the time the trial came up, McMath had faced eight other gubernatorial candidates in the July primary,[95] a run-off and general election and had become Arkansas's governor-elect.[96]

---

[92] *Rochester Democrat and Chronicle*, 1 February 1948.

[93] *Sentinel-Record*, 6 July 1948.

[94] *Arkansas Democrat*, 14 February 1948.

[95] *Sentinel-Record*, 29 July 1948.

[96] Ibid., 21 November 1948.

Garland County and Hot Springs have been subjected to a number of very intense and heated political races. The first election of Leo P. McLaughlin as mayor in 1927 was unequalled, for its "mud-slinging" and bitterness. And, of course, the county's election of 1946, at which time the political machine lost its tenacious hold on the electorate had been fiercely fought and was unparalleled in its intensity. But in some ways the election of 1948 closely resembled the other two as it was "hotly" contested along the "open-town" versus "closed-town" issue. Not only were the issues "hashed and rehashed," but the personal integrity of the candidates were questioned and brought into play.

The prosecuting attorney's race again became the focus of the local campaign. When State Senator Ernest Maner said he intended to support Walter Hebert because he was an independent and "not indebted to any political faction," Maner came under a scathing attack from candidate Hurst.

"The people of Hot Springs," Hurst told an audience, "will remember that Senator Ernest Maner began his political career within the ranks of Garland county's former machine organization. The machine sent him to the House of Representatives where he did their bidding. Then they sent him to the Senate."[97]

When Hurst said that if something wasn't done to "open" the city a bit, "Grass will be growing in the streets," he brought comment from one of his opponents that at least there should be a run on lawn mower sales.

"Surely the grass that one of my opponents said would grow in the streets must be very valuable," candidate Julian Glover answered, and went on to give statistics reflecting only a slight decrease in bank deposits had occurred since gambling had ceased. He cited that retail sales had increased in 1947 over 1946. He stated, "Gambling is not the basis of a community economy and that gamblers follow the crowd instead of the crowd following gambling."[98]

Milan Creighton, PBA candidate for sheriff, was unusually sharp in his attacks on Sheriff I.G. Brown, now being sponsored by the GIL. He accused Brown of being "impetuous, immature, having a lack of knowledge and lack of ethical standards and accepted rules of procedure and good conduct."[99]

He charged I.G. Brown with appearing "uninvited and unwanted" at a PBA sponsored rally at Morning Star Methodist Church east of town. The former football coach had just walked out in a "mine field" with that accusation as a large advertisement appeared almost immediately in the local newspapers completely refuting Creighton's statement. The ad was signed by Sunday School officers, Secretary and Treasurer, the Board of Trustees and several

---

[97] Ibid., 6 July 1948.
[98] Ibid., 7 July 1948.
[99] Ibid., 6 July 1948.

dozens members of the church. The article stated, "Sheriff Brown was Most Definitely Invited." It went on to describe how individuals in the parking lot of the church had attempted to disrupt Brown's talk. "The only infantile, emotionally immature actions exhibited last Friday evening were brought about by a horn-blowing barrage which was designed to prevent fellow citizens inside the church from hearing the noble truth from Sheriff Brown. The horn-blowing barrage was premeditated and executed by certain members of the PBA, and we are sincerely ashamed of their actions."[100]

Creighton, seemingly caught in an untruth, replied that several of the church members weren't even registered to vote in the election.

During the later stages of the election, I.G. Brown told the Hot Springs *Sentinel-Record* of an attempt by the gambling faction to get him to withdraw from the race. He said he had been offered $100,000 to withdraw his candidacy. "I could have crossed my fingers and become a wealthy man, but I did not," he said. "My honor is not for sale."[101]

The PBA portrayed itself in a cartoon as a knight equipped with sword and shield slaying a dragon with letters imposed across its back, "Get In Line" (GIL).

The Government Improvement League countered with a cartoon of its own. The drawing, quite well done, reflected the launching of a patched up boat with the name "P.B.A." on its bow and was manned by a crew of well known local politicians and former Administration supporters. Standing boldly in the center was the captain labled "McLaughlin" with a caption over him of "McMath should see me now." The heading was descriptive, "Same Old Boat --just a new name--Set For Another 20 year cruise."

Personal attacks between the contestants became sharper and vicious, accusing each other of the lack of ability, integrity and civic responsibility to hold office. Every day during the political race the papers were filled with campaign advertisements. Each day, charges and counter charges were hurled by the candidates. Challenges for debates were issued and rejected. It seemed the entire election was totally out of control.

Finally, Dr. John L. Dodge, pastor of First Baptist Church and "unanimously" supported by the Hot Springs Ministerial Alliance tried to put things into perspective, at least he hoped to reach the voter who may have been confused by all the rhetoric. He took to the airwaves over radio station KTHS and appealed to the people to "Think Before You Vote, but Vote." He pointed out that Plato had said centuries before, "The penalty good men pay for indifference to public affairs is to be ruled by evil men."

---

[100] Ibid., 7 July 1948

[101] Ibid., 8 July 1948. It was rumored that the offer had been made through former gangster Owney Madden.

Dr. Dodge went on to say, "I have heard expressions something like the following: 'This is a Resort Center, therefore it is necessary to have and tolerate a certain amount of gambling. We must have places of recreation for our visitors." "This is a Resort Center, but my fellow-citizen, because of this fact does it license the citizens to resort to unlawful and ungodly vice? "It seems to me," Dr. Dodge told his audience, "that the question before the citizens of our City, County and District are: What type of visitors do we desire in this Resort Center? Do we want the gangsters from New York? Do we want thugs from the alleys of Chicago? Do we want the racketeers from Hell's Elbow in New Orleans? If so, then let's have gambling dens. Or, do we want good, clean, law abiding Christian visitors from all over the world? Do we desire visitors who will add something to the moral and spiritual well being of our Community? If those are the type visitors we desire, do you think gambling will influence and attract them to come here?"[102]

The preferential primary, July 27, 1948, answered only a few questions, but it had narrowed the field. Heavy voting statewide had eliminated seven men from the field of nine in the gubernatorial race leaving the Spa's Sidney McMath to face attorney Jack Holt of Little Rock. The PBA organization was disappointed in the race for governor as it had supported James "Uncle Mac" MacKrell, who came in third. That was because the organization could not get a commitment from either Sid McMath or Jack Holt that if elected governor they would shut their eyes over any gambling being conducted in this county. The PBA had over estimated its influence with local voters relative to the governor's race. After one of the PBA rallies it announced a straw vote had been taken in the gubernatorial race, which had nine candidates, and claimed that "playboy" John Lonsdale, Jr., had polled 3,178 votes and Sid McMath only 2.[103] That was foolish thinking! In the Garland County primary McMath actually polled 4,801 and Lonsdale 699. McMath more that doubled his nearest opponent, Jack Holt who drew 2,195.[104]

In the local prosecuting attorney's race Q. Byrum Hurst came in first in the primary but he would have to face R. Julian Glover in the runoff. Hurst had received heavy support in the old McLaughlin's strongholds, the Second and Fifth wards.

Incumbent Sheriff I.G. Brown would face the scrappy Milan Creighton, who wanted the position passionately and campaigned for the August runoff, on the "Anything goes" theory.[105]

---

[102] Ibid., 25 July 1948.

[103] Ibid., 7 July 1948.

[104] Ibid., 29 July 1948.

[105] Creighton had headed a committee trying to obtain a new stadium in Central Arkansas where the University of Arkansas would play some of its games. Even though the group of business and sportsmen from the Spa met the money and land requirements the entire

The Democratic runoff was scheduled for August 10 and it was a long, hot day for not only the contestants, but the poll workers and voters alike. Q.Byrum Hurst must have been terribly disappointed in the runoff as he saw his primary margin of over 1,000 votes dissipate and by 2:00 A.M. there was only one vote separating him from his opponent, Julian Glover.[106] Hurst had again ran up some large figures in the Second and Fifth wards, but Glover's strong showing in the other wards had narrowed the vote. By the time all returns were received Glover had surged ahead, winning the vote in both Garland and Montgomery counties by a margin of 860 votes.[107]

On election eve night, Milan Creighton, candidate for sheriff, speaking at a PBA rally held at Whittington Park, let the voters know where he and his organization stood and left no doubt as to his position on an "open" town. He totally supported this policy.[108] As Hurst had done, Creighton carried the old black wards but was beaten badly in the others. Brown won easily.

With the defeat of both Hurst and Creighton and the fact that Circuit Judge Clyde H. Brown, who opposed the "open" town policy and would not be up for reelection for two years, there remained little the gambling community could do. Not only had they no one in key-offices in the court house, the new governor elect, Sidney McMath had not changed his position on "no gambling."

With the summer and fall elections behind him and while waiting to be sworn in as governor, Sidney McMath prepared to try Leo P. McLaughlin on a second charge. The second trial was based on an indictment charging McLaughlin, as mayor of Hot Springs, with the misuse of public funds by paying a salary to his brother George, to which the state maintained he was not entitled.

There just didn't seem the interest or excitement surrounding this trial as the previous one exactly a year before. For one thing it went over the same ground that the one involving George McLaughlin had. Oh, the "actors" were the same as they played their parts and again center stage would be dominated by Prosecuting Attorney, now governor-elect, Sidney McMath and defendant,

---

county was disappointed when the stadium was awarded to Little Rock whose bid was not as great. Creighton had worked very hard for the project.

[106] Ibid., 11 August 1948.

[107] Ibid., 12 August 1948.

[108] Ibid., 10 August 1948.

former Mayor Leo P. McLaughlin.

In trying to evade the state penitentiary McLaughlin's defense team subpoenaed a total of 39 witnesses.[109] Many of these had testified in the George McLaughlin trial which ended with a hung jury. After all testimony had been heard, Prosecutor McMath addressed the jury and pointed out, "George McLaughlin was not a police clerk, neither was he a chief clerk nor a police investigator. There was no ordinance creating such an office. Verne Ledgerwood, municipal judge for 34 years didn't even know he was on the city payroll. Emmett Jackson, city clerk, didn't know what his duties were. Commissioner of Public Safety Weldon Rasberry, head of the police department said if George had any duties with that department he didn't know what they were. Even George's wife, Mrs. Fannie McLaughlin, didn't know what he was doing. As close as man and wife are don't you think in all those years he would have told her he was doing any special investigations?"[110]

McMath pointed out illegal activities of George McLaughlin during this time. "George was supposed to be a special investigator in December 1945. He was violating the law every day of his life by his interest in the operation of a gambling house, inconsistent with any duties he might have had with the police department.

"As director of the police force, Leo would have known what George was doing. He knew he was operating a horse book in the Southern Club because he received rent from Otis McCraw of $75.00 a month as administrator for the W. S. Jacobs' estate. He knew who the tenants were."[111]

Leo McLaughlin assisted in his own defense and asked for and received permission to address the jury. This was Leo at his best--he made himself look pitiful and paraphrased the Golden Rule. "This is the most serious moment in my life," he told them. "I had just as soon have 21 years as five years. I am 60 years old now. I would die in the penitentiary anyway. I would rather have you tie my hands behind me and hang me to a post than convict me of something like this. If you convict me, you will take the rest of my life from me. There isn't much left after a man or woman reaches 60. McMath has no evidence. He hopes by spilling all his oratory he can win this case. Don't let him benumb your minds. Do unto me as you would have me do unto you."[112]

Maybe there just wasn't enough evidence to convict Leo McLaughlin. Or maybe some of the jury saw this "old" man almost begging for his life and decided that this was not Montgomery County's problem to solve: --it had been dumped on them. And perhaps some of the jury may have believed that

---

[109] Ibid., 16 November 1948.
[110] Ibid., 21 November 1948.
[111] Ibid.
[112] Ibid.

by convicting Leo they might be burdened by a "guilt-trip," especially if he died in prison as he had predicted. Or, had the "cattle buyers" former Judge Earl Witt said he had arranged and described to Shirley Jean Abbott and her Mother, really gotten to the jury and influenced their decision?[113]

At any rate, after the case had gone to the jury and been in its hands for a few hours, Foreman M.J. Lewis, Jr., informed Judge Maupin Cummings that it was hopelessly deadlocked 9-3, in favor of acquittal. Judge Cummings declared it a mistrial.

Prosecuting Attorney Sidney McMath, who had only one month left to serve in that capacity, announced he was dropping the fourteen remaining charges against Leo P. McLaughlin.

McMath said, "The prosecuting attorney's office has fulfilled its duty in the prosecution of these cases. I do not feel there is justification for putting the county to the additional expense of further trials. I, therefore, respectfully request permission of the court to *nolle prosse* the remaining indictments against Leo P. McLaughlin."[114] The court agreed.

With the charges against him dropped, no longer was Leo the humble man he had presented to the jury. Boldly, he declared to the press and everyone that was listening that all of the charges against him had been "politically motivated" and that he had never spent "one-red cent of the city's money that had not been justified."

While McLaughlin may have felt he had "beaten" McMath in their personal encounter in court, he clearly realized that the ex-Marine Colonel had smashed his prized political machine and in essence had "opened the gate and turned Leo out to pasture!"

[113] *The Bookmaker's Daughter*, Shirley Abbott, Ticknor & Fields, New York (1991), p. 216.

[114] Ibid.

It was not easy an easy adjustment when Leo P. McLaughlin was no longer in the limelight and the center of attention in city affairs. Since he was no longer mayor he received no invitations to speak at conventions and meetings held at the Arlington or Majestic hotels. He missed meeting the trains bringing some dignitary to town when he might present that individual with a large "key to the city." And because he no longer was the city's chief executive officer he did not have a police escort when he ventured forth in his little sulky pulled by his bays *Scotch* and *Soda*. In fact, he restricted his buggy rides mainly to side streets in the Second Ward. There, he had many supporters who would wave at him and call to him, "Hi, Mr. Leo." McLaughlin would always wave back and sometimes he would stop and chat for a few minutes with an old acquaintance or supporter, but never alighting from his mount or buggy.

Leo continued to live in the McLaughlin home at 820 Malvern. With only his two sisters, Stella and Elizabeth, left, the seventeen-room house, equipped with five baths, was quite large for the three of them.

Stella McLaughlin — ca. 1950

The McLaughlin Home

Two years after Leo P. McLaughlin died, his two remaining sisters, Elizabeth and Stella, moved from the family's stately old mansion. Almost immediately, vandals ransacked the home looking for what they believed to be Leo's hidden money.

Brother George and his wife, Fannie, lived just two houses away. With gambling shut-down and his "cushy" undercover job gone, George entered in to business with one of his brothers-in-law, James Mahaffey. The two operated the Red Ball Liquor store on Malvern Avenue for several years. Fannie, of course was employed at the Leo N. Levi Memorial Hospital.[1]

Leo continued to maintain an office in the Arkansas National Building for several years. He really did not have a great amount of business, but he was

---

[1] By 1951, Fannie McLaughlin had become Administrator of this hospital. She succeeded Miss Regina Kaplan, who headed the institution for 35 years. Sentinel-Record, 31 December 1950.

still one of the better divorce lawyers in the Spa. When a client showed up with a case that required considerable preparation or was a bit complicated, he would some times turn the matter over to an energetic young lawyer he had "taken under his wing," Earl Lane. Lane was glad to get the case and would share the fee with McLaughlin.[2]

The ex-mayor missed being at city hall where there had been endless activity, but realizing he was no longer welcome, he seldom ventured to that area. He did spend considerable time sitting on a bench in a corridor or outside the Garland County court house. This way he did keep in some contact with people with whom he once had business or knew. He did notice that many of his old acquaintance were either avoiding him or had stopped coming by and mentioned this to Verne Ledgerwood. "I told him," Ledgerwood said, "That's just human nature. When you are not in power and able to do favors for people, they stop coming."[3]

He had tried to hold onto the chairmanship of the county Democratic Central Committee to keep his hand in politics, but after twenty-four new "conservatives" were elected, he resigned.[4] His influence could still be evidenced in the 1948 election by PBA candidates Milan Creighton and Q. Byrum Hurst polling such large margins in McLaughlin's strongest wards, the Second and Fifth. On election day, Leo P. McLaughlin had seated himself outside one of the polls on Malvern Avenue, calling almost every voter by name.

McLaughlin and Verne Ledgerwood attempted to orchestrate a coup two years later by trying to install Roy Raef, one of the "old-guard," as chairman in the local democratic organization. The political duo of McLaughlin and Ledgerwood had assembled a group of their supporters on the committee including C. Floyd Huff, who had defended Leo in his trials, Charles Hallsell, chairman of the Board of Equalization under McLaughlin, former sheriff Marion Anderson, and Owney Madden, the ex-mobster from New York.

The "Liberals" as the news services referred to the group, had also gone out into the county and obtained pledges from twenty-seven newly-elected committeemen "that they would support the liberal's candidate, Roy Raef, for chairman."[5] The caucus was chaired by Verne Ledgerwood. The plan was to try to force a vote for the leadership of the Central Committee before any other vote was taken. At this point they believed they had a slight margin over their more conservative democrats. Their plan was discovered and thwarted.

---

[2] LAT - Earl Lane.
[3] LAT - Verne Ledgerwood.
[4] *Arkansas Gazette*, 1 December 1948.
[5] Ibid., 20 August 1950.

When Third Ward Committeeman F.W. Jones "stepped in for the liberals and moved that election of Committee officers be held before the (12) vacant seats were filled," and in a correct parliamentary procedure, Committee Chairman Jacob King ruled Jones was out of order. He proceeded to hold an election on the vacancies, and the "coup" was history--McLaughlin and Ledgerwood had lost any chance to regain power in the Democratic organization. It was really the last political battle for the pair, a rare defeat.

Oh, there were rumors for a time that McLaughlin was planning to come out of retirement and run for office. But that was all there was to it - just rumors. When *Arkansas Democrat* Staff Writer Roy Bosson heard that Leo might be considering another run for mayor, he called him at his home and asked him if it was true? "I hadn't given it any thought," he replied, "I've been busy taking care of my law practice." But, then as so often when the subject was brought up, he told the newsman, "Several people have approached me on the subject in my office and on the street, but I haven't encouraged any of them at all."[6]

The Hot Springs Sentinel-Record reported six years after he had left office that "former Mayor Leo P. McLaughlin is strongly considering an attempted political comeback next summer as a candidate for prosecuting attorney of the Eighteenth Judicial district."[7]

Again, just rumors. It seemed to be an ego thing with Leo--he desired to be wanted, but there just didn't seem to be enough supporters! As one of Roy Bosson's old contacts, described as one of "the more powerful old-line liberals said, "There are too many old sores unhealed for Leo to make much headway. Besides we have a good mayor, Floyd Housley, who is liberal and popular with the people."[8]

Leo P. McLaughlin left office a bitter and unhappy man. Not only had he seen his great power over almost all areas of the city's life erased, but he had to endure two trials that had threatened to send him to the penitentiary. Undoubtedly, the expense of five lawyers had a considerable impact of his wealth, which would have been most "painful," as most people viewed the ex-mayor as having been a greedy man. And to top it off, he had seen "the crown-jewel" of what he believed to be his legacy, the new airport bearing his name, changed and his proud name chiseled from its marbled floor.[9] As far as Leo was concerned, that was the "final straw."

He had received strong support from various members of his

---

[6] *Arkansas Democrat,* 26 October 1951.

[7] *Sentinel-Record,* 13 January 1952.

[8] *Arkansas Democrat,* 26 October 1951.

[9] LAT - Jimmy Dowds. Dowds said that McLaughlin would not have been more anguished "if he had been crucified and nails driven through his hands," than to have his name ripped off the airport.

Administration and the political machine bearing his name which encompassed the city hall and the entire county courthouse. No one, even in time of crisis, had rendered him stronger support or had been more loyal than his old school mate, Verne Ledgerwood. Ledgerwood had preferred the fringes of the spot-light of publicity, rather than the direct rays, in which McLaughlin had loved to bask. One sore spot McLaughlin had with Verne, was that Ledgerwood did not "lie" on the witness stand for his brother, George McLaughlin. Ledgerwood's veracity was supported by all others acquainted with George.

However, in spite of that, it was a bit of a surprise not only to the acquaintances of both men but to the general public, when in early 1956 Leo McLaughlin filed a "tax-payers" suit naming Verne S. Ledgerwood, Floyd Housley, Emmett Jackson, J.M. Lowrey and Fred Shelton, all a part or former supporters of his Administration.[10] What had occurred to cause Leo to act in such a manner? Especially so against life long and close associates?

Leo had learned that Mayor Floyd Housley and City Clerk Emmett Jackson, in concert with County Judge James Lowrey and County Clerk Shelton, had instituted a pension plan for Verne S. Ledgerwood, who had served the Spa and county for thirty-four years. The Arkansas State Legislature had passed Act 160 in 1953, which allowed cities to pension municipal judges one-half their salary, after serving a required number of years. Since Ledgerwood easily had met the required length of service, Mayor Housley and City Clerk Emmett Jackson erred in instituting the pension without benefit of a city Ordinance by the City Council, as the Act required. They further misinterpreted Act 160 by establishing the pension rate based on the salary of the municipal judge at the time the Act was passed. When Ledgerwood resigned he was drawing $200 monthly. When the Act was passed the local municipal judge's salary had been raised to $350. Housley and Jackson, without an ordinance by the City Council, began paying Verne Ledgerwood a pension of not $100 per month, but $175, another mistake.

Switching circuits, Chancellor Sam Garrett brought in a prominent jurist from southeast Arkansas, Carleton Harris. Judge Harris made short order of the matter, ruling, "I am accordingly convinced that Judge Ledgerwood is not qualified to receive benefits provided by Act 160 and any compensation received by him under the provisions of said Act, was improperly and illegally drawn. I cannot conceive as how anyone can legally draw a pension based upon anyone's salary but his own."[11]

Well, Leo had been correct, however, he had by his attitude and the suit

---

[10] Garland Chancery Court Records, Case # 30,089, Leo P. McLaughlin v. Verne S. Ledgerwood, Floyd A. Housley, Emmett Jackson, J.M. Lowrey and Fred Shelton.

[11] Ibid., Opinion, 2 March 1956.

severed ties to several people who had once been very close to him. That included Ledgerwood and those named in the suit as well as the two capable lawyers who had represented them, Richard M. Ryan and Earl J. Lane, who believed Verne's many years service had entitled him to a pension.

Those who knew the two men, Ledgerwood and McLaughlin, did not believe it to be truly a taxpayer's suit, but a case of jealousy on the part of the former mayor. It had been the final act to rupture any friendship existing between the two men. When Leo was hospitalized seriously ill a short time later, Verne did not visit him. "We just didn't have anything left in common," Ledgerwood said.

The two remaining McLaughlin men, George and Leo, were both suffering ill health during the 1950s. George had been discovered to have cancer of the colon and prostate and after a colostomy by Dr. H. King Wade, Sr., lived for a couple of years. Then he suffered a coronary occlusion and on September 30, 1957, George Joseph McLaughlin quietly slipped beyond the veil. He was laid to rest in the family plot at Calvary Cemetery.

Leo McLaughlin continued to look forward to each spring as his days were full of activity with the opening of each Oaklawn season. The Leo P. McLaughlin Handicap was generally the featured race each opening day and Leo could generally be found in his box, which still bears his name, "holding court." Over the years he had entertained many famous celebrities and the rich and famous. Stella some times accompanied him. But, Leo, Elizabeth and Stella did not entertain in their home and they seldom had visitors. At the track, however, the likes of former New York mayor, and Leo's idol, Jimmy Walker and his wife had shared his box. Once, when Leo had met the couple at the train a photographer wanted to photograph the trio. Walker had insisted that Leo stand between them saying, "Let Leo between us as a mayor is always in the middle."

He had also welcomed U.S. Senator A.B. "Happy" Chandler, of Kentucky, and later the Commissioner of Baseball; Judge Joseph Sabath of Chicago and the Racing Commissioner of Kentucky, General J. Fred Mills.

When the "Lum" of Lum and Abner, radio and movie-star, Chet Lauck, came to town he and McLaughlin got along well. Lauck, also an admirer of "horseflesh," was shown about town and invited to view the fine stable of horses of the Mayor.[12]

Leo truly enjoyed the spring season and it seemed to temporarily boost his spirits and restore his zest for life.

---

[12] After Chet Lauck retired from the movies and his Vice President of Public Relations with Continental Oil Company, he settled and lived out his days in Hot Springs. He was appointed chairman of the Arkansas State Racing Commission and served in that capacity for several years. His wife, Harriet, was a decorator.

Mayor McLaughlin welcomes former New York Mayor Jimmy Walker and Mrs. Walker

On pleasant evenings he would saddle one of his horses and either ride toward Rix School or through the streets of "Tin-Can Hill," or perhaps exercise his steeds at his trotting track on the old Park Hotel grounds.

In the summer of 1947 a number of horse lovers, members of the Garland County Fair Association, organized the county's first horse show. County Judge Q. Byrum Hurst headed the group with several well known names from the past filling its committee, Arch Cooper, Ben Murray, Dr. Allen Power, Mrs. B.H. Dye and Samuel Kirsch. Dr. R.C. Turk was elected to be the Ringmaster of the First Annual Horse Show. The event was scheduled for the Whittington Park Speedway, July 2.[13] Leo McLaughlin entered one of his favorite 5-gaited horses, *Belle of Killarney*.[14] Leo, still a fine horseman, elected to ride his horse, but failed to place in the first three categories.

One year the horse show met at Rix Stadium. By 1950 the Hot Springs Horse Show Association had built a stadium on the Belvedere Country property. McLaughlin entered and rode *County Clare*, another talented 5-gaited mare.[15]

As Leo's health began to decline in 1951 his interest and attention to his horses also waned and he began decreasing his stable. When he became quite ill in early 1958, he summoned a life-long acquaintance to his stable. He and Holden H. Blahut had been fellow students at St. Mary's Academy on

---

[13] *Sentinel-Record*, 18 June 1947.

[14] Official Program, First Annual Hot Springs Horse Show, 2 July 1947.

[15] *New Era*, 21 June 1950.

Whittington Avenue in the 1890s.[16] Blahut had become a veterinarian and had looked after and treated Leo's horses for years. Blahut had been elected to the city council in 1924 and remained through the entire McLaughlin years. He had always been supportive of Leo's policies.

The job Leo had for Blahut was not something pleasurable for the ex-mayor. He had called for the veterinarian to "put-down" or euthanize his beloved team of *Scotch* and *Soda*. The two beautiful matched bays were well over twenty years-old and no longer able to pull the little buggy in which their master loved to ride. McLaughlin knew no one would want them at their age and was afraid they might be abused. It must have been very painful for the proud ex-mayor to lose something he truly loved.

Leo's health problems continued to increase and in January 1957 he had become "very ill" and was rushed to the St. Joeseph's hospital suffering from nephritis, an inflammation of his kidneys. He had had kidney problems over the years and had been under the treatment of Dr. George C. Coffey. At this time he came under the primary treatment of Dr. E. Driver Rowland for hypertension.

Continuing to suffer from chronic nephritis Leo was hospitalized in early April 1958 with severe influenza, but his condition was not believed to be serious. However, he failed to respond fully to treatment. Rallying a bit and feeling a little better, McLaughlin sent word for his old opponent on the Democratic Central Committee, Jacob King to come see him. The two men had not gotten along very well and King was truly surprised at the request. But being a forgiving and Christian gentleman, and totally unaware as to why Leo would summon him, responded by going to his bedside. Jacob King, an accountant, was queried by McLaughlin on some new tax laws which Congress had passed and which he did not understand. Apparently Leo had the confidence in Jacob King's character and reliability to know he would help him in spite of their past differences.[17]

Stella, who had attended every day of her brother's two trials and had carried sack lunches for them to share, sat in his hospital room each day making certain Leo was comfortable and ordering the nurses about when she thought he was not getting the best of attention. She carefully screened his few visitors.

For five weeks he steadily lost strength, suffering from uremia or kidney poisoning. Several blood transfusions were necessary and a few of his old acquaintances, summoned by Stella, came by and donated blood.[18] For several days Leo lay quietly in a coma and finally on May 5, 1958, the third son of John Henry and Bridget Russell McLaughlin, quietly passed from this world

---

[16] *Sentinel-Record*, 29 June 1936.

[17] Taped interview - Jacob King.

[18] Former State Senator Bud Canada advised the writer that he was one of the donors.

at the age of 69 years and 11 months.[19]

Rosary service was held at the McLaughlin home. A private funeral service was conducted at St. Mary's Catholic Church and Leo was buried in a plot in line with his parents and five other brothers and sisters. No birth date or record of his death appears on the simple stone, only the name, "Leo Patrick."

Leo McLaughlin's obituaries were cloaked with many of the inaccuracies which had existed during his entire life. Both local newspapers, *The Hot Springs Sentinel-Record* and *The Hot Springs New Era*, as well as the two state papers *The Arkansas Gazette* and *Arkansas Democrat* printed that "He had a record of never having lost a personal election contest. This, of course, was not true as he had lost one election as city attorney and had run for city commissioner when he came in twelfth in a twenty-man race. Also, it was reported he had been married twice, whereas he actually had three marriages. Another mistake, commonly compounded over the years was that he was a graduate of the University of Arkansas and even a member of the Razorback football team even though his tenure at that institution had lasted only two weeks. One publication even went so far as to state he had been a "star player." It is little wonder that erroneous statements as these continued as Leo had never tried to dispel or correct any of them. He had been very quick, however to correct any news item if it was critical of him or his Administration in any way.

It was his flamboyancy and style which had drawn attention from the meager details of his failed marriages and personal life and shrouded him with a bit of mystery. He stood out in a crowd, always immaculately dressed, with a handkerchief and lapel flower and his hat was always at a rakish angle. And when he brazenly rode his sulky down Central Avenue behind his high-stepping horses fitted with beautifully trimmed harness he was "Mr. Hot Springs" on display and all but his bitterest enemies basked proudly in the city's high profile mayor.

And in many respects, Leo had been an effective mayor. When he had taken the job as the city's chief executive officer in 1927, the city was heavily in debt. Few streets were paved and the entire utility system was in deplorable condition. Through his programs he paved dozens of streets during his twenty-year tenure as mayor and partially solved the downtown flooding problem. It took a number of years, but he led the city to a solid financial basis -this in the midst of the worst Depression this country had ever seen. He had not built any parks or replaced the aging city auditorium and city hall, but he had been frugal with the city's funds. Though the amount of money collected from the gambling community in fines assessed was small in comparison to

---

[19] Bureau of Vital Statistics, State of Arkansas Death Certificate, # 58-005895. Also, Caruth Funeral Home Record, # 4921. It is interesting to note that several newspapers had either miscalculated his age or had accepted a previous erroneously quoted age of 67.

The Last Boutonniere

the overall take, it did help maintain the city during trying years. How much money the "grateful" gamblers poured into Leo's pockets has always been debated, however it must have been quite substantial.

His Administration had been filled with controversy and scandal--yet he survived it for twenty years. He had gained control and had misused the entire election procedure with fraudulent poll tax lists to perpetuate his political machine. McLaughlin had been supported by the gambling community and through corruptness in his relationship with this element had undoubtedly become rich and greedy. Near the end of his career, he had appeared almost childish and whinney in the controversy over naming the airport. This damaged him more politically than he admitted.

He and his family were not known to be charitable and left no direct heirs. It does seem a pity that a man who had such an influence over the city and its affairs for so many years is so slightly remembered and does not even have a street or park bearing his name. It seems the voters were totally unforgiving!

The two remaining sisters, Elizabeth McLaughlin and Stella McLaughlin Snyder, continued to reside in the family residence at 820 Malvern Avenue after Leo's death. The large home with shrubbery blowing and scraping against the window screens must have seemed spooky and scary at times. The two women did report to the police on occasions they believed burglars or prowlers were about and on their property. These may not have been idle fantasies as stories were being told around town and perhaps wildly exaggerated concerning the size of Leo's wealth and speculation went unchecked as to what he had done with it? This was a subject, it seems, that dwelled on several minds in the community.

Less than two years after the ex-mayor's death, his two sisters rented an apartment at the Majestic Hotel. They were able to get their meals there and would feel secure with people close around them.

Almost from the moment the McLaughlin sisters moved to the Majestic, their large home on Malvern Avenue became the target of vandals and treasure seekers. These prowlers dug up the backyard, the stable and garage looking for buried loot. They broke in the windows and doors of the silent old mansion hoping it would be the road to riches. They tore the paper from the walls and pried open the sheathing. Fireplace mantles and hearths were broken up. Each tread on the stairs was pried up to uncover any possible hiding place. Carpets and draperies were ripped apart. Closets and floors were torn apart.

Light and electrical fixtures were pulled loose. The attic was thoroughly ransacked and torn apart.

Fortunately, Elizabeth and Stella had sold some of the better furniture before the wrecking began Pieces left behind were torn asunder by the plunderers. Sadly, they placed the house and large lots on sale. At that time gambling in the city had made a comeback and good commercial property was at a premium. It was announced that George King, Jr. of Beverly Hills, California had made an offer to the sisters of $225,000, as he wanted to build a large, new modern motel. The two women agreed to accept the offer.[20] Before the owner could take charge of the property under a 45-day waiting period, Stella and Elizabeth backed out, apparently thinking the treasure seekers might find something on the property that was valuable. But, after satisfying themselves that if any treasure had been located there the vandals had already discovered it, they proceeded to sell. A large Safeway Super-Market (Later Harvest Foods) was constructed on the site.

To have their home, where they had resided so many years, literally destroyed must have been extremely painful and devastating to the two sisters It was nothing however compared to what they would face a few days after the house had sold. Stella received a call from the caretaker of Calvary Cemetery requesting she come out. When she drove up to the McLaughlin family plot she was horrified to see that during the previous night grave robbers had uncovered Leo's grave. The vandals had cut open his metal casket with an acetylene torch and pulled her brother's remains out, apparently looking for the money they had never found on the McLaughlin property. It was a macabre event to say the least. Stella went ballistic, ranting, raving and threatening dire curses and plagues upon those responsible. The caretaker summoned James Dowds, who was in charge of the cemetery. Dowds was very sympathetic with Stella and was able to calm her down. He convinced her that the less said concerning the grave desecration, the better. The body was re-buried. There was no publicity of the event, although a number of people became aware of it.[21]

The two sisters lived at the hotel for seven years. On September 22, 1967 Elizabeth McLaughlin, who had never married, passed away and was buried in the family plot at Calvary Cemetery.[22]

Stella McLaughlin Snyder was now left alone. She had no blood relations only a sister-in-law, Fannie McLaughlin, George's widow.

---

[20] *Sentinel-Record*, 11 September 1961.

[21] LAT - James Dowds.

[22] Elizabeth McLaughlin was 88 years old when she died. She left an estate of $31,80 in cash and Government bonds and an appraised property of $101,300. Probate Court Record Garland County Arkansas, Case # 11,133.

Leo P. McLaughlin died in 1958. Several months after he was buried, the sexton of Calvary Cemetery discovered the former mayor's grave site had been desecrated. Here, James Dowds, who was in charge of the cemetery, tries to calm Stella McLaughlin Snyder, Leo's sister.

At that time Fannie was living in the Suburban Apartments with her widowed sister, Hannah Norwood. The two Benedict sisters invited Stella to join them, which she did. When another of the Benedict sisters lost her husband, the four women moved to a home on Robinwood Drive.[23]

On June 2, 1971, Stella McLaughlin Snyder died at home. She, too was buried in the McLaughlin family plot.[24]

Stella, who like the rest of her family had never been very charitable, left $5,000 to the Good Shepherd Convent and to her sister-in-law Fannie Benedict McLaughlin, described as a "Family friend," she willed the balance of her estate, $668,852.73.[25]

It is a remarkable fact that of this "pioneer" family in early Hot Springs composed of eight children who reached adulthood only three were married and there were no children born to them. Stella was the "last limb" on the McLaughlin family tree.[26]

---

[23] Fannie Benedict McLaughlin, died at the age of 85 at El Dorado, Arkansas, where she had moved to be near her nephew, Norwood Phillips. She was buried at Arlington Cemetery in El Dorado.

[24] *Sentinel-Record*, 3 June 1971, and Caruth Funeral Records.

[25] Garland County Probate Records, 3 June 1971, Case # 12,522. Undoubtedly this figure included much of Leo's wealth, which was mainly tied up in government bonds. Several people who were closely acquainted with Leo McLaughlin believed he had left safety deposit boxes filled with money. These were supposedly in cities like Memphis, St. Louis, Chicago and Louisville, where he visited quite often. Verne Ledgerwood discounted this theory, saying "Leo was too smart for that and had his funds invested in government bonds." It is strange that Leo being a lawyer, never made a will!

[26] The three who married were Leo, three times, Stella once and George, once. Only George's marriage to Fannie was a success and lasted.

Vernal S. Ledgerwood said he had enjoyed his thirty-four years of service to the City of Hot Springs and Garland county as its first municipal judge. Pleasing to him was the fact that working out of city hall he had been at the center of activity those many years.[27] For several years before he left the bench, his wife, Bess, had been trying to convince him to retire, however, he had stayed on.

As he watched the G.I. organization dismantle their political machine by a sweeping victory of all county offices he began to change his mind that it was time to go. He would later admit that it was a time to change and said the political machine had fallen under its own weight. When Leo P. McLaughlin, who was under siege facing charges and indictments handed down by the Grand Jury, decided not to run again for mayor, Verne made up his mind. He still had a year to go on his term, but announced he was retiring from the bench.

While Ledgerwood had not been indicted by the Grand Jury, he had not escaped completely. In August 1947, eight months after the indictments of Leo and George McLaughlin, Jay Rowland, Ed Spear and others, Prosecuting Attorney Sidney McMath did file *information* charges against him.[28] The *information* named Ledgerwood "with being an accessory to operating a gambling house."[29] He was charged "with having aided and abetted in the operation of gambling houses in Hot Springs and Garland county, said offense being committed between January 1, 1946 to December 28, 1946."[30]

Ledgerwood immediately denied the charges and lashed back at the prosecuting attorney as he said, "Within the past six weeks several hundred people have solicited me to run for prosecuting attorney, when Mr. McMath's term expires, or to run for mayor when Mr. Ricks' term expires; could this be Mr. McMath's way in making me carry some weight in case I should decide to run for some political office?"[31]

But Verne Ledgerwood need not have worried. When the prosecuting

---

[27] LAT - Verne Ledgerwood.

[28] *Information* under law is a charge or charges under oath of a criminal offense, not by indictment of a grand jury, but by a public officer such as Prosecuting Attorney Sidney McMath.

[29] *Arkansas Gazette*, 3 August 1947, and *Sentinel-Record*, same date.

[30] Ibid. Places and operators named specifically were: Blue Ribbon Club, operated by Lewis Larson, George Pakis and Gordon Henderson. Tulsa Club, Milwaukee Bar and Lone Star Bar, all operated by Walter Weldon. Ohio Club, operated by Otis and Otho McCraw. Citizens Club, operated by Louis Longinotti and G.H. Britt. Main Cigar Store, operated by Fred Nichols and David Clark. Reno Club, operated by Erbert O. Wheatley. White Front Club, operated by A. J. "Tony" Karston. Southern Club, operated by Arch Ledgerwood and Jack McJunkin. Belvedere Club, operated by Arch Ledgerwood and Jack McJunkin. Tower Club, operated by Arch Ledgerwood and Jack McJunkin. Cameo Club, operated by Will Page, Sr. and Will Page, Jr.

[31] *Sentinel-Record*, 3 August 1947.

attorney's office was unsuccessful in convicting Leo McLaughlin on two tries and dropped all charges against him there was little chance the much more popular Ledgerwood would be convicted of any of the allegations. All charges were quietly *nol prossed* and dropped and McMath went on to a successful run for governor.

With the pressure of the threat of old "transgressions" behind him, Verne was set to enjoy life. He did "keep his hand in politics" for awhile, staying in the background and was an influence behind the electing of Floyd Housley as mayor when Earl Ricks failed to run again. He and Bess were comfortable having a good income from his apartment house and investments. He had benefitted from his father's estate and had been willed some stocks and bonds by a grateful client.[32] In fact, that client, a physician and his wife left property to the couple in Hot Springs and in eastern Arkansas.[33] Ledgerwood believed in investing in "blue stocks and bonds." He said he and Leo P. McLaughlin had once had a discussion about the best or safest investments. McLaughlin, according to Ledgerwood, had preferred government and municipal bonds to corporate stocks. Both men had been very conservative in their spending.

For several years during World War II, when gasoline rationing was at its tightest, Verne and Bess had moved from their lake home to an apartment at the Como Hotel, where they were close friends to the owners, Al and Gladys Reynolds. The two couples often played cards together.

They resided after that at a home at 1803 Central Avenue which had previously been owned by Dr. James Dennis and his wife Elizabeth. During the latter part of that decade, they embarked on designing and building the house of their dreams. The pink brick house located at 721 Prospect was completed in 1959. It was located on a beautifully landscaped lot and was spacious in area. Verne left much of the planning up to Bess, but was insistent that a study be included on the lower level and he moved his old roll-top desk into it. Here, the couple enjoyed living and entertaining their many friends each Christmas season with an egg nog party. Verne, a "tee-totaller," sometimes invited Earl Lane to "attend bar" and to do the honors.

In 1962 Tulane University at New Orleans invited Verne to attend the 50th anniversary of his graduating class. Ten years later, Hubert E. Longnecker, President of Tulane, presented him with a 60th year certificate of recognition.[34]

For several years after his retirement from public office, Verne and his brother continued to share and maintain an office on the 3rd floor of the First

---

[32] J.J. Ledgerwood had died in 1943. The eldest brother, Archie Ledgerwood, who had been closely associated with the gambling casinos, passed away 2 June 1958.

[33] LAT - Verne Ledgerwood.

[34] Observance of the 60th Anniversary of The University's Class of 1912, was presented in June 1972. The certificate is in possession of V.S. Ledgerwood's niece, Dora Jane Ledgerwood Ellis.

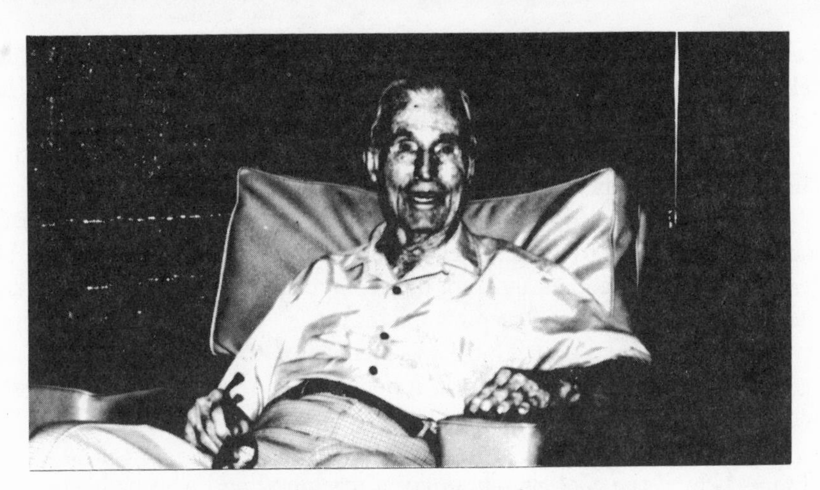

Vernal Snell Ledgerwood — 1980

Federal Building (originally Citizens Bank Building). There the two brothers, laughed, drank coffee, plotted and planned their next assault upon the tarpons off the Florida Keys, the black bass of Lake Hamilton or the ducks in the rice paddies of Arkansas County. The two brothers and a couple of their "cronies" had even gone frog hunting, and in "a three-hour period" had caught ninety-six bull frogs.[35]

Then tragedy struck the two Ledgerwood families. On November 24, 1972, Cecil lost his wife and Dora Jane, her Mother, Theresa Marie Turk Ledgerwood. Only slightly more than three months later, Verne was widowed when Bess passed away.

Bess had been ill for some time, but on February 27, 1973, Verne took her out for a ride. Returning home, they drove over West Mountain. "She loved to look at our home as we came off of the mountain," he said. "That day, just as we sighted the house, she just suddenly fell over in my arms and died."[36] It was just eight months short of Verne's and Bess's 60th wedding anniversary!

In the early 1930s, shortly after Lakes Catherine and Hamilton had been built, Verne Ledgerwood fished almost every day. Even when he reached his 80th birthday, he was still managing "to wet a hook" about 200 days a year. He had invested $1,000, along with twenty other men in a duck camp near Stuttgart, Arkansas. It was an organization much like the "Last Man Club." As members either resigned from the club, or died, the remaining members would purchase their share. After many years, Verne had worked, or lived, himself to the top as ranking member and it became known as "the

---

[35] *Sentinel-Record*, 18 May 1969.

[36] LAT - Verne Ledgerwood.

Ledgerwood Duck Club."[37] The club house was modernly equipped with television, telephone and had access to two large duck ponds. He and his friends spent many enjoyable days there.

The friends of Verne "feted" the judge, and his brother Cecil, with a surprise dinner at the club, following his eightieth birthday.[38]

Verne continued to be active for several years. He had always exercised daily and continued to cut his lawn and trim the hedges into his nineties. He read the local newspapers and kept himself apprised of local happenings and read the *Reader's Digest* to "keep his mind alert."

Reaching his mid-nineties, he was persuaded to hire a "care-giver" or companion. Donald Whitt, a local resident, filled that position for several months.

Vernal Snell Ledgerwood, who had quite often been referred to as the "brains behind the McLaughlin political machine," and who had kept it on course for so many years, died in a local hospital, March 2, 1986, just six-weeks short of his 97th birthday. The man who had been born in Greenwood County Kansas, was laid to rest with a simple service, in Greenwood Cemetery, Hot Springs, Arkansas. With Calvary Cemetery on one side and Greenwood on the other, Third Street separated the grave sites of two of the most fascinating politicians this county ever produced, and whose lives had a most profound effect upon the citizens of this area for over two decades---Leo and Verne.[39]

---

[37] *Sentinel-Record*, 18 May 1969.

[38] Ibid. Some of those participating in preparing the dinner and entertainment were Darrel Sims, Bill Mears, Joe Kaufman, Nick Burrell, Earl Robbins, Van Lyell and Ish Beam.

[39] Cecil Ledgerwood followed his brother in death later that year, 18 December 1986. Only the talented Dora Jane Ledgerwood Ellis remains as "The Last Limb."

EPILOGUE

1947-1967: The Turbulent Years

For eighty years politics in the Spa had to face the question of "open-town" versus "closed-town." The deposing of the McLaughlin political machine had hardly changed the issue. The problem still lay there, festering like a sore boil, never going away. For twenty years following the "G.I. Revolt," as it was sometimes called, the gambling problem kept the city of Hot Springs in a turmoil!

Some of the gamblers who had owned or worked in the clubs had always depended on the business as an occupation and hardly knew what else to do. A few retired. Others headed west to Las Vegas or Reno, Nevada where gambling was beginning to flourish. Those left behind worked in pool halls, beer parlors and other associated businesses hoping gaming like the legendary Phoenix bird would rise from the ashes of the political defeat and be resurrected. Hope for these was on the horizon, even if they could not see it.

The local elections of 1950-1952, just about wiped out those elected officials claiming tie-ins to the former G.I. organization. One of the principal positions, held by Circuit Judge Clyde H. Brown, was opposed in 1952 by ex-McLaughlin "team-player" Curtis Ridgway. The liberal faction strongly supported Ridgway while Governor Sid McMath tried to come to the rescue of his ex-law partner, but to no avail as Brown went down to defeat. Ridgway's unexpected death, as a result of a cerebral hemorrhage, a few days after the election compounded the local political problem.[1]

Floyd C. "Babe" Huff, who had been one of Leo P. McLaughlin's defense attorneys was urged by the liberal faction to run for the office.[2] The defeated democratic incumbent, Clyde H. Brown, then announced as an independent candidate for the circuit judges position he had held for the past four years.[3]

---

[1] *Arkansas Gazette*, 16 August 1950/ Ridgway won 6,426 votes to 5,987 for Brown, *Arkansas Gazette*, 9 August 1950.

[2] *Sentinel-Record*, 6 September 1950.

[3] Ibid., 6 September 1950.

Huff prevailed, winning the election over Brown and was supported by the liberal faction in the Spa. Again, Brown was supported by his old friend Governor Sidney McMath, but was ineffective as Sid's popularity had suffered in Garland County over his opposition to gambling.

In that same election, incumbent Sheriff I.G. Brown, another road block to wide-open gambling, lost to Will Lowe, who had also been closely aligned with the old McLaughlin faction.

Over at city hall, Mayor Earl T. Ricks had decided not to run for office again in 1949 and was replaced by Floyd A. Housley, who secured the victory over a field of six candidates.[4] Housley was often referred to as "The Friendly Mayor," and he was, having friends in all sectors of the community. He took the position that he had no gambling problem. "There is nothing," he said, "For me to do about gambling in Hot Springs. The sheriff, the prosecuting attorney, the circuit judge and the governor of Arkansas have said there will be no gambling in Hot Springs as long as they're in office. That takes it out of the hands of the mayor of the city."[5]

But Housley was flexible as that was how he stayed in office for ten years. When the liberals regained most of the key county offices and the casinos and clubs began to reopen he was cooperative. However, when "unfavorable national publicity," was brought on the Spa because of the reporting of "wide-spread gambling activities," Housley ordered the police to "crack down" on what he called "two-bit bookies."[6] The local raids did not seem to bother the larger clubs.

After announcing his intention to run for a sixth term, he was stricken with a heart attack and died while driving on Park Avenue.[7] Housley's administration had been one of activity and much had been accomplished under his leadership. New and vastly superior lighting on the major streets had taken place; the erection of permanent street markers and the paving of 150 blocks had greatly improved the streets in the suburbs. Improvements at the airport had been made, including the resealing and extension of the airport runways to accommodate larger planes. And there were others.

At the time of his death, the filing deadline had passed and the only other candidate to have announced for the office was Seventh Ward alderman, Dan Wolf. Wolf, the owner and operator of a small bus line had not been

---

4 Ibid., 6 April 1949. Ricks accepted the appointment offered him by Governor Sidney McMath as State Adjutant General. Ricks had backed Bill Seiz, who came in second in the six-man mayor's race.

5 *Arkansas Democrat*, 10 April 1949.

6 *New Era*, 3 May 1949.

7 *Sentinel-Record*, 22 September 1959.

considered a serious opponent of incumbent Mayor Housley. There was speculation on whether other prospective candidates might be permitted to file under the unusual circumstances. That idea was dispelled as then Circuit Judge Plummer E. Dobbs ruled Wolf would be the only nominee in the November election and that "write-in" votes for any other persons would not be permitted.[8] As it turned out, Dan Wolf took the job seriously and became a high-profile mayor, attending every business opening and community event, very adequately representing the City of Hot Springs in special functions.

Wolf, who claimed he wasn't superstitious, but really was, insisted on being sworn in to office at exactly 11:16 in the morning. He said the number 16 was his "lucky number." He had filed for office on the 16th of the month and had a "number of personal business matters started on the 16th which were culminated successfully." And, oh yes, he just happened to reside at 1616 Central Avenue, where lots of nice things had happened to him.

Both mayors Housley and Wolf had been attuned to the needs and desires of the business community. Neither tried to be dictatorial like Leo P. McLaughlin and neither tried to run the city as a military unit as had Earl Ricks. Both men worked with the city council and both received good cooperation. And both had the same efficient and helpful secretary--Hilda Shuffield.[9] If the need or desire of the business community was for wide-open gambling Housley and Wolf worked with "the boys." If there was no flood of protests and criticism, it was okay with them. They believed that if the gambling cliques were to operate under the sanction of the city and county government, they had to bear a larger share of the financial burden.

One of Housley's last acts in office was to help set the machinery in motion for a bond issue to build a new auditorium.[10] To support the taxation of the Spa's citizens a city ordinance was passed to tax the gambling houses, open bars (also illegal in Arkansas) and any other public or private establishments which dealt in services more or less illegal.[11] The tax was first set on large casinos at $500 monthly; $200 on smaller establishments, and any place having a bar was $50 unless it was a "fraternal club," which had an assessed figure of $25. Each slot machine had a required monthly fee of $5. Clubs with bingo

---

[8] *New Era*, 16 October 1959.

[9] Mrs. Shuffield kept scrapbooks in a professional manner for both mayors. These are a part of the Garland County Historical Society's archives and have been invaluable in our research.

[10] *Sentinel Record*, 22 September 1959.

[11] *Fort Worth Star-Telegram*, 10 December 1962.

games were taxed $50 monthly.[12]

The funds received from this tax were referred to as an "amusement tax," and the city was quick to explain to any inquisitive reporters that it was not a "licensing fee," for what was obviously an illegal activity. By 1962, only four years after the "amusement tax" had been recognized, the city clerk reported the fund totaled over $315,000."[13] The money was rolling in at a pace of over $6,000 a month. The proceeds were placed in a special fund handled by City Clerk Emmett Jackson, and designated toward the construction of a new city hall, central fire station and a civic auditorium to be built on the old Rock Island Railroad property. This arrangement seemed to have salved the conscience of the community.

Just how had the Spa reached the point where wide-open gambling had not only made a comeback, but actually exceeded that of a decade before? It was an interesting journey.

During Governor Sidney McMath's second term, a delegation of twenty-one businessmen, "representing a faction in Hot Springs favoring open gambling visited him." The spokesman of the group was Clyde Halk, who asked the governor for a "hands-off policy" and the relaxing of gambling restrictions in the resort. At first, the appeal was to allow the clubs to open and operate just during the up-coming racing season.

McMath, who was considering running for a third term and needed both financial and voter support, acknowledged he was aware that "The people of Hot Springs had defeated in last summer's elections those officials who stood for a closed-town policy and had elected officials who favor a liberalized viewpoint.

"You and I know," continued the Governor, "That regardless of how Hot Springs people feel, it still doesn't change the basic laws of the state which prohibit gambling."

But then it seemed as if the Governor weakened his stand as he said, "Gambling is your problem over there," and promised there would be no state interference unless the situation constituted a state-wide problem.[14]

McMath most certainly had in mind that the delegation would return to the Spa and would urge conservative measures and restraint in reopening the town. And probably most of the delegation had that in mind, also. However many small bar and tavern operators viewed the situation as an opportunity

---

[12] *Sentinel-Record*, 18 1960. City records later revealed that "The Belvedere Club, paid a monthly tax of $1,440 to operate its casino, bar and 84 slot machines in early 1964." During that same period the Vapors "operated more than five gaming tables at $750 per month." *Sentinel Record*, 12 October 1987.

[13] *St. Louis Post-Dispatch, 3 July 1962.*

[14] *Sentinel-Record*, 14 February 1951.

for them to "get involved." The word "moderation" is almost unknown in most gambler's vocabulary and it was "damn the torpedoes and full steam ahead."

Like a herd of longhorn cattle stampeded by a bolt of lighting new bars and clubs sprang up selling illegal mixed drinks and providing some sort of gaming from dice to roulette and poker. Slots appeared in bars and dives all over the county and at least one grocery store featured a "one-armed bandit."[15] Places like the Trade Winds, Benny's Pizza, Baby Grand, Cliff's Drive-In, Ruby's Tavern, Joker Lounge, Carousel Club, Pastime Bar, Black Orchid, Night Train and Top Cat clubs took on new life and made available slots for their customers. In a few short years a total of eighty-nine places having gambling of some sort were registered in the county. No doubt, there were some who were not registered.

Well-known eateries, Coy's, Williams Restaurant, Colonial Steak House and King's Sandwich Shop had from one to eight machines. Even the V.F.W. and American Legion Clubs shined up eleven of the hungry slots for their members.[16]

Without a strong hand to guide the gambling community it ran amok and totally out of control. **Bookies Operate Almost in Open At Hot Springs,** headlines in one state paper reported.[17] Friction between some of the large clubs' owners and some of the new and smaller organizations occurred. Two factions, both liberal, developed, one supported by the municipal judge and the other by the circuit judge.

An examination of the city docket by reporter Bill Farley of the *Arkansas Gazette* revealed the names of eight individuals who "forfeited" fines of $128.00 each for gaming. None of the names were of individuals listed in the *City Directory* or local telephone books. Were the boys playing the old game of using fictitious names? Municipal Judge Lloyd Darnell, who had been backed by one liberal faction, shrugged away the question and said he "was not familiar" with the men or the cases.[18]

As the gambling in Garland County became widespread and disorganized, stories began to circulate that organized crime was interested in moving in to Hot Springs and becoming involved in the free-wheeling activities. The *Arkansas Democrat* even ran a story speculating that because there was no

---

[15] Ibid., 27 August 1961. By this time a report came out reflecting 441 gaming device stamps had been issued for machines in Garland County.

[16] From a list found in 1994 and sent to Ken Wheatley from William C. Gilliam, attorney at Malvern, Arkansas, 18 March 1994. A copy was designated to the late Inez Cline. The list was for slot machines which had paid tax stamps as required by federal law.

[17] *Arkansas Gazette*, 29 September 1951.

[18] Ibid.

"gambling czar" like the late W.S. Jacobs to hold "the boys in line," New York mobster and gambler Frank Costello was being brought in to correct the situation.

Costello, referred to by one writer as the "Prime Minister" of the underworld, had been a frequent visitor to the Spa. He had appeared in town in late 1950 and had several suites of rooms registered to him at the Jack Tar Motor Hotel. Accompanying him that trip were such well known underworld figures as Eddie Barrick, George Uffner, Phil Farber and Julie Pedell.

Circuit Judge Floyd C. Huff was not amused at the *Democrat's* story and said, "It is so ridiculous as to hardly deserve a denial. There is absolutely no basis for it at all. The trouble here is state politics. Such stories as this are the result of agitation and the source of much of it is former Mayor Leo P. McLaughlin."[19] The *Democrat* stated it had based the story "on a usually reliable New York source."

Governor McMath, upon reading the *Democrat's* story commented, "I can't believe that Costello has any such plans. However, if he does entertain any such ideas he had best forget them because the people of Arkansas will not tolerate the establishment of an underworld stronghold in this state."[20]

When Frank Costello read the Associated Press article in an eastern newspaper, he sat down and addressed a letter to the editor of the *Hot Springs Sentinel Record* and advised that the story was only a rumor and that he had no such plans. He commented that he had been a regular visitor in the Spa for over twenty-five years and "I have found enjoyment and pleasure in its wonderful climate and medicinal baths and waters and fine and hospitable people." He added, "I never have had the remotest idea of engaging in or being connected with the gambling business in Hot Springs or any place in Arkansas--directly or indirectly."[21]

It was also rumored that Judge C. Floyd Huff, who was closely involved and supported by one faction of the local liberal gambling organization, sent word to Costello to the effect that if outside interests tried to become involved in the local situation, the entire county operation would be closed.

From time to time McMath had called attention to and warned of well known gamblers assembling in Hot Springs. "They are not there to take the baths," he cautioned.[22]

When the story got out that reported the "lord high executioner" of Murder,

---

[19] *Sentinel-Record*, 14 November 1951. While Huff had represented the ex-mayor in his trials, the two men had a falling-out.

[20] *New Era*, 6 November 1951.

[21] *Sentinel-Record*, 14 November 1951.

[22] Ibid., 6 August 1950.

Inc., Albert Anastasia, was being forced out of New York and intended to move to the Spa to "avoid being rubbed out," the entire community became alarmed. Again, Circuit Judge Huff spoke out, "We're not going to have him here. "If he thinks he can run away from New York mobsters and run down here he can do his running in some other direction."[23] Assistant Chief of Police John Ermey added, "He (Anastasia) might retire in one of our city jail cells until he changed his mind about staying here. It would be easy enough to place a vagrancy charge against him and move him on his way." Prosecuting Attorney Julian Glover agreed, saying, "I do not want anyone here of doubtful character. That includes Anastasia."[24]

Other gang lords and mobsters were linked to Hot Springs between the years of 1950-1964. Meyer Lansky, called the "Godfather's Godfather,"a mathematical genius," and major figure in the National Crime Syndicate continued to vacation in the Spa. Joseph A. Doto, a.k.a. "Joe Adonis," identified as "one of the big three of New York's professional gambling empire," stayed several weeks at the Arlington, golfing and relaxing.[25] Philadelphia numbers racket boss, Harry Stromberg, came several times in the early 1950s. So did Art Samish, called the gambling czar of the West Coast. Kansas City mobsters Tony Gizzio and Gus Gargotta showed up in the Spa. Gargotta's brother had just come to an untimely end as a result of an underworld misunderstanding.[26]

Carlos Marcello, referred to as the head of Syndicate Operations in New Orleans and his chief "strong arm" Joe Perretto, were frequent visitors to the Spa during this period. It was said Marcello was known as Frank Costello's principal distributor of racing wire information in the South. It was through this communication avenue that Owney Madden, the Spa's "retired" mobster, became the principal and only supplier of racing results in the city. Madden had established a central distribution point in the Ritter Hotel, on Exchange

---

[23] Ibid., 21 November 1951. An editorial in the referenced newspaper referred to Anastasia as a "cold blooded gangster who escaped trial for a Murder, Inc., slaying in 1941 when Abe Reles, a key witness, plunged to his death from a Coney Island hotel window. Reles was in custody of the police at the time." The editorial stated, "Hot Springs does not want Anastasia or any of his ilk. Hot Springs must not become the dumping ground for the scum of the world."

[24] Ibid. Anastasia was murdered October 25, 1957, in the barbershop of the Park-Sheraton Hotel in Manhattan. The killing was encouraged by mobster Vito Genovese and supposedly carried out by Carlo Gambino and Joe Bandy.

[25] *Arkansas Gazette*, 22 October 1950. The other two gambling New York kingpins were Frank Costello and Frank Erickson.

[26] Ibid.

Street, which was owned by his close friend, Attorney Q. Byrum Hurst.[27]

Salvatore Gilomar "Sam" Giancana, head of the Chicago Mafia operations, whose many criminal ties were being closely monitored by the Chicago FBI office for possible prosecution came calling.[28] When he suddenly made a trip to the Spa, local Special Agent Clay T. White was notified and he and other agents were assigned to watch his activities. It turned out, according to Agent White, that the McGuire Sisters were performing at the Vapors Club, and Giancana merely was "love-struck" over the beautiful Phyliss, who admitted, "He hasn't gotten anything going here. He just came because of me."[29] Giancana came to a violent end in 1975. After a dinner party at his Oak Park, Illinois home, he was found shot to death. His slayer was never found.[30]

It wasn't the occasional mobster or gangster visiting the area which concerned the boys at city hall or the court house. What really made them nervous was when reports were received that an Apalachin-type meeting of underworld figures had taken place or was about to meet.[31] When that occurred they were concerned that the "big boys" intended to "muscle-in" on the local illegal gambling operation. Then, they immediately went in to a defensive mode.

One such story appeared in the *Chicago Daily News* reporting a meeting of mobsters from Chicago, New York, Cleveland and California "had taken place (at Hot Springs) lasting ten days from February 14 and wound up abruptly February 24 when the participants learned they were being observed by local and federal authorities." The meeting, according to the Chicago newspaper had been to select the successor to Anthony J. "Big Tuna" Accardo, reputed underworld boss at Chicago. It once had been reported that Accardo had scheduled a meeting of crime bosses in the Spa several years before but had

---

[27] Taped Interview with Q. Byrum Hurst, 28 March 1998. Also, *The English Godfather.*

[28] *The Crime Encyclopedia,* 28-29.

[29] Taped Interview of Clayburn T. White, by Orval E. Allbritton, 25 July 2002. Special Agent White, of the FBI was Resident Agent at Hot Springs for twenty-three years. He became the Director of the State Crime Lab under appointment by Governor David Pryor. Later, he served six uninterrupted terms as Garland County Sheriff and was never beaten in an election.

[30] *The Crime Encyclopedia,* 32.

[31] The Apalachin conclave was a meeting in 1957 of major crime members who assembled in upstate New York three weeks after the demise of Albert Anastasia. To the horror of the underworld the meeting was accidentally discovered by a local policeman who called other officers in to investigate. Major crime figures tried to flee through the woods on foot and by driving across fields. Some were not taken into custody and escaped but dozens were to their consternation. See, Peter Maas, *The Valachi Papers,* G.P. Putnam & Sons, New York (1968), 250-255.

canceled when it was discovered before hand.[32] All local officials, including Mayor Dan Wolf, Police Chief Milford Sanders and Prosecuting Attorney David Whittington claimed to have no information that such a meeting had been held.[33]

Ten years earlier, in 1951, United States Senator Estes Kefauver (D-Tenn.) of the Senate Crime Investigating Committee had described Hot Springs as a "meeting place" of the nation's big-time crime operators. New York gambler Frank Costello had been questioned by the Kefauver committee about one of his recent visits to Hot Springs three weeks before when he supposedly had met with Charles "Lucky" Luciano, Arthur Samish, of California, Tony Gizzo, Kansas City, and others. When questioned about the Southern Club where Costello and others were entertained by Owney Madden, the New York mobster, replied, "I have no information about the operation of the Southern Club."[34]

The "esteemed" Senator from Tennessee said that so many major national crime figures had made visits to the Spa it had been dubbed "as the nation's number two gathering spot for men of Costello's reputation." Kefauver said Florida had an edge on Arkansas "in this respect."[35]

Before the senate committee was finished, Kefauver had declared Hot Springs to be the number one and largest "illegal operation" in the nation.

The Kefauver committee was followed by the McClellan Crime Committee, headed by Arkansas' own senior senator, John McClellan. The Senator had always had a "right-friendly" attitude toward Hot Springs which had regularly contributed a very substantial democratic vote and had always enriched his re-election fund with campaign donations. The gambling community had especially been appreciative of his efforts and had been generous in their gifts. The McClellan committee hammered away "against wickedness in Chicago, New Jersey and other cities outside the chairman's home state."[36] Others accused McClellan of being "soft" on the wide-open illegal gambling taking place in his own state. The feisty senator from Arkansas bristled and promptly subpoenaed Owney Madden and one of his employees. Both men made the long flight to Washington, D.C. And, both declined to answer the committee's questions, taking the Fifth Amendment.

When a Federal grand Jury met at Fort Smith and investigated the gambling in Arkansas scores of Spa citizens were subpoenaed. The jubilant headlines

---

[32] *Chicago Sun-Times*, 12 February 1963.-

[33] *Arkansas Democrat*, 2 March 1961.

[34] *Arkansas Gazette*, 21 March 1951.

[35] Ibid.

[36] *Chicago Sun-Times*, 12 February 1963, article by Ray Brennan, correspondent.

of the jury's findings in the *Sentinel Record* proclaimed **U. S. Jury Gives Spa Clean Bill In Probe of Gambling.** State Senator Q. Byrum Hurst proudly gave his approval of the findings as he said, "I am delighted to know the federal laws were found not to have been violated in the local operation of this entertainment industry."[37]

That endorsement was not exactly the summary of the grand jury's findings. Despite the jubilant news, what generally was unknown was how close the Federal grand jury had come to indicting some of the gambling owners, and their protectors, city and county officials. Just how close were these to indictments? Only one vote!

In mid-July 1962, the annual FBI crime report was released and reflected Hot Springs as having the highest crime rate of any city in the state.[38] Mayor Dan Wolf immediately took issue with the figures and tried to place a different "spin" to the statistics, although everyone acknowledged it is difficult to argue against facts and figures.

In spite of probes and investigations by federal grand juries and crime committees, the Spa continued to "rock-and-roll" through this era much like a run-away train on a dead-end track. The club operators seemed to have everything in place for the good times to continue. They had a liberal mayor in Dan Wolf, a close supporter in municipal judge Earl Mazander, a more than sympathetic circuit judge in Plummer E. Dobbs. The latter had told churchmen and reporters "he was *unaware* of *any* gambling taking place" though he had been seen in such establishments and would maintain this attitude until a bomb wrecked the front porch of his home one morning. And most importantly, a five term governor in Orval Faubus, who had often proclaimed a "hands-off" policy regarding gambling. But as in the song in Meredith Wilson's *The Music Man*, there was "trouble in River City."

There was still no one person who could be looked upon as being the "head" or the "czar" of the gambling community as W.S. Jacobs had been. The nearest was probably H. Dane Harris, who had built the new Vapors Club on Park Avenue in 1959 where Phillips Drive-In had been located. Harris had a large interest in Club Belvedere and the Tower Club in addition to the Vapors. He had been in partnership in the Southern Club with Owney Madden's wife, Agnes Demby Madden and the two had sold their interests to Dino Soncini, George and Jack Pakis and Gene Stonecipher.[39] One of Harris' backers was reported to be Harry Hastings, Sr., owner of a large liquor

---

[37] *Sentinel-Record*, 14 December 1962.

[38] *Arkansas Gazette*, 13 July 1962.

[39] Ibid., 10 February 1956. Also, *Sentinel-Record*, same date. Only a few days before this transaction, Mrs. Caroline McJunkin had sold the 40 percent interest owned by her husband's estate to those same buyers.

Dane Harris, owner of the Vapors and Belvedere Clubs and Fred Mark Palmer — 1978
Courtesy of Fred Mark Palmer

distributing company at Little Rock.[40] Hastings was also a close friend of Governor Orval Faubus and acted as a "go-between" and sometimes "bagman."[41] Several of the clubs' owners followed the lead set by Harris.

But there were several small club owners who resented Harris and refused to cooperate in some of the "civic" undertakings sponsored bythe larger clubs to create and maintain the goodwill of the community. These rifts within the "liberal" faction were divisive and at times actually caused a shutdown of the Spa's activities.

In late December 1958, a group of "handbooks, gambling places and club's selling mixed drinks were closed," based on the fact that "operators of a number of establishments had backed the wrong candidates" in the previous elections. *Sentinel-Record* reporter Edna Lee Howe, wrote "certain supporters of successful candidates in this year's elections were now demanding to be cut-

[40] H. Dane Harris was born 14 September 1918 and died 9 June 1981.

[41] *Faubus*, by Roy Reed, 318.

in on the spoils from the gambling." Another reporter said the "outs want in and the ins want to keep the outs, out."

In 1960 another shutdown occurred because of "selfishness on everybody's part as to what they're to receive from the gambling." As one gambler referred to the political climate, it was "just a big shake-down."[42]

The shut-downs caused by factional differences were especially expensive to some of the larger clubs which had big name performers scheduled for their entertainment shows which they used to bring in the gamblers. For instance, one week, Rowan and Martin were scheduled at the Southern Club; Teresa Brewer at Belvedere; and Eleanor Powell at the Vapors.[43] Even some of the smaller clubs had floor shows featuring named entertainers such as Sally Rand, the aging fan-dancer, appearing at the Palms Club and the Junoesque figured Dagmar at the Tower Club. Generally these shows did not support themselves and were subsidized by the gaming going on at the clubs.

When the gambling was closed, many of the shows had to be canceled. Frequently this caused a large loss of income especially when a star performer had a guaranteed contract.

Sometimes the factional disputes caused other problems. Over the years there were several instances where explosives were strategically placed to convey "a message" to a club owner or politician. Some exploded, others did not, but each left an impression nevertheless.

In January 1951, Norwood Phillips, one of the owners of the Southern Club discovered a package of dynamite on the front porch of his home on Hobson Avenue. Fortunately, the fuse had not been lit.[44] Phillips could think of no suspect to the act, saying " I don't believe I have an enemy in the world." But, obviously he did! Another "unexploded" bomb was found a few years later on the front lawn of Gerald Vanderslice on Prospect.

A bomb under the hood of an Oldsmobile, owned by Prosecuting Attorney David Whittington, shook awake the Alcorn Street neighborhood and damaged the vehicle but injured no one.[45]

Then there were three bombings that appeared to be related to the Whittington incident. The Vapors Club, on January 4, 1963 received extensive damage as a result of a blast from a bomb causing thirty-three injuries as a school for new croupiers was being held. Also the home of the owner, H. Dane Harris on Trivista, was rocked by an explosion resulting in considerable damage and caused great concern. When another explosion wrecked the front

---

[42] *Sentinel-Record*, 18 December 1962.

[43] Ibid., 16 February 1964.

[44] Ibid., 12 January 1951.

[45] Ibid., 23 April 1963.

The Southern Club

porch of Circuit Judge P.E. Dobbs' home and shook the Dell Street neighborhood, things appeared to be getting serious. Dobbs, who had said he was unaware of any gambling going on or other problems and had refused to call the grand jury at the urging of various citizen groups, to investigate any illegal activities, joined Dane Harris in each putting up a $2,500 reward. Others donated to the fund until over ten-thousand dollars was subscribed. Circuit Judge P.E. Dobbs also decided two terms were enough for him and he did not announce for reelection. He left to be straightened out an unbelievable encumbered case load for his successor, Judge Henry Britt.

There were a number of people who believed that Las Vegas gamblers were trying to discourage Hot Springs from enlarging its operations by trying to pass an amendment to the State Constitution legalizing gambling in Garland County. Neither Jack Pakis, owner of the Southern Club or FBI Agent Clay White shared this view. Pakis said, "Those people (gamblers in Las Vegas) were our friends. They offered to help us in our campaign to get Amendment 55 passed. They offered to send money and also to send people to help us get the word out."

FBI Agent White investigated several of the bombings and was of the opinion they had been the work of the owner of a small club who was disgruntled and considered a "hothead" who believed he was being treated unfairly by the operators of some of the larger ones and also the local authorities. The agent said, "We were pretty positive on who had done the

The Tower Club opened in the 1940s. One of its early owners was Jack McJunkin, a city fireman sponsored by Mayor Leo P. McLaughlin. It was razed about 1998.

Slot machines at the Tower Club — ca. 1960

job, but just could not establish enough evidence to get an indictment."[46]

Neither the shutdowns from political actions, factional disputes or the bombings could stop the gambling in the Spa. That much was certain. Each interruption was shrugged off and the gambling would reopen on a larger scale than before. The gambling operations and the book making establishments were more numerous and wide-opened than they had been in the days of W.S. Jacobs and Leo P. McLaughlin, but they were not as well-controlled.

But there were events taking place in other parts of the country which would finally affect the local situation. These were the senate hearings in Washington, D.C. With Senator John F. Kennedy and little brother Bobby grabbing the headlines for their activities, having pushed Chairman John L. McClellan into the background --it was quite a show.

Bobby Kennedy was serving as Counsel for the McClellan committee's investigation into labor and criminal racketeering. The hearings were some of the first to be televised live and people were glued to their television sets as young Kennedy's shrill voice questioned labor leaders and mob bosses unmercifully. Bobby was described by one Teamster attorney as "a sadistic little monster."[47]

After Bobby Kennedy got a good look into the sordid businesses of the various mobs and other criminal elements, such as "wide-open illegal gambling," he set out to encourage Congress to pass wide-sweeping anti-crime bills. He said, "The point I want to make is this: If we do not on a national scale attack organized criminals with weapons and techniques as effective as their own, they will destroy us."[48]

When his brother John was elected president and Robert was appointed Attorney General he was at last in a position from which he felt he could combat the underworld and its many vices. Bobby wanted to be known as a "crime-buster." His actions caused a lot of people to believe that Robert Kennedy was "meaner than a junk-yard dog." The boys in the illegal clubs, casinos and bookies soon agreed.

The new laws restricted the number of people who could be brought in from out-of-state to work in the clubs and casinos. Restrictions were tightened to prevent slot machines and even parts from coming in from out of state. Officials, city, county and state were made more accountable for their actions or inaction toward illegal operations and activities.

Bobby Kennedy, as attorney general, ordered the FBI to closely investigate

---

[46] Taped interview of FBI Special Agent Clay T. White.

[47] Victor Lasky, *J.F.K., The Man and the Myth,* The MacMillan Co., New York (1960), Twelfth Printing.

[48] Robert F. Kennedy, *The Enemy Within;* Popular Library, New York (1960), 228 - 253.

all illegal gambling activities throughout the country and especially at Hot Springs. As many as thirty agents were working at a time in the Spa, many undercover.[49] Detailed reports covering every phase of the illegal activities going in the Spa were sent to the Justice Department in Washington, D.C. for its review.

On 16 February 1964, FBI Special Agent Clay White received a call from the Little Rock Field office informing him that two high-ranking officials would be in Hot Springs on the following day and he was told to meet with them and accord them every courtesy. The next day White met with William Hundley, chief of the United States Department of Justice Organized Crime and Racketeering section, and Edward T. Joyce, head of the Gambling section.

The two visitors requested Special Agent White to escort them to several of the gambling casinos. The trio started out and White took them to the Southern, Vapors, and Belvedere clubs and to several smaller ones. There were crowds of people, some three or four deep around the dice and roulette tables. Even though the two Justice Department officials had read numerous FBI reports of the gambling operations in the Spa they were quite impressed at how wide-open and unrestricted they were.

Hundley and Joyce requested Agent White to call a press conference for the following day.[50] Joining William Hundley and Edward T. Joyce at the press conference was United States Attorney for the Western District of Arkansas, Charles Conway.

Hundley, acting as spokesman, announced the U. S. Justice Department was "conducting an intensive investigation of Hot Springs gambling, the largest illegal gambling in any state."[51] He further informed the news conference that "The Justice Department is looking for violations of (the) 1961 federal laws against bringing equipment or people across state lines for gambling purposes."[52] Hundley referred to information provided by ex-mobster Joseph Valachi, who had testified before a congressional committee on the operations of the Cosa Nostra crime syndicate and had mentioned Hot Springs as having been a gathering spot for Chicago and New York hoodlums.[53]

---

[49] Taped interview with Special Agent Clay White.

[50] Ibid.

[51] *New Era*, 18 February 1964.

[52] *Texarkana Gazette*, 19 February 1964.

[53] Ibid. Valachi, had been a high ranking member of the Don Vito Genovese crime family. When he fell into disfavor with members of Cosa Nostra, and to save his life, he became a government witness. See Peter Mass, *The Valachi Papers*, G.P. Putnam's Sons, New York (1968).

Local officials tried to put their best "spin" on the federal probe, pointing out that Joseph Valachi had not been to the Spa since the 1930s and that Hundley's "suspicions about outside interests being involved in the gambling" was totally incorrect as the local operators were financed "all by local Arkansas money."[54]

Well, that was some support, but the local boys were badly shaken--what could they do to protect themselves and their interests? Could or would the Governor help? After all, he reportedly had been accepting "contributions" from the Hot Springs gamblers for the past ten years. Just how much "support" had Faubus received? Roy Reed, author of *Faubus, The Life and Times of an American Prodigal*, quotes sources as believing "election-year contributions amounted to at least fifty thousand dollars," and "a routine pay-off month by month ran to about seventy-five thousand dollars a year."[55] Other sources estimated the Governor's share, for his "umbrella of safety" to have cost the gambling community from fifty to one hundred thousand dollars a year. A governor's support did not come cheap!

To be sure, Governor Faubus wanted to help, however he had some major problems. He was getting "heat" from ministerial groups, not only from Hot Springs, of which he paid scant attention, but others from Saline, Jefferson and Pulaski counties. Also, for the first time he knew he was headed for a "dog-fight" in running for his sixth term as he would be facing a strong Republican opponent, Winthrop Rockefeller, who had deep pockets so far as campaign expenses were concerned, and who would utilize the gambling problem in the Spa as an issue.

While the clubs' and casinos' owners were contemplating what action they should take, the Arkansas House of Representatives, took the matter into their hands. A house resolution, introduced by Rep. Roy Galyean of Benton County, urged "local officials to stop illegal gambling in the state." The resolution passed 91-3, when a roll call vote was requested. Only Garland County's two representatives, Nathan Schoenfeld and Ray Smith, Jr., joined by G.D. Smith, of Jefferson County, were the measure's only opponents.[56]

The action by the legislature has been given the credit over the years as being the "prod" that Governor Faubus needed to close down the illegal gambling in Hot Springs. That was not totally correct, although it did help to make up the Governor's mind. But it was not the only consideration he gave to the problem. Faubus was not afraid to "face down" an obstacle to his will or neatly side step it. Controversy did not intimidate him and he was difficult

---

[54] *Texarkana Gazette*, 19 February 1964. Also, *Saturday Evening Post*, "No Dice in Hot Springs," 19 September 1964, an article by John Skow, 78.

[55] *Faubus*, 318.

[56] *Sentinel-Record*, 29 March 1964.

to "pin-down." Remember, he once said, "Just because I said it, doesn't make it so." It had not been a timid individual who had ordered the National Guard to stop integration at Central High School in Little Rock in 1957, and who had defied the federal government until President Eisenhower nationalized the Guard and sent in the 101st Airborne to control the situation. And Faubus was not cowed by the Resolution passed by the legislature. He just used it to his own advantage in looking to his sixth campaign.

The other thing to aid the Governor in making up his mind was when he received word, possibly direct from one of the head gamblers, H. Dane Harris, but quite possibly from Faubus' long-time hunting and fishing buddy, Harry Hastings, Sr. Faubus was told that it was time to "pull the plug," and close down the gambling.[57]

Why would they do this? It was obvious with the federal investigative probe underway at that time and with agents swarming over the Spa gathering evidence that continuing to operate as they had been was much like playing "Russian Roulette." If the clubs and owners kept going as they were, someone most likely would end up in a federal penitentiary. And there was another reason. Several of the small clubs' and bars' owners were at odds with Harris and the other large casino owners, refusing to cooperate, and probably would not voluntarily close down. They probably would respond to an order from the governor.

Faubus, who had never sent the State Police on a raiding party to Hot Springs, agreed with this understanding.[58] Only thirty-six hours after the Resolution had been passed by the State Legislature, Governor Faubus issued a "crisp gubernatorial order which abruptly ended open gambling at Hot Springs, March 28."[59]

On Saturday night, March 28, business in the Spa was described "booming as never before." The races at Oaklawn Park were approaching their last week. They had enjoyed record crowds. The motels and hotels were full and the restaurants were doing a "land-office business." It was reported the Belvedere, Vapors, Southern, Tower and Palms had "standing room only."[60] The clubs all stayed open later than their 2:00 a.m. closing hour, but late patrons could see the employees were stowing and packing items preparing to close down the operation. By 4:00 a.m., all was darkened.

As the casinos locked their doors, many of the visitors in the Spa who were

---

[57] Taped interview - Clay White.

[58] There had been a couple of State Police raids in 1956, however those had been prompted by Attorney General Tom Gentry and not Orval Faubus.

[59] *Arkansas Democrat*, 29 March 1964. This was an Associated Press article written by John Robert Starr, Bureau Chief.

[60] *Sentinel-Record*, 29 March 1964.

registered through the following week, began checking out of their accommodations and heading home.

New trendy motels had sprung up during the last nine years' boom. Others, like Walter Hudlow's 80-unit Ramada was just getting under construction when the casinos closed.[61] Owners worried what effect the shut-down would have on their investments?

Almost by the time the last light was turned off in the gaming rooms, Senator Q. Byrum Hurst was announcing a petition campaign to get an amendment on the November ballot as an initiated act to legalize gambling in the Spa.[62] The petitions were obtained and Amendment 55, called the Garland County Lawful Wagering Amendment was readied for the voters. It had to be voted on state wide and a large campaign and drive was planned.

The *Sentinel-Record* commenced a series of articles supposedly to give the voters an unbiased view of the pros and cons of legalized gambling. A reporter was assigned to research the experiences of areas that had legalized gaming. Various individuals in gambling centers such as Las Vegas were interviewed. Perhaps to the readers of that era the reports may have appeared to be unbiased. To the reader of today they definitely seem to be slanted toward pro-gambling.

Even the effort of the Hot Springs Chamber of Commerce in putting out a "Fact-O-Gram" on Amendment 55 was quite obviously sharply slanted in favor of gambling. It is noticeably clear that no mention was made of any downside effects legalized gambling can have on a community. Everything is painted "rosy." Out of the nine questions the brochure poses and the answers given as "Fact" gives a utopian picture of the bill "and why the Amendment is so important to everyone in Arkansas."[63]

It was an "easy sell" to the citizens of Garland County as the Amendment passed locally by a vote of 15,348 to 5,825. But the remainder of the state had not swallowed all the propaganda as Amendment 55 was "beat like a yard-dog," by over one-hundred thousand votes. It was a bitter and expensive defeat for the proponents of gaming.

State Senator Hurst was not through, however, as he said he would introduce a bill in the legislature to legalize gambling in Garland County. Governor Orval Faubus could read the will of the people in a vote about as well as any Arkansas politician ever, and told the Senator that if the bill reached his desk he would veto it. Disappointed, Hurst never submitted it.

But secretly, Faubus was sympathetic with the clubs at Hot Springs. He had

---

[61] Ibid, 19 April 1964.

[62] *Arkansas Gazette*, 29 March 1964.

[63] Hot Springs Chamber of Commerce Public Information Committee undated brochure. Copy on file at GCHS.

been questioned in a public meeting of the Pulaski County Ministerial Association if he could keep the casinos closed with the defeat of Amendment 55. He answered, "Yes, and I will."[64]

Some of the "boys" at Hot Springs were hurting and trying to get his permission to reopen the clubs, and he knew he had to be careful. He also had another reason to be lenient with the situation at the Spa. Realizing after he entered his sixth term as governor, that his tenure was running out and since he was planning to build a house--a big house, one over 200 feet long on top of a mountain in his beloved Madison County, he needed money, a lot of money.[65]

Soon after January 1, 1965, in spite of an overwhelming popular vote against the gambling amendment, the word was quietly passed down, "Its o.k. to open, but boys, keep it low key. If you get in trouble there'll be little help from Little Rock."

The Governor refused to acknowledge that some of the casinos and clubs had reopened. Roy Reed wrote in his analytical biography, "Faubus maintained a kind of amazed innocence." Reed cites that one reporter interviewing the Governor at the Arlington Hotel in Hot Springs was assured that the gambling was closed. The reporter, after the interview, strolled across Central Avenue and entered the Southern Club and found it operating wide-open.[66] During this time, the Governor told reporters that he had sent the State Police investigators to clubs at Little Rock and Hot Springs and they "had been unable to find any gambling." Another investigative reporter wrote, "The slot machines are back," having counted 72 in the Vapors, the Southern Club and the Turf Club. Three days later, the count was up to 85 in those same three clubs. Black jack games had returned to the White Front and Showboat clubs.[67]

But time was running out for wide-open illegal gambling in the Spa. In the fall of 1966 Winthrop "Win" Rockefeller, was elected governor. He was an extremely wealthy man who had moved to Arkansas to obtain a divorce, liked the state and stayed. He invested millions of dollars in various industries and bought a mountain top ranch at Petit Jean. Rockefeller involved himself in politics and completely energized the Republican Party into a formidable organization for the first time in the state's history. In his campaign for governor he let it be clearly known he was totally against illegal gambling. He

---

[64] *Arkansas Gazette*, 25 July 1970. This was an editorial and a summary of Orval Faubus' handling of the gambling situation during his 12-year tenure as governor.

[65] *Pine Bluff Commercial*, 9 March 1966.

[66] Reed - *Faubus*, 320.

[67] *Arkansas Gazette*, 5 March & 8 March 1965.

was serious about this campaign promise and because of his immense personal wealth, he was above the level of bribery.

Many of the clubs had retreated under the guise of "private clubs," believing they might be protected from state police raids. It was wishful thinking. The "required" membership into the clubs was so shallow it was as if they didn't exist. Some of the clubs handed out membership cards on the street, others at the door. A few had a membership enrollment sheet, but after a time they did not even bother with this.

Several newspapers closely monitored the new governor's actions toward gambling. Cliff McIntyre, an *Arkansas Democrat* staff writer did considerable research into the illegal activities at Hot Springs. He learned that 129 individuals were holders of federal tax stamps for coin operated gambling devices.[68] As the article explained, each stamp could represent *any* number of machines. A gambling stamp cost $250 a year. The Internal Revenue Service had issued 441 tax stamps to residents of Garland County in 1961. The stamps covered coin operated devices and ranged from the Southern Club partnership of Dino Soncini, George and Jack Pakis and Gene Stonecipher with 62; The Vapors Club with 38; and down to one machine each for Jackson's Fish Market, Gee's Villanova Restaurant and Joe's Red Rose on Albert Pike.[69] Using statistics provided by the McCelllan and Kefauver Congressional Investigating Committees, each machine would provide an estimated $50 per week for its owner.[70]

Shortly after his inauguration in 1967, Governor Rockefeller sent a letter to both Mayor Dan Wolf, of Hot Springs and Mayor William F. Laman of North Little Rock and all law enforcement in Garland and Pulaski counties. He advised he had been apprised that illegal gambling was being conducted in their respective cities and requested an "immediate investigation by you is called for."[71] Rockefeller said he wasn't trying to "pick-on" the two counties, but that local authorities had the primary responsibility for controlling gambling. "However," he add, "if gambling is permitted on an open, notorious and continuing basis, it becomes an affront to the people of Arkansas and is a matter of state concern." "If gambling again becomes flagrant, I will move on my own initiative," he declared. "If it becomes obnoxious to the people, it behooves the governor to act."[72]

At Hot Springs, Garland County Sheriff, Eugene "Bud" Canada warned the

---

[68] *Arkansas Democrat,* 15 January 1967.

[69] *Arkansas Gazette,* 29 August 1961.

[70] *Arkansas Democrat,* 5 January 1967.,

[71] *Arkansas Gazette,* 13 January 1967.

[72] Ibid.

private clubs they "must adhere to the law."

At only one place did the sheriff's request meet with refusal and the operator of the Ohio Club was arrested and the place closed.[73]

How far would the Governor go to close down the gambling? The question was would he do anything--was it just politics as usual and he would do nothing? Again the state newspapers, *The Arkansas Gazette* and *Arkansas Democrat* led the way and made their own investigation.

The *Democrat's* Cliff McIntyre reported dice tables, roulette wheels and 31 slot machines were in full swing at the Bridge Street Club. The Ohio Club had 21 tables, two dice tables and seven slot machines bringing in the customers. He reported, "it was virtually impossible to get a table to see Mickey Rooney at the Vapors and its casino was so over crowded "expectant gamblers," were being referred to the White Front Club.[74]

The Governor had read enough. If reporters could find such wide-open illegal gambling the local authorities certainly should have been able to locate such places and closed them down. He did not set a deadline until the 20th of February for "all gambling operations to cease." The deadline came and went in Garland County, club owners testing the resolve of the state's chief executive. Those in Pulaski County who were operating bookies decided the Governor was not bluffing and shut their doors.

At Hot Springs, Senator Hurst said he believed the state had no legal grounds to raid the private clubs as he "contended that private clubs enjoy the same constitutional protection as private homes." Rockefeller did not agree with Hurst's legal assessment of the situation and had conferred with the Attorney General and he said, "The private club law may not be as effective a legal defense as some would have us believe."

The *Democrat's* Cliff McIntyre had become a "thorn-in-the-flesh" to the gambling concerns in the Spa. The paper received two threatening letters, anonymous of course, indicating bodily harm would befall the reporters if they persisted in "reviling my city."[75]

That same day, McIntyre wrote he had visited the Palms, a night club across Central Avenue from Oaklawn Park racetrack and described how quickly it filled up with people following the races until there was "standing room only." Even though the Palms was considered a "private club," the *Democrat* reporter had been successful in walking in without a membership card or being challenged by anyone. From the reporter's vantage point inside the club, he could see State Police officers directing traffic in front of the racetrack.

---

[73] *Sentinel-Record*, 15 January 1967.

[74] *Arkansas Democrat*, 28 February 1967.

[75] Ibid.

That did it. Governor Rockefeller's patience was at an end--he ordered Col. Herman E. Lindsey, State Police Director to "end gambling."[76]

On March 1, 1967, the Arkansas State Police, members of the Hot Springs Police Department and Sheriff and deputies of the Garland County sheriff's office swooped down on eight clubs. Opps--there had been a leak! No gambling paraphernalia was found at the Ohio, White Front, Bridge Street, Palms, Citizens, Cliff's Drive In and Oasis clubs. Only at the Cameo Club did they discovered a dismantled dice table.[77] The "Boys" had been tipped off!

Just a day or two earlier, investigators had gone into those clubs and made a list of equipment in use. For instance, at the Bridge Street Club, they had observed three dice tables, three blackjack or "21" tables, 30 slot machines and one roulette table. The other clubs had similar gambling equipment. A list of the equipment was presented to Municipal Judge Earl Mazander, who issued the warrants.[78]

To say that State Police Director Lindsey was unhappy with the results is to put it mildly. He announced he was delegating authority to Major Bill Struebing, head of the Criminal Investigation Division, (CID) and Captain Kenneth McKee, commander of the uniformed Highway Patrol, "to act at will," in enforcing gambling laws, "without further contact with this office."[79] He further urged reporters to advise the State Police of gambling violations they uncovered prior to publication.

The next raids were conducted by State Police personnel only, hitting the Palms, Shamrock and Frontier clubs. Then the hunting got better!

On March 10, plain-clothed State Police raided three Hot Springs establishments and arrested their owners. These three "private clubs, were popular eateries, Coy's Steak House, Jud's Steak House and the Hornsby House. They seized a total of 17 slot machines, dice and "21" tables. The officers carted off the confiscated equipment to Little Rock.

After other raids, Municipal Judge Earl Mazander got into the act, ordering the State Police to return the contraband to Hot Springs and set a deadline as March 24.[80] He even charged Maj. Struebing of the State Police with contemp, but later dropped the charges.

State Attorney General Joe Purcell, cited Act 176 of 1963, the so-called private club law under which "private clubs and any charitable organization operates, as providing provisions for revoking club charters when a club

---

[76] *Arkansas Gazette*, 28 February 1967.

[77] *New Era*, *Arkansas Gazette*, 2 March 1967.

[78] *Arkansas Gazette*, 2 March 1967.

[79] Ibid.

[80] *New Era*, 13 March 1967.

violates state laws, becomes a public nuisance or ceases to operate within the scope of its charter."[81]

Purcell proceeded to file petitions in Pulaski Circuit Court to revoke the charters of several of the clubs. He asked for, and was granted, a court order to impound the equipment as evidence.[82] Inasmuch as Judge Mazander had represented two of the defendants previously in his private practice, he disqualified himself from the hearing the cases.[83]

Maj. Bill Struebing and his crew struck unexpectedly again on March 18 and confiscated equipment at the Citizens Club and were carrying the feared, "search and destroy" warrant, issued by Circuit Judge Henry M. Britt. There was no argument over what to do with the confiscated equipment as the troopers carried it directly to a gravel pit and destroyed it by fire. They presented photographic film as evidence to Police Chief Ermey.[84]

The State Police's CID unit was beginning to inflict major damage on the Spa's gambling community by destroying expensive equipment. Help was sought from State Senator Q. Byrum Hurst, who along with Senator Guy "Mutt" Jones of Conway, tried to eliminate the CID unit by "bogging down" the department's annual appropriation in committee.[85] In fact, Hurst introduced a bill to "abolish the State Police's Criminal Investigative Division. The Division has been conducting a series of raids on alleged gambling establishments in Garland County."[86]

When Senator Hurst introduced the bill to abolish the CID, he said it "was not directed at the Hot Springs situation and that it was unfortunate it is timed that way."[87] Hurst told reporters, "The State Police was created to patrol the highways," and that the CID was interfering with local law enforcement.[88]

While several other senators had expressed dissatisfaction with the CID, it would not have been prudent to remove this unit from the availability of support to local law enforcement agencies for complicated investigations. The measure to do away with the unit was not perceived to be a good move and was blocked in committee, although Senator Hurst was able to prevent its budget from being increased.

---

[81] *Arkansas Gazette*, 21 March 1967.

[82] Ibid.

[83] *New Era*, 21 March 1967.

[84] *Arkansas Gazette*, 20 March 1967.

[85] *Sentinel-Record*, 30 March 1967.

[86] Ibid. Also, *Arkansas Gazette*, 29 March 1967.

[87] *Arkansas Gazette*, 29 March 1967.

[88] *Arkansas Democrat*, 30 March 1967.

The likeable Hurst fought hard for his friends and constituents around the clubs. In 1957, he and Max Howell, Ellis M. Fagan and Artie Gregory of Pulaski County, had introduced a bill in the senate to legalize gambling. Before the bill came to a vote there was a big "flap" about vote-buying. Two other solons advised they had been offered $500 to vote for the bill. As a result, "the 1957 bill died."[89] In 1959, Senator Hurst placed another legalized gambling bill in the senate "hopper." It was similar to the bill two years earlier. It, too, was "shot down."

Two years later, in 1961, three crime commission bills were introduced. They would have allowed the commission to investigate any areas in the state where it appeared local law enforcement was not dealing with illegal activities. All three bills were opposed by Senator Hurst and his pal, Rep. Van Dalsem, and they were successful in blocking the measure.

When Rep. Nap Murphy, of West Memphis, introduced a bill to create a special division within the state police to *enforce* the gambling laws, Senator Q. Byrum Hurst led the Garland County delegation "in amending it to death."[90] Then came Hurst's Amendment 55 in 1964, which was soundly defeated in a state wide vote.

But if the Senator was one thing, he was persistent. In 1967, along with Senators Oscar Alagood, Max Howell and Dan Sprick, all of Little Rock, they introduced a bill that would "set up a five member Arkansas Crime Commission which would have control of gambling of any kind in private clubs in the state.[91] Of course, tied to the commission bill was a provision to legalize gambling in Garland County, but to limit casino type gambling to only four clubs. It was not explained who the "favored four" might be. The Senator "sweetened" the pot over the provisions of the failed Amendment 55. In that amendment, the State of Arkansas' take was to be limited to 3½ - 5 percent. The latest bill was more generous, allowing 8 percent, and taxing each of the four casinos $10,000, a bargain.[92]

The failure of Amendment 55, three years earlier had apparently faded in the memory of the state legislature as the gambling bill surprisedly passed both houses. There was almost immediately a loud cry of opposition and indignation from around the state. Editor Leroy Tyron of *The Dermott News* wrote, "Never do we remember a time when a state legislative group disregarded the expressed wishes of the people more so than last week when our legislature passed the legalized gambling bill for Garland County." There

---

[89] Ibid., 16 March 1967.

[90] Ibid.

[91] *New Era*, 27 1967.

[92] Ibid.

were others who wrote pointedly of the legislature's "apparent mental relapse."[93]

Governor Rockefeller let the bill lay on his desk "simmering." Some of the solons thought he'd indicated he would sign the bill, "if both houses passed it." He reminded them he had made his position on gambling "very, very clear" in 1964 when he said he was morally opposed to gambling and that he had not changed his position. He told a gathering of 200 people he hoped they would talk to their senators and representatives and let them know how the constituents felt about the gambling bill, as he "was giving them a chance to recall the bill that would legalize limited casino gambling in Hot Springs."[94]

The Governor believed he had read the "pulse" of the people correctly and just before the legalized gambling bill became law, he vetoed it.

Another brouhaha occurred when Pulaski-Perry County Representative Gayle Windsor placed those in the legislature who had voted for the bill under a cloud of suspicion as he revealed "he had been offered ten-bills or $1,000 to vote for it." Those members rose in resentment at the implication.[95] They professed an air of innocence, *demanding* a grand jury investigation.

Gambling in Hot Springs had suffered a mortal blow with the governor's veto. Even some of the law makers and sponsors had second thoughts and wished they had been more prudent in casting their vote. Senator Oscar Alagood, of Little Rock, who had joined Hurst in sponsoring the bill, made a complete turn-around in his opinion and said, "I've had some second thoughts in the last two or three weeks. I'm not too sure at this moment that the legalization of gambling is the answer. Gambling is rather insidious. It can spread, and it has some ramifications that aren't good at all."[96]

At Hot Springs, several of the small-time gamblers began trying to do business "from hotel room to hotel room."[97] The Hot Springs Police Department joined in and began closing down some of the small clubs and making arrests as they tried furtively to reopen. They hit the Palms, the Question Mark Lounge and Cliff's Drive In on April 1st. All gambling equipment was confiscated and destroyed.

---

[93] *Arkansas, Gazette*, 12 March 1967, The Arkansas Press, "In The Aftermath of That Casino Gambling Bill." This column gave excerpts from fifteen editorials from over the state--all critical of the legislature's action.

[94] *Arkansas Democrat*, 6 March 1967.

[95] *The Magnolia Daily Banner*, 7 March 1967. Also, *Arkansas Democrat*, 26 March 1967.

[96] *Arkansas Gazette*, 1 November 1967.

[97] *Arkansas Democrat*, 30 March 1967.

A truck loaded with confiscated slot machines seized by State Police in a raid on a barn in Bellaire Addition — 1967.
Courtesy of Bob Brown

The end of the line for 111 slot machines seized by State Police. The machines were doused with diesel and burned in 1967, signaling the end of an era.
Courtesy of Bob Brown

Through the summer and fall of 1967, the State Police made numerous raids, confiscating dozens of slot machines and destroying them. Municipal Judge Mazander began ordering confiscated slot machines and other devices to be destroyed.[98]

A new State Police Director, Lynn Davis, an ex-FBI agent, led his men on raids of the Ohio, Bridge Street, Citizens and White Front clubs on August 17. Judge Mazander ordered the contraband of 25 slot machines, six dice tables, six "21" tables and a large quantity of poker chips to be burned.[99]

In November the State Police raided the Spa Amusement Company on Second Street and seized a number of slot machines. It appeared that not only were machines being repaired, but new ones were being manufactured to get around the federal laws. More shocking to the State Police was the fact they discovered through the serial numbers that 15 of those were identified as being machines supposedly destroyed by local police on September 22.[100] Charges were made against the Chief of Police and Assistant Chief of failing to destroy the equipment as ordered. Both denied any impropierty. They were supported by Judge Mazander, who said after his own personal investigation, "I can see no basis of a court hearing or other action against Police Chief John Ermey or Assistant Joe Crain."[101] Everyone knew that had the officers looked the other way and permitted the machines to "live." They were just trying to keep their jobs--that was how things worked in those days.

The recovered slots were destroyed a second time by State Police, using sledge hammers and diesel fuel.[102] The slot machines which had been so numerous and highly visible in the gambling operations were quickly disappearing as police raided the clubs that were foolish enough to try to open.

The Benton, Arkansas Police Department found a trailer parked in a gravel pit outside of town and secured a search warrant and discovered 38 machines inside. The trailer was registered to a Hot Springs business owned by some club owners.[103]

The State Police "hit the jackpot" in a little red barn behind a residence in trendy Bellaire in the Spa. One hundred and eleven machines were seized. These would not be "recycled" as they were run over and mangled by a bulldozer, burned and buried.

---

[98] Ibid., 25 March 1967.

[99] *Arkansas Gazette*, 23 September 1967.

[100] *Sentinel-Record*, 17 November 1967.

[101] *New Era*, 18 November 1967.

[102] Ibid., 20 November 1967.

[103] Ibid., 26 September 1967.

Over three hundred of the Mills "High-tops," Criss Cross, Watling "Rol-A-Tops," and "Superbells" coin operated slots had been confiscated and destroyed.[104] They were irreplaceable as there was a federal statute prohibiting new machines or parts from being brought in state.

By the end of 1967, the back of illegal gambling had been broken. The large clubs--Southern, Belvedere and the Vapors--tried to hold on as supper clubs, but their fate was sealed. As wide-open, free wheeling gambling casinos only their memories linger on.

The great old Belvedere became a country club and golf course. The main building's demise came a few years later. The historic old Southern Club, dating back to near the turn of the century, was sold and became a wax museum. Dane Harris, gambling king-pin, was lured to Turkey and opened a large casino, but had many problems from that foreign government. His plush Vapors Club was closed and sold and operates today as a church.

Predictions that without gambling Hot Springs would "dry-up" and "wither-away," have happily not come to pass. In fact, with the commercialization of the lakes, Mid-America Park, Magic Springs Amusement Park, the art colony and various festivals, have enticed families to visit the Spa by the thousands. As Hot Springs' colorful history slowly recedes into the ages, its future has never seemed brighter! The secret of its survival and endurance from fires, floods and political wars is its strongest asset--its resilient and wonderful people!

---

[104] *The Coin Slot*, October 1982 issue.